Excel® 2019

BIBLE

Michael Alexander
Dick Kusleika
Previously by John Walkenbach

WILEY

Excel® 2019 Bible

Published by
John Wiley & Sons, Inc.
10475 Crosspoint Boulevard
Indianapolis, IN 46256
www.wiley.com

Copyright © 2019 by John Wiley & Sons, Inc., Indianapolis, Indiana

Published simultaneously in Canada

ISBN: 978-1-119-51478-7
ISBN: 978-1-119-51477-0 (ebk)
ISBN: 978-1-119-51476-3 (ebk)

For general information on our other products and services please contact our Customer Care Department within the United States at (877) 762-2974, outside the United States at (317) 572-3993 or fax (317) 572-4002.

Wiley publishes in a variety of print and electronic formats and by print-on-demand. Some material included with standard print versions of this book may not be included in e-books or in print-on-demand. If this book refers to media such as a CD or DVD that is not included in the version you purchased, you may download this material at http://booksupport.wiley.com. For more information about Wiley products, visit www.wiley .com.

Library of Congress Control Number: 2018954472

Printed in Singapore
M003323_170122

About the Authors

Michael Alexander is a Microsoft Certified Application Developer (MCAD) and author of several books on advanced business analysis with Microsoft Access and Microsoft Excel. He has more than 20 years of experience consulting and developing Microsoft Office solutions. Mike has been named a Microsoft MVP for his ongoing contributions to the Excel community. You can find Mike at www.datapigtechnologies.com.

Dick Kusleika is a 12-time Microsoft Excel MVP and has been working with Microsoft Office for more than 20 years. Dick develops Access- and Excel-based solutions for his clients and has conducted training seminars on Office products in the United States and Australia. Dick also writes a popular Excel-related blog at www.dailydoseofexcel.com.

John Walkenbach is a best-selling Excel author who has published more than 50 spreadsheet books. He lives amid the saguaros, javelinas, rattlesnakes, bobcats, and Gila monsters in Southern Arizona, but the critters are mostly scared away by his clawhammer banjo playing. For more information, Google him.

About the Technical Editors

Jordan Goldmeier is an internationally recognized analytics professional and data visualization expert, author, speaker, and CEO. He is the owner of Cambia Factor, a data consulting agency, and the author of *Advanced Excel Essentials* (Apress, 2014) and co-author of *Dashboards for Excel* (Apress, 2015), both on developing advanced analytics with Excel. He has consulted with and provided training for the NATO Training Mission, Pentagon, Air Force and Navy, Financial Times, and the University of Cincinnati, among others. His work has been cited by and quoted in the Associated Press, Bloomberg BusinessWeek, Dice News, and American Express OPEN Forum. He holds the prestigious MVP award from Microsoft since 2013, and he is an owner and producer of Excel.TV, an online community devoted to sharing stories, setbacks, and lessons from experts and practitioners in Excel, business intelligence, big data, and analytics. He has provided technical editing and review for Wiley, O'Reilly, and others.

Joyce J. Nielsen has worked in the publishing industry for more than 25 years as an author, development editor, technical editor, and project manager specializing in Microsoft Office, Windows, Internet, and general technology titles for leading educational and retail publishers. She is the author or co-author of more than 40 computer books and has edited several hundred IT publications and more than 2,000 online articles. Joyce holds a bachelor of science degree in quantitative business analysis from Indiana University's Kelley School of Business in Bloomington. Joyce currently resides in Arizona.

Doug Holland is an architect evangelist at Microsoft Corporation, working with partners to drive digital transformation through technologies such as the Microsoft Cloud, Office 365, and HoloLens. He holds a master's degree in software engineering from Oxford University and lives in Northern California with his wife and five children.

Guy Hart-Davis is the author of an improbable number of computer books on a bizarre range of topics. If you had been wondering who was responsible for the *Word 2000 Developer's Handbook*, *AppleScript: A Beginner's Guide*, *iMac Portable Genius*, or *Samsung Galaxy S8 Maniac's Guide*, you need wonder no more.

Credits

Project Editor
Gary Schwartz

Technical Editors
Jordan Goldmeier
Joyce J. Nielsen
Doug Holland
Guy Hart-Davis

Production Editor
Barath Kumar Rajasekaran

Copy Editor
Kim Wimpsett

Production Manager
Kathleen Wisor

Content Enablement and Operations Manager
Pete Gaughan

Marketing Manager
Christie Hilbrich

Associate Publisher
Jim Minatel

Senior Editorial Assistant
Devon Lewis

Project Coordinator, Cover
Brent Savage

Proofreader
Amy J. Schneider

Indexer
John Sleeva

Cover Designer
Wiley

Cover Image
iStockphoto.com/Aleksandar

Acknowledgments

Our deepest thanks to the professionals at John Wiley & Sons for all the hours of work put into bringing this book to life. Thanks also to Jordan Goldmeier, Joyce Nielsen, Doug Holland, and Guy Hart-Davis for suggesting numerous improvements to the examples and text in this book. A special thank-you goes out to our families for putting up with all the time spent locked away on this project. Finally, we'd like to thank John Walkenbach for his many years of work on the previous editions of this book. His efforts in curating Excel knowledge have been instrumental, not only in helping millions of Excel users to achieve their learning goals but in inspiring countless Excel MVPs to share their expertise with the Excel community.

Contents at a Glance

Contents

Contents

Contents

Contents

Contents

Part II: Working with Formulas and Functions 205

Contents

Contents

Part III: Creating Charts and Other Visualizations   443

Chapter 20: Getting Started with Excel Charts 445

Contents

Contents

Contents

Contents

Contents

Part V: Understanding Power Pivot and Power Query   781

Contents

Introduction

W elcome to the world of Excel. Okay, that's a bit cheesy. But if you look around the business world, the financial world, the manufacturing world, and any other industry you can think of, you will see people using Excel. Excel is everywhere. It is by far the most popular program in the history of business applications. So, we truly are living in a world of Excel. This is probably why you've picked up this book. You need a way to accelerate your learning and get up to speed quickly.

Well, worry not, dear reader. Whether you're boning up on Excel for a new job (congratulations, by the way), for a school project, or just for home use, this book is perfect for you.

In this book, we've organized everything that one would need to know to get up and running quickly with Excel. And we've made certain that this book contains many useful examples and lots of tips and tricks that cover all of the essential aspects of Excel—from the basics to more advanced topics.

Is This Book for You?

This book is designed to enhance the skillset of users at all levels (beginning, intermediate, and even advanced users).

Start at the beginning if you're new to Excel. Part I covers everything you'll need to get familiar entering data, managing workbooks, formatting worksheets, and printing. You can then move on to Part II, where you'll discover the ins and outs of Excel formulas.

If you're a seasoned analyst, hoping to enhance your data visualization and analytic toolset, check out Part III and Part IV. We've included many examples and tips for analyzing data and creating visually appealing Excel dashboards.

If you've been working with an earlier version of Excel, this book is for you too! Part V covers the new Power Pivot and Power Query toolsets. In the past, these features were free Microsoft add-ins that were used peripherally. Now they've become an essential part of how Excel manages data and interacts with external data sources.

If you want to learn the basics of Visual Basic for Applications (VBA) programming, you'll find what you need in Part VI. The topic of VBA is a rich one that deserves its own book, so we have also written *Excel 2019 Power Programming with VBA* (Wiley, 2019). Nonetheless, this book offers a robust set of chapters that will get you started leveraging VBA to automate and enhance your Excel solutions.

Software Versions

This book was written for the desktop version of Microsoft® Excel 2019 for Windows. Please note that this book is not applicable to Microsoft® Excel for Mac.

Excel is available in several versions, including a web version and a version for tablets and phones. Though this book was written for the desktop version of Excel, much of the information here will also apply to the web and tablet versions. Excel 2016 and Excel 2013 users will also find the information in this book relevant.

If you are using the Office 365 version of Excel, you may very well see features in your version of Excel that are not covered here. Over the last few years, Microsoft has adopted an agile release cycle, releasing updates to Office 365 practically on a monthly basis. This is great news for those who love seeing new features added to Excel. It's not so great if you're trying to document the features of these tools in a book.

Our assumption is that Microsoft will continue to add new bells and whistles to Excel at a rapid pace after publication of this book. Thus, you may encounter new functionality not covered in this book. That being said, Excel has a broad feature set, much of which is stable and here to stay. So, even though changes will be made to Excel, they won't be so drastic as to turn this book into a doorstop. The core functionality covered in these chapters will remain relevant—even if the mechanics change a bit.

Conventions Used in This Book

Take a minute to scan this section to learn some of the typographical and organizational conventions that this book uses.

Excel commands

Excel uses a context-sensitive Ribbon system. The words along the top (such as File, Insert, Page Layout, and so on) are known as *tabs*. Click a tab, and the Ribbon displays the commands for the selected tab. Each command has a name, which is (usually) displayed next to or below the icon. The commands are arranged in groups, and the group name appears at the bottom of the Ribbon.

The convention we use is to indicate the tab name, followed by the group name, followed by the command name. So, the command used to toggle word wrap within a cell is indicated as follows:

> Home ➪ Alignment ➪ Wrap Text

You'll learn more about the Ribbon user interface in Chapter 1, "Introducing Excel."

Typographical conventions

Anything that you're supposed to type using the keyboard appears in a **`bold monospaced font`**. Lengthy input usually appears on a separate line. Here's an example:

```
="Part Name: " &VLOOKUP(PartNumber,PartList,2)
```

Names of the keys on your keyboard appear in normal type. When two keys should be pressed simultaneously, they're connected with a plus sign, like this: "Press Ctrl+C to copy the selected cells."

The four "arrow" keys are collectively known as the navigation keys.

Excel built-in worksheet functions appear in monospaced font in uppercase like this: "Note the SUMPRODUCT function used in cell C20."

Mouse conventions

You'll come across some of the following mouse-related terms, which are all standard fare:

Mouse pointer   This is the small graphic figure that moves on-screen when you move your mouse. The mouse pointer is usually an arrow, but it changes shape when you move to certain areas of the screen or when you're performing certain actions.

Point   Move the mouse so that the mouse pointer is on a specific item; for example, "Point to the Save button on the toolbar."

Click   Press the left mouse button once and release it immediately.

Right-click   Press the right mouse button once and release it immediately. The right mouse button is used in Excel to open shortcut menus that are appropriate for whatever is currently selected.

Double-click   Press the left mouse button twice in rapid succession.

Drag   Press the left mouse button and keep it pressed while you move the mouse. Dragging is often used to select a range of cells or to change the size of an object.

For Touchscreen Users

If you happen to be using one of these devices, you probably already know the basic touch gestures.

This book doesn't cover specific touchscreen gestures, but these three guidelines should work most of the time:

- When you read "click," you should tap. Quickly touching and releasing your finger on a button is the same as clicking it with a mouse.
- When you read "double-click," tap twice. Touching twice in rapid succession is equivalent to double-clicking.
- When you read "right-click," press and hold your finger on the item until a menu appears. Tap an item on the pop-up menu to execute the command.

Make sure you enable Touch mode from the Quick Access toolbar. Touch mode increases the spacing between the Ribbon commands, making it less likely that you'll touch the wrong command. If the Touch mode command is not in your Quick Access toolbar, touch the rightmost control and select Touch/Mouse Mode. This command toggles between normal mode and Touch mode.

How This Book Is Organized

Notice that the book is divided into six main parts.

Part I: Getting Started with Excel This part consists of eight chapters that provide background about Excel. These chapters are considered required reading for Excel newcomers, but even experienced users will probably find some new information here.

Part II: Working with Formulas and Functions The chapters in Part II cover everything that you need to know to become proficient with performing calculations in Excel.

Part III: Creating Charts and Other Visualizations The chapters in Part III describe how to create effective charts. In addition, you'll find chapters on the conditional formatting visualization features, Sparkline graphics, and a chapter with lots of tips on integrating graphics into your worksheet.

Part IV: Managing and Analyzing Data Data analysis is the focus of the chapters in Part IV. Here you'll find chapters focusing on data validation, pivot tables, conditional analyses, and more.

Part V: Understanding Power Pivot and Power Query The chapters in Part V take an indepth look at the functionality found in Power Pivot and Power Query. Here you'll discover how to develop powerful reporting solutions with Power Pivot, as well as how to leverage Power Query to automate and steps for cleaning and transforming data.

Part VI: Automating Excel Part VI is for those who want to customize Excel for their own use or who are designing workbooks or add-ins that are to be used by others. It starts with an introduction to recording macros and VBA programming, and then it provides coverage of UserForms, events, and add-ins.

How to Use This Book

This book is obviously not meant to be read cover to cover. Instead, it's a reference book that you can consult when you need help with the following situations:

- You're stuck while trying to do something.
- You need to do something that you've never done before.
- You have some time on your hands, and you're interested in learning something new about Excel.

The index is comprehensive, and each chapter typically focuses on a single broad topic. Don't be discouraged if some of the material is over your head. Most users get by just fine by using only a small subset of Excel's total capabilities. In fact, the 80/20 rule applies here: 80 percent of Excel users use only 20 percent of its features. However, knowing only 20 percent of Excel's features still gives you a lot of power at your fingertips.

What's on the Website

This book contains many examples, and you can download the workbooks for those examples from the Web. The files are arranged in directories that correspond to the chapters.

The URL is www.wiley.com/go/excel2019bible.

Please note that the URL is case sensitive, so use all lowercase letters.

Part I

Getting Started with Excel

The chapters in this part are intended to provide essential background information for working with Excel. Here you'll see how to make use of the basic features that are required for every Excel user. If you've used Excel (or even a different spreadsheet program) in the past, much of this information may seem like review. Even so, it's likely that you'll find quite a few new tricks and techniques in these chapters.

Introducing Excel

This chapter is an introductory overview of Excel 2019. If you're already familiar with a previous version of Excel, reading (or at least skimming) this chapter is still a good idea.

Understanding What Excel Is Used For

Excel is the world's most widely used spreadsheet software and is part of the Microsoft Office suite. Other spreadsheet software is available, but Excel is by far the most popular and has been the world standard for many years.

Much of the appeal of Excel is its versatility. Excel's forte, of course, is performing numerical calculations, but Excel is also useful for nonnumeric applications. Here are just a few uses for Excel:

Crunching numbers Create budgets, tabulate expenses, analyze survey results, and perform just about any type of financial analysis you can think of.

Creating charts Create a variety of highly customizable charts.

Organizing lists Use the row-and-column layout to store lists efficiently.

Manipulating text Clean up and standardize text-based data.

Accessing other data Import data from a variety of sources.

Creating graphical dashboards Summarize a large amount of business information in a concise format.

Creating graphics and diagrams Use shapes and SmartArt to create professional-looking diagrams.

Automating complex tasks Perform a tedious task with a single mouse click with Excel's macro capabilities.

Looking at What's New in Excel 2019

Here's a quick summary of what's new in Excel 2019, relative to Excel 2016. Keep in mind that this book deals only with the desktop version of Excel. The mobile and online versions do not necessarily have the same set of features.

New charts   Two new chart types, Funnel Chart and Map Chart, are available in Excel 2019. See Part III, "Creating Charts and Other Visualizations," for more information on all of the chart types available.

Enhanced AutoComplete   When you start typing a function name, AutoComplete will show you a list of functions that start with what you typed. In Excel 2019, AutoComplete tries to give you a better list. If you type =Day, you no longer just get DAY and DAYS360. Now you also get NETWORKDAYS, TODAY, and many more.

Power Query and Power Pivot   Excel 2019 adds many new minor features including several new connectors, new filter options, and new transform options. See Part V, "Understanding Power Pivot and Power Query," for details on working with these new features.

No CSV warnings   Excel 2019 will no longer warn you that you'll lose features if you save as a CSV file.

Icons   The Insert tab in Excel 2019 contains an Icons control with many premade icons for you to use.

SVG images   In Excel 2019, you can insert Scalable Vector Graphic (SVG) images and even convert them into shapes.

Deselect cells   If you've ever selected multiple cells by holding down the Ctrl key and you accidentally selected too many, you'll appreciate this new feature. Instead of starting over, you can Ctrl+click a selected cell to deselect it.

PivotTable layout   You can save your preferred PivotTable settings as a default layout, and all new PivotTables you create will automatically have those settings.

Understanding Workbooks and Worksheets

You perform the work you do in Excel in a *workbook*. You can have as many *workbooks* open as you need, and each one appears in its own window. By default, Excel workbooks use an `.xlsx` file extension.

> **NOTE**
>
> In old versions of Excel, every workbook opened in a single Excel window. Beginning with Excel 2013, each workbook opens in its own window. This change makes Excel work more like other Office applications and gives you the opportunity to put different workbooks on different monitors more easily.

Each workbook contains one or more worksheets, and each worksheet consists of individual cells. Each cell can contain a number, a formula, or text. A worksheet also has an invisible drawing layer, which holds charts, images, and diagrams. Objects on the drawing layer sit over the top of the cells, but they are not *in* the cells like a number or formula. Each worksheet in a workbook is accessible by clicking the tab at the bottom of the workbook window. In addition, a workbook can store chart sheets: a chart sheet displays a single chart and is accessible by clicking a tab.

Newcomers to Excel are often intimidated by all of the different elements that appear within Excel's window. After you become familiar with the various parts, it all starts to make sense and you'll feel right at home.

Figure 1.1 shows you the more important bits and pieces of Excel. As you look at the figure, refer to Table 1.1 for a brief explanation of the items shown.

FIGURE 1.1

The Excel screen has many useful elements that you will use often.

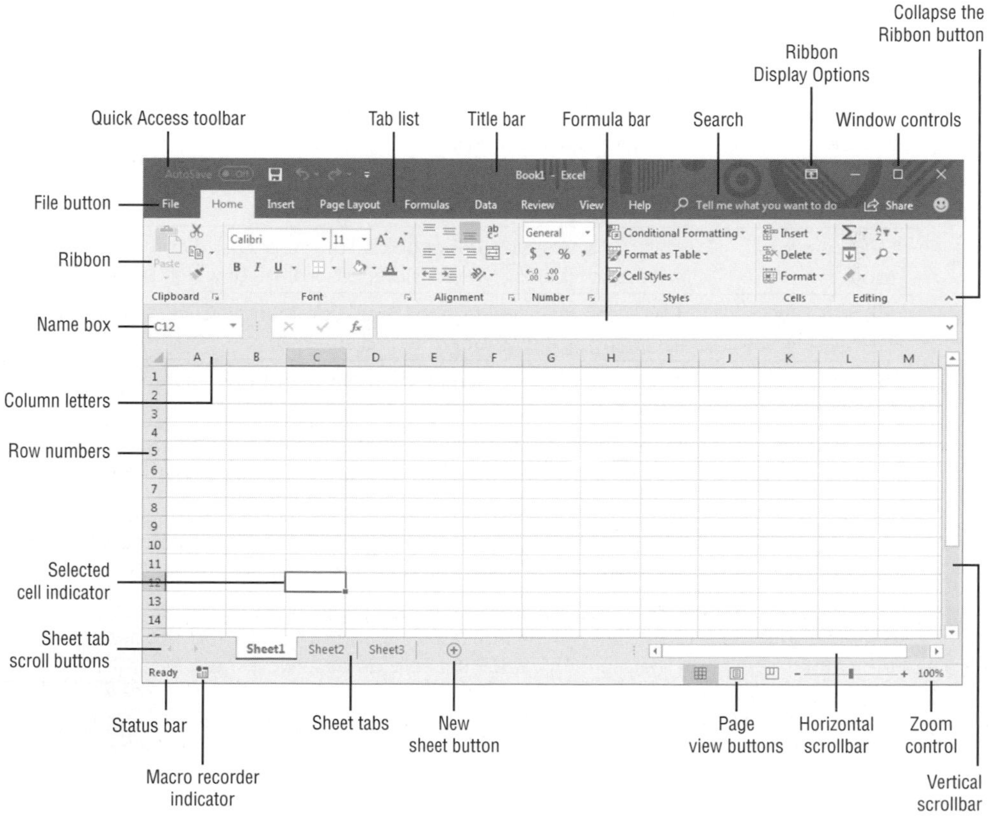

TABLE 1.1 **Parts of the Excel Screen That You Need to Know**

Name	Description
Collapse the Ribbon button	Click this button to hide the Ribbon temporarily. Double-click any Ribbon tab to make the Ribbon remain visible. Ctrl+F1 is the shortcut key that does the same task.
Column letters	Letters range from A to XFD—one for each of the 16,384 columns in the worksheet. You can click a column heading to select an entire column or click between the columns to change the column width.
File button	Click this button to open Backstage view, which contains many options for working with your document (including printing) and setting Excel options.
Formula bar	When you enter information or formulas into a cell, it appears in this bar.
Horizontal scrollbar	Use this tool to scroll the sheet horizontally.
Macro recorder indicator	Click to start recording a Visual Basic for Applications (VBA) macro. The icon changes while your actions are being recorded. Click again to stop recording.
Name box	This box displays the active cell address or the name of the selected cell, range, or object.
New Sheet button	Add a new worksheet by clicking the New Sheet button (which is displayed after the last sheet tab).
Page View buttons	Click these buttons to change the way the worksheet is displayed.
Quick Access toolbar	This customizable toolbar holds commonly used commands. The Quick Access toolbar is always visible, regardless of which tab is selected.
Ribbon	This is the main location for Excel commands. Clicking an item in the tab list changes the Ribbon that is displayed.
Ribbon Display Options	A drop-down control that offers three options related to displaying the Ribbon.
Row numbers	Numbers range from 1 to 1,048,576—one for each row in the worksheet. You can click a row number to select an entire row or click between the row numbers to change the row height.
Search	The Search control is a magnifying glass with the caption "Tell me what you want to do." Use this control to identify commands or have Excel issue a command automatically.
Selected cell indicator	This dark outline indicates the currently selected cell or range of cells. (There are 17,179,869,184 cells on each worksheet.)

Name	Description
Sheet tabs	Each of these notebook-like tabs represents a different sheet in the workbook. A workbook can have any number of sheets, and each sheet has its name displayed in a sheet tab.
Sheet tab scroll buttons	Use these buttons to scroll the sheet tabs to display tabs that aren't visible. You can also right-click to get a list of sheets.
Status bar	This bar displays various messages as well as the status of the Num Lock, Caps Lock, and Scroll Lock keys on your keyboard. It also shows summary information about the range of cells selected. Right-click the status bar to change the information displayed.
Tab list	Use these commands to display a different Ribbon, similar to a menu.
Title bar	This displays the name of the program and the name of the current workbook. It also holds the Quick Access toolbar (on the left) and some control buttons that you can use to modify the window (on the right).
Vertical scrollbar	Use this to scroll the sheet vertically.
Window controls	These are three controls for minimizing the current window, maximizing or restoring the current window, and closing the current window, which are common to virtually all Windows applications.
Zoom control	Use this to zoom your worksheet in and out.

Moving around a Worksheet

This section describes various ways to navigate the cells in a worksheet.

Every worksheet consists of rows (numbered 1 through 1,048,576) and columns (labeled A through XFD). Column labeling works like this: After column Z comes column AA, which is followed by AB, AC, and so on. After column AZ comes BA, BB, and so on. After column ZZ is AAA, AAB, and so on.

The intersection of a row and a column is a single cell, and each cell has a unique address made up of its column letter and row number. For example, the address of the upper-left cell is A1. The address of the cell at the lower right of a worksheet is XFD1048576.

At any given time, one cell is the active cell. The active cell is the cell that accepts keyboard input, and its contents can be edited. You can identify the active cell by its darker border, as shown in Figure 1.2. If more than one cell is selected, the dark border surrounds the entire selection, and the active cell is the light-colored cell within the border. Its address appears in the Name box. Depending on the technique that you use to navigate through a workbook, you may or may not change the active cell when you navigate.

FIGURE 1.2

The active cell is the one with the dark border—in this case, cell C8.

◢	A	B	C	D
1		This Year	Last Year	
2	January	8,580	7,815	
3	February	8,715	8,190	
4	March	8,830	9,318	
5	April	7,620	7,779	
6	May	8,950	8,531	
7	June	7,798	9,150	
8	July	8,156	8,360	
9				
10				
11				

The row and column headings of the active cell appear in a different color to make it easier to identify the row and column of the active cell.

> **NOTE**
>
> Excel 2019 is also available for devices that use a touch interface. This book assumes you have a traditional keyboard and mouse, so it doesn't cover the touch-related commands. Note that the drop-down control in the Quick Access toolbar has a Touch/Mouse Mode command. In Touch mode, the Ribbon and Quick Access toolbar icons are placed further apart.

Navigating with your keyboard

Not surprisingly, you can use the standard navigational keys on your keyboard to move around a worksheet. These keys work just as you'd expect: the down arrow moves the active cell down one row, the right arrow moves it one column to the right, and so on. PgUp and PgDn move the active cell up or down one full window. (The actual number of rows moved depends on the number of rows displayed in the window.)

> **TIP**
>
> You can use the keyboard to scroll through the worksheet without changing the active cell by turning on Scroll Lock, which is useful if you need to view another area of your worksheet and then quickly return to your original location. Just press Scroll Lock and use the navigation keys to scroll through the worksheet. When you want to return to the original position (the active cell), press Ctrl+Backspace and then press Scroll Lock again to turn it off. When Scroll Lock is turned on, Excel displays Scroll Lock in the status bar at the bottom of the window.

The Num Lock key on your keyboard controls the way the keys on the numeric keypad behave. When Num Lock is on, the keys on your numeric keypad generate numbers. Many keyboards have a separate set of navigation (arrow) keys located to the left of the numeric keypad. The state of the Num Lock key doesn't affect these keys.

Table 1.2 summarizes all the worksheet movement keys available in Excel.

TABLE 1.2 Excel Worksheet Movement Keys

Key	Action
Up arrow (↑)	Moves the active cell up one row
Down arrow (↓) or Enter	Moves the active cell down one row
Left arrow (←) or Shift+Tab	Moves the active cell one column to the left
Right arrow (→) or Tab	Moves the active cell one column to the right
PgUp	Moves the active cell up one screen
PgDn	Moves the active cell down one screen
Alt+PgDn	Moves the active cell right one screen
Alt+PgUp	Moves the active cell left one screen
Ctrl+Backspace	Scrolls the screen so that the active cell is visible
↑*	Scrolls the screen up one row (active cell does not change)
↓*	Scrolls the screen down one row (active cell does not change)
←*	Scrolls the screen left one column (active cell does not change)
→*	Scrolls the screen right one column (active cell does not change)

* With Scroll Lock on

Navigating with your mouse

To change the active cell by using the mouse, just click another cell and it becomes the active cell. If the cell that you want to activate isn't visible in the workbook window, you can use the scrollbars to scroll the window in any direction. To scroll one cell, click either of the arrows on the scrollbar. To scroll by a complete screen, click either side of the scrollbar's scroll box. To scroll faster, drag the scroll box or right-click anywhere on the scrollbar for a menu of shortcuts.

TIP

If your mouse has a wheel, you can use it to scroll vertically. Also, if you click the wheel and move the mouse in any direction, the worksheet scrolls automatically in that direction. The more you move the mouse, the faster you scroll.

Press Ctrl while you use the mouse wheel to zoom the worksheet. If you prefer to use the mouse wheel to zoom the worksheet without pressing Ctrl, choose File ➪ Options and select the Advanced section. Place a check mark next to the Zoom on Roll with IntelliMouse check box.

Using the scrollbars or scrolling with your mouse doesn't change the active cell. It simply scrolls the worksheet. To change the active cell, you must click a new cell after scrolling.

Using the Ribbon

In Office 2007, Microsoft debuted the *Ribbon*, a collection of icons at the top of the screen that replaced the traditional menus and toolbars. The words above the icons are known as *tabs*: the Home tab, the Insert tab, and so on. Most users find that the Ribbon is easier to use than the old menu system; it can also be customized to make it even easier to use. (See Chapter 8, "Customizing the Excel User Interface.")

The Ribbon can be either hidden or visible—it's your choice. To toggle the Ribbon's visibility, press Ctrl+F1 (or double-click a tab at the top). If the Ribbon is hidden, it temporarily appears when you click a tab and hides itself when you click in the worksheet. The title bar has a control named Ribbon Display Options (next to the Minimize button). Click the control, and choose one of three Ribbon options: Auto-Hide Ribbon, Show Tabs, or Show Tabs and Commands.

Ribbon tabs

The commands available in the Ribbon vary, depending upon which tab is selected. The Ribbon is arranged into groups of related commands. Here's a quick overview of Excel's tabs:

Home You'll probably spend most of your time with the Home tab selected. This tab contains the basic Clipboard commands, formatting commands, style commands, commands to insert and delete rows or columns, plus an assortment of worksheet editing commands.

Insert Select this tab when you need to insert something into a worksheet—a table, a diagram, a chart, a symbol, and so on.

Page Layout This tab contains commands that affect the overall appearance of your worksheet, including some settings that deal with printing.

Formulas Use this tab to insert a formula, name a cell or a range, access the formula auditing tools, or control the way Excel performs calculations.

Data Excel's data-related commands are on this tab, including data validation commands.

Review This tab contains tools to check spelling, translate words, add comments, or protect sheets.

View The View tab contains commands that control various aspects of how a sheet is viewed. Some commands on this tab are also available in the status bar.

Developer This tab isn't visible by default. It contains commands that are useful for programmers. To display the Developer tab, choose File ➪ Options and then select Customize

Ribbon. In the Customize the Ribbon section on the right, make sure that Main Tabs is selected in the drop-down control and place a check mark next to Developer.

Help   This tab provides ways to get help, make suggestions, and access other aspects of Microsoft's community.

Add-Ins   This tab is visible only if you loaded an older workbook or add-in that customizes the menu or toolbars. Because menus and toolbars are no longer available in Excel 2019, these user interface customizations appear on the Add-Ins tab.

The preceding list contains the standard Ribbon tabs. Excel may display additional Ribbon tabs based on what's selected or resulting from add-ins that are installed.

> **NOTE**
>
> Although the File button shares space with the tabs, it's not actually a tab. Clicking the File button displays a different screen (known as Backstage view), where you perform actions with your documents. This screen has commands along the left side. To exit the Backstage view, click the back-arrow button in the upper-left corner.

The appearance of the commands on the Ribbon varies, depending on the width of the Excel window. When the Excel window is too narrow to display everything, the commands adapt; some of them might seem to be missing, but the commands are still available. Figure 1.3 shows the Home tab of the Ribbon with all controls fully visible. Figure 1.4 shows the Ribbon when Excel's window is made narrower. Notice that some of the descriptive text is gone, but the icons remain. Figure 1.5 shows the extreme case when the window is made very narrow. Some groups display a single icon; however, if you click the icon, all the group commands are available to you.

FIGURE 1.3

The Home tab of the Ribbon

FIGURE 1.4

The Home tab when Excel's window is made narrower

FIGURE 1.5

The Home tab when Excel's window is made very narrow

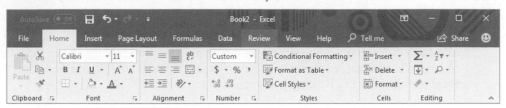

Contextual tabs

In addition to the standard tabs, Excel includes contextual tabs. Whenever an object (such as a chart, a table, or a SmartArt diagram) is selected, specific tools for working with that object are made available in the Ribbon.

Figure 1.6 shows the contextual tabs that appear when a chart is selected. In this case, it has two contextual tabs: Design and Format. Notice that the contextual tabs contain a description (Chart Tools) in Excel's title bar. When contextual tabs appear, you can, of course, continue to use all of the other tabs.

FIGURE 1.6

When you select an object, contextual tabs contain tools for working with that object.

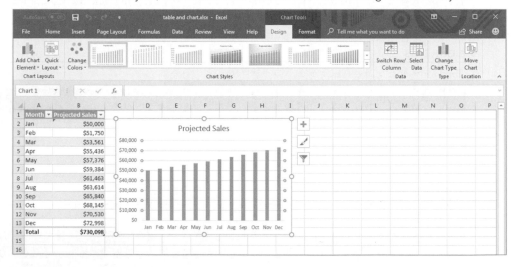

Types of commands on the Ribbon

When you hover your mouse pointer over a Ribbon command, you'll see a ScreenTip that contains the command's name and a brief description. For the most part, the commands in the Ribbon work just as you would expect. You'll find several different styles of commands on the Ribbon.

Simple buttons   Click the button, and it does its thing. An example of a simple button is the Increase Font Size button in the Font group of the Home tab. Some buttons perform the action immediately; others display a dialog box so that you can enter additional information. Button controls may or may not be accompanied by a descriptive label.

Toggle buttons   A toggle button is clickable and conveys some type of information by displaying two different colors. An example is the Bold button in the Font group of the Home tab. If the active cell isn't bold, the Bold button displays in its normal color. If the active cell is already bold, the Bold button displays a different background color. If you click the Bold button, it toggles the Bold attribute for the selection.

Simple drop-downs   If the Ribbon command has a small down arrow, the command is a drop-down. Click it, and additional commands appear below it. An example of a simple drop-down is the Conditional Formatting command in the Styles group of the Home tab. When you click this control, you see several options related to conditional formatting.

Split buttons   A split button control combines a one-click button with a drop-down. If you click the button part, the command is executed. If you click the drop-down part (a down arrow), you choose from a list of related commands. An example of a split button is the Merge & Center command in the Alignment group of the Home tab (see Figure 1.7). Clicking the left part of this control merges and centers text in the selected cells. If you click the arrow part of the control (on the right), you get a list of commands related to merging cells.

FIGURE 1.7

The Merge & Center command is a split button control.

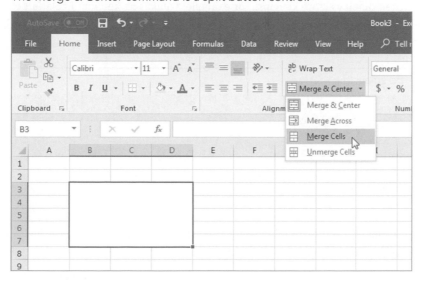

Check boxes   A check box control turns something on or off. An example is the Gridlines control in the Show group of the View tab. When the Gridlines check box is checked, the sheet displays gridlines. When the control isn't checked, the gridlines don't appear.

Spin buttons   Excel's Ribbon has only one spin button control: the Scale To Fit group of the Page Layout tab. Click the top part of the spin button to increase the value; click the bottom part of the spin button to decrease the value.

Some of the Ribbon groups contain a small icon in the bottom-right corner, known as a *dialog box launcher.* For example, if you examine the groups in the Home tab, you find dialog box launchers for the Clipboard, Font, Alignment, and Number groups—but not the Styles, Cells, and Editing groups. Click the icon, and Excel displays a dialog box or task pane. The dialog box launchers often provide options that aren't available in the Ribbon.

Accessing the Ribbon by using your keyboard

At first glance, you may think that the Ribbon is completely mouse centric. After all, the commands don't display the traditional underlined letter to indicate the Alt+keystrokes. But in fact, the Ribbon is very keyboard friendly. The trick is to press the Alt key to display the pop-up keytips. Each Ribbon control has a letter (or series of letters) that you type to issue the command.

> **TIP**
> You don't need to hold down the Alt key while you type keytip letters.

Figure 1.8 shows how the Home tab looks after you press the Alt key to display the keytips and then the H key to display the keytips for the Home tab. If you press one of the keytips, the screen then displays more keytips. For example, to use the keyboard to align the cell contents to the left, press Alt, followed by H (for Home), and then AL (for Align Left).

FIGURE 1.8

Pressing Alt displays the keytips.

Nobody will memorize all of these keys, but if you're a keyboard fan, it takes just a few times before you memorize the keystrokes required for commands that you use frequently.

After you press Alt, you can also use the left- and right-arrow keys to scroll through the tabs. When you reach the proper tab, press the down arrow to enter the Ribbon. Then use left- and right-arrow keys to scroll through the Ribbon commands. When you reach the command you need, press Enter to execute it. This method isn't as efficient as using the keytips, but it's a quick way to take a look at the commands available.

TIP

Often, you'll want to repeat a particular command. Excel provides a way to simplify that. For example, if you apply a particular style to a cell (by choosing Home ⇨ Styles ⇨ Cell Styles), you can activate another cell and press Ctrl+Y (or F4) to repeat the command.

Searching for Commands

Excel 2019 has a Search box for finding commands. This box has a magnifying glass icon with the caption "Tell me what you want to do." It is situated to the right of the Ribbon tabs. If you're unsure of where to find a command, try typing it in the box. For example, if you want to insert a hyperlink on the current worksheet, activate the box and type **hyperlink**. Excel displays a list of potentially relevant commands and some help topics. If you see the command you want, click it (or use the arrow keys and press Enter). The command is executed. In this example, the Link split button is the top hit, which you normally find at Insert ⇨ Links ⇨ Link.

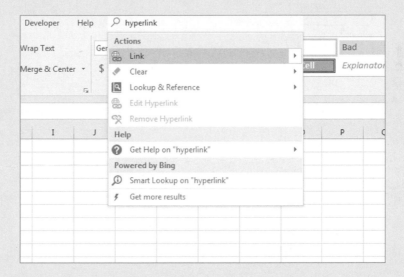

This feature may be helpful for newcomers who are still getting familiar with the Ribbon commands.

Using Shortcut Menus

In addition to the Ribbon, Excel features many shortcut menus, which you access by right-clicking just about anything within Excel. Shortcut menus don't contain every relevant command, just those that are most commonly used for whatever is selected.

As an example, Figure 1.9 shows the shortcut menu that appears when you right-click a cell in a table. The shortcut menu appears at the mouse-pointer position, which makes selecting a command fast and efficient. The shortcut menu that appears depends on what you're doing at the time. For example, if you're working with a chart, the shortcut menu contains commands that are pertinent to the selected chart element.

FIGURE 1.9

Right-click to display a shortcut menu of commands you're most likely to use.

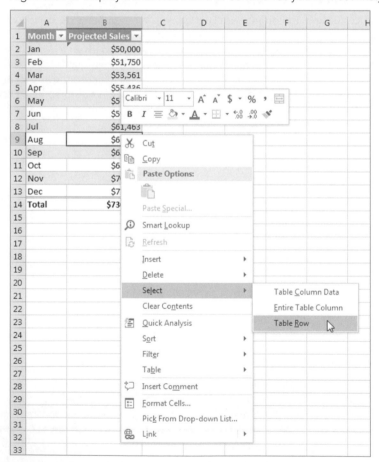

The box above the shortcut menu—the Mini toolbar—contains commonly used tools from the Home tab. The Mini toolbar was designed to reduce the distance your mouse has to travel around the screen. Just right-click, and common formatting tools are within an inch of your mouse pointer. The Mini toolbar is particularly useful when a tab other than Home is displayed. If you use a tool on the Mini toolbar, the toolbar remains displayed in case you want to perform other formatting on the selection.

Customizing Your Quick Access Toolbar

The Ribbon is fairly efficient, but many users prefer to have certain commands available at all times without having to click a tab. The solution is to customize your Quick Access toolbar. Typically, the Quick Access toolbar appears on the left side of the title bar, above the Ribbon. Alternatively, you can display the Quick Access toolbar below the Ribbon; just right-click the Quick Access toolbar and choose Show Quick Access Toolbar Below The Ribbon.

Displaying the Quick Access toolbar below the Ribbon provides a bit more room for icons, but it also means that you see one less row of your worksheet.

By default, the Quick Access toolbar contains four tools: AutoSave, Save, Undo, and Redo. You can customize the Quick Access toolbar by adding other commands that you use often or removing the default controls. To add a command from the Ribbon to your Quick Access toolbar, right-click the command and choose Add to Quick Access Toolbar. If you click the down arrow to the right of the Quick Access toolbar, you see a drop-down menu with some additional commands that you might want to place in your Quick Access toolbar.

Excel has quite a few commands (mostly obscure ones) that aren't available on the Ribbon. In most cases, the only way to access these commands is to add them to your Quick Access toolbar. Right-click the Quick Access toolbar, and choose Customize Quick Access Toolbar. You see the Excel Options dialog box, as shown in Figure 1.10. This section of the Excel Options dialog box is your one-stop shop for Quick Access toolbar customization.

 See Chapter 8 for more information about customizing your Quick Access toolbar.

Changing Your Mind

You can reverse almost every action in Excel by using the Undo command, located on the Quick Access toolbar. Click Undo (or press Ctrl+Z) after issuing a command in error, and it's as if you never issued the command. You can reverse the effects of the past 100 actions that you performed.

If you click the arrow on the right side of the Undo button, you see a list of the actions that you can reverse. Click an item in that list to undo that action and all the subsequent actions you performed.

The Redo button, also on the Quick Access toolbar, performs the opposite of the Undo button: Redo reissues commands that have been undone. If nothing has been undone, this command is not available.

FIGURE 1.10

Add new icons to your Quick Access toolbar by using the Quick Access Toolbar section of the Excel Options dialog box.

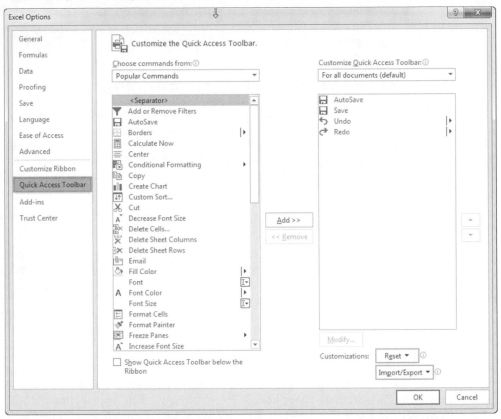

> **CAUTION**
>
> You can't reverse every action, however. Generally, anything that you do using the File button can't be undone. For example, if you save a file and realize that you've overwritten a good copy with a bad one, Undo can't save the day. You're just out of luck unless you have a backup of the file. Also, changes made by a macro can't be undone. In fact, executing a macro that changes the workbook clears the Undo list.

Working with Dialog Boxes

Many Excel commands display a dialog box, which is simply a way of getting more information from you. For example, if you choose Review ⇨ Protect ⇨ Protect Sheet, Excel can't carry out the command until you tell it what parts of the sheet you want to protect. Therefore, it displays the Protect Sheet dialog box, shown in Figure 1.11.

FIGURE 1.11

Excel uses a dialog box to get additional information about a command.

Excel dialog boxes vary in the way they work. You'll find two types of dialog boxes.

Typical dialog box   A modal dialog box takes the focus away from the spreadsheet. When this type of dialog box is displayed, you can't do anything in the worksheet until you dismiss the dialog box. Clicking OK performs the specified actions, and clicking Cancel (or pressing Esc) closes the dialog box without taking any action. Most Excel dialog boxes are this type.

Stay-on-top dialog box   A modeless dialog box works in a manner similar to a toolbar. When a modeless dialog box is displayed, you can continue working in Excel, and the dialog box remains open. Changes made in a modeless dialog box take effect immediately. An example of a modeless dialog box is the Find and Replace dialog box. You can leave this dialog box open while you continue to use your worksheet. A modeless dialog box has a Close button but no OK button.

Most people find working with dialog boxes to be quite straightforward and natural. If you've used other programs, you'll feel right at home. You can manipulate the controls either with your mouse or directly from the keyboard.

Navigating dialog boxes

Navigating dialog boxes is generally easy—you simply click the control that you want to activate.

Although dialog boxes were designed with mouse users in mind, you can also use the keyboard. Every dialog box control has text associated with it, and this text always has one underlined letter (called a *hot key* or an *accelerator key*). You can access the control from the keyboard by pressing Alt and then the underlined letter. You can also press Tab to cycle through all of the controls on a dialog box. Pressing Shift+Tab cycles through the controls in reverse order.

> **TIP**
>
> When a control that accepts text entry is selected, a cursor appears in the control. For drop-down and spin button controls, the default text is highlighted. Use Alt+down arrow to drop the list down or up, and use the down arrows to change the spin button value. For all other controls, a dotted outline surrounds the control to let you know that it's selected. You can use the spacebar to activate a selected control.

Using tabbed dialog boxes

Several Excel dialog boxes are "tabbed" dialog boxes; that is, they include notebook-like tabs, each of which is associated with a different panel.

When you select a tab, the dialog box changes to display a new panel containing a new set of controls. The Format Cells dialog box, shown in Figure 1.12, is a good example. It has six tabs, which makes it functionally equivalent to six different dialog boxes.

Tabbed dialog boxes are quite convenient because you can make several changes in a single dialog box. After you make all of your setting changes, click OK or press Enter.

> **TIP**
>
> To select a tab by using the keyboard, press Ctrl+PgUp or Ctrl+PgDn, or simply press the first letter of the tab that you want to activate.

Using Task Panes

Another user interface element is the *task pane*. Task panes appear automatically in response to several commands. For example, to work with a picture that you've inserted, right-click the image and choose Format Picture. Excel responds by displaying the Format Picture task pane, as shown in Figure 1.13. The task pane is similar to a dialog box except that you can keep it visible as long as you like.

FIGURE 1.12

Use the dialog box tabs to select different functional areas of the dialog box.

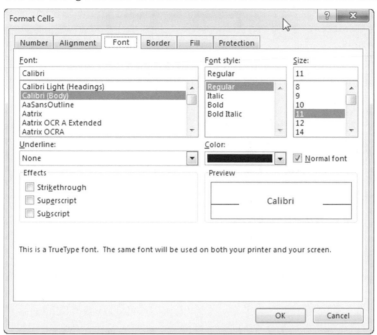

Many of the task panes are complex. The Format Picture task pane has four icons along the top. Clicking an icon changes the command lists displayed next. Click an item in a command list, and it expands to show the options.

There's no OK button in a task pane. When you're finished using a task pane, click the Close button (X) in the upper-right corner.

By default, a task pane is docked on the right side of the Excel window, but you can move it anywhere you like by clicking its title bar and dragging. Excel remembers the last position, so the next time you use that task pane, it will be right where you left it. To re-dock the task pane, double-click the task pane's title bar.

TIP

If you prefer to use your keyboard to work within a task pane, you may find that common dialog box keys such as Tab, spacebar, the arrow keys, and Alt key combinations don't seem to work. The trick is to press F6. After doing so, you'll find that the task pane works well using only a keyboard. For example, use the Tab key to activate a section title and then press Enter to expand the section.

FIGURE 1.13

The Format Picture task pane, docked on the right side of the window

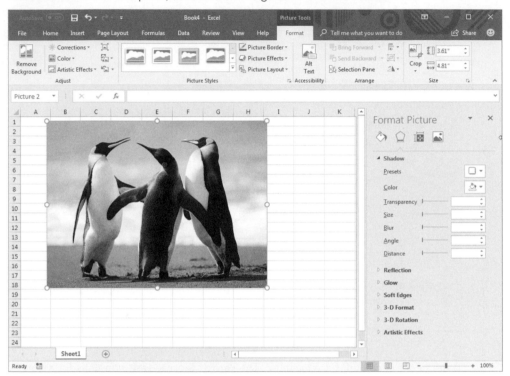

Creating Your First Excel Workbook

This section presents an introductory hands-on session with Excel. If you haven't used Excel, you may want to follow along on your computer to get a feel for how this software works.

In this example, you create a simple monthly sales projection table plus a chart that depicts the data.

Getting started on your worksheet

Start Excel and make sure you have an empty workbook displayed. To create a new, blank workbook, press Ctrl+N (the shortcut key for File ➪ New ➪ Blank Workbook).

The sales projection will consist of two columns of information. Column A will contain the month names, and column B will store the projected sales numbers. You start by entering some descriptive titles into the worksheet. Here's how to begin:

1. Select cell A1 (the upper-left cell in the worksheet) by using the navigation (arrow) keys, if necessary. The Name box displays the cell's address.

2. Type **Month** into cell A1 and press Enter. Depending on your setup, either Excel moves the selection to a different cell or the pointer remains in cell A1.

3. Select cell B1, type **Projected Sales**, and press Enter. The text extends beyond the cell width, but don't worry about that for now.

Filling in the month names

In this step, you enter the month names in column A.

1. **Select cell A2 and type Jan (an abbreviation for January).** At this point, you can enter the other month name abbreviations manually, or you can let Excel do some of the work by taking advantage of the AutoFill feature.

2. **Make sure that cell A2 is selected.** Notice that the active cell is displayed with a heavy outline. At the bottom-right corner of the outline, you'll see a small square known as the *fill handle*. Move your mouse pointer over the fill handle, click, and drag down until you've highlighted from cell A2 down to cell A13.

3. **Release the mouse button, and Excel automatically fills in the month names.**

Your worksheet should resemble the one shown in Figure 1.14.

FIGURE 1.14

Your worksheet after you've entered the column headings and month names

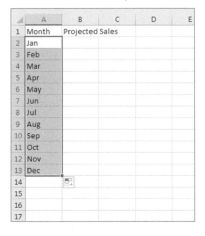

Entering the sales data

Next, you provide the sales projection numbers in column B. Assume that January's sales are projected to be $50,000 and that sales will increase by 3.5 percent in each subsequent month.

1. **Select cell B2 and type** `50000`, **the projected sales for January.** You could type a dollar sign and comma to make the number more legible, but you do the number formatting a bit later.

2. **To enter a formula to calculate the projected sales for February, move to cell B3 and type the following:**

   =B2*103.5%

   When you press Enter, the cell displays `51750`. The formula returns the contents of cell B2, multiplied by 103.5%. In other words, February sales are projected to be 103.5% of the January sales—a 3.5% increase.

3. **The projected sales for subsequent months use a similar formula, but rather than retype the formula for each cell in column B, take advantage of the AutoFill feature.** Make sure that cell B3 is selected. Click the cell's fill handle, drag down to cell B13, and release the mouse button.

At this point, your worksheet should resemble the one shown in Figure 1.15. Keep in mind that, except for cell B2, the values in column B are calculated with formulas. To demonstrate, try changing the projected sales value for the initial month, January (in cell B2). You'll find that the formulas recalculate and return different values. All of these formulas depend on the initial value in cell B2.

FIGURE 1.15

Your worksheet after you've created the formulas

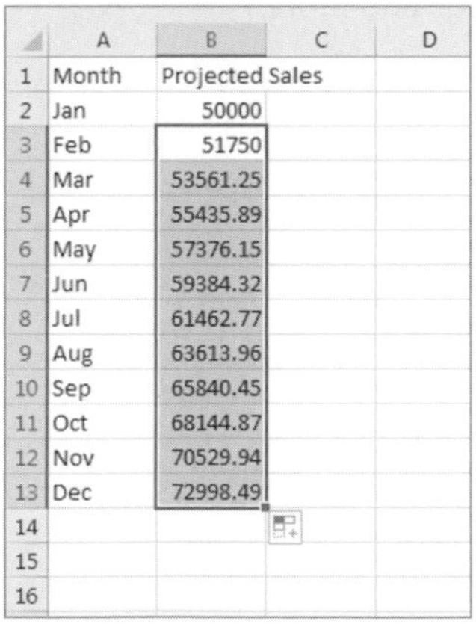

	A	B	C	D
1	Month	Projected Sales		
2	Jan	50000		
3	Feb	51750		
4	Mar	53561.25		
5	Apr	55435.89		
6	May	57376.15		
7	Jun	59384.32		
8	Jul	61462.77		
9	Aug	63613.96		
10	Sep	65840.45		
11	Oct	68144.87		
12	Nov	70529.94		
13	Dec	72998.49		
14				
15				
16				

Formatting the numbers

The values in the worksheet are difficult to read because they aren't formatted. In this step, you apply a number format to make the numbers easier to read and more consistent in appearance.

1. **Select the numbers by clicking cell B2 and dragging down to cell B13.** Don't drag the fill handle this time, though, because you're selecting cells, not filling a range.

2. **Access the Ribbon and choose Home.** In the Number group, click the drop-down Number Format control (it initially displays General), and select Currency from the list. The numbers now display with a currency symbol and two decimal places. That's much better, but the decimal places aren't necessary for this type of projection.

3. **Make sure that the range B2:B13 is selected, choose Home ⇨ Number, and click the Decrease Decimal button.** One of the decimal places disappears. Click that button a second time, and the values are displayed with no decimal places.

Making your worksheet look a bit fancier

At this point, you have a functional worksheet, but it could use some help in the appearance department. Converting this range to an "official" (and attractive) Excel table is a snap.

1. **Activate any cell within the range A1:B13.**

2. **Choose Insert ⇨ Tables ⇨ Table.** Excel displays the Create Table dialog box to make sure that it guessed the range properly.

3. **Click OK to close the Create Table dialog box.** Excel applies its default table formatting and displays its Table Tools ⇨ Design contextual tab.

Your worksheet should look like Figure 1.16.

FIGURE 1.16

Your worksheet after you've converted the range to a table

	A	B	C
1	Month	Projected Sales	
2	Jan	$50,000	
3	Feb	$51,750	
4	Mar	$53,561	
5	Apr	$55,436	
6	May	$57,376	
7	Jun	$59,384	
8	Jul	$61,463	
9	Aug	$63,614	
10	Sep	$65,840	
11	Oct	$68,145	
12	Nov	$70,530	
13	Dec	$72,998	
14			
15			

If you don't like the default table style, just select another one from the Table Tools ⇨ Design ⇨ Table Styles group. Notice that you can get a preview of different table styles by moving your mouse over the Ribbon. When you find one you like, click it, and the style will be applied to your table.

See Chapter 4, "Working with Excel Ranges and Tables," for more information on Excel tables.

Summing the values

The worksheet displays the monthly projected sales, but what about the total projected sales for the year? Because this range is a table, it's simple.

1. **Activate any cell in the table.**
2. **Choose Table Tools ⇨ Design ⇨ Table Style Options ⇨ Total Row.** Excel automatically adds a new row to the bottom of your table, including a formula that calculates the total of the Projected Sales column.
3. **If you'd prefer to see a different summary formula (for example, average), click cell B14 and choose a different summary formula from the drop-down list.**

Creating a chart

How about a chart that shows the projected sales for each month?

1. **Activate any cell in the table.**
2. **Choose Insert ⇨ Charts ⇨ Recommended Charts.** Excel displays some suggested chart type options.
3. **In the Insert Chart dialog box, click the second recommended chart (a column chart), and click OK.** Excel inserts the chart in the center of the window. To move the chart to another location, click its border and drag it.
4. **Click the chart and choose a style using the Chart Tools ⇨ Design ⇨ Chart Styles options.**

Figure 1.17 shows the worksheet with a column chart. Your chart may look different, depending on the chart style you selected.

 This workbook is available on this book's website at www.wiley.com/go/excel2019bible. The filename is table and chart.xlsx.

Printing your worksheet

Printing your worksheet is easy (assuming that you have a printer attached and that it works properly).

1. **Make sure that the chart isn't selected.** If a chart is selected, the chart will print on a page by itself. To deselect the chart, just press Esc or click any cell.
2. **To make use of Excel's handy Page Layout view, click the Page Layout button on the right side of the status bar.** Excel displays the worksheet page by page so that you can easily see how your printed output will look. In Page Layout view, you can tell immediately whether the chart is too wide to fit on one page. If the chart is too

wide, click and drag a corner of the chart to resize it or just move the chart below the table of numbers.

FIGURE 1.17

The table and chart

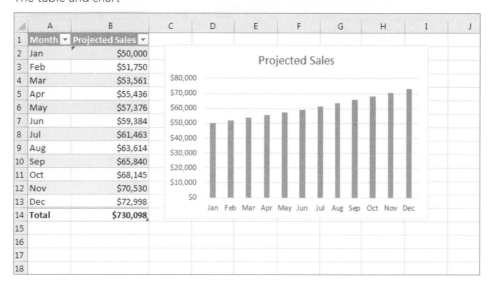

3. **When you're ready to print, choose File ⇨ Print.** At this point, you can change some print settings. For example, you can choose to print in landscape rather than portrait orientation. Make the change, and you see the result in the preview window.

4. **When you're satisfied, click the large Print button in the upper-left corner.** The page is printed, and you're returned to your workbook.

Saving your workbook

Until now, everything that you've done has occurred in your computer's memory. If the power should fail, all may be lost—unless Excel's AutoRecover feature happened to kick in. It's time to save your work to a file on your hard drive.

1. **Click the Save button on the Quick Access toolbar.** (This button looks like an old-fashioned floppy disk, popular in the previous century.) Because the workbook hasn't been saved yet and still has its default name, Excel responds with a Backstage screen that lets you choose the location for the workbook file. The Backstage screen lets you save the file to an online location or to your local computer.

2. **Click Browse.** Excel displays the Save As dialog box.

3. **In the File Name field, enter a name (such as `Monthly Sales Projection`).** If you like, you can specify a different location.
4. **Click Save or press Enter.** Excel saves the workbook as a file. The workbook remains open so that you can work with it some more.

> **NOTE**
> By default, Excel saves a backup copy of your work automatically every 10 minutes. To adjust the AutoRecover setting (or turn it off), choose File ⇨ Options and click the Save tab of the Excel Options dialog box. However, you should never rely on Excel's AutoRecover feature. Saving your work frequently is a good idea.

If you've followed along, you probably have realized that creating this workbook was not difficult. But, of course, you've barely scratched the surface of Excel. The remainder of this book covers these tasks (and many, many more) in much greater detail.

CHAPTER

2

Entering and Editing Worksheet Data

IN THIS CHAPTER

Understanding the types of data you can use

Entering text and values into your worksheets

Entering dates and times into your worksheets

Modifying and editing information

Using built-in and custom number formats

This chapter describes what you need to know about entering and modifying data in your worksheets. As you'll see, Excel doesn't treat all data equally. Therefore, you need to learn about the various types of data you can use in an Excel worksheet.

Exploring Data Types

An Excel workbook file can hold any number of worksheets, and each worksheet is made up of more than 17 billion cells. A cell can hold any of four basic types of data.

- A numeric value
- Text
- A formula
- An error

A worksheet can also hold charts, diagrams, pictures, buttons, and other objects. These objects aren't contained in cells. Instead, they reside on the worksheet's drawing layer, which is an invisible layer on top of each worksheet.

 Error values are discussed throughout Part II, "Working with Formulas and Functions."

Numeric values

Numeric values represent a quantity of some type: sales amounts, number of employees, atomic weights, test scores, and so on. Values also can be dates (Feb 26, 2019) or times (such as 3:24 AM).

Excel can display values in many different formats. In the "Applying Number Formatting" section later in this chapter, you'll see how different format options can affect the display of numeric values.

Excel's Numeric Limitations

You may be curious about the types of values Excel can handle. In other words, how large can a number be? How accurate are large numbers?

Excel's numbers are precise up to 15 digits. For example, if you enter a large value, such as 123,456,789,123,456,789 (18 digits), Excel actually stores it with only 15 digits of precision. This 18-digit number displays as 123,456,789,123,456,000. This precision may seem quite limiting, but in practice, it rarely causes any problems.

One situation in which the 15-digit precision can cause a problem is when entering credit card numbers. Most credit card numbers are 16 digits, but Excel can handle only 15 digits, so it substitutes a zero for the last credit card digit. Even worse, you may not even realize that Excel made the card number invalid. The solution? Enter the credit card numbers as text. The easiest way is to preformat the cell as Text. (Choose Home ⇨ Number, and choose Text from the Number Format drop-down list.) Or you can precede the credit card number with an apostrophe. Either method prevents Excel from interpreting the entry as a number.

Here are some of Excel's other numeric limits:

Largest positive number: 9.9E+307

Smallest negative number: −9.9E+307

Smallest positive number: 2.2251E−308

Largest negative number: −2.2251E−308

These numbers are expressed in scientific notation. For example, the largest positive number is "9.9 times 10 to the 307th power"—in other words, 99 followed by 306 zeros. Keep in mind, though, that this number has only 15 digits of precision.

Text entries

Most worksheets also include text in some of the cells. Text can serve as data (for example, a list of employee names), labels for values, headings for columns, or instructions about the worksheet. Text is often used to clarify what the values in a worksheet mean or where the numbers came from.

Text that begins with a number is still considered text. For example, if you type **12 Employees** into a cell, Excel considers the entry to be text rather than a numeric value. Consequently, you can't use this cell for numeric calculations. If you need to indicate that the number 12 refers to employees, enter **12** into a cell and then type **Employees** into the cell to the right.

Formulas

Formulas are what make a spreadsheet a spreadsheet. Excel enables you to enter flexible formulas that use the values (or even text) in cells to calculate a result. When you enter a formula into a cell, the formula's result appears in the cell. If you change any of the cells used by a formula, the formula recalculates and shows the new result.

Formulas can be simple mathematical expressions, or they can use some of the powerful functions that are built into Excel. Figure 2.1 shows an Excel worksheet set up to calculate a monthly loan payment. The worksheet contains values, text, and formulas. The cells in column A contain text. Column B contains four values and two formulas. The formulas are in cells B6 and B10. Column D, for reference, shows the actual contents of the cells in column B.

FIGURE 2.1

You can use values, text, and formulas to create useful Excel worksheets.

	A	B	C	D	E
1	**Loan Payment Calculator**				
2					
3				**Column B Contents**	
4	Purchase Amount:	$475,000		475000	
5	Down Payment Pct:	20%		0.2	
6	Loan Amount:	$380,000		=B4*(1-B5)	
7	Term (months):	360		360	
8	Interest Rate (APR):	6.25%		0.0625	
9					
10	**Monthly Payment:**	$2,339.73		=PMT(B8/12,B7,-B6)	
11					
12					

 This workbook, named `loan payment calculator.xlsx`, is available on this book's website at www.wiley.com/go/excel2019bible.

 You can find out much more about formulas in Part II, "Working with Formulas and Functions."

Entering Text and Values into Your Worksheets

If you've ever worked in a Windows application, you'll find that entering data into worksheet cells is simple and intuitive. And while there are differences in how Excel stores and displays the different data types, for the most part it just works.

Entering numbers

To enter a numeric value into a cell, select the appropriate cell, type the value, and then press Enter, Tab, or one of the arrow navigation keys. The value is displayed in the cell and appears in the Formula bar when the cell is selected. You can include decimal points and currency symbols when entering values, along with plus signs, minus signs, percent signs, and commas (to separate thousands). If you precede a value with a minus sign or enclose it in parentheses, Excel considers it to be a negative number.

Entering text

Entering text into a cell is just as easy as entering a value: activate the cell, type the text, and then press Enter or a navigation key. A cell can contain a maximum of about 32,000 characters—more than enough to store a typical chapter in this book. Even though a cell can hold a huge number of characters, you'll find that it's not actually possible to display all of these characters.

> **TIP**
>
> If you type an exceptionally long text entry into a cell, the Formula bar may not show all the text. To display more of the text in the Formula bar, click the bottom of the Formula bar and drag down to increase the height (see Figure 2.2). Also useful is the Ctrl+Shift+U keyboard shortcut. Pressing this key combination toggles the height of the Formula bar to show either one row or the previous size.

FIGURE 2.2

The Formula bar, expanded in height to show more information in the cell

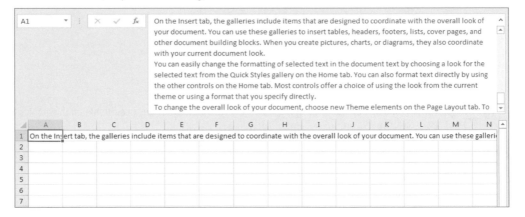

What happens when you enter text that's longer than its column's current width? If the cells to the immediate right are blank, Excel displays the text in its entirety, appearing to spill the entry into adjacent cells. If an adjacent cell isn't blank, Excel displays as much of the text as possible. (The full text is contained in the cell; it's just not displayed.) If you need to display a long text string in a cell that's adjacent to a nonblank cell, you have a few choices.

- Edit your text to make it shorter.
- Increase the width of the column (drag the border in the column letter display).
- Use a smaller font.
- Wrap the text within the cell so that it occupies more than one line. Choose Home ⇨ Alignment ⇨ Wrap Text to toggle wrapping on and off for the selected cell or range.

Using Enter mode

The left side of Excel's status bar normally displays "Ready," indicating that Excel is ready for you to enter or edit the worksheet. If you start typing numbers or text in a cell, the status bar changes to display "Enter" to indicate you're in *Enter mode*. The most common modes for Excel to be in are Ready, Enter, and Edit. See "Modifying Cell Contents" later in this chapter for more information about Edit mode.

In Enter mode, you are actively entering something into a cell. As you type, the text shows in the cell and in the Formula bar. You haven't actually changed the contents of the cell until you leave Enter mode, which commits the value to the cell. To leave Enter mode, you can press Enter, Tab, or just about any navigation key on your keyboard (like PageUp or Home). The value you typed is committed to the cell, and the status bar changes back to say "Ready."

You can also leave Enter mode by pressing the Esc key. Pressing Esc ignores your changes and returns the cell to its previous value.

Entering Dates and Times into Your Worksheets

Excel treats dates and times as special types of numeric values. Dates and times are values that are formatted so that they appear as dates or times. If you work with dates and times, you need to understand Excel's date and time system.

Entering date values

Excel handles dates by using a serial number system. The earliest date that Excel understands is January 1, 1900. This date has a serial number of 1. January 2, 1900, has a serial number of 2, and so on. This system makes it easy to deal with dates in formulas. For example, you can enter a formula to calculate the number of days between two dates.

Most of the time, you don't have to be concerned with Excel's serial number date system. You can simply enter a date in a common date format, and Excel takes care of the details behind the scenes. For example, if you need to enter June 1, 2019, you can enter the date by typing **June 1, 2019** (or use any of several different date formats). Excel interprets your entry and stores the value 43617, which is the serial number for that date.

> **NOTE**
> The date examples in this book use the U.S. English system. Your Windows regional settings will affect the way Excel interprets a date that you've entered. For example, depending on your regional date settings, June 1, 2019, may be interpreted as text rather than a date. In such a case, you need to enter the date in a format that corresponds to your regional date settings—for example, 1 June, 2019.

 For more information about working with dates, see Chapter 12, "Using Formulas with Dates and Times."

Entering time values

When you work with times, you extend Excel's date serial number system to include decimals. In other words, Excel works with times by using fractional days. For example, the date serial number for June 1, 2019, is `43617`. Noon on June 1, 2019 (halfway through the day), is represented internally as `43617.5` because the time fraction is added to the date serial number to get the full date/time serial number.

Again, you normally don't have to be concerned with these serial numbers or fractional serial numbers for times. Just enter the time into a cell in a recognized format. In this case, type **June 1, 2019 12:00**.

 See Chapter 12 for more information about working with time values.

Modifying Cell Contents

After you enter a value or text into a cell, you can modify it in several ways.

- Delete the cell's contents.
- Replace the cell's contents with something else.
- Edit the cell's contents.

> **NOTE**
> You can also modify a cell by changing its formatting. However, formatting a cell affects only a cell's appearance. Formatting doesn't affect the cell's contents. Later sections in this chapter cover formatting.

Deleting the contents of a cell

To delete the contents of a cell, just click the cell and press the Delete key. To delete more than one cell, select all of the cells that you want to delete and then press Delete. Pressing Delete removes the cell's contents but doesn't remove any formatting (such as bold, italic, or a different number format) that you may have applied to the cell.

For more control over what gets deleted, you can choose Home ➪ Editing ➪ Clear. This command's drop-down list has six choices.

Clear All   Clears everything from the cell—its contents, formatting, and cell comment (if it has one).

Clear Formats   Clears only the formatting and leaves the value, text, or formula.

Clear Contents   Clears only the cell's contents and leaves the formatting. This has the same effect as pressing Delete.

Clear Comments   Clears the comment (if one exists) attached to the cell.

Clear Hyperlinks   Removes hyperlinks contained in the selected cells. The text and formatting remain, so the cell still looks like it has a hyperlink, but it no longer functions as a hyperlink.

Remove Hyperlinks   Removes hyperlinks in the selected cells, including the cell formatting.

> **NOTE**
>
> Clearing formats doesn't clear the background colors in a range that has been designated as a table unless you've replaced the table style background colors manually. See Chapter 4, "Working with Excel Ranges and Tables," for more about tables.

Replacing the contents of a cell

To replace the contents of a cell with something else, just activate the cell and type your new entry, which replaces the previous contents. Any formatting applied to the cell remains in place and is applied to the new content.

You can also replace cell contents by dragging and dropping or by copying and pasting data from another cell. In both cases, the cell formatting will be replaced by the format of the new data. To avoid pasting formatting, choose Home ➪ Clipboard ➪ Paste ➪ Values (V), or Home ➪ Clipboard ➪ Paste ➪ Formulas (F).

Editing the contents of a cell

If the cell contains only a few characters, replacing its contents by typing new data usually is easiest. However, if the cell contains lengthy text or a complex formula and you need to make only a slight modification, you probably want to edit the cell rather than re-enter information.

When you want to edit the contents of a cell, you can use one of the following ways to enter Edit mode:

- **Double-click the cell** to edit the cell contents directly in the cell.
- **Select the cell and press F2** to edit the cell contents directly in the cell.

- **Select the cell that you want to edit and then click inside the Formula bar** to edit the cell contents in the Formula bar.

You can use whichever method you prefer. Some people find editing directly in the cell easier; others prefer to use the Formula bar to edit a cell.

> **NOTE**
>
> The Advanced tab of the Excel Options dialog box contains a section called Editing Options. These settings affect how editing works. (To access this dialog box, choose File ⇨ Options.) If the Allow Editing Directly in Cells option isn't enabled, you can't edit a cell by double-clicking. In addition, pressing F2 allows you to edit the cell in the Formula bar (not directly in the cell).

All of these methods cause Excel to go into Edit mode. (The word Edit appears at the left side of the status bar at the bottom of the window.) When Excel is in Edit mode, the Formula bar enables two icons: Cancel (the X) and Enter (the check mark). Figure 2.3 shows these two icons. Clicking the Cancel icon cancels editing without changing the cell's contents. (Pressing Esc has the same effect.) Clicking the Enter icon completes the editing and enters the modified contents into the cell. (Pressing Enter has the same effect, except that clicking the Enter icon doesn't change the active cell.)

FIGURE 2.3

When you're editing a cell, the Formula bar enables two new icons: Cancel (X) and Enter (check mark).

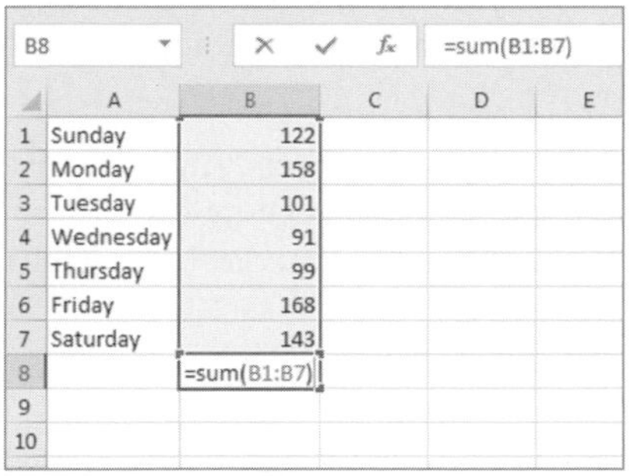

When you begin editing a cell, the insertion point appears as a vertical bar, and you can perform the following tasks:

- **Add new characters at the location of the insertion point.** Move the insertion point by doing one of the following:
  - Using the navigation keys to move within the cell
  - Pressing Home to move the insertion point to the beginning of the cell
  - Pressing End to move the insertion point to the end of the cell

- **Select multiple characters.** Press Shift while you use the navigation keys.
- **Select characters while you're editing a cell.** Use the mouse. Just click and drag the mouse pointer over the characters that you want to select.
- **Delete a character to the left of the insertion point.** The Backspace key deletes the selected text or the character to the left of the insertion point if no characters are selected.
- **Delete a character to the right of the insertion point.** The Delete key also deletes the selected text. If no text is selected, it deletes the character to the right of the insertion point.

Learning some handy data-entry techniques

You can simplify the process of entering information into your Excel worksheets and make your work go quite a bit faster by using a number of useful tricks, which are described in the following sections.

Automatically moving the selection after entering data

By default, Excel automatically selects the next cell down when you press the Enter key after entering data into a cell. To change this setting, choose File ➪ Options and click the Advanced tab (see Figure 2.4). The check box that controls this behavior is labeled After pressing Enter, move selection. If you enable this option, you can choose the direction in which the selection moves (down, left, up, or right).

Selecting a range of input cells before entering data

When a range of cells is selected, Excel automatically selects the next cell in the range when you press Enter, even if you disabled the After pressing Enter, move selection option. If the selection consists of multiple rows, Excel moves down the column; when it reaches the end of the selection in the column, it moves to the first selected cell in the next column.

To skip a cell, just press Enter without entering anything. To go backward, press Shift+Enter. If you prefer to enter the data by rows rather than by columns, press Tab rather than Enter. Excel continues to cycle through the selected range until you select a cell outside the range. Any of the navigation keys, like the arrow keys or the Home key, will change the selected range. If you want to navigate within the selected range, you have to stick to Enter and Tab.

Using Ctrl+Enter to place information into multiple cells simultaneously

If you need to enter the same data into multiple cells, Excel offers a handy shortcut. Select all of the cells that you want to contain the data; enter the value, text, or formula; and then press Ctrl+Enter. The same information is inserted into each cell in the selection.

FIGURE 2.4

You can use the Advanced tab in Excel Options to select a number of helpful input option settings.

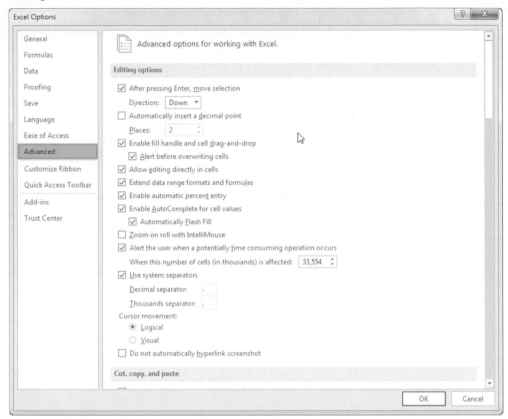

Changing modes

You can press F2 to change between Enter mode and Edit mode. For example, if you're typing a long sentence in Enter mode and you realize that you spelled a word wrong, you can press F2 to change to Edit mode. In Edit mode, you can move through the sentence with your arrow keys to fix the misspelled word. You can also use the Ctrl+arrow keys to move one word at a time instead of one character at a time. You can continue to enter text in Edit mode or return to Enter mode by pressing F2 again, after which the navigation keys can be used to move to a different cell.

Entering decimal points automatically

If you need to enter lots of numbers with a fixed number of decimal places, Excel has a useful tool that works like some old adding machines. Access the Excel Options dialog box and click the Advanced tab. Select the Automatically Insert a Decimal Point check box and make sure that the Places box is set for the correct number of decimal places for the data you need to enter.

When this option is set, Excel supplies the decimal points for you automatically. For example, if you specify two decimal places, entering **12345** into a cell is interpreted as 123.45. To restore things to normal, just clear the Automatically Insert a Decimal Point check box in the Excel Options dialog box. Changing this setting doesn't affect any values that you already entered.

CAUTION

The fixed decimal places option is a global setting and applies to all workbooks (not just the active workbook). If you forget that this option is turned on, you can easily end up entering incorrect values—or cause some major confusion if someone else uses your computer.

Using AutoFill to enter a series of values

The Excel AutoFill feature makes inserting a series of values or text items in a range of cells easy. It uses the *fill handle* (the small box at the lower right of the active cell). You can drag the fill handle to copy the cell or automatically complete a series.

Figure 2.5 shows an example. Enter **1** into cell A1, and enter **3** into cell A2. Then select both cells and drag down the fill handle to create a linear series of odd numbers. The figure also shows an icon that, when clicked, displays some additional AutoFill options. This icon appears only if the Show Paste Options button when content is pasted option is selected in the Advanced tab of the Excel Options dialog box.

FIGURE 2.5

This series was created by using AutoFill.

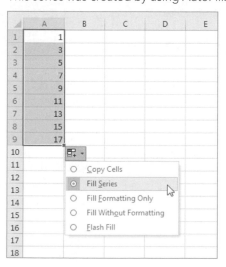

Excel uses the cells' data to guess the pattern. If you start with 1 and 2, it will guess you want each cell to go up by 1. If, as in the previous example, you start with 1 and 3, it guesses that you want the increment to be 2. Excel does a good job of guessing date patterns too. If you start with 1/31/2019 and 2/28/2019, it will fill the last day of the successive months.

> **TIP**
>
> If you drag the fill handle while you press and hold the right mouse button, Excel displays a shortcut menu with additional fill options. You can also use Home ⇨ Editing ⇨ Fill for even more control over automatically filling a range.

Using AutoComplete to automate data entry

The Excel AutoComplete feature makes entering the same text into multiple cells easy. With AutoComplete, you type the first few letters of a text entry into a cell, and Excel automatically completes the entry based on other entries that you already made in the column. Besides reducing typing, this feature ensures that your entries are spelled correctly and are consistent.

Here's how it works: Suppose you're entering product information into a column. One of your products is named Widgets. The first time you enter **Widgets** into a cell, Excel remembers it. Later, when you start typing **Widgets** in that same column, Excel recognizes it by the first few letters and finishes typing it for you. Just press Enter, and you're done. To override the suggestion, just keep typing.

AutoComplete also changes the case of letters for you automatically. If you start entering **widgets** (with a lowercase *w*) in the second entry, Excel makes the *w* uppercase to be consistent with the previous entry in the column.

> **TIP**
>
> You also can access a mouse-oriented version of AutoComplete by right-clicking the cell and choosing Pick from Drop-Down List from the shortcut menu. Excel then displays a drop-down box that has all of the text entries in the current column, and you just click the one that you want.

Keep in mind that AutoComplete works only within a contiguous column of cells. If you have a blank row, for example, AutoComplete identifies only the cell contents below the blank row.

Sometimes, Excel will use AutoComplete to try to finish a word when you don't want it to do so. If you type **canister** in a cell and then below it type the shorter word **can**, Excel will attempt to AutoComplete the entry to *canister*. When you want to type a word that starts with the same letters as an AutoComplete entry but is shorter, simply press the Delete key when you've reached the end of the word and then press Enter or a navigation key.

If you find the AutoComplete feature distracting, you can turn it off by using the Advanced tab of the Excel Options dialog box. Remove the check mark from the Enable AutoComplete for Cell Values box.

Forcing text to appear on a new line within a cell

If you have lengthy text in a cell, you can force Excel to display it in multiple lines within the cell: press Alt+Enter to start a new line in a cell.

When you add a line break, Excel automatically changes the cell's format to Wrap Text. But unlike normal text wrap, your manual line break forces Excel to break the text at a specific place within the text, which gives you more precise control over the appearance of the text than if you rely on automatic text wrapping.

> **TIP**
>
> To remove a manual line break, edit the cell and press Delete when the insertion point is located at the end of the line that contains the manual line break. You won't see any symbol to indicate the position of the manual line break, but the text that follows it will move up when the line break is deleted.

Using AutoCorrect for shorthand data entry

You can use the AutoCorrect feature to create shortcuts for commonly used words or phrases. For example, if you work for a company named Consolidated Data Processing Corporation, you can create an AutoCorrect entry for an abbreviation, such as *cdp*. Then, whenever you type **cdp** and take an action to trigger AutoCorrect (such as typing a space, pressing Enter, or selecting a different cell), Excel automatically changes the text to Consolidated Data Processing Corporation.

Excel includes quite a few built-in AutoCorrect terms (mostly to correct common misspellings), and you can add your own. To set up your custom AutoCorrect entries, access the Excel Options dialog box (choose File ➪ Options) and click the Proofing tab. Then click the AutoCorrect Options button to display the AutoCorrect dialog box. In the dialog box, click the AutoCorrect tab, check the Replace Text as You Type option, and then enter your custom entries. (Figure 2.6 shows an example.) You can set up as many custom entries as you like. Just be careful not to use an abbreviation that might appear normally in your text.

> **TIP**
>
> Excel shares your AutoCorrect list with other Microsoft Office applications. For example, any AutoCorrect entries you created in Word also work in Excel.

FIGURE 2.6

AutoCorrect allows you to create shorthand abbreviations for text you enter often.

Entering numbers with fractions

Most of the time, you'll want noninteger values to be displayed with decimal points. But Excel can also display values with fractions. To enter a fractional value into a cell, leave a space between the whole number and the fraction. For example, to enter 6 7/8, enter **6 7/8** and then press Enter. When you select the cell, 6.875 appears in the Formula bar, and the cell entry appears as a fraction. If you have a fraction only (for example, 1/8), you must enter a zero first, like this—**0 1/8**—or Excel will likely assume that you're entering a date. When you select the cell and look at the Formula bar, you see 0.125. In the cell, you see 1/8.

Using a form for data entry

Many people use Excel to manage lists in which the information is arranged in rows. Excel offers a simple way to work with this type of data through the use of a data entry form that Excel can create automatically. This data form works with either a normal range of data or a range that has been designated as a table. (Choose Insert ➪ Tables ➪ Table.) Figure 2.7 shows an example.

FIGURE 2.7

Excel's built-in data form can simplify many data-entry tasks.

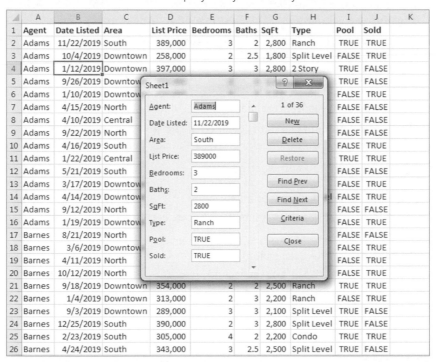

Unfortunately, the command to access the data form is not on the Ribbon. To use the data form, you must add it to your Quick Access toolbar or add it to the Ribbon. Here's how to add this command to your Quick Access toolbar:

1. **Right-click the Quick Access toolbar and choose Customize Quick Access Toolbar.** The Quick Access Toolbar panel of the Excel Options dialog box appears.

2. **In the Choose Commands From drop-down list, choose Commands Not in the Ribbon.**

3. **In the list box on the left, select Form.**

4. **Click the Add button to add the selected command to your Quick Access toolbar.**

5. **Click OK to close the Excel Options dialog box.**

After you perform these steps, a new icon appears on your Quick Access toolbar.

To use a data entry form, follow these steps:

1. **Arrange your data so that Excel can recognize it as a table by entering headings for the columns into the first row of your data entry range.**

2. **Select any cell in the table, and click the Form button on your Quick Access toolbar.** Excel displays a dialog box customized to your data (refer to Figure 2.7).

3. **Fill in the information.** Press Tab to move between the text boxes. If a cell contains a formula, the formula result appears as text (not as an edit box). In other words, you can't modify formulas using the data entry form.

4. **When you complete the data form, click the New button.** Excel enters the data into a row in the worksheet and clears the dialog box for the next row of data.

You can also use the form to edit existing data.

Entering the current date or time into a cell

If you need to date-stamp or time-stamp your worksheet, Excel provides two shortcut keys that do this task for you:

- **Current date:** Ctrl+; (semicolon)
- **Current time:** Ctrl+Shift+; (semicolon)

To enter both the date and time, press Ctrl+;, type a space, and then press Ctrl+Shift+;.

The date and time are from the system time in your computer. If the date or time isn't correct in Excel, use the Windows Settings to make the adjustment.

> **NOTE**
>
> When you use either of these shortcuts to enter a date or time into your worksheet, Excel enters a static value into the worksheet. In other words, the date or time entered doesn't change when the worksheet is recalculated. In most cases, this setup is probably what you want, but you should be aware of this limitation. If you want the date or time display to update, use one of these formulas:
> =TODAY()
> =NOW()

Applying Number Formatting

Applying number formatting changes the appearance of values contained in cells. Excel provides a variety of number formatting options. In the following sections, you will see how to use many of Excel's formatting options to improve the appearance and readability of your worksheets quickly.

> **TIP**
>
> The formatting that you apply works with the selected cell or cells. Therefore, you need to select the cell (or range of cells) before applying the formatting. Also remember that changing the number format does not affect the underlying value. Number formatting affects only the appearance.

Values that you enter into cells normally are unformatted. In other words, they simply consist of a string of numerals. Typically, you want to format the numbers so that they're easier to read or are more consistent in terms of the number of decimal places shown.

Figure 2.8 shows a worksheet that has two columns of values. The first column consists of unformatted values. The cells in the second column are formatted to make the values easier to read. The third column describes the type of formatting applied.

FIGURE 2.8

Use numeric formatting to make it easier to understand what the values in the worksheet represent.

	A	B	C	D
1				
2	Unformatted	Formatted	Type	
3	1200	$1,200.00	Currency	
4	0.231	23.1%	Percentage	
5	43603	5/18/2019	Short Date	
6	43603	Saturday, May 18, 2019	Long Date	
7	123439832	$ 123,439,832.00	Accounting	
8	5559832	555-9832	Phone Number	
9	434988723	434-98-8723	Social Security Number	
10	0.552	1:14:53 PM	Time	
11	0.25	1/4	Fraction	
12	12332354090	1.23E+10	Scientific	
13				
14				

 This workbook is available on this book's website at www.wiley.com/go/excel2019bible. The file is named number formatting.xlsx.

> **TIP**
>
> If you select a cell that has a formatted value, the Formula bar displays the value in its unformatted state because the formatting affects only the way the value appears in the cell—not the actual value contained in the cell. There are a few exceptions, however. When you enter a date or a time, Excel always displays the value as a date or a time, even though it's stored internally as a value. Also, values that use the Percentage format display with a percent sign in the Formula bar.

Using automatic number formatting

Excel is able to perform some formatting for you automatically. For example, if you enter **12.2%** into a cell, Excel knows that you want to use a percentage format and applies it for you automatically. If you use commas to separate thousands (such as 123,456), Excel applies comma formatting for you. And if you precede your value with a dollar sign, the cell is formatted for currency (assuming that the dollar sign is your system currency symbol).

Anything you enter that can possibly be construed as a date will be treated as such. And depending on how you enter it, Excel will choose a date format to match. If you enter **1/31/2020**, Excel will interpret that as a date and format the cell as 1/31/2020 (just as it was entered). If you enter **Jan 31, 2020**, Excel will the format it as 31-Jan-20 (if you omit the comma, Excel won't recognize it as a date). The less obvious example of entering **1-31** causes Excel to display 31-Jan. If you need to enter **1-31** in a cell and it's not supposed to be a date, type an apostrophe (') first.

> **TIP**
>
> A handy default feature in Excel makes entering percentage values into cells easier. If a cell is formatted to display as a percent, you can simply enter a normal value (for example, 12.5 for 12.5%). To enter values less than 1%, precede the value with a zero (for example, 0.52 for 0.52%). If this automatic percent entry feature isn't working (or if you prefer to enter the actual value for percents), access the Excel Options dialog box and click the Advanced tab. In the Editing Options section, locate the Enable Automatic Percent Entry check box and add or remove the check mark.

Formatting numbers by using the Ribbon

The Home ⇨ Number group in the Ribbon contains controls that let you quickly apply common number formats.

The Number Format drop-down list contains 11 common number formats (see Figure 2.9). Additional options in the Home ⇨ Number group include an Accounting Number Format drop-down list (to select a currency format), a Percent Style button, and a Comma Style button. The group also contains a button to increase the number of decimal places and another to decrease the number of decimal places.

When you select one of these controls, the active cell takes on the specified number format. You also can select a range of cells (or even entire rows or columns) before clicking these buttons. If you select more than one cell, Excel applies the number format to all of the selected cells.

Using shortcut keys to format numbers

Another way to apply number formatting is to use shortcut keys. Table 2.1 summarizes the shortcut-key combinations that you can use to apply common number formatting to the selected cells or range. Notice that these Ctrl+Shift characters are located together, in the lower left of your keyboard.

FIGURE 2.9

You can find number formatting commands in the Number group of the Home tab.

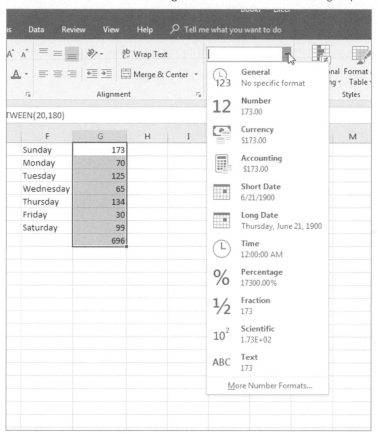

TABLE 2.1   Number Formatting Keyboard Shortcuts

Key Combination	Formatting Applied
Ctrl+Shift+~	General number format (that is, unformatted values)
Ctrl+Shift+$	Currency format with two decimal places (negative numbers appear in red and inside parentheses)
Ctrl+Shift+%	Percentage format, with no decimal places
Ctrl+Shift+^	Scientific notation number format, with two decimal places
Ctrl+Shift+#	Date format with the day, month, and year
Ctrl+Shift+@	Time format with the hour, minute, and AM or PM
Ctrl+Shift+!	Two decimal places, thousands separator, and a hyphen for negative values

Formatting numbers by using the Format Cells dialog box

In most cases, the number formats that are accessible from the Number group on the Home tab are just fine. Sometimes, however, you want more control over how your values appear. Excel offers a great deal of control over number formats through the use of the Format Cells dialog box, as shown in Figure 2.10. For formatting numbers, you need to use the Number tab.

FIGURE 2.10

When you need more control over number formats, use the Number tab of the Format Cells dialog box.

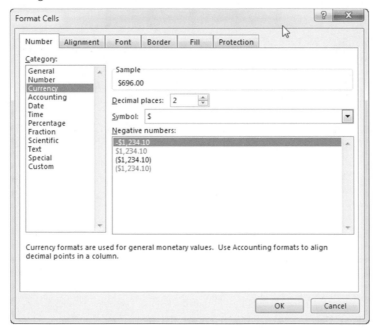

You can bring up the Format Cells dialog box in several ways. Start by selecting the cell or cells that you want to format and then do one of the following:

- Choose Home ⇨ Number and click the small dialog box launcher icon (in the lower-right corner of the Number group).
- Choose Home ⇨ Number, click the Number Format drop-down list, and choose More Number Formats from the drop-down list.
- Right-click the cell, and choose Format Cells from the shortcut menu.
- Press Ctrl+1.

The Number tab of the Format Cells dialog box displays 12 categories of number formats. When you select a category from the list box, the right side of the tab changes to display options appropriate to that category.

The Number category has three options that you can control: the number of decimal places displayed, whether to use a thousands separator, and how you want negative numbers displayed. The Negative Numbers list box has four choices (two of which display negative values in red), and the choices change depending on the number of decimal places and whether you choose to separate thousands.

The top of the tab displays a sample of how the active cell will appear with the selected number format (visible only if a cell with a value is selected). After you make your choices, click OK to apply the number format to all of the selected cells.

When Numbers Appear to Add Incorrectly

Applying a number format to a cell doesn't change the value—it only changes how the value appears in the worksheet. For example, if a cell contains 0.874543, you may format it to appear as 87%. If that cell is used in a formula, the formula uses the full value (0.874543), not the displayed value (87%).

In some situations, formatting may cause Excel to display calculation results that appear incorrect, such as when totaling numbers with decimal places. For example, if values are formatted to display two decimal places, you may not see the actual numbers used in the calculations. But because Excel uses the full precision of the values in its formula, the sum of the two values may appear to be incorrect.

Several solutions to this problem are available. You can format the cells to display more decimal places. You can use the ROUND function on individual numbers and specify the number of decimal places to which Excel should round. Or, you can instruct Excel to change the worksheet values to match their displayed format. To do so, access the Excel Options dialog box and click the Advanced tab. Check the Set Precision as Displayed check box (located in the When Calculating This Workbook section).

CAUTION

Selecting the Set Precision as Displayed option changes the numbers in your worksheets to match their appearance on-screen permanently. This setting applies to all sheets in the active workbook. Most of the time, this option is *not* what you want. Make sure you understand the consequences of using the Set Precision as Displayed option.

 Chapter 9, "Introducing Formulas and Functions," discusses ROUND and other built-in functions.

The following are the number format categories, along with some general comments:

General   The default format; it displays numbers as integers, as decimals, or in scientific notation if the value is too wide to fit in the cell.

Number   Enables you to specify the number of decimal places, whether to use a comma to separate thousands, and how to display negative numbers (with a minus sign, in red, in parentheses, or in red and in parentheses).

Currency   Enables you to specify the number of decimal places, choose a currency symbol, and specify how to display negative numbers (with a minus sign, in red, in parentheses, or in red and in parentheses). This format always uses a comma to separate thousands.

Accounting   Differs from the Currency format in that the currency symbols always align vertically.

Date   Enables you to choose from several different date formats.

Time   Enables you to choose from several different time formats.

Percentage   Enables you to choose the number of decimal places and always displays a percent sign.

Fraction   Enables you to choose from among nine fraction formats.

Scientific   Displays numbers in exponential notation (with an E): 2.00E+05 = 200,000; 2.05E+05 = 205,000. You can choose the number of decimal places to display to the left of E. The second example can be read as "2.05 times 10 to the fifth."

Text   When applied to a value, causes Excel to treat the value as text (even if it looks like a number). This feature is useful for such items as part numbers and credit card numbers.

Special   Contains additional number formats. In the U.S. version of Excel, the additional number formats are Zip Code, Zip Code +4, Phone Number, and Social Security Number.

Custom   Enables you to define custom number formats that aren't included in any other category.

> **TIP**
>
> If a cell displays a series of hash marks (such as #########), it usually means that the column isn't wide enough to display the value in the number format that you selected. Either make the column wider or change the number format. Hashmarks also indicate a negative time value or an invalid date (that is, a date prior to January 1, 1900).

Adding your own custom number formats

Sometimes you may want to display numerical values in a format that isn't included in any of the other categories. If so, the answer is to create your own custom format. Basic custom number formats contain four sections separated by semicolons. Those four sections determine how a number will be formatted if it is a positive value, negative value, a zero, or text.

Performing Basic Worksheet Operations

IN THIS CHAPTER

Understanding Excel worksheet basics

Controlling your views

Manipulating the rows and columns

This chapter covers some basic information regarding workbooks, worksheets, and windows. You'll discover tips and techniques to help you take control of your worksheets and help you to work more efficiently.

Learning the Fundamentals of Excel Worksheets

In Excel, each file is called a *workbook*, and each workbook can contain one or more worksheets. You may find it helpful to think of an Excel workbook as a binder and worksheets as pages in the binder. As with a binder, you can view a particular sheet, add new sheets, remove sheets, rearrange sheets, and copy sheets.

A workbook can hold any number of sheets, and these sheets can be either worksheets (sheets consisting of rows and columns) or chart sheets (sheets that hold a single chart). A worksheet is what people usually think of when they think of a spreadsheet.

The following sections describe the operations that you can perform with windows and worksheets.

Working with Excel windows

Each Excel workbook file that you open is displayed in a window. A window is the operating system's container for that workbook. You can open as many Excel workbooks as necessary at the same time.

Each Excel window has five icons at the right side of its title bar. From left to right, they are Account, Ribbon Display Options, Minimize, Maximize (or Restore Down), and Close.

An Excel window can be in one of the following states:

Maximized   Fills the entire screen. To maximize a window, click its Maximize button.

Minimized   Hidden but still open. To minimize a window, clicks its Minimize button.

Restored   Visible but smaller than the whole screen. To restore a maximized window, click its Restore Down button. To restore a minimized window, click its icon in the Windows taskbar. A window in this state can be resized and moved.

If you work with more than one workbook simultaneously (which is quite common), you need to know how to move, resize, close, and switch among the workbook windows.

Moving and resizing windows

To move a window, click and drag its title bar with your mouse. If it's maximized, it will change to a restored state. If it's already in a restored state, it will maintain its current size.

To resize a window, click and drag any of its borders until it's the size that you want it to be. When you position the mouse pointer on a window's border, the mouse pointer changes to a double arrow, which lets you know that you can now click and drag to resize the window. To resize a window horizontally and vertically at the same time, click and drag any of its corners.

If you want all of your workbook windows to be visible (that is, not obscured by another window), you can move and resize the windows manually, or you can let Excel do it for you. Choosing View ➪ Window ➪ Arrange All displays the Arrange Windows dialog box, as shown in Figure 3.1. This dialog box has four window arrangement options. Just select the one that you want and click OK. Windows that are minimized aren't affected by this command.

FIGURE 3.1

Use the Arrange Windows dialog box to arrange all open nonminimized workbook windows quickly.

Switching among windows

At any given time, one (and only one) workbook window is the active window. The active window accepts your input, and it is the window on which your commands work. The active window appears at the top of the stack of windows. To work in a workbook in a different window, you need to make that window active. You can make a different window the active window in several ways.

- **Click another window if it's visible.** The window you click moves to the top and becomes the active window. This method isn't possible if the current window is maximized.
- **Press Ctrl+Tab to cycle through all open windows until the window that you want to work with appears on top as the active window.** Pressing Shift+Ctrl+Tab cycles through the windows in the opposite direction.
- **Choose View ➪ Window ➪ Switch Windows, and select the window that you want from the drop-down list (the active window has a check mark next to it).** This menu can display as many as nine windows. If you have more than nine workbook windows open, choose More Windows (which appears below the nine window names).
- **Click the corresponding Excel icon in the Windows taskbar.**

You might be one of the many people who prefer to do most work with maximized workbook windows, which enables you to see more cells and eliminates the distraction of other workbook windows getting in the way. At times, however, viewing multiple windows is preferred. For example, displaying two windows is more efficient if you need to compare information in two workbooks or if you need to copy data from one workbook to another.

> **TIP**
>
> You also can display a single workbook in more than one window. For example, if you have a workbook with two work-sheets, you may want to display each worksheet in a separate window to compare the two sheets. All of the window manipulation procedures described previously still apply. See "Viewing a worksheet in multiple windows" later in this chapter.

Closing windows

If you have multiple windows open, you may want to close those windows that you no longer need. Excel offers several ways to close the active window.

- Choose File ⇨ Close.
- Click the Close button (the X icon) on the right side of the workbook window's title bar.
- Press Alt+F4.
- Press Ctrl+W.

When you close a workbook window, Excel checks whether you have made any changes since the last time you saved the file. If you have made changes, Excel prompts you to save the file before it closes the window. If you haven't, the window closes without a prompt from Excel.

Sometimes you will be prompted to save a workbook even if you've made no changes to it. This occurs if your workbook contains any *volatile* functions. Volatile functions recalculate every time the workbook recalculates. For example, if a cell contains =NOW(), you will be prompted to save the workbook because the NOW function updated the cell with the current date and time.

Activating a worksheet

At any given time, one workbook is the active workbook, and one sheet is the active sheet in the active workbook. To activate a different sheet, just click its sheet tab, which is located at the bottom of the workbook window. You also can use the following shortcut keys to activate a different sheet:

- **Ctrl+PgUp** activates the previous sheet, if one exists.
- **Ctrl+PgDn** activates the next sheet, if one exists.

If your workbook has many sheets, all of its tabs may not be visible. Use the tab scrolling controls (see Figure 3.2) to scroll the sheet tabs. Clicking the scrolling controls scrolls one tab at a time, and Ctrl+clicking scrolls to the first or last sheet. The sheet tabs share space with the worksheet's horizontal scrollbar. You also can drag the tab split control (to the left of the horizontal scrollbar) to display more or fewer tabs. Dragging the tab split control simultaneously changes the number of visible tabs and the size of the horizontal scrollbar.

FIGURE 3.2

Use the tab scrolling controls to activate a different worksheet or to see additional worksheet tabs.

Tab scrolling controls ———

> **TIP**
>
> When you right-click any of the tab scrolling controls, Excel displays a list of all sheets in the workbook. You can quickly activate a sheet by double-clicking it in the list.

Adding a new worksheet to your workbook

Worksheets can be an excellent organizational tool. Instead of placing everything on a single worksheet, you can use additional worksheets in a workbook to separate various workbook elements logically. For example, if you have several products whose sales you track individually, you may want to assign each product to its own worksheet and then use another worksheet to consolidate your results.

Here are four ways to add a new worksheet to a workbook:

- Click the New Sheet control, which is the plus sign icon located to the right of the last visible sheet tab. A new sheet is added after the active sheet.
- Press Shift+F11. A new sheet is added before the active sheet.
- From the Ribbon, choose Home ➪ Cells ➪ Insert ➪ Insert Sheet. A new sheet is added before the active sheet.
- Right-click a sheet tab, choose Insert from the shortcut menu, and select the General tab of the Insert dialog box that appears. Then select the Worksheet icon and click OK. A new sheet is added before the active sheet.

Deleting a worksheet you no longer need

If you no longer need a worksheet or if you want to get rid of an empty worksheet in a workbook, you can delete it in either of two ways.

- Right-click its sheet tab and choose Delete from the shortcut menu.
- Activate the unwanted worksheet and choose Home ➪ Cells ➪ Delete ➪ Delete Sheet.

If the worksheet is not empty, Excel asks you to confirm that you want to delete the sheet (see Figure 3.3).

3

FIGURE 3.3

Excel's warning that you might be losing some data

Changing the name of a worksheet

The default names that Excel uses for worksheets—Sheet1, Sheet2, and so on—are generic and nondescriptive. To make it easier to locate data in a multisheet workbook, you'll want to make the sheet names more descriptive.

These are three ways to change a sheet's name:

- From the Ribbon, choose Home ➪ Cells ➪ Format ➪ Rename Sheet.
- Double-click the sheet tab.
- Right-click the sheet tab and choose Rename Sheet.

Excel highlights the name on the sheet tab so that you can edit the name or replace it with a new name. While editing a sheet name, all of the normal text selection techniques work, such as Home, End, arrow keys, and Shift+arrow keys. Press Enter when you're finished editing and the focus will be back on the active cell.

Sheet names can contain as many as 31 characters, and spaces are allowed. However, you can't use the following characters in sheet names:

:	Colon
/	Slash
\	Backslash
[ ]	Square brackets

?	Question mark
*	Asterisk

Keep in mind that a longer worksheet name results in a wider tab, which takes up more space on-screen. Therefore, if you use lengthy sheet names, you won't be able to see as many sheet tabs without scrolling the tab list.

Changing a sheet tab color

Excel allows you to change the background color of your worksheet tabs. For example, you may prefer to color-code the sheet tabs to make identifying the worksheet's contents easier.

To change the color of a sheet tab, choose Home ⇨ Cells ⇨ Format ⇨ Tab Color, or right-click the tab and choose Tab Color from the shortcut menu. Then select the color from the color palette. You can't change the text color, but Excel will choose a contrasting color to make the text visible. For example, if you make a sheet tab black, Excel will display white text.

If you change a sheet tab's color, the tab shows a gradient from that color to white when the sheet is active. When a different sheet is active, the whole tab appears in the selected color.

Rearranging your worksheets

You may want to rearrange the order of worksheets in a workbook. If you have a separate worksheet for each sales region, for example, arranging the worksheets in alphabetical order might be helpful. You can also move a worksheet from one workbook to another and create copies of worksheets, either in the same workbook or in a different workbook.

You can move a worksheet in the following ways:

- Right-click the sheet tab and choose Move or Copy to display the Move or Copy dialog box (see Figure 3.4). Use this dialog box to specify the location for the sheet.
- From the Ribbon, choose Home ⇨ Cells ⇨ Format ⇨ Move or Copy Sheet. This shows the same dialog box as the previous method.
- Click the worksheet tab and drag it to its desired location. When you drag, the mouse pointer changes to a small sheet icon, and a small arrow indicates where the sheet will be placed when you release the mouse button. To move a worksheet to a different workbook by dragging, both workbooks must be visible.

Copying the worksheet is similar to moving it. If you use one of the options that shows the Move or Copy dialog box, select the Create a copy check box. To drag and create a copy, hold down the Ctrl key while you drag the worksheet tab. The mouse pointer will change to a small sheet icon with a plus sign on it.

FIGURE 3.4

Use the Move or Copy dialog box to move or copy worksheets in the same or another work-book.

If you move or copy a worksheet to a workbook that already has a sheet with the same name, Excel changes the name to make it unique. For example, Sheet1 becomes Sheet1 (2). You probably want to rename the copied sheet to give it a more meaningful name. (See "Changing the Name of a Worksheet" earlier in this chapter.)

Hiding and unhiding a worksheet

In some situations, you may want to hide one or more worksheets. Hiding a sheet may be useful if you don't want others to see it or if you just want to get it out of the way. When a sheet is hidden, its sheet tab is also hidden. You can't hide all of the sheets in a workbook; at least one sheet must remain visible.

To hide a worksheet, choose Home ⇨ Cells ⇨ Format ⇨ Hide & Unhide ⇨ Hide Sheet, or right-click its sheet tab and choose Hide. The active worksheet (or selected worksheets) will be hidden from view.

To unhide a hidden worksheet, choose Home ⇨ Cells ⇨ Format ⇨ Hide & Unhide ⇨ Unhide Sheet, or right-click any sheet tab and choose Unhide. Excel opens the Unhide dialog box, which lists all hidden sheets. Choose the sheet that you want to redisplay, and click OK. You can't select multiple sheets from this dialog box, so you need to repeat the command for each sheet that you want to unhide. When you unhide a sheet, it appears in its previous position among the sheet tabs.

Preventing Sheet Actions

To prevent others from unhiding hidden sheets, inserting new sheets, renaming sheets, copying sheets, or deleting sheets, protect the workbook's structure.

1. **Choose Review ⇨ Protect ⇨ Protect Workbook.**
2. **In the Protect Structure and Windows dialog box, select the Structure option.**
3. **Provide a password (optional) and click OK.**

After performing these steps, several commands will no longer be available from the Ribbon or when you right-click a sheet tab: Insert, Delete Sheet, Rename Sheet, Move or Copy Sheet, Tab Color, Hide Sheet, and Unhide Sheet. Be aware, however, that this is a weak security measure. Cracking this particular protection feature is relatively easy.

Controlling the Worksheet View

As you add more information to a worksheet, you may find that navigating and locating what you want becomes more difficult. Excel includes a few options that enable you to view your sheet, and sometimes multiple sheets, more efficiently. This section discusses a few additional worksheet options at your disposal.

Zooming in or out for a better view

Normally, everything you see onscreen is displayed at 100%. You can change the zoom percentage from 10% (very tiny) to 400% (huge). Using a small zoom percentage can help you get a bird's-eye view of your worksheet to see how it's laid out. Zooming in is useful if you have trouble deciphering tiny type. Zooming doesn't change the font size specified for the cells, so it has no effect on printed output.

 Excel contains separate options for changing the size of your printed output. (Use the controls in the Page Layout ⇨ Scale to Fit Ribbon group.) See Chapter 7, "Printing Your Work," for details.

You can change the zoom factor of the active worksheet window by using any of these three methods:

- Use the Zoom slider located on the right side of the status bar. Click and drag the slider, and your screen transforms instantly.
- Press Ctrl and use the wheel button on your mouse to zoom in or out.

3

■ Choose View ⇨ Zoom ⇨ Zoom, which displays a dialog box with some zoom options.

Also in the Zoom Ribbon group is a 100% button to return to 100% zoom quickly and a Zoom to Selection button to change the zoom so that whatever cells you have selected take up the whole window (but still limited to the 10–400% zoom range).

> **TIP**
>
> Zooming affects only the active worksheet window, so you can use different zoom factors for different worksheets. Also, if you have a worksheet displayed in two different windows, you can set a different zoom factor for each of the windows.

 If your worksheet uses named ranges (see Chapter 4, "Working with Excel Ranges and Tables"), zooming your worksheet to 39% or less displays the name of the range overlaid on the cells. Viewing named ranges in this manner is useful for getting an overview of how a worksheet is laid out.

Viewing a worksheet in multiple windows

Sometimes, you may want to view two different parts of a worksheet simultaneously—perhaps to make referencing a distant cell in a formula easier. Or you may want to examine more than one sheet in the same workbook simultaneously. You can accomplish either of these actions by opening a new view to the workbook, using one or more additional windows.

To create and display a new view of the active workbook, choose View ⇨ Window ⇨ New Window.

Excel displays a new window for the active workbook, similar to the one shown in Figure 3.5. In this case, each window shows a different worksheet in the workbook. Notice the text in the windows' title bars: climate data.xlsx - 1 and climate data.xlsx - 2. To help you keep track of the windows, Excel appends a hyphen and a number to each window.

> **TIP**
>
> If the workbook is maximized when you create a new window, you may not even notice that Excel created the new window. If you look at the Excel title bar, though, you'll see that the workbook title now has - 2 appended to the name. Choose View ⇨ Window ⇨ Arrange All and then choose one of the Arrange options in the Arrange Windows dialog box to display the open windows. If you select the Windows of Active Workbook check box, only the windows of the active workbook are arranged.

A single workbook can have as many views (that is, separate windows) as you want. Each window is independent. In other words, scrolling to a new location in one window doesn't cause scrolling in the other window(s). However, if you make changes to the worksheet shown in a particular window, those changes are also made in all views of that worksheet.

You can close these additional windows when you no longer need them. For example, clicking the Close button on the active window's title bar closes the active window but doesn't close the other windows for the workbook. If you have unsaved changes, Excel will prompt you to save only when you close the last window.

> **TIP**
>
> Multiple windows make copying or moving information from one worksheet to another easier. You can use Excel's drag-and-drop procedures to copy or move ranges.

FIGURE 3.5

Use multiple windows to view different sections of a workbook at the same time.

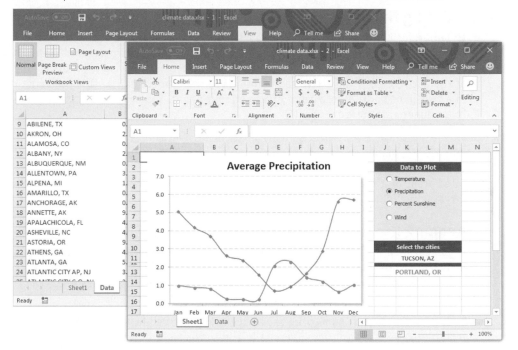

Comparing sheets side by side

In some situations, you may want to compare two worksheets that are in different windows. The View Side by Side feature makes this task a bit easier.

First, make sure that the two sheets are displayed in separate windows. (The sheets can be in the same workbook or in different workbooks.) If you want to compare two sheets in the same workbook, choose View ⇨ Window ⇨ New Window to create a new window for the active workbook. Activate the first window; then choose View ➪ Window ➪ View Side by Side. If more than two windows are open, you see a dialog box that lets you select the window for the comparison. The two windows are tiled to fill the entire screen.

When using the Compare Side by Side feature, scrolling in one of the windows also scrolls the other window. If you don't want this simultaneous scrolling, choose View ➪ Window ➪ Synchronous Scrolling (which is a toggle). If you have rearranged or moved the windows, choose View ➪ Window ➪ Reset Window Position to restore the windows to the initial side-by-side arrangement. To turn off the side-by-side viewing, choose View ➪ Window ➪ View Side by Side again.

Keep in mind that this feature is for manual comparison only. Unfortunately, Excel doesn't provide a way to identify the differences between two sheets automatically.

Splitting the worksheet window into panes

If you prefer not to clutter your screen with additional windows, Excel provides another option for viewing multiple parts of the same worksheet. Choosing View ➪ Window ➪ Split splits the active worksheet into two or four separate panes. The split occurs at the location of the active cell. If the active cell pointer is in row 1 or column A, this command results in a two-pane split; otherwise, it gives you four panes. You can use the mouse to drag the individual panes to resize them.

Figure 3.6 shows a worksheet split into four panes. Notice that row numbers aren't continuous. The top panes show rows 9 through 14, and the bottom panes show rows 107 through 121. In other words, splitting panes enables you to display in a single window widely separated areas of a worksheet. To remove the split panes, choose View ➪ Window ➪ Split again (or double-click the split bar).

Keeping the titles in view by freezing panes

If you set up a worksheet with column headings or descriptive text in the first column, this identifying information won't be visible when you scroll down or to the right. Excel provides a handy solution to this problem: freezing panes. Freezing panes keeps the column or row headings visible while you're scrolling through the worksheet.

To freeze panes, start by moving the active cell to the cell below the row that you want to remain visible while you scroll vertically and to the right of the column that you want to remain visible while you scroll horizontally. Then choose View ➪ Window ➪ Freeze Panes and select the Freeze Panes option from the drop-down list. Excel inserts dark lines to indicate the frozen rows and columns. The frozen rows and columns remain visible while you scroll throughout the worksheet. To remove the frozen panes, choose View ➪ Window ➪ Freeze Panes, and select the Unfreeze Panes option from the drop-down list.

Figure 3.7 shows a worksheet with frozen panes. In this case, rows 4:7 and column A are frozen in place. (Cell B8 was the active cell when the View ⇨ Window ⇨ Freeze Panes command was used.) This technique allows you to scroll down and to the right to locate some information while keeping the column titles and the column A entries visible.

FIGURE 3.6

You can split the worksheet window into two or four panes to view different areas of the worksheet at the same time.

	A	B	C	D	E	F	G	H	I	J
9	ABILENE, TX	0.97	1.13	1.41	1.67	2.83	3.06	1.69	2.63	2.
10	AKRON, OH	2.49	2.28	3.15	3.39	3.96	3.55	4.02	3.65	3.
11	ALAMOSA, CO	0.25	0.21	0.46	0.54	0.70	0.59	0.94	1.19	0.
12	ALBANY, NY	2.71	2.27	3.17	3.25	3.67	3.74	3.50	3.68	3.
13	ALBUQUERQUE, NM	0.49	0.44	0.61	0.50	0.60	0.65	1.27	1.73	1.
14	ALLENTOWN, PA	3.50	2.75	3.56	3.49	4.47	3.99	4.27	4.35	4.
107	GRAND ISLAND, NE	0.54	0.68	2.04	2.61	4.07	3.72	3.14	3.08	2.
108	GRAND JUNCTION, CO	0.60	0.50	1.00	0.86	0.98	0.41	0.66	0.84	0.
109	GRAND RAPIDS, MI	2.03	1.53	2.59	3.48	3.35	3.67	3.56	3.78	4.
110	GREAT FALLS, MT	0.68	0.51	1.01	1.40	2.53	2.24	1.45	1.65	1.
111	GREATER CINCINNATI AP	2.92	2.75	3.90	3.96	4.59	4.42	3.75	3.79	2.
112	GREEN BAY, WI	1.21	1.01	2.06	2.56	2.75	3.43	3.44	3.77	3.
113	GREENSBORO-WNSTN-SA	3.54	3.10	3.85	3.43	3.95	3.53	4.44	3.71	4.
114	GREENVILLE-SPARTANBUF	4.41	4.24	5.31	3.53	4.59	3.92	4.65	4.08	3.
115	GUAM, PC	5.58	5.11	4.24	4.16	6.39	6.28	11.66	16.17	13.
116	GULKANA,AK	0.45	0.52	0.36	0.22	0.59	1.54	1.82	1.80	1.
117	HARRISBURG, PA	3.18	2.88	3.58	3.31	4.60	3.99	3.21	3.24	3.
118	HARTFORD, CT	3.84	2.96	3.88	3.86	4.39	3.85	3.67	3.98	4.
119	HAVRE, MT	0.47	0.36	0.70	0.87	1.84	1.90	1.51	1.20	1.
120	HELENA, MT	0.52	0.38	0.63	0.91	1.78	1.82	1.34	1.29	1.
121	HILO, HI	9.74	8.86	14.35	12.54	8.07	7.36	10.71	9.78	9.

Most of the time you'll want to freeze either the first row or the first column. The View ⇨ Window ⇨ Freeze Panes drop-down list has two additional options: Freeze Top Row and Freeze First Column. Using these commands eliminates the need to position the active cell before freezing panes.

TIP

If you designated a range to be a table (by choosing Insert ⇨ Tables ⇨ Table), you may not even need to freeze panes. When you scroll down, Excel displays the table column headings in place of the column letters. Figure 3.8 shows an example. The table headings replace the column letters only when a cell within the table is selected.

FIGURE 3.7

Freeze certain columns and rows to make them remain visible while you scroll the worksheet.

	A	G	H	I	J	K	L
4	Normal Monthly Precipita						
5	NORMALS 1971-2000						
6							
7	284 CITIES	JUN	JUL	AUG	SEP	OCT	NOV
36	BETTLES,AK	1.43	2.10	2.54	1.82	1.08	0.90
37	BIG DELTA,AK	2.38	2.77	2.11	1.03	0.73	0.59
38	BILLINGS, MT	1.89	1.28	0.85	1.34	1.26	0.75
39	BINGHAMTON, NY	3.80	3.49	3.35	3.59	3.02	3.32
40	BIRMINGHAM AP,AL	3.78	5.09	3.48	4.05	3.23	4.63
41	BISHOP, CA	0.21	0.17	0.13	0.28	0.20	0.44
42	BISMARCK, ND	2.59	2.58	2.15	1.61	1.28	0.70
43	BLOCK IS.,RI	2.77	2.62	3.00	3.19	3.04	3.77
44	BLUE HILL, MA	3.93	3.74	4.06	4.13	4.42	4.64
45	BOISE, ID	0.74	0.39	0.30	0.76	0.76	1.38
46	BOSTON, MA	3.22	3.06	3.37	3.47	3.79	3.98
47	BRIDGEPORT, CT	3.57	3.77	3.75	3.58	3.54	3.65
48	BRISTOL-JHNSN CTY-KNGS	3.89	4.21	3.00	3.08	2.30	3.08
49	BROWNSVILLE, TX	2.93	1.77	2.99	5.31	3.78	1.75
50	BUFFALO, NY	3.82	3.14	3.87	3.84	3.19	3.92
51	BURLINGTON, VT	3.43	3.97	4.01	3.83	3.12	3.06
52	BURNS,OR	0.66	0.40	0.45	0.50	0.72	1.11
53	CAPE HATTERAS, NC	3.82	4.95	6.56	5.68	5.31	4.93

FIGURE 3.8

When using a table, scrolling down displays the table headings where the column letters normally appear.

	284 CITIES	JAN	FEB	MAR	APR	MAY	JUN	JUL	AUG	SEP	OCT
25	BALTIMORE, MD	3.47	3.02	3.93	3	3.89	3.43	3.85	3.74	3.98	3.16
26	BARROW, AK	0.12	0.12	0.09	0.12	0.12	0.32	0.87	1.04	0.69	0.39
27	BATON ROUGE, LA	6.19	5.1	5.07	5.56	5.34	5.33	5.96	5.86	4.84	3.81
28	BECKLEY, WV	3.23	2.96	3.63	3.42	4.39	3.92	4.78	3.45	3.23	2.64
29	BETHEL, AK	0.62	0.51	0.67	0.65	0.85	1.6	2.03	3.02	2.31	1.43
30	BETTLES,AK	0.84	0.61	0.55	0.38	0.85	1.43	2.1	2.54	1.82	1.08
31	BIG DELTA,AK	0.34	0.41	0.22	0.2	0.77	2.38	2.77	2.11	1.03	0.73
32	BILLINGS, MT	0.81	0.57	1.12	1.74	2.48	1.89	1.28	0.85	1.34	1.26
33	BINGHAMTON, NY	2.58	2.46	2.97	3.49	3.55	3.8	3.49	3.35	3.59	3.02
34	BIRMINGHAM AP,AL	5.45	4.21	6.1	4.67	4.83	3.78	5.09	3.48	4.05	3.23
35	BISHOP, CA	0.88	0.97	0.62	0.24	0.26	0.21	0.17	0.13	0.28	0.2
36	BISMARCK, ND	0.45	0.51	0.85	1.46	2.22	2.59	2.58	2.15	1.61	1.28
37	BLOCK IS.,RI	3.68	3.04	3.99	3.72	3.4	2.77	2.62	3	3.19	3.04
38	BLUE HILL, MA	4.78	4.06	4.79	4.32	3.79	3.93	3.74	4.06	4.13	4.42
39	BOISE, ID	1.39	1.14	1.41	1.27	1.27	0.74	0.39	0.3	0.76	0.76

Monitoring cells with a Watch Window

In some situations, you may want to monitor the value in a particular cell as you work. As you scroll throughout the worksheet, that cell may disappear from view. A feature known as a Watch Window can help. A Watch Window displays the value of any number of cells in a handy window that's always visible.

To display the Watch Window, choose Formulas ⇨ Formula Auditing ⇨ Watch Window. The Watch Window is actually a task pane, and you can dock it to the side of the window or drag it and make it float over the worksheet.

To add a cell to watch, click Add Watch and specify the cell that you want to watch. The Watch Window displays the value in that cell. You can add any number of cells to the Watch Window. Figure 3.9 shows the Watch Window monitoring four cells in different worksheets.

FIGURE 3.9

Use the Watch Window to monitor the value in one or more cells.

Book	Sheet	N...	Cell	Value	Formula
Status Reports.xlsx	Totals		F8	564,798	=SUM(F2:F7)
Status Reports.xlsx	Operations		F8	594,987	=SUM(F2:F7)
Status Reports.xlsx	Marketing		F8	574,743	=SUM(F2:F7)
Status Reports.xlsx	Manufacturi...		F8	677,931	=SUM(F2:F7)

TIP

Double-click a cell in the Watch Window to select that cell immediately. This works only if the watched cell is in the active workbook.

Working with Rows and Columns

This section discusses worksheet operations that involve complete rows and columns (rather than individual cells). Every worksheet has exactly 1,048,576 rows and 16,384 columns, and these values can't be changed.

NOTE

If you open a workbook that was created in a version of Excel prior to Excel 2007, the workbook is opened in Compatibility Mode. These workbooks have 65,536 rows and 256 columns. If you would like to increase the number of rows and columns, save the workbook as an Excel `.xlsx` or `.xlsm` file and then reopen it.

Inserting rows and columns

Although the number of rows and columns in a worksheet is fixed, you can still insert and delete rows and columns if you need to make room for additional information. These operations don't change the number of rows or columns. Instead, inserting a new row moves down the other rows to accommodate the new row. The last row is simply removed from the worksheet if it's empty. Inserting a new column shifts the columns to the right, and the last column is removed if it's empty.

> **NOTE**
>
> If the last row isn't empty, you can't insert a new row. Similarly, if the last column contains information, Excel doesn't let you insert a new column. In either case, attempting to add a row or column displays the dialog box shown in Figure 3.10.

FIGURE 3.10

You can't add a new row or column if it causes nonblank cells to move off the worksheet.

To insert a new row or rows, use either of these methods:

- Select an entire row or multiple rows by clicking the row numbers in the worksheet border. Right-click and choose Insert from the shortcut menu.
- Move the active cell to the row that you want to insert and then choose Home ⇨ Cells ⇨ Insert ⇨ Insert Sheet Rows. If you select multiple cells in the column, Excel inserts additional rows that correspond to the number of cells selected in the column and moves the rows below the insertion down.

To insert a new column or columns, use either of these methods:

- Select an entire column or columns by clicking the column letters in the worksheet border. Right-click and choose Insert from the shortcut menu.
- Move the active cell to the column that you want to insert and then choose Home ⇨ Cells ⇨ Insert ⇨ Insert Sheet Columns. If you select multiple cells in the row, Excel inserts additional columns that correspond to the number of cells selected in the row.

You can also insert cells rather than just rows or columns. Select the range into which you want to add new cells and then choose Home ⇨ Cells ⇨ Insert ⇨ Insert Cells (or right-click the selection and choose Insert). To insert cells, you must shift the existing cells to the right or down. Therefore, Excel displays the Insert dialog box shown in Figure 3.11 so that you can specify the direction in which you want to shift the cells. Notice that this dialog box also enables you to insert entire rows or columns.

FIGURE 3.11

You can insert partial rows or columns by using the Insert dialog box.

Deleting rows and columns

You may also want to delete rows or columns in a worksheet. For example, your sheet may contain old data that is no longer needed, or you may want to remove empty rows or columns.

To delete a row or rows, use either of these methods:

- Select an entire row or multiple rows by clicking the row numbers in the worksheet border. Right-click and choose Delete from the shortcut menu.
- Move the active cell to the row that you want to delete and then choose Home ⇨ Cells ⇨ Delete ⇨ Delete Sheet Rows. If you select multiple cells in the column, Excel deletes all rows in the selection.

Deleting columns works in a similar way.

If you discover that you accidentally deleted a row or column, select Undo from the Quick Access toolbar (or press Ctrl+Z) to undo the action.

> **TIP**
>
> You can use the shortcut keys Ctrl+ (plus sign) and Ctrl+ (minus sign) to insert and delete rows, columns, or cells. If you have an entire row or entire column selected, those shortcuts will insert or delete the entire row or column. If the selection isn't an entire row or column, the Insert Cells dialog is displayed.

Changing column widths and row heights

Often, you'll want to change the width of a column or the height of a row. For example, you can make columns narrower to show more information on a printed page. Or you may want to increase row height to create a "double-spaced" effect.

Excel provides several ways to change the widths of columns and the height of rows.

Changing column widths

Column width is measured in terms of the number of characters of a monospaced font that will fit into the cell's width. By default, each column's width is 8.43 units, which equates to 64 pixels (*px*).

TIP

If hash symbols (#) fill a cell that contains a numerical value, the column isn't wide enough to accommodate the information in the cell. Widen the column to solve the problem.

Before you change the column width, you can select multiple columns so that the width will be the same for all selected columns. To select multiple columns, either click and drag in the column border or press Ctrl while you select individual columns. To select all columns, click the button where the row and column headers intersect. You can change column widths by using any of the following techniques:

- Drag the right-column border with the mouse until the column is the desired width.
- Choose Home ➪ Cells ➪ Format ➪ Column Width and enter a value in the Column Width dialog box.
- Choose Home ➪ Cells ➪ Format ➪ AutoFit Column Width to adjust the width of the selected column so that the widest entry in the column fits. Instead of selecting an entire column, you can just select cells in the column, and the column is adjusted based on the widest entry in your selection.
- Double-click the right border of a column header to set the column width automatically to the widest entry in the column.

TIP

To change the default width of all columns, choose Home ➪ Cells ➪ Format ➪ Default Width. This command displays a dialog box into which you enter the new default column width. All columns that haven't been previously adjusted take on the new column width.

CAUTION

After you manually adjust a column's width, Excel will no longer automatically adjust the column to accommodate longer numerical entries. If you enter a long number that displays as hash symbols (#), you need to change the column width manually.

Changing row heights

Row height is measured in points (a standard unit of measurement in the printing trade—72 pts is equal to 1 inch). The default row height using the default font is 15 pts, or 20 pixels (*px*).

The default row height can vary, depending on the font defined in the Normal style. In addition, Excel automatically adjusts row heights to accommodate the tallest font in the row. So, if you change the font size of a cell to 20 pts, for example, Excel makes the row taller so that the entire text is visible.

You can set the row height manually, however, by using any of the following techniques. As with columns, you can select multiple rows:

- Drag the lower row border with the mouse until the row is the desired height.
- Choose Home ⇨ Cells ⇨ Format ⇨ Row Height and enter a value (in points) in the Row Height dialog box.
- Double-click the bottom border of a row to set the row height automatically to the tallest entry in the row. You can also choose Home ⇨ Cells ⇨ Format ⇨ AutoFit Row Height for this task.

Changing the row height is useful for spacing out rows and is almost always preferable to inserting empty rows between lines of data.

Hiding rows and columns

In some cases, you may want to hide particular rows or columns. Hiding rows and columns may be useful if you don't want users to see particular information or if you need to print a report that summarizes the information in the worksheet without showing all the details.

 Chapter 27, "Creating and Using Worksheet Outlines," discusses another way to summarize worksheet data without showing all the details—worksheet outlining.

To hide rows in your worksheet, select the row or rows that you want to hide by clicking in the row header on the left. Then right-click and choose Hide from the shortcut menu. Or, you can use the commands on the Home ⇨ Cells ⇨ Format ⇨ Hide & Unhide menu.

To hide columns, use the same technique, but start by selecting columns rather than rows.

TIP

You can also drag the row or column's border to hide the row or column. You must drag the border in the row or column heading. Drag the bottom border of a row upward or the right border of a column to the left.

A hidden row is actually a row with its height set to zero. Similarly, a hidden column has a column width of zero. When you use the navigation keys to move the active cell, cells in hidden rows or columns are skipped. In other words, you can't use the navigation keys to move to a cell in a hidden row or column.

Notice, however, that Excel displays a narrow column heading for hidden columns and a narrow row heading for hidden rows. You can click and drag the column heading to make the column wider—and make it visible again. For a hidden row, click and drag the small row heading to make the row visible.

Another way to unhide a row or column is to choose Home ⇨ Editing ⇨ Find & Select ⇨ Go To (or use one of its two shortcut keys: F5 or Ctrl+G) to select a cell in a hidden row or column. For example, if column A is hidden, you can press F5 and go to cell A1 (or any other cell in column A) to move the active cell to the hidden column. Then you can choose Home ⇨ Cells ⇨ Format ⇨ Hide & Unhide ⇨ Unhide Columns.

Working with Excel Ranges and Tables

IN THIS CHAPTER

Understanding Excel cells and ranges

Selecting cells and ranges

Copying or moving ranges

Using names to work with ranges

Adding comments to cells

Working with Tables

Most of the work you do in Excel involves cells and ranges. Understanding how best to manipulate cells and ranges will save you time and effort. This chapter discusses a variety of techniques that are essential for Excel users.

Understanding Cells and Ranges

A *cell* is a single element in a worksheet that can hold a value, some text, or a formula. A cell is identified by its address, which consists of its column letter and row number. For example, cell D9 is the cell in the fourth column and the ninth row.

A group of one or more cells is called a *range*. You designate a range address by specifying its upper-left cell address and its lower-right cell address, separated by a colon.

Here are some examples of range addresses:

C24	A range that consists of a single cell.
A1:B1	Two cells that occupy one row and two columns.
A1:A100	100 cells in column A.
A1:D4	16 cells (four rows by four columns).
C1:C1048576	An entire column of cells; this range also can be expressed as C:C.
A6:XFD6	An entire row of cells; this range also can be expressed as 6:6.
A1:XFD1048576	All cells in a worksheet. This range also can be expressed as either A:XFD or 1:1048576.

Selecting ranges

To perform an operation on a range of cells in a worksheet, you must first select the range. For example, if you want to make the text bold for a range of cells, you must select the range and then choose Home ⇨ Font ⇨ Bold (or press Ctrl+B).

When you select a range, the cells appear highlighted. The exception is the active cell, which remains its normal color. Figure 4.1 shows an example of a selected range (A4:D8) in a worksheet. Cell A4, the active cell, is in the selected range but not highlighted.

FIGURE 4.1

When you select a range, it appears highlighted, but the active cell within the range is not highlighted.

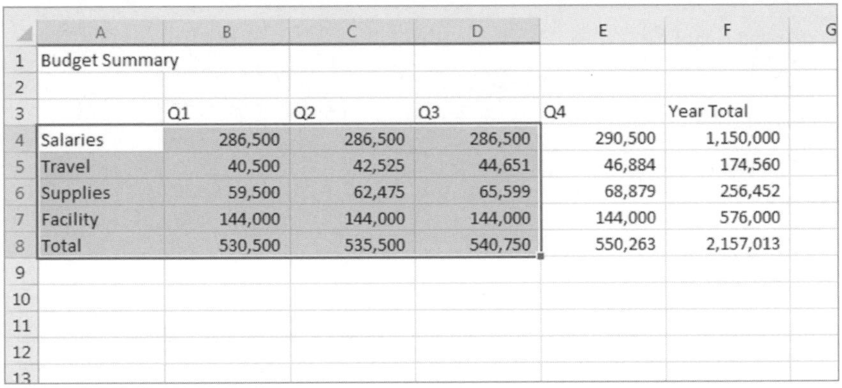

	A	B	C	D	E	F	G
1	Budget Summary						
2							
3		Q1	Q2	Q3	Q4	Year Total	
4	Salaries	286,500	286,500	286,500	290,500	1,150,000	
5	Travel	40,500	42,525	44,651	46,884	174,560	
6	Supplies	59,500	62,475	65,599	68,879	256,452	
7	Facility	144,000	144,000	144,000	144,000	576,000	
8	Total	530,500	535,500	540,750	550,263	2,157,013	
9							
10							
11							
12							
13							

You can select a range in several ways:

- Left-click and drag over the range. If you drag to the end of the window, the worksheet will scroll.
- Press the Shift key while you use the navigation keys to select a range.
- Press F8 to enter Extend Selection mode (Extend Selection appears in the status bar). In this mode, click the lower-right cell of the range or use the navigation keys to extend the range. Press F8 again to exit Extend Selection mode.
- Type the cell or range address into the Name box (located to the left of the Formula bar) and press Enter. Excel selects the cell or range that you specified.
- Choose Home ⇨ Editing ⇨ Find & Select ⇨ Go To (or press F5 or Ctrl+G) and enter a range's address manually in the Go To dialog box. When you click OK, Excel selects the cells in the range that you specified.

> **TIP**
>
> While you're selecting a range that contains more than one cell, Excel displays the number of rows and columns in your selection in the Name box (which is to the left of the Formula bar). When you finish making the selection, the Name box reverts to showing the address of the active cell.

Selecting complete rows and columns

Often, you'll need to select an entire row or column. For example, you may want to apply the same numeric format or the same alignment options to an entire row or column. You can select entire rows and columns in much the same manner as you select ranges:

- Click the row or column header to select a single row or column or click and drag for multiple rows or columns.
- To select multiple (nonadjacent) rows or columns, click the first row or column header and then hold down the Ctrl key while you click the additional row or column header that you want.
- Press Ctrl+spacebar to select the column(s) of the currently selected cells. Press Shift+spacebar to select the row(s) of the currently selected cells.

TIP

Press Ctrl+A to select all cells in the worksheet, which is the same as selecting all rows and all columns. If the active cell is within a contiguous range, Ctrl+A will just select that range. In that case, press Ctrl+A again to select all of the cells in the worksheet. You can also click the area at the intersection of the row and column headers to select all cells.

Selecting noncontiguous ranges

Most of the time, the ranges that you select are contiguous—a single rectangle of cells. Excel also enables you to work with noncontiguous ranges, which consist of two or more ranges (or single cells) that aren't necessarily adjacent to each other. Selecting noncontiguous ranges is also known as a *multiple selection*. If you want to apply the same formatting to cells in different areas of your worksheet, one approach is to make a multiple selection. When the appropriate cells or ranges are selected, the formatting that you select is applied to all of them. Figure 4.2 shows a noncontiguous range selected in a worksheet. Three ranges are selected: B3:E3, B6:C8, and cell F15.

You can select a noncontiguous range in the same ways that you select a contiguous range with a few minor differences. Instead of simply clicking and dragging for contiguous ranges, hold down the Ctrl key while you click and drag. If you're selecting a range using the arrow keys, press Shift+F8 to enter Add or Remove Selection mode (that term will appear in the status bar). Press Shift+F8 again to exit Add or Remove Selection mode. Anywhere you type the range manually, such as in the Name box or the Go To dialog box, simply separate the noncontiguous ranges with a comma. For example, typing `A1:A10, C5:C6` will select those two noncontiguous ranges.

NOTE

Noncontiguous ranges differ from contiguous ranges in several important ways. One major difference is that you can't use drag-and-drop methods (described later) to move or copy noncontiguous ranges.

4

FIGURE 4.2

Excel enables you to select noncontiguous ranges.

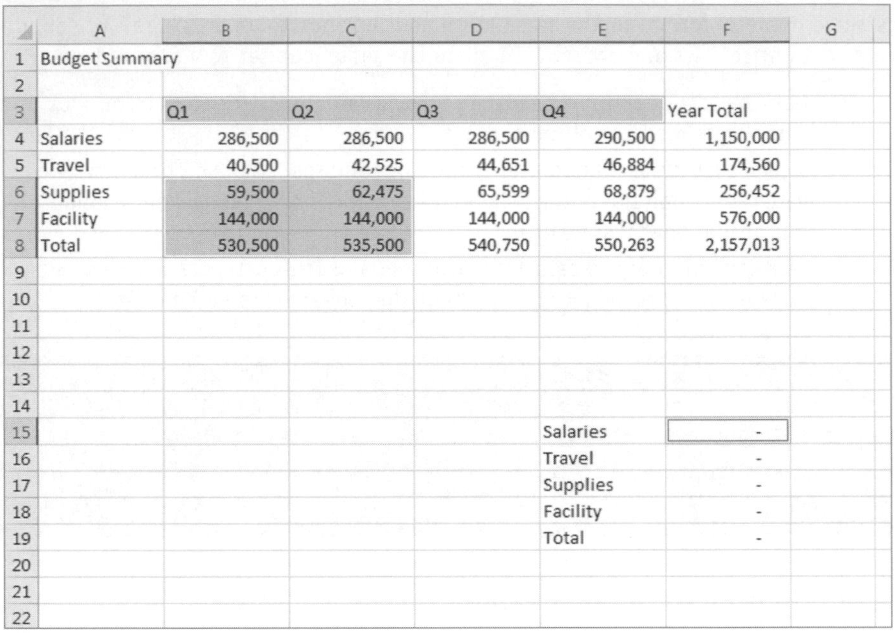

	A	B	C	D	E	F	G
1	Budget Summary						
2							
3		Q1	Q2	Q3	Q4	Year Total	
4	Salaries	286,500	286,500	286,500	290,500	1,150,000	
5	Travel	40,500	42,525	44,651	46,884	174,560	
6	Supplies	59,500	62,475	65,599	68,879	256,452	
7	Facility	144,000	144,000	144,000	144,000	576,000	
8	Total	530,500	535,500	540,750	550,263	2,157,013	
9							
10							
11							
12							
13							
14							
15					Salaries	-	
16					Travel	-	
17					Supplies	-	
18					Facility	-	
19					Total	-	
20							
21							
22							

Selecting multisheet ranges

In addition to two-dimensional ranges on a single worksheet, ranges can extend across multiple worksheets to be three-dimensional ranges.

Suppose you have a workbook set up to track budgets. One approach is to use a separate worksheet for each department, making it easy to organize the data. You can click a sheet tab to view the information for a particular department.

Figure 4.3 shows a simplified example. The workbook has four sheets: Totals, Operations, Marketing, and Manufacturing. The sheets are laid out identically. The only difference is the values. The Totals sheet contains formulas that compute the sum of the corresponding items in the three departmental worksheets.

FIGURE 4.3

The worksheets in this workbook are laid out identically.

	A	B	C	D	E	F	G	H
1	Operations							
2								
3		Q1	Q2	Q3	Q4	Year Total		
4	Salaries	128,500	128,500	128,500	132,500	518,000		
5	Travel	18,500	19,425	20,396	21,416	79,737		
6	Supplies	16,000	16,800	17,640	18,522	68,962		
7	Facility	23,000	23,000	23,000	23,000	92,000		
8	Total	186,000	187,725	189,536	195,438	758,699		
9								
10								
11								
12								
13								
14								
15								
16								

Tabs: Totals | **Operations** | Marketing | Manufacturing

Ready — 100%

 This workbook, named `budget.xlsx`, is available on this book's website at `www.wiley.com/go/excel2019bible`.

Assume that you want to apply formatting to the sheets—for example, to make the column headings bold with background shading. One (albeit not-so-efficient) approach is to format the cells in each worksheet separately. A better technique is to select a multisheet range and format the cells in all the sheets simultaneously. The following is a step-by-step example of multisheet formatting using the workbook shown in Figure 4.3:

1. Activate the Totals worksheet by clicking its tab.

2. Select the range B3:F3.

3. Press Shift and click the Manufacturing sheet tab. This step selects all worksheets between the active worksheet (Totals) and the sheet tab that you click—in essence, a three-dimensional range of cells (see Figure 4.4). When multiple sheets are selected, the workbook window's title bar displays Group to remind you that you've selected a group of sheets and that you're in Group mode.

FIGURE 4.4

In Group mode, you can work with a three-dimensional range of cells that extend across multiple worksheets.

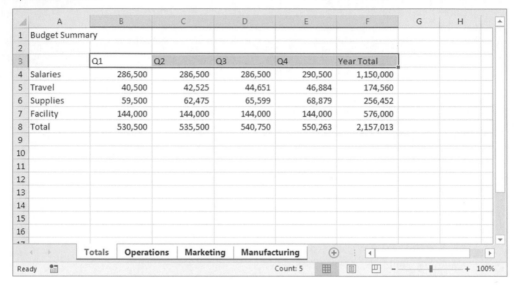

4. Choose Home ⇨ Font ⇨ Bold and then choose Home ⇨ Font ⇨ Fill Color to apply a colored background. Excel applies the formatting to the selected range across the selected sheets.

5. Click one of the other sheet tabs. This step selects the sheet and cancels Group mode; Group is no longer displayed in the title bar.

When a workbook is in Group mode, any changes that you make to cells in one worksheet also apply to the corresponding cells in all of the other grouped worksheets. You can use this to your advantage when you want to set up a group of identical worksheets because any labels, data, formatting, or formulas you enter are automatically added to the same cells in all of the grouped worksheets.

NOTE

When Excel is in Group mode, some commands are disabled and can't be used. For example, in the preceding example, you can't convert all of these ranges to tables by choosing Insert ⇨ Tables ⇨ Table.

In general, selecting a multisheet range is a simple two-step process: select the range in one sheet and then select the worksheets to include in the range. To select a group of contiguous worksheets, select the first worksheet in the group and then press Shift and click the sheet tab of the last worksheet that you want to include in the selection. To select individual worksheets, select one of the worksheets in the group and then press Ctrl and click the sheet tab of each additional worksheet that you want to select. If all of the worksheets in a workbook aren't laid out the same, you can skip the sheets that you don't want to format. When you make the selection, the sheet tabs of the selected sheets display in bold with underlined text, and Excel displays Group in the title bar.

TIP

To select all sheets in a workbook, right-click any sheet tab and choose Select All Sheets from the shortcut menu.

CAUTION

When sheets are grouped, you are making changes to sheets you can't see. Before you group sheets, be sure you understand what changes you intend to make and how that will affect all the sheets in the group. When you're done, don't forget to ungroup the sheets. You can overwrite data on the other sheets if you start typing on the active sheet while in Group mode.

Selecting special types of cells

As you use Excel, you may need to locate specific types of cells in your worksheets. For example, wouldn't it be handy to be able to locate every cell that contains a formula—or perhaps all of the formula cells that depend on the active cell? Excel provides an easy way to locate these and many other special types of cells: select a range and choose Home ➪ Editing ➪ Find & Select ➪ Go To Special to display the Go To Special dialog box, as shown in Figure 4.5.

FIGURE 4.5

Use the Go To Special dialog box to select specific types of cells.

After you make your choice in the dialog box, Excel selects the qualifying subset of cells in the current selection. Often, this subset of cells is a multiple selection. If no cells qualify, Excel lets you know with the message `No cells were found`.

> **TIP**
>
> If you bring up the Go To Special dialog box with only one cell selected, Excel bases its selection on the entire used area of the worksheet. Otherwise, the selection is based on the selected range.

Table 4.1 offers a description of the options available in the Go To Special dialog box.

TABLE 4.1 Go To Special Options

Option	What it does
Comments	Selects the cells that contain a cell comment.
Constants	Selects all nonempty cells that don't contain formulas. Use the check boxes under the Formulas option to choose which types of nonformula cells to include.
Formulas	Selects cells that contain formulas. Qualify this by selecting the type of result: numbers, text, logical values (TRUE or FALSE), or errors.
Blanks	Selects all empty cells. If a single cell is selected when the dialog box displays, this option selects the empty cells in the used area of the worksheet.
Current Region	Selects a rectangular range of cells around the active cell. This range is determined by surrounding blank rows and columns. You can also press Ctrl+Shift+*.
Current Array	Selects the entire array. (See Chapter 18, "Understanding and Using Array Formulas," for more on arrays.)
Objects	Selects all embedded objects on the worksheet, including charts and graphics.
Row Differences	Analyzes the selection and selects cells that are different from other cells in each row.
Column Differences	Analyzes the selection and selects the cells that are different from other cells in each column.
Precedents	Selects cells that are referred to in the formulas in the active cell or selection (limited to the active sheet). You can select either direct precedents or precedents at all levels. (See Chapter 19, "Making Your Formulas Error-Free," for more information.)
Dependents	Selects cells with formulas that refer to the active cell or selection (limited to the active sheet). You can select either direct dependents or dependents at all levels. (See Chapter 19 for more information.)

Option	What it does
Last Cell	Selects the bottom-right cell in the worksheet that contains data or formatting. For this option, the entire worksheet is examined, even if a range is selected when the dialog box displays.
Visible Cells Only	Selects only visible cells in the selection. This option is useful when dealing with a filtered list or a table.
Conditional Formats	Selects cells that have a conditional format applied (by choosing Home ⇨ Styles ⇨ Conditional Formatting). The All option selects all such cells. The Same option selects only the cells that have the same conditional formatting as the active cell.
Data Validation	Selects cells that are set up for data entry validation (by choosing Data ⇨ Data Tools ⇨ Data Validation). The All option selects all such cells. The Same option selects only the cells that have the same validation rules as the active cell.

TIP

When you select an option in the Go To Special dialog box, be sure to note which suboptions become available. The placement of these suboptions can be misleading. For example, when you select Constants, the suboptions under Formulas become available to help you further refine the results. Likewise, the suboptions under Dependents also apply to Precedents, and those under Data Validation also apply to Conditional Formats.

Selecting cells by searching

Another way to select cells is to choose Home ⇨ Editing ⇨ Find & Select ⇨ Find (or press Ctrl+F), which allows you to select cells by their contents. The Find and Replace dialog box is shown in Figure 4.6. This figure illustrates additional options that are available when you click the Options button.

FIGURE 4.6

The Find and Replace dialog box, with its options displayed

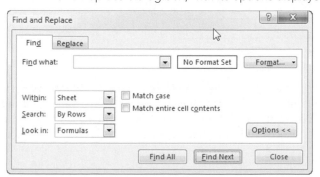

Enter the text you're looking for; then click Find All. The dialog box expands to display all of the cells that match your search criteria. For example, Figure 4.7 shows the dialog box after Excel has located all cells that contain the text supplies. You can click an item in the list, and the screen will scroll so that you can view the cell in context. To select all of the cells in the list, first select any single item in the list. Then press Ctrl+A to select them all.

FIGURE 4.7

The Find and Replace dialog box, with its results listed

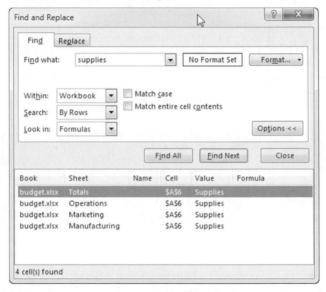

The Find and Replace dialog box supports two wildcard characters:

?	Matches any single character
*	Matches any number of characters

Wildcard characters also work with values when the Match Entire Cell Contents option is selected. For example, searching for 3* locates all cells that contain a value that begins with 3. Searching for 1?9 locates all three-digit entries that begin with 1 and end with 9. Searching for *00 locates values that end with two zeros.

TIP

To search for a question mark or an asterisk, precede the character with a tilde (~). For example, the following search string finds the text *NONE*:

~*NONE~*

If you need to search for the tilde character, use two tildes.

If your searches don't seem to be working correctly, double-check these three options:

Match Case   If this check box is selected, the case of the text must match exactly. For example, searching for smith does not locate Smith.

Match Entire Cell Contents   If this check box is selected, a match occurs if the cell contains only the search string (and nothing else). For example, searching for Excel doesn't locate a cell that contains Microsoft Excel. When using wildcard characters, an exact match is not required.

Look In   This drop-down list has three options: Values, Formulas, and Comments. The Formulas option looks only at the text that makes up the formula or the contents of the cell if there is no formula. The Values option looks at the cell value and the results, not the text, of the formula. If, for example, Formulas is selected, searching for 900 doesn't find a cell that contains the formula =899+1 but will find a cell with a value of 900. The Values option will find both of those cells.

Copying or Moving Ranges

As you create a worksheet, you may find it necessary to copy or move information from one location to another. Excel makes copying or moving ranges of cells easy. Here are some common things that you might do:

- Copy a cell to another location.
- Copy a cell to a range of cells. The source cell is copied to every cell in the destination range.
- Copy a range to another range.
- Move a range of cells to another location.

The primary difference between copying and moving a range is the effect of the operation on the source range. When you copy a range, the source range is unaffected. When you move a range, the contents are removed from the source range.

NOTE

Copying a cell normally copies the cell's contents, any formatting that is applied to the original cell (including conditional formatting and data validation), and the cell comment (if it has one). When you copy a cell that contains a formula, the cell references in the copied formulas are changed automatically to be relative to their new destination.

Copying or moving consists of two steps (although shortcut methods are available):

1. Select the cell or range to copy (the source range), and copy it to the Clipboard. To move the range instead of copying it, cut the range instead of copying it.

2. Select the cell or range that will hold the copy (the destination range), and paste the Clipboard contents.

CAUTION

When you paste information, Excel overwrites any cells that get in the way without warning you. If you find that pasting overwrote some essential cells, choose Undo from the Quick Access toolbar (or press Ctrl+Z).

CAUTION

When you copy a cell or range, Excel surrounds the copied area with a thick-dashed border. As long as that border remains visible, the copied information is available for pasting. If you press Esc to cancel the border, Excel removes the information from the Clipboard.

Because copying (or moving) is used so often, Excel provides many different methods. We discuss each method in the following sections. Copying and moving are similar operations, so we point out only important differences between the two.

Copying by using Ribbon commands

Choosing Home ➪ Clipboard ➪ Copy transfers a copy of the selected cell or range to the Windows Clipboard and the Office Clipboard. After performing the copy part of this operation, select the destination cell and choose Home ➪ Clipboard ➪ Paste.

Instead of choosing Home ➪ Clipboard ➪ Paste, you can just activate the destination cell and press Enter. If you use this technique, Excel removes the copied information from the Clipboard so that it can't be pasted again.

If you're copying a range, you don't need to select an entire same-sized range before you click the Paste button. You only need to activate the upper-left cell in the destination range.

TIP

The Home ➪ Clipboard ➪ Paste control contains a drop-down arrow that, when clicked, gives you additional paste option icons. The paste preview icons are explained later in this chapter (see "Pasting in special ways").

About the Office Clipboard

Whenever you cut or copy information from a Windows program, Windows stores the information on the Windows Clipboard, which is an area of your computer's memory. Each time that you cut or copy information, Windows replaces the information previously stored on the Clipboard with the new information that you cut or copied. The Windows Clipboard can store data in a variety of formats. Because Windows manages information on the Clipboard, it can be pasted to other Windows applications, regardless of where it originated.

Microsoft Office has its own Clipboard (the Office Clipboard), which is available only in Office programs. To view or hide the Office Clipboard, click the dialog box launcher in the bottom-right corner of the Home ➪ Clipboard group.

Whenever you cut or copy information in an Office program, such as Excel or Word, the program places the information on both the Windows Clipboard and the Office Clipboard. However, the program treats information on the Office Clipboard differently from the way it treats information on the Windows Clipboard. Instead of replacing information on the Office Clipboard, the program appends the information to the Office Clipboard. With multiple items stored on the Clipboard, you can then paste the items either individually or as a group.

You can find out more about this feature (including an important limitation) in "Using the Office Clipboard to paste" later in this chapter.

Copying by using shortcut menu commands

If you prefer, you can use the following shortcut menu commands for copying and pasting:

- Right-click the range and choose Copy (or Cut) from the shortcut menu to copy the selected cells to the Clipboard.
- Right-click and choose Paste from the shortcut menu that appears to paste the Clipboard contents to the selected cell or range.

For more control over how the pasted information appears, right-click the destination cell and use one of the Paste icons in the shortcut menu (see Figure 4.8).

Instead of using Paste, you can just activate the destination cell and press Enter. If you use this technique, Excel removes the copied information from the Clipboard so that it can't be pasted again.

Copying by using shortcut keys

The copy and paste operations also have shortcut keys associated with them:

- Ctrl+C copies the selected cells to both the Windows Clipboard and the Office Clipboard.
- Ctrl+X cuts the selected cells to both the Windows Clipboard and the Office Clipboard.
- Ctrl+V pastes the Windows Clipboard contents to the selected cell or range.

4

FIGURE 4.8

The Paste icons on the shortcut menu provide more control over how the pasted information appears.

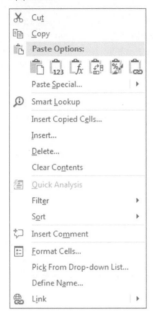

Using Paste Options Buttons When Inserting and Pasting

Some cell and range operations—specifically inserting, pasting, and filling cells by dragging—result in the display of Paste Options buttons. For example, if you copy a range and then paste it to a different location using Home ➪ Clipboard ➪ Paste, a drop-down options list appears at the lower right of the pasted range. Click the list (or press Ctrl), and you see the options shown in the following figure. These options enable you to specify how the data should be pasted, such as values only or formatting only. In this case, using the Paste Options buttons is an alternative to using options in the Paste Special dialog box. (Read more about Paste Special in the upcoming section "Using the Paste Special dialog box.")

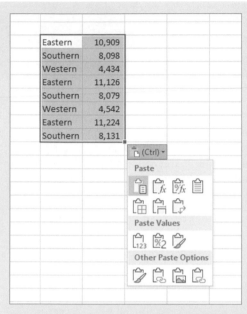

To disable this feature, choose File ➪ Options and click the Advanced tab. Remove the check mark from the two options labeled Show Paste Options Button When Content Is Pasted and Show Insert Options Buttons.

Copying or moving by using drag-and-drop

Excel also enables you to copy or move a cell or range by dragging. Unlike other methods of copying and moving, dragging and dropping does not place any information on either the Windows Clipboard or the Office Clipboard.

> **CAUTION**
>
> The drag-and-drop method of moving does offer one advantage over the cut-and-paste method: Excel warns you if a drag-and-drop move operation will overwrite existing cell contents. Oddly, you do not get a warning if a drag-and-drop copy operation will overwrite existing cell contents.

To copy using drag-and-drop, select the cell or range that you want to copy, press Ctrl, and move the mouse to one of the selection's borders. (The mouse pointer is augmented with a small plus sign.) Then drag the selection to its new location while you continue to hold down the Ctrl key. The original selection remains behind, and Excel makes a new copy when you release the mouse button.

To move a range using drag-and-drop, don't press Ctrl while dragging the border.

4

Copying to adjacent cells

Often, you need to copy a cell to an adjacent cell or range. This type of copying is quite common when you're working with formulas. For example, if you're working on a budget, you might create a formula to add the values in column B. You can use the same formula to add the values in the other columns. Rather than re-enter the formula, you can copy it to the adjacent cells.

Excel provides additional options for copying to adjacent cells. To use these commands, activate the cell that you're copying and extend the cell selection to include the cells to which you're copying. Then issue the appropriate command from the following list for one-step copying:

- Home ⇨ Editing ⇨ Fill ⇨ Down (or Ctrl+D) copies the cell to the selected range below.
- Home ⇨ Editing ⇨ Fill ⇨ Right (or Ctrl+R) copies the cell to the selected range to the right.
- Home ⇨ Editing ⇨ Fill ⇨ Up copies the cell to the selected range above.
- Home ⇨ Editing ⇨ Fill ⇨ Left copies the cell to the selected range to the left.

None of these commands places information on either the Windows Clipboard or the Office Clipboard.

Copying a range to other sheets

You can use the copy procedures described previously to copy a cell or range to another worksheet, even if the worksheet is in a different workbook. You must, of course, activate the other worksheet before you select the location to which you want to copy.

Excel offers a quicker way to copy a cell or range and paste it to other worksheets in the same workbook:

1. **Select the range to copy.**
2. **Press Ctrl and click the sheet tabs for the worksheets to which you want to copy the information.** Excel displays Group in the workbook's title bar.
3. **Choose Home ⇨ Editing ⇨ Fill ⇨ Across Worksheets.** A dialog box appears to ask you what you want to copy (All, Contents, or Formats).
4. **Make your choice and then click OK.** Excel copies the selected range to the selected worksheets; the new copy occupies the same cells in the selected worksheets as the original occupies in the initial worksheet.

> **CAUTION**
>
> Be careful with the Home ⇨ Editing ⇨ Fill ⇨ Across Worksheets command because Excel doesn't warn you when the destination cells contain information. You can quickly overwrite lots of cells with this command and not even realize it. So make sure that you check your work, and use Undo if the result isn't what you expected.

Using the Office Clipboard to paste

Whenever you cut or copy information in an Office program such as Excel, you can place the data on both the Windows Clipboard and the Office Clipboard. When you copy information to the Office Clipboard, you append the information to the Office Clipboard instead of replacing what is already there. With multiple items stored on the Office Clipboard, you can then paste the items either individually or as a group.

To use the Office Clipboard, you first need to open it. Use the dialog box launcher on the bottom right of the Home ⇨ Clipboard group to toggle the Clipboard task pane on and off.

4

> **TIP**
>
> To make the Clipboard task pane open automatically, click the Options button near the bottom of the task pane and choose the Show Office Clipboard Automatically option.

After you open the Clipboard task pane, select the first cell or range that you want to copy to the Office Clipboard and copy it by using any of the preceding techniques. Repeat this process, selecting the next cell or range that you want to copy. As soon as you copy the information, the Office Clipboard task pane shows you the number of items that you've copied and a brief description (it will hold up to 24 items). Figure 4.9 shows the Office Clipboard with five copied items (four from Excel and one from Word).

FIGURE 4.9

Use the Clipboard task pane to copy and paste multiple items.

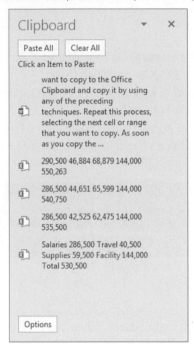

When you're ready to paste information, select the cell into which you want to paste information. To paste an individual item, click it in the Clipboard task pane. To paste all of the items that you've copied, click the Paste All button (which is at the top of the Clipboard task pane). The items are pasted, one after the other. The Paste All button is probably more useful in Word for situations in which you copy text from various sources and then paste it all at once.

You can clear the contents of the Office Clipboard by clicking the Clear All button.

The following items about the Office Clipboard and how it functions are worth noting:

- Excel pastes the contents of the Windows Clipboard (the last item you copied to the Office Clipboard) when you paste by choosing Home ➪ Clipboard ➪ Paste, by pressing Ctrl+V, or by right-clicking and choosing Paste from the shortcut menu.

- The last item that you cut or copied appears on both the Office Clipboard and the Windows Clipboard.
- Clearing the Office Clipboard also clears the Windows Clipboard.

> **CAUTION**
>
> The Office Clipboard has a serious problem that limits its usefulness for Excel users: if you copy a range that contains formulas, the formulas are not transferred when you paste from the Clipboard task pane to a different range. Only the values are pasted. Furthermore, Excel doesn't even warn you about this fact.

Pasting in special ways

You may not always want to copy everything from the source range to the destination range. For example, you may want to copy only the formula results rather than the formulas themselves. Or you may want to copy the number formats from one range to another without overwriting any existing data or formulas.

To control what is copied into the destination range, choose Home ⇨ Clipboard ⇨ Paste and use the drop-down menu shown in Figure 4.10. When you hover your mouse pointer over an icon, you'll see a preview of the pasted information in the destination range. Click the icon to use the selected paste option.

FIGURE 4.10

Excel offers several pasting options, with preview. Here, the information is copied from E4:G7 and is being pasted beginning at cell F11 using the Transpose option.

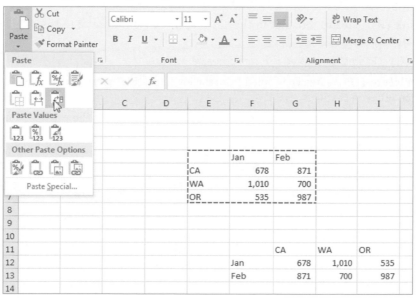

The paste options are as follows:

Paste (P)   Pastes the cell's contents, formula, formats, and data validation from the Windows Clipboard.

Formulas (F)   Pastes formulas but not formatting.

Formulas & Number Formatting (O)   Pastes formulas and number formatting only.

Keep Source Formatting (K)   Pastes formulas and all formatting.

No Borders (B)   Pastes everything except borders that appear in the source range.

Keep Source Column Widths (W)   Pastes formulas and duplicates the column width of the copied cells.

Transpose (T)   Changes the orientation of the copied range. Rows become columns, and columns become rows. Any formulas in the copied range are adjusted so that they work properly when transposed.

Merge Conditional Formatting (G)   This icon is displayed only when the copied cells contain conditional formatting. When clicked, it merges the copied conditional formatting with any conditional formatting in the destination range.

Values (V)   Pastes the results of formulas. The destination for the copy can be a new range or the original range. In the latter case, Excel replaces the original formulas with their current values.

Values & Number Formatting (A)   Pastes the results of formulas plus the number formatting.

Values & Source Formatting (E)   Pastes the results of formulas plus all formatting.

Formatting (R)   Pastes only the formatting of the source range.

Paste Link (N)   Creates formulas in the destination range that refer to the cells in the copied range.

Picture (U)   Pastes the copied information as a picture.

Linked Picture (I)   Pastes the copied information as a "live" picture that is updated if the source range is changed.

Paste Special   Displays the Paste Special dialog box (described in the next section).

> **NOTE**
>
> After you paste, you're offered another chance to change your mind. A Paste Options drop-down appears at the lower right of the pasted range. Click it (or press Ctrl), and you see the paste option icons again.

Using the Paste Special dialog box

For yet another pasting method, choose Home ⇨ Clipboard ⇨ Paste ⇨ Paste Special to display the Paste Special dialog box (see Figure 4.11). You can also right-click and choose Paste Special from the shortcut menu to display this dialog box. This dialog box has several options, some of which are identical to the buttons in the Paste drop-down menu. The options that are different are explained in the following list.

FIGURE 4.11

The Paste Special dialog box

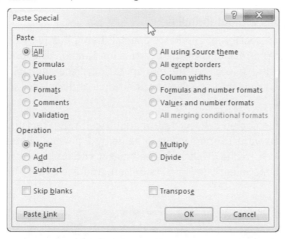

> **NOTE**
>
> Excel actually has several different Paste Special dialog boxes, each with different options. The one displayed depends on what's copied. This section describes the Paste Special dialog box that appears when a range or cell has been copied.

> **TIP**
>
> For the Paste Special command to be available, you need to copy a cell or range. (Choosing Home ⇨ Clipboard ⇨ Cut doesn't work.)

Comments   Copies only the cell comments from a cell or range. This option doesn't copy cell contents or formatting.

Validation   Copies the validation criteria so that the same data validation will apply. Data validation is applied by choosing Data ⇨ Data Tools ⇨ Data Validation.

All using Source theme   Pastes everything but uses the formatting from the document theme of the source. This option is relevant only if you're pasting information from a different workbook, and the workbook uses a different document theme than the active workbook.

Column widths   Pastes only column width information.

All merging conditional formats   Merges the copied conditional formatting with any conditional formatting in the destination range. This option is enabled only when you're copying a range that contains conditional formatting.

In addition, the Paste Special dialog box enables you to perform other operations, described in the following sections.

Performing mathematical operations without formulas

The option buttons in the Operation section of the Paste Special dialog box let you perform an arithmetic operation on values and formulas in the destination range. For example, you can copy a range to another range and select the Multiply operation. Excel multiplies the corresponding values in the source range and the destination range and replaces the destination range with the new values.

This feature also works with a single copied cell, pasted to a multicell range. Assume that you have a range of values, and you want to increase each value by 5 percent. Enter **105%** into any blank cell and copy that cell to the Clipboard. Then select the range of values and bring up the Paste Special dialog box. Select the Multiply option, and each value in the range is multiplied by 105%.

> **CAUTION**
>
> If the destination range contains formulas, the formulas are also modified. In many cases, this is not what you want.

Skipping blanks when pasting

The Skip Blanks option in the Paste Special dialog box prevents Excel from overwriting cell contents in your paste area with blank cells from the copied range. This option is useful if you're copying a range to another area but don't want the blank cells in the copied range to overwrite existing data.

Transposing a range

The Transpose option in the Paste Special dialog box changes the orientation of the copied range. Rows become columns, and columns become rows. Any formulas in the copied range are adjusted so that they work properly when transposed. Note that you can use this check box with the other options in the Paste Special dialog box. Figure 4.12 shows an example of a horizontal range (A1:D5) that was transposed to a different range (A7:E10).

> **TIP**
>
> If you click the Paste Link button in the Paste Special dialog box, you create formulas that link to the source range. As a result, the destination range automatically reflects changes in the source range.

FIGURE 4.12

Transposing a range changes the orientation as the information is pasted into the worksheet.

	A	B	C	D	E	F
1		January	February	March		
2	Region 1	31,601	34,855	38,091		
3	Region 2	25,117	31,583	35,696		
4	Region 3	39,493	33,010	34,590		
5	Region 4	33,867	34,367	39,683		
6						
7		Region 1	Region 2	Region 3	Region 4	
8	January	31,601	25,117	39,493	33,867	
9	February	34,855	31,583	33,010	34,367	
10	March	38,091	35,696	34,590	39,683	
11						
12						
13						

Using Names to Work with Ranges

Dealing with cryptic cell and range addresses can sometimes be confusing, especially when you work with formulas, which we cover in Chapter 9, "Introducing Formulas and Functions." Fortunately, Excel allows you to assign descriptive names to cells and ranges. For example, you can give a cell a name such as Interest_Rate, or you can name a range JulySales. Working with these names (rather than cell or range addresses) has several advantages:

- A meaningful range name (such as Total_Income) is much easier to remember than a cell address (such as AC21).
- Entering a name is less error prone than entering a cell or range address, and if you type a name incorrectly in a formula, Excel will display a #NAME? error.
- You can quickly move to areas of your worksheet either by using the Name box, located at the left side of the Formula bar (click the arrow to drop down a list of defined names), or by choosing Home ⇨ Editing ⇨ Find & Select ⇨ Go To (or pressing F5 or Ctrl+G) and specifying the range name.
- Creating formulas is easier. You can paste a cell or range name into a formula by using Formula AutoComplete.

 See Chapter 9 for information on Formula AutoComplete.

- Names make your formulas more understandable and easier to use. A formula such as =Income–Taxes is certainly more intuitive than =D20–D40.

Creating range names in your workbooks

Excel provides several methods that you can use to create range names. Before you begin, however, you should be aware of a few rules:

- Names can't contain spaces. You may want to use an underscore character to simulate a space (such as Annual_Total).
- You can use any combination of letters and numbers, but the name must begin with a letter, underscore, or backslash. A name can't begin with a number (such as 3rdQuarter) or look like a cell address (such as QTR3). If these are desirable names, though, you can precede the name with an underscore or a backslash, for example, _3rd Quarter and \QTR3.
- Symbols—except for underscores, backslashes, and periods—aren't allowed.
- Names are limited to 255 characters, but it's a good practice to keep names as short as possible yet still meaningful.

> **CAUTION**
>
> Excel also uses a few names internally for its own use. Although you can create names that override Excel's internal names, you should avoid doing so. To be on the safe side, avoid using the following for names: Print_Area, Print_Titles, Consolidate_Area, and Sheet_Title. To delete a range name or rename a range, see "Managing names" later in this chapter.

Using the Name box

The fastest way to create a name is to use the Name box (to the left of the Formula bar). Select the cell or range to name, click the Name box, and type the name. Press Enter to create the name. (You must press Enter to actually record the name; if you type a name and then click in the worksheet, Excel doesn't create the name.)

If you type an invalid name (such as `May21`, which happens to be a cell address, MAY21), Excel activates that address and doesn't warn you that the name is not valid. If the name you type includes an invalid character, Excel displays an error message. If a name already exists, you can't use the Name box to change the range to which that name refers. Attempting to do so simply selects the range.

The Name box is a drop-down list and shows all names in the workbook. To choose a named cell or range, click the arrow on the right side of the Name box and choose the name. The name appears in the Name box, and Excel selects the named cell or range in the worksheet.

Using the New Name dialog box

For more control over naming cells and ranges, use the New Name dialog box. Start by selecting the cell or range that you want to name. Then choose Formulas ➪ Defined Names

⇨ Define Name. Excel displays the New Name dialog box, shown in Figure 4.13. Note that this is a resizable dialog box. Click and drag a border to change the dimensions.

FIGURE 4.13

Create names for cells or ranges by using the New Name dialog box.

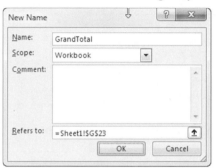

Type a name in the Name text field (or use the name that Excel proposes, if any). The selected cell or range address appears in the Refers To text field. Use the Scope drop-down list to indicate the scope for the name. The scope indicates where the name will be valid, and it's either the entire workbook or the worksheet in which the name is defined. If you like, you can add a comment that describes the named range or cell. Click OK to add the name to your workbook and close the dialog box.

Using the Create Names from Selection dialog box

You may have a worksheet that contains text that you want to use for names for adjacent cells or ranges. For example, you may want to use the text in column A to create names for the corresponding values in column B. Excel makes this task easy.

To create names by using adjacent text, start by selecting the name text and the cells that you want to name. (These items can be individual cells or ranges of cells.) The names must be adjacent to the cells that you're naming. (A multiple selection is allowed.) Then choose Formulas ⇨ Defined Names ⇨ Create from Selection. Excel displays the Create Names from Selection dialog box, shown in Figure 4.14.

The check marks in the Create Names from Selection dialog box are based on Excel's analysis of the selected range. For example, if Excel finds text in the first row of the selection, it proposes that you create names based on the top row. If Excel didn't guess correctly, you can change the check boxes. Click OK, and Excel creates the names. Using the data in Figure 4.14, Excel creates the seven named ranges shown in Figure 4.15.

FIGURE 4.14

Use the Create Names from Selection dialog box to name cells using labels that appear in the worksheet.

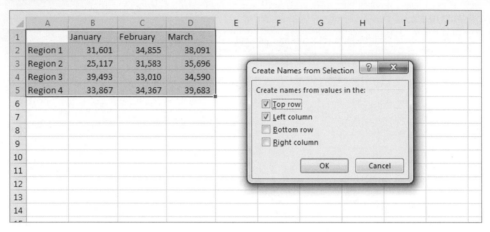

FIGURE 4.15

Use the Name Manager to work with range names.

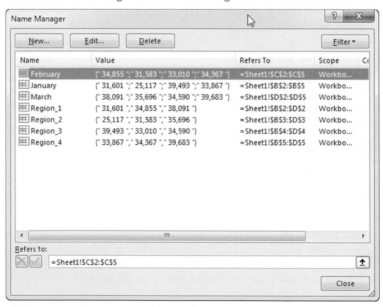

> **NOTE**
>
> If the text contained in a cell would result in an invalid name, Excel modifies the name to make it valid. For example, if a cell contains the text Net Income (which is invalid for a name because it contains a space), Excel converts the space to an underscore character. If Excel encounters a value or a numeric formula where text should be, however, it doesn't convert it to a valid name. It simply doesn't create a name, and it does not inform you of that fact.

> **CAUTION**
>
> If the upper-left cell of the selection contains text and you choose the Top Row and Left Column options, Excel uses that text for the name of the entire range, excluding the top row and left column. So, after Excel creates the names, take a minute to make sure that they refer to the correct ranges. If Excel creates a name that is incorrect, you can delete or modify it by using the Name Manager (described next).

Managing names

A workbook can have any number of named cells and ranges. If your workbook has many names, you should know about the Name Manager, which is shown in Figure 4.15.

The Name Manager appears when you choose Formulas ⇨ Defined Names ⇨ Name Manager (or press Ctrl+F3). The Name Manager has the following features:

Displays information about each name in the workbook   You can resize the Name Manager dialog box, widen the columns to show more information, and even rearrange the order of the columns. You can also click a column heading to sort the information by the column.

Allows you to filter the displayed names   Clicking the Filter button lets you show only those names that meet certain criteria. For example, you can view only the worksheet-level names.

Provides quick access to the New Name dialog box   Click the New button to create a new name without closing the Name Manager.

Lets you edit names   To edit a name, select it in the list, and then click the Edit button. You can change the name itself, modify the Refers To range, or edit the comment.

Lets you quickly delete unneeded names   To delete a name, select it in the list and click Delete.

> **CAUTION**
>
> Be extra careful when deleting names. If the name is used in a formula, deleting the name causes the formula to become invalid. (It displays #NAME?.) It seems logical that Excel would replace the name with its actual address, but that doesn't happen. However, deleting a name can be undone, so if you find that formulas return #NAME? after you delete a name, choose Undo from the Quick Access toolbar (or press Ctrl+Z) to get the name back.

If you delete the rows or columns that contain named cells or ranges, the names contain an invalid reference. For example, if cell A1 on Sheet1 is named Interest and you delete row 1 or column A, the name Interest then refers to =Sheet1!#REF! (an erroneous reference). If you use the name Interest in a formula, the formula displays #REF!.

> **TIP**
>
> To create a list of names in a worksheet, first select a cell in an empty area of your worksheet. The list is created at the active cell position and overwrites any information at that location. Press F3 to display the Paste Name dialog box, which lists all of the defined names, and then click the Paste List button. Excel creates a list of all names in the workbook and their corresponding addresses.

Adding Comments to Cells

Documentation that explains certain elements in the worksheet can often be helpful. One way to document your work is to add comments to cells. This feature is useful when you need to describe a particular value or explain how a formula works.

To add a comment to a cell, select the cell and use any of these actions:

- Choose Review ⇨ Comments ⇨ New Comment.
- Right-click the cell and choose Insert Comment from the shortcut menu.
- Press Shift+F2.

Excel inserts a comment that points to the active cell. Initially, the comment consists of your name, as specified in the General tab of the Excel Options dialog box (choose File ⇨ Options to display this dialog box). If you like, you can delete your name from the comment. Enter the text for the cell comment and then click anywhere in the worksheet to hide the comment. You can change the size of the comment by clicking and dragging any of its borders. Figure 4.16 shows a cell with a comment.

Cells that have a comment display a small red triangle in the upper-right corner. When you move the mouse pointer over a cell that contains a comment, the comment becomes visible.

You can force a comment to be displayed even when the mouse is not hovering over the cell. Right-click the cell and choose Show/Hide Comments. Although this command refers to "comments" (plural), it affects only the comment in the active cell. To return to normal (make the comment appear only when its cell is activated or the mouse pointer hovers over it), right-click the cell and choose Hide Comment.

FIGURE 4.16

You can add comments to cells to help point out specific items in your worksheets.

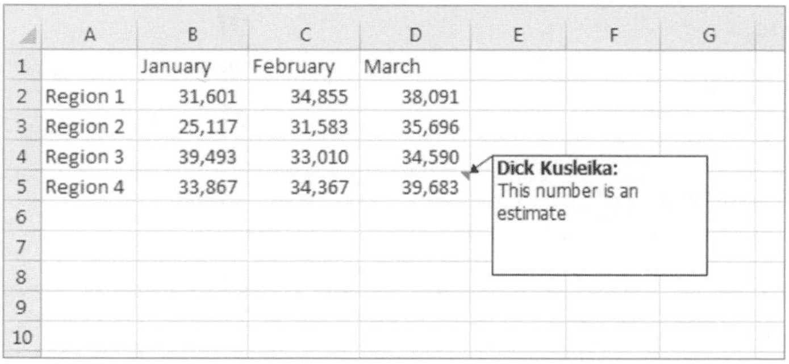

◢	A	B	C	D	E	F	G
1		January	February	March			
2	Region 1	31,601	34,855	38,091			
3	Region 2	25,117	31,583	35,696			
4	Region 3	39,493	33,010	34,590			
5	Region 4	33,867	34,367	39,683			
6							
7							
8							
9							
10							

> Dick Kusleika:
> This number is an estimate

Formatting comments

If you don't like the default look of cell comments, you can make some changes. Right-click the cell and choose Edit Comment. Select the text in the comment and use the commands of the Font and the Alignment groups (on the Home tab) to make changes to the comment's appearance.

For even more formatting options, right-click the comment's border and choose Format Comment from the shortcut menu. Excel responds by displaying the Format Comment dialog box, which allows you to change many aspects of its appearance, including color, border, and margins.

4

FIGURE 4.17

This comment contains a graphics image.

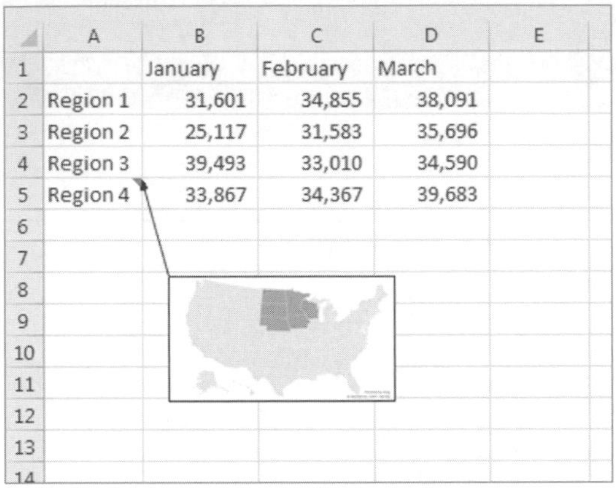

	A	B	C	D	E
1		January	February	March	
2	Region 1	31,601	34,855	38,091	
3	Region 2	25,117	31,583	35,696	
4	Region 3	39,493	33,010	34,590	
5	Region 4	33,867	34,367	39,683	
6					
7					
8					
9					
10					
11					
12					
13					
14					

An Alternative to Cell Comments

You can make use of Excel's Data Validation feature (see Chapter 26, "Using Data Validation") to add a different type of comment to a cell. This type of comment appears automatically when the cell is selected. Follow these steps:

1. **Select the cell that will contain the comment.**
2. **Choose Data ⇨ Data Tools ⇨ Data Validation.** The Data Validation dialog box appears.
3. **Click the Input Message tab.**
4. **Make sure that the Show Input Message When Cell Is Selected check box is selected.**
5. **Type your comment in the Input Message box.**
6. **(Optional) Type a title in the Title box.** This text will appear in bold at the top of the message.
7. **Click OK to close the Data Validation dialog box.**

After you perform these steps, the message appears when the cell is activated, and it disappears when any other cell is activated.

Note that this message isn't a "real" comment. For example, a cell that contains this type of message doesn't display a comment indicator, and it's not affected by any of the commands used to work with cell comments. In addition, you can't format these messages in any way, and you can't print them.

Changing a comment's shape

Cell comments are rectangular, but they don't have to be. To change the shape of a cell comment, make sure that it's visible (right-click the cell and select Edit Comment). Then click the comment's border to select it as a Shape (or Ctrl+click the comment to select it as a Shape). Type **Change Shape** into the Tell Me What You Want to Do box, and choose a new shape for the comment. Figure 4.18 shows a cell comment with a nonstandard shape.

FIGURE 4.18

Cell comments don't have to be rectangles.

⊿	A	B	C	D	E	F	G	H	I
1		January	February	March					
2	Region 1	31,601	34,855	38,091					
3	Region 2	25,117	31,583	35,696					
4	Region 3	39,493	33,010	34,590					
5	Region 4	33,867	34,367	39,683					
6									
7						Dick Kusleika:			
8						This number is an estimate			
9									
10									
11									
12									
13									
14									

Reading comments

To read all comments in a workbook, choose Review ⇨ Comments ⇨ Next. Keep clicking Next to cycle through all of the comments in a workbook. Choose Review ⇨ Comments ⇨ Previous to view the comments in reverse order.

See Chapter 7, "Printing Your Work," for information about including comments on your printouts.

Hiding and showing comments

If you want all cell comments to be visible (regardless of the location of the mouse), choose Review ⇨ Comments ⇨ Show All Comments. This command is a toggle; select it again to hide all cell comments.

To toggle the display of an individual comment, select its cell and then choose Review ⇨ Comments ⇨ Show/Hide Comment.

Editing comments

To edit the text in a comment, activate the cell, right-click, and then choose Edit Comment from the shortcut menu. Or select the cell and press Shift+F2. After you make your changes, click any cell.

Deleting comments

To delete a cell comment, activate the cell that contains the comment and then choose Review ➪ Comments ➪ Delete. Or right-click and then choose Delete Comment from the shortcut menu.

Working with Tables

A *table* is a specially designated area of a worksheet. When you designate a range as a table, Excel gives it special properties that make certain operations easier and that help prevent errors.

The purpose of a table is to enforce some structure around your data. If you're familiar with a table in a database (like Microsoft Access), then you already understand the concept of structured data. If not, don't worry. It's not difficult.

In a table, each row contains information about a single entity. In a table that holds employee information, each row will contain information about one employee (such as name, department, and hire date). Each column contains the same piece of information for each employee. The same column that holds the hire date for the first employee holds the hire date for all the other employees.

Understanding a table's structure

Figure 4.19 shows a simple table. The various components of a table are described in the following sections.

FIGURE 4.19

The areas that make up a table

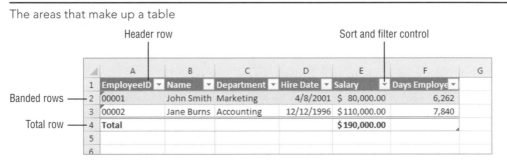

 This workbook, named `EmployeeTable.xlsx`, is available on this book's website at `www.wiley.com/go/excel2019bible`.

The header row

The *header row* is generally colored differently than the other rows. The names in the header identify the columns. If you have a formula that refers to a table, the header row will determine how the column is referred to. For example, the Days Employed column contains a formula that refers to the Hire Date column (column D). The formula is =NOW()-[@[Hire Date]]. If your table is longer than one screen, the header row will replace the normal column headers in Excel when you scroll down.

 See Chapter 17 to learn about special table referencing in formulas.

The header also contains *Filter Buttons*. These drop-downs work exactly like Excel's normal AutoFilter feature. You can use them to sort and filter the table's data.

The data body

The *data body* is one or more rows of data. By default, the rows are *banded*, that is, formatted with alternating colors. When you add new data to the table, the formatting of the existing data is applied to the new data. For example, if a column is formatted as Text, that column in the new row will also be formatted as Text. The same is true for conditional formatting.

It's not just formatting that applies to the new data. If a column contains a formula, that formula is automatically inserted into the new row. Data validation will also be transferred. You can make a fairly robust data entry area knowing that the table structure will apply to new data.

One of the best features of tables is that as the data body expands, anything that refers to the table will expand automatically. If you were to base a pivot table or a chart on your table, the pivot table or chart would adjust as you added or deleted rows from the table.

The total row

The *total row* is not visible by default when you create a table. To show the total row, check the Total Row check box on the Table Tools Design Ribbon. When you show the total row, the text Total is placed in the first column. You can change this to another value or to a formula.

Each cell in the total row has a drop-down arrow with a list of common functions. It's no accident that the list of functions resembles the arguments for the SUBTOTAL function. When you select a function from the list, Excel inserts a SUBTOTAL formula in the cell. The SUBTOTAL function ignores filtered cells, so the total will change if you filter the table.

4

In addition to the list of functions, there is a More Functions option at the bottom of the drop-down list. Selecting this option shows the Insert Function dialog box and makes all of Excel's functions available to you. Beyond that, you can simply type whatever formula you want in the total row.

The resizing handle

At the bottom right of the last cell in the table is the *resizing handle*. You can drag this handle to change the size of the table. Increasing the length of the table adds blank rows, copying down formatting, formulas, and data validation. Increasing the width of the table adds new columns with generic names like Column1, Column2, and so forth. You can change those names to something more meaningful.

Decreasing the size of the table simply changes what data is considered part of the table. It does not delete any data, formatting, formulas, or data validation. If you want to change what's in your table, you're better off deleting the columns and rows as you would any range rather than trying to do it with the resizing handle.

Creating a table

Most of the time, you'll create a table from an existing range of data. However, Excel also allows you to create a table from an empty range so that you can fill in the data later. The following instructions assume that you already have a range of data that's suitable for a table:

1. **Make sure the range doesn't contain any completely blank rows or columns; otherwise, Excel will not guess the table range correctly.**

2. **Select any cell within the range.**

3. **Choose Insert ⇨ Tables ⇨ Table (or press Ctrl+T).** Excel responds with its Create Table dialog box, shown in Figure 4.20. Excel tries to guess the range, as well as whether the table has a header row. Most of the time, it guesses correctly. If not, make your corrections before you click OK.

The range is converted to a table (using the default table style), and the Table Tools Design tab of the Ribbon appears.

> **NOTE**
>
> Excel may not guess the table's dimensions correctly if the table isn't separated from other information by at least one empty row or column. If Excel guesses incorrectly, just specify the exact range for the table in the Create Table dialog box. Better yet, click Cancel and rearrange your worksheet such that the table is separated from your other data by at least one blank row or column.

To create a table from an empty range, select the range and choose Insert ⇨ Tables ⇨ Table. Excel creates the table, adds generic column headers (such as Column1 and Column2), and applies table formatting to the range. Almost always, you'll want to replace the generic column headers with more meaningful text.

FIGURE 4.20

Use the Create Table dialog box to verify that Excel guessed the table dimensions correctly.

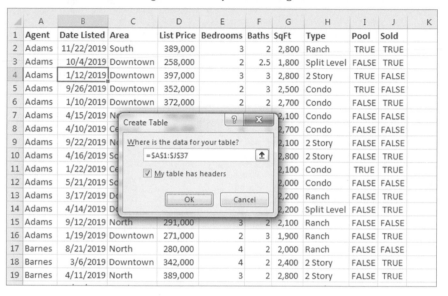

	A	B	C	D	E	F	G	H	I	J	K
1	Agent	Date Listed	Area	List Price	Bedrooms	Baths	SqFt	Type	Pool	Sold	
2	Adams	11/22/2019	South	389,000	3	2	2,800	Ranch	TRUE	TRUE	
3	Adams	10/4/2019	Downtown	258,000	2	2.5	1,800	Split Level	FALSE	TRUE	
4	Adams	1/12/2019	Downtown	397,000	3	3	2,800	2 Story	TRUE	FALSE	
5	Adams	9/26/2019	Downtown	352,000	2	3	2,500	Condo	TRUE	FALSE	
6	Adams	1/10/2019	Downtown	372,000	2	2	2,700	Condo	FALSE	TRUE	
7	Adams	4/15/2019	N				2,100	Condo	FALSE	FALSE	
8	Adams	4/10/2019	C				2,700	Condo	FALSE	FALSE	
9	Adams	9/22/2019	N				2,100	2 Story	FALSE	FALSE	
10	Adams	4/16/2019	S				2,800	2 Story	FALSE	TRUE	
11	Adams	1/22/2019	C				2,100	Condo	TRUE	TRUE	
12	Adams	5/21/2019	S				2,000	Condo	FALSE	FALSE	
13	Adams	3/17/2019	D				2,200	Ranch	FALSE	TRUE	
14	Adams	4/14/2019	D				2,200	Split Level	FALSE	TRUE	
15	Adams	9/12/2019	North	291,000	3	2	2,100	Ranch	FALSE	FALSE	
16	Adams	1/19/2019	Downtown	271,000	2	3	1,900	Ranch	FALSE	TRUE	
17	Barnes	8/21/2019	North	280,000	4	2	2,000	Ranch	FALSE	FALSE	
18	Barnes	3/6/2019	Downtown	342,000	4	2	2,400	2 Story	FALSE	TRUE	
19	Barnes	4/11/2019	North	389,000	3	2	2,800	2 Story	FALSE	TRUE	

Create Table

Where is the data for your table?

=$A$1:$J$37

☑ My table has headers

OK   Cancel

Adding data to a table

If your table doesn't have a total row, the easiest way to enter data is simply to start typing in the row just below the table. When you enter something in a cell, Excel automatically expands the table and applies the formatting, formulas, and data validation to the new row. You can also paste a value in the next row. In fact, you could paste several rows' worth of data and the table will expand to accommodate.

If your table does have a total row, you can't use that technique. In that case, you can insert rows into a table just like you would insert a row into any range. To insert a row, select a cell or the entire row and choose Home ⇨ Cells ⇨ Insert. When the selected range is inside a table, you'll see new entries on the Insert menu that deal with tables specifically. When you use these, the table is changed, but the data outside the table is unaffected.

When the selected cell is inside a table, the shortcut keys Ctrl– (minus sign) and Ctrl+ (plus sign) work on the table only and not on data outside the table. Moreover, as opposed to when you're not in a table, those shortcuts work on the whole table row or column regardless of whether you've selected the whole row or column.

Sorting and filtering table data

Each item in the header row of a table contains a drop-down arrow known as a *Filter Button*. When clicked, the Filter Button displays sorting and filtering options (see Figure 4.21).

4

FIGURE 4.21

Each column in a table has sorting and filtering options.

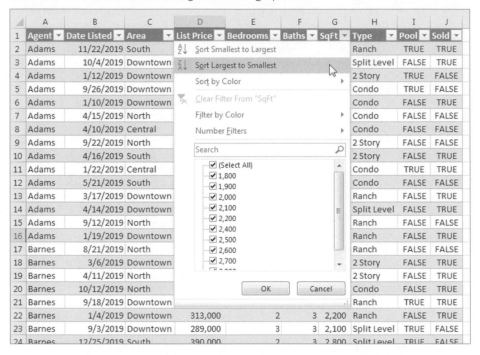

Sorting a table

Sorting a table rearranges the rows based on the contents of a particular column. You may want to sort a table to put names in alphabetical order. Or, maybe you want to sort your sales staff by the total sales made.

To sort a table by a particular column, click the Filter Button in the column header and choose one of the sort commands. The exact command varies, depending on the type of data in the column.

You can also select Sort by Color to sort the rows based on the background or text color of the data. This option is relevant only if you've overridden the table style colors with custom formatting.

You can sort on any number of columns. The trick is to sort the least significant column first and then proceed until the most significant column is sorted last. For example, in the real estate table, you may want to sort the list by agent. And within each agent's group, sort the rows by area. Then within each area, sort the rows by list price. For this type of sort, first sort by the List Price column, then sort by the Area column, and then sort by the Agent column. Figure 4.22 shows the table sorted in this manner.

FIGURE 4.22

A table after performing a three-column sort

	Agent	Date Listed	Area	List Price	Bedrooms	Baths	SqFt	Type	Pool	Sold
2	Adams	1/22/2019	Central	295,000	4	3.5	2,100	Condo	TRUE	TRUE
3	Adams	4/10/2019	Central	384,000	4	2	2,700	Condo	FALSE	FALSE
4	Adams	10/4/2019	Downtown	258,000	2	2.5	1,800	Split Level	FALSE	TRUE
5	Adams	1/19/2019	Downtown	271,000	2	3	1,900	Ranch	FALSE	TRUE
6	Adams	4/14/2019	Downtown	310,000	3	3.5	2,200	Split Level	FALSE	TRUE
7	Adams	3/17/2019	Downtown	312,000	4	3	2,200	Ranch	FALSE	TRUE
8	Adams	9/26/2019	Downtown	352,000	2	3	2,500	Condo	TRUE	FALSE
9	Adams	1/10/2019	Downtown	372,000	2	2	2,700	Condo	FALSE	TRUE
10	Adams	1/12/2019	Downtown	397,000	3	3	2,800	2 Story	TRUE	FALSE
11	Adams	9/22/2019	North	288,000	3	2	2,100	2 Story	FALSE	FALSE
12	Adams	4/15/2019	North	289,000	2	2	2,100	Condo	FALSE	FALSE
13	Adams	9/12/2019	North	291,000	3	2	2,100	Ranch	FALSE	FALSE
14	Adams	5/21/2019	South	282,000	2	3	2,000	Condo	FALSE	FALSE
15	Adams	4/16/2019	South	388,000	4	3	2,800	2 Story	FALSE	TRUE
16	Adams	11/22/2019	South	389,000	3	2	2,800	Ranch	TRUE	TRUE
17	Barnes	11/18/2019	Downtown	275,000	3	2	2,000	Ranch	TRUE	TRUE
18	Barnes	9/3/2019	Downtown	289,000	3	3	2,100	Split Level	TRUE	FALSE
19	Barnes	1/4/2019	Downtown	313,000	2	3	2,200	Ranch	FALSE	TRUE
20	Barnes	3/6/2019	Downtown	342,000	4	2	2,400	2 Story	FALSE	TRUE
21	Barnes	9/18/2019	Downtown	354,000	2	2	2,500	Ranch	TRUE	TRUE
22	Barnes	8/21/2019	North	280,000	4	2	2,000	Ranch	FALSE	FALSE
23	Barnes	10/12/2019	North	300,000	2	2.5	2,100	Condo	FALSE	TRUE
24	Barnes	4/11/2019	North	389,000	3	2	2,800	2 Story	FALSE	TRUE
25	Barnes	2/23/2019	South	305,000	4	2	2,200	Condo	TRUE	TRUE
26	Barnes	4/24/2019	South	343,000	3	2.5	2,500	Split Level	TRUE	FALSE
27	Barnes	12/25/2019	South	390,000	2	3	2,800	Split Level	TRUE	FALSE
28	Bennet	9/10/2019	Central	340,000	3	3	2,400	2 Story	TRUE	FALSE
29	Bennet	9/18/2019	Central	395,000	3	2	2,800	2 Story	FALSE	TRUE
30	Bennet	7/8/2019	Downtown	343,000	3	2	2,500	2 Story	FALSE	FALSE
31	Bennet	5/15/2019	Downtown	379,000	2	3	2,700	Condo	TRUE	FALSE
32	Bennet	3/19/2019	Downtown	385,000	4	3.5	2,800	2 Story	TRUE	FALSE

Another way of performing a multiple-column sort is to use the Sort dialog box (choose Home ⇨ Editing ⇨ Sort & Filter ⇨ Custom Sort). Or right-click any cell in the table and choose Sort ⇨ Custom Sort from the shortcut menu.

In the Sort dialog box, use the drop-down lists to specify the sort specifications. In this example, you start with Agent. Then click the Add Level button to insert another set of search controls. In this new set of controls, specify the sort specifications for the Area column. Then add another level and enter the specifications for the List Price column. Figure 4.23 shows the dialog box after entering the specifications for the three-column sort. This technique produces the same sort as described previously in this section.

FIGURE 4.23

Using the Sort dialog box to specify a three-column sort

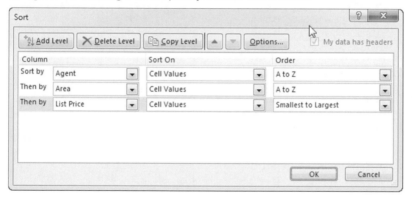

Filtering a table

Filtering a table refers to displaying only the rows that meet certain conditions. (The other rows are hidden.)

Note that entire worksheet rows are hidden. Therefore, if you have other data to the left or right of your table, that information may also be hidden when you filter the table. If you plan to filter your list, don't include any other data to the left or right of your table.

Using the real estate table, assume that you're interested only in the data for the Downtown area. Click the Filter Button in the Area row header and remove the check mark from Select All, which deselects everything. Then place a check mark next to Downtown and click OK. The table, shown in Figure 4.24, is now filtered to display only the listings in the Downtown area. Notice that some of the row numbers are missing. These rows are hidden and contain data that does not meet the specified criteria.

FIGURE 4.24

This table is filtered to show the information for only one area.

	A	B	C	D	E	F	G	H	I	J
1	Agent	Date Listed	Area	List Price	Bedrooms	Baths	SqFt	Type	Pool	Sold
4	Adams	10/4/2019	Downtown	258,000	2	2.5	1,800	Split Level	FALSE	TRUE
5	Adams	1/19/2019	Downtown	271,000	2	3	1,900	Ranch	FALSE	TRUE
6	Adams	4/14/2019	Downtown	310,000	3	3.5	2,200	Split Level	FALSE	TRUE
7	Adams	3/17/2019	Downtown	312,000	4	3	2,200	Ranch	FALSE	TRUE
8	Adams	9/26/2019	Downtown	352,000	2	3	2,500	Condo	TRUE	FALSE
9	Adams	1/10/2019	Downtown	372,000	2	2	2,700	Condo	FALSE	TRUE
10	Adams	1/12/2019	Downtown	397,000	3	3	2,800	2 Story	TRUE	FALSE
17	Barnes	11/18/2019	Downtown	275,000	3	2	2,000	Ranch	TRUE	TRUE
18	Barnes	9/3/2019	Downtown	289,000	3	3	2,100	Split Level	TRUE	FALSE
19	Barnes	1/4/2019	Downtown	313,000	2	3	2,200	Ranch	FALSE	TRUE
20	Barnes	3/6/2019	Downtown	342,000	4	2	2,400	2 Story	FALSE	TRUE
21	Barnes	9/18/2019	Downtown	354,000	2	2	2,500	Ranch	TRUE	TRUE
30	Bennet	7/8/2019	Downtown	343,000	3	2	2,500	2 Story	FALSE	FALSE
31	Bennet	5/15/2019	Downtown	379,000	2	3	2,700	Condo	TRUE	FALSE

Also notice that the Filter Button in the Area column now shows a different graphic—an icon that indicates the column is filtered.

You can filter by multiple values in a column using multiple check marks. For example, to filter the table to show only Downtown and Central, place a check mark next to both values in the drop-down list in the Area row header.

You can filter a table using any number of columns. For example, you may want to see only the Downtown listings in which the Type is Condo. Just repeat the operation using the Type column. The table then displays only the rows in which the Area is Downtown and the Type is Condo.

For additional filtering options, select Text Filters (or Number Filters, if the column contains values). The options are fairly self-explanatory, and you have a great deal of flexibility in displaying only the rows in which you're interested. For example, you can display rows in which the List Price is greater than or equal to $200,000 and less than $300,000 (see Figure 4.25).

4

FIGURE 4.25

Specifying a more complex numeric filter

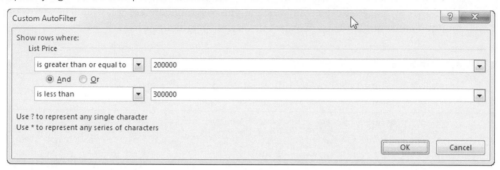

Also, you can right-click a cell and use the Filter command on the shortcut menu. This menu item leads to several additional filtering options that enable you to filter data based on the contents of the selected cell or by formatting.

NOTE

As you may expect, when you use filtering, the total row is updated to show the total only for the visible rows.

When you copy data from a filtered table, only the visible data is copied. In other words, rows that are hidden by filtering aren't copied. This filtering makes it easy to copy a subset of a larger table and paste it to another area of your worksheet. Keep in mind, though, that the pasted data is not a table—it's just a normal range. You can, however, convert the copied range to a table.

To remove filtering for a column, click the drop-down in the row header and select Clear Filter. If you've filtered using multiple columns, it may be faster to remove all filters by choosing Home ⇨ Editing ⇨ Sort & Filter ⇨ Clear.

Filtering a table with slicers

Another way to filter a table is to use one or more *slicers*. This method is less flexible but more visually appealing. Slicers are particularly useful when the table will be viewed by novices or those who find the normal filtering techniques too complicated. Slicers are very visual, and it's easy to see exactly what type of filtering is in effect. A disadvantage of slicers is that they take up a lot of room on the screen.

To add one or more slicers, activate any cell in the table and choose Table Tools Design ⇨ Tools ⇨ Insert Slicer. Excel responds with a dialog box that displays each header in the table (see Figure 4.26).

FIGURE 4.26

Use the Insert Slicers dialog box to specify which slicers to create.

Place a check mark next to the field(s) that you want to filter. You can create a slicer for each column, but that's rarely needed. In most cases, you'll want to be able to filter the table by only a few fields. Click OK, and Excel creates a slicer for each field you specified.

A slicer contains a button for every unique item in the field. In the real estate listing example, the slicer for the Agent field contains 14 buttons because the table has records for 14 different agents.

> **NOTE**
>
> Slicers may not be appropriate for columns that contain numeric data. For example, the real estate listing table has 78 different values in the List Price column. Therefore, a slicer for this column would have 78 buttons (and there's no way to group the values into numeric ranges). This is an example of how a slicer is not as flexible as normal filtering using Filter Buttons.

To use a slicer, just click one of the buttons. The table displays only the rows that have a value that corresponds to the button. You can also press Ctrl to select multiple buttons and press Shift to select a continuous group of buttons, which would be useful for selecting a range of List Price values.

If your table has more than one slicer, it's filtered by the selected buttons in each slicer. To remove filtering for a particular slicer, click the Clear Filter icon in the upper-right corner of the slicer.

Use the tools in the Slicer Tools Options Ribbon to change the appearance or layout of a slicer. You have quite a bit of flexibility.

Figure 4.27 shows a table with two slicers. The table is filtered to show only the records for Adams, Barnes, Chung, and Hamilton in the Downtown area.

FIGURE 4.27

The table is filtered by two slicers.

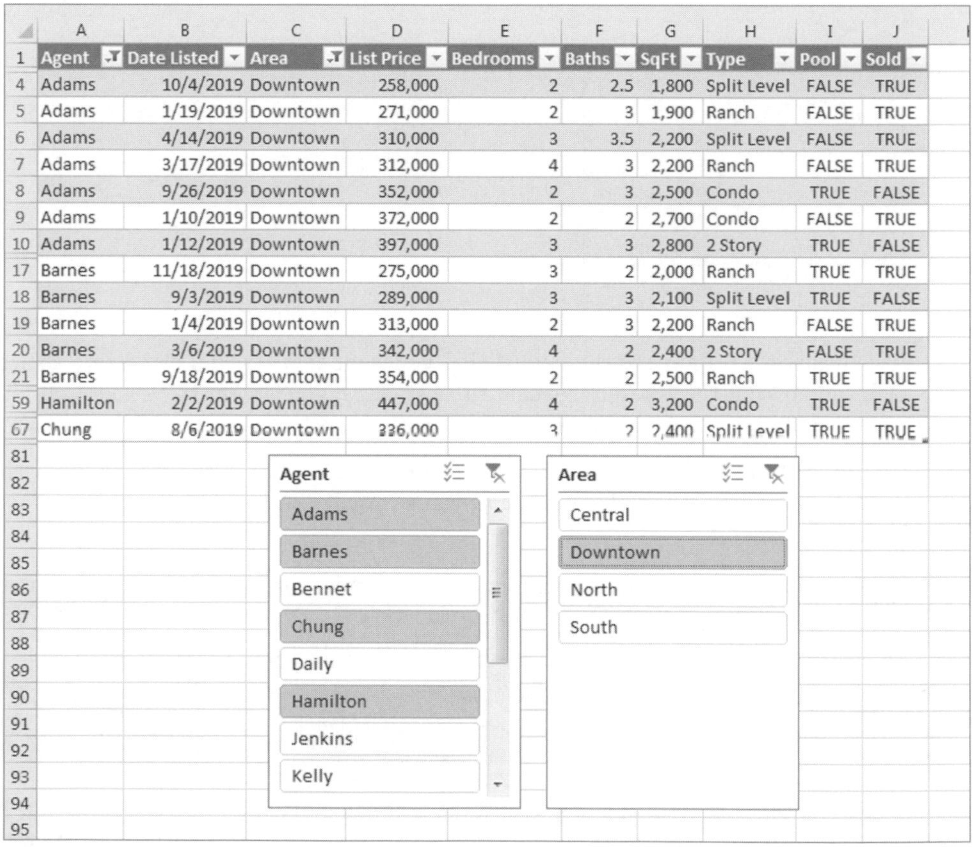

	A	B	C	D	E	F	G	H	I	J
1	Agent	Date Listed	Area	List Price	Bedrooms	Baths	SqFt	Type	Pool	Sold
4	Adams	10/4/2019	Downtown	258,000	2	2.5	1,800	Split Level	FALSE	TRUE
5	Adams	1/19/2019	Downtown	271,000	2	3	1,900	Ranch	FALSE	TRUE
6	Adams	4/14/2019	Downtown	310,000	3	3.5	2,200	Split Level	FALSE	TRUE
7	Adams	3/17/2019	Downtown	312,000	4	3	2,200	Ranch	FALSE	TRUE
8	Adams	9/26/2019	Downtown	352,000	2	3	2,500	Condo	TRUE	FALSE
9	Adams	1/10/2019	Downtown	372,000	2	2	2,700	Condo	FALSE	TRUE
10	Adams	1/12/2019	Downtown	397,000	3	3	2,800	2 Story	TRUE	FALSE
17	Barnes	11/18/2019	Downtown	275,000	3	2	2,000	Ranch	TRUE	TRUE
18	Barnes	9/3/2019	Downtown	289,000	3	3	2,100	Split Level	TRUE	FALSE
19	Barnes	1/4/2019	Downtown	313,000	2	3	2,200	Ranch	FALSE	TRUE
20	Barnes	3/6/2019	Downtown	342,000	4	2	2,400	2 Story	FALSE	TRUE
21	Barnes	9/18/2019	Downtown	354,000	2	2	2,500	Ranch	TRUE	TRUE
59	Hamilton	2/2/2019	Downtown	447,000	4	2	3,200	Condo	TRUE	FALSE
67	Chung	8/6/2019	Downtown	336,000	3	2	2,400	Split Level	TRUE	TRUE

Agent slicer: Adams, Barnes, Bennet, Chung, Daily, Hamilton, Jenkins, Kelly (Adams, Barnes, Chung, Hamilton selected)

Area slicer: Central, Downtown, North, South (Downtown selected)

Changing the table's appearance

When you create a table, Excel applies the default table style. The actual appearance depends on which document theme is used in the workbook (see Chapter 5, "Formatting Worksheets"). If you prefer a different look, you can easily apply a different table style.

Select any cell in the table and choose Table Tools Design ➪ Table Styles. The Ribbon shows one row of styles, but if you click the More button at the bottom of the scrollbar to the right, the Table Styles group expands, as shown in Figure 4.28. The styles are grouped into three categories: Light, Medium, and Dark. Notice that you get a "live" preview as you move your mouse among the styles. When you see one you like, just click to make it permanent. And yes, some are really ugly and practically illegible.

> **TIP**
>
> To change the default table style for the workbook, right-click the style in the Table Styles group and choose Set As Default from the shortcut menu. Subsequent tables that you create in that workbook will use that style.

FIGURE 4.28

Excel offers many different table styles.

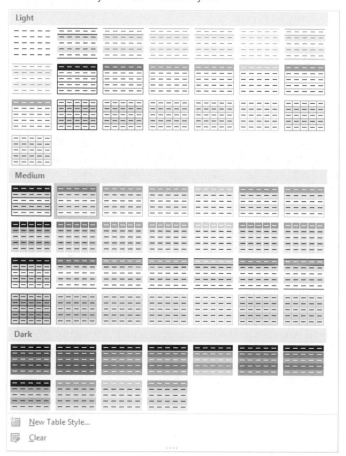

For a different set of color choices, choose Page Layout ⇨ Themes ⇨ Themes to select a different document theme.

 For more information about themes, see Chapter 5.

You can change some elements of the style by using the check box controls in the Table Tools Design ⇨ Table Style Options group. These controls determine whether various elements of the table are displayed and whether some formatting options are in effect:

Header Row   Toggles the display of the header row.

Total Row   Toggles the display of the total row.

First Column   Toggles special formatting for the first column. Depending on the table style used, this command might have no effect.

Last Column   Toggles special formatting for the last column. Depending on the table style used, this command might have no effect.

Banded Rows   Toggles the display of banded (alternating color) rows.

Banded Columns   Toggles the display of banded columns.

Filter Button   Toggles the display of the drop-down buttons in the table's header row.

> **TIP**
>
> If applying table styles isn't working, it's probably because the range was already formatted before you converted it to a table. Table formatting doesn't override normal formatting. To clear existing background fill colors, select the entire table and choose Home ⇨ Font ⇨ Fill Color ⇨ No Fill. To clear existing font colors, choose Home ⇨ Font Font Color ⇨ Automatic. To clear existing borders, choose Home ⇨ Font ⇨ Borders ⇨ No Border. After you issue these commands, the table styles should work as expected.

If you'd like to create a custom table style, choose Table Tools Design ⇨ Table Styles ⇨ New Table Style to display the New Table Style dialog box shown in Figure 4.29. You can customize any or all of the 12 table elements. Select an element from the list, click Format, and specify the formatting for that element. When you're finished, give the new style a name and click OK. Your custom table style will appear in the Table Styles gallery in the Custom category.

Custom table styles are available only in the workbook in which they were created. However, if you copy a table that uses a custom style to a different workbook, the custom style will be available in the other workbook.

FIGURE 4.29

Use this dialog box to create a new table style.

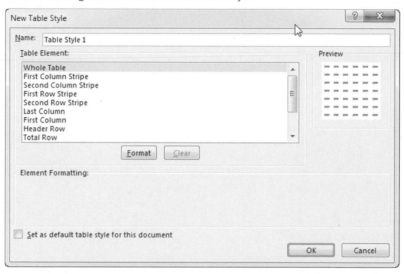

TIP

If you want to make changes to an existing table style, locate it in the Ribbon and right-click and then choose Duplicate from the shortcut menu. Excel displays the Modify Table Style dialog box with all of the settings from the specified table style. Make your changes, give the style a new name, and click OK to save it as a custom table style.

Formatting Worksheets

IN THIS CHAPTER

Understanding how formatting can improve your worksheets

Getting to know the formatting tools

Using formatting in your worksheets

Using conditional formatting

Using named styles for easier formatting

Understanding document themes

Formatting your worksheet is more than just making your worksheet pretty. Proper formatting can help users understand the purpose of the worksheet and help prevent data entry errors.

Stylistic formatting isn't essential for every workbook that you develop, especially if it's only for your own use. On the other hand, it takes only a few moments to apply some simple formatting and, after you apply it, the formatting will remain in place without further effort on your part.

Getting to Know the Formatting Tools

Figure 5.1 shows how even simple formatting can significantly improve a worksheet's readability. The unformatted worksheet (on the left) is perfectly functional but not very readable compared to the formatted worksheet (on the right).

This workbook is available on this book's website at www.wiley.com/go/excel2019bible. The file is named loan payments.xlsx.

The Excel cell formatting tools are available in three locations.

- On the Home tab of the Ribbon
- On the Mini toolbar that appears when you right-click a selected range or a cell
- From the Format Cells dialog box

FIGURE 5.1

Simple formatting can greatly improve the appearance of your worksheet.

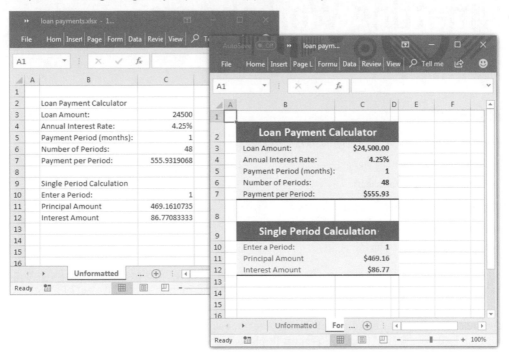

In addition, many common formatting commands have keyboard shortcuts.

Using the formatting tools on the Home tab

The Home tab of the Ribbon provides quick access to the most commonly used formatting options. Start by selecting the cell or range you want to format. Then use the appropriate tool in the Font, Alignment, or Number group.

Using these tools is intuitive, and the best way to familiarize yourself with them is to experiment. Enter some data, select some cells, and then click the controls to change the appearance. Note that some of these controls are actually drop-down lists. Click the small arrow on the button, and the button expands to display your choices.

Using the Mini toolbar

When you right-click a cell or a range selection, you get a shortcut menu. In addition, the Mini toolbar appears above or below the shortcut menu. Figure 5.2 shows how this toolbar looks. The Mini toolbar for cell formatting contains the most commonly used controls from the Home tab of the Ribbon.

FIGURE 5.2

The Mini toolbar appears above or below the right-click shortcut menu.

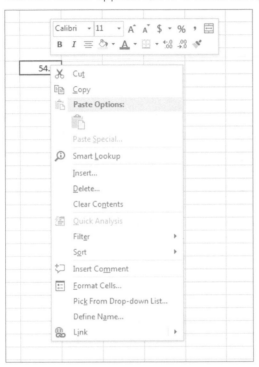

If you use a tool on the Mini toolbar, the shortcut menu disappears, but the toolbar remains visible so that you can apply other formatting to the selected cells. To hide the Mini toolbar, just click in any cell or press Esc.

Using the Format Cells dialog box

The formatting controls available on the Home tab of the Ribbon are sufficient most of the time, but some types of formatting require that you use the Format Cells dialog box. This tabbed dialog box lets you apply nearly any type of stylistic formatting and number formatting. The formats that you choose in the Format Cells dialog box apply to the selected cells. Later sections in this chapter cover the tabs of the Format Cells dialog box.

After selecting the cell or range to format, you can display the Format Cells dialog box by using any of the following methods:

- Press Ctrl+1.
- Click the dialog box launcher in Home ⇨ Font, Home ⇨ Alignment, or Home ⇨ Number. (The dialog box launcher is the small downward-pointing arrow icon

displayed to the right of the group name in the Ribbon.) When you display the Format Cells dialog box using a dialog box launcher, the dialog box is displayed with the appropriate tab visible.

- Right-click the selected cell or range and choose Format Cells from the shortcut menu.
- Click the More command in some of the drop-down controls in the Ribbon. For example, the Home ⇨ Font ⇨ Border drop-down includes an item named More Borders.

The Format Cells dialog box contains six tabs: Number, Alignment, Font, Border, Fill, and Protection. The following sections contain more information about the formatting options available in this dialog box.

Formatting Your Worksheet

Excel offers most of the same formatting options as other Office applications like Word or PowerPoint. As you might expect, cell-related formatting like fill color and borders feature more prominently in Excel than some of the other applications.

Using fonts to format your worksheet

You can use different fonts, font sizes, or text attributes in your worksheets to make various parts, such as the headers for a table, stand out. You also can adjust the font size. For example, using a smaller font allows for more information on a single screen or printed page.

By default, Excel uses the 11-point (pt) Calibri font. A font is described by its typeface (Calibri, Cambria, Arial, Times New Roman, Courier New, and so on) as well as by its size, measured in points. (Seventy-two points equal one inch.) Excel's row height, by default, is 15 pt. Therefore, 11-pt type entered into 15-pt rows leaves a small amount of blank space between the characters in vertically adjacent rows.

> **TIP**
>
> If you haven't manually changed a row's height, Excel automatically adjusts the row height based on the tallest text that you enter into the row.

> **TIP**
>
> If you plan to distribute a workbook to other users, remember that Excel does not embed fonts. Therefore, you should stick with the standard fonts that are included with Windows or Microsoft Office. If you open a workbook and your system doesn't have the font used in the workbook, Windows attempts to use a similar font. Sometimes this attempt works okay; other times it doesn't.

Use the Font and Font Size tools in the Font group on the Home tab of the Ribbon (or on the Mini toolbar) to change the font or size for selected cells.

You also can use the Font tab in the Format Cells dialog box to choose fonts, as shown in Figure 5.3. This tab enables you to control several other font attributes that aren't available elsewhere. Besides choosing the font, you can change the font style (bold, italic), underlining, color, and effects (strikethrough, superscript, or subscript). If you select the Normal Font check box, Excel displays the selections for the font defined for the Normal style. We discuss styles later in this chapter (see "Using Named Styles for Easier Formatting").

FIGURE 5.3

The Font tab of the Format Cells dialog box gives you many additional font attribute options.

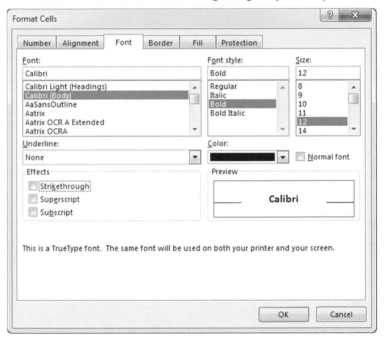

Figure 5.4 shows several examples of font formatting. In this figure, gridlines were turned off to make the underlining more visible. Notice, in the figure, that Excel provides four different underlining styles. In the two nonaccounting underline styles, only the cell contents are underlined. In the two accounting underline styles, the entire width of the cells is always underlined.

5

FIGURE 5.4

You can choose many different font formatting options for your worksheets.

If you prefer to keep both hands on the keyboard, you can use the following shortcut keys to format a selected range quickly:

- Ctrl+B: Bold
- Ctrl+I: Italic
- Ctrl+U: Underline
- Ctrl+5: Strikethrough

These shortcut keys act as a toggle. For example, you can turn bold on and off by repeatedly pressing Ctrl+B.

Using Multiple Formatting Styles in a Single Cell

If a cell contains text (as opposed to a value or a formula), you can apply formatting to individual characters in the cell. To do so, switch to Edit mode (press F2, or double-click the cell) and then select the characters that you want to format. You can select characters either by dragging the mouse over them or by pressing the Shift key as you press the left or right arrow key.

This technique is useful if you need to apply superscript or subscript formatting to a few characters in the cell (refer to Figure 5.4 for examples).

After you select the characters to format, use any of the standard formatting techniques, including options in the Format Cells dialog box. To display the Format Cells dialog box when editing a cell, press Ctrl+1. The changes apply only to the selected characters in the cell. This technique doesn't work with cells that contain values or formulas.

Changing text alignment

The contents of a cell can be aligned horizontally and vertically. By default, Excel aligns numbers to the right and text to the left. All cells use bottom alignment by default.

Overriding these defaults is a simple matter. The most commonly used alignment commands are in the Alignment group on the Home tab of the Ribbon. Use the Alignment tab of the Format Cells dialog box for even more options (see Figure 5.5).

FIGURE 5.5

The full range of alignment options is available on the Alignment tab of the Format Cells dialog box.

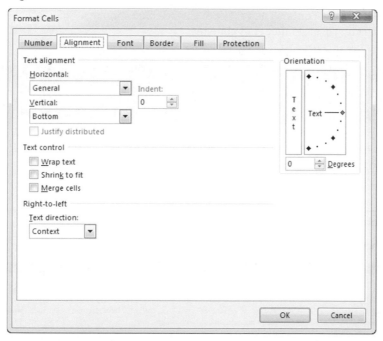

Choosing horizontal alignment options

Horizontal alignment options, which control how cell contents are distributed across the width of the cell (or cells), are available from the Format Cells dialog box.

General Aligns numbers to the right, aligns text to the left, and centers logical and error values. This option is the default horizontal alignment.

Left Aligns the cell contents to the left side of the cell. If the text is wider than the cell, the text spills over to the cell on the right. If the cell on the right isn't empty, the text is truncated and not completely visible. This is also available on the Ribbon.

Center Centers the cell contents in the cell. If the text is wider than the cell, the text spills over to cells on either side if they're empty. If the adjacent cells aren't empty, the text is truncated and not completely visible. This is also available on the Ribbon.

5

Right   Aligns the cell contents to the right side of the cell. If the text is wider than the cell, the text spills over to the cell on the left. If the cell on the left isn't empty, the text is truncated and not completely visible. This is also available on the Ribbon.

Fill   Repeats the contents of the cell until the cell's width is filled. If cells to the right also are formatted with Fill alignment, they also are filled.

Justify   Justifies the text to the left and right of the cell. This option is applicable only if the cell is formatted as wrapped text and uses more than one line.

Center Across Selection   Centers the text over the selected columns. This option is useful for centering a heading over a number of columns.

Distributed   Distributes the text evenly across the selected column.

> **NOTE**
>
> If you choose Left, Right, or Distributed, you can also adjust the Indent setting, which adds horizontal space between the cell border and the text.

Figure 5.6 shows examples of text that uses three types of horizontal alignment: Left, Justify, and Distributed (with an indent).

FIGURE 5.6

The same text, displayed with three types of horizontal alignment

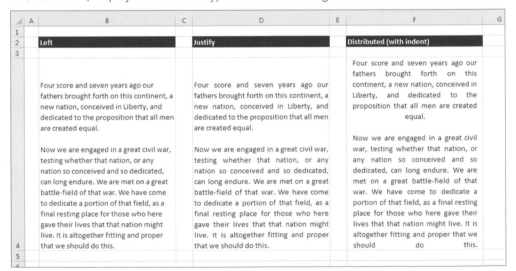

If you want to experiment with text alignment settings, this workbook is available at this book's website at www.wiley.com/go/excel2019bible. **The file is named** `text alignment.xlsx`.

Choosing vertical alignment options

Vertical alignment options typically aren't used as often as horizontal alignment options. In fact, these settings are useful only if you've adjusted row heights so that they're considerably taller than normal.

Here are the vertical alignment options available in the Format Cells dialog box:

Top   Aligns the cell contents to the top of the cell. This is also available on the Ribbon.

Center   Centers the cell contents vertically in the cell. This is also available on the Ribbon.

Bottom   Aligns the cell contents to the bottom of the cell. This is also available on the Ribbon. This option is the default vertical alignment.

Justify   Justifies the text vertically in the cell; this option is applicable only if the cell is formatted as wrapped text and uses more than one line. This setting can be used to increase the line spacing.

Distributed   Distributes the text evenly vertically in the cell.

Wrapping or shrinking text to fit the cell

If you have text too wide to fit the column width but you don't want that text to spill over into adjacent cells, you can use either the Wrap Text option or the Shrink to Fit option to accommodate that text. The Wrap Text option is also available on the Ribbon.

The Wrap Text option displays the text on multiple lines in the cell, if necessary. Use this option to display lengthy headings without having to make the columns too wide and without reducing the size of the text.

The Shrink to Fit option reduces the size of the text so that it fits into the cell without spilling over to the next cell. The times that this command is useful seem to be rare. Unless the text is just slightly too long, the result is almost always illegible.

NOTE
If you apply Wrap Text formatting to a cell, you can't use the Shrink to Fit formatting.

Merging worksheet cells to create additional text space

A handy formatting option is the ability to merge two or more cells. When you merge cells, you don't combine the contents of cells. Rather, you combine a group of cells into a single cell that occupies the same space. The worksheet shown in Figure 5.7 contains four sets of merged cells. Range C2:I2 has been merged into a single cell and so have ranges J2:P2, B4:B8, and B9:B13. In the latter two cases, the text orientation has also been changed (see "Displaying text at an angle" later in this chapter).

5

FIGURE 5.7

Merge worksheet cells to make them act as if they were a single cell.

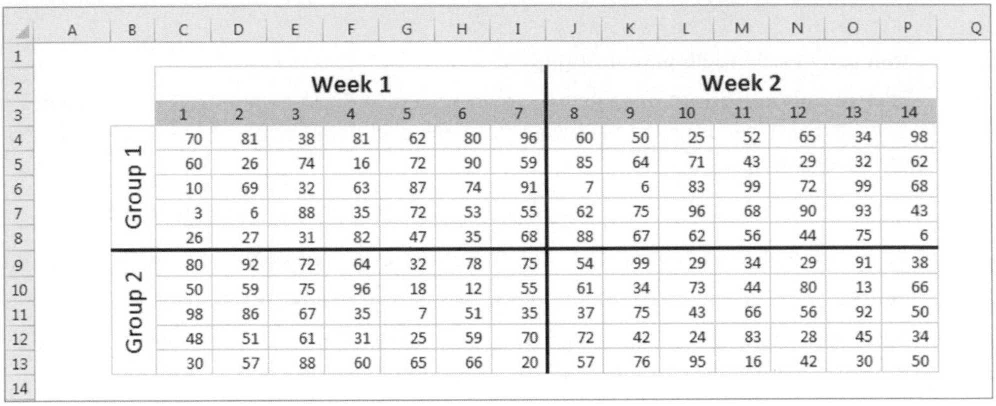

◢	A	B	C	D	E	F	G	H	I	J	K	L	M	N	O	P	Q
1																	
2						Week 1							Week 2				
3			1	2	3	4	5	6	7	8	9	10	11	12	13	14	
4			70	81	38	81	62	80	96	60	50	25	52	65	34	98	
5		Group 1	60	26	74	16	72	90	59	85	64	71	43	29	32	62	
6			10	69	32	63	87	74	91	7	6	83	99	72	99	68	
7			3	6	88	35	72	53	55	62	75	96	68	90	93	43	
8			26	27	31	82	47	35	68	88	67	62	56	44	75	6	
9			80	92	72	64	32	78	75	54	99	29	34	29	91	38	
10		Group 2	50	59	75	96	18	12	55	61	34	73	44	80	13	66	
11			98	86	67	35	7	51	35	37	75	43	66	56	92	50	
12			48	51	61	31	25	59	70	72	42	24	83	28	45	34	
13			30	57	88	60	65	66	20	57	76	95	16	42	30	50	
14																	

You can merge any number of cells occupying any number of rows and columns. In fact, you can merge all 17 billion cells in a worksheet into a single cell—although there probably isn't a good reason to do so, except maybe to play a trick on a co-worker.

The range that you intend to merge should be empty, except for the upper-left cell. If any of the other cells that you intend to merge are not empty, Excel displays a warning. If you continue, all of the data (except in the upper-left cell) will be deleted.

You can use the Alignment tab of the Format Cells dialog box to merge cells, but using the Merge & Center control in the Alignment group on the Ribbon (or on the Mini toolbar) is simpler. To merge cells, select the cells that you want to merge and then click the Merge & Center button. The cells will be merged, and the content in the upper-left cells will be centered horizontally. The Merge & Center button acts as a toggle. To unmerge cells, select the merged cells and click the Merge & Center button again.

After you merge cells, you can change the alignment to something other than Center by using the controls in the Home ⇨ Alignment group.

The Home ⇨ Alignment ⇨ Merge & Center control contains a drop-down list with these additional options:

Merge Across   When a multirow range is selected, this command creates multiple merged cells—one for each row.

Merge Cells   Merges the selected cells without applying the Center attribute.

Unmerge Cells   Unmerges the selected cells.

Displaying text at an angle

In some cases, you may want to create more visual impact by displaying text at an angle within a cell. You can display text horizontally, vertically, or at any angle between 90 degrees up and 90 degrees down.

From the Home ➪ Alignment ➪ Orientation drop-down list, you can apply the most common text angles. For more control, use the Alignment tab of the Format Cells dialog box. In the Format Cells dialog box (refer to Figure 5.5), use the Degrees spinner control—or just drag the red pointer in the gauge. You can specify a text angle between –90 and +90 degrees.

Figure 5.8 shows an example of text displayed at a 45-degree angle.

FIGURE 5.8

Rotate text for additional visual impact.

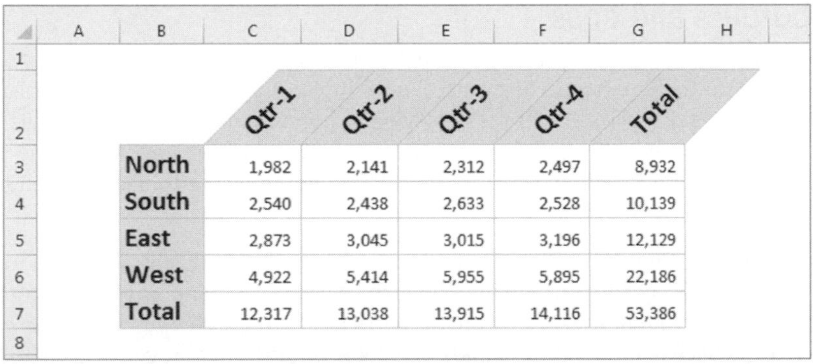

	Qtr-1	Qtr-2	Qtr-3	Qtr-4	Total
North	1,982	2,141	2,312	2,497	8,932
South	2,540	2,438	2,633	2,528	10,139
East	2,873	3,045	3,015	3,196	12,129
West	4,922	5,414	5,955	5,895	22,186
Total	12,317	13,038	13,915	14,116	53,386

NOTE

Rotated text may look a bit distorted on-screen, but the printed output is usually of much better quality.

Using colors and shading

Excel provides the tools to create some colorful worksheets. You can change the color of the text or add colors to the backgrounds of the worksheet cells. Prior to Excel 2007, workbooks were limited to a palette of 56 colors. Since then, Microsoft has increased the number of colors to more than 16 million.

You control the color of the cell's text by choosing Home ➪ Font ➪ Font Color. Control the cell's background color by choosing Home ➪ Font ➪ Fill Color. Both of these color controls are also available on the Mini toolbar, which appears when you right-click a cell or range.

TIP
To hide the contents of a cell, make the background color the same as the font text color. The cell contents are still visible in the Formula bar when you select the cell. Keep in mind, however, that some printers may override this setting, and the text may be visible when printed.

Even though you have access to a lot of colors, you might want to stick with the ten theme colors (and their light/dark variations) displayed in the various color selection controls. In other words, avoid using the More Color option, which lets you select a color. Why? First, those ten colors were chosen because they "go together." (Well, at least somebody thought they did.) Another reason involves document themes. If you switch to a different document theme for your workbook, nontheme colors aren't changed. In some cases, the result may be less than pleasing aesthetically. (See "Understanding Document Themes" later in this chapter for more information about themes.)

Adding borders and lines

Borders (and lines within the borders) are another visual enhancement that you can add around groups of cells. Borders are often used to group a range of similar cells or to delineate rows or columns. Excel offers 13 preset styles of borders, as you can see in the Home ➪ Font ➪ Borders drop-down list shown in Figure 5.9. This control works with the selected cell or range and enables you to specify which, if any, border style to use for each border of the selection.

You may prefer to draw borders rather than select a preset border style. To do so, use the Draw Border or Draw Border Grid command from the Home ➪ Font ➪ Borders drop-down list. Selecting either command lets you create borders by dragging your mouse. Use the Line Color or Line Style command to change the color or style. When you're finished drawing borders, press Esc to cancel the border-drawing mode.

Another way to apply borders is to use the Border tab of the Format Cells dialog box, which is shown in Figure 5.10. One way to display this dialog box is to select More Borders from the Borders drop-down list.

Before you display the Format Cells dialog box, select the cell or range to which you want to add borders. Then, in the Format Cells dialog box, choose a line style and color and then choose the border position for the line style by clicking one or more of the Border icons. (These icons are toggles.)

Notice that the Border tab has three preset icons, which can save you some clicking. If you want to remove all borders from the selection, click None. To put an outline around the selection, click Outline. To put borders inside the selection, click Inside.

FIGURE 5.9

Use the Borders drop-down list to add lines around worksheet cells.

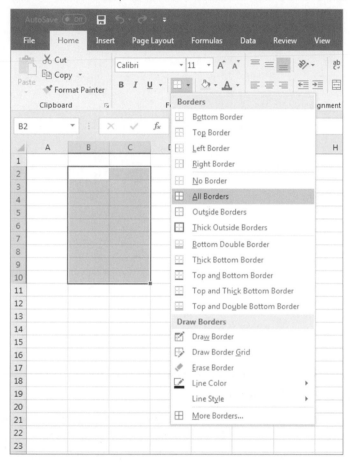

Excel displays the selected border style in the dialog box; there is no live preview in the worksheet. You can choose different styles for different border positions; you can also choose a color for the border. Using this dialog box may require some experimentation, but you'll get the hang of it.

When you apply two diagonal lines, the cells look like they've been crossed out.

TIP

If you use border formatting in your worksheet, you may want to turn off the grid display to make the borders more pronounced. Choose View ⇨ Show ⇨ Gridlines to toggle the gridline display.

5

FIGURE 5.10

Use the Border tab of the Format Cells dialog box for more control over cell borders.

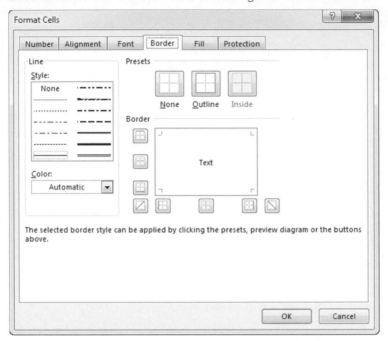

Copying Formats by Painting

Perhaps the quickest way to copy the formats from one cell to another cell or range is to use the Format Painter button (the button with the paintbrush image) of the Home ⇨ Clipboard group.

1. **Select the cell or range that has the formatting attributes that you want to copy.**

2. **Click the Format Painter button.** The mouse pointer changes to include a paintbrush.

3. **Select the cells to which you want to apply the formats.**

4. **Release the mouse button, and Excel applies the same set of formatting options that were in the original range.**

If you double-click the Format Painter button, you can paint multiple areas of the worksheet with the same formats. Excel applies the formats that you copy to each cell or range that you select. To get out of Paint mode, click the Format Painter button again (or press Esc).

Using Conditional Formatting

You can apply *conditional formatting* to a cell so that the cell looks different depending on its contents. Conditional formatting is a useful tool for visualizing numeric data. In some cases, conditional formatting may be a viable alternative to creating a chart.

Conditional formatting lets you apply cell formatting selectively and automatically, based on the contents of the cells. For example, you can apply conditional formatting in such a way that all negative values in a range have a light-yellow background color. When you enter or change a value in the range, Excel examines the value and checks the conditional formatting rules for the cell. If the value is negative, the background is shaded; otherwise, no formatting is applied.

Specifying conditional formatting

To apply a conditional formatting rule to a cell or range, select the cells and then use one of the commands from the Home ⇨ Styles ⇨ Conditional Formatting drop-down list to specify a rule. The choices are as follows:

Highlight Cells Rules   Examples include highlighting cells that are greater than a particular value, are between two values, contain a specific text string, contain a date, or are duplicated.

Top/Bottom Rules   Examples include highlighting the top ten items, the items in the bottom 20 percent, and the items that are above average.

Data Bars   Applies graphic bars directly in the cells, proportional to the cell's value.

Color Scales   Applies background color, proportional to the cell's value.

Icon Sets   Displays icons directly in the cells. The icons depend on the cell's value.

New Rule   Enables you to specify other conditional formatting rules, including rules based on a logical formula.

Clear Rules   Deletes all the conditional formatting rules from the selected cells.

Manage Rules   Displays the Conditional Formatting Rules Manager dialog box in which you create new conditional formatting rules, edit rules, or delete rules.

Using graphical conditional formats

This section describes the three conditional formatting options that display graphics: data bars, color scales, and icon sets. These types of conditional formatting can be useful for visualizing the values in a range.

Using data bars

The data bars conditional format displays horizontal bars directly in the cell. The length of the bar is based on the value of the cell relative to the other values in the range.

5

Figure 5.11 shows an example of data bars. It's a list of tracks on 39 Bob Dylan albums, with the length of each track in column D. With data bar conditional formatting applied to column D, you can tell at a glance which tracks are longer.

FIGURE 5.11

The length of the data bars is proportional to the track length in the cell in column D.

	A	B	C	D
1	Artist	Album	Title	Length
2	Bob Dylan	Infidels	Jokerman	0:06:19
3	Bob Dylan	Modern Times	When The Deal Goes Down	0:05:04
4	Bob Dylan	Infidels	Don't Fall Apart On Me Tonight	0:05:56
5	Bob Dylan	Blonde On Blonde	Leopard-Skin Pill-Box Hat	0:04:00
6	Bob Dylan	Under the Red Sky	2 X 2	0:03:36
7	Bob Dylan	Highway 61 Revisited	Just Like Tom Thumb's Blues	0:05:32
8	Bob Dylan	Self Portrait	She Belongs to Me	0:02:43
9	Bob Dylan	New Morning	New Morning	0:03:59
10	Bob Dylan	Planet Waves	Forever young	0:04:57
11	Bob Dylan	30th Anniversary Concert	Emotionally Yours	0:05:43
12	Bob Dylan	Good As I Been to You	Canadee-I-O	0:04:23
13	Bob Dylan	Down in the Groove	When Did You Leave Heaven	0:02:13
14	Bob Dylan	Street Legal	We Better Talk This Over	0:04:04
15	Bob Dylan	The Times They Are A-Changin'	North Country Blues	0:04:33
16	Bob Dylan	30th Anniversary Concert	Foot Of Pride	0:08:47
17	Bob Dylan	Time Out of Mind	Til I Fell in Love with You	0:05:17
18	Bob Dylan	Knocked Out Loaded	Under Your Spell	0:03:56
19	Bob Dylan	Another Side of Bob Dylan	To Ramona	0:03:52
20	Bob Dylan	Time Out of Mind	Million Miles	0:05:52
21	Bob Dylan	Another Side of Bob Dylan	I Don't Believe You	0:04:22
22	Bob Dylan	Tell Tale Signs (Disc 2)	Cross The Green Mountain	0:08:14
23	Bob Dylan	Empire Burlesque	I'll Remember You	0:04:14
24	Bob Dylan	Slow Train Coming	Gonna Change My Way of Thinking	0:05:28
25	Bob Dylan	Together Through Life	I Feel A Change Comin' On	0:05:25
26	Bob Dylan	30th Anniversary Concert	Introduction	0:00:55
27	Bob Dylan	The Times They Are A-Changin'	The Lonesome Death Of Hattie Carroll	0:05:47
28	Bob Dylan	Bob Dylan	House of the Risin' Sun	0:05:18
29	Bob Dylan	The Freewheelin' Bob Dylan	Corrina, Corrina	0:02:44
30	Bob Dylan	World Gone Wrong	World Gone Wrong	0:03:58

 The examples in this section are available on this book's website at www.wiley.com/go/ excel2019bible. The workbook is named data bars examples.xlsx.

TIP

When you adjust the column width, the bar lengths adjust accordingly. The differences among the bar lengths are more prominent when the column is wider.

Excel provides quick access to 12 data bar styles via Home ➪ Styles ➪ Conditional Formatting ➪ Data Bars. For additional choices, click the More Rules option, which displays the New Formatting Rule dialog box. Use this dialog box to

- Show the bar only. (Hide the numbers.)
- Specify Minimum and Maximum values for the scaling.
- Change the appearance of the bars.

- Specify how negative values and the axis are handled.
- Specify the direction of the bars.

> **NOTE**
>
> Oddly, if you add data bars using one of the 12 data bar styles, the colors used for data bars are not theme colors. If you apply a new document theme, the data bar colors do not change. However, if you add the data bars by using the New Formatting Rule dialog box, the colors you choose are theme colors.

Using color scales

The color scale conditional formatting option varies the background color of a cell based on the cell's value relative to other cells in the range.

Figure 5.12 shows examples of color scale conditional formatting. The example on the left depicts monthly sales for three regions. Conditional formatting was applied to the range B4:D15. The conditional formatting uses a three-color scale, with red for the lowest value, yellow for the midpoint, and green for the highest value. Values in between are displayed using a color within the gradient. It's clear that the Central region consistently has lower sales volumes, but the conditional formatting doesn't help identify monthly differences for a particular region.

FIGURE 5.12

Two examples of color scale conditional formatting

	A	B	C	D	E	F	G	H	I
1	A single conditional formatting rule					A separate rule for each region			
2									
3	Month	Western	Central	Eastern		Month	Western	Central	Eastern
4	January	214,030	103,832	225,732		January	214,030	103,832	225,732
5	February	224,948	105,498	217,703		February	224,948	105,498	217,703
6	March	219,210	105,312	218,783		March	219,210	105,312	218,783
7	April	217,347	101,842	221,332		April	217,347	101,842	221,332
8	May	208,045	106,716	231,296		May	208,045	106,716	231,296
9	June	200,201	106,928	232,567		June	200,201	106,928	232,567
10	July	204,767	107,134	222,910		July	204,767	107,134	222,910
11	August	198,639	107,753	223,328		August	198,639	107,753	223,328
12	September	198,558	110,017	235,186		September	198,558	110,017	235,186
13	October	197,498	105,267	239,329		October	197,498	105,267	239,329
14	November	198,213	109,227	234,400		November	198,213	109,227	234,400
15	December	197,343	104,054	243,325		December	197,343	104,054	243,325
16									

The example on the right shows the same data, but conditional formatting was applied to each region separately. This approach facilitates comparisons within a region and can identify high or low sales months.

Neither one of these approaches is necessarily better. The way you set up conditional formatting depends entirely on what you're trying to visualize.

This workbook, named `color scale example.xlsx`, **is available on this book's website at** `www. wiley.com/go/excel2019bible`.

Excel provides six two-color scale presets and six three-color scale presets, which you can apply to the selected range by choosing Home ⇨ Styles ⇨ Conditional Formatting ⇨ Color Scales.

To customize the colors and other options, choose Home ⇨ Styles ⇨ Conditional Formatting ⇨ Color Scales ⇨ More Rules, and the New Formatting Rule dialog box, shown in Figure 5.13, appears. Adjust the settings, and watch the Preview box to see the effects of your changes.

FIGURE 5.13

Use the New Formatting Rule dialog box to customize a color scale.

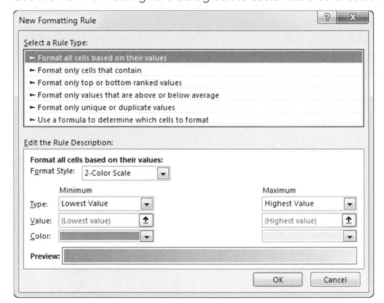

Using icon sets

Yet another conditional formatting option is to display an icon in the cell. The icon displayed depends on the value of the cell.

To assign an icon set to a range, select the cells and choose Home ⇨ Styles ⇨ Conditional Formatting ⇨ Icon Sets. Excel provides 20 icon sets from which you may choose. The number of icons in the sets ranges from three to five. You can't create a custom icon set.

Figure 5.14 shows an example that uses an icon set. The symbols graphically depict the status of each project, based on the value in column C.

FIGURE 5.14

Using an icon set to indicate the status of projects

	A	B	C	D
1		Project Status Report		
2				
3		Project	Pct Completed	
4		Project 1	95%	
5		Project 2	100%	
6		Project 3	50%	
7		Project 4	0%	
8		Project 5	20%	
9		Project 6	80%	
10		Project 7	100%	
11		Project 8	0%	
12		Project 9	0%	
13		Project 10	50%	
14				

The icon set example in this section is available on this book's website at www.wiley.com/go/ excel2019bible. The workbook is named icon set examples.xlsx.

By default, the symbols are assigned using percentiles. For a three-symbol set, the items are grouped into three percentiles. For a four-symbol set, they're grouped into four percentiles. For a five-symbol set, the items are grouped into five percentiles.

If you would like more control over how the icons are assigned, choose Home ⇨ Styles ⇨ Conditional Formatting ⇨ Icon Sets ⇨ More Rules to display the New Formatting Rule dialog box. To modify an existing rule, choose Home ⇨ Styles ⇨ Conditional Formatting ⇨ Manage Rules. Then select the rule to modify and click the Edit Rule button.

Figure 5.15 shows how to modify the icon set rules such that only projects that are 100 percent complete get the check mark icons. Projects that are 0 percent complete get the X icon. All other projects get no icon.

5

FIGURE 5.15

Changing the icon assignment rule

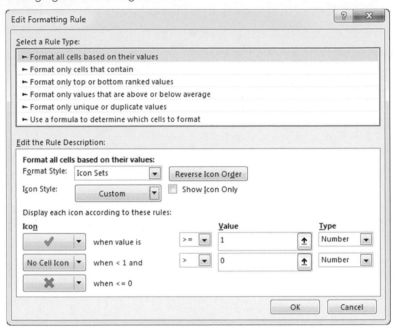

Figure 5.16 shows the project status list after making this change.

FIGURE 5.16

Using a modified rule and eliminating an icon makes the table more readable.

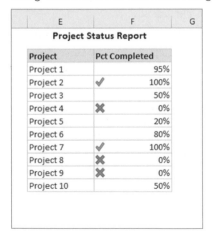

Creating formula-based rules

The graphical conditional formats are generally used to show a cell in relation to other, nearby cells. Formula-based rules generally apply to one cell independently. The same rule may apply to many cells, but each cell is considered on its own.

The Highlight Cells Rules and Top/Bottom Rules options under the Conditional Formatting Ribbon control are commonly used shortcuts for formula-based rules. If you choose Home ⇨ Styles ⇨ Conditional Formatting ⇨ New Rule, Excel displays the New Formatting Rule dialog box. You saw this dialog box in the previous section when the built-in graphical conditional formats needed tweaking. The entry Format Only Cells that Contain is another shortcut for a formula-based rule.

The last entry in the New Formatting Rule dialog box is Use a Formula to Determine Which Cells to Format. This is the entry you choose if none of the other shortcuts does what you want. It provides maximum flexibility for creating a rule.

NOTE

The formula must be a logical one that returns either TRUE or FALSE. If the formula evaluates to TRUE, the condition is satisfied, and the conditional formatting is applied. If the formula evaluates to FALSE, the conditional formatting is not applied.

Understanding relative and absolute references

If the formula that you enter into the New Formatting Rule or Edit Formatting Rule dialog box contains a cell reference, that reference is considered a relative reference based on the upper-left cell in the selected range.

For example, suppose that you want to set up a conditional formatting condition that applies shading to cells in range A1:B10 only if the cell contains text. None of Excel's conditional formatting options can do this task, so you need to create a formula that will return TRUE if the cell contains text and FALSE otherwise. Follow these steps:

1. Select the range A1:B10, and make sure that cell A1 is the active cell.
2. Choose Home ⇨ Styles ⇨ Conditional Formatting ⇨ New Rule. The New Formatting Rule dialog box appears.
3. Click the Use a Formula to Determine Which Cells to Format rule type.
4. Enter the following formula into the Formula box:

   `=ISTEXT(A1)`
5. Click the Format button. The Format Cells dialog box appears.
6. From the Fill tab, specify the cell shading that will be applied if the formula returns TRUE.
7. Click OK to return to the New Formatting Rule dialog box (see Figure 5.17).

FIGURE 5.17

Creating a conditional formatting rule based on a formula

8. Click OK to close the New Formatting Rule dialog box.

Notice that the formula entered in step 4 contains a relative reference to the upper-left cell in the selected range.

Generally, when entering a conditional formatting formula for a range of cells, you'll use a reference to the active cell, which is typically the upper-left cell in the selected range. One exception is when you need to refer to a specific cell. For example, suppose that you select range A1:B10 and you want to apply formatting to all cells in the range that exceed the value in cell C1. Enter this conditional formatting formula:

```
=A1>$C$1
```

In this case, the reference to cell C1 is an absolute reference; it will not be adjusted for the cells in the selected range. In other words, the conditional formatting formula for cell A2 looks like this:

```
=A2>$C$1
```

The relative cell reference is adjusted, but the absolute cell reference is not.

Conditional formatting formula examples

Each of these examples uses a formula entered directly into the New Formatting Rule dialog box, after selecting the Use a Formula to Determine Which Cells to Format rule type. You decide the type of formatting that you apply conditionally.

Identifying weekend days

Excel provides a number of conditional formatting rules that deal with dates, but it doesn't let you identify dates that fall on a weekend. Use this formula to identify weekend dates:

```
=OR(WEEKDAY(A1)=7,WEEKDAY(A1)=1)
```

This formula assumes that a range is selected and that cell A1 is the active cell.

Highlighting a row based on a value

Figure 5.18 shows a worksheet that contains a conditional formula in the range A3:G28. If a name entered in cell B1 is found in the first column, the entire row for that name is highlighted.

FIGURE 5.18

Highlighting a row, based on a matching name

	A	B	C	D	E	F	G	H
1	Name:	Noel						
2								
3	Alice	7	118	61	55	85	26	
4	Bob	198	134	180	3	132	63	
5	Carl	2	46	59	63	59	26	
6	Denise	190	121	12	26	68	97	
7	Elvin	174	42	176	68	124	14	
8	Francis	129	114	83	103	129	129	
9	George	9	128	24	44	139	108	
10	Harald	168	183	200	167	134	83	
11	Ivan	165	141	95	91	100	144	
12	June	116	171	109	84	148	15	
13	Kathy	131	43	197	82	103	163	
14	Larry	139	30	171	122	34	196	
15	Mary	31	171	185	162	171	17	
16	Noel	78	126	190	78	123	2	
17	Oliver	157	98	100	75	137	10	
18	Patrick	120	144	106	39	39	119	
19	Quincey	156	200	58	74	37	76	
20	Raul	58	147	160	182	11	79	
21	Shiela	79	183	5	161	104	23	
22	Todd	91	54	100	174	198	78	
23	Ursula	53	140	188	58	54	36	
24	Vince	121	13	2	139	148	101	
25	Walter	132	65	123	129	174	90	
26	Xenu	162	127	86	51	164	35	

The conditional formatting formula is

```
=$A3=$B$1
```

5

Notice that a mixed reference is used for cell A3. Because the column part of the reference is absolute, the comparison is always done using the contents of column A.

Displaying alternate-row shading

The conditional formatting formula that follows was applied to the range A1:D18, as shown in Figure 5.19, to apply shading to alternate rows:

```
=MOD(ROW(),2)=0
```

FIGURE 5.19

Using conditional formatting to apply formatting to alternate rows

▲	A	B	C	D	E
1	582	652	340	172	
2	634	592	103	429	
3	994	523	914	484	
4	455	175	649	771	
5	588	577	638	849	
6	718	151	645	825	
7	409	262	450	781	
8	433	587	150	733	
9	654	745	165	733	
10	430	648	7	722	
11	304	276	567	394	
12	215	336	595	646	
13	889	148	38	756	
14	888	850	291	342	
15	438	429	739	429	
16	59	869	822	680	
17	145	193	793	168	
18	877	788	859	111	
19					

Alternate row shading can make your spreadsheets easier to read. If you add or delete rows within the conditional formatting area, the shading is updated automatically.

This formula uses the ROW function (which returns the row number) and the MOD function (which returns the remainder of its first argument divided by its second argument). For cells in even-numbered rows, the MOD function returns 0, and cells in that row are formatted.

For alternate shading of columns, use the COLUMN function instead of the ROW function.

Creating checkerboard shading

The following formula is a variation on the example in the preceding section. It applies formatting to alternate rows and columns, creating a checkerboard effect.

```
=MOD(ROW(),2)=MOD(COLUMN(),2)
```

Shading groups of rows

Here's another row shading variation. The following formula shades alternate groups of rows. It produces four shaded rows, followed by four unshaded rows, followed by four more shaded rows, and so on.

```
=MOD(INT((ROW()-1)/4)+1,2)=1
```

Figure 5.20 shows an example.

FIGURE 5.20

Conditional formatting produces these groups of alternating shaded rows.

	A	B	C	D	E
1	91	100	463	200	
2	341	203	442	443	
3	404	262	378	120	
4	37	195	285	22	
5	235	9	258	252	
6	38	125	207	58	
7	41	375	214	383	
8	455	59	221	498	
9	285	327	418	314	
10	38	401	22	211	
11	171	394	89	80	
12	193	132	42	240	
13	139	108	478	83	
14	179	123	230	434	
15	261	186	158	403	
16	359	418	292	353	
17	105	417	290	421	
18	361	379	400	212	
19	236	174	198	208	
20	19	199	83	267	
21	227	214	84	207	
22	189	102	122	308	
23					

For different sizes groups, change the 4 to some other value. For example, use this formula to shade alternate groups of two rows:

```
=MOD(INT((ROW()-1)/2)+1,2)=1
```

Working with conditional formats

This section describes some additional information about conditional formatting that you may find useful.

5

Managing rules

The Conditional Formatting Rules Manager dialog box is useful for checking, editing, deleting, and adding conditional formats. First select any cell in the range that contains conditional formatting. Then choose Home ⇨ Styles ⇨ Conditional Formatting ⇨ Manage Rules.

You can specify as many rules as you like by clicking the New Rule button. Cells can even use data bars, color scales, and icon sets at the same time.

Copying cells that contain conditional formatting

Conditional formatting information is stored with a cell much like standard formatting information is stored with a cell. As a result, when you copy a cell that contains conditional formatting, you also copy the conditional formatting.

> **TIP**
>
> To copy only the formatting (including conditional formatting), copy the cells and then use the Paste Special dialog box and select the Formats option, or choose Home ⇨ Clipboard ⇨ Paste ⇨ Formatting (R).

If you insert rows or columns within a range that contains conditional formatting, the new cells have the same conditional formatting.

Deleting conditional formatting

When you press Delete to delete the contents of a cell, you don't delete the conditional formatting for the cell (if any). To remove all conditional formats (as well as all other cell formatting), select the cell and then choose Home ⇨ Editing ⇨ Clear ⇨ Clear Formats. Or, choose Home ⇨ Editing ⇨ Clear ⇨ Clear All to delete the cell contents and the conditional formatting.

To remove only conditional formatting (and leave the other formatting intact), choose Home ⇨ Styles ⇨ Conditional Formatting ⇨ Clear Rules and choose one of the available options.

Locating cells that contain conditional formatting

You can't always tell, just by looking at a cell, whether it contains conditional formatting. You can, however, use the Go To Special dialog box to select such cells.

1. Choose Home ⇨ Editing ⇨ Find & Select ⇨ Go To Special. The Go To Special dialog box appears.
2. In the Go To Special dialog box, select the Conditional Formats option.
3. To select all cells on the worksheet containing conditional formatting, select the All option; to select only the cells that contain the same conditional formatting as the active cell, select the Same option.
4. Click OK. Excel selects the cells for you.

Using Named Styles for Easier Formatting

One of the most underutilized features in Excel is named styles. *Named styles* make it easy to apply a set of predefined formatting options to a cell or range. In addition to saving time, using named styles helps to ensure a consistent look.

A style can consist of settings for up to six attributes:

- Number format
- Alignment (vertical and horizontal)
- Font (type, size, and color)
- Borders
- Fill
- Cell protection (locked and hidden)

The real power of styles is apparent when you change a component of a style. All cells that use that named style automatically incorporate the change. Suppose that you apply a particular style to a dozen cells scattered throughout your worksheet. Later, you realize that these cells should have a font size of 14 pt rather than 12 pt. Rather than change each cell, simply edit the style. All cells with that particular style change automatically.

Applying styles

Excel includes a good selection of predefined named styles that work in conjunction with document themes. Figure 5.21 shows the effect of choosing Home ⇨ Styles ⇨ Cell Styles. Note that this display is a live preview—as you move your mouse over the style choices, the selected cell or range temporarily displays the style. When you see a style you like, click it to apply the style to the selection.

NOTE

If Excel's window is wide enough, you won't see the Cell Styles command in the Ribbon. Instead, you'll see four or more formatted style boxes. Click the drop-down arrow to the right of these boxes to display all of the defined styles.

NOTE

By default, all cells use the Normal style. If you modify the Normal style, all cells that haven't been assigned a different style will reflect the new formatting.

FIGURE 5.21

Excel displays samples of predefined cell styles.

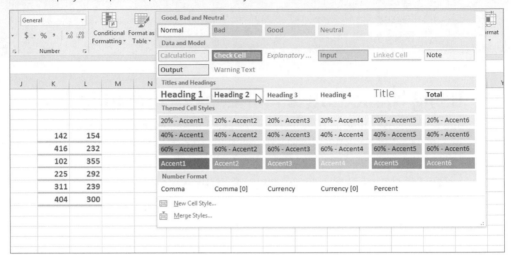

After you apply a style to a cell, you can apply additional formatting to it by using any formatting method discussed in this chapter. Formatting modifications that you make to the cell don't affect other cells that use the same style.

You have quite a bit of control over styles. In fact, you can do any of the following:

- Modify an existing style.
- Create a new style.
- Merge styles from another workbook into the active workbook.

The following sections describe these procedures.

Modifying an existing style

To change an existing style, choose Home ⇨ Styles ⇨ Cell Styles. Right-click the style that you want to modify and choose Modify from the shortcut menu. Excel displays the Style dialog box, as shown in Figure 5.22. In this example, the Style dialog box shows the settings for the Office theme Normal style—which is the default style for all cells. The style definitions vary, depending on which document theme is active.

Here's a quick example of how you can use styles to change the default font used throughout your workbook:

1. Choose Home ⇨ Styles ⇨ Cell Styles. Excels displays the list of styles for the active workbook.
2. Right-click Normal and choose Modify. Excel displays the Style dialog box (refer to Figure 5.22), with the current settings for the Normal style.

3. Click the Format button. Excel displays the Format Cells dialog box.

4. Click the Font tab, and choose the font and size that you want as the default.

5. Click OK to return to the Style dialog box. Notice that the Font item displays the font choice you made.

6. Click OK again to close the Style dialog box.

FIGURE 5.22

Use the Style dialog box to modify named styles.

The font for all cells that use the Normal style changes to the font that you specified. You can change any formatting attributes for any style.

Creating new styles

In addition to using Excel's built-in styles, you can create your own styles. This feature can be quite handy because it enables you to apply your favorite formatting options quickly and consistently.

To create a new style, follow these steps:

1. Select a cell, and apply all the formatting that you want to include in the new style. You can use any of the formatting that is available in the Format Cells dialog box.

2. After you format the cell to your liking, choose Home ⇨ Styles ⇨ Cell Styles, and choose New Cell Style. Excel displays its Style dialog box (refer to Figure 5.22), along with a proposed generic name for the style. Note that Excel displays the words By Example to indicate that it's basing the style on the current cell.

3. Enter a new style name in the Style Name field. The check boxes display the current formats for the cell. By default, all check boxes are selected.

4. (Optional) If you don't want the style to include one or more format categories, remove the check(s) from the appropriate check box(es).

5. Click OK to create the style and to close the dialog box.

After you perform these steps, the new custom style is available when you choose Home ⇨ Styles ⇨ Cell Styles. Custom styles are available only in the workbook in which they were created. To copy your custom styles to another workbook, see the section that follows.

> **NOTE**
> The Protection option in the Style dialog box controls whether users will be able to modify cells for the selected style. This option is effective only if you've also turned on worksheet protection by choosing Review ⇨ Protect ⇨ Protect Sheet.

Merging styles from other workbooks

Custom styles are stored with the workbook in which they were created. If you've created some custom styles, you probably don't want to go through all of the work required to create copies of those styles in each new Excel workbook. A better approach is to merge the styles from a workbook in which you previously created them.

To merge styles from another workbook, open both the workbook that contains the styles that you want to merge and the workbook that will contain the merged styles. Activate the second workbook, choose Home ⇨ Styles ⇨ Cell Styles, and then choose Merge Styles. Excel displays the Merge Styles dialog box that shows a list of all open workbooks. Select the workbook that contains the styles you want to merge and click OK. Excel copies custom styles from the workbook that you selected into the active workbook.

Controlling styles with templates

When you start Excel, it loads with several default settings, including the settings for stylistic formatting. If you spend a lot of time changing the default elements for every new workbook, you should know about templates.

Here's an example. You may prefer that gridlines aren't displayed in worksheets. And maybe you prefer Wrap Text to be the default setting for alignment. Templates provide an easy way to change defaults.

The trick is to create a workbook with the Normal style modified in the way you want it. Then save the workbook as a template (with an .xltx extension). After doing so, you can choose this template as the basis for a new workbook.

 Refer to Chapter 6, "Understanding Excel Files and Templates," for more information about templates.

Understanding Document Themes

In an attempt to help users create more professional-looking documents, the Office design-ers incorporated a feature known as *document themes*. Using themes is an easy (and almost foolproof) way to specify the colors, fonts, and a variety of graphic effects in a document. Best of all, changing the entire look of your document is a breeze. A few mouse clicks is all that it takes to apply a different theme and change the look of your workbook.

Importantly, the concept of themes is incorporated into other Office applications. Therefore, a company can easily create a standard and consistent look for all of its documents.

> **NOTE**
>
> Themes don't override specific formatting that you apply. For example, assume that you apply the Accent1 named style to a range. Then you change the font color for a few cells in that range. If you change to a different theme, the manually applied font colors won't be modified to use the new theme font colors. Bottom line: If you plan to take advantage of themes, stick with the default formatting choices.

Figure 5.23 shows a worksheet that contains a SmartArt diagram, a table, a chart, a range formatted with the Title named style, and a range formatted with the Explanatory Text named style. These items all use the default theme, which is the Office theme.

FIGURE 5.23

The elements in this worksheet use the default theme.

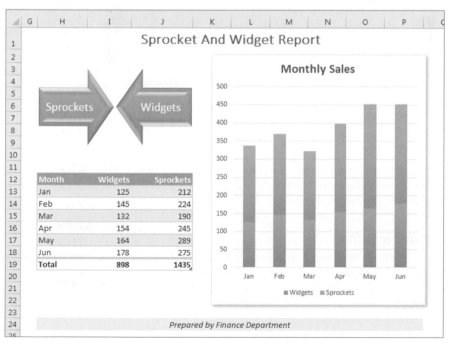

Figure 5.24 shows the same worksheet after applying a different document theme. The different theme changed the fonts, the colors (which may not be apparent in the figure), and the graphics effects for the SmartArt diagram.

FIGURE 5.24

The worksheet after applying a different theme

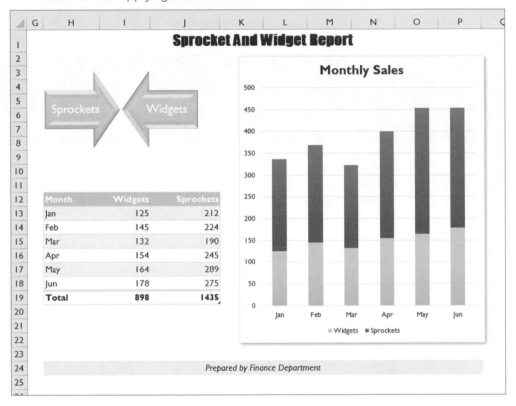

 If you'd like to experiment with using various themes, the workbooks shown in Figure 5.23 and Figure 5.24 are available on this book's website at www.wiley.com/go/excel2019bible. The file is named theme examples.xlsx.

Applying a theme

Figure 5.25 shows the theme choices that appear when you choose Page Layout ⇨ Themes ⇨ Themes. This display is a live preview. As you move your mouse over the theme choices, the active worksheet displays the theme. When you see a theme you like, click it to apply the theme to all worksheets in the workbook.

FIGURE 5.25

Built-in Excel theme choices

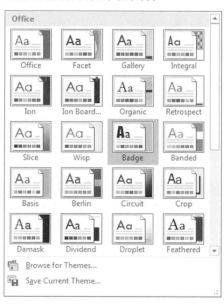

When you specify a particular theme, the gallery choices for various elements reflect the new theme. For example, the chart styles that you can choose from vary, depending on which theme is active.

Customizing a theme

Notice that the Themes group on the Page Layout tab contains three other controls: Colors, Fonts, and Effects. You can use these controls to change just one of the three components of a theme. For example, you might like the colors and effects in the Office theme but would prefer different fonts. To change the font set, apply the Office theme and then specify your preferred font set by choosing Page Layout ⇨ Themes ⇨ Fonts.

5

Each theme uses two fonts (one for headers and one for the body), and in some cases these two fonts are the same. If none of the theme choices is suitable, choose Page Layout ➪ Themes ➪ Fonts ➪ Customize Fonts to specify the two fonts that you prefer (see Figure 5.26).

FIGURE 5.26

Use this dialog box to specify two fonts for a theme.

TIP

When you choose Home ➪ Font ➪ Font, the two fonts for the current theme are listed first in the drop-down list.

Choose Page Layout ➪ Themes ➪ Colors to select a different set of colors. And, if you're so inclined, you can even create a custom set of colors by choosing Page Layout ➪ Themes ➪ Colors ➪ Customize Colors. This command displays the Create New Theme Colors dialog box, as shown in Figure 5.27. Note that each theme consists of twelve colors. Four of the colors are for text and backgrounds, six are for accents, and two are for hyperlinks. As you specify different colors, the preview panel in the dialog box updates.

NOTE

Theme effects operate on graphics elements, such as SmartArt, shapes, and charts. You can choose a different set of theme effects, but you can't customize theme effects.

FIGURE 5.27

If you're feeling creative, you can specify a set of custom colors for a theme.

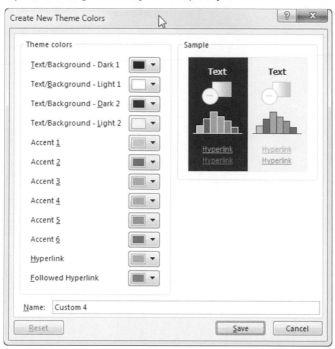

If you've customized a theme using different fonts or colors, you can save the new theme by choosing Page Layout ⇨ Themes ⇨ Save Current Theme. Your customized themes appear in the theme list in the Custom category. Other Office applications, such as Word and PowerPoint, can use these theme files.

5

Understanding Excel Files and Templates

IN THIS CHAPTER

Creating a new workbook

Opening an existing workbook

Saving and closing workbooks

Working with templates

This chapter describes the operations that you perform with workbook files: opening, saving, closing, and so on. It discusses how Excel uses files and provides an overview of the various types of files. Most of the file operations discussed here occur in the *Backstage view*, the screen that you see when you click the File button above the Excel Ribbon. It also discusses templates, a special kind of workbook file.

Creating a New Workbook

When you start Excel 2019, it displays a Start screen that lists recently used files and shows templates that you can use as the basis for a new workbook. One of the template options is Blank Workbook, which gives you an empty workbook. Figure 6.1 shows a portion of the Start screen.

> **TIP**
> If you prefer to skip the Start screen and always start with an empty workbook, choose File ⇨ Options. In the Excel Options dialog box, click the General tab and remove the check mark from the option labeled Show the Start Screen When This Application Starts.

After you start Excel and create a blank workbook, the empty workbook is called *Book1*. This workbook exists only in memory, and it hasn't been saved to disk. By default, this workbook contains one worksheet named Sheet1. If you're starting a project from scratch, you can use this blank workbook. By the way, you can change the default number of sheets in a new workbook by using the General tab of the Excel Options dialog box.

FIGURE 6.1

Choosing Blank Workbook from Excel's Start screen

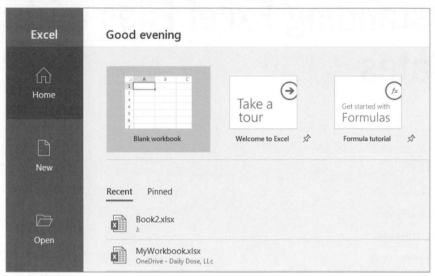

While you're working in Excel, you can create a new (empty) workbook at any time. Excel provides two ways to create a new workbook:

- Choose File ➪ New, which displays a screen that lets you create a blank workbook or a workbook based on a template. To create a new blank workbook, click Blank Workbook.
- Press Ctrl+N. This shortcut is the fastest way to start a new workbook if you're not using a template.

Opening an Existing Workbook

Here are some of the ways to open a workbook that's already been saved:

- Choose File ➪ Open ➪ Recent and then select the file that you want from the list on the right. Only the most recently used files are listed. You can specify the number of files to display (maximum of 50) in the Advanced section of the Excel Options dialog box.
- Choose File ➪ Open and choose a location from the list on the left. The locations will vary depending on which "places" you've set up. You may see cloud-based options. One of the options is always This PC. You can navigate to your files directly using the list, or you can click Browse to display the Open dialog box, which gives you many more options.

- Locate the Excel workbook file via a File Explorer file list. Just double-click the file-name (or icon), and the workbook opens in Excel. If Excel isn't running, Windows automatically starts Excel and loads the workbook file.

> **TIP**
>
> When you choose File ⇨ Open ⇨ Recent, each file in the recent workbooks list displays a pushpin icon on the right when you hover the mouse pointer over the filename. Click the pushpin icon, and that file becomes "pinned" to the list and will always appear at the top of the list. This handy feature ensures that important files always appear on the recent workbooks list—even if you haven't opened the file recently.
>
> Also, notice that you can right-click a workbook in the list and choose Remove from List. Choose Clear Unpinned Workbooks to clear the list and start fresh.

To open a workbook from the Open dialog box, use the folder tree display on the left to locate the folder that contains the file and then select the workbook file from the list on the right. You can resize the Open dialog box by using the control in the lower-right corner. After you locate and select the file, click Open, and the file opens. Or just double-click the filename to open it.

Notice that the Open button is actually a drop-down list. Click the arrow, and you see these additional options:

Open Opens the file normally.

Open Read-Only Opens the selected file in read-only mode. When a file is opened in this mode, you can't save changes with the original filename.

Open as Copy Opens a copy of the selected file. If the file is named budget.xlsx, the workbook that opens is named Copy(1)budget.xlsx.

Open in Browser Opens the file in your default web browser. If the file can't be opened in a browser, this option is disabled.

Open in Protected View Opens the file in a special mode that doesn't allow editing. In this view, most of the Excel Ribbon commands are disabled. Read more about this new feature in the nearby sidebar "About Protected View."

Open and Repair Attempts to open a file that may be damaged and recover information contained in it.

Show Previous Versions Applies to documents stored where version histories are maintained, as on OneDrive or SharePoint Online.

> **TIP**
>
> In the Open dialog box, you can hold down the Ctrl key and select multiple workbooks. When you click Open, all of the selected workbook files open.
>
> Right-clicking a filename in the Open dialog box displays a shortcut menu with many extra Windows commands. For example, you can copy, delete, or rename the file; modify its properties; and so on.

About Protected View

Excel 2010 introduced a security feature known as Protected View. Although it might seem like Excel is trying to keep you from opening your own files, Protected View is all about protecting you from malware. Malware refers to something that can harm your system. Hackers have figured out several ways to manipulate Excel files in a way that harmful code can be executed. Protected View essentially prevents these types of attacks by opening a file in a protected environment (a *sandbox*).

If you open an Excel workbook that you downloaded from the Web, you'll see a colorful message above the Formula bar. In addition, the Excel title bar displays [Protected View]. Choose File ⇨ Info to find out why Excel opened the file in Protected View.

If you're certain that the file is safe, click Enable Editing. If you don't enable editing, you'll be able to view the contents of the workbook, but you won't be able to make any changes to it.

If the workbook contains macros, you'll see another message after you enable editing: Security Warning. Macros have been disabled. If you're sure that the macros are harmless, click Enable Content.

By default, Protected View kicks in for the following:

- Files downloaded from the Internet
- Attachments opened from Outlook
- Files open from potentially unsafe locations, such as your Temporary Internet Files folder
- Files that are blocked by File Block Policy (a Windows feature that allows administrators to define potentially dangerous files)
- Files that have a digital signature that has expired

In some situations, you don't care about working with the document. You just want to print it. In that case, choose File ⇨ Print and then click the Enable Printing button.

Also, note that you can copy a range of cells from a workbook in Protected View and paste it into a different workbook.

You have some control over the types of files that trigger Protected View. To change the settings, choose File ⇨ Options and click Trust Center. Then click the Trust Center Settings button and click the Protected View tab in the Trust Center dialog box.

Filtering filenames

Near the bottom-right corner of the Open dialog box is a button with a drop-down list. When the Open dialog box is displayed, this button shows All Excel Files (and a long list of file extensions). The Open dialog box displays only those files that match the extensions. In other words, you see only standard Excel files.

If you want to open a file of a different type, click the arrow in the drop-down list and select the file type that you want to open. This changes the filtering and displays only files of the type that you specify.

You can also type a filter directly in the File Name box. For example, typing the following will display only files that have an `.xlsx` extension (press Enter after typing the filter): **`*.xlsx`**.

Choosing your file display preferences

The Open dialog box can display your workbook filenames in several styles: as a list, with complete details, as icons, and so on. You control the style by clicking the More Options arrow (in the upper-right corner) and then selecting a display style from the drop-down list.

Opening Workbooks Automatically

Many people work on the same workbooks each day. If this describes you, you'll be happy to know that Excel can open specific workbook files automatically whenever you start Excel. Any workbooks placed in the XLStart folder open automatically.

The location of the XLStart folder varies, depending on your Windows version. To determine the location of the XLStart folder on your system, follow these steps:

1. Choose File ➪ Options, and select the Trust Center tab.
2. Click the Trust Center Settings button. The Trust Center dialog box appears.
3. In the Trust Center dialog box, select the Trusted Locations tab. You'll see a list of trusted locations.
4. Look in the path for the location described as User Startup. The path might look something like this:

`C:\Users\<username>\AppData\Roaming\Microsoft\Excel\XLSTART\`

Another XLStart folder may be located here:

`C:\Program Files\Microsoft Office\root\Office16\XLSTART\`

Any workbook files (excluding template files) stored in either of these XLStart folders open automatically when Excel starts. If one or more files open automatically from an XLStart folder, Excel won't start with a blank workbook.

You can specify an alternate startup folder in addition to the XLStart folder. Choose File ➪ Options and select the Advanced tab. Scroll down to the General section, and enter a new folder name in the At Startup, Open All Files In field. Then when you start Excel, it automatically opens all workbook files in both the XLStart folders and the alternate folder that you specified.

Saving a Workbook

When you're working in Excel, your workbook is vulnerable to day-ruining events such as power failures and system crashes. Therefore, you should save your work often. Saving a file takes only a few seconds, but re-creating lost work can take many hours.

Excel provides four ways to save your workbook:

- Click the Save icon on the Quick Access toolbar. (It looks like an old-fashioned floppy disk.)
- Press Ctrl+S.
- Press Shift+F12.
- Choose File ⇨ Save.

CAUTION

Saving a file overwrites the previous version of the file on your hard drive. If you open a workbook and then completely mess it up, don't save the file. Instead, close the workbook without saving it and then reopen the good copy.

If your workbook has already been saved, it's saved again using the same filename in the same location. If you want to save the workbook to a new file or to a different location, choose File ⇨ Save As (or press F12).

If your workbook has never been saved, you'll be taken to the Save As pane in the Backstage view. Here you can choose a location, such as on your PC or in your OneDrive account—if you have one. You enter the filename in the right pane and click Save, or you can click the Browse button to show the Save As dialog box, where you can change the folder and type the filename. A new (unsaved) workbook has a default name, such as Book1 or Book2. Although Excel allows you to use these generic workbook names for filenames, you'll almost always want to specify a more descriptive filename in the Save As dialog box.

The Save As dialog box is similar to the Open dialog box. Select the desired folder in the folder list on the left. After you select the folder, enter the filename in the File Name field. You don't need to specify a file extension—Excel adds it automatically, based on the file type specified in the Save as Type field. By default, files are saved in the standard Excel file format, which uses an .xlsx file extension.

TIP

To change the default file format for saving files, choose File ⇨ Options to access the Excel Options dialog box. Click the Save tab and change the setting for the Save Files in This Format option. For example, if your workbooks must be compatible with older versions of Excel (versions before Excel 2007), you can change the default format to Excel 97–2003 Workbook (*.xls). Doing so eliminates the need to select the older file type every time you save a new workbook.

CAUTION

If your workbook contains VBA macros, saving it with an .xlsx file extension will erase all of the macros. It must be saved with an .xlsm extension (or saved in the XLS or XLSB format). If your workbook has macros, Excel will still propose to save it as an XLSX file. In other words, Excel suggests a file format that will destroy your macros! It will, however, warn you that the macros will be lost.

If a file with the same name already exists in the location that you specify, Excel asks whether you want to overwrite that file with the new file. Be careful! You can't recover the previous file after you overwrite it.

NEW FEATURE
When you saved a workbook as a comma-separated values (CSV) file in previous versions, Excel would display a dialog box warning you that some data may be lost. CSV files are simple text files and don't store formulas or formatting. The problem with the warning is that it would appear even if you didn't have formulas or formatting, and it would appear every single time you saved the CSV file. In Excel 2019, the dialog box was replaced with a yellow status bar that includes the option Don't Show Again. The new status bar is much less invasive and a welcome change for users who deal with CSV files.

Using AutoRecover

If you've used computers for any length of time, you've probably lost some work. You forgot to save a file, or maybe the power went out and your unsaved work was lost. Or maybe you were working on something and didn't think it was important, so you closed the file without saving. Of course, later you realized that it was *indeed* important. Excel's AutoRecover feature might make these types of "d'oh!" moments less frequent.

As you work in Excel, your work is periodically saved automatically. It happens in the background so you don't even know that it's happening. If necessary, you can access these autosaved versions of your work. This even applies to workbooks that you never explicitly saved.

The AutoRecover feature consists of two components:

- Versions of a workbook are saved automatically, and you can view them.
- Workbooks that you closed without saving are saved as draft versions.

Recovering versions of the current workbook

To see whether any previous versions of the active workbook are available, choose File ⇨ Info. The Manage Workbook section lists the available old versions (if any) of the current workbook. In some cases, more than one autosaved version will be listed. In other cases, no autosaved versions will be available. Figure 6.2 shows a workbook with two recovery points.

You can open an autosaved version by clicking its name. Remember that opening an autosaved version won't automatically replace the current version of your workbook. Therefore, you can decide whether the autosaved version is preferable to the current version. Or you can just copy some information that may have been accidentally deleted and paste it to your current workbook.

When you close the workbook, the autosaved versions are deleted.

FIGURE 6.2

You can recover to older versions of your workbook.

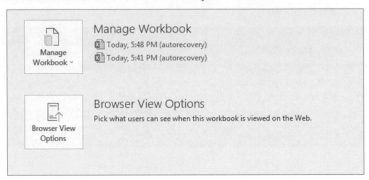

Recovering unsaved work

When you close a workbook without saving your changes, Excel asks whether you're sure. If that unsaved workbook has an autosaved version, the Are You Sure dialog box informs you of that fact.

To recover a workbook that you closed without saving, choose File ⇨ Info ⇨ Manage Workbook ⇨ Recover Unsaved Workbooks. You'll see a list of all draft versions of your workbooks. You can open them and (if you're lucky) recover something that you needed. Note that the unsaved workbooks are stored in the XLSB file format and are read-only files. If you want to save one of these files, you need to provide a new name.

Draft versions are deleted after four days or when you edit the file.

Configuring AutoRecover

Normally, AutoRecover files are saved every ten minutes. You can adjust the AutoRecover save time in the Save tab of the Excel Options dialog box. You can specify a save interval between 1 and 120 minutes.

If you work with sensitive documents, you might prefer that previous versions aren't saved automatically on your computer. The Save tab of the Excel Options dialog box lets you disable this feature completely or disable it just for a specific workbook.

File-Naming Rules

Excel workbook files are subject to the same rules that apply to other Windows files. A filename can be up to 255 characters, including spaces. This length enables you to give meaningful names to your files. You can't, however, use any of the following characters in your filenames:

\ (slash)	? (question mark)
: (colon)	* (asterisk)
" (quote)	< (less than)
> (greater than)	| (vertical bar)

You can use uppercase and lowercase letters in your names to improve readability, but the filenames aren't case sensitive. For example, My 2019 Budget.xlsx and MY 2019 BUDGET.xlsx are equivalent names.

Password-Protecting a Workbook

In some cases, you may want to specify a password for your workbook. When a user attempts to open a password-protected workbook, a password must be entered before the file is opened.

To set a password for a workbook, follow these steps:

1. Choose File ➪ Info and click the Protect Workbook button. This button displays some additional options in a drop-down list.

2. Choose Encrypt with Password from the list. Excel displays the Encrypt Document dialog box, as shown in Figure 6.3.

FIGURE 6.3

The Encrypt Document dialog box is where you specify a password for your workbook.

3. Enter the password, click OK, and then enter it again.

4. Click OK and save the workbook.

When you reopen the workbook, you'll be prompted for a password.

> **CAUTION**
>
> Passwords are case sensitive. Be careful when using password protection because it's impossible to open the workbook (using normal methods) if you forget the password. Also, remember that Excel passwords can be cracked, so it's not a perfect security measure.

Organizing Your Files

If you have hundreds of Excel files, you might have a problem locating the workbook that you need. Using descriptive filenames can help. Using folders and subfolders (with descriptive names) also makes it easier to find the particular file you need. In some cases, though, that's not enough.

Fortunately, Excel lets you assign a variety of descriptive information (sometimes known as *metadata*) to a workbook. These are known as document properties. This information includes such items as the author, tags, and categories.

When you choose File ➪ Info, you can view (or modify) the document properties for the active workbook. This information is shown on the right side of the screen.

> **TIP**
>
> To access even more properties for your workbook, click the down arrow on Properties and choose Advanced Properties.

Other Workbook Info Options

The Info pane of Backstage view displays more file-related options. To display this pane, choose File ➪ Info. These options, described in the following sections, may be useful if you plan to distribute your workbook to others. Note that not all workbooks display all of the options described in the following sections. Only the relevant options are shown.

Protect Workbook options

The File ➪ Info ➪ Protect Workbook drop-down list contains the following options:

Always Open Read-Only Use this option to save the file as read-only to prevent changes.

Encrypt with Password Use this command to specify a password that is required to open the workbook. (See "Password-Protecting a Workbook" earlier in this chapter.)

Protect Current Sheet   This command lets you protect various elements of a worksheet. It displays the same dialog box as the Review ⇨ Protect ⇨ Protect Sheet command.

Protect Workbook Structure   This command lets you protect the structure of a workbook. It displays the same dialog box as Review ⇨ Protect ⇨ Protect Workbook.

Restrict Access   If your organization uses the Azure Rights Management System, you can connect your workbook to it and get more granular options for protecting it.

Add a Digital Signature   This command allows you to "sign" a workbook digitally so that users can trust that you signed it.

Mark as Final   Use this option to designate the workbook as "final." The document is saved as a read-only file to prevent changes. This isn't a security feature. Rather, the Mark as Final command is useful to let others know that you're sharing a completed version of a workbook.

 See Chapter 34, "Protecting Your Work," for more information about protecting worksheets, protecting workbooks, and using digital signatures.

Check for Issues options

The File ⇨ Info ⇨ Check for Issues drop-down list contains the following options:

Inspect Document   This command displays the Document Inspector dialog box. The Document Inspector can alert you to some potentially private information that may be contained in your workbook—perhaps information that's contained in hidden rows or columns or hidden worksheets. If you plan to make a workbook available to a large audience, it's an excellent idea to use the Document Inspector for a final check.

Check Accessibility   This command checks the workbook for potential problems that might occur for people with disabilities. The results of the check are displayed in a task pane in the workbook.

Check Compatibility   This command is useful if you need to save your workbook in an older file format. It displays a helpful Compatibility Checker dialog box that lists potential compatibility problems. This dialog box also appears when you save a workbook using an older file format.

Manage Workbook options

If Excel automatically saved previous versions of your workbook, you can recover one of the earlier versions.

Browser View options

If your workbook will be viewed in a web browser, you can specify which sheets and other objects will be viewable.

Compatibility Mode section

If the active workbook is an old workbook opened in compatibility mode, you'll see the Compatibility Mode section in the Info pane. To convert the workbook to the current Excel file format, click the Convert button.

> **CAUTION**
>
> Be aware that this command deletes the original version of the file, which seems like a rather drastic measure. It's probably wise to make a copy of your workbook before you use this command.

Closing Workbooks

After you're finished with a workbook, you can close it to free the memory that it uses. Other workbooks will remain open. When you close the last open workbook, you also close Excel.

You can close a workbook by using any of the following methods:

- Choose File ➪ Close.
- Click the Close button (the X) in the right corner of the window's title bar.
- Press Ctrl+F4.
- Press Ctrl+W.

If you've made any changes to your workbook since it was last saved, Excel asks whether you want to save the changes to the workbook before closing it.

Safeguarding Your Work

Nothing is more frustrating than spending hours creating a complicated Excel workbook only to have it destroyed by a power failure, a hard drive crash, or even human error. Fortunately, protecting yourself from these disasters is not a difficult task.

Earlier in the chapter, we discussed the AutoRecover feature that makes Excel save a backup copy of your workbook at regular intervals (see "Using AutoRecover"). AutoRecover is a good idea, but it certainly isn't the only backup protection you should use. If a workbook is important, you need to take extra steps to ensure its safety. The following backup options help ensure the safety of individual files:

Keep a backup copy of the file on the same drive   Although this option offers some protection if you make a mess of the workbook, it won't do you any good if the entire hard drive crashes.

Keep a backup copy on a different hard drive   This method assumes, of course, that your system has more than one hard drive. This option offers more protection than the preceding method because the likelihood that both hard drives will fail is remote. If the entire system is destroyed or stolen, however, you're out of luck.

Keep a backup copy on a network server   This method assumes that your system is connected to a server on which you can write files. This method is fairly safe. If the network server is located in the same building, however, you're at risk if the entire building burns down or is otherwise destroyed.

Keep a backup copy on an Internet backup site   Several websites specialize in storing backup files.

Keep a backup copy on a removable medium   This is probably the safest method. Using a removable medium, such as a USB drive, enables you to physically take the backup to another location. So if your system (or the entire building) is damaged, your backup copy remains intact.

Working with Templates

A *template* is essentially a model that serves as the basis for something else. An Excel template is a special type of workbook that's used as the basis to create other workbooks. This section discusses some of the templates available from Microsoft, and it describes how to create your own template files. Creating a template takes some time, but in the long run, doing so may save you a lot of work.

Exploring Excel templates

The best way to become familiar with Excel template files is to jump in and try a few. Excel 2019 gives you quick access to hundreds of template files.

TIP

Examining templates is also a good way to learn about Excel. You may discover some techniques that you can incorporate into your own work.

Viewing templates

To explore the Excel templates, choose File ➪ New. The template thumbnails displayed on the screen that appears are just a small sampling of those that are available. Click one of the suggested search terms, or enter a descriptive word and search for more.

NOTE

The searching is done at Microsoft Office Online, so you must be connected to the Internet to search for templates.

For example, enter `invoice` and click the Search button. Excel displays many thumbnails. You can narrow the search by using the category filters on the right.

Figure 6.4 shows the results of a template search for `invoice`.

FIGURE 6.4

The New page in Backstage view allows you to search for templates.

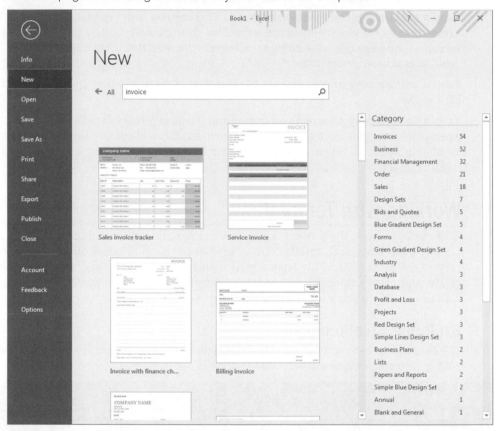

> **NOTE**
>
> Microsoft Office Online has a variety of templates. Some are better than others, so if you download a few duds, don't give up. Even though a template may not be perfect, you may be able to modify it to meet your needs. Modifying an existing template is often easier than creating a workbook from scratch.

Creating a workbook from a template

To create a workbook based on a template, just locate a template that looks like it might do the job and click the thumbnail. Excel displays a box with a larger image, the source for the template, and some additional information. If it still looks good, click the Create button. Otherwise, click one of the arrows to view details for the next (or previous) template in the list.

When you click the Create button, Excel downloads the template and then creates a new workbook based on that template.

What you do next depends on the template. Every template is different, but most are self-explanatory. Some workbooks require customization. Just replace the generic information with your own information.

6

> **NOTE**
>
> It's important to understand that you're not working with the template file. Instead, you're working with a workbook that was created from the template file. If you make any changes, you're not changing the template—you're changing the workbook that's based on the template. After you download a template from Microsoft Office Online, that template is saved for future use. (You won't have to download it again.) Downloaded templates appear as thumbnails when you choose File ⭢ New.

Figure 6.5 shows a workbook created from a template. This workbook needs to be customized in several areas. But if this template will be used again, it's more efficient to customize the template rather than every workbook created from the template.

FIGURE 6.5

A workbook created from a template

If you want to save the newly created workbook, click the Save button. Excel proposes a filename based on the template's name, but you can use any filename you like.

Modifying a template

A template file that you download is just like a workbook file. You can open a template file, make changes to it, and then resave it. For example, with the invoice template shown in Figure 6.5, you may want to modify the template so that it shows your company information and logo and uses your actual sales tax rate. Then, when you use that template in the future, the workbook created from it will already be customized.

To open a template for editing, choose File ⇨ Open (not File ⇨ New) and locate the template file (it will have an `.xltx`, `.xltm`, or `.xlt` extension). When you open a template file by choosing File ⇨ Open, you're opening the actual template file—you are *not* creating a workbook from the template file.

One way to find the location of your downloaded template files is to look at your trusted locations list:

1. Choose File ⇨ Options. The Excel Options dialog box appears.
2. Choose Trust Center, and click the Trust Center Settings button. The Trust Center dialog box appears.
3. In the Trust Center dialog box, choose Trusted Locations. You'll see a list of trusted locations. Downloaded templates are stored in the location described as User Templates. If you want to modify (or delete) a downloaded template, this is where you'll find it.

On my system, downloaded templates are stored here:

```
C:\Users\<username>\AppData\Roaming\Microsoft\Templates\
```

After you've made changes to the template, use File ⇨ Save to save the template file. Future workbooks that you create from this template will use the modified version of the template.

Using default templates

Excel supports three types of templates:

The default workbook template   This type is used as the basis for new workbooks.

The default worksheet template   This type is used as the basis for new worksheets inserted into a workbook.

Custom workbook templates   Usually, these ready-to-run workbooks include formulas, but they can be as simple or as complex as you like. Typically, these templates are set up so that a user can simply plug in values and get immediate results. The Microsoft Office Online templates (discussed earlier in this chapter) are examples of this type of template.

The default workbook and default worksheet templates are discussed in this section. Custom workbook templates are discussed in the next section.

Using the workbook template to change workbook defaults

Every new workbook that you create starts out with some default settings. For example, the workbook has one worksheet, the worksheet has gridlines, the page header and footer are blank, text appears in the font defined in the default Normal style, columns are 8.43 units wide, and so on. If you're not happy with any of the default workbook settings, you can change them by creating a workbook template.

Making changes to Excel's default workbook is fairly easy to do, and it can save you lots of time in the long run. Here's how to change Excel's workbook defaults:

1. **Open a new workbook.**

2. **Add or delete sheets to give the workbook the number of worksheets that you want.**

3. **Make any other changes that you want to make, which can include column widths, named styles, page setup options, and many of the settings that are available in the Excel Options dialog box.** To change the default formatting for cells, choose Home ⇨ Styles ⇨ Cell Styles and then modify the settings for the Normal style. For example, you can change the default font, size, or number format.

4. **When your workbook is set up to your liking, choose File ⇨ Save As ⇨ Browse.** The Save As dialog box appears.

5. **Select Excel Template (*.xltx) from the Save As Type list.** If your template contains VBA macros, select Excel Macro-Enabled Template (*.xltm).

6. **Enter** book **for the filename.**

> **CAUTION**
>
> Excel will offer a name, such as Book1.xltx. You must change this name to book.xltx (or book.xltm) if you want Excel to use your template to set the workbook defaults.

7. Save the file in your XLStart folder (not in the Templates folder that Excel proposes).

8. Close the template file.

After you perform the preceding steps, the new default workbook is based on the book.xltx (or book.xltm) workbook template. You can create a workbook based on your template by using any of these methods:

- Press Ctrl+N.
- Open Excel without first selecting a workbook to open. This option works only if you disable the option to show the Start screen when Excel starts. This option is specified in the General tab of the Excel Options dialog box. (Choose File ⇨ Options to display the Excel Options dialog box.)

Creating a worksheet template

You can also create a single sheet template named `sheet.xltx`. Use the same procedure described for `book.xltx`. The `sheet.xltx` template is used when you insert a new worksheet.

Editing your template

After you create your `book.xltx` template, you may discover that you need to change it. You can open the template file and edit it just like any other workbook. After you make your changes, save the file to its original location and close it.

Resetting the default workbook

If you create a `book.xltx` (or `book.xltm`) file and then decide that you'd rather use the standard default settings, simply delete (or rename) the `book.xltx` (or `book.xltm`) template file. Excel then uses its built-in default settings for new workbooks.

Using custom workbook templates

The `book.xltx` template discussed in the preceding section is a special type of template that determines default settings for new workbooks. This section discusses other types of templates, referred to as *custom workbook templates*, which are simply workbooks that you set up as the basis for new, specific types of workbooks.

Creating custom templates

Creating a custom workbook template can eliminate repeating work. Assume that you create a monthly sales report that consists of your company's sales by region, plus several summary calculations and charts. You can create a template file that consists of everything except the input values. Then when it's time to create your report, you can open a workbook based on the template, fill in the blanks, and be finished.

When you create a workbook that's based on a template, the default workbook name is the template name with a number appended. For example, if you create a new workbook based on a template named `Sales Report.xltx`, the workbook's default name is `Sales Report1.xlsx`. The first time you save a workbook created from a template, Excel displays the Save As dialog box so that you can give the workbook a different name if you want to.

A custom template is essentially a normal workbook. It can use any Excel feature, such as charts, formulas, and macros. Usually, a template is set up so that the user can enter values and get immediate results. In other words, most templates include everything but the data, which the user enters.

> **NOTE**
> If your template contains macros, it must be saved as an Excel Macro-Enabled Template, with an `.xltm` extension.

Locking Formula Cells in a Template File

If novices are going to use the template, you might consider locking all the formula cells to make sure that the formulas aren't deleted or modified. By default, all cells are locked and can't be changed when the worksheet is protected. The following steps describe how to unlock the nonformula cells:

1. Choose Home ⇨ Editing ⇨ Find & Select ⇨ Go To Special. The Go To Special dialog box appears.
2. Select Constants and click OK. This step selects all nonformula cells.
3. Press Ctrl+1. The Format Cells dialog box appears.
4. Select the Protection tab.
5. Remove the check mark from the Locked check box.
6. Click OK to close the Format Cells dialog box.
7. Choose Review ⇨ Protect ⇨ Protect Sheet. The Protect Sheet dialog box appears.
8. Specify a password (optional) and click OK.

After you perform these steps, you can't modify the formula cells unless the sheet is unprotected.

Saving your custom templates

To save a workbook as a template, choose File ⇨ Save As ⇨ Browse and select Excel Template (`*.xltx`) from the Save as Type drop-down list. If the workbook contains any VBA macros, select Excel Macro-Enabled Template (`*.xltm`). Save the template in your `Templates` folder—which Excel automatically suggests—or a folder within that `Templates` folder.

If you later discover that you want to modify the template, choose File ⇨ Open to open and edit the template.

Using custom templates

To create a workbook based on a custom template, choose File ⇨ New and then click Personal (below the search box). You'll see thumbnails of all your custom worksheet templates (plus others). Click a template, and Excel creates a workbook based on the template.

Printing Your Work

IN THIS CHAPTER

Changing your worksheet view

Adjusting your print settings for better results

Preventing some cells from being printed

Using the Custom Views feature

Creating PDF files

Despite predictions of the "paperless office," paper remains an excellent way to carry information around and share it with others, particularly if there's no electricity or Wi-Fi where you're going. Some of the worksheets that you develop with Excel will end up as hard-copy reports, and you'll want them to look as good as possible. You'll find that printing from Excel is quite easy and that you can generate attractive, well-formatted reports with minimal effort. In addition, Excel has many options that give you a great deal of control over the printed page. These options are explained in this chapter.

Doing Basic Printing

If you want to print a copy of a worksheet with no fuss and bother, use the Quick Print option. One way to access this command is to choose File ⇨ Print (which displays the Print pane of Backstage view) and then click the Print button. The keyboard shortcut Ctrl+P has the same effect as File ⇨ Print. When you use Ctrl+P to show the Backstage view, the Print button has the focus, so you can simply press Enter to print.

If you like the idea of one-click printing, take a few seconds to add a new button to your Quick Access toolbar. Click the downward-pointing arrow on the right of the Quick Access toolbar and then choose Quick Print from the drop-down list. Excel adds the Quick Print icon to your Quick Access toolbar.

Clicking the Quick Print button prints the current worksheet on the currently selected printer, using the default print settings. If you've changed any of the default print settings (by using the Page Layout tab), Excel uses the new settings; otherwise, it uses the following default settings:

- Prints the active worksheet (or all selected worksheets), including any embedded charts or objects
- Prints one copy

- Prints the entire active worksheet
- Prints in portrait mode
- Doesn't scale the printed output
- Uses letter-size paper with 0.75-inch margins for the top and bottom and 0.70-inch margins for the left and right margins (for the U.S. version)
- Prints with no headers or footers
- Doesn't print cell comments
- Prints with no cell gridlines
- For wide worksheets that span multiple pages, prints down and then over

When you print a worksheet, Excel prints only the active area of the worksheet. In other words, it won't print all 17 billion cells—just those that have data in them. If the worksheet contains any embedded charts or other graphic objects (such as SmartArt or shapes), they're also printed.

Using Print Preview

When you choose File ➪ Print (or press Ctrl+P), Backstage view displays a preview of your printed output, exactly as it will be printed. Initially, Excel displays the first page of your printed output. To view subsequent pages, use the page controls along the bottom of the preview pane (or use the vertical scrollbar along the right side of the screen).

The Print Preview window has a few other commands (at the bottom) that you can use while previewing your output. For multipage printout, use the page number controls to jump quickly to a particular page. The Show Margins button toggles the display of margins, and Zoom to Page ensures that a complete page is displayed.

When the Show Margins option is in effect, Excel adds markers to the preview that indicate column borders and margins. You can drag the column or margin markers to make changes that appear onscreen. Changes that you make to column widths in preview mode are also made in the actual worksheet.

Print Preview is certainly useful, but you may prefer to use Page Layout view to preview your output (see "Changing Your Page View").

Changing Your Page View

Page Layout view shows your worksheet divided into pages. In other words, you can visualize your printed output while you work.

Page Layout view is one of three worksheet views, which are controlled by the three icons on the right side of the status bar. You could also use the commands in the View ➪ Workbook Views group on the Ribbon to switch views. The three view options are

Normal The default view of the worksheet. This view may or may not show page breaks.

Page Layout Shows individual pages.

Page Break Preview   Allows you to adjust page breaks manually.

Just click one of the icons to change the view. You can also use the Zoom slider to change the magnification from 10% (a very tiny, bird's-eye view) to 400% (very large, for showing fine detail).

The following sections describe how these views can help with printing.

Normal view

Most of the time when you work in Excel, you use Normal view. Normal view can display page breaks in the worksheet. The page breaks are indicated by horizontal and vertical dotted lines. These page break lines adjust automatically if you change the page orientation, add or delete rows or columns, change row heights, change column widths, and so on. For example, if you find that your printed output is too wide to fit on a single page, you can adjust the column widths (keeping an eye on the page break display) until the columns are narrow enough to print on one page.

> **NOTE**
>
> Page breaks aren't displayed until you print (or preview) the worksheet at least one time. Page breaks are also displayed if you set a print area by choosing Page Layout ⇨ Page Setup ⇨ Print Area.

> **TIP**
>
> If you'd prefer not to see the page break display in Normal view, choose File ⇨ Options and select the Advanced tab. Scroll down to the Display Options for This Worksheet section and remove the check mark from Show Page Breaks. This setting applies only to the active worksheet. Unfortunately, the option to turn off page break display is not on the Ribbon, and it's not even available for inclusion on the Quick Access toolbar.

Figure 7.1 shows a worksheet in Normal view, zoomed out to show multiple pages. Notice the dotted lines that indicate page breaks.

Page Layout view

Unlike the preview in Backstage view (choose File ⇨ Print), Page Layout view is not a view-only mode. You have complete access to all Excel commands. In fact, you can use Page Layout view all of the time if you like.

Figure 7.2 shows a worksheet in Page Layout view, zoomed out to show multiple pages. Notice that the page header and footer (if any) appear on each page. If you've specified any repeated rows and columns, they also display—giving you a true preview of the printed output.

FIGURE 7.1

In Normal view, dotted lines indicate page breaks.

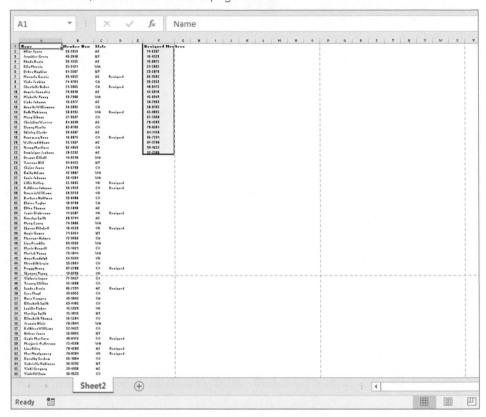

> **TIP**
>
> If you move the mouse to the corner of a page while in Page Layout view, you can click to hide the white space in the margins. Doing so gives you all of the advantages of Page Layout view, but you can see more information on-screen because the unused margin space is hidden.

Page Break Preview

Page Break Preview displays the worksheet and the page breaks. Figure 7.3 shows an example. This view mode is different from Normal view mode with page breaks turned on. The key difference is that you can drag the page breaks. You can also drag the edges of the print area to change its size (if you've set a print area). Unlike Page Layout view, Page Break Preview does not display headers and footers.

FIGURE 7.2

In Page Layout view, the worksheet resembles printed pages.

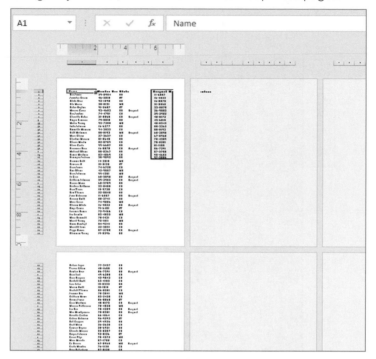

When you enter Page Break Preview, Excel performs the following:

- Changes the zoom factor so that you can see more of the worksheet
- Displays the page numbers overlaid on the pages
- Displays the current print range with a white background; nonprinting areas appear with a gray background
- Displays all page breaks as draggable dashed lines

When you change the page breaks by dragging, Excel automatically adjusts the scaling so that the information fits on the pages, per your specifications.

TIP

In Page Break Preview, you still have access to all Excel commands. You can change the zoom factor if you find the text to be too small.

To exit Page Break Preview, just click one of the other View icons on the right side of the status bar.

FIGURE 7.3

Page Break Preview mode gives you a bird's-eye view of your worksheet and shows exactly where the page breaks occur.

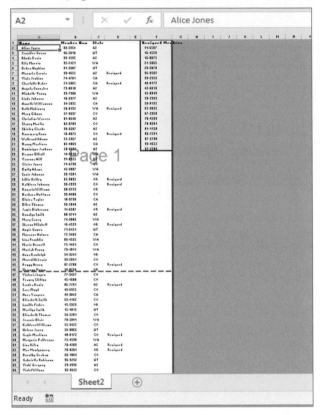

Adjusting Common Page Setup Settings

Clicking the Quick Print button (or choosing File ➪ Print ➪ Print) may produce acceptable results in many cases, but a little tweaking of the print settings can often improve your printed reports. You can adjust print settings in three places:

- The Print settings screen in Backstage view, displayed when you choose File ➪ Print.
- The Page Layout tab of the Ribbon.
- The Page Setup dialog box, displayed when you click the dialog launcher in the lower-right corner of the Page Layout ➪ Page Setup group on the Ribbon. You can also access the Page Setup dialog box from the Print settings screen in Backstage view.

Table 7.1 summarizes the locations where you can make various types of print-related adjustments in Excel 2019.

TABLE 7.1   Where to Change Printer Settings

Setting	Print Settings Screen	Page Layout Tab of Ribbon	Page Setup Dialog Box
Number of copies	X		
Printer to use	X		
What to print	X		
Pages to print	X		
Specify worksheet print area		X	X
1-sided or 2-sided	X		
Collated	X		
Orientation	X	X	X
Paper size	X	X	X
Adjust margins	X	X	X
Specify manual page breaks		X	
Specify repeating rows or columns			X
Set print scaling	X	X	X
Print or hide gridlines		X	X
Print or hide row and column headings		X	X
Specify the first page number			X
Center output on page			X
Specify header/footers and options			X
Specify how to print cell comments			X
Specify page order			X
Specify black-and-white output			X
Specify how to print error cells			X
Launch Printer Properties dialog box	X		X

Table 7.1 might make printing seem more complicated than it really is. The key point to remember is this: if you can't find a way to make a particular adjustment, it's probably available from the Page Setup dialog box.

Choosing your printer

To switch to a different printer or output device, choose File ⇨ Print, and use the drop-down control in the Printer section to select a different installed printer.

> **NOTE**
>
> To adjust printer settings, click the Printer Properties link to display a property box for the selected printer. The exact dialog box that you see depends on the printer. The Properties dialog box lets you adjust printer-specific settings, such as the print quality and the paper source. In most cases, you won't have to change any of these settings, but if you're having print-related problems, you may want to check the settings.

Specifying what you want to print

Sometimes you may want to print only part of the worksheet rather than the entire active area. Or you may want to reprint selected pages of a report without printing all the pages. Choose File ⇨ Print, and use the controls in the Settings section to specify what to print.

You have several options:

Print Active Sheets Prints the active sheet or sheets that you selected. (This option is the default.) You can select multiple sheets to print by pressing Ctrl and clicking the sheet tabs. If you select multiple sheets, Excel begins printing each sheet on a new page.

Print Entire Workbook Prints the entire workbook, including chart sheets.

Print Selection Prints only the range that you selected before choosing File ⇨ Print.

Print Selected Chart Appears only if a chart is selected. If this option is chosen, only the chart will be printed.

Print Selected Table Appears only if the cell pointer is within a table (created by choosing Insert ⇨ Tables ⇨ Table) when the Print Setting screen is displayed. If this option is chosen, only the table will be printed.

> **TIP**
>
> You can also choose Page Layout ⇨ Page Setup ⇨ Print Area ⇨ Set Print Area to specify the range(s) to print. Before you choose this command, select the range(s) that you want to print. To clear the print area, choose Page Layout ⇨ Page Setup ⇨ Print Area ⇨ Clear Print Area. To override the print area, select the Ignore Print Area check box in the list of Print What options.

> **NOTE**
>
> The print area does not have to be a single range. You can select multiple areas before you set the print area. Each area will print on a separate page.

If your printed output uses multiple pages, you can select which pages to print by indicating the number of the first and last pages to print by using Pages controls in the Settings section. You can either use the spinner controls or type the page numbers in the edit boxes.

Changing page orientation

Page orientation refers to the way output is printed on the page. Choose Page Layout ⇨ Page Setup ⇨ Orientation ⇨ Portrait to print tall pages (the default) or Page Layout ⇨ Page Setup ⇨ Orientation ⇨ Landscape to print wide pages. Landscape orientation is useful when you have a wide range that doesn't fit on a vertically oriented page.

If you change the orientation, the on-screen page breaks adjust automatically to accommodate the new paper orientation.

Page orientation settings are also available when you choose File ⇨ Print.

Specifying paper size

Choose Page Layout ⇨ Page Setup ⇨ Size to specify the paper size you're using. The paper size settings are also available when you choose File ⇨ Print.

NOTE
Even though Excel displays a variety of paper sizes, your printer may not be capable of using all of them.

Printing multiple copies of a report

Use the Copies control at the top of the Print tab in Backstage View to specify the number of copies to print. Just enter the number of copies you want and then click Print.

TIP
If you're printing multiple copies of a report, make sure that the Collated option is selected so that Excel prints the pages in order for each set of output. If you're printing only one page, Excel ignores the Collated setting.

Adjusting the page margins

Margins are the unprinted areas along the sides, top, and bottom of a printed page. Excel provides four "quick margin" settings; you can also specify the exact margin size you require. All printed pages have the same margins. You can't specify different margins for different pages.

In Page Layout view, a ruler is displayed above the column header and to the left of the row header. Use your mouse to drag the margins in the ruler. Excel adjusts the page display immediately. Use the horizontal ruler to adjust the left and right margins, and use the vertical ruler to adjust the top and bottom margins.

From the Page Layout ⇨ Page Setup ⇨ Margins drop-down list, you can select Normal, Wide, Narrow, or the Last Custom Setting. These options are also available when you choose

File ⇨ Print. If none of these settings does the job, choose Custom Margins to display the Margins tab of the Page Setup dialog box, as shown in Figure 7.4.

FIGURE 7.4

The Margins tab of the Page Setup dialog box

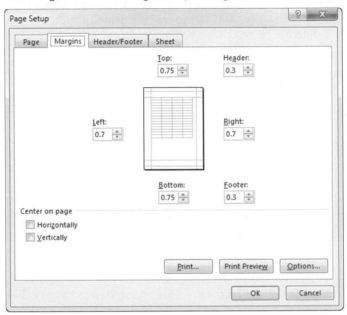

To change a margin, click the appropriate spinner (or you can enter a value directly). The margin settings that you specify in the Page Setup dialog box will then be available in the Page Layout ⇨ Page Setup ⇨ Margins drop-down list, referred to as Last Custom Setting.

NOTE

The Preview box in the center of the Page Setup dialog box is a bit deceiving because it doesn't really show you how your changes look in relation to the page; instead, it displays a darker line to let you know which margin you're adjusting.

You can also adjust margins in the preview window in Backstage view (choose File ⇨ Print). Click the Show Margins button in the bottom-right corner to display the margins in the preview pane. Then drag the margin indicators to adjust the margins.

In addition to the page margins, you can adjust the distance of the header from the top of the page and the distance of the footer from the bottom of the page. These settings should be less than the corresponding margin; otherwise, the header or footer may overlap with the printed output.

By default, Excel aligns the printed page at the top and left margins. If you want the output to be centered vertically or horizontally, select the appropriate check box in the Center on Page section of the Margins tab.

Understanding page breaks

When printing lengthy reports, controlling where pages break is often important. For example, you probably don't want a row to print on a page by itself, nor do you want a table header row to be the last line on a page. Fortunately, Excel gives you precise control over page breaks.

Excel handles page breaks automatically, but sometimes you may want to force a page break—either a vertical or a horizontal one—so that the report prints the way you want. For example, if your worksheet consists of several distinct sections, you may want to print each section on a separate sheet of paper.

Inserting a page break

To insert a horizontal page break line, move the cell pointer to the cell that will begin the new page. Make sure you place the pointer in column A, though; otherwise, you'll insert a vertical page break and a horizontal page break. For example, if you want row 14 to be the first row of a new page, select cell A14. Then choose Page Layout ⇨ Page Setup ⇨ Breaks ⇨ Insert Page Break.

> **NOTE**
>
> Page breaks are visualized differently, depending on which view mode you're using. (See "Changing Your Page View" earlier in this chapter.)

To insert a vertical page break line, move the cell pointer to the cell that will begin the new page. In this case, though, make sure to place the pointer in row 1. Choose Page Layout ⇨ Page Setup ⇨ Breaks ⇨ Insert Page Break to create the page break.

Removing manual page breaks

To remove a page break that you've added, move the cell pointer to the first row beneath (or the first column to the right of) the manual page break and then choose Page Layout ⇨ Page Setup ⇨ Breaks ⇨ Remove Page Break.

To remove all manual page breaks in the worksheet, choose Page Layout ⇨ Page Setup ⇨ Breaks ⇨ Reset All Page Breaks.

Printing row and column titles

If your worksheet is set up with titles in the first row and descriptive names in the first column, it can be difficult to identify data that appears on printed pages where those titles don't appear. To resolve this problem, you can choose to print selected rows or columns as titles on each page of the printout.

Row and column titles serve pretty much the same purpose on a printout as frozen panes do in navigating within a worksheet. Keep in mind, however, that these features are independent of each other. In other words, freezing panes doesn't affect the printed output.

 See Chapter 3, "Performing Basic Worksheet Operations," for more information on freezing panes.

CAUTION

Don't confuse print titles with headers; these are two different concepts. Headers appear at the top of each page and contain information, such as the worksheet name, date, or page number. Row and column titles describe the data being printed, such as field names in a database table or list.

You can specify particular rows to repeat at the top of every printed page or particular columns to repeat at the left of every printed page. To do so, choose Page Layout ⇨ Page Setup ⇨ Print Titles. Excel displays the Sheet tab of the Page Setup dialog box, as shown in Figure 7.5.

FIGURE 7.5

Use the Sheet tab of the Page Setup dialog box to specify rows or columns that will appear on each printed page.

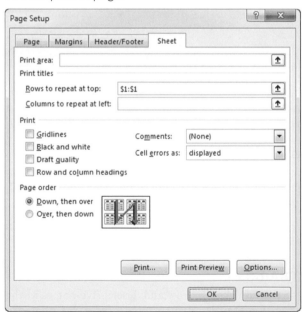

Activate the appropriate box (either Rows to Repeat at Top or Columns to Repeat at Left) and then select the rows or columns in the worksheet. Or you can enter these references manually. For example, to specify rows 1 and 2 as repeating rows, enter **1:2**.

NOTE

When you specify row and column titles and use Page Layout view, these titles will repeat on every page (just as when the document is printed). However, the cells used in the title can be selected only on the page in which they first appear.

Scaling printed output

In some cases, you may need to force your printed output to fit on a specific number of pages. You can do so by enlarging or reducing the size. To enter a scaling factor, choose Page Layout ➪ Scale to Fit ➪ Scale. You can scale the output from 10% up to 400%. To return to normal scaling, enter **100%**.

To force Excel to print using a specific number of pages, choose Page Layout ➪ Scale to Fit ➪ Width and Page Layout ➪ Scale to Fit ➪ Height. When you change either one of these settings, the corresponding scale factor is displayed in the Scale control.

CAUTION

Excel doesn't ensure legibility. It will gladly scale your output to be so small that no one can read it.

Printing cell gridlines

Typically, cell gridlines aren't printed. If you want your printout to include the gridlines, choose Page Layout ➪ Sheet Options ➪ Gridlines ➪ Print.

Alternatively, you can insert borders around some cells to simulate gridlines. Change the border color to White Background 1, 25% Darker to get a pretty good simulation of a gridline. To change the color, choose Home ➪ Font ➪ Borders ➪ More Borders. Make sure you change the color before you apply the border.

 See Chapter 5, "Formatting Worksheets," for information about borders.

Printing row and column headers

By default, row and column headers for a worksheet are not printed. If you want your printout to include these items, choose Page Layout ➪ Sheet Options ➪ Headings ➪ Print.

Using a background image

Would you like to have a background image on your printouts? Unfortunately, you can't. You may have noticed the Page Layout ➪ Page Setup ➪ Background command. This button displays a dialog box that lets you select an image to display as a background. Placing this control among the other print-related commands is misleading. Background images placed on a worksheet are never printed.

> **TIP**
>
> In lieu of a true background image, you can insert WordArt, a shape, or a picture on your worksheet and then adjust its transparency. Then copy the image to all printed pages. Alternatively, you can insert an object in a page header or footer. (See the sidebar "Inserting a Watermark.")

Inserting a Watermark

A *watermark* is an image (or text) that appears on each printed page. A watermark can be a faint company logo or a word such as DRAFT. Excel doesn't have an official command to print a watermark, but you can add a watermark by inserting a picture in the page header or footer. Here's how:

1. **Locate an image on your hard drive that you want to use for the watermark.**
2. **Choose View ⇨ Workbook Views ⇨ Page Layout View.**
3. **Click the center section of the header.**
4. **Choose Header & Footer Tools ⇨ Design ⇨ Header & Footer Elements ⇨ Picture.** The Insert Pictures dialog box appears.
5. **Click Browse and locate the image from step 1 (or locate a suitable image from other sources listed).**
6. **Click outside the header to see your image.**
7. **To center the image in the middle of the page, click the center section of the header and add some carriage returns before the `&[Picture]` code.** You'll need to experiment to determine the number of carriage returns required to push the image into the body of the document.
8. **If you need to adjust the image (for example, make it lighter), click the center section of the header and then choose Header & Footer Tools ⇨ Design ⇨ Header & Footer Elements ⇨ Format Picture. Use the Image controls in the Picture tab of the Format Picture dialog box to adjust the image.** You may need to experiment with the settings to make sure that the worksheet text is legible.

The accompanying figure shows an example of a header image (a copyright symbol) used as a watermark. You can do a similar thing with text, but you don't get the same formatting controls, such as controlling the brightness and contrast.

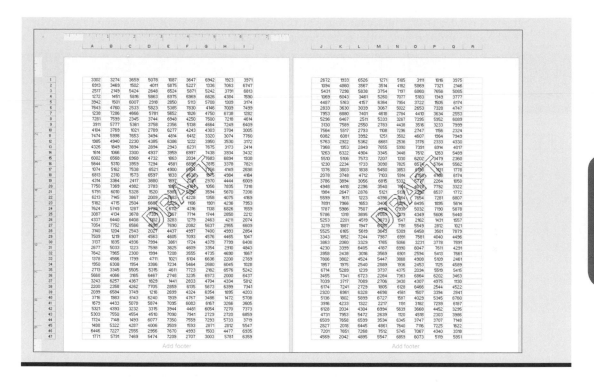

7

Adding a Header or a Footer to Your Reports

A header is information that appears at the top of each printed page. A footer is information that appears at the bottom of each printed page. By default, new workbooks do not have headers or footers.

You can specify headers and footers by using the Header/Footer tab of the Page Setup dialog box. Or, you can simplify the task by switching to Page Layout view, where you can click the section labeled Click to Add Header or Click to Add Footer.

> **NOTE**
>
> If you're working in Normal view, you can choose Insert ➪ Text ➪ Header & Footer. Excel switches to Page Layout view and activates the center section of the page header.

You can then type the information and apply any type of formatting you like. Note that headers and footers consist of three sections: left, center, and right. For example, you can create a header that prints your name at the left margin, the worksheet name centered in the header, and the page number at the right margin.

> **TIP**
>
> If you want a consistent header or footer for all your documents, create a `book.xltx` template with your headers or footers specified. A `book.xltx` template is used as the basis for new workbooks.

 See Chapter 6, "Understanding Excel Files and Templates," for details on creating a template.

When you activate the header or footer section in Page Layout view, the Ribbon displays a new contextual tab: Header & Footer Tools ⇨ Design. Use the controls on this tab to work with headers and footers.

Selecting a predefined header or footer

You can choose from a number of predefined headers or footers by using either of the two drop-down lists in the Header & Footer Tools ⇨ Design ⇨ Header & Footer group. Notice that some items in these lists consist of multiple parts, separated by a comma. Each part goes into one of the three header or footer sections (left, center, or right). Figure 7.6 shows an example of a header that uses all three sections.

FIGURE 7.6

This three-part header is one of Excel's predefined headers.

	A	B	C	D	E	F	G	H	I
	Confidential				6/10/2018				Page 1
1	2129	2304	3157	4820	6028	2564	6484	4790	6859
2	2952	6181	5158	4017	6087	3490	4583	6917	6842
3	1154	1709	1882	6982	7853	6597	4338	3322	1498
4	1524	6836	5469	4434	6114	1353	3122	7848	3350
5	3622	4152	6793	2183	1793	7893	4469	5614	4043
6	7559	6333	2853	1200	2977	6675	1759	1384	4710
7	1032	2359	6831	1474	6537	1768	6775	3505	2714
8	3838	7506	1037	2633	1359	3691	2606	3079	4766
9	5161	6395	4687	6180	5997	4766	2097	5719	3547
10	7394	7348	6581	4038	2670	3150	4435	6449	7753
11	7227	6869	7309	5948	6961	2268	1230	6342	4064
12	6320	1510	6273	1035	6226	6143	7459	6048	3048
13	6557	2771	1261	6267	6702	7746	5964	1134	1531
14	3617	7637	7236	4493	7315	2800	2870	4967	1205
15	3797	1930	2085	1296	5934	1999	7482	1840	4328
16	7779	7684	6041	6887	7371	2950	5032	2564	7602
17	4592	7157	2750	2737	6787	7445	7039	4887	7550
18	6924	6978	5609	7759	5341	1625	5369	4362	2039
19	6978	7823	3881	5946	7228	2831	6652	4338	5071
20	5891	3381	2076	3722	2737	2583	4714	7997	2882
21	5158	6383	2731	4558	2802	1633	2283	5134	4606
22	2306	1579	6156	6963	1279	3166	7650	3958	1943
23	1986	1007	1874	4943	7020	1789	7740	3632	1771

Understanding header and footer element codes

When a header or footer section is activated, you can type whatever text you like into the section. Or to insert variable information, you can insert any of several element codes by clicking a button in the Header & Footer Tools ➪ Design ➪ Header & Footer Elements group. Each button inserts a code into the selected section. For example, to insert the current date, click the Current Date button. Table 7.2 lists the buttons and their functions.

TABLE 7.2 Header and Footer Buttons and Their Functions

Button	Code	Function
Page Number	&[Page]	Displays the page number
Number of Pages	&[Pages]	Displays the total number of pages to be printed
Current Date	&[Date]	Displays the current date
Current Time	&[Time]	Displays the current time
File Path	&[Path]&[File]	Displays the workbook's complete path and filename
File Name	&[File]	Displays the workbook name
Sheet Name	&[Tab]	Displays the sheet's name
Picture	&[Picture]	Enables you to add a picture
Format Picture	Not applicable	Enables you to change an added picture's settings

You can combine text and codes and insert as many codes as you like into each section.

NOTE

If the text that you enter uses an ampersand (&), you must enter the ampersand twice (because Excel uses an ampersand to signal a code). For example, to enter the text Research & Development into a section of a header or footer, type Research && Development.

You can also use different fonts and sizes in your headers and footers. Just select the text you want to change and then use the formatting tools in the Home ➪ Font group. Or use the controls on the Mini toolbar, which appears automatically when you select the text. If you don't change the font, Excel uses the font defined for the Normal style.

TIP

You can use as many lines as you like. Press Enter to force a line break for multiline headers or footers. If you use multiline headers or footers, you may need to adjust the top or bottom margin so that the text won't overlap with the worksheet data. (See "Adjusting the page margins" earlier in this chapter.)

Unfortunately, you can't print the contents of a specific cell in a header or footer. For example, you may want Excel to use the contents of cell A1 as part of a header. To do so, you need to enter the cell's contents manually—or write a VBA macro to perform this operation before the sheet is printed.

Exploring other header and footer options

When a header or footer is selected in Page Layout view, the Header & Footer ⇨ Design ⇨ Options group contains controls that let you specify other options:

Different First Page If checked, you can specify a different header/footer for the first printed page.

Different Odd & Even Pages If checked, you can specify a different header/footer for odd and even pages.

Scale with Document If checked, the font size in the header and footer will be sized accordingly if the document is scaled when printed. This option is enabled by default.

Align with Page Margins If checked, the left header and footer will be aligned with the left margin, and the right header and footer will be aligned with the right margin. This option is enabled by default.

> **NOTE**
>
> If you check either of the Different First Page or Different Odd & Even Pages checkboxes, you can no longer use the predefined headers and footers. You must use the Custom Header and Custom Footer buttons.

Exploring Other Print-Related Topics

The following sections cover some additional topics related to printing from Excel.

Copying Page Setup settings across sheets

Each Excel worksheet has its own print setup options (orientation, margins, headers and footers, and so on). These options are specified in the Page Setup group of the Page Layout tab.

When you add a new sheet to a workbook, it contains the default page setup settings. Here's an easy way to transfer the settings from one worksheet to additional worksheets:

1. **Activate the sheet that contains the desired setup information.** This is the source sheet.
2. **Select the target sheets, and Ctrl+click the sheet tabs of the sheets that you want to update with the settings from the source sheet.**
3. **Click the dialog box launcher in the lower-right corner of the Page Layout ⇨ Page Setup group.**

4. **When the Page Setup dialog box appears, click OK to close it.**

5. **Ungroup the sheets by right-clicking any selected sheet and choosing Ungroup Sheets from the shortcut menu.** Because multiple sheets are selected when you close the Page Setup dialog box, the settings of the source sheet will be transferred to all target sheets.

> **NOTE**
>
> Two settings located on the Sheet tab of the Page Setup dialog box are not transferred: Print Area and Print Titles. In addition, pictures in the header or footer are not transferred.

Preventing certain cells from being printed

If your worksheet contains confidential information, you may want to print the worksheet but not the confidential parts. You can use several techniques to prevent certain parts of a worksheet from printing:

Hide rows or columns   When you hide rows or columns, the hidden rows or columns aren't printed. Choose Home ⇨ Cells ⇨ Format drop-down list to hide the selected rows or columns.

Hide cells or ranges by making the text color the same color as the background color   You can hide cells or ranges by making the text color the same color as the background color. Be aware, however, that this method may not work for all printers.

Hide cells or ranges by using a custom number format   You can hide cells by using a custom number format that consists of three semicolons (; ; ;). See Chapter 2, "Entering and Editing Worksheet Data," for more information about using custom number formats.

Mask an area   You can mask a confidential area of a worksheet by covering it with a rectangle shape. Choose Insert ⇨ Illustrations ⇨ Shapes and click Rectangle Shape. You'll probably want to adjust the fill color to match the cell background and remove the border.

If you find that you must regularly hide data before you print certain reports, consider using the Custom Views feature, discussed later in this chapter. (See "Creating custom views of your worksheet.") This feature allows you to create a named view that doesn't show the confidential information.

Preventing objects from being printed

To prevent objects on the worksheet (such as charts, shapes, and SmartArt) from being printed, you need to access the Properties tab of the object's Format dialog box (see Figure 7.7):

1. **Right-click the object and choose Format *xxxx* from the shortcut menu.** (*xxxx* varies, depending on the object.)

2. **In the Format dialog box that opens for the object, click the Size & Properties icon.**

3. **Expand the Properties section of the dialog box.**

4. **Remove the check mark for Print Object.**

FIGURE 7.7

Use the Properties tab of the object's Format dialog box to prevent objects from printing.

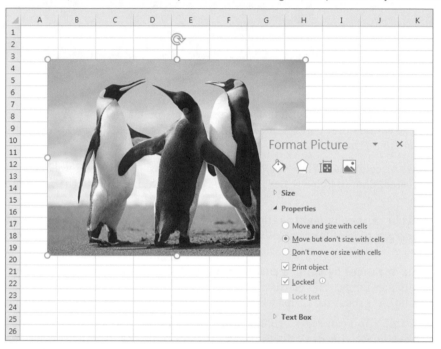

> **NOTE**
>
> For a chart, you must right-click the chart's chart area (the background of the chart). Or double-click the chart's border to display the Format Chart Area dialog box. Then expand the Properties section and remove the check mark from Print Object.

Creating custom views of your worksheet

If you need to create several different printed reports from the same Excel workbook, setting up the specific settings for each report can be a tedious job. For example, you may need to print a full report in landscape mode for your boss. Another department may require a simplified report using the same data but with some hidden columns in portrait mode. You can simplify the process by creating custom named views of your worksheets that include the proper settings for each report.

The Custom Views feature enables you to give names to various views of your worksheet. You can quickly switch among these named views. A view includes settings for the following:

- Print settings, as specified in the Page Layout ⇨ Page Setup, Page Layout ⇨ Scale to Fit, and Page ⇨ Page Setup ⇨ Sheet Options groups
- Hidden rows and columns
- The worksheet view (Normal, Page Layout, Page Break preview)
- Selected cells and ranges
- The active cell
- The zoom factor
- Window sizes and positions
- Frozen panes

If you find that you're constantly fiddling with these settings before printing and then changing them back, using named views can save you some work.

> **CAUTION**
>
> Unfortunately, the Custom Views feature doesn't work if the workbook (not just the worksheet) contains at least one table, created using Insert ⇨ Tables ⇨ Table. When a workbook that contains a table is active, the Custom View command is disabled. This severely limits the usefulness of the Custom Views feature.

To create a named view, follow these steps:

1. **Set up the view settings the way you want them.** For example, hide some columns.
2. **Choose View ⇨ Workbook Views ⇨ Custom Views.** The Custom Views dialog box appears.
3. **Click the Add button.** The Add View dialog box (shown in Figure 7.8) appears.

FIGURE 7.8

Use the Add View dialog box to create a named view.

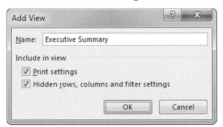

4. **Provide a descriptive name.** You can also specify what to include in the view by using the two check boxes. For example, if you don't want the view to include print settings, remove the check mark from Print Settings.

5. **Click OK to save the named view.**

Then when you're ready to print, open the Custom Views dialog box to see all named views. To select a particular view, just select it from the list and click the Show button. To delete a named view from the list, click the Delete button.

Creating PDF files

The PDF file format is widely used as a way to present information in a read-only manner, with precise control over the layout. If you need to share your work with someone who doesn't have Excel, creating a PDF is often a good solution. Free software to display PDFs is available from a number of sources.

> **NOTE**
> Excel can create PDFs, but it can't open them. Word 2019 can create and open PDFs.

XPS is another "electronic paper" format, developed by Microsoft as an alternative to the PDF format. At this time, there is little third-party support for the XPS format.

To save a worksheet in PDF or XPS format, choose File ➪ Export ➪ Create PDF/XPS Document ➪ Create a PDF/XPS. Excel displays its Publish as PDF or XPS dialog box, in which you can specify a filename and location and set some other options.

Customizing the Excel User Interface

IN THIS CHAPTER

Customizing the Quick Access toolbar

Customizing the Ribbon

A software program's user interface consists of all the ways that the user interacts with the software. In Excel, the user interface consists of the following:

- The Ribbon
- The Quick Access toolbar
- Right-click shortcut menus
- Dialog boxes
- Task panes
- Keyboard shortcuts

This chapter describes how to make changes to two Excel user interface components: the Quick Access toolbar and the Ribbon. You might want to customize these elements to make Excel more suited to the way you use it.

Customizing the Quick Access Toolbar

The Quick Access toolbar is always visible, regardless of which Ribbon tab is selected. After you customize the Quick Access toolbar, your frequently used commands will always be one click away.

> **NOTE**
>
> The only situation in which the Quick Access toolbar is not visible is in full-screen mode, which is enabled by clicking the Ribbon Display Options button in the Excel title bar and choosing Auto-Hide Ribbon. To display the Quick Access toolbar (and Ribbon) temporarily in full-screen mode, click the title bar or press the Alt key. To cancel full-screen mode, click the Ribbon Display Options button in the Excel title bar and choose Show Tabs or Show Tabs and Commands.

About the Quick Access toolbar

By default, the Quick Access toolbar is located on the left side of the Excel title bar, above the Ribbon (see Figure 8.1). Unless you customize it, this toolbar includes four tools:

AutoSave   Periodically saves workbooks that have already been saved to OneDrive or SharePoint

Save   Saves the active workbook

Undo   Reverses the effect of the last action

Redo   Reverses the effect of the last undo

FIGURE 8.1

The default location for the Quick Access toolbar is on the left side of the Excel title bar.

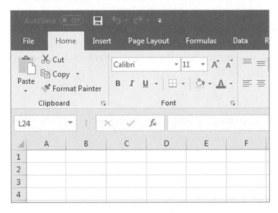

If you prefer, you can move the Quick Access toolbar below the Ribbon. To do so, right-click the Quick Access toolbar and choose Show Quick Access Toolbar Below the Ribbon. Moving the Quick Access toolbar below the Ribbon uses additional vertical space on your screen. In other words, you'll be able to see one or two fewer rows of your worksheet if you move the Quick Access toolbar from its default location. Unlike traditional toolbars, the Quick Access toolbar cannot be made free floating, so you can't move it to a convenient location. It always appears either above or below the Ribbon.

Commands on the Quick Access toolbar always appear as small icons with no text. An exception to this rule is drop-down controls that display text. For example, if you add the Font control from the Home ⇨ Font group, it appears as a drop-down control in the Quick Access toolbar. When you hover your mouse pointer over an icon, you see a ScreenTip showing the name of the command and a brief description.

You can customize the Quick Access toolbar by adding or removing commands. If you find that you use some Excel commands frequently, you can make these commands easily accessible by adding them to your Quick Access toolbar. You can also rearrange the order of the icons.

As far as we can tell, there is no limit to the number of commands that you can add. The Quick Access toolbar always displays only a single line of icons. If the number of icons exceeds the Excel window width, it displays an additional icon at the end: More Controls. Click the More Controls icon, and the hidden Quick Access toolbar icons appear in a pop-up window.

Adding new commands to the Quick Access toolbar

You can add a new command to the Quick Access toolbar in three ways:

- **Click the Quick Access toolbar drop-down control, which is located on the right side of the Quick Access toolbar (see Figure 8.2).** The list contains a few commonly used commands. Select a command from the list, and Excel adds it to your Quick Access toolbar.

FIGURE 8.2

This drop-down list is one way to add a new command to the Quick Access toolbar.

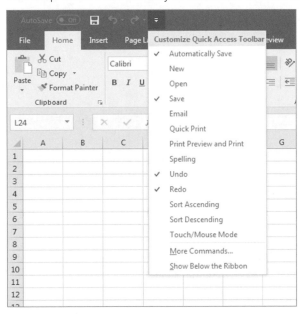

- **Right-click any control on the Ribbon and choose Add to Quick Access Toolbar.** The control is added to your Quick Access toolbar, positioned to the right of the last control.

- **Use the Quick Access Toolbar tab in the Excel Options dialog box.** A quick way to access this dialog box is to right-click any Ribbon control and choose Customize Quick Access Toolbar.

The remainder of this section discusses the Quick Access Toolbar tab of the Excel Options dialog box, as shown in Figure 8.3.

FIGURE 8.3

Use the Quick Access Toolbar tab in the Excel Options dialog box to customize the Quick Access toolbar.

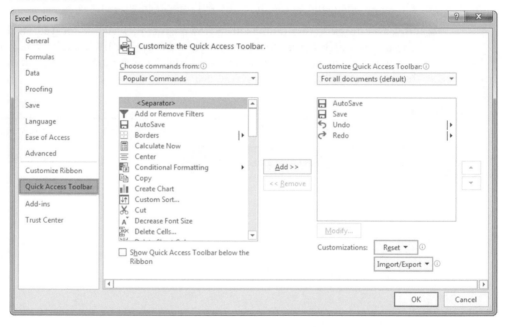

The left side of the dialog box displays a list of Excel commands, and the right side shows the commands currently on your Quick Access toolbar. Above the command list on the left is the Choose Commands From drop-down list, from which you can filter the list. Select an item from the drop-down list, and the list displays only the commands for that item. In Figure 8.3, the list shows commands in the Popular Commands category.

Some of the items in the drop-down list are as follows:

Popular Commands   Displays commands that Excel users commonly use.

Commands Not in the Ribbon   Displays a list of commands that you can't access from the Ribbon. Many, but not all, are obsolete or not very useful.

All Commands   Displays a complete list of Excel commands.

Macros   Displays a list of all available macros.

File Tab   Displays the commands available in the Backstage view.

Home Tab   Displays all commands available when the Home tab is active.

In addition, the Choose Commands From drop-down list contains an item for every other tab, including the contextual tabs (for example, the additional tabs that are displayed when a chart is selected). To add an item to your Quick Access toolbar, select it from the list on the left and then click Add. The command appears in the list on the right. At the top of each list is an item called <Separator>. Adding this item to your Quick Access toolbar results in a vertical bar to help you group commands.

The commands are listed in alphabetical order. Sometimes you need to do some guessing to find a particular command.

TIP

By default, Quick Access toolbar customizations are visible for all documents. You can create a Quick Access toolbar configuration that's specific to a particular workbook. In other words, the commands on the Quick Access toolbar appear only when a particular workbook is active. Start by activating the workbook and then display the Quick Access Toolbar tab of the Excel Options dialog box. When you add a command to the Quick Access toolbar, use the drop-down list in the upper right to specify whether the change is for all workbooks or just the active workbook.

When you select Macros from the Choose Commands From drop-down, Excel lists all available macros. You can attach a macro to a Quick Access toolbar icon so that when you click the icon, the macro is executed. If you add a macro to your Quick Access toolbar, you can click the Modify button to change the text and choose a different icon for the macro.

When you finish making your Quick Access toolbar customizations, click OK to close the Excel Options dialog box. The new icon(s) will appear on the Quick Access toolbar.

TIP

The only times you ever need to use the Quick Access Toolbar tab of the Excel Options dialog box is when you want to add a command that's not on the Ribbon, add a command that executes a macro, or rearrange the order of the icons. In all other situations, it's much easier to locate the command in the Ribbon, right-click the command, and choose Add to Quick Access Toolbar.

Other Quick Access toolbar actions

Other Quick Access toolbar actions include the following:

Rearranging the Quick Access toolbar icons   If you want to change the order of your Quick Access toolbar icons, you can do so from the Quick Access Toolbar tab of the Excel Options dialog box. Select the command and then use the Up and Down arrow buttons on the right to move the icon.

Removing Quick Access toolbar icons   The easiest way to remove an icon from your Quick Access toolbar is to right-click the icon and choose Remove from Quick Access Toolbar. You can also use the Quick Access Toolbar tab of the Excel Options dialog box. Just select the command in the list on the right and click Remove.

Resetting the Quick Access toolbar   If you want to return the Quick Access toolbar to its default state, display the Quick Access Toolbar tab of the Excel Options dialog box and click the Reset button. Then choose Reset Only Quick Access Toolbar. The Quick Access toolbar then displays its four default commands.

CAUTION

You can't undo resetting the Quick Access toolbar.

Sharing User Interface Customizations

In the Excel Options dialog box, the Quick Access Toolbar tab and the Customize Ribbon tab both have an Import/Export button. You can use this button to save and open files that contain user interface customizations. For example, you might create a new Ribbon tab and want to share it with your officemates.

Click the Import/Export button, and you get two options:

Import Customization File   You're prompted to locate the file. Before you load a file, you're asked whether you want to replace all existing Ribbon and Quick Access toolbar customizations.

Export All Customizations   You're prompted to provide a filename and location for the file.

The information is stored in a file that has an exportedUI extension.

Unfortunately, importing and exporting are not implemented very well. Excel doesn't allow you to save or load only the Quick Access toolbar customizations or only the Ribbon customizations. Both types of customizations are exported and imported. Therefore, you can't share your Quick Access toolbar customizations without also sharing your Ribbon customizations.

TIP

Commands on the Quick Access toolbar are assigned numbers for shortcut keys. For example, the shortcut Alt+1 executes the first command on the Quick Access toolbar. After the ninth command, the shortcuts change to 09, 08, 07.... After the 18th command, the shortcuts change to 0A, 0B, 0C.... And after Alt+0Z, Excel stops assigning shortcuts.

Customizing the Ribbon

The Ribbon is Excel's primary user interface component. It consists of tabs along the top. When you click a tab, it displays a set of relevant commands, and the commands are arranged in groups.

Why you may want to customize the Ribbon

Most users have no need to customize the Ribbon. If you find that you tend to use the same command over and over, though—and you're constantly clicking tabs to access these commands—you might benefit from customizing the Ribbon in such a way that the commands you need are on the same tab.

What can be customized

You can customize tabs on the Ribbon by

- Adding new custom tabs
- Deleting custom tabs
- Changing the order of the tabs
- Changing the name of tabs
- Hiding built-in tabs

You can customize groups on the Ribbon by

- Adding new custom groups
- Adding commands to custom groups
- Removing commands from custom groups
- Removing groups from tabs
- Moving a group to a different tab
- Changing the order of the groups within a tab
- Changing the name of a group

Those are fairly comprehensive lists of customization options, but there are some actions that you can't do:

- Remove built-in tabs (but you can hide them)
- Remove specific commands from built-in groups (but you *can* remove entire groups)
- Change the order of commands in a built-in group

> **NOTE**
>
> Unfortunately, you can't use VBA macros to customize the Ribbon (or Quick Access toolbar). However, developers can write RibbonX code and store it in workbook files. When the file is opened, the Ribbon is modified to display new commands. Writing RibbonX code is relatively complicated and beyond the scope of this book.

8

How to customize the Ribbon

Customizing the Ribbon is done via the Customize Ribbon panel of the Excel Options dialog box (see Figure 8.4). The quickest way to display this dialog box is to right-click anywhere on the Ribbon and choose Customize the Ribbon.

FIGURE 8.4

The Customize Ribbon tab of the Excel Options dialog box

Creating a new tab

If you'd like to create a new tab, click the New Tab button. Excel creates a tab named New Tab (Custom) and a new group in the tab named New Group (Custom).

You'll almost always want to give the tab (and the group) better names. Select the item and click Rename. Use the Move Up and Move Down arrow buttons on the right to reposition the new tab, if necessary.

> **NOTE**
>
> You don't need to add a new tab just because you want to add new commands to the Ribbon. You can create a new group for an existing tab.

Creating a new group

To create a new group, select the tab that will hold the new group and click the New Group button. Excel creates a new group named New Group (Custom). Use the Rename button to provide a more descriptive name, and use the Move Up and Move Down arrow buttons on the right to reposition the group within the tab.

Adding commands to a new group

Adding commands to the Ribbon is similar to adding commands to the Quick Access toolbar, which we described earlier in this chapter. Commands that you add must be placed in a new group. Here's the general procedure:

1. **Use the Choose Commands From drop-down list on the left to display various groups of commands.**
2. **Select the command in the list box on the left.**
3. **Use the Customize the Ribbon drop-down list on the right to choose a group of tabs.** Main Tabs refers to the tabs that are always visible; Tool Tabs refers to the contextual tabs that appear when a particular object is selected.
4. **In the list box on the right, select the tab and the group where you want to put the command.** You'll need to click the plus-sign control to expand the tab name so that it displays its group names.

> **NOTE**
> You can add commands only to groups that you've created.

5. **Click the Add button to add the selected command from the left to the selected group on the right.**

To rearrange the order of tabs, groups, or commands, select the item and use the Move Up and Move Down buttons on the right. Note that you can move a group into a different tab.

> **NOTE**
> Although you can't remove a built-in tab, you can hide the tab by clearing the check box next to its name.

Figure 8.5 shows a part of a customized Ribbon. In this case, two groups were added to the View tab (to the right of the Macros group): Extra Commands (with three new commands) and Speech (with five new commands).

FIGURE 8.5

The View tab, with two new groups added

8

Resetting the Ribbon

To restore all or part of the Ribbon to its default state, right-click any part of the Ribbon and choose Customize the Ribbon from the shortcut menu. Excel displays the Customize Ribbon tab of the Excel Options dialog box. Click the Reset button to display two options: Reset Only Selected Ribbon Tab and Reset All Customizations. If you choose the latter, the Ribbon will be returned to its default state, and you'll lose any Quick Access toolbar customizations that you made.

Part II

Working with Formulas and Functions

Formulas and worksheet functions are essential to manipulating data and obtaining useful information from your Excel workbooks. The chapters in this part present a wide variety of formula examples that use many Excel functions.

IN THIS PART

Introducing Formulas and Functions

Formulas are what make a spreadsheet program so useful. If it weren't for formulas, a spreadsheet would simply be a fancy word processing document that has great support for tabular information.

You use formulas in your Excel worksheets to calculate results from the data stored in the worksheet. When data changes, the formulas calculate updated results with no extra effort on your part. This chapter introduces formulas and functions and helps you to get up to speed with this important element.

Understanding Formula Basics

A formula consists of special code entered into a cell. It performs a calculation of some type and returns a result that is displayed in the cell. Formulas use a variety of operators and worksheet functions to work with values and text. The values and text used in formulas can be located in other cells, which makes changing data easy and gives worksheets their dynamic nature. For example, you can see multiple scenarios quickly by changing the data in a worksheet and letting your formulas do the work.

A formula always begins with an equal sign and can contain any of these elements:

- Mathematical operators, such as + (for addition) and * (for multiplication)
- Cell references (including named cells and ranges)
- Values or text
- Worksheet functions (such as SUM and AVERAGE)

After you enter a formula, the cell displays the calculated result of the formula. The formula itself appears in the Formula bar when you select the cell, however.

Here are a few examples of formulas:

`=150*.05`	Multiplies 150 times 0.05. This formula uses only values, and it always returns the same result. You could just enter the value 7.5 into the cell, but using a formula provides information on how the value was calculated.
`=A3`	Displays the value in cell A3. No calculation is performed on A3.
`=A1+A2`	Adds the values in cells A1 and A2.
`=Income-Expenses`	Subtracts the value in the cell named Expenses from the value in the cell named Income.
`=SUM(A1:A12)`	Adds the values in the range A1:A12, using the SUM function.
`=A1=C12`	Compares cell A1 with cell C12. If the cells are the same, the formula returns TRUE; otherwise, it returns FALSE.

Note that every formula begins with an equal sign (=). The initial equal sign allows Excel to distinguish a formula from plain text.

Using operators in formulas

Excel formulas support a variety of operators. Operators are symbols that indicate what mathematical (or logical) operation you want the formula to perform. Table 9.1 lists the operators that Excel recognizes. In addition to these, Excel has many built-in functions that enable you to perform additional calculations.

TABLE 9.1   Operators Used in Formulas

Operator	Name
+	Addition
−	Subtraction
*	Multiplication
/	Division
^	Exponentiation
&	Concatenation
=	Logical comparison (equal to)
>	Logical comparison (greater than)
<	Logical comparison (less than)
>=	Logical comparison (greater than or equal to)

Operator	Name
<=	Logical comparison (less than or equal to)
<>	Logical comparison (not equal to)

You can, of course, use as many operators as you need to perform the desired calculation.

Here are some examples of formulas that use various operators:

Formula	What It Does
="Part-"&"23A"	Joins (concatenates) the two text strings to produce Part-23A.
=A1&A2	Concatenates the contents of cell A1 with cell A2. Concatenation works with values as well as text. If cell A1 contains 123 and cell A2 contains 456, this formula would return the text 123456. Note that the result of concatenation is always formatted as text.
=6^3	Raises 6 to the third power (216).
=216^(1/3)	Raises 216 to the power of 1/3. This is mathematically equivalent to calculating the cube root of 216, which is 6.
=A1<A2	Returns TRUE if the value in cell A1 is less than the value in cell A2. Otherwise, it returns FALSE. Logical comparison operators also work with text. If A1 contains Bill and A2 contains Julia, the formula would return TRUE because Bill comes before Julia in alphabetical order.
=A1<=A2	Returns TRUE if the value in cell A1 is less than or equal to the value in cell A2. Otherwise, it returns FALSE.

Understanding operator precedence in formulas

When Excel calculates the value of a formula, it uses certain rules to determine the order in which the various parts of the formula are calculated. You need to understand these rules so that your formulas produce accurate results.

Table 9.2 lists the Excel operator precedence. This table shows that exponentiation has the highest precedence (performed first) and logical comparisons have the lowest precedence (performed last).

TABLE 9.2 Operator Precedence in Excel Formulas

Symbol	Operator	Precedence
^	Exponentiation	1
*	Multiplication	2
/	Division	2

Continues

TABLE 9.2 *(continued)*

Symbol	Operator	Precedence
+	Addition	3
−	Subtraction	3
&	Concatenation	4
=	Equal to	5
<	Less than	5
>	Greater than	5

You can use parentheses to override Excel's built-in order of precedence. Expressions within parentheses are always evaluated first. For example, the following formula uses parentheses to control the order in which the calculations occur. In this case, cell B3 is subtracted from cell B2, and the result is multiplied by cell B4:

```
=(B2-B3)*B4
```

If you enter the formula without the parentheses, Excel computes a different answer. Because multiplication has a higher precedence, cell B3 is multiplied by cell B4. This result is then subtracted from cell B2, which isn't what was intended.

The formula without parentheses looks like this:

```
=B2-B3*B4
```

> **TIP**
>
> It's good practice to use parentheses even when they aren't strictly necessary. Doing so helps to clarify what the formula is intended to do. For example, the following formula makes it perfectly clear that B3 should be multiplied by B4 and the result subtracted from cell B2. Without the parentheses, you would need to remember Excel's order of precedence.
>
> ```
> =B2-(B3*B4)
> ```

You can also nest parentheses within formulas—that is, put them inside other parentheses. If you do so, Excel evaluates the most deeply nested expressions first—and then works its way out. Here's an example of a formula that uses nested parentheses:

```
=((B2*C2)+(B3*C3)+(B4*C4))*B6
```

This formula has four sets of parentheses—three sets are nested inside the fourth set. Excel evaluates each nested set of parentheses and then sums the three results. This result is then multiplied by the value in cell B6.

Although the preceding formula uses four sets of parentheses, only the outer set is really necessary. If you understand operator precedence, it should be clear that you can rewrite this formula as follows:

=(B2*C2+B3*C3+B4*C4)*B6

Most would agree that using the extra parentheses makes the calculation much clearer.

Note that operators at the same level of precedence, such as multiplication and division, are evaluated from left to right (unless parentheses would indicate a different order).

Every left parenthesis, of course, must have a matching right parenthesis. If you have many levels of nested parentheses, keeping them straight can sometimes be difficult. If the parentheses don't match, Excel displays a message explaining the problem, and it won't let you enter the formula.

CAUTION

In some cases, if your formula contains mismatched parentheses, Excel may propose a correction to your formula. Figure 9.1 shows an example of a proposed correction. You may be tempted simply to accept Excel's suggestion, but be careful—in many cases, the proposed formula, although syntactically correct, isn't the formula you intended, and it will produce an incorrect result.

FIGURE 9.1

Excel sometimes suggests a syntactically correct formula, but not the formula you had in mind.

TIP

When you're editing a formula, Excel lends a hand in helping you match parentheses by displaying matching parentheses in the same color.

Using functions in your formulas

Many formulas that you create use worksheet functions. These functions enable you to greatly enhance the power of your formulas and perform calculations that are difficult (or even impossible) if you use only the operators discussed previously. For example, you can use the TAN function to calculate the tangent of an angle. You can't do this complicated calculation by using the mathematical operators alone.

Examples of formulas that use functions

A worksheet function can simplify a formula significantly.

Here's an example. To calculate the average of the values in ten cells (A1:A10) without using a function, you'd have to construct a formula like this:

```
=(A1+A2+A3+A4+A5+A6+A7+A8+A9+A10)/10
```

Not very pretty, is it? Even worse, you would need to edit this formula if you added another cell to the range. Fortunately, you can replace this formula with a much simpler one that uses one of Excel's built-in worksheet functions, AVERAGE:

```
=AVERAGE(A1:A10)
```

The following formula demonstrates how using a function can enable you to perform calculations that are not otherwise possible. Say that you need to determine the largest value in a range. A formula can't tell you the answer without using a function. Here's a formula that uses the MAX function to return the largest value in the range A1:D100:

```
=MAX(A1:D100)
```

Functions also can sometimes eliminate manual editing. Assume that you have a worksheet that contains 1,000 names in cells A1:A1000 and the names appear in all-capital letters. Your boss sees the listing and informs you that the names will be mail-merged with a form letter. Use of all-uppercase letters is not acceptable; for example, JOHN F. SMITH must now appear as John F. Smith. You could spend the next several hours re-entering the list (ugh), or you could use a formula, such as the following, which uses the PROPER function to convert the text in cell A1 to the proper case:

```
=PROPER(A1)
```

Enter this formula once in cell B1 and then copy it down to the next 999 rows. Then select B1:B1000 and choose Home ⇨ Clipboard ⇨ Copy to copy the range. Next, with B1:B1000 still selected, choose Home ⇨ Clipboard ⇨ Paste Values (V) to convert the formulas to values. Delete the original column, and you've just accomplished several hours of work in less than a minute.

> **TIP**
>
> You can also use Excel's Flash Fill feature to make this type of transformation, without formulas. See Chapter 25, "Importing and Cleaning Data," for more about Flash Fill.

One last example should convince you of the power of functions. Suppose you have a worksheet that calculates sales commissions. If the salesperson sold $100,000 or more of product, the commission rate is 7.5 percent; otherwise, the commission rate is 5.0 percent. Without using a function, you would have to create two different formulas and make sure you use the correct formula for each sales amount. A better solution is to write a formula that uses the IF function to ensure that you calculate the correct commission, regardless of sales amount:

```
=IF(A1<100000,A1*5%,A1*7.5%)
```

This formula performs some simple decision-making. The formula checks the value of cell A1, which contains the sales amount. If this value is less than 100,000, the formula returns cell A1 multiplied by 5 percent. Otherwise, it returns what's in cell A1 multiplied by 7.5 percent. This example uses three arguments, separated by commas. We discuss this in the next section, "Function arguments."

Function arguments

In the preceding examples, you may have noticed that all of the functions used parentheses. The information inside the parentheses is the list of arguments.

Functions vary in the way they use arguments. Depending on what it has to do, a function may use one of the following:

- No arguments
- One argument
- A fixed number of arguments
- An indeterminate number of arguments
- Optional arguments

An example of a function that doesn't use an argument is the NOW function, which returns the current date and time. Even if a function doesn't use an argument, you must still provide a set of empty parentheses, like this:

```
=NOW()
```

If a function uses more than one argument, separate each argument with a comma. The examples at the beginning of the chapter used cell references for arguments. Excel is quite flexible when it comes to function arguments, however. An argument can consist of a cell reference, literal values, literal text strings, expressions, and even other functions. Here are some examples of functions that use various types of arguments:

Cell reference: =SUM(A1:A24)
Literal value: =SQRT(121)
Literal text string: =PROPER("john f. smith")
Expression: =SQRT(183+12)
Other functions: =SQRT(SUM(A1:A24))

More about functions

All told, Excel includes more than 450 built-in functions. And if that's not enough, you can download or purchase additional specialized functions from third-party suppliers—and even create your own custom functions (by using VBA) if you're so inclined.

Some users feel a bit overwhelmed by the sheer number of functions, but you'll probably find that you use only a dozen or so on a regular basis. And as you'll see, the Excel Insert Function dialog box (described later in this chapter) makes it easy to locate and insert a function, even if it's not one that you use frequently.

 You'll find many examples of Excel's built-in functions throughout Part II, "Working with Formulas and Functions." Chapter 43, "Creating Custom Worksheet Functions," covers the basics of creating custom functions with VBA.

Entering Formulas into Your Worksheets

Every formula must begin with an equal sign to inform Excel that the cell contains a formula rather than text. Excel provides two ways to enter a formula into a cell: manually or by pointing to cell references. The following sections discuss each method in detail.

Excel provides additional assistance when you create formulas by displaying a drop-down list that contains function names and range names. The items displayed in the list are determined by what you've already typed. For example, if you're entering a formula and then type the letters SU, you'll see the drop-down list shown in Figure 9.2. If you type an additional letter, the list is shortened to show only the matching functions. To have Excel autocomplete an entry in that list, use the navigation keys to highlight the entry and then press Tab. Notice that highlighting a function in the list also displays a brief description of the function. See the next sidebar, "Using Formula AutoComplete," for an example of how this feature works.

FIGURE 9.2

Excel displays a drop-down list when you enter a formula.

Using Formula AutoComplete

The Formula AutoComplete feature makes entering formulas easier than ever. Simply start typing your formula, and Excel will help by presenting you with a list of the possible options and arguments available. In this example, Excel is presenting the options for the SUBTOTAL function.

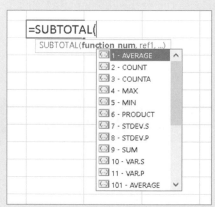

Formula AutoComplete includes the following items (and each type is identified by an icon):

- Excel built-in functions.
- User-defined functions (functions defined by the user through VBA or other methods).
- Defined names (cells or range named using the Formulas ⇨ Defined Names ⇨ Define Name command).
- Enumerated arguments that use a value to represent an option. (Only a few functions use such arguments, and SUBTOTAL is one of them.)
- Table structure references (used to identify portions of a table).

9

Entering formulas manually

Entering a formula manually involves, well, entering a formula manually. In a selected cell, you type an equal sign (=) followed by the formula. As you type, the characters appear in the cell and in the Formula bar. You can, of course, use all of the normal editing keys when entering a formula.

Entering formulas by pointing

Even though you can enter formulas by typing in the entire formula, Excel provides another method of entering formulas that is generally easier, faster, and less error prone. This method still involves some manual typing, but you can simply point to the cell references instead of typing their values manually. For example, to enter the formula =A1+A2 into cell A3, follow these steps:

1. **Select cell A3.**

2. **Type an equal sign (=) to begin the formula.** Notice that Excel displays Enter in the status bar (lower left of your screen).

3. **Press the up arrow twice.** As you press this key, Excel displays a dashed border around cell A1, and the cell reference appears in cell A3 and in the Formula bar. In addition, Excel displays Point in the status bar.

4. **Type a plus sign (+).** A solid color border replaces the dashed border of A1, and Enter reappears in the status bar.

5. **Press the up arrow again.** The dashed border encompasses cell A2 and adds that cell address to the formula.

6. **Press Enter to complete the formula.**

> **TIP**
>
> When creating a formula by pointing, you can also point to the data cells by using your mouse.

Pasting range names into formulas

If your formula uses named cells or ranges, you can either type the name in place of the address or choose the name from a list and have Excel insert the name for you automatically. Three ways to insert a name into a formula are available:

- Select the name from the drop-down list. To use this method, you must know at least the first character of the name. When you're entering the formula, type the first character and then select the name from the drop-down list.

- Press F3. The Paste Name dialog box appears. Select the name from the list and then click OK (or just double-click the name). Excel enters the name into your formula. If no names are defined, pressing F3 has no effect.

- Click the Use in Formula drop-down on the Formulas tab (Defined Names group). This command is available while you are in edit mode, and it allows you to select from the available range names.

See Chapter 4, "Working with Excel Ranges and Tables," for information about creating names for cells and ranges.

Inserting functions into formulas

The easiest way to enter a function into a formula is to use Formula AutoComplete (the drop-down list that Excel displays while you type a formula). To use this method, however, you must know at least the first character of the function's name.

Another way to insert a function is to use tools in the Function Library group on the Formulas tab on the Ribbon (see Figure 9.3). This method is especially useful if you can't remember which function you need. When entering a formula, click the function category (Financial, Logical, Text, and so on) to get a list of the functions in that category. Click the function that you want, and Excel displays its Function Arguments dialog box. This is where you enter the function's arguments. In addition, you can click the Help on This Function link to learn more about the selected function.

FIGURE 9.3

You can insert a function by selecting it from one of the function categories.

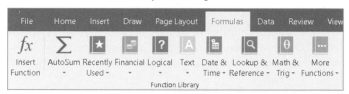

Yet another way to insert a function into a formula is to use the Insert Function dialog box (see Figure 9.4). You can access this dialog box in several ways:

- Choose Formulas ⇨ Function Library ⇨ Insert Function.
- Use the Insert Function command, which appears at the bottom of each drop-down list in the Formulas ⇨ Function Library group.
- Click the Insert Function icon, which is directly to the left of the Formula bar. This button displays fx.
- Press Shift+F3.

The Insert Function dialog box shows a drop-down list of function categories. Select a category, and the functions in that category are displayed in the list box. To access a function that you recently used, select Most Recently Used from the drop-down list.

If you're not sure which function you need, you can search for the appropriate function by using the Search for a Function field at the top of the dialog box.

1. **Enter your search terms and click Go.** You get a list of relevant functions. When you select a function from the Select a Function list, Excel displays the function (and its argument names) in the dialog box along with a brief description of what the function does.

FIGURE 9.4

The Insert Function dialog box

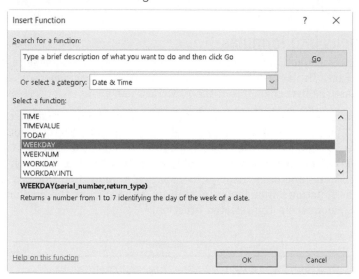

2. **When you locate the function you want to use, highlight it and click OK.** Excel then displays its Function Arguments dialog box, as shown in Figure 9.5.

FIGURE 9.5

The Function Arguments dialog box

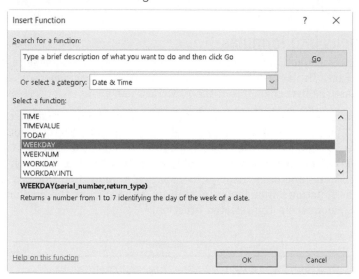

3. **Specify the arguments for the function.** The Function Arguments dialog box will vary, depending on the function that you are inserting, and it will show one text box for each of the function's arguments. To use a cell or range reference as an

argument, you can enter the address manually or click inside the argument box and then select (that is, point to) the cell or range in the sheet.

4. **After you specify all of the function arguments, click OK.**

TIP

Yet another way to insert a function while you're entering a formula is to use the Function List to the left of the Formula bar. When you're entering or editing a formula, the space typically occupied by the Name box displays a list of the functions that you've used most recently (if any). After you select a function from this list, Excel displays the Function Arguments dialog box.

Function entry tips

Here are some additional tips to keep in mind when you use the Insert Function dialog box to enter functions:

- You can use the Insert Function dialog box to insert a function into an existing formula. Just edit the formula and move the insertion point to the location at which you want to insert the function. Then open the Insert Function dialog box (using any of the methods described earlier) and select the function.

- You can also use the Function Arguments dialog box to modify the arguments for a function in an existing formula. Click the function in the Formula bar and then click the Insert Function button (the fx button, to the left of the Formula bar).

- If you change your mind about entering a function, click the Cancel button.

- The number of boxes that you see in the Function Arguments dialog box depends on the number of arguments used in the function you selected. If a function uses no arguments, you won't see any boxes. If the function uses a variable number of arguments (such as the AVERAGE function), Excel adds a new box every time you enter an optional argument. Note that required arguments appear in bold, while optional arguments are not bold.

- As you provide arguments in the Function Arguments dialog box, the value of each argument is displayed to the right of each box.

- A few functions, such as INDEX, have more than one form. If you choose such a function, Excel displays another dialog box that lets you choose which form you want to use.

- As you become familiar with the functions, you can bypass the Insert Function dialog box and type the function name directly. Excel prompts you with argument names as you enter the function.

Editing Formulas

After you enter a formula, you can (of course) edit it. You may need to edit a formula if you make some changes to your worksheet and then have to adjust the formula to accommodate the changes. Or the formula may return an error value, in which case you need to edit the formula to correct the error.

Notice that Excel color-codes the range addresses and ranges when you're entering or editing a formula. This helps you quickly spot the cells that are used in a formula.

Here are some of the ways to get into cell edit mode:

- Double-click the cell, which enables you to edit the cell contents directly in the cell.
- Press F2, which enables you to edit the cell contents directly in the cell.
- Select the cell that you want to edit and then click in the Formula bar. This enables you to edit the cell contents in the Formula bar.
- If the cell contains a formula that returns an error, Excel will display a small triangle in the upper-left corner of the cell. Activate the cell, and you'll see an error indicator. Click the error indicator, and you can choose one of the options for correcting the error. (The options will vary according to the type of error in the cell.)

> **TIP**
>
> You can control whether Excel displays these formula error indicators in the Formulas section of the Excel Options dialog box. To display this dialog box, choose File ⇨ Options. If you remove the check mark from Enable Background Error Checking, Excel no longer displays these error indicators.

While you're editing a formula, you can select multiple characters either by dragging the mouse cursor over them or by pressing Shift while you use the navigation keys.

> **TIP**
>
> If you have a formula that you can't seem to edit correctly, you can convert the formula to text and tackle it again later. To convert a formula to text, just remove the initial equal sign (=). When you're ready to try again, type the initial equal sign to convert the cell contents back to a formula.

Using Cell References in Formulas

Most formulas that you create include references to cells or ranges. These references enable your formulas to work dynamically with the data contained in those cells or ranges. For example, if your formula refers to cell A1 and you change the value contained in A1, the formula result changes to reflect the new value. If you didn't use references in your formulas, you would need to edit the formulas themselves to change the values used in the formulas.

Using relative, absolute, and mixed references

When you use a cell (or range) reference in a formula, you can use three types of references:

Relative   The row and column references can change when you copy the formula to another cell because the references are actually offsets from the current row and column. By default, Excel creates relative cell references in formulas.

Absolute   The row and column references don't change when you copy the formula because the reference is to an actual cell address. An absolute reference uses two dollar signs in its address: one for the column letter and one for the row number (for example, $A$5).

Mixed   Either the row or the column reference is relative, and the other is absolute. Only one of the address parts is absolute (for example, $A4 or A$4).

The type of cell reference is important only if you plan to copy the formula to other cells. The following examples illustrate this point.

Figure 9.6 shows a simple worksheet. The formula in cell D2, which multiplies the quantity by the price, is

    =B2*C2

FIGURE 9.6

Copying a formula that contains relative references

This formula uses relative cell references. Therefore, when the formula is copied to the cells below it, the references adjust in a relative manner. For example, the formula in cell D3 is

    =B3*C3

But what if the cell references in D2 contained absolute references, like this?

    =$B$2*$C$2

In this case, copying the formula to the cells below would produce incorrect results. The formula in cell D3 would be the same as the formula in cell D2.

Now we'll extend the example to calculate sales tax, which is stored in cell B7 (see Figure 9.7). In this situation, the formula in cell D2 is

    =(B2*C2)*$B$7

FIGURE 9.7

Formula references to the sales tax cell should be absolute.

| D2 | ▾ | : | ✕ | ✓ | *fx* | =B2*C2*$B$7 | | |

◢	A	B	C	D	E
1	Item	Quantity	Price	Sales Tax	Total
2	Chair	4	$125.00	$37.50	
3	Desk	4	$695.00		
4	Lamp	3	$39.95		
5					
6					
7	Sales Tax:	7.50%			

The quantity is multiplied by the price, and the result is multiplied by the sales tax rate stored in cell B7. Notice that the reference to B7 is an absolute reference. When the formula in D2 is copied to the cells below it, cell D3 will contain this formula:

    =(B3*C3)*$B$7

Here, the references to cells B2 and C2 were adjusted, but the reference to cell B7 was not, which is exactly what you want because the address of the cell that contains the sales tax never changes.

Figure 9.8 demonstrates the use of mixed references. The formulas in the C3:F7 range calculate the area for various lengths and widths. Here's the formula in cell C3:

    =$B3*C$2

FIGURE 9.8

Using mixed cell references

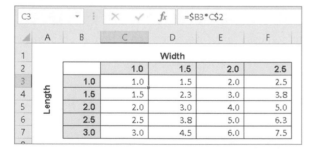

| C3 | ▾ | : | ✕ | ✓ | *fx* | =$B3*C$2 | |

◢	A	B	C	D	E	F
1				Width		
2			1.0	1.5	2.0	2.5
3		1.0	1.0	1.5	2.0	2.5
4	Length	1.5	1.5	2.3	3.0	3.8
5		2.0	2.0	3.0	4.0	5.0
6		2.5	2.5	3.8	5.0	6.3
7		3.0	3.0	4.5	6.0	7.5

Notice that both cell references are mixed. The reference to cell B3 uses an absolute reference for the column ($B), and the reference to cell C2 uses an absolute reference for the row ($2). As a result, this formula can be copied down and across, and the calculations will be correct. For example, the formula in cell F7 is

    =$B7*F$2

If C3 used either absolute or relative references, copying the formula would produce incorrect results.

 A workbook that demonstrates the various types of references is available on this book's website at www.wiley.com/go/excel2019bible. **The file is named** `cell references.xlsx`.

> **NOTE**
> When you cut and paste a formula (move it to another location), the cell references in the formula aren't adjusted. Again, this is usually what you want to happen. When you move a formula, you generally want it to continue to refer to the original cells.

Changing the types of your references

You can enter nonrelative references (that is, absolute or mixed) manually by inserting dollar signs in the appropriate positions of the cell address. Or you can use a handy shortcut: the F4 key. When you've entered a cell reference (by typing it or by pointing), you can press F4 repeatedly to have Excel cycle through all four reference types.

For example, if you enter =A1 to start a formula, pressing F4 converts the cell reference to =$A$1. Pressing F4 again converts it to =A$1. Pressing it again displays =$A1. Pressing it one more time returns to the original =A1. Keep pressing F4 until Excel displays the type of reference that you want.

> **NOTE**
> When you name a cell or range, Excel (by default) uses an absolute reference for the name. For example, if you give the name `SalesForecast` to B1:B12, the Refers To box in the New Name dialog box lists the reference as $B$1:$B$12. This is almost always what you want. If you copy a cell that has a named reference in its formula, the copied formula contains a reference to the original name.

Referencing cells outside the worksheet

Formulas can also refer to cells in other worksheets—and the worksheets don't even have to be in the same workbook. Excel uses a special type of notation to handle these types of references.

Referencing cells in other worksheets

To use a reference to a cell in another worksheet in the same workbook, use this format:

```
=SheetName!CellAddress
```

In other words, precede the cell address with the worksheet name followed by an exclamation point. Here's an example of a formula that uses a cell on the Sheet2 worksheet:

```
=A1*Sheet2!A1
```

9

This formula multiplies the value in cell A1 on the current worksheet by the value in cell A1 on Sheet2.

> **TIP**
>
> If the worksheet name in the reference includes one or more spaces, you must enclose it in single quotation marks. (Excel does that automatically if you use the point-and-click method when creating the formula.) For example, here's a formula that refers to a cell on a sheet named All Depts:

```
=A1*'All Depts'!A1
```

Referencing cells in other workbooks

To refer to a cell in a different workbook, use this format:

```
=[WorkbookName]SheetName!CellAddress
```

In this case, the workbook name (in square brackets), the worksheet name, and an exclamation point precede the cell address. The following is an example of a formula that uses a cell reference in the Sheet1 worksheet in a workbook named Budget:

```
=[Budget.xlsx]Sheet1!A1
```

If the workbook name in the reference includes one or more spaces, you must enclose it (and the sheet name and square brackets) in single quotation marks. For example, here's a formula that refers to a cell on Sheet1 in a workbook named Budget For 2019:

```
=A1*'[Budget For 2019.xlsx]Sheet1'!A1
```

When a formula refers to cells in a different workbook, the other workbook doesn't have to be open. If the workbook is closed, however, you must add the complete path to the reference so that Excel can find it. Here's an example:

```
=A1*'C:\My Documents\[Budget For 2019.xlsx]Sheet1'!A1
```

A linked file can also reside on another system that's accessible on your corporate network. The following formula refers to a cell in a workbook in the files directory of a computer named DataServer:

```
='\\DataServer\files\[budget.xlsx]Sheet1'!$D$7
```

 See Chapter 28, "Linking and Consolidating Worksheets," for more information about linking workbooks.

> **TIP**
>
> To create formulas that refer to cells in a different worksheet, point to the cells instead of entering their references manually. Excel takes care of the details regarding the workbook and worksheet references. The workbook you're referencing in your formula must be open if you're going to use the pointing method.

> **NOTE**
>
> If you point to a different worksheet or workbook when creating a formula, you'll notice that Excel always inserts absolute cell references. Therefore, if you plan to copy the formula to other cells, make sure that you change the cell references to relative before you copy.

Using Formulas in Tables

A table is a specially designated range of cells, set up with column headers. In this section, we describe how formulas work with tables.

 See Chapter 4, "Working with Excel Ranges and Tables" for an introduction to the Excel table features.

Summarizing data in a table

Figure 9.9 shows a simple table with three columns. We entered the data and then converted the range to a table by choosing Insert ⇨ Tables ⇨ Table. Note that we didn't define any names, but the table is named Table1 by default.

FIGURE 9.9

A simple table with three columns of information

	A	B	C	D
1				
2		Month	Projected	Actual
3		Jan	4,000	3,255
4		Feb	4,000	4,102
5		Mar	4,000	3,982
6		Apr	5,000	4,598
7		May	5,000	5,873
8		Jun	5,000	4,783
9		Jul	5,000	5,109
10		Aug	6,000	5,982
11		Sep	6,000	6,201
12		Oct	7,000	6,833
13		Nov	8,000	7,983
14		Dec	9,000	9,821
15				

 This workbook is available on this book's website at www.wiley.com/go/excel2019bible. It is named table formulas.xlsx.

If you'd like to calculate the total projected and total actual sales, you don't even need to write a formula. Simply click a button to add a row of summary formulas to the table:

1. **Activate any cell in the table.**

2. **Place a check mark next to Table Tools Design ⇨ Table Style Options ⇨ Total Row.** Excel adds a total row to the table and displays the sum of each numeric column.

3. **To change the type of summary formula, activate a cell in the total row and use the drop-down list to change the type of summary formula to use (see Figure 9.10).** For example, to calculate the average of the Actual column, select AVERAGE from the drop-down list in cell D15. Excel creates this formula:

   =SUBTOTAL(101,[Actual])

FIGURE 9.10

A drop-down list enables you to select a summary formula for a table column.

Month	Projected	Actual
Jan	4,000	3,255
Feb	4,000	4,102
Mar	4,000	3,982
Apr	5,000	4,598
May	5,000	5,873
Jun	5,000	4,783
Jul	5,000	5,109
Aug	6,000	5,982
Sep	6,000	6,201
Oct	7,000	6,833
Nov	8,000	7,983
Dec	9,000	9,821
Total	68,000	68,522

None
Average
Count
Count Numbers
Max
Min
Sum
StdDev
Var
More Functions...

For the SUBTOTAL function, 101 is an enumerated argument that represents AVERAGE. The second argument for the SUBTOTAL function is the column name in square brackets. Using the column name within brackets creates "structured" references within a table. (We discuss this further in the upcoming section "Referencing data in a table.")

NOTE
You can toggle the total row display via Table Tools Design ⇨ Table Style Options ⇨ Total Row. If you turn it off, the summary options you selected will be displayed again when you turn it back on.

Using formulas within a table

In many cases, you'll want to use formulas within a table to perform calculations that use other columns in the table. For example, in the table shown in Figure 9.10, you may want a column that shows the difference between the Actual and Projected amounts. To add this formula, follow these steps:

1. **Activate cell E2 and type Difference for the column header.** After you press Enter, Excel automatically expands the table for you to include the new column.

2. **Move to cell E3 and type an equal sign to signify the beginning of a formula.**

3. **Press the left arrow key.** Excel displays [@Actual], which is the column heading, in the Formula bar.

4. **Type a minus sign and then press the left arrow key twice.** Excel displays [@Projected] in your formula.

5. **Press Enter to end the formula.** Excel copies the formula to all rows in the table.

Figure 9.11 shows the table with the new column.

FIGURE 9.11

The Difference column contains a formula.

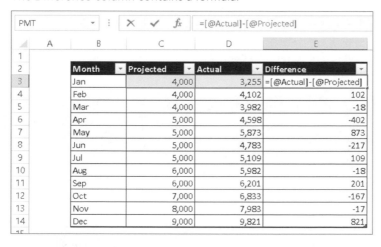

Examine the table, and you will find this formula for all cells in the Difference column:

    = [@Actual] - [@Projected]

Although the formula was entered into the first row of the table, that's not necessary. Any time a formula is entered into an empty table column, it will automatically fill all of the cells in that column. If you need to edit the formula, Excel will automatically copy the edited formula to the other cells in the column.

NOTE

The at symbol (@) that precedes the column header represents "this row." So `[@Actual]` means "the value in the Actual column in this row."

These steps use the pointing technique to create the formula. Alternatively, you could have entered the formula manually using standard cell references rather than column headers. For example, you could have entered the following formula in cell E3:

```
=D3-C3
```

If you type the cell references, Excel will still copy the formula to the other cells automatically.

One thing should be clear, however, about formulas that use the column headers instead of cell references—they're much easier to understand.

TIP

To override the automatic column formulas, access the Proofing tab of the Excel Options dialog box. Click AutoCorrect Options and then select the AutoFormat As You Type tab in the AutoCorrect dialog box. Remove the check mark from Fill Formulas in Tables to Create Calculated Columns.

Referencing data in a table

Excel offers some other ways to refer to data that's contained in a table by using the table name and column headers.

NOTE

Remember that you don't need to create names for tables and columns. The data in the table itself has a range name, which is created automatically when you create the table (for example, `Table1`), and you can refer to data within the table by using the column headers, which are not range names.

You can, of course, use standard cell references to refer to data in a table, but using the table name and column headers has a distinct advantage: the names adjust automatically if the table size changes by adding or deleting rows. In addition, formulas that use table names and column headers will adjust automatically if you change the name of the table or give a new name to a column.

Refer to the table shown in Figure 9.11. This table is named `Table1`. To calculate the sum of all of the data in the table, enter this formula into a cell outside the table:

```
=SUM(Table1)
```

This formula will return the sum of all of the data (excluding calculated total row values, if any), even if rows or columns are added or deleted. And if you change the name of `Table1`,

Excel will adjust formulas that refer to that table automatically. For example, if you renamed `Table1` to `AnnualData` (by using the Name Manager or by choosing Table Tools Design ⇨ Properties ⇨ Table Name), the preceding formula would change to

    =SUM(AnnualData)

Most of the time, a formula will refer to a specific column in the table. The following formula returns the sum of the data in the `Actual` column:

    =SUM(Table1[Actual])

Notice that the column name is enclosed in square brackets. Again, the formula adjusts automatically if you change the text in the column heading.

Even better, Excel provides some helpful assistance when you create a formula that refers to data within a table. Figure 9.12 shows the formula AutoComplete helping to create a formula by showing a list of the elements in the table. Notice that, in addition to the column headers in the table, Excel lists other table elements that you can reference: `#All`, `#Data`, `#Headers`, `#Totals`, and `@ - This Row`.

FIGURE 9.12

The formula AutoComplete feature is useful when creating a formula that refers to data in a table.

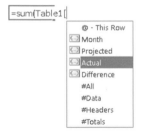

Correcting Common Formula Errors

Sometimes when you enter a formula, Excel displays a value that begins with a hash mark (#). This is a signal that the formula is returning an error value. You have to correct the formula (or correct a cell that the formula references) to get rid of the error display.

> **TIP**
>
> If the entire cell is filled with hash-mark characters, the column isn't wide enough to display the value. You can either widen the column or change the number format of the cell.

In some cases, Excel won't even let you enter an erroneous formula. For example, the following formula is missing the closing parenthesis:

```
=A1*(B1+C2
```

If you attempt to enter this formula, Excel informs you that you have unmatched parentheses, and it proposes a correction. Often, the proposed correction is accurate, but you can't count on it.

Table 9.3 lists the types of error values that may appear in a cell that has a formula. Formulas may return an error value if a cell to which they refer has an error value. This is known as the *ripple effect*—a single error value can make its way into lots of other cells that contain formulas that depend on that one cell.

TABLE 9.3 **Excel Error Values**

Error Value	Explanation
#DIV/0!	The formula is trying to divide by zero. Because Excel applies a value of 0 to empty cells, this error also occurs when the formula attempts to divide by a cell that is blank or has a value of 0.
#NAME?	The formula uses a name that Excel doesn't recognize. This can happen if you delete a name that's used in the formula, if you misspell a name and then hit Enter, or if you have unmatched quotes when using text.
#N/A	The formula is referring (directly or indirectly) to a cell that uses the NA function to signal that data is not available. For instance, the following formula returns an #N/A error if the A1 is empty: =IF(A1="", NA(), A1)
	Some lookup functions (for example, VLOOKUP and MATCH) can also return #N/A when they do not find a match.
#NULL!	The formula uses an intersection of two ranges that don't intersect. (This concept is described later in the chapter.)
#NUM!	A problem with a value exists; for example, you specified a negative number as an argument where a positive number is required.
#REF!	The formula refers to a cell that isn't valid. This can happen if the cell has been deleted from the worksheet.
#VALUE!	The formula includes an argument or operand of the wrong type. (An operand is a value or cell reference that a formula uses to calculate a result.)

Handling circular references

When you're entering formulas, you may occasionally see a warning message indicating that the formula you just entered will result in a circular reference. A *circular reference* occurs when a formula refers to its own cell—either directly or indirectly. For example, you create a circular reference if you enter =A1+A2+A3 into cell A3 because the formula in cell

A3 refers to cell A3. Every time the formula in A3 is calculated, it must be calculated again because A3 has changed. The calculation could go on forever.

When you get the circular reference message after entering a formula, Excel gives you two options:

- Click OK to enter the formula as is.
- Click Help to see a help screen about circular references.

Regardless of which option you choose, Excel displays a message on the left side of the status bar to remind you that a circular reference exists.

CAUTION

Excel won't tell you about a circular reference if the Enable Iterative Calculation setting is in effect. You can check this setting in the Formulas section of the Excel Options dialog box. If Enable Iterative Calculation is turned on, Excel performs the circular calculation exactly the number of times specified in the Maximum Iterations field (or until the value changes by less than 0.001 or whatever value is in the Maximum Change field). In a few situations, you may use a circular reference intentionally. In these cases, the Enable Iterative Calculation setting must be on. However, it's best to keep this setting turned off so that you're warned of circular references. Usually, a circular reference indicates an error that you must correct.

Often, a circular reference is quite obvious and easy to identify and correct. But when a circular reference is indirect (as when a formula refers to another formula that refers to yet another formula that refers to the original formula), it may require a bit of detective work to get to the problem.

Specifying when formulas are calculated

You've probably noticed that Excel calculates the formulas in your worksheet immediately. If you change any cells that the formula uses, Excel displays the formula's new result with no effort on your part. All of this happens when Excel's Calculation mode is set to Automatic. In Automatic Calculation mode (which is the default mode), Excel follows these rules when it calculates your worksheet:

- When you make a change—enter or edit data or formulas, for example—Excel calculates immediately those formulas that depend on new or edited data.
- If Excel is in the middle of a lengthy calculation, it temporarily suspends the calculation when you need to perform other worksheet tasks; it resumes calculating when you're finished with your other worksheet tasks.
- Formulas are evaluated in a natural sequence. In other words, if a formula in cell D12 depends on the result of a formula in cell D24, Excel calculates cell D24 before calculating cell D12.

Sometimes, however, you may want to control when Excel calculates formulas. For example, if you create a worksheet with thousands of complex formulas, you may find that processing can slow to a snail's pace while Excel does its thing. In such a case, set Excel's

9

calculation mode to Manual, which you can do by choosing Formulas ⇨ Calculation ⇨ Calculation Options ⇨ Manual.

> **TIP**
>
> If your worksheet uses any large data tables, you may want to select the Automatic Except for Data Tables option. Large data tables calculate notoriously slowly. A data table is not the same as a table created by choosing Insert ⇨ Tables ⇨ Table.

 See Chapter 31, "Performing Spreadsheet What-If Analysis," for more on data tables.

When you're working in Manual Calculation mode, Excel displays Calculate in the status bar when you have any uncalculated formulas. You can use the following shortcut keys to recalculate the formulas:

F9: Calculates the formulas in all open workbooks.

Shift+F9: Calculates only the formulas in the active worksheet. Other worksheets in the same workbook aren't calculated.

Ctrl+Alt+F9: Forces a complete recalculation of all formulas.

Ctrl+Alt+Shift+F9: Rebuilds the calculation dependency tree and performs a complete recalculation.

> **NOTE**
>
> Excel's Calculation mode isn't specific to a particular worksheet. When you change the Calculation mode, it affects all open workbooks, not just the active workbook.

Using Advanced Naming Techniques

Using range names can make your formulas easier to understand and modify and even help prevent errors. Dealing with a meaningful name such as AnnualSales is much easier than dealing with a range reference, such as AB12:AB68.

 See Chapter 4, "Working with Excel Ranges and Tables," for basic information regarding working with names.

Excel offers a number of advanced techniques that make using names even more useful. We discuss these techniques in the sections that follow. This information is for those who are interested in exploring some of the aspects of Excel that most users don't even know about.

Using names for constants

Many Excel users don't realize that you can give a name to an item that doesn't appear in a cell. For example, if formulas in your worksheet use a sales tax rate, you would probably insert the tax rate value into a cell and use this cell reference in your formulas. To make things easier, you would probably also name this cell something similar to `SalesTax`.

Here's how to provide a name for a value that doesn't appear in a cell:

1. **Choose Formulas ⇨ Defined Names ⇨ Define Name.** The New Name dialog box appears.
2. **Enter the name (in this case, `SalesTax`) into the Name field.**
3. **Select a scope in which the name will be valid (either the entire workbook or a specific worksheet).**
4. **Click the Refers To text box, delete its contents, and replace the old contents with a value (such as** `.075`**).**
5. **(Optional) Use the Comment box to provide a comment about the name.**
6. **Click OK to close the New Name dialog box and create the name.**

You just created a name that refers to a constant rather than a cell or range. Now if you type `=SalesTax` into a cell that's within the scope of the name, this simple formula returns `0.075`—the constant that you defined. You can also use this constant in a formula, such as `=A1*SalesTax`.

TIP

A constant also can be text. For example, you can define a constant for your company's name.

NOTE

Named constants don't appear in the Name box or in the Go To dialog box. This makes sense because these constants don't reside anywhere tangible. They do appear in the drop-down list that's displayed when you enter a formula. This is handy because you use these names in formulas.

Using names for formulas

In addition to creating named constants, you can create named formulas. Like a named constant, a named formula doesn't reside in a cell.

You create named formulas the same way that you create named constants—by using the New Name dialog box. For example, you might create a named formula that calculates the monthly interest rate from an annual rate; Figure 9.13 shows an example. In this case, the name `MonthlyRate` refers to the following formula:

```
=Sheet3!$B$1/12
```

FIGURE 9.13

Excel allows you to name a formula that doesn't exist in a worksheet cell.

When you use the name MonthlyRate in a formula, it uses the value in B1 divided by 12. Notice that the cell reference is an absolute reference.

Naming formulas gets more interesting when you use relative references rather than absolute references. When you use the pointing technique to create a formula in the Refers To field of the New Name dialog box, Excel always uses absolute cell references—which is unlike its behavior when you create a formula in a cell.

For example, activate cell B1 on Sheet1 and create the name Cubed for the following formula:

```
=Sheet1!A1^3
```

In this example, the relative reference points to the cell to the left of the cell in which the name is used. Therefore, make certain that cell B1 is the active cell before you open the New Name dialog box; this is important. The formula contains a relative reference. When you use this named formula in a worksheet, the cell reference is always relative to the cell that contains the formula. For example, if you enter **=Cubed** into cell D12, cell D12 displays the contents of cell C12 raised to the third power. (C12 is the cell directly to the left of cell D12.)

Using range intersections

This section describes a concept known as *range intersections* (individual cells that two ranges have in common). Excel uses an intersection operator—a space character—to determine the overlapping references in two ranges. Figure 9.14 shows a simple example.

The formula in cell B9 is

```
=C1:C6 A3:D3
```

This formula returns 13, the value in cell C3—that is, the value at the intersection of the two ranges.

The intersection operator is one of three reference operators used with ranges. Table 9.4 lists these operators.

FIGURE 9.14

You can use a range intersection formula to determine values.

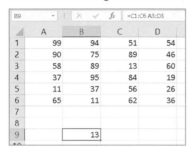

TABLE 9.4   Reference Operators for Ranges

Operator	What It Does
: (colon)	Specifies a range.
, (comma)	Specifies the union of two ranges. This operator combines multiple range references into a single reference.
Space	Specifies the intersection of two ranges. This operator produces cells that are common to two ranges.

The real value of knowing about range intersections is apparent when you use names. Examine Figure 9.15, which shows a table of values. We selected the entire table and then chose Formulas ⇨ Defined Names ⇨ Create from Selection to create names automatically by using the top row and the left column.

FIGURE 9.15

With names, using a range intersection formula to determine values is even more helpful.

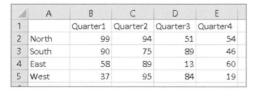

Excel created the following eight names:

North	=Sheet1!$B$2:$E$2	Quarter1	=Sheet1!$B$2:$B$5
South	=Sheet1!$B$3:$E$3	Quarter2	=Sheet1!$C$2:$C$5
West	=Sheet1!$B$4:$E$4	Quarter3	=Sheet1!$D$2:$D$5
East	=Sheet1!$B$5:$E$5	Quarter4	=Sheet1!$E$2:$E$5

With these names defined, you can create formulas that are easy to read and use. For example, to calculate the total for Quarter 4, just use this formula:

    =SUM(Quarter4)

To refer to a single cell, use the intersection operator. Move to any blank cell and enter the following formula:

    =Quarter1 West

This formula returns the value for the first quarter for the West region. In other words, it returns the value that exists where the Quarter1 range intersects with the West range. Naming ranges in this manner can help you create very readable formulas.

Applying names to existing references

When you create a name for a cell or a range, Excel doesn't automatically use the name in place of existing references in your formulas. For example, suppose you have the following formula in cell F10:

    =A1-A2

If you later define a name Income for A1 and Expenses for A2, Excel won't automatically change your formula to =Income-Expenses. Replacing cell or range references with their corresponding names is fairly easy, however.

To apply names to cell references in formulas after the fact, start by selecting the range that you want to modify. Then choose Formulas ➪ Defined Names ➪ Define Name ➪ Apply Names. The Apply Names dialog box appears. Select the names you want to apply by clicking them and then click OK. Excel replaces the range references with the names in the selected cells.

Working with Formulas

In this section, we offer a few additional tips and pointers relevant to formulas.

Not hard-coding values

When you create a formula, think twice before you use any specific value in the formula. For example, if your formula calculates sales tax (which is 6.5%), you may be tempted to enter a formula, such as the following:

    =A1*.065

A better approach is to insert the sales tax rate in a cell—and use the cell reference. Or you can define the tax rate as a named constant, using the technique presented earlier in this chapter. Doing so makes modifying and maintaining your worksheet easier. For example, if the sales tax rate changed to 6.75%, you would have to modify every formula that used the old value. If you store the tax rate in a cell, however, you simply change that one cell, and Excel updates all the formulas.

Using the Formula bar as a calculator

If you need to perform a quick calculation, you can use the Formula bar as a calculator. For example, enter the following formula but don't press Enter:

```
=(145*1.05)/12
```

If you press Enter, Excel enters the formula into the cell. But because this formula always returns the same result, you may prefer to store the formula's result rather than the formula itself. To do so, press F9 and watch the result appear in the Formula bar. Press Enter to store the result in the active cell. (This technique also works if the formula uses cell references or worksheet functions.)

Making an exact copy of a formula

When you copy a formula, Excel adjusts its cell references when you paste the formula to a different location. Sometimes you may want to make an exact copy of the formula. One way to do this is to convert the cell references to absolute values, but this isn't always desirable. A better approach is to select the formula in Edit mode and then copy it to the Clipboard as text. You can do this in several ways. Here's a step-by-step example of how to make an exact copy of the formula in A1 and copy it to A2:

1. **Double-click A1 (or press F2) to get into Edit mode.**
2. **Drag the mouse to select the entire formula.** You can drag from left to right or from right to left. To select the entire formula with the keyboard, press End, followed by Shift+Home.
3. **Choose Home ⇨ Clipboard ⇨ Copy (or press Ctrl+C).** This copies the selected text (which will become the copied formula) to the Clipboard.
4. **Press Esc to leave Edit mode.**
5. **Select cell A2.**
6. **Choose Home ⇨ Clipboard ⇨ Paste (or press Ctrl+V) to paste the text into cell A2.**

You can also use this technique to copy just part of a formula, if you want to use that part in another formula. Just select the part of the formula that you want to copy by dragging the mouse and then use any of the available techniques to copy the selection to the Clipboard. You can then paste the text to another cell.

Formulas (or parts of formulas) copied in this manner won't have their cell references adjusted when they're pasted into a new cell. That's because the formulas are being copied as text, not as actual formulas.

9

TIP

You can also convert a formula to text by adding an apostrophe (') in front of the equal sign. Then copy the cell as usual and paste it to its new location. Remove the apostrophe from the pasted formula, and it will be identical to the original formula. Don't forget to remove the apostrophe from the original formula.

Converting formulas to values

In certain scenarios, you may want to use formulas to get to an answer and then convert those formulas to actual values. For example, if you use the RANDBETWEEN function to create a set of random numbers and you don't want Excel to recalculate those random numbers each time you press Enter, you can convert the formulas to values. Just follow these steps:

1. **Select A1:A20.**
2. **Choose Home ⇨ Clipboard ⇨ Copy (or press Ctrl+C).**
3. **Choose Home ⇨ Clipboard ⇨ Paste Values (V).**
4. **Press Esc to cancel Copy mode.**

Using Formulas for Common Mathematical Operations

IN THIS CHAPTER

Calculating percentages

Rounding numbers

Counting values in a range

M ost Excel analysts working in the corporate world will be asked to perform mathematical operations that provide insight into key operational metrics. In this chapter, you'll get to explore a few mathematical operations commonly used in the world of business analytics.

Calculating Percentages

Calculations such as percent of totals, variance to budget, and running totals are the cornerstone of any basic business analysis. In this section, you'll explore some examples of formulas that will help with these types of analyses.

 This book's website, www.wiley.com/go/excel2019bible, includes a copy of the sample workbook for this chapter. The file is named Mathematical Formulas.xlsx.

Calculating percent of goal

When someone asks you to calculate a percent of goal, they are simply asking you to compare the actual performance against a stated goal. The math involved in this calculation is simple: divide the actual by the goal. This will give you a percentage value that represents how much of the goal has been achieved. For instance, if your goal is to sell 100 widgets and you sell 80 widgets, your percent of goal is 80% (80/100).

Figure 10.1 shows a list of regions with a column for goals and a column for actuals. Note that the formula in cell E5 simply divides the value in the Actual column by the value in the Goal column.

    =D5/C5

FIGURE 10.1

Calculating the percent of goal

	A	B	C	D	E
1					
2					
3					
4		Region	Goal	Actual	Percent of Goal
5		North	$509,283	$553,887	=D5/C5
6		South	$483,519	$511,115	106%
7		East	$640,603	$606,603	95%
8		West	$320,312	$382,753	119%

There isn't much to this formula. You're simply using cell references to divide one value by another. You can enter the formula one time in the first row (cell E5 in this case) and then copy that formula down to every other row in your table.

Alternatively, if you need to compare actuals to a common goal, you can set up a model like the one shown in Figure 10.2. In this model, each region does not have its own goal. Instead, you're comparing the values in the Actual column to a single goal found in cell B3.

    =C6/$B$3

FIGURE 10.2

Calculating the percent of goal using a common goal

	A	B	C	D
1				
2		Common Goal		
3		$700,000		
4				
5		Region	Actual	Percent of Goal
6		North	$553,887	=C6/$B$3
7		South	$511,115	73%
8		East	$606,603	87%
9		West	$382,753	55%

Note that the cell reference to the common goal is entered as an absolute reference ($B$3). Using the dollar symbols locks the reference to the goal in place, ensuring that the cell reference pointing to the common goal does not adjust as you copy the formula down.

See Chapter 9, "Introducing Formulas and Functions," for more information on absolute and relative cell references.

Calculating percent variance

A *variance* is an indicator of the difference between one number and another. To understand this, imagine that you sold 120 widgets one day, and on the next day, you sold 150 widgets. The difference in sales in actual terms is easy to see; you sold 30 more widgets on the second day. 150 widgets minus 120 widgets gives you a unit variance of +30.

So, what is a percent variance? This is essentially the percentage difference between the benchmark number (120) and the new number (150). You calculate the percent variance by subtracting the benchmark number from the new number and then dividing that result by the benchmark number. In this example, (150-120)/120 = 25%. The percent variance tells us that you sold 25% more widgets than on the previous day.

Figure 10.3 demonstrates how to translate this into a formula. The formula in E4 calculates the percent variance between current year sales and previous year sales.

    =(D4-C4)/C4

FIGURE 10.3

Calculating the percent variance between current year sales and previous year sales

	A	B	C	D	E
1					
2					
3		Region	Prior Year	Current Year	Percent Variance
4		North	$509,283	$553,887	=(D4-C4)/C4
5		South	$483,519	$511,115	6%
6		East	$640,603	$606,603	-5%
7		West	$320,312	$382,753	19%

The one thing to note about this formula is the use of parentheses. By default, Excel's order of operations states that division must be done before subtraction. But if we let that happen, we would get an erroneous result. Wrapping the first part of the formula in parentheses ensures that Excel performs subtraction before the division.

You can simply enter the formula one time in the first row (cell E4 in this case) and then copy that formula down to every other row in your table.

 See Chapter 9, "Introducing Formulas and Functions," for a detailed explanation of the order of operator precedence.

An alternative formula for calculating percent variance is simply to divide the current year sales by the previous year sales and then subtract 1. Because Excel performs division operations before subtraction, you don't have to use parentheses with this alternative formula.

    =D4/C4-1

10

Calculating percent variance with negative values

In the previous section, "Calculating percent variance," you discovered how to calculate a percent variance. This works beautifully in most cases. However, when the benchmark value is a zero or less, the formula breaks down.

For example, imagine you're starting a business and expect to take a loss during the first year. So, you give yourself a budget of negative $10,000. Now imagine that after your first year, you actually made money, earning $12,000. Calculating the percent variance between your actual revenue and budgeted revenue would give you –220%. You can try it on a calculator. 12,000 minus –10,000 divided by –10,000 equals –220%.

How can you say that your percent variance is –220% when you clearly made money? Well, the problem is that when your benchmark value is a negative number, the math inverts the results, causing numbers to look wacky. This is a real problem in the corporate world, where budgets can often be negative values.

The fix is to leverage the ABS function to negate the negative benchmark value:

```
=(C4-B4)/ABS(B4)
```

Figure 10.4 uses this formula in cell E4, illustrating the different results you get when using the standard percent variance formula and the improved percent variance formula.

FIGURE 10.4

Using the ABS function will give you an accurate percent variance when dealing with negative values.

◢	A	B	C	D	E
1					
2					
3		Budget	Actual	Standard Percent Variance	Improved Percent Variance
4		-10,000	12,000	-220%	220%

Excel's ABS function returns the absolute value for any number you pass to it. Entering =ABS(-100) into cell A1 would return 100. The ABS function essentially makes any number a non-negative number. Using ABS in this formula negates the effect of the negative benchmark (the negative 10,000 budget in our example) and returns the correct percent variance.

> **TIP**
>
> You can use safely use this formula for all of your percent variance needs because it works with any combination of positive and negative numbers.

Calculating a percent distribution

Percent distribution is a measure of how a metric (such as total revenue) is distributed among the component parts that make up the total. As you can see in Figure 10.5, the calculation is relatively simple. You divide each component part by the total. In this example, we have a cell that contains the total revenue (cell C9). We then divide each region's revenue by the total to get a percent distribution for each region.

FIGURE 10.5

Calculating a percent distribution of revenue across regions

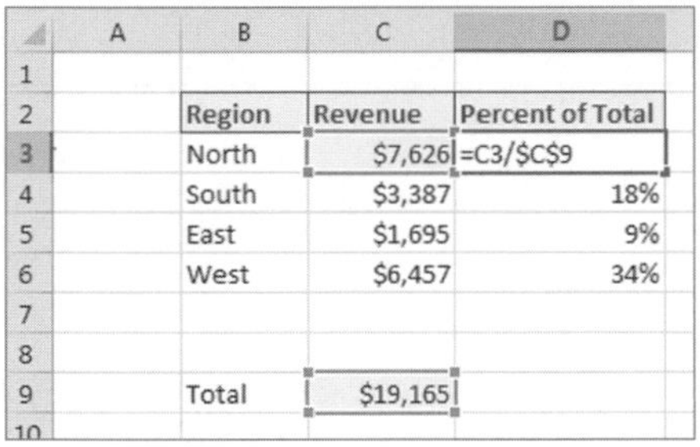

	A	B	C	D
1				
2		Region	Revenue	Percent of Total
3		North	$7,626	=C3/$C$9
4		South	$3,387	18%
5		East	$1,695	9%
6		West	$6,457	34%
7				
8				
9		Total	$19,165	
10				

There isn't much to this formula. You're simply using cell references to divide each component value by the total. The one thing to note is that the cell reference to the total is entered as an absolute reference ($C$9). Using the dollar symbols locks the reference in place, ensuring that the cell reference pointing to the total value does not adjust as you copy the formula down.

You don't have to dedicate a separate cell to an actual total value. You can simply calculate the total on the fly within the percent distribution formula. Figure 10.6 demonstrates how you can use the SUM function in place of a cell dedicated to holding a total value. The SUM function adds together any numbers you pass to it.

FIGURE 10.6

Calculating percent distribution with the SUM function

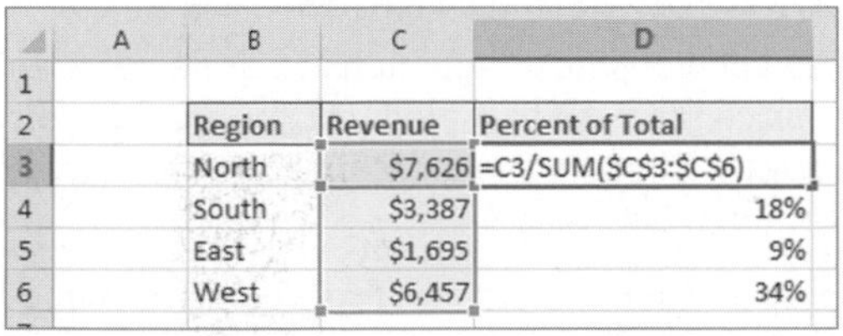

	A	B	C	D
1				
2		Region	Revenue	Percent of Total
3		North	$7,626	=C3/SUM($C$3:$C$6)
4		South	$3,387	18%
5		East	$1,695	9%
6		West	$6,457	34%

Again, note the use of absolute references in the SUM function. This ensures that the SUM range stays locked as you copy the formula down.

```
=C3/SUM($C$3:$C$6)
```

Calculating a running total

Some organizations like to see a running total as a mechanism to analyze the changes in a metric as a period of time progresses. Figure 10.7 illustrates a running total of units sold for January through December. The formula used in cell D3 is copied down to each month.

```
=SUM($C$3:C3)
```

FIGURE 10.7

Calculating a running total

▲	A	B	C	D
1				
2			Units Sold	Running Total
3		January	78	=SUM($C$3:C3)
4		February	63	141
5		March	38	179
6		April	17	196
7		May	84	280
8		June	63	343
9		July	32	375
10		August	20	395
11		September	98	493
12		October	63	556
13		November	75	631
14		December	75	706

In this formula, the SUM function is used to add up all of the units from cell C3 to the current row. The trick to this formula is the absolute reference ($C$3). Placing an absolute reference in the reference for the first value of the year locks that value down. This ensures that as the formula is copied down, the SUM function will always capture and add the units from the first value to the value on the current row.

Applying a percent increase or decrease to values

A common task for an Excel analyst is to apply a percentage increase or decrease to a given number. For instance, when applying a price increase to a product, you would typically raise the original price by a certain percent. When giving a customer a discount, you would decrease that customer's rate by a certain percent.

Figure 10.8 illustrates how to apply a percent increase and decrease using a simple formula. In cell E5, we're applying a 10% price increase to Product A. In cell E9, we're giving a 20% discount to Customer A.

FIGURE 10.8

Applying a percent increase and decrease using a simple formula

	A	B	C	D	E
1					
2					
3					
4			Unit Cost	Price Increase	Final Price
5		Product A	100	10%	=C5*(1+D5)
6					
7					
7					
8			Cost per Service	Percent Discount	Discounted Cost
9		Customer A	1000	20%	=C9*(1-D9)

To increase a number by a percentage amount, multiply the original amount by 1 plus the percent of increase. In the example in Figure 10.8, Product A is getting a 10% increase. So, we first add 1 to the 10%. This gives us 110%. We then multiply the original price of 100 by 110%. This calculates to the new price of 110.

To decrease a number by a percentage amount, multiply the original amount by 1, which is the percent discount. In the example in Figure 10.8, Customer A is getting a 20% discount. So, we first subtract 20% from 1. This gives us 80%. We then multiply the original 1000 cost per service by 80%. This calculates to the new rate of 800.

Note the use of parentheses in the formulas. By default, Excel's order of operations states that multiplication must be done before addition or subtraction. But if we let that happen, we would get an erroneous result. Wrapping the second part of the formula in parentheses ensures that Excel performs the multiplication last.

Dealing with divide-by-zero errors

In mathematics, division by zero is impossible. One way to understand why it's impossible is to consider what happens when you divide a number by another.

Division is really nothing more than fancy subtraction. For example, 10 divided by 2 is the same as starting with 10 and continuously subtracting 2 as many times as needed to get to zero. In this case, you would need to continuously subtract 2 five times.

$$10 - 2 = 8$$
$$8 - 2 = 6$$
$$6 - 2 = 4$$
$$4 - 2 = 2$$
$$2 - 2 = 0$$

So, 10/2 = 5.

Now if you tried to do this with 10 divided by 0, you would never get anywhere because 10 − 0 is 10 all day long. You'd be sitting there subtracting 0 until your calculator dies.

10

$$10 - 0 = 10$$
$$10 - 0 = 10$$
$$10 - 0 = 10$$
$$10 - 0 = 10$$
...infinity

Mathematicians call the result you get when dividing any number by zero *undefined*. Software like Excel simply gives you an error when you try to divide by zero. In Excel, when you divide a number by zero, you get the #DIV/0! error.

You can avoid this by telling Excel to skip the calculation if your denominator is a zero. Figure 10.9 illustrates how to do this by wrapping the division operation in Excel's IF function.

    =IF(C4=0, 0, D4/C4)

FIGURE 10.9

Using the IF function to avoid a division-by-zero error

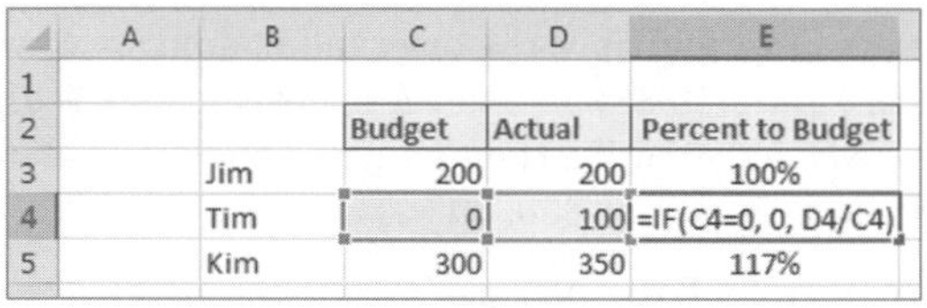

▲	A	B	C	D	E
1					
2			Budget	Actual	Percent to Budget
3		Jim	200	200	100%
4		Tim	0	100	=IF(C4=0, 0, D4/C4)
5		Kim	300	350	117%

The IF function has three arguments: the condition, what to do if the condition is true, and what to do if the condition is false.

The condition argument in this example is that the budget in C4 is equal to zero (C4 0). Condition arguments must be structured to return TRUE or FALSE, which usually means there is a comparison operation (such as an equal sign or greater-than sign) or another worksheet function that returns TRUE of FALSE (like ISERR or ISBLANK).

If our condition argument returns TRUE, the second argument of the IF function is returned to the cell. Our second argument is 0, meaning that we simply want a zero displayed if the budget number in cell C4 is a zero.

If the condition argument is not zero, the third argument takes effect. In our third argument, we tell Excel to perform the division calculation (D4/C4).

So, this formula basically says if C4 equals 0, then return a 0; otherwise, return the result of D4/C4.

Rounding Numbers

Oftentimes, your customers will want to look at clean, round numbers. Inundating a user with decimal values and unnecessary digits for the sake of precision can actually make your reports harder to read. For this reason, you may consider using Excel's rounding functions.

In this section, you'll explore some of the techniques that you can leverage to apply rounding to your calculations.

Rounding numbers using formulas

Excel's ROUND function is used to round a given number to a specified number of digits. The ROUND function takes two arguments: the original value and number of digits to round to.

Passing 0 as the second argument tells Excel to remove all decimal places and round the integer portion of the number based on the first decimal place. For instance, this formula rounds to 94:

```
=ROUND(94.45,0)
```

Passing a 1 as the second argument tells Excel to round to one decimal based on the value of the second decimal place. For example, this formula rounds to 94.5:

```
=ROUND(94.45,1)
```

You can also pass a negative number to the second argument, telling Excel to round based on values to the left of the decimal point. The following formula, for example, returns 90:

```
=ROUND(94.45,-1)
```

You can force rounding in a particular direction using the ROUNDUP or ROUNDDOWN function.

This ROUNDDOWN formula rounds 94.45 down to 94:

```
=ROUNDDOWN(94.45,0)
```

This ROUNDUP formula rounds 94.45 up to 95:

```
=ROUNDUP(94.45,0)
```

Rounding to the nearest penny

In some industries, it is common practice to round a dollar amount to the nearest penny. Figure 10.10 demonstrates how rounding a dollar amount up or down to the nearest penny can affect the resulting number.

10

FIGURE 10.10

Rounding to the nearest penny

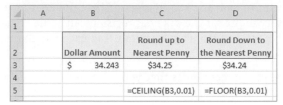

	A	B	C	D
1				
2		Dollar Amount	Round up to Nearest Penny	Round Down to the Nearest Penny
3		$ 34.243	$34.25	$34.24
4				
5			=CEILING(B3,0.01)	=FLOOR(B3,0.01)

You can round to the nearest penny by using the CEILING or FLOOR function.

The CEILING function will round a number up to the nearest multiple of significance that you pass to it. This comes in handy when you need to override the standard rounding protocol with your own business rules. For instance, you can force Excel to round 123.222 to 124 by using the CEILING function with a significance of 1.

```
=CEILING(123.222,1)
```

So, passing a .01 as the significance tells the CEILING function to round up to the nearest penny.

If you wanted to round up to the nearest nickel, you can use .05 as the significance. For instance, the following formula returns 123.15:

```
=CEILING(123.11,.05)
```

The FLOOR function works the same way except it forces a rounding down to the nearest significance. The following example function rounds 123.19 down to the nearest nickel, giving you 123.15 as the result:

```
=FLOOR(123.19,.05)
```

Rounding to significant digits

In some financial reports, figures are presented in significant digits. The idea is that when you're dealing with numbers in the millions, there is no need to inundate a report with superfluous numbers for the sake of showing precision down to the tens, hundreds, and thousands place.

For instance, instead of showing the number 883,788, you could choose to round the number to one significant digit. This would mean displaying the same number as 900,000. Rounding 883,788 to two significant digits would show the number as 880,000.

In essence, you're deeming that a particular number's place is significant enough to show. The rest of the number can be replaced with zeros. This may feel like it could introduce problems, but when dealing with large enough numbers, any number below a certain significance would be inconsequential.

Figure 10.11 demonstrates how you can implement a formula that rounds numbers to a given number of significant digits.

FIGURE 10.11

Rounding numbers to one significant digit

	A	B	C	D	E
1					
2					Significant Digits
3					1
4		Raw Number	Significant Digits		
5		605,390	=ROUND(B5,LEN(INT(ABS(B5)))*-1+$E$3)		
6		900,942	900,000		
7		591,007	600,000		
8		491,235	500,000		
9		883,788	900,000		
10		952,687	1,000,000		
11		(332,602)	-300,000		

Let's take a moment to see how this works.

Excel's ROUND function is used to round a given number to a specified number of digits. The ROUND function takes two arguments: the original value and number of digits to round to.

Passing a negative number to the second argument tells Excel to round based on significant digits to the left of the decimal point. The following formula, for example, returns 9500:

```
=ROUND(9489,-2)
```

Changing the significant digits argument to –3 will return a value of 9000.

```
=ROUND(9489,-3)
```

This works great, except what if we have numbers on differing scales? That is to say, what if some of our numbers are millions while others are hundreds of thousands? If we wanted to display all of our numbers in one significant digit, we would need to build a different ROUND function for each number to account for the differing significant digits argument that we would need for each type of number.

To help solve this, we can replace our hard-coded significant digits argument with a formula that calculates what that number should be.

Imagine that our number is –2330.45. We can use this formula as the significant digits argument in our ROUND function:

```
LEN(INT(ABS(-2330.45)))*-1+2
```

This formula first wraps our number within the ABS function, effectively removing any negative symbol that may exist. It then wraps that result in the INT function, stripping

10

out any decimals that may exist. Finally, it wraps that result in the LEN function to get a measure of how many digits are in the number without any decimals or negation symbols.

In the example, this part of the formula results in 4. If you take the number –2330.45 and strip away the decimals and negative symbol, you have four digits left.

This number is then multiplied by –1 to make it a negative number, and it is then added to the number of significant digits we are seeking. In this example, 4*-1+2 = –2.

Again, this formula will be used as the second argument for our ROUND function. Enter this formula into Excel, and you'll round this number to –2300 (two significant digits).

```
=ROUND(-2330.45,LEN(INT(ABS(-2330.45)))*-1+2)
```

You can then replace this formula with cell references that point to the source number and cell that holds the number of desired significant digits. This what you saw in Figure 10.11.

```
=ROUND(B5,LEN(INT(ABS(B5)))*-1+$E$3)
```

Counting Values in a Range

Excel provides several functions to count the values in a range: COUNT, COUNTA, and COUNTBLANK. Each of these functions provides a different method of counting based on whether the values are numbers, numbers and text, or blank.

Figure 10.12 illustrates the different kinds of counting that you can perform. In row 12, we are using the COUNT function to count only the exams where students have passed. In column H, we are using the COUNTA function to count all of the exams taken by a student. In column I, we are using the COUNTBLANK function to count only those exams that have not yet been taken.

FIGURE 10.12

A demonstration of counting cells

	Math	English	Science	History	Exams Taken By Each Student	Exams Remaining
Student 1	Fail		1		2	2
Student 2	1	1	1		3	1
Student 3		1	1	1	3	1
Student 4	Fail		Fail		2	2
Student 5	1	1	1	Fail	4	0

How many students passed each exam.			
Math	English	Art	History
2	3	4	1

The COUNT function will count only numeric values in a given range. It requires only a single argument where you pass a range of cells. For example, this formula will count only those cells in range C4:C8 that contain a numeric value:

```
=COUNT(C4:C8)
```

The COUNTA function will count any cell that is not blank. This function can be used when counting cells that contain any combination of numbers and text. It requires only a single argument where you pass a range of cells. For instance, this formula will count all of the nonblank cells in range C4:F4:

```
=COUNTA(C4:F4)
```

The COUNTBLANK function will count only the blank cells in a given range. It requires only a single argument where you pass a range of cells. For instance, this formula will count all of the blank cells in range C4:F4:

```
=COUNTBLANK(C4:F4)
```

Using Excel's Conversion Functions

You may work at a company where it's important to know how many cubic yards can be covered by a gallon of material or how many cups are needed to fill an Imperial gallon.

You can use Excel's CONVERT function to produce a conversion table containing every possible type of conversion you need for a set of measures. Figure 10.13 illustrates a conversion table created using nothing but Excel's CONVERT function.

FIGURE 10.13

Creating a unit-of-measure conversion table

	C	D	E	F	G	H	I
1							
2				Teaspoon	Tablespoon	Fluid ounce	Cup
3				tsp	tbs	oz	cup
4		Teaspoon	tsp	=CONVERT(1,$E4,F$3)	0.33	0.17	0.02
5		Tablespoon	tbs	3.00	1.00	0.50	0.06
6		Fluid ounce	oz	6.00	2.00	1.00	0.13
7		Cup	cup	48.00	16.00	8.00	1.00
8		U.S. pint	us_pt	96.00	32.00	16.00	2.00
9		U.K. pint	uk_pt	115.29	38.43	19.22	2.40
10		Quart	qt	192.00	64.00	32.00	4.00
11		Imperial quart	uk_qt	230.58	76.86	38.43	4.80
12		Gallon gal	gal	768.00	256.00	128.00	16.00

10

With this table, you can get a quick view of the conversions from one unit of measure to another. You can see that it takes 48 teaspoons to make a cup, 2.4 cups to make an English pint, and so forth.

The CONVERT function requires three arguments: a number value, the unit you're converting from, and the unit you're converting to. For instance, to convert 100 miles into kilometers, you can enter this formula to get the answer 160.93:

```
=CONVERT(100,"mi",  "km")
```

You can use the following formula to convert 100 gallons into liters. This will give you the result 378.54.

```
=CONVERT(100,"gal",  "l")
```

You'll notice the conversion codes for each unit of measure. These codes are specific and must be entered exactly how Excel expects to see them. Entering a CONVERT formula using gallon or GAL instead of the expected gal will return an error.

Luckily, Excel provides a tooltip as you start entering your CONVERT function, letting you pick the correct unit codes from a list.

You can refer to Excel's help files on the CONVERT function to get a list of valid units of measure conversion codes.

Once you have the codes in which you are interested, you can enter them in a matrix-style table like the one you saw in Figure 10.13. In the top-left cell in your matrix, enter a formula that points to the appropriate conversion code for the matrix row and matrix column.

Be sure to include the absolute references necessary to lock the references to the conversion codes. For the codes located in the matrix row, lock to the column reference. For the codes located in matrix column, lock the row reference.

```
=CONVERT(1,$E4,F$3)
```

At this point, you can simply copy your formula across the entire matrix.

CHAPTER
11

Using Formulas to Manipulate Text

IN THIS CHAPTER

Seeing how Excel handles text entered into cells

Exploring Excel worksheet functions that handle text

Getting examples of advanced text formulas

Oftentimes, the work you do with Excel not only involves calculating numbers but also includes transforming and shaping data to fit your data models. Many of these activities include manipulating text strings. This chapter will highlight some of the common text transformation exercises an Excel analyst performs and in the process give you a sense of some of the text-based functions that Excel has to offer.

Working with Text

When you enter data into a cell, Excel immediately goes to work and determines whether you're entering a formula, a number (including a date or time), or anything else. That "anything else" is considered text.

> **NOTE**
> You may hear the term *string* used instead of *text*. You can use these terms interchangeably. Sometimes they even appear together, as in *text string*.

A single cell can hold up to 32,000 characters—more than the number of characters in this chapter.

But Excel is not a word processor, and there's no reason why anyone would need to come even close to that number of characters in a cell.

If you need to display lots of text in a worksheet, consider using a text box. Choose Insert ⇨ Text ⇨ Text Box, click the worksheet to create the text box, and then start typing. Working with large amounts of text in a text box is easier than editing cells. In addition, you can easily move, resize, or change the dimensions of a text box. However, if you need to work with the text using formulas and functions, the text must reside in cells.

When a Number Isn't Treated as a Number

If you import data into Excel, you may be aware of a common problem: sometimes the imported values are treated as text.

Depending on your error-checking settings, Excel may display error indicators to identify numbers stored as text. An error indicator appears as a green triangle in the upper-left corner of cells. In addition, an icon appears next to the cell. Activate the cell and click the icon, which expands to show a list of options. To force the number to be treated as an actual number, select Convert to Number from the list of options.

To control which error-checking rules are in effect, choose File ⇨ Options and then select the Formulas tab. You can enable any or all of the nine error types listed under Error Checking Rules.

Here's another way to convert these non-numbers to actual values. Activate any empty cell and choose Home ⇨ Clipboard ⇨ Copy (or press Ctrl+C). Then select the range that contains the values you need to fix. Choose Home ⇨ Clipboard ⇨ Paste Special. In the Paste Special dialog box, select the Add operation and then click OK. This procedure essentially adds zero to each cell—and, in the process, forces Excel to treat the non-numbers as actual values.

Using Text Functions

Excel has an excellent assortment of worksheet functions that can handle text. You can access these functions just where you'd expect: from the Text control in the Function Library group of the Formulas tab.

Many of the text functions are not limited to text: They can also operate with cells that contain numeric values. You'll find that Excel is very accommodating when it comes to treatinq numbers as text.

The examples discussed in this section demonstrate some common (and useful) things you can do with text. You may need to adapt some of these examples for your own use.

 This book's website, www.wiley.com/go/excel2019bible, includes a copy of the sample workbook for this chapter. The file is named Text Formulas.xlsx.

Joining text strings

One of the more basic text manipulation actions that you can do is joining text strings together. In the example shown in Figure 11.1, we are creating a full name column by joining together first and last names.

FIGURE 11.1

Joining first and last names

	A	B	C	D
1				
2		FirstName	LastName	Full Name
3		Guy	Gilbert	=B3&" "&C3
4		Kevin	Brown	Kevin Brown
5		Roberto	Tamburello	Roberto Tamburello
6		Rob	Walters	Rob Walters
7		Thierry	Alexander	Thierry Alexander
8		David	Bradley	David Bradley
9		JoLynn	Dobney	JoLynn Dobney
10		Ruth	Ellerbrock	Ruth Ellerbrock
11		Doris	Hartwig	Doris Hartwig
12		John	Campbell	John Campbell

This example illustrates the use of the ampersand (&) operator. The ampersand operator tells Excel to concatenate values with one another. As you can see in Figure 11.1, you can join cell values with text of your own. In this example, we are joining the values in cells B3 and C3 separated by a space (created by entering a space in quotes).

Excel 2019 introduces the new TEXTJOIN function to provide an easier way to handle more complex scenarios. This new function requires just a few arguments:

```
TEXTJOIN(delimiter,ignore_empty_values,text)
```

The first argument is the character that you want placed between the cells that you are joining. If you type a comma as the "delimiter," the function will place a comma between the joined values.

The second argument determines what to do when Excel encounters an empty cell. You can either set this argument to TRUE, telling Excel to ignore empty cells, or set it to FALSE. The best way to think about this argument is how you want Excel to place your chosen delimiter. Setting this argument to TRUE will ensure that Excel does not add extra commas between your joined text because of blank cells in the selected range.

The third argument is the text to be joined. This can be a simple text string, or it can be an array of strings like a range of cells. The TEXTJOIN function requires as least one value or cell reference in this argument.

Figure 11.2 demonstrates how you can use the TEXTJOIN function to easily pull together the first name, last name, and middle initial for each person in the table.

FIGURE 11.2

Using the TEXTJOIN function

	A	B	C	D	E
13					
14					
15		FirstName	Middle Initial	LastName	TEXTJOIN
16		Guy	H.	Gilbert	=TEXTJOIN(" ",TRUE,B16:D16)
17		Kevin	P.	Brown	Kevin P. Brown
18		Roberto	B.	Tamburello	Roberto B. Tamburello
19		Rob	A.	Walters	Rob A. Walters
20		Thierry	D.	Alexander	Thierry D. Alexander
21		David		Bradley	David Bradley
22		JoLynn		Dobney	JoLynn Dobney
23		Ruth	T.	Ellerbrock	Ruth T. Ellerbrock
24		Doris	W.	Hartwig	Doris W. Hartwig
25		John		Campbell	John Campbell

Setting text to sentence case

Excel provides three useful functions to change the text to upper, lower, or proper case. As you can see in rows 6, 7, and 8 illustrated in Figure 11.3, these functions require nothing more than a pointer to the text that you want to be converted. As you might guess, the UPPER function converts text to all uppercase, the LOWER function converts text to all lowercase, and the PROPER function converts text to title case (the first letter of every word is capitalized).

FIGURE 11.3

Converting text into upper, lower, proper, and sentence case

	A	B	C
1			
3			
4			The QUICK brown FOX JUMPS over the lazy DOG.
5			
6		=UPPER(C6)	THE QUICK BROWN FOX JUMPS OVER THE LAZY DOG.
7		=LOWER(C7)	the quick brown fox jumps over the lazy dog.
8		=PROPER(C8)	The Quick Brown Fox Jumps Over The Lazy Dog.
9			
10		=UPPER(LEFT(C4,1))&LOWER(RIGHT(C4,LEN(C4)-1))	The quick brown fox jumps over the lazy dog.

What Excel lacks is a function to convert text to sentence case (where only the first letter of the first word is capitalized). But as you can see in Figure 11.3, you can use the following formula to force text into sentence case:

    =UPPER(LEFT(C4,1))&LOWER(RIGHT(C4,LEN(C4)-1))

If you take a look at this formula closely, you can see that it's made up of two parts that are joined by the ampersand.

The first part uses Excel's LEFT function.

```
UPPER(LEFT(C4,1))
```

The LEFT function allows you to extract a given number of characters from the left of a given text string. The LEFT function requires two arguments: the text string you are evaluating and the number of characters you need to be extracted from the left of the text string. In this case, we are extracting the left one character from the text in cell C4. We are then making it uppercase by wrapping it in the UPPER function.

The second part is a bit trickier. Here we are using Excel's RIGHT function:

```
LOWER(RIGHT(C4,LEN(C4)-1))
```

Like the LEFT function, the RIGHT function requires two arguments: the text you are evaluating and the number of characters you need to be extracted from the right of the text string. In this case, however, we can't just give the RIGHT function a hard-coded number for the second argument. We have to calculate that number by subtracting 1 from the entire length of the text string. We subtract 1 to account for the first character, which is already uppercase thanks to the first part of the formula.

The LEN function is used to get the entire length of the text string. We subtract 1 from that, and we have the number of characters needed for our RIGHT function.

We can finally pass all of that to the LOWER function to make everything but the first character lowercase.

Joining the two parts together gives us our sentence case:

```
=UPPER(LEFT(C4,1))&LOWER(RIGHT(C4,LEN(C4)-1))
```

Removing spaces from a text string

If you pull data in from external databases and legacy systems, you will no doubt encounter text that contains extra spaces. Sometimes these extra spaces are found at the beginning of the text, at the end of the text, or even between text strings (as in cell B6 shown in Figure 11.4).

Extra spaces are generally evil because they can cause problems in lookup formulas, charting, column sizing, and printing.

Figure 11.4 illustrates how you can remove superfluous spaces by using the TRIM function.

FIGURE 11.4

Removing excess spaces from text

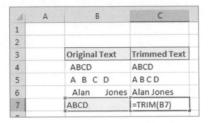

The TRIM function is relatively straightforward. Simply give it some text and it will remove all spaces from the text except for single spaces between words.

As with other functions, you can nest the TRIM function in other functions to clean up your text while applying some other manipulation. For instance, this function trims the text in cell A1 and converts it to uppercase all in one step:

```
=UPPER(TRIM(A1))
```

It's important to note that the TRIM function was designed to trim only the ASCII space character from text. The ASCII space character has a code value of 32. In the Unicode character set, however, there is an additional space character called the *nonbreaking space character*. This character is commonly used in web pages and has the Unicode value of 160.

The TRIM function is designed to handle only CHAR(32) space characters. It cannot, by itself, handle CHAR(160) space characters. To handle this kind of space, you'll need to utilize the SUBSTITUTE function to find CHAR(160) space characters and replace them with CHAR(32) space characters so that the TRIM function can fix them. You can accomplish this all at one time in the following formula:

```
=TRIM(SUBSTITUTE(A4,CHAR(160),CHAR(32)))
```

For a detailed look at the SUBSTITUTE function, see the section "Substituting text strings" in this chapter.

Extracting parts of a text string

One of the most important techniques for manipulating text in Excel is the ability to extract specific portions of text. Using Excel's LEFT, RIGHT, and MID functions, you can do things like this:

- Convert nine-digit postal codes into five-digit postal codes
- Extract phone numbers without the area code
- Extract parts of employee or job codes for use somewhere else

Figure 11.5 demonstrates how using the LEFT, RIGHT, and MID functions can help easily accomplish these tasks.

FIGURE 11.5

Using the LEFT, RIGHT, and MID functions

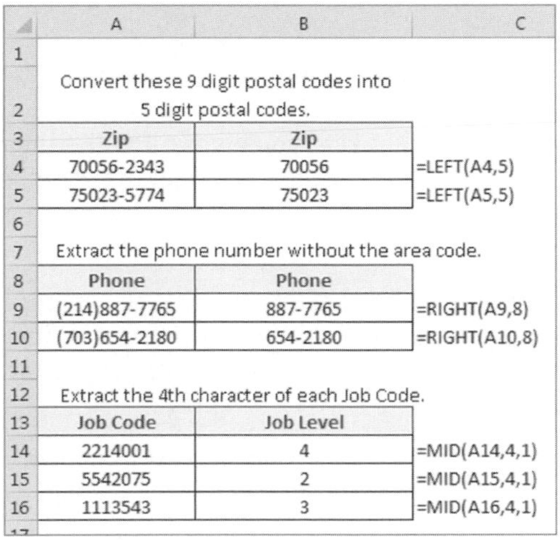

▲	A	B	C
1			
2	Convert these 9 digit postal codes into 5 digit postal codes.		
3	Zip	Zip	
4	70056-2343	70056	=LEFT(A4,5)
5	75023-5774	75023	=LEFT(A5,5)
6			
7	Extract the phone number without the area code.		
8	Phone	Phone	
9	(214)887-7765	887-7765	=RIGHT(A9,8)
10	(703)654-2180	654-2180	=RIGHT(A10,8)
11			
12	Extract the 4th character of each Job Code.		
13	Job Code	Job Level	
14	2214001	4	=MID(A14,4,1)
15	5542075	2	=MID(A15,4,1)
16	1113543	3	=MID(A16,4,1)

The LEFT function allows you to extract a given number of characters from the left of a given text string. The LEFT function requires two arguments: the text you are evaluating and the number of characters you need to be extracted from the left of the text string. In this example, we are extracting the left five characters from the value in cell A4:

=LEFT(A4,5)

The RIGHT function allows you to extract a given number of characters from the right of a given text string. The RIGHT function requires two arguments: the text string you are evaluating and the number of characters you need to be extracted from the right of the text string. In this example, we are extracting the right eight characters from the value in cell A9:

=RIGHT(A9,8)

The MID function allows you to extract a given number of characters from the middle of a given text string. The MID function requires three arguments: the text string you are evaluating, the character position in the text string from where to start the extraction, and the number of characters you need to be extracted. In this example, we are starting at the fourth character in our text string and extracting one character:

=MID(A14,4,1)

Finding a particular character in a text string

Excel's LEFT, RIGHT, and MID functions work great for extracting text, but only if you know the exact position of the characters you are targeting. What can you do when you don't know exactly where to start the extraction? For example, if you had the following list of product codes, how would you go about extracting all of the text after the hyphens?

PRT-432

COPR-6758

SVCCALL-58574

The LEFT function wouldn't work because you need the right few characters. The RIGHT function alone wouldn't work because you need to tell it exactly how many characters to extract from the right of the text string. Any number that you give will pull either too many or too few characters from the text. The MID function alone wouldn't work because you need to tell it exactly where in the text to start extracting. Again, any number you give will pull either too many or too few characters from the text.

The reality is that you will often need to find specific characters to get the appropriate starting position for the extraction. This is where Excel's FIND function comes in handy. With the FIND function, you can get the position number of a particular character and use that character position in other operations.

In the example shown in Figure 11.6, we use the FIND function in conjunction with the MID function to extract the middle numbers from a list of product codes. As you can see from the formula, we find the position of the hyphen and use that to feed the MID function.

```
=MID(B3,FIND("-",B3)+1,2)
```

FIGURE 11.6

Using the FIND function to extract data based on the position of the hyphen

⊿	A	B	C
1			
2		Product Code	Extract the Numbers
3		PWR-16-Small	=MID(B3,FIND("-",B3)+1,2)
4		PW-18-Medium	18
5		PW-19-Large	19
6		CWS-22-Medium	22
7		CWTP-44-Large	44
8			

The FIND function has two required arguments. The first argument is the text you want to find. The second argument is the text you want to search. By default, the FIND function will return the position number of the character you are trying to find. If the text you are searching contains more than one of your search characters, the FIND function will return the position number of the first encounters.

For instance, the following formula will search for a hyphen in the text string PWR-16-Small. The result will be a number 4 because the first hyphen it encounters is the fourth character in the text string.

```
=FIND("-","PWR-16-Small")
```

You can use the FIND function as an argument in a MID function to extract a set number of characters after the position number returned by the FIND function.

Entering this formula in a cell will give you the two numbers after the first hyphen found in the text. Note the +1 in the formula. This ensures that you move over one character to get to the text after the hyphen.

```
=MID("PWR-16-Small",FIND("-","PWR-16-Small")+1, 2)
```

Finding the second instance of a character

By default, the FIND function returns the position number of the first instance of the character for which you are searching. If you want the position number of the second instance, you can use the optional Start_Num argument. This argument lets you specify the character position in the text string to start the search.

For example, this formula will return the position number of the second hyphen because we're telling the FIND function to start searching at position 5 (after the first hyphen):

```
=FIND("-","PWR-16-Small",5)
```

To do this dynamically (without knowing where to start the search), you can nest a FIND function as the Start_Num argument in another FIND function. You can enter this formula into Excel to get the position number of the second hyphen:

```
=FIND("-","PWR-16-Small",FIND("-","PWR-16-Small")+1)
```

Figure 11.7 demonstrates a real-world example of this concept. Here we are extracting the size attribute from the product code by finding the second instance of the hyphen and using that position number as the starting point in the MID function. The formula shown in cell C3 is as follows:

```
=MID(B3,FIND("-",B3,FIND("-",B3)+1)+1,10000)
```

FIGURE 11.7

Nesting the FIND function to extract everything after the second hyphen

⊿	A	B	C
1			
2		Product Code	Extract the Size Designation
3		PWR-16-Small	=MID(B3,FIND("-",B3,FIND("-",B3)+1)+1,10000)
4		PW-18-Medium	Medium
5		PW-19-Large	Large
6		CWS-22-Medium	Medium
7		CWTP-44-Large	Large
8			

This formula tells Excel to find the position number of the second hyphen, move over one character, and then extract the next 10,000 characters. Of course, there aren't 10,000 characters, but this ensures that everything after the second hyphen is pulled.

Substituting text strings

There are cases when it's helpful to substitute some text with other text. One such case is where you encounter the annoying apostrophe S ('S) quirk that you get with the PROPER function. To see what we mean, enter this formula into Excel:

```
=PROPER("STARBUCK'S COFFEE")
```

This formula is meant to convert the given text into title case (where the first letter of every word is capitalized). The actual result of the formula is this:

```
Starbuck'S Coffee
```

Note how the PROPER function capitalizes the S after the apostrophe—annoying to say the least.

However, with a little help from Excel's SUBSTITUTE function, you can avoid this annoyance. Figure 11.8 shows the fix using the following formula:

```
=SUBSTITUTE(PROPER(SUBSTITUTE(B4,"'","qzx")),"qzx","'")
```

FIGURE 11.8

Fixing the apostrophe S issue with the SUBSTITUTE function

Our formula uses the SUBSTITUTE function, which requires three arguments: the target text, the old text you want to be replaced, and the new text to use as the replacement.

As you look at the full formula, you'll note there are two SUBSTITUTE functions in use. This formula is actually two formulas (one nested in the other). The first formula is the part that reads as follows:

```
PROPER(SUBSTITUTE(B4,"'","qzx"))
```

In this part, we are using the SUBSTITUTE function to replace the apostrophe (') with qzx. This may seem like a crazy thing to do, but there is some method here. The PROPER function will essentially capitalize any letter coming directly after a symbol. Here, we are tricking the PROPER function by substituting the apostrophe with a benign set of letters that are unlikely to be strung together in the original text.

The second formula actually wraps the first. This formula substitutes the benign qzx with an apostrophe:

```
=SUBSTITUTE(PROPER(SUBSTITUTE(B4,"'","qzx")),"qzx","'")
```

So, the entire formula replaces the apostrophe with qzx, performs the PROPER function, and then reverts the qzx to an apostrophe.

Counting specific characters in a cell

A useful trick is to be able to count the number of times a specific character exists in a text string. The technique for doing this in Excel is relatively clever. If you wanted to count the number of times the letter *s* appears in the word *Mississippi*, for example, you could count them by hand, of course, but systematically, you could follow these general steps:

1. **Measure the character length of the word *Mississippi* (11 characters).**
2. **Measure the character length after removing every letter *s* (7 characters).**
3. **Subtract the adjusted length from the original length.**

After performing these steps, you'll accurately conclude that the letter *s* occurs four times in the word *Mississippi*.

A real-world use for this technique of counting specific characters is to calculate a word count in Excel. In Figure 11.9, you'll see the following formula used to count the number of words entered in cell B4 (nine words in this case):

```
=LEN(B4)-LEN(SUBSTITUTE(B4," ",""))+1
```

FIGURE 11.9

Calculating the number of words in a cell

This formula essentially follows the steps mentioned earlier in the setup for this section. The formula first uses the LEN function to measure the length of the text in cell B4:

```
LEN(B4)
```

It then uses the SUBSTITUTE function to remove the spaces from the text:

```
SUBSTITUTE(B4," ","")
```

Wrapping the SUBSTITUTE function in a LEN function gives us the length of the text without the spaces. Note that we have to add one (+1) to that answer to account for the fact that the last word will not have an associated space:

    LEN(SUBSTITUTE(B4," ",""))+1

Subtracting the adjusted length from the original length gives us our word count:

    =LEN(B4)-LEN(SUBSTITUTE(B4," ",""))+1

Adding a line break within a formula

When creating charts in Excel, it's sometimes useful to force line breaks for the purpose of creating better visualizations. Take the chart shown in Figure 11.10, for example. Here you see a chart where the x-axis labels include the data value for each sales rep. This comes in handy when you don't want to inundate your chart with data labels.

FIGURE 11.10

The x-axis labels in this chart include a line break and a reference to the data values.

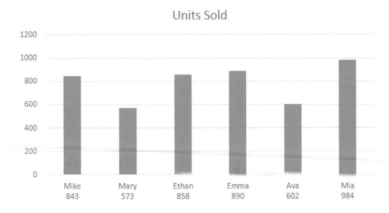

The secret to this trick is the use of the CHAR() function within a formula that makes up your chart labels (see Figure 11.11).

Every character in Excel has an associated American National Standards Institute (ANSI) character code. The ANSI character code is a Windows system code set that defines the characters you see on your screen. The ANSI character set consists of 255 characters, numbering from 1 to 255. The uppercase letter *A* is character 65. The number 9 is character 57.

Even nonprinting characters have codes. The code for a space is 32. The code for a line break is 10.

FIGURE 11.11

Using the CHAR() function to force a line break between the sales rep name and the data value

⁄	A	B	C
1			
2			Units Sold
3	Mike	=A3&CHAR(10)&C3	843
4	Mary	Mary573	573
5	Ethan	Ethan858	858
6	Emma	Emma890	890
7	Ava	Ava602	602
8	Mia	Mia984	984

You can call up any character in a formula by using the CHAR() function. In the example shown in Figure 11.11, we are calling up the line break character and joining it with the values in cells A3 and C3:

```
=A3&CHAR(10)&C3
```

The cell itself won't show the line break unless you have applied wrap text. But even if you haven't, any chart using this kind of formula will display the data returned by the formula with the line breaks.

Cleaning strange characters from text fields

When importing data from external data sources like text files or web feeds, strange characters may come in with your data. Instead of trying to clean these up manually, you can use Excel's CLEAN function (see Figure 11.12).

FIGURE 11.12

Cleaning data with the CLEAN function

⁄	A	B	C
1			
2		Store	Cleaned Text
3		Detroit (Store #1)▯▯▯▯▯	=TRIM(CLEAN(B3))
4		Detroit (Store #2)▯▯▯▯▯	Detroit (Store #2)
5		Detroit (Store #3)▯▯▯▯▯	Detroit (Store #3)
6		Charlotte (Store #1)▯▯▯▯▯	Charlotte (Store #1)
7		Charlotte (Store #2)▯▯▯▯▯	Charlotte (Store #2)
8		Charlotte (Store #3)▯▯▯▯▯	Charlotte (Store #3)

The CLEAN function removes nonprintable characters from any text you pass to it. You can wrap the CLEAN function within the TRIM function to remove unprintable characters and excess spaces at the same time.

```
=TRIM(CLEAN(B3))
```

Padding numbers with zeros

In many cases, the work you do in Excel ends up in other database systems within the organization. Those database systems often have field length requirements that mandate a certain number of characters. A common technique for ensuring that a field consists of a set number of characters is to pad data with zeros.

Padding data with zeros is a relatively easy concept. If you have a Customer ID field that must be 10 characters long, you essentially would need to add enough zeros to fulfill that requirement. So, Customer ID 2345 would need be padded with six zeros, making that ID 2345000000.

Cell C4 shown in Figure 11.13 uses this formula to pad the Customer ID fields with zeros:

```
=LEFT(B4&"0000000000",10)
```

FIGURE 11.13

Padding Customer ID fields to 10 characters

⊿	A	B	C
1			
2			
3		Customer ID	Pad to 10 characters
4		5381656	=LEFT(B4&"0000000000", 10)
5		832	8320000000
6		23	2300000000
7		290	2900000000
8		2036	2036000000
9		5965	5965000000
10		6	6000000000
11		7457	7457000000
12		2903	2903000000
13		6137	6137000000

The formula shown in Figure 11.13 first joins the value in cell B4 and a text string composed of 10 zeros. This effectively creates a new text string that guarantees a Customer ID value with 10 zeros.

We then use the LEFT function to extract the left 10 characters of that new text string.

Formatting the numbers in a text string

It's not uncommon to have reporting that joins text with numbers. For example, you may have a requirement to display a line in your report that summarizes a salesperson's results like this:

```
John Hutchison: $5,000
```

The problem is that when you join numbers in a text string, the number formatting does not follow. Look at Figure 11.14, for example. Note how the numbers in the joined string do not adopt the formatting of the source cells.

FIGURE 11.14

Numbers joined with text do not inherently adopt number formatting.

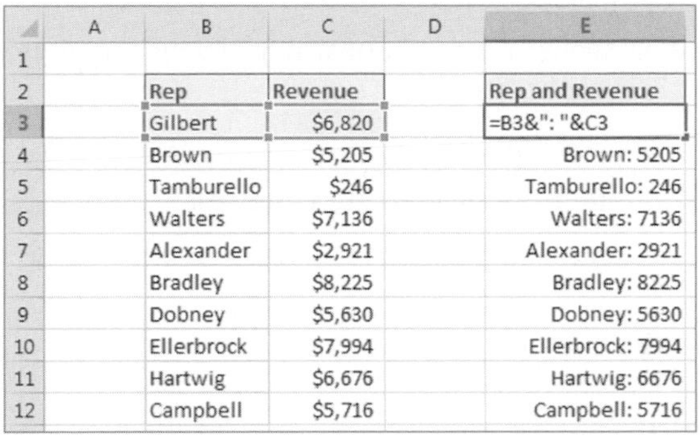

	A	B	C	D	E
1					
2		Rep	Revenue		Rep and Revenue
3		Gilbert	$6,820		=B3&": "&C3
4		Brown	$5,205		Brown: 5205
5		Tamburello	$246		Tamburello: 246
6		Walters	$7,136		Walters: 7136
7		Alexander	$2,921		Alexander: 2921
8		Bradley	$8,225		Bradley: 8225
9		Dobney	$5,630		Dobney: 5630
10		Ellerbrock	$7,994		Ellerbrock: 7994
11		Hartwig	$6,676		Hartwig: 6676
12		Campbell	$5,716		Campbell: 5716

To solve this problem, you'll have to wrap the cell reference for your number value in the TEXT function. Using the TEXT function, you can apply the needed formatting on the fly. The formula shown in Figure 11.15 resolves the issue.

```
=B3&": "&TEXT(C3,"$0,000")
```

FIGURE 11.15

Using the TEXT function lets you format numbers joined with text.

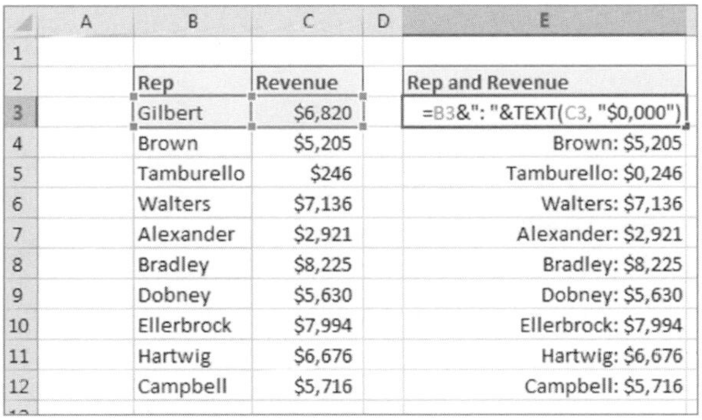

	A	B	C	D	E
1					
2		Rep	Revenue		Rep and Revenue
3		Gilbert	$6,820		=B3&": "&TEXT(C3, "$0,000")
4		Brown	$5,205		Brown: $5,205
5		Tamburello	$246		Tamburello: $0,246
6		Walters	$7,136		Walters: $7,136
7		Alexander	$2,921		Alexander: $2,921
8		Bradley	$8,225		Bradley: $8,225
9		Dobney	$5,630		Dobney: $5,630
10		Ellerbrock	$7,994		Ellerbrock: $7,994
11		Hartwig	$6,676		Hartwig: $6,676
12		Campbell	$5,716		Campbell: $5,716

The TEXT function requires two arguments: a value and a valid Excel format. You can apply any formatting that you want to a number as long as it's a format that Excel recognizes. For example, you can enter this formula into Excel to display $99:

```
=TEXT(99.21,"$#,###")
```

You can enter this formula into Excel to display 9921%:

```
=TEXT(99.21,"0%")
```

You can enter this formula into Excel to display 99.2:

```
=TEXT(99.21,"0.0")
```

An easy way to get the syntax for a particular number format in which you're interested is to look at the Number Format screen. Follow these steps:

1. **Right-click any cell and select Format Cell.**
2. **On the Number Format tab, select the formatting you need.**
3. **Select Custom from the Category list on the left of the Number Format dialog box.**
4. **Copy the syntax found in the Type input box.**

Using the DOLLAR function

If the number value you're joining with text is a dollar figure, you can use the simpler DOLLAR function. This function applies the regional currency format to the given text.

The DOLLAR function has two basic arguments: the number value and the number of decimals you want to display.

```
=B3&":  "&DOLLAR(C3,0)
```

Using Formulas with Dates and Times

IN THIS CHAPTER

Getting an overview of dates and times in Excel

Using Excel date-related functions

Working with Excel time-related functions

Many worksheets contain dates and times in cells. For example, you might track information by date or create a schedule based on time. Beginners often find that working with dates and times in Excel can be frustrating. To work with dates and times, you need a good understanding of how Excel handles time-based information. This chapter provides the information you need to create powerful formulas that manipulate dates and times.

> **NOTE**
>
> The dates in this chapter correspond to the U.S. English language date format: month/day/year. For example, the date 3/1/1952 refers to March 1, 1952, not January 3, 1952. We realize that this setup may seem illogical, but that's the way Americans have been trained. We trust that the non-American readers of this book can make the adjustment.

Understanding How Excel Handles Dates and Times

This section presents a quick overview of how Excel deals with dates and times. It covers Excel's date and time serial number system. It also provides some tips for entering and formatting dates and times.

Understanding date serial numbers

To Excel, a date is simply a number. More precisely, a date is a serial number that represents the number of days since the fictitious date of January 0, 1900. A serial number of 1 corresponds to January 1, 1900; a serial number of 2 corresponds to January 2, 1900; and so on. This system makes it possible to create formulas that perform calculations with dates. For example, you can create a formula to calculate the number of days between two dates (just subtract one from the other).

Excel supports dates from January 1, 1900, through December 31, 9999 (serial number = 2,958,465).

You may wonder about January 0, 1900. This nondate (which corresponds to date serial number 0) is actually used to represent times that aren't associated with a particular day. This concept becomes clear later in this chapter. (See "Entering times.")

To view a date serial number as a date, you must format the cell as a date. Choose Home ⇨ Number ⇨ Number Format. This drop-down control provides you with two date formats. To select from additional date formats, see "Formatting dates and times" later in this chapter.

Choose Your Date System: 1900 or 1904

Excel supports two date systems: the 1900 date system and the 1904 date system. Which system you use in a workbook determines what date serves as the basis for dates. The 1900 date system uses January 1, 1900, as the day assigned to date serial number 1. The 1904 date system uses January 1, 1904, as the base date. By default, Excel for Windows uses the 1900 date system, and pre-2011 versions of Excel for Mac use the 1904 date system.

Excel for Windows supports the 1904 date system for compatibility with older Mac files. You can choose the date system for the active workbook in the Advanced section of the Excel Options dialog box. (It's in the When Calculating This Workbook section.) Generally, you should use the default 1900 date system. And you should exercise caution if you use two different date systems in workbooks that are linked. For example, assume that Book1 uses the 1904 date system and contains the date 1/15/1999 in cell A1. Assume that Book2 uses the 1900 date system and contains a link to cell A1 in Book1. Book2 displays the date as 1/14/1995. Both workbooks use the same date serial number (34713), but they're interpreted differently.

One advantage to using the 1904 date system is that it enables you to display negative time values. With the 1900 date system, a calculation that results in a negative time (for example, 4:00 PM–5:30 PM) cannot be displayed. When using the 1904 date system, the negative time displays as –1:30 (that is, a difference of 1 hour and 30 minutes).

Entering dates

You can enter a date directly as a serial number (if you know the serial number) and then format it as a date. More often, you enter a date by using any of several recognized date formats. Excel automatically converts your entry into the corresponding date serial number (which it uses for calculations), and it applies the default date format to the cell so that it displays as an actual date rather than as a cryptic serial number.

For example, if you need to enter June 18, 2018, into a cell, you can enter the date by typing `June 18, 2018` (or any of several different date formats). Excel interprets your entry and stores the value 43269, the date serial number for that date. It also applies the default date format, so the cell contents may not appear exactly as you typed them.

12

> **NOTE**
>
> Depending on your regional settings, entering a date in a format such as June 18, 2018, may be interpreted as a text string. In such a case, you need to enter the date in a format that corresponds to your regional settings, such as 18 June 2018.

When you activate a cell that contains a date, the Formula bar shows the cell contents formatted by using the default date format—which corresponds to your system's short date format. The Formula bar doesn't display the date's serial number. If you need to find out the serial number for a particular date, format the cell with the General format.

> **TIP**
>
> To change the default date format, you need to change a systemwide setting. From the Windows Control Panel, select Clock and Region and then click Region to open the Region dialog box. The exact procedure varies, depending on the version of Windows you use. Look for the drop-down list that lets you change the Short Date format. The setting you choose determines the default date format that Excel uses to display dates in the Formula bar.

Excel is rather flexible when it comes to recognizing dates entered into a cell. It's not perfect, however. If you attempt to enter a date that lies outside the supported date range, Excel interprets it as text. If you attempt to format a serial number that lies outside the supported range as a date, the value displays as a series of hash marks (#########).

Searching for Dates

If your worksheet uses many dates, you may need to search for a particular date by using the Find and Replace dialog box (Home ➪ Editing ➪ Find & Select ➪ Find, or Ctrl+F). Excel is rather picky when it comes to finding dates. You must enter the date as it appears in the Formula bar. For example, if a cell contains a date formatted to display as June 19, 2016, the date appears in the Formula bar using your system's short date format (for example, 6/19/2016). Therefore, if you search for the date as it appears in the cell, Excel won't find it. But it will find the cell if you search for the date in the format that appears in the Formula bar.

Understanding time serial numbers

When you need to work with time values, you extend the Excel date serial number system to include decimals. In other words, Excel works with time by using fractional days. For example, the date serial number for June 1, 2016, is 42522. Noon (halfway through the day) is represented internally as 42522.5.

The serial number equivalent of one minute is approximately 0.00069444. The following formula calculates this number by multiplying 24 hours by 60 minutes and dividing the result into 1. The denominator consists of the number of minutes in a day (1,440).

```
=1/(24*60)
```

Similarly, the serial number equivalent of one second is approximately 0.00001157, obtained by the following formula:

```
=1/(24*60*60)
```

In this case, the denominator represents the number of seconds in a day (86,400).

In Excel, the smallest unit of time is one 1,000th of a second. The time serial number shown here represents 23:59:59.999 (one 1,000th of a second before midnight):

```
0.99999999
```

Table 12.1 shows various times of day along with each associated time serial number.

TABLE 12.1 Times of Day and Their Corresponding Serial Numbers

Time of Day	Time Serial Number
12:00:00 AM (midnight)	0.00000000
1:30:00 AM	0.06250000
7:30:00 AM	0.31250000
10:30:00 AM	0.43750000
12:00:00 PM (noon)	0.50000000
1:30:00 PM	0.56250000
4:30:00 PM	0.68750000
6:00:00 PM	0.75000000
9:00:00 PM	0.87500000
10:30:00 PM	0.93750000

Entering times

As with entering dates, you normally don't have to worry about the actual time serial numbers. Just enter the time into a cell using a recognized format. Table 12.2 shows some examples of time formats that Excel recognizes.

TABLE 12.2 Time Entry Formats Recognized by Excel

Entry	Excel Interpretation
11:30:00 AM	11:30 AM
11:30:00 AM	11:30 AM
11:30 PM	11:30 PM
11:30	11:30 AM
13:30	1:30 PM

Because the preceding samples don't have a specific day associated with them, Excel uses a date serial number of 0, which corresponds to the nonday January 0, 1900. Often, you'll want to combine a date and time. Do so by using a recognized date entry format, followed by a space, and then a recognized time entry format. For example, if you enter **6/18/2016 11:30** into a cell, Excel interprets it as 11:30 AM on June 18, 2016. Its date/time serial number is 42539.47917.

When you enter a time that exceeds 24 hours, the associated date for the time increments accordingly. For example, if you enter **25:00:00** into a cell, it's interpreted as 1:00 AM on January 1, 1900. The day part of the entry increments because the time exceeds 24 hours. Keep in mind that a time value without a date uses January 0, 1900, as the date.

Similarly, if you enter a date and a time (and the time exceeds 24 hours), the date you entered is adjusted. If you enter **9/18/2016 25:00:00**, for example, it's interpreted as 9/19/2016 1:00:00 AM

If you enter a time only (without an associated date) into an unformatted cell, the maximum time you can enter into a cell is 9999:59:59 (just less than 10,000 hours). Excel adds the appropriate number of days. In this case, 9999:59:59 is interpreted as 3:59:59 PM on 02/19/1901. If you enter a time that exceeds 10,000 hours, the entry is interpreted as a text string rather than a time.

Formatting dates and times

You have a great deal of flexibility in formatting cells that contain dates and times. For example, you can format the cell to display the date part only, the time part only, or both the date and time parts.

You format dates and times by selecting the cells and then using the Number tab of the Format Cells dialog box. To display this dialog box, click the dialog box launcher icon in the Number group of the Home tab, or click the Number Format control and choose More Number Formats from the list that appears.

The Date category shows built-in date formats, and the Time category shows built-in time formats. Some formats include both date and time displays. Just select the desired format from the Type list and then click OK.

> **TIP**
>
> When you create a formula that refers to a cell containing a date or a time, Excel sometimes automatically formats the formula cell as a date or a time. Often, this automation is helpful; at other times, it's completely inappropriate and downright annoying. To return the number formatting to the default General format, choose Home ➪ Number ➪ Number Format and choose General from the drop-down list. Or just press Ctrl+Shift+~ (tilde).

Problems with dates

Excel has some problems when it comes to dates. Many of these problems stem from the fact that Excel was designed many years ago. Excel designers basically emulated the Lotus 1-2-3 program's limited date and time features, which contain a nasty bug that was duplicated intentionally in Excel (described next). If Excel were being designed from scratch today, I'm sure it would be much more versatile in dealing with dates. Unfortunately, users are currently stuck with a product that leaves much to be desired in the area of dates.

Excel's leap year bug

A leap year, which occurs every four years, contains an additional day (February 29). Specifically, years that are evenly divisible by 100 are not leap years, unless they are also evenly divisible by 400. Although the year 1900 was not a leap year, Excel treats it as such. In other words, when you type 2/29/1900 into a cell, Excel interprets it as a valid date and assigns a serial number of 60.

If you type 2/29/1901, however, Excel correctly interprets it as a mistake and doesn't convert it to a date. Instead, it simply makes the cell entry a text string.

How can a product used daily by millions of people contain such an obvious bug? The answer is historical. The original version of Lotus 1-2-3 contained a bug that caused it to treat 1900 as a leap year. When Excel was released some time later, the designers knew about this bug and chose to reproduce it in Excel to maintain compatibility with Lotus 1-2-3 worksheet files.

Why does this bug still exist in later versions of Excel? Microsoft asserts that the disadvantages of correcting this bug outweigh the advantages. If the bug were eliminated, it would mess up millions of existing workbooks. In addition, correcting this problem would possibly affect compatibility between Excel and other programs that use dates. As it stands, this bug really causes very few problems because most users don't use dates prior to March 1, 1900.

Pre-1900 dates

The world, of course, didn't begin on January 1, 1900. People who use Excel to work with historical information often need to work with dates before January 1, 1900. Unfortunately, the only way to work with pre-1900 dates is to enter the date into a cell as text. For example, you can enter July 4, 1776, into a cell, and Excel won't complain.

> **TIP**
>
> If you plan to sort information by old dates, you should enter your text dates with a four-digit year, followed by a two-digit month, and then a two-digit day—for example, 1776-07-04. You won't be able to work with these text strings as dates, but this format will enable accurate sorting.

Using text as dates works in some situations, but the main problem is that you can't perform manipulation on a date that's entered as text. For example, you can't change its numeric formatting, you can't determine on which day of the week this date occurred, and you can't calculate the date that occurs seven days later.

Inconsistent date entries

You need to be careful when entering dates by using two digits for the year. When you do so, Excel has some rules that determine which century to use.

Two-digit years between 00 and 29 are interpreted as 21st-century dates, and two-digit years between 30 and 99 are interpreted as 20th-century dates. For example, if you enter 12/15/28, Excel interprets your entry as December 15, 2028. But if you enter 12/15/30, Excel sees it as December 15, 1930, because Windows uses a default boundary year of 2029. You can keep the default as is or change it via the Windows Control Panel. From the Region dialog box, click the Additional Settings button to display the Customize Format dialog box. Select the Date tab and then specify a different year.

> **TIP**
> The best way to avoid any surprises is to simply enter all years using all four digits for the year.

Using Excel's Date and Time Functions

Excel has quite a few functions that work with dates and times. These functions are accessible by choosing Formulas ⇨ Function Library ⇨ Date & Time.

These functions leverage the fact that, beneath the covers, dates and times are nothing more than a numbering system. This opens the door for all kinds of cool formula-driven analyses. In this section, you'll walk through some of these cool analyses. Along the way, you'll pick up a few techniques that will help you create your own formulas.

 This book's website, www.wiley.com/go/excel2019bible, includes a copy of the sample workbook for this chapter. The file is named Dates and Times.xlsx.

Getting the current date and time

Instead of typing the current date and time, you can use one of two Excel functions. The TODAY function returns the current date:

    =TODAY()

The NOW() function returns the current date along with the current time:

    =NOW()

Both the TODAY and NOW functions return date serial numbers that represent the current system date and time. The TODAY function assumes 12 PM as the time, while the NOW function returns the actual time.

It's important to note that both of these functions will automatically recalculate each time you change or open your workbook, so don't use these functions as a timestamp of record.

You can use the TODAY function as part of a text string by wrapping it in the TEXT function with some date formatting. This formula will display text that will return today's date in Month Day, Year format.

```
="Today is "&TEXT(TODAY(),"mmmm d, yyyy")
```

 For more details on using the TEXT function, see the section called "Formatting the numbers in a text string" in Chapter 11.

Calculating age

One of the easiest ways to calculate the age of anything is to use Excel's DATEDIF function. This function makes calculating any kind of date comparisons a breeze.

To calculate a person's age using the DATEDIF function, you can enter a formula like this:

```
=DATEDIF("5/16/1972",TODAY(),"y")
```

You can, of course, reference a cell that contains a date:

```
=DATEDIF(B4,TODAY(),"y")
```

The DATEDIF function calculates the number of days, months, or years between two dates. It requires three arguments—a start date, an end date, and a time unit.

The time units are defined by a series of codes listed in Table 12.3.

TABLE 12.3 DATEDIF **Time Unit Codes**

Code	What It Returns
"y"	The number of complete years in the period.
"m"	The number of complete months in the period.
"d"	The number of days in the period.
"md"	The difference between the days in start_date and end_date. The months and years of the dates are ignored.
"ym"	The difference between the months in start_date and end_date. The days and years of the dates are ignored.
"yd"	The difference between the days of start_date and end_date. The years of the dates are ignored.

Using these time codes, you can easily calculate the number of years, months, and days between two dates. If someone was born on May 16, 1972, you could find that person's age in years, months, and days using these respective formulas:

```
=DATEDIF("5/16/1972",TODAY(),"y")
=DATEDIF("5/16/1972",TODAY(),"m")
=DATEDIF("5/16/1972",TODAY(),"d")
```

Calculating the number of days between two dates

One of the most common date calculations performed in the corporate world is figuring the number of days between two dates. Project management teams use it to measure performance against a milestone, HR departments use it to measure time to fill a requisition, and finance departments use it to track receivables aging. Luckily, it's one of the easiest calculations to perform thanks to the handy DATEDIF function.

Figure 12.1 demonstrates a sample report that uses the DATEDIF function to calculate the number of days outstanding for a set of invoices.

FIGURE 12.1

Calculating the number of days between today and the invoice date

	Invoice Date	Days Outstanding
3	Invoice Date	Days Outstanding
4	25-Jun-18	=DATEDIF(C4,TODAY(),"d")
5	04-Jun-18	70
6	04-Jun-18	70
7	22-Apr-18	113
8	31-Mar-18	135
9	28-Mar-18	138

Looking at Figure 12.1, you'll see the formula in cell D4 is as follows:

```
=DATEDIF(C4,TODAY(),"d")
```

This formula uses the DATEDIF function with the time code d. This tells Excel to return the number of days based on the start date (C4) and the end date (TODAY).

Calculating the number of workdays between two dates

Oftentimes when reporting on the elapsed number of days between a start date and end date, it's not appropriate to count the weekends in the final number of days. Operations are typically shut down on the weekends, so you would want to avoid counting those days.

You can use Excel's NETWORKDAYS function to calculate the number of days between a start date and end date excluding weekends.

As you can see in Figure 12.2, the NETWORKDAYS function is used in cell E4 to calculate the number of workdays between 1/1/2019 and 12/31/2019.

FIGURE 12.2

Calculating the number of workdays between two dates

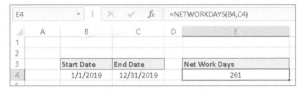

This formula is fairly straightforward. The NETWORKDAYS function has two required arguments: a start date and an end date. If your start date is in cell B4 and your end date is in cell C4, this formula would return the number of workdays (excluding Saturdays and Sundays):

    =NETWORKDAYS(B4,C4)

Using NETWORKDAYS.INTL

The one drawback to using the NETWORKDAYS function is that it defaults to excluding Saturday and Sunday. But what if you work in a region where the weekends are actually Fridays and Saturdays? Or worse yet, what if your weekends only include Sundays?

Excel has you covered with the NETWORKDAYS.INTL function. In addition to the required start and end dates, this function has an optional third argument—a weekend code. The weekend code allows you to specify which days to exclude as a weekend day.

As you enter the NETWORKDAYS.INTL function, Excel displays a menu as soon as you go into the third argument (see Figure 12.3). Simply select the appropriate weekend code and press Enter.

FIGURE 12.3

NETWORKDAY.INTL allows you to specify which days to exclude as weekend days.

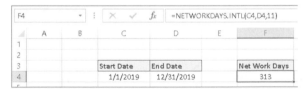

Generating a list of business days excluding holidays

When creating dashboards and reports in Excel, it's often useful to have a helper table that contains a list of dates that represent business days (that is, dates that are not weekends or holidays). This kind of a helper table can help assist in calculations like revenue per business day, units per business day, and so on.

One of the easiest ways to generate a list of business days is to use the WORKDAY.INTL function. Start with a spreadsheet that contains the last date of the previous year and a list of your organization's holidays. As you can see in Figure 12.4, your list of holidays should be formatted dates.

FIGURE 12.4

Start with a sheet containing the last date of the previous year and a list of holidays.

	A	B	C	D
1				
2				
3		12/31/2012		Holidays
4				1/1/2013
5				1/21/2013
6				3/29/2013
7				3/31/2013
8				5/31/2013
9				7/4/2013
10				9/1/2013
11				10/14/2013
12				11/28/2013
13				12/24/2013
14				12/25/2013
15				12/31/2013

In the cell beneath the last date of the previous year, enter this formula:

```
=WORKDAY.INTL(B3,1,1,$D$4:$D$15)
```

At this point, you can copy the formula down to create as many business days as you need (see Figure 12.5).

FIGURE 12.5

Creating a list of business days

	A	B	C	D
1				
2				
3		12/31/2012		Holidays
4		=WORKDAY.INTL(B3,1,1,$D$4:$D$15)		1/1/2013
5		1/3/2013		1/21/2013
6		1/4/2013		3/29/2013
7		1/7/2013		3/31/2013
8		1/8/2013		5/31/2013
9		1/9/2013		7/4/2013
10		1/10/2013		9/1/2013
11		1/11/2013		10/14/2013
12		1/14/2013		11/28/2013
13		1/15/2013		12/24/2013
14		1/16/2013		12/25/2013
15		1/17/2013		12/31/2013

The WORKDAY.INTL function returns a workday date based on the number of days you tell it to increment. This function has two required arguments and two optional arguments:

Start Date (required) This argument is the date to start from.

Days (required) This argument is the number of days from the start date that you want returned.

Weekends (optional) By default, the WORKDAY.INTL function excludes Saturdays and Sundays, but this third argument allows you to specify which weekdays to exclude as a weekend day. As you enter the WORKDAY.INTL function, Excel displays a menu where you can select the appropriate weekend code.

Holidays (optional) This argument allows you to give Excel a list of dates to exclude in addition to the weekend days.

In this example, we are telling Excel to start from 12/31/2012 and then increment up 1 to give us the next business day after our start date. For our optional arguments, we specify that we need to exclude Saturdays and Sundays, along with the holidays listed in cells $D$4:$D$15.

```
=WORKDAY.INTL(B3,1,1,$D$4:$D$15)
```

Be sure to lock down the range for your list of holidays with absolute references so that it remains locked as you copy your formula down.

Extracting parts of a date

Although it may seem trivial, it's often helpful to pick out a specific part of a date. For example, you may need to filter all records that have order dates within a certain month or all employees who have time allocated to Saturdays. In these situations, you would need to pull out the month and workday number from the formatted dates.

Excel provides a simple set of functions to parse dates out into their component parts. These functions are as follows:

YEAR extracts the year from a given date.

MONTH extracts the month from a given date.

DAY extracts the month day number from a given date.

WEEKDAY returns the weekday number for a given date.

WEEKNUM returns the week number for a given date.

Figure 12.6 demonstrates the use of these functions to parse the date in cell C3 into its component parts.

These functions are fairly straightforward.

The YEAR function returns a four-digit number that corresponds to the year of a specified date. This formula returns 2015.

```
=YEAR("5/16/2015")
```

FIGURE 12.6

Extract the parts of a date.

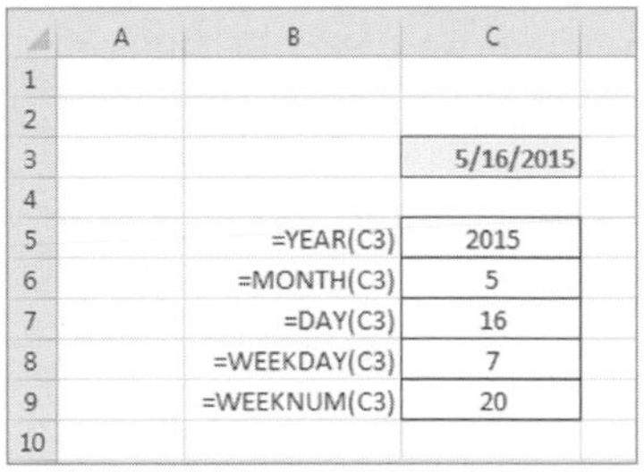

▲	A	B	C	
1				
2				
3			5/16/2015	
4				
5		=YEAR(C3)	2015	
6		=MONTH(C3)	5	
7		=DAY(C3)	16	
8		=WEEKDAY(C3)	7	
9		=WEEKNUM(C3)	20	
10				

The MONTH function returns a number between 1 and 12 that corresponds to the month of a specified date. This formula returns 5.

```
=MONTH("5/16/2015")
```

The DAY function returns a number between 1 and 31 that corresponds to the day of the month represented in a specified date. This formula returns 16.

```
=DAY("5/16/2015")
```

The WEEKDAY function returns a number from 1 to 7 that corresponds to the day of the week (Sunday through Saturday) on which the given date falls. If the date falls on a Sunday, the number 1 is returned. If the date falls on a Monday, the number 2 is returned, and so on. This formula returns 7 because 5/16/2015 falls on a Saturday.

```
=WEEKDAY("5/16/2015")
```

This function actually has an optional return_type argument that lets you define which day of the week holds the first position. As you enter the WEEKDAY function, Excel displays a menu where you can select the appropriate return_type code.

You can adjust the formula so that the return values 1 through 7 represent Monday through Sunday. In this case, the formula would return 6, so Saturdays are now tagged as the 6th day of the week.

```
=WEEKDAY("5/16/2015",2)
```

The WEEKNUM function returns the week number in the year for the week in which the specified date occurs. This formula returns 20 because 5/16/2015 falls within week 20 in 2015.

```
=WEEKNUM("5/16/2015")
```

This function actually has an optional return_type argument that lets you specify which day of the week defines the start of the week. By default, the WEEKNUM function defines the start of the week as Sunday. As you enter the WEEKNUM function, Excel displays a menu where you can select a different return_type code.

12

Calculating number of years and months between dates

In some cases, you'll be asked to express the difference between two dates in years and months. In these cases, you can create a text string using two DATEDIF functions.

Cell C4 shown in Figure 12.7 contains the following formula:

```
=DATEDIF(A4,B4,"Y") & " Years, " & DATEDIF(A4,B4,"YM") & " Months"
```

FIGURE 12.7

Showing the years and months between dates

	A	B	C	D
	=DATEDIF(A4,B4,"Y") & " Years, " & DATEDIF(A4,B4,"YM") & " Months"			
1				
2				
3	Start Date	End Date	Number of Years and Months	
4	11/23/1960	5/13/2014	53 Years, 5 Months	
5	10/25/1944	5/13/2014	69 Years, 6 Months	
6	4/14/1920	5/13/2014	94 Years, 0 Months	
7	8/28/1940	5/13/2014	73 Years, 8 Months	
8	8/5/1987	5/13/2014	26 Years, 9 Months	
9	8/24/1982	5/13/2014	31 Years, 8 Months	
10	3/17/1959	5/13/2014	55 Years, 1 Months	
11	4/6/1961	5/13/2014	53 Years, 1 Months	
12	6/5/1944	5/13/2014	69 Years, 11 Months	
13	3/15/1930	5/13/2014	84 Years, 1 Months	
14	9/29/1921	5/13/2014	92 Years, 7 Months	
15	5/10/1953	5/13/2014	61 Years, 0 Months	

We accomplish this task by using two DATEDIF functions joined in a text string with the ampersand (&) operator.

The first DATEDIF function calculates the number of years between the start and end dates by passing the year time unit (Y)

```
DATEDIF(A4,B4,"Y")
```

The second DATEDIF function uses the YM time unit to calculate the number of months ignoring the year portion of the date:

```
DATEDIF(A4,B4,"YM")
```

We join these two functions with some text of our own to let the users know which number represents years and which represents months:

```
=DATEDIF(A4,B4,"Y") & " Years, " & DATEDIF(A4,B4,"YM") & " Months"
```

Converting dates to Julian date formats

Julian dates are often used in manufacturing environments as a timestamp and quick reference for batch number. This type of date coding allows retailers, consumers, and service agents to identify when a product was made and thus the age of the product. Julian dates are also used in programming, the military, and astronomy.

Different industries have their own variations on Julian dates, but the most commonly used variation is made up of two parts: a two-digit number representing the year and the number of elapsed days in the year. For example, the Julian date for 1/1/1960 would be 601. The Julian date for 12/31/2014 would be 14365.

Excel has no built-in function to convert a standard date to a Julian date, but Figure 12.8 illustrates how a formula can be used to accomplish the task.

```
=RIGHT(YEAR(A4),2)& A4-DATE(YEAR(A4),1,0)
```

FIGURE 12.8

Converting standard dates into Julian dates

	A	B
1		
2		
3	Standard Date	Julian Date
4	1/1/1960	=RIGHT(YEAR(A4),2)&A4-DATE(YEAR(A4),1,0)
5	10/25/1944	44299
6	4/14/1920	20105
7	8/28/1940	40241
8	8/5/1987	87217
9	8/24/1982	82236
10	3/17/1959	5976
11	4/6/1961	6196
12	6/5/1944	44157
13	3/15/1930	3074
14	9/29/2000	00273
15	5/10/2014	14130

This formula is really two formulas joined as a text string using the ampersand (&).

The first formula uses the RIGHT function to extract the right two digits of the year number. Note we are using the YEAR function to pull out the year portion from the actual date.

```
=RIGHT(YEAR(A4),2)
```

For more details on using the RIGHT function, see the section called "Extracting parts of a text string" in Chapter 11.

The second formula is a bit trickier. Here we have to find out how many days have elapsed since the beginning of the year. For this, we first need to subtract the target date from the last day of the previous year.

```
A4-DATE(YEAR(A4),1,0)
```

You'll note the use of the DATE function. The DATE function allows us to build a date on the fly using three arguments: the year, the month, and the day. The year can be any whole number from 1900 to 9999. The month and date can be any positive or negative number. For example, this formula would return the date serial number for December 1, 2013:

```
=DATE(2013, 12, 1)
```

Note that in our Julian date formula, we are using a zero as our day argument. When you use 0 as the day argument, you are telling Excel that you want the day before the 1st of the given month. In this example, the day before January 1 is December 31. For instance, entering this formula into a blank cell will return December 31, 1959:

```
=DATE(1960,1,0)
```

Joining our two formulas together with an ampersand brings the Julian date together:

```
=RIGHT(YEAR(A4),2)& A4-DATE(YEAR(A4),1,0)
```

Calculating the percent of year completed and remaining

When building Excel reports and dashboards, oftentimes it's beneficial to calculate the percent of the year that has elapsed and what percent remains. These percentages can be used in other calculations or simply as a notification for your audience.

Figure 12.9 shows a sample of this concept. Note in the Formula bar that we are using the YEARFRAC function.

FIGURE 12.9

Calculating the percent of the year completed

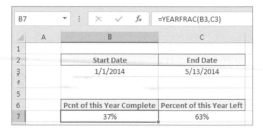

The YEARFRAC function simply requires a start date and an end date. Once it has those two variables, it calculates the fraction of the year representing the number of days between the start date and end date.

```
=YEARFRAC(B3,C3)
```

To get the percent remaining, as shown in cell C7 of Figure 12.9, simply subtract 1 from the YEARFRAC formula:

```
=1-YEARFRAC(B3,C3)
```

Returning the last date of a given month

A common need when working with dates is to calculate dynamically the last date in a given month. Although the last day for most months is fixed, the last day for February varies depending on whether the given year is a leap year.

Figure 12.10 illustrates how to get the last date in February for each date given in order to see which years are leap years.

FIGURE 12.10

Calculating the last day of each date

	A	B	C
1			
2		First Day of February	Last Day of February
3		2/1/1999	=DATE(YEAR(B3),MONTH(B3)+1,0)
4		2/1/2000	2/29/2000
5		2/1/2001	2/28/2001
6		2/1/2002	2/28/2002
7		2/1/2003	2/28/2003
8		2/1/2004	2/29/2004
9		2/1/2005	2/28/2005
10		2/1/2006	2/28/2006
11		2/1/2007	2/28/2007
12		2/1/2008	2/29/2008
13		2/1/2009	2/28/2009
14		2/1/2010	2/28/2010
15		2/1/2011	2/28/2011
16		2/1/2012	2/29/2012

The DATE function lets you build a date on the fly using three arguments: the year, the month, and the day. The year can be any whole number from 1900 to 9999. The month and date can be any positive or negative number.

For example, this formula would return the date serial number for December 1, 2013:

```
=DATE(2013, 12, 1)
```

When you use 0 as the day argument, you are telling Excel that you want the day before the 1st of the month. For instance, entering this formula into a blank cell will return February 29, 2000:

```
=DATE(2000,3,0)
```

In our example, instead of hard-coding the year and month, we use the YEAR function to get the desired year and the MONTH function to get the desired month. We add 1 to the month so that we go into the next month. This way, when we use 0 as the day, we get the last day of the month in which we're actually interested.

```
=DATE(YEAR(B3),MONTH(B3)+1,0)
```

As you look at Figure 12.10, keep in mind that you can use the formula to get the last day of any month, not just February.

Using the EOMONTH function

The EOMONTH function is an easy alternative to using the DATE function. With the EOMONTH function, you can get the last date of any future or past month. All you need is two arguments: a start date and the number of months in the future or past.

For example, this formula will return the last day of April 2015:

```
=EOMONTH("1/1/2015", 3)
```

Specifying a negative number of months will return a date in the past. This formula will return the last day of October 2014:

```
=EOMONTH("1/1/2015", -3)
```

You can combine the EOMONTH function with the TODAY function to get the last day of the current month.

```
=EOMONTH(TODAY(),0)
```

Calculating the calendar quarter for a date

Believe it or not, there is no built-in function to calculate quarter numbers in Excel. If you need to calculate into which calendar quarter a specific date falls, you'll need to create your own formula.

Figure 12.11 demonstrates the following formula used for calculating calendar quarters:

```
=ROUNDUP(MONTH(B3)/3,0)
```

FIGURE 12.11

Calculating calendar quarters

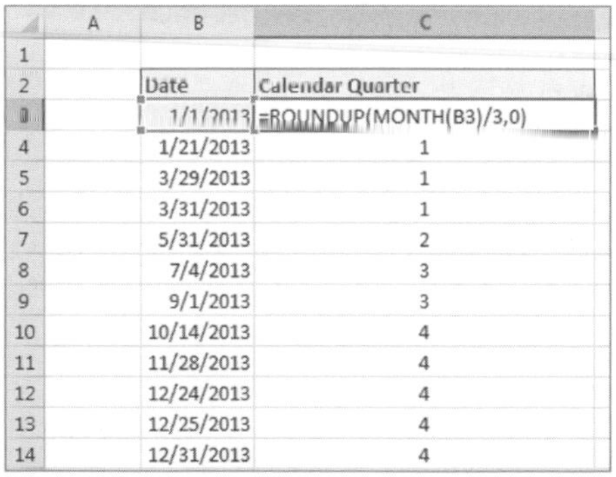

	A	B	C
1			
2		Date	Calendar Quarter
3		1/1/2013	=ROUNDUP(MONTH(B3)/3,0)
4		1/21/2013	1
5		3/29/2013	1
6		3/31/2013	1
7		5/31/2013	2
8		7/4/2013	3
9		9/1/2013	3
10		10/14/2013	4
11		11/28/2013	4
12		12/24/2013	4
13		12/25/2013	4
14		12/31/2013	4

The secret to this formula is simple math. Here you're dividing the month number for the given month by 3 and then rounding that number up to the nearest integer. For instance, let's say you want to calculate the quarter into which August falls. Since August is the 8th month of the year, you could divide 8 by 3. That would give you the answer 2.66. Round that number up, and you get 3. Thus, August is in the third quarter of the calendar year.

The following formula does the same thing. We're using the MONTH function to extract the month number from the given date and the ROUNDUP function to force rounding up.

=ROUNDUP(MONTH(B3)/3,0)

Calculating the fiscal quarter for a date

Many of us work in organizations where the fiscal year does not start in January. Instead, it starts in October or April or any other month. In these organizations, the fiscal quarters can't be calculated in the same way as calendar quarters.

Figure 12.12 demonstrates a clever formula for converting a date into a fiscal quarter using the CHOOSE function. In this example, we're calculating the fiscal quarters when our fiscal year starts in April. The formula seen in the Formula bar shows the following:

=CHOOSE(MONTH(B3),4,4,4,1,1,1,2,2,2,3,3,3)

FIGURE 12.12

Calculating fiscal quarters

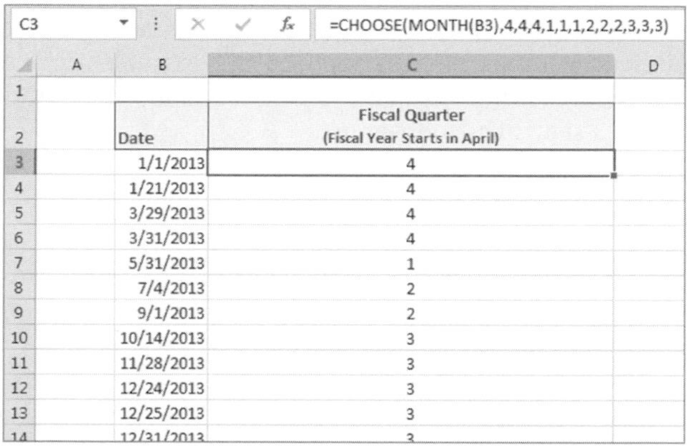

	A	B	C	D
			=CHOOSE(MONTH(B3),4,4,4,1,1,1,2,2,2,3,3,3)	
1				
2		Date	Fiscal Quarter (Fiscal Year Starts in April)	
3		1/1/2013	4	
4		1/21/2013	4	
5		3/29/2013	4	
6		3/31/2013	4	
7		5/31/2013	1	
8		7/4/2013	2	
9		9/1/2013	2	
10		10/14/2013	3	
11		11/28/2013	3	
12		12/24/2013	3	
13		12/25/2013	3	
14		12/31/2013	3	

The CHOOSE function returns an answer from a list of choices based on a position number. If you were to enter the formula =CHOOSE(2, "Gold", "Silver", "Bronze", "Coupon"), you would get Silver because Silver is the second choice in your list of choices. Replace the 2 with a 4, and you would get Coupon, the fourth choice.

The CHOOSE function's first argument is a required index number. This argument is a number from 1 to as many choices as you list in the next set of arguments. The index number determines which of the next arguments is returned.

The next 254 arguments (only the first one is required) defines your choices and determines what is returned when an index number is provided. If the index number is 1, the first choice is returned. If the index number is 2, the second choice is returned.

The idea here is to use the CHOOSE function to pass a date to a list of quarter numbers:

=CHOOSE(MONTH(B3),4,4,4,1,1,1,2,2,2,3,3,3)

The formula shown in cell C3 (see Figure 12.12) tells Excel to use the month number for the given date and select a quarter that corresponds to that number. In this case, since the month is January, Excel returns the first choice (January is the first month). The first choice happens to be a 4. January is in the fourth fiscal quarter.

Let's say that your company's fiscal year starts in October instead of April. You can easily compensate for this by simply adjusting your list of choices to correlate with your fiscal year's start month.

```
=CHOOSE(MONTH(B3),2,2,2,3,3,3,4,4,4,1,1,1)
```

Returning a fiscal month from a date

In some organizations, the operationally recognized months don't start on the 1st and end on the 30th or 31st. Instead, they have specific days marking the beginning and end of a month. For instance, you may work in an organization where each fiscal month starts on the 21st and ends on the 20th of the next month. In these organizations, it's important to be able to translate a standard date into their own fiscal months.

Figure 12.13 demonstrates a formula for converting a date into a fiscal month using the EOMONTH function in conjunction with the TEXT function. In this example, we're calculating the fiscal month where our fiscal month starts on the 21st and ends on the 20th of the next month. The formula in cell C3 shows the following:

```
=TEXT(EOMONTH(B3-20,1),"mmm")
```

FIGURE 12.13

Calculating fiscal months

	A	B	C
1			
2		Date	Fiscal Month [Starts on the 21st and ends on the 20th of the Next Month]
3		1/1/2013	=TEXT(EOMONTH(B3-20,1),"mmm")
4		1/1/2013	Jan
5		1/21/2013	Feb
6		3/20/2013	Mar
7		3/31/2013	Apr
8		4/21/2013	May
9		6/20/2013	Jun
10		6/21/2013	Jul
11		7/21/2013	Aug
12			

In this formula, we're first taking our date (in B3) and going back 20 days by subtracting 20. Then we are using that new date in the EOMONTH function to get the last day next month:

```
EOMONTH(B3-20,1)
```

We then wrap that in a TEXT function to format the resulting date into a three-letter month name:

```
TEXT(EOMONTH(B3-20,1),"mmm")
```

Calculating the date of the Nth weekday of the month

Many analytical processes rely on knowing the dates of specific events. For example, if payroll processing occurs the second Friday of every month, it's beneficial to know which dates in the year represent the second Friday of each month.

Using the date functions covered thus far in this chapter, you can build dynamic date tables that automatically provide you with the key dates you need.

Figure 12.14 illustrates such a table. In this table, formulas calculate the Nth weekday for each month listed. The idea is to fill in the years and months you need and then tell it what number occurrence of each weekday you are seeking. In this example, cell B2 shows that we are looking for the second occurrence of each weekday.

FIGURE 12.14

A dynamic date table calculating the Nth occurrence of each weekday

	A	B	C	D	E	F	G	H	I
1		Nth Occurence							
2		2							
3									
4			1	2	3	4	5	6	7
5	YEAR	MONTH	Nth Sun of the Month	Nth Mon of the Month	Nth Tues of the Month	Nth Wed of the Month	Nth Thur of the Month	Nth Fri of the Month	Nth Sat of the Month
6	2014	1	1/12/2014	1/13/2014	1/14/2014	1/8/2014	1/9/2014	1/10/2014	1/11/2014
7	2014	2	2/9/2014	2/10/2014	2/11/2014	2/12/2014	2/13/2014	2/14/2014	2/8/2014
8	2014	3	3/9/2014	3/10/2014	3/11/2014	3/12/2014	3/13/2014	3/14/2014	3/8/2014
9	2014	4	4/13/2014	4/14/2014	4/8/2014	4/9/2014	4/10/2014	4/11/2014	4/12/2014
10	2014	5	5/11/2014	5/12/2014	5/13/2014	5/14/2014	5/8/2014	5/9/2014	5/10/2014
11	2014	6	6/8/2014	6/9/2014	6/10/2014	6/11/2014	6/12/2014	6/13/2014	6/14/2014
12	2014	7	7/13/2014	7/14/2014	7/8/2014	7/9/2014	7/10/2014	7/11/2014	7/12/2014
13	2014	8	8/10/2014	8/11/2014	8/12/2014	8/13/2014	8/14/2014	8/8/2014	8/9/2014
14	2014	9	9/14/2014	9/8/2014	9/9/2014	9/10/2014	9/11/2014	9/12/2014	9/13/2014
15	2014	10	10/12/2014	10/13/2014	10/14/2014	10/8/2014	10/9/2014	10/10/2014	10/11/2014
16	2014	11	11/9/2014	11/10/2014	11/11/2014	11/12/2014	11/13/2014	11/14/2014	11/8/2014
17	2014	12	12/14/2014	12/8/2014	12/9/2014	12/10/2014	12/11/2014	12/12/2014	12/13/2014

Cell C6 (see Figure 12.14) contains the following formula:

```
=DATE($A6,$B6,1)+C$4-WEEKDAY(DATE($A6,$B6,1))+($B$2-(C$4>=WEEKDAY(DATE($A6,$B6,1))))*7
```

This formula applies some basic math to calculate which date within the month should be returned given a specific week number and occurrence.

To use the table in Figure 12.14, simply enter the years and months you are targeting, starting in cells A6 and B6. Then adjust the occurrence number you need in cell B2.

If you are looking for the first Monday of each month, enter a **1** in cell B2 and look in the Monday column. If you are looking for the third Thursday of each month, enter a **3** in cell B2 and look in the Thursday column.

Calculating the date of the last weekday of the month

You can leverage the functions covered in this chapter thus far to build a dynamic date table that automatically provides you with the last instance of a given weekday. For instance, Figure 12.15 illustrates a table that calculates the last Sunday, Monday, Tuesday, and so forth for each month listed.

FIGURE 12.15

A dynamic date table calculating the last weekday in each month

	A	B	C	D	E	F	G	H	I
1									
2			7	6	5	4	3	2	1
3	YEAR	MONTH	Last Sun of the Month	Last Mon of the Month	Last Tues of the Month	Last Wed of the Month	Last Thurs of the Month	Last Fri of the Month	Last Sat of the Month
4	2014	1	1/26/2014	1/27/2014	1/28/2014	1/29/2014	1/30/2014	1/31/2014	1/25/2014
5	2014	2	2/23/2014	2/24/2014	2/25/2014	2/26/2014	2/27/2014	2/28/2014	2/22/2014
6	2014	3	3/30/2014	3/31/2014	3/25/2014	3/26/2014	3/27/2014	3/28/2014	3/29/2014
7	2014	4	4/27/2014	4/28/2014	4/29/2014	4/30/2014	4/24/2014	4/25/2014	4/26/2014
8	2014	5	5/25/2014	5/26/2014	5/27/2014	5/28/2014	5/29/2014	5/30/2014	5/31/2014
9	2014	6	6/29/2014	6/30/2014	6/24/2014	6/25/2014	6/26/2014	6/27/2014	6/28/2014
10	2014	7	7/27/2014	7/28/2014	7/29/2014	7/30/2014	7/31/2014	7/25/2014	7/26/2014
11	2014	8	8/31/2014	8/25/2014	8/26/2014	8/27/2014	8/28/2014	8/29/2014	8/30/2014
12	2014	9	9/28/2014	9/29/2014	9/30/2014	9/24/2014	9/25/2014	9/26/2014	9/27/2014
13	2014	10	10/26/2014	10/27/2014	10/28/2014	10/29/2014	10/30/2014	10/31/2014	10/25/2014
14	2014	11	11/30/2014	11/24/2014	11/25/2014	11/26/2014	11/27/2014	11/28/2014	11/29/2014
15	2014	12	12/28/2014	12/29/2014	12/30/2014	12/31/2014	12/25/2014	12/26/2014	12/27/2014

Cell C4 (see Figure 12.15) contains the following formula:

```
=DATE($A4,$B4+1,1)- WEEKDAY(DATE($A4,$B4+1,C$2))
```

This formula applies some basic math to calculate which date within the month should be returned given a specific year, month, and week number.

To use the table in Figure 12.15, simply enter the years and months that you are targeting, starting in cells A4 and B4. The idea is to use this table in your Excel models as a place to which you can link or simply copy from to get the dates you need.

Extracting parts of a time

It's often helpful to pick out a specific part of a time. Excel provides a simple set of functions to parse time out into its component parts. These functions are as follows:

HOUR extracts the hour portion of a given time value.

MINUTE extracts the minute portion of a given time value.

SECOND extracts the second portion of a given time value.

Figure 12.16 demonstrates the use of these functions to parse the time in cell C3 into its component parts.

FIGURE 12.16

Extract the parts of a time.

◢	A	B	C
1			
2			
3			6:15:27 AM
4			
5		=HOUR(C3)	6
6		=MINUTE(C3)	15
7		=SECOND(C3)	27
8			

These functions are fairly straightforward.

The HOUR function returns a number between 0 and 23 corresponding to the hour of a given time. This formula returns 6.

```
=HOUR("6:15:27 AM")
```

The MINUTE function returns a number between 0 and 59 corresponding to the minutes of a given time. This formula returns 15.

```
=MINUTE("6:15:27 AM")
```

The SECOND function returns a number between 0 and 59 corresponding to the seconds of a given time. This formula returns 27.

```
=SECOND("6:15:27 AM")
```

Calculating elapsed time

One of the more common calculations done with time values is calculating elapsed time, that is, how many hours and minutes between a start time and an end time.

The table in Figure 12.17 shows a list of start and end times, along with calculated elapsed times. Look at Figure 12.17, and you can see that the formula in cell D4 is as follows:

```
=IF(C4< B4, 1 + C4 - B4, C4 - B4)
```

To get the elapsed time between a start and end time, all you need to do is to subtract the start time from the end time. There is a catch, however. If the end time is less than the start time, you have to assume that the clock has been running for a full 24-hour period, effectively looping back the clock.

In these cases, you have to add a 1 to the time to represent a full day. This ensures that you don't have negative elapsed times.

In our elapsed time formula, we use an IF function to check whether the end time is less than the start time. If so, we add a 1 to our simple subtraction. If not, we can just do the subtraction.

```
=IF(C4< B4, 1 + C4 - B4, C4 - B4)
```

FIGURE 12.17

Calculating elapsed time

	A	B	C	D
1				
2				
3		Start Time	End Time	Elapsed Minutes:Seconds
4		8:57:50 AM	10:04:39 AM	=IF(C4< B4, 1 + C4 - B4, C4 - B4)
5		4:35:20 PM	4:23:23 PM	23:48
6		8:24:35 AM	4:14:36 PM	7:50
7		3:10:39 PM	9:50:59 AM	18:40
8		2:33:22 PM	2:01:49 PM	23:28
9		8:42:35 AM	11:16:31 AM	2:33
10		11:20:24 AM	9:36:17 AM	22:15
11		3:56:53 PM	2:05:17 PM	22:08
12		3:33:16 PM	10:46:08 AM	19:12
13		12:41:54 PM	1:18:37 PM	0:36
14		11:30:07 AM	11:19:15 AM	23:40

 For more details on the IF function, see "Checking if a simple condition is met" in Chapter 13.

Rounding time values

It's often necessary to round time to a particular increment. For instance, if you're a consultant, you may always want to round time up to the next 15-minute increment or down to 30-minute increments.

Figure 12.18 demonstrates how you can round to 15- and 30-minute increments.

FIGURE 12.18

Rounding time values to 15- and 30-minute increments

	A	B	C	D	E	F
1						
2						
3		Start Time	End Time	Elapsed Minutes:Seconds	Round Up to Nearest 15 Minutes	Round Down to Nearest 30 minutes
4		8:49:12 AM	10:03:56 AM	1:14	10:15	10:00
5		10:58:31 AM	10:18:55 AM	23:20	10:30	10:00
6		9:23:37 AM	1:48:26 PM	4:24	14:00	13:30
7		8:39:16 AM	4:40:22 PM	8:01	16:45	16:30
8						

The formula in cell E4 is as follows:

```
=ROUNDUP(C4*24/0.25,0)*(0.25/24)
```

The formula in cell F4 is as follows:

```
=ROUNDDOWN(C4*24/0.5,0)*(0.5/24)
```

You can round a time value to the nearest hour by multiplying the time by 24, passing that value to the ROUNDUP function, and then dividing the result by 24. For instance, this formula would return 7:00:00 AM:

```
=ROUNDUP("6:15:27"*24,0)/24
```

To round up to 15-minute increments, you simply divide 24 by 0.25 (a quarter). This formula would return 6:30:00 AM:

```
=ROUNDUP("6:15:27"*24/0.25,0)*(0.25/24)
```

To round down to 30-minute increments, divide 24 by 0.5 (a half). This formula would return 6:00:00 AM:

```
=ROUNDDOWN("6:15:27"*24/0.5,0)*(0.5/24)
```

 For more details on the ROUNDDOWN and ROUNDUP functions, see Chapter 10, "Using Formulas for Common Mathematical Operations."

Converting decimal hours, minutes, or seconds to a time

It's not uncommon to get a feed from an external source where the times are recorded in decimal hours. For example, for 1 hour and 30 minutes, you see 1.5 instead of the standard 1:30. You can easily correct this by dividing the decimal hour by 24 and then formatting the result as a time.

Figure 12.19 shows some example decimal hours and the converted times.

FIGURE 12.19

Converting decimal hours to hours and minutes

⊿	A	B	C
1			
2		Decimal Hours	Hours:Minutes
3		11.50	=B3/24
4		13.75	13:45
5		18.25	18:15
6		11.35	11:21
7		12.45	12:27
8		15.60	15:36
9		18.36	18:21
10		18.56	18:33
11		21.83	21:49

Dividing the decimal hour by 24 will result in a decimal that Excel recognizes as a time value.

To convert decimal minutes into time, divide the number by 1440. This formula will return 1:04 (one hour and four minutes):

```
=64.51/1440
```

To convert decimal seconds into time, divide the number by 86400. This formula will return 0:06 (six minutes):

```
=390.45/86400
```

Adding hours, minutes, or seconds to a time

Because time values are nothing more than a decimal extension of the date serial number system, you can add two time values together to get a cumulative time value. In some cases, you may want to add a set number of hours and minutes to an existing time value. In these situations, you can use the TIME function.

Cell D4 in Figure 12.20 contains this formula:

```
=C4+TIME(5,30,0)
```

In this example, we're adding 5 hours and 30 minutes to all of the times in the list.

FIGURE 12.20

Adding a set number of hours and minutes to an existing time value

	A	B	C	D
1				
2				
3			Start Time	End time if working 5 hours and 30 minutes
4			3:00:52 PM	=C4+TIME(5,30,0)
5			3:43:03 PM	9:13:03 PM
6			12:30:14 PM	6:00:14 PM
7			8:08:53 AM	1:38:53 PM
8			11:33:56 AM	5:03:56 PM
9			3:55:18 PM	9:25:18 PM

The TIME function lets you build a time value on the fly using three arguments: hour, minute, and second. For example, this formula would return the time value 2:30:30 PM:

```
=TIME(14,30,30)
```

To add a certain number of hours to an existing time value, simply use the TIME function to build a new time value and then add them together. This formula adds 30 minutes to the existing time, resulting in a time value of 3:00 PM:

```
="2:30:00 PM" + TIME(0, 30, 0)
```

Using Formulas for Conditional Analysis

IN THIS CHAPTER

Understanding conditional analysis

Performing conditional calculations

E xcel provides several worksheet functions for performing conditional analysis. You'll use some of those functions in this chapter. Conditional analysis means performing different actions depending on whether a condition is met.

Understanding Conditional Analysis

A condition is a value or expression that returns TRUE or FALSE. Based on the value of the condition, a formula can branch into two separate calculations. That is, when the condition returns TRUE, one value or expression is evaluated while the other is ignored. A FALSE condition reverses the flow of the formula, and the first value or expression is ignored while the other is evaluated.

In this section, you'll explore some of the logical functions available in Excel.

 This book's website, www.wiley.com/go/excel2019bible, includes a copy of the sample workbook for this chapter. The file is named Conditional Analysis.xlsx.

Checking if a simple condition is met

Figure 13.1 shows a list of states and six monthly gas prices. For each price, say you want to determine whether that state's price in that month is above or below the average of all the states for the same month. For higher than average prices, you will report "High" and for lower than average "Low." A grid below the data will be used to report the results.

```
=IF(C3>AVERAGE(C$3:C$11),"High","Low")
```

FIGURE 13.1

Monthly gas prices by state

	C14			f_x	=IF(C3>AVERAGE(C$3:C$11),"High","Low")				
	A	B	C	D	E	F	G	H	I
1									
2		State	Aug-13	Sep-13	Oct-13	Nov-13	Dec-13	Jan-14	
3		California	3.919	3.989	3.829	3.641	3.642	3.666	
4		Colorado	3.569	3.582	3.410	3.231	3.122	3.238	
5		Florida	3.614	3.558	3.388	3.377	3.516	3.486	
6		Massachusetts	3.761	3.703	3.518	3.419	3.520	3.527	
7		Minnesota	3.577	3.540	3.318	3.143	3.113	3.272	
8		New York	3.933	3.879	3.700	3.633	3.736	3.734	
9		Ohio	3.542	3.512	3.317	3.231	3.281	3.336	
10		Texas	3.509	3.383	3.180	3.104	3.171	3.187	
11		Washington	3.855	3.767	3.567	3.373	3.348	3.366	
12									
13									
14		California	High	High	High	High	High	High	
15		Colorado	Low	Low	Low	Low	Low	Low	
16		Florida	Low	Low	Low	High	High	High	
17		Massachusetts	High	High	High	High	High	High	
18		Minnesota	Low	Low	Low	Low	Low	Low	
19		New York	High	High	High	High	High	High	
20		Ohio	Low	Low	Low	Low	Low	Low	
21		Texas	Low	Low	Low	Low	Low	Low	
22		Washington	High	High	High	High	Low	Low	
23									

The IF function is the most basic conditional analysis function in Excel. It has three arguments: the condition, what to do if the condition is true, and what to do if the condition is false.

The condition argument in this example is C3>AVERAGE(C$3:C$11). Condition arguments must be structured to return TRUE or FALSE, and this usually means that there is a comparison operation (like an equal sign or greater-than sign) or another worksheet function that returns TRUE or FALSE (like ISERR or ISBLANK). The example condition has a greater-than sign and compares the value in C3 to the average of all the values in C3:C11.

If our condition argument returns TRUE, the second argument of the IF function is returned to the cell. The second argument is High, and since the value in C3 is indeed larger than the average, cell C14 shows the word High.

Cell C15 compares the value in C4 to the average. Because it is lower, the condition argument returns FALSE, and the third argument is returned. Cell C15 shows Low, the third argument of the IF function.

Checking for multiple conditions

Simple conditions like the one shown in Figure 13.1 can be strung together. This is known as *nesting* functions. The value_if_true and value_if_false arguments can contain simple conditions of their own. This allows you to test more than one condition where subsequent conditions are dependent on the first one.

Figure 13.2 shows a spreadsheet with two user input fields for the type of automobile and a property of that automobile type. The properties are listed in two ranges below the user input fields. When the user selects the type and property, we want a formula to report whether the user has identified a coupe, a sedan, a pickup, or an SUV.

```
=IF(E2="Car",IF(E3="2-door","Coupe","Sedan"),IF(E3="Has
Bed","Pickup","SUV"))
```

FIGURE 13.2

A model for selecting an automobile

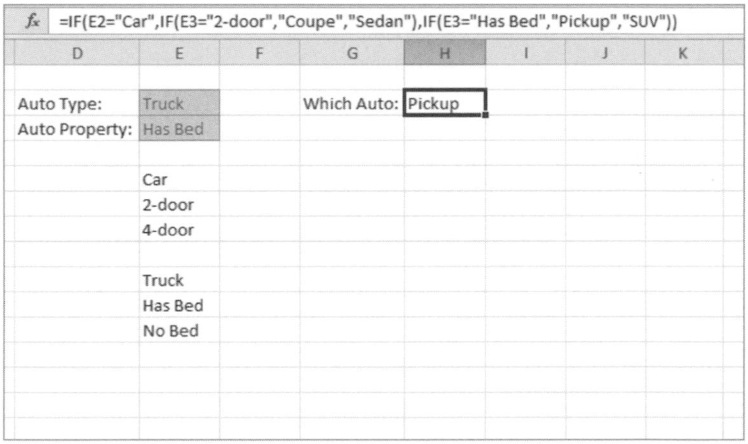

With some conditional analysis, the result of the first condition causes the second condition to change. In this case, if the first condition is Car, the second condition is 2-door or 4-door. But if the first condition is Truck, the second condition changes to either Has Bed or No Bed.

You've seen that Excel provides the IF function to perform conditional analysis. You can also nest IF functions; that is, you can use another IF function as an argument to the first IF function when you need to check more than one condition. In this example, the first IF checks the value of E2. Rather than returning a value if TRUE, the second argument is another IF formula that checks the value of cell E3. Similarly, the third argument doesn't simply return a value of FALSE, but it contains a third IF function that also evaluates cell E3.

In Figure 13.2, the user has selected Truck. The first IF returns FALSE because E2 doesn't equal Car and the FALSE argument is evaluated. In that argument, E3 is seen to be equal to Has Bed and the TRUE condition (Pickup) is returned. If the user had selected No Bed, the FALSE condition (SUV) would have been the result.

Validating conditional data

The user input fields in Figure 13.2 are actually data validation lists. The user can make selections from a drop-down box rather than typing in the values. The data validation in cell E3 uses an interesting technique with an INDIRECT function to change its list depending on the value in E2.

There are two named ranges in the worksheet. The range named Car points to E6:E7, and the range named Truck points to E10:E11. The names are identical to choices in the E2 data validation list. Figure 13.3 shows the Data Validation dialog box for cell E3. The source is an INDIRECT function with E2 as the argument.

FIGURE 13.3

Data validation using INDIRECT

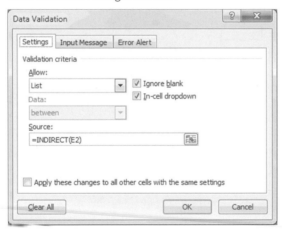

The INDIRECT function takes a text argument that it resolves into a cell reference. In this case, since E2 is Truck, the formula becomes =INDIRECT("Truck"). Because Truck is a named range, INDIRECT returns a reference to E10:E11, and the values in those cells become the choices. If E2 contained Car, INDIRECT would return E6:E7, and those values become the choices.

One problem with this type of conditional data validation is that when the value in E2 is changed, the value in E3 does not change. The choices in E3 change, but the user still has to select from the available choices or your formulas may return inaccurate results.

Looking up values

When you have too many nested IF functions, your formulas can become long and hard to manage. Figure 13.4 shows a slightly different setup to the auto-selector model. Instead of hard-coding the results in nested IF functions, the results are entered into the cells next to their properties (for example, Sedan is entered in the cell next to 4-door).

FIGURE 13.4

A different auto-selector model

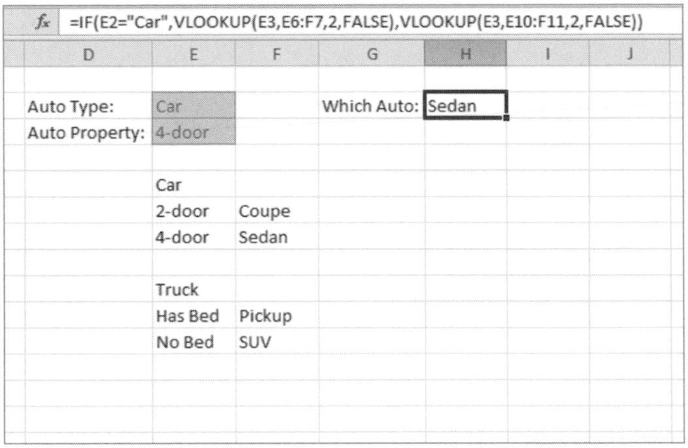

f_x =IF(E2="Car",VLOOKUP(E3,E6:F7,2,FALSE),VLOOKUP(E3,E10:F11,2,FALSE))

D	E	F	G	H	I	J
Auto Type:	Car		Which Auto:	Sedan		
Auto Property:	4-door					
	Car					
	2-door	Coupe				
	4-door	Sedan				
	Truck					
	Has Bed	Pickup				
	No Bed	SUV				

The new formula is as follows:

    =IF(E2="Car",VLOOKUP(E3,E6:F7,2,FALSE),VLOOKUP(E3,E10:F11,2,FALSE))

This formula can now be used to return the automobile. The IF condition is the same, but now a TRUE result looks up the proper value in E6:E7, and a FALSE result looks it up in E10:F11. You can learn more about VLOOKUP in Chapter 14.

Checking if Condition1 AND Condition2 are met

In addition to nesting conditional functions, they can be evaluated together inside an AND function. This is useful when two or more conditions need to be evaluated at the same time to determine where the formula should branch.

Figure 13.5 shows a listing of inventory items, their quantities, and the discount that applies when they are sold. The inventory items are structured with three sections divided by hyphens. The first section is the department; the second section determines whether the item is a part, a subassembly, or a final assembly; and the third condition is a unique four-digit number. We want to assign a discount of 10 percent only to those items that are in Department 202 and are final assemblies. All other items have no discount.

    =IF(AND(LEFT(B3,3)="202",MID(B3,5,3)="FIN"),10%,0%)

The IF function returns 10 percent if TRUE and 0 percent if FALSE. For the condition argument (the first argument), you need an expression that returns TRUE if both the first section of the item number is 202 and the second section is FIN. Excel provides the AND function to accomplish this. The AND function takes up to 255 logical arguments separated by commas. Logical arguments are expressions that return either TRUE or FALSE. For this example, we're using only two logical arguments.

FIGURE 13.5

An inventory listing

fx	=IF(AND(LEFT(B3,3)="202",MID(B3,5,3)="FIN"),10%,0%)				
A	B	C	D	E	F
1					
2	Inventory Item	Quantity	Discount		
3	202-PRT-3013	76	0%		
4	201-FIN-1452	69	0%		
5	202-FIN-8206	12	10%		
6	201-FIN-8238	79	0%		
7	203-FIN-8882	16	0%		
8	202-PRT-9587	87	0%		
9	203-FIN-4614	97	0%		
10	201-PRT-2478	25	0%		
11	202-SUB-1955	14	0%		
12	201-SUB-8641	67	0%		
13	202-FIN-9069	40	10%		
14	202-PRT-7937	61	0%		
15	201-SUB-3124	70	0%		
16	203-SUB-4369	16	0%		
17	202-FIN-6273	74	10%		
18	203-SUB-3972	85	0%		
19	203-PRT-3335	84	0%		
20	201-SUB-1022	48	0%		
21	203-FIN-3507	17	0%		
22	203-SUB-8304	31	0%		
23					
24					

The first logical argument, LEFT(B3,3)="202", returns TRUE if the first three characters of B3 are equal to 202. The second logical argument, MID(B3,5,3)="FIN", returns TRUE if the three digits starting at the fifth position are equal to FIN. Text manipulation functions are discussed in Chapter 11.

With the AND function, all logical arguments must return TRUE for the entire function to return TRUE. If even one of the logical arguments returns FALSE, then the AND function returns FALSE. Table 13.1 shows the results of the AND function with two logical arguments.

TABLE 13.1 A Truth Table for the AND Function

First Logical Argument	Second Logical Argument	Result of AND Function
TRUE	TRUE	TRUE
TRUE	FALSE	FALSE
FALSE	TRUE	FALSE
FALSE	FALSE	FALSE

In cell D3, the first logical condition returns TRUE because the first three characters of the item number are 202. The second logical condition returns FALSE because the middle section of the item number is PRT, not FIN. According to Table 13.1, a TRUE condition and a FALSE condition return FALSE, and 0 percent is the result. Cell D5, on the other hand, returns TRUE because both logical conditions return TRUE.

Referring to logical conditions in cells

The AND function in Figure 13.5 includes two logical conditions that evaluate to TRUE or FALSE. The arguments to AND can also reference cells as long as those cells evaluate to TRUE or FALSE. When building a formula with the AND function, it can be useful to break out the logical conditions into their own cells. In Figure 13.6, the inventory listing is modified to show two extra columns. These columns can be inspected to understand why a particular item does or does not get the discount.

FIGURE 13.6

A modified inventory listing

	A	B	C	D	E	F	G
					fx =IF(AND(D3,E3),10%,0%)		
1							
2		Inventory Item	Quantity	IsDept202	IsFinalAssembly	Discount	
3		202-PRT-3013	76	TRUE	FALSE	0%	
4		201-FIN-1452	69	FALSE	TRUE	0%	
5		202-FIN-8206	12	TRUE	TRUE	10%	
6		201-FIN-8238	79	FALSE	TRUE	0%	
7		203-FIN-8882	16	FALSE	TRUE	0%	
8		202-PRT-9587	87	TRUE	FALSE	0%	
9		203-FIN-4614	97	FALSE	TRUE	0%	
10		201-PRT-2478	25	FALSE	FALSE	0%	
11		202-SUB-1955	14	TRUE	FALSE	0%	
12		201-SUB-8641	67	FALSE	FALSE	0%	
13		202-FIN-9069	40	TRUE	TRUE	10%	
14		202-PRT-7937	61	TRUE	FALSE	0%	
15		201-SUB-3124	70	FALSE	FALSE	0%	
16		203-SUB-4369	16	FALSE	FALSE	0%	
17		202-FIN-6273	74	TRUE	TRUE	10%	
18		203-SUB-3972	85	FALSE	FALSE	0%	
19		203-PRT-3335	84	FALSE	FALSE	0%	
20		201-SUB-1022	48	FALSE	FALSE	0%	
21		203-FIN-3507	17	FALSE	TRUE	0%	
22		203-SUB-8304	31	FALSE	FALSE	0%	
23							
24							

With these modifications, the result doesn't change, but the formula becomes

```
=IF(AND(D3,E3),10%,0%)
```

Checking if Condition1 OR Condition2 are met

In Figure 13.6, we applied a discount to certain products based on their item number. In this example, we want to expand the number of products eligible for the discount. As before, only final assembly products will get the discount, but the departments will be expanded to include both department 202 and department 203. Figure 13.7 shows the inventory list and the new discount schedule.

```
=IF(AND(OR(LEFT(B3,3)="202",LEFT(B3,3)="203"),MID(B3,5,3)="
FIN"),10%,0%)
```

FIGURE 13.7

A revised discount scheme

	A	B	C	D	E	F	G	H
		_fx_	=IF(AND(OR(LEFT(B9,3)="202",LEFT(B9,3)="203"),MID(B9,5,3)="FIN"),10%,0%)					
1								
2		Inventory Item	Quantity	Discount				
3		202-PRT-3013	76	0%				
4		201-FIN-1452	69	0%				
5		202-FIN-8206	12	10%				
6		201-FIN-8238	79	0%				
7		203-FIN-8882	16	10%				
8		202-PRT-9587	87	0%				
9		203-FIN-4614	97	10%				
10		201-PRT-2478	25	0%				
11		202-SUB-1955	14	0%				
12		201-SUB-8641	67	0%				
13		202-FIN-9069	40	10%				
14		202-PRT-7937	61	0%				
15		201-SUB-3124	70	0%				
16		203-SUB-4369	16	0%				
17		202-FIN-6273	74	10%				
18		203-SUB-3972	85	0%				
19		203-PRT-3335	84	0%				
20		201-SUB-1022	48	0%				
21		203-FIN-3507	17	10%				
22		203-SUB-8304	31	0%				

We've expanded the conditional argument to the IF function to account for the changes in the discount scheme. The AND function is restrictive because all of the arguments must be TRUE for AND to return TRUE. Conversely, the OR function is inclusive. With OR, if any one of the arguments is TRUE, the entire function returns TRUE. In this example, we've nested an OR function inside the AND function—we've made it one of the arguments. Table 13.2 shows a truth table for how our nested functions work.

Cell D9 in Figure 13.7 shows a previously undiscounted product that receives a discount under the new scheme. The OR section, OR(LEFT(B9,3)="202",LEFT(B9,3)="203"), returns TRUE because one of its arguments returns TRUE.

TABLE 13.2   A Truth Table for an OR Function Nested in an AND Function

OR Logical 1	OR Logical 2	OR Result	AND Logical 2	Final Result
TRUE	TRUE	TRUE	TRUE	TRUE
TRUE	FALSE	TRUE	TRUE	TRUE
FALSE	TRUE	TRUE	TRUE	TRUE
FALSE	FALSE	FALSE	TRUE	FALSE
TRUE	TRUE	TRUE	FALSE	FALSE
TRUE	FALSE	TRUE	FALSE	FALSE
FALSE	TRUE	TRUE	FALSE	FALSE
FALSE	FALSE	FALSE	FALSE	FALSE

Performing Conditional Calculations

Simple conditional functions like IF generally work on only one value or cell at a time. Excel provides some different conditional functions for aggregating data, such as summing or averaging.

In this section, you'll dive into some of the techniques for applying calculations based on a given set of conditions.

Summing all values that meet a certain condition

Figure 13.8 shows a listing of accounts with positive and negative values. We want to sum all of the negative balances, which we will later compare to the sum of all the positive balances to ensure that they are equal. Excel provides the SUMIF function to sum values based on a condition.

```
=SUMIF(C3:C12,"<0")
```

SUMIF takes each value in C3:C12 and compares it to the condition (the second argument in our function). If the value is less than zero, it meets the condition and is included in the sum. If it is zero or greater, the value is ignored. Text values and blank cells are also ignored. For the example in Figure 13.8, cell C3 is evaluated first. Because it is greater than zero, it is ignored. Next, cell C4 is evaluated. It meets our condition of being less than zero, so it is added to the total. This continues for each cell. When it's complete, cells C4, C7, C8, C9, and C11 are included in the sum, and the others are not.

The second argument of SUMIF, the condition to be met, has quotes around it. Because we're using a less-than sign for this example, we have to create a string that represents the expression.

FIGURE 13.8

Summing values less than zero

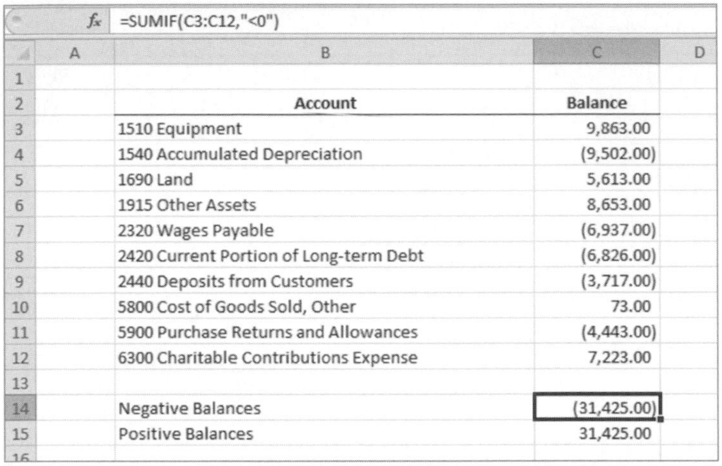

	fx	=SUMIF(C3:C12,"<0")		
	A	B	C	D
1				
2		Account	Balance	
3		1510 Equipment	9,863.00	
4		1540 Accumulated Depreciation	(9,502.00)	
5		1690 Land	5,613.00	
6		1915 Other Assets	8,653.00	
7		2320 Wages Payable	(6,937.00)	
8		2420 Current Portion of Long-term Debt	(6,826.00)	
9		2440 Deposits from Customers	(3,717.00)	
10		5800 Cost of Goods Sold, Other	73.00	
11		5900 Purchase Returns and Allowances	(4,443.00)	
12		6300 Charitable Contributions Expense	7,223.00	
13				
14		Negative Balances	(31,425.00)	
15		Positive Balances	31,425.00	
16				

The SUMIF function has an optional third argument called the sum_range. So far, we've been applying the condition to the very numbers we are summing. By using the third argument, we can sum a range of numbers but apply our conditions to a different range. Figure 13.9 shows a listing of regions and their associated sales. To sum the sales for the East region, use the formula =SUMIF(B2:B11,"East",C2:C11).

FIGURE 13.9

List of regions and sales values

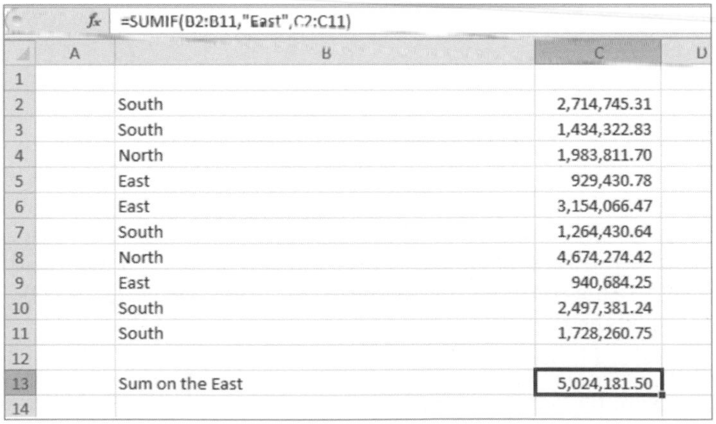

	fx	=SUMIF(B2:B11,"East",C2:C11)		
	A	B	C	D
1				
2		South	2,714,745.31	
3		South	1,434,322.83	
4		North	1,983,811.70	
5		East	929,430.78	
6		East	3,154,066.47	
7		South	1,264,430.64	
8		North	4,674,274.42	
9		East	940,684.25	
10		South	2,497,381.24	
11		South	1,728,260.75	
12				
13		Sum on the East	5,024,181.50	
14				

Summing greater than zero

Figure 13.8 also shows the total of all the positive balances. The formula for that calculation is =SUMIF(C3:C12,">0"). Note that the only difference between this formula and our example formula is the expression string. Instead of "<0" as the second argument, this formula has ">0".

We don't have to include zero in our calculation because we're summing and zero never changes a sum. If, however, we were interested in summing numbers greater or less than 1,000, we couldn't simply use "<1000" and ">1000" as our second arguments because we would never include anything that was exactly 1,000.

When you use greater than or less than a nonzero number in a SUMIF, make either the greater than a greater than or equal to, such as ">=1000", or the less than a less than or equal to, such as "<=1000". Don't use the equal sign for both; just use one. This will ensure that you include any numbers that are exactly 1,000 in one or the other calculation but not both.

The syntax needed to use your comparison operators can be tricky. Table 13.3 lists a set of simple rules that can help you get it right every time.

TABLE 13.3 Simple Rules for Using Comparison Operators

To Set a Condition...	...Follow These Rules	For Example
Equal to a number or cell reference	Don't use an equal sign or any double quotes.	=SUMIF(A1:A10,3)
Equal to a string	Don't use an equal sign, but put the string in quotes.	=SUMIF(A1:A10,"book")
Nonequal comparison to a number	Put both the operator and the number in double quotes.	=SUMIF(A1:A10,">=50")
Nonequal comparison to a string	Put both the operator and the string in double quotes.	=SUMIF(A1:A10,"<>Payroll")
Nonequal comparison to a cell reference or formula	Put the operator in double quotes and concatenate the cell reference or formula with the ampersand (&).	=SUMIF(A1:A10,"<"&C1)

You can use the TODAY function (to get the current date), or most other functions, in the second argument. Figure 13.10 shows a listing of dates and values. To sum a range of numbers that correspond to today, use the formula =SUMIF(B3:B11,TODAY(),C3:C11). To sum only those values that are today or before, concatenate the less-than-or-equal-to sign to the function, such as =SUMIF(B3:B11,"<="&TODAY(),C3:C11).

FIGURE 13.10

SUMIF using the TODAY function

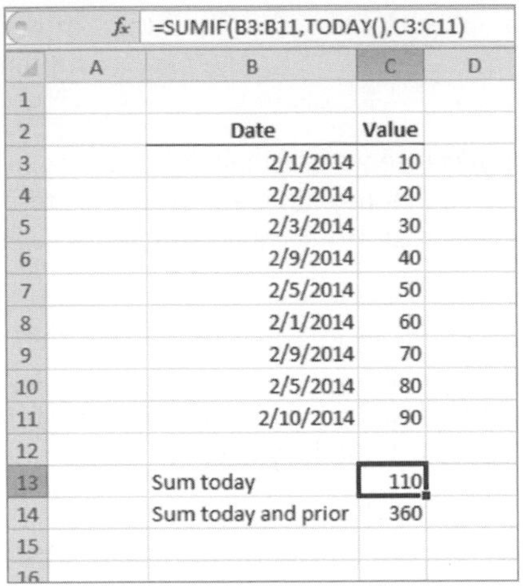

	fx	=SUMIF(B3:B11,TODAY(),C3:C11)		
	A	B	C	D
1				
2		Date	Value	
3		2/1/2014	10	
4		2/2/2014	20	
5		2/3/2014	30	
6		2/9/2014	40	
7		2/5/2014	50	
8		2/1/2014	60	
9		2/9/2014	70	
10		2/5/2014	80	
11		2/10/2014	90	
12				
13		Sum today	110	
14		Sum today and prior	360	
15				
16				

There are two wildcard characters that you can use in the condition argument to SUMIF. The question mark (?) represents any single character, and the asterisk (*) represents zero, one, or any number of characters. The formula =SUMIF(B2:B11,"?o*",C2:C11) will sum all the values in C2:C11 that correspond to the values in B2:B11 where the second character is a lowercase *o*. If we apply that formula to the data in Figure 13.9, we will get the sum for sales in both the North and South regions because both have a lowercase *o* as the second letter and East does not.

Summing all values that meet two or more conditions

The limitation of SUMIF shown in Figure 13.9 is that it works with only one condition. The SUMIFS function can be used when more than one condition is needed.

Figure 13.11 shows a partial listing of countries and their gross domestic product (GDP) from 2000 to 2009. We want to total Brazil's GDP from 2003 to 2006. Excel's SUMIFS worksheet function is used to sum values where two or more conditions must be met, such as Country and Year in this example.

    =SUMIFS(D3:D212,B3:B212,G3,C3:C212,">="&G4,C3:C212,"<="&G5)

SUMIFS arguments start with the range that contains the value that you want to sum. The remaining arguments are in pairs that follow the pattern *criteria_range, criteria*. Because of the way that the arguments are laid out, SUMIFS will always have an odd number of arguments. The first criteria pair is required—without at least one condition, SUMIFS would be no different than SUM. The remaining pairs of conditions, up to 126 of them, are optional.

    =SUMIFS(D3:D212,B3:B212,G3,C3:C212,">="&G4,C3:C212,"<="&G5)

FIGURE 13.11

A partial listing of countries and their gross domestic product

fx		=SUMIFS(D3:D212,B3:B212,G3,C3:C212,">="&G4,C3:C212,"<="&G5)						

	A	B	C	D	E	F	G
1							
2		Country	Year	GDP			
3		Australia	2000	399,594		Country	Brazil
4		Australia	2001	377,207		Start Year	2003
5		Australia	2002	423,676		End Year	2006
6		Australia	2003	539,162			
7		Australia	2004	654,968		Total GDP	3,187,415
8		Australia	2005	730,729		Using SUMPRODUCT	3,187,415
9		Australia	2006	777,933			
10		Australia	2007	945,364			
11		Australia	2008	1,051,261			
12		Australia	2009	993,349			
13		Belgium	2000	233,354			
14		Belgium	2001	232,686			
15		Belgium	2002	253,689			
16		Belgium	2003	312,285			
17		Belgium	2004	362,160			
18		Belgium	2005	378,006			
19		Belgium	2006	400,337			
20		Belgium	2007	460,280			
21		Belgium	2008	509,765			
22		Belgium	2009	474,580			
23		Brazil	2000	644,734			
24		Brazil	2001	554,185			
25		Brazil	2002	506,043			
26		Brazil	2003	552,383			
27		Brazil	2004	663,734			
28		Brazil	2005	882,043			
29		Brazil	2006	1,089,255			
30		Brazil	2007	1,366,854			
31		Brazil	2008	1,653,538			
32		Brazil	2009	1,622,311			
33		Canada	2000	739,451			

In this example, each cell in D3:D212 is added to the total only if the corresponding values in B3:B212 and C3:C212 meet their respective conditions. The condition for B3:B212 is that it matches whatever is in cell G3. There are two year conditions because we need to define the lower bound and upper bound of our year range. The lower bound is in cell G4, and the upper bound is in cell G5. Those two cells are concatenated with greater than or equal to and less than or equal to, respectively, to create the year conditions. Only if all three conditions are true is the value included in the total.

Summing if values fall between a given date range

One way that you can use SUMIF with two or more conditions is to add or subtract multiple SUMIF calculations. If the two conditions operate on the same range, this is an effective way to use multiple conditions. When you want to test different ranges, the formulas get tricky because you have to make sure you don't double count values.

Figure 13.12 shows a list of dates and amounts. We want to find the sum of the values that are between June 23 and June 29, inclusive. The starting and ending dates will be put in cells F4 and F5, respectively.

```
=SUMIF(B3:B20,"<="&F5,C3:C20)-SUMIF(B3:B20,"<"&F4,C3:C20)
```

FIGURE 13.12

Summing values that are between two dates

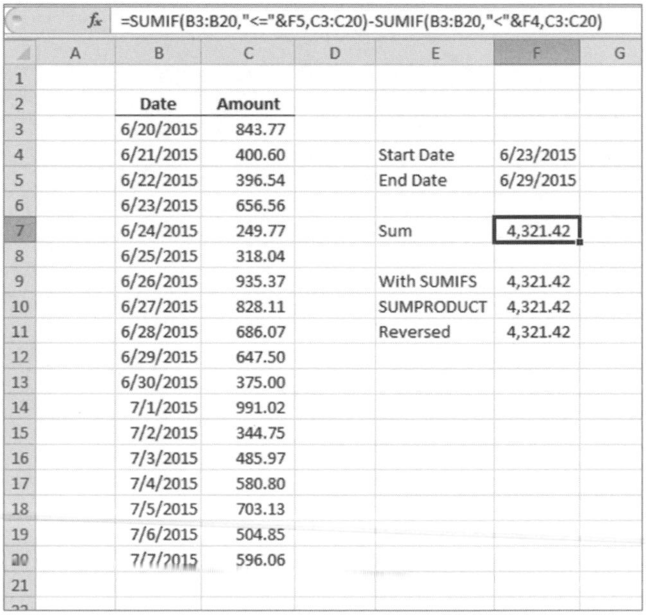

	A	B	C	D	E	F	G
	fx	=SUMIF(B3:B20,"<="&F5,C3:C20)-SUMIF(B3:B20,"<"&F4,C3:C20)					
1							
2		Date	Amount				
3		6/20/2015	843.77				
4		6/21/2015	400.60		Start Date	6/23/2015	
5		6/22/2015	396.54		End Date	6/29/2015	
6		6/23/2015	656.56				
7		6/24/2015	249.77		Sum	4,321.42	
8		6/25/2015	318.04				
9		6/26/2015	935.37		With SUMIFS	4,321.42	
10		6/27/2015	828.11		SUMPRODUCT	4,321.42	
11		6/28/2015	686.07		Reversed	4,321.42	
12		6/29/2015	647.50				
13		6/30/2015	375.00				
14		7/1/2015	991.02				
15		7/2/2015	344.75				
16		7/3/2015	485.97				
17		7/4/2015	580.80				
18		7/5/2015	703.13				
19		7/6/2015	504.85				
20		7/7/2015	596.06				
21							

This technique subtracts one SUMIF from another to get the desired result. The first SUMIF, SUMIF(B3:B20,"<="&F5,C3:C20), returns the sum of the values less than or equal to the date in F5, June 29 in this example. The conditional argument is the less-than-or-equal-to operator concatenated to the cell reference F5. If that was the whole formula, the result would be 5,962.33. But we want only values that are also greater than or equal to June 23. That means we want to exclude values that are less than June 23. The second SUMIF achieves that. Sum everything less than or equal to the later date, and subtract everything less than the earlier date to get the sum of values between the two dates.

Using SUMIFS

You may even find SUMIFS to be more intuitive than the subtraction technique. The formula =SUMIFS(C3:C20,B3:B20,"<="&F5,B3:B20,">="&F4) sums the values in C3:C20 that correspond to the values in B3:B20 that meet the criteria pairs. The first criteria pair is identical to the first `SUMIF` criteria, `"<="&F5`. The second criteria pair limits the dates to greater than or equal to the start date.

Getting a count of values that meet a certain condition

Summing values isn't the only aggregation you can do in Excel. Like `SUMIF` and `SUMIFS`, Excel provides functions for conditionally counting values in a range.

In Figure 13.13, there is a partial listing of countries and their gross domestic product from 2000 to 2009. We want to know how many times the GDP was greater than or equal to 1 million. The criteria to be applied will be in cell G3.

```
=COUNTIF(D3:D212,G3)
```

FIGURE 13.13

A partial listing of countries and their gross domestic product

fx =COUNTIF(D3:D212,G3)

	A	B	C	D	E	F	G	H
1								
2		Country	Year	GDP				
3		Australia	2000	399,594		Criterion	>=1000000	
4		Australia	2001	377,207				
5		Australia	2002	423,676		Count	96	
6		Australia	2003	539,162				
7		Australia	2004	654,968		Between	500000	
8		Australia	2005	730,729		And	1000000	
9		Australia	2006	777,933				
10		Australia	2007	945,364		Count	62	
11		Australia	2008	1,051,261				
12		Australia	2009	993,349		SUMPRODUCT	96	
13		Belgium	2000	233,354				
14		Belgium	2001	232,686				
15		Belgium	2002	253,689				
16		Belgium	2003	312,285				
17		Belgium	2004	362,160				
18		Belgium	2005	378,006				
19		Belgium	2006	400,337				
20		Belgium	2007	460,280				
21		Belgium	2008	509,765				
22		Belgium	2009	474,580				
23		Brazil	2000	644,734				
24		Brazil	2001	554,185				
25		Brazil	2002	506,043				
26		Brazil	2003	552,383				
27		Brazil	2004	663,734				
28		Brazil	2005	882,043				
29		Brazil	2006	1,089,255				

The `COUNTIF` function works in a similar manner as the `SUMIF` function from Figure 13.9. The obvious difference, as the name suggests, is that it counts entries that meet the criteria rather than sum them. Another difference is that there is no optional third argument as there is in SUMIF. With SUMIF, you can sum a range that's different from the range to which the criterion is applied. But with COUNTIF, that wouldn't make sense because counting a different range would get the same result.

The formula in this example uses a slightly different technique to construct the criteria argument. The string concatenation occurs all in cell G3 rather than in the function's second argument. If we had done it the same as SUMIF in Figure 13.11, the second argument would look like ">=1000000" or ">="&G3 rather than just pointing to G3. You may also note that the formula in G3, =">="&10^6, uses the exponent operator, or caret (^), to calculate 1 million. Representing large numbers using the caret can help reduce errors caused by miscounting the number of zeros that you typed.

Getting a count of values that meet two or more conditions

The SUMIF function has its COUNTIF cousin. Of course, Microsoft couldn't introduce SUMIFS for summing multiple conditions without also introducing COUNTIFS to count them.

In Figure 13.14, there is a list of Alpine Skiing medalists from the 1972 Winter Olympics. We would like to know how many silver medalists have an ö in their name. The letter we're looking for is typed in cell I3 and the type of medal in cell I4.

```
=COUNTIFS(C3:C20,"*"&I3&"*",F3:F20,I4)
```

FIGURE 13.14

1972 Alpine Skiing Olympic medalists

	A	B	C	D	E	F	G	H	I	J
				f_x	=COUNTIFS(C3:C20,"*"&I3&"*",F3:F20,I4)					
1										
2		Event	Athlete	Country	Result	Medal				
3		Downhill Men	Bernhard Russi	SUI	01:51.4	GOLD		Name contains	ö	
4		Downhill Men	Roland Collombin	SUI	01:52.1	SILVER		Medal Won	SILVER	
5		Downhill Men	Heini Messner	AUT	01:52.4	BRONZE		Count	3	
6		Slalom Men	Francisco Fernández	ESP	01:49.3	GOLD		SUMPRODUCT	3	
7		Slalom Men	Gustav Thöni	ITA	01:50.3	SILVER				
8		Slalom Men	Roland Thöni	ITA	01:50.3	BRONZE		T	84	
9		Giant Slalom Men	Gustav Thöni	ITA	03:09.6	GOLD		h	104	
10		Giant Slalom Men	Edmund Bruggmann	SUI	03:10.7	SILVER		ö	246	
11		Giant Slalom Men	Werner Mattle	SUI	03:11.0	BRONZE		n	110	
12		Downhill Women	Marie-Thérès Nadig	SUI	01:36.7	GOLD		i	105	
13		Downhill Women	Annemarie Moser-Pröll	AUT	01:37.0	SILVER				
14		Downhill Women	Susan Corrock	USA	01:37.7	BRONZE				
15		Slalom Women	Barbara Cochran	USA	01:31.2	GOLD				
16		Slalom Women	Danièlle Debernard	FRA	01:31.3	SILVER				
17		Slalom Women	Florence Steurer	FRA	01:32.7	BRONZE				
18		Giant Slalom Women	Marie-Thérès Nadig	SUI	01:29.9	GOLD				
19		Giant Slalom Women	Annemarie Moser-Pröll	AUT	01:30.8	SILVER				
20		Giant Slalom Women	Wiltrud Drexel	AUT	01:32.4	BRONZE				
21										

The criteria_range and criteria arguments come in pairs just like in SUMIFS. Whereas SUMIFS will always have an odd number of arguments, COUNTIFS will always have an even number.

The first criteria_range argument is the list of athlete names in C3:C20. The matching criteria argument, "*"&I3&"*", surrounds whatever is in I3 with asterisks. Asterisks are wildcard characters in COUNTIFS that stand for zero, one, or more characters of any kind. By including an asterisk both before and after the character, we're asking Excel to count all of the names that include that character anywhere within the name. That is, we don't care if there are zero, one, or more characters before ö, and we don't care if there are zero, one, or more characters after ö as long as that character is in there somewhere.

The second criteria_range, criteria argument pair counts those entries in F3:F20 that are SILVER (the value typed into I4). Only those rows where both the first argument pair and the second argument pair match (only rows where the athlete's name contains ö *and* the medal won was silver) are counted. In this example, Gustav Thöni won the silver in the Men's Slalom, and Annemarie Moser-Pröll placed in both the Women's Downhill and the Women's Giant Slalom for a count of three.

Finding nonstandard characters

The ö was typed into cell I3 by holding down the Alt key and typing 0246 on the numeric keyboard. Don't try to type those numbers on the number keys across the top of your keyboard because it won't work. The number 246 is the ASCII code that represents ö. Every character in this chapter has an ASCII code.

In cells H8:I12 in Figure 13.14, you can see a small table of characters and their codes. In cell H8, the formula =MID($C$8,ROW(),1) returns the eighth character from the name in cell C8. (The eighth character was chosen somewhat haphazardly. It was somewhere before the character we're looking for but not too far away.) That formula is copied down a few rows until the character we want to inspect shows up. The character we want is in H10. The dollar signs in $C$8 anchor that cell reference so that it doesn't change as the formula is copied. The ROW() function without an argument returns the row of whatever cells it's in. As the formula is copied down, ROW() returns 8, 9, 10, and so on.

In cell I8 is the formula =CODE(H8). The CODE worksheet function returns the ASCII code for the letter that's passed in. In this example, we can see that a capital T is ASCII code 84, a lowercase i is ASCII code 105, and ö is ASCII code 246. Armed with that knowledge, we can hold down the Alt key and type the code to use that character anywhere we want.

Getting the average of all numbers that meet a certain condition

After summing and counting, taking an average of a range of numbers is the next most common aggregator. The average, also known as the *arithmetic mean*, is the sum of the numbers divided by the count of the numbers.

Figure 13.15 once again shows the medalists' results from the 1972 Winter Olympics. We want to determine the average result but only for those skiers from Switzerland. The country code is entered in cell I3 so that it can be easily changed to a different country.

```
=AVERAGEIF(D3:D20,I3,E3:E20)
```

FIGURE 13.15

Averaging results based on a country

	A	B	C	D	E	F	G	H	I
			fx	=AVERAGEIF(D3:D20,I3,E3:E20)					
2		Event	Athlete	Country	Result	Medal			
3		Downhill Men	Bernhard Russi	SUI	01:51.4	GOLD		Country	SUI
4		Downhill Men	Roland Collombin	SUI	01:52.1	SILVER			
5		Downhill Men	Heini Messner	AUT	01:52.4	BRONZE		Average Result	02:12.0
6		Slalom Men	Francisco Fernández	ESP	01:49.3	GOLD		SUMIF and COUNTIF	02:12.0
7		Slalom Men	Gustav Thöni	ITA	01:50.3	SILVER			
8		Slalom Men	Roland Thöni	ITA	01:50.3	BRONZE			
9		Giant Slalom Men	Gustav Thöni	ITA	03:09.6	GOLD			
10		Giant Slalom Men	Edmund Bruggmann	SUI	03:10.7	SILVER			
11		Giant Slalom Men	Werner Mattle	SUI	03:11.0	BRONZE			
12		Downhill Women	Marie-Thérès Nadig	SUI	01:36.7	GOLD			
13		Downhill Women	Annemarie Moser-Pröll	AUT	01:37.0	SILVER			
14		Downhill Women	Susan Corrock	USA	01:37.7	BRONZE			
15		Slalom Women	Barbara Cochran	USA	01:31.2	GOLD			
16		Slalom Women	Danièlle Debernard	FRA	01:31.3	SILVER			
17		Slalom Women	Florence Steurer	FRA	01:32.7	BRONZE			
18		Giant Slalom Women	Marie-Thérès Nadig	SUI	01:29.9	GOLD			
19		Giant Slalom Women	Annemarie Moser-Pröll	AUT	01:30.8	SILVER			
20		Giant Slalom Women	Wiltrud Drexel	AUT	01:32.4	BRONZE			
21									
22									
23									

Excel provides the AVERAGEIF function to accomplish just what we want. Like its cousin, the SUMIF function, AVERAGEIF has a criteria_range and a criteria argument. The final argument is the range to average. In this example, each cell in E3:E20 is either included in or excluded from the average depending on whether the corresponding cell in D3:D20 meets the criteria.

If no rows meet the criteria in AVERAGEIF, the function returns the #DIV/0! error.

Getting the average of all numbers that meet two or more conditions

Microsoft introduced AVERAGEIFS along with SUMIFS and COUNTIFS to allow you to average a range of numbers based on more than one condition.

Continuing our analysis of skiing times, Figure 13.16 shows some results of the 1972 Winter Olympics. In this case, we want to determine the average time based on more than one condition. The country, gender, and medal are entered into cells I3:I5. We want to average only those results that meet all three criteria.

```
=AVERAGEIFS(E3:E20,D3:D20,I3,B3:B20,"*"&I4,F3:F20,I5)
```

FIGURE 13.16

Averaging on three conditions

	A	B	C	D	E	F	G	H	I
			f_x	=AVERAGEIFS(E3:E20,D3:D20,I3,B3:B20,"*"&I4,F3:F20,I5)					
1									
2		Event	Athlete	Country	Result	Medal			
3		Downhill Men	Bernhard Russi	SUI	01:51.4	GOLD		Country	SUI
4		Downhill Men	Roland Collombin	SUI	01:52.1	SILVER		Gender	Women
5		Downhill Men	Heini Messner	AUT	01:52.4	BRONZE		Medal	GOLD
6		Slalom Men	Francisco Fernández	ESP	01:49.3	GOLD		Average Result	01:33.3
7		Slalom Men	Gustav Thöni	ITA	01:50.3	SILVER		SUMIF and COUNTIF	01:33.3
8		Slalom Men	Roland Thöni	ITA	01:50.3	BRONZE			
9		Giant Slalom Men	Gustav Thöni	ITA	03:09.6	GOLD			
10		Giant Slalom Men	Edmund Bruggmann	SUI	03:10.7	SILVER			
11		Giant Slalom Men	Werner Mattle	SUI	03:11.0	BRONZE			
12		Downhill Women	Marie-Thérès Nadig	SUI	01:36.7	GOLD			
13		Downhill Women	Annemarie Moser-Pröll	AUT	01:37.0	SILVER			
14		Downhill Women	Susan Corrock	USA	01:37.7	BRONZE			
15		Slalom Women	Barbara Cochran	USA	01:31.2	GOLD			
16		Slalom Women	Danièlle Debernard	FRA	01:31.3	SILVER			
17		Slalom Women	Florence Steurer	FRA	01:32.7	BRONZE			
18		Giant Slalom Women	Marie-Thérès Nadig	SUI	01:29.9	GOLD			
19		Giant Slalom Women	Annemarie Moser-Pröll	AUT	01:30.8	SILVER			
20		Giant Slalom Women	Wiltrud Drexel	AUT	01:32.4	BRONZE			
21									

13

The AVERAGEIFS function is structured similarly to the SUMIFS function. The first argument is the range to average, and it's followed by up to 127 pairs of criteria_range/criteria arguments. The three criteria pairs are as follows:

- D3:D20,I3 includes only those rows where the country code is SUI.
- B3:B20,"*"&I4 includes only those rows where the event name ends with the word Women.
- F3:F20,I5 includes only those rows where the medal is GOLD.

When all three conditions are met, the time in the Result column is averaged.

Using Formulas for Matching and Lookups

IN THIS CHAPTER

Introducing formulas that look up values in a table

Identifying the worksheet functions used to perform lookups

Delving into more sophisticated lookup formulas

This chapter discusses various techniques that you can use to look up a value in a range of data. Excel has three worksheet functions (LOOKUP, VLOOKUP, and HLOOKUP) designed for this task, but you may find that these functions don't quite cut it.

In this chapter you'll explore many lookup examples, including alternative techniques that go well beyond the Excel program's normal lookup capabilities.

Introducing Lookup Formulas

A lookup formula returns a value from a table by looking up another related value. A common telephone directory (remember those?) provides a good analogy. If you want to find a person's telephone number, you first locate the name (look it up) and then retrieve the corresponding number.

> **NOTE**
>
> We use the term *table* to describe any rectangular range of data. The range does not necessarily need to be an "official" table, as created by choosing Insert ▷ Tables ▷ Table.

Several Excel functions are useful when writing formulas to look up information in a table. Table 14.1 describes these functions.

TABLE 14.1 **Functions Used in Lookup Formulas**

Function	Description
CHOOSE	Returns a specific value from a list of values supplied as arguments.
HLOOKUP	Horizontal lookup. Searches for a value in the top row of a table and returns a value in the same column from a row you specify in the table.
IF	Returns one value if a condition you specify is TRUE and returns another value if the condition is FALSE.
IFERROR	If the first argument returns an error, the second argument is evaluated and returned. If the first argument does not return an error, then it is evaluated and returned.
INDEX	Returns a value (or the reference to a value) from within a table or range.
LOOKUP	Returns a value from either a one-row or one-column range. Another form of the LOOKUP function works like VLOOKUP but is restricted to returning a value from the last column of a range.
MATCH	Returns the relative position of an item in a range that matches a specified value.
OFFSET	Returns a reference to a range that is a specified number of rows and columns from a cell or range of cells.
VLOOKUP	Vertical lookup. Searches for a value in the first column of a table and returns a value in the same row from a column that you specify in the table.

Leveraging Excel's Lookup Functions

Finding data in a list or table is central to many Excel formulas. Excel provides several functions to assist in looking up data vertically, horizontally, left to right, and right to left. By nesting some of these functions, you can write a formula that looks up the correct data even after the layout of your table changes.

Let's take a look at some of the more common ways to utilize Excel's lookup functions.

 This book's website, www.wiley.com/go/excel2019bible, includes a copy of the sample workbook for this chapter. The file is named Performing Lookups.xlsx.

Looking up an exact value based on a left lookup column

Many tables are arranged so that the key piece of data, the data that makes a certain row unique, is in the far-left column. While Excel has many lookup functions, VLOOKUP was designed for just that situation. Figure 14.1 shows a table of employees. We want to fill out a simplified paystub form by pulling the information from this table when an employee's ID is selected.

FIGURE 14.1

A table of employee information

	A	B	C	D	E	F	G	H	I	J
1										
2		ID	Employee Name	Address	Frequency	Salary	Tax Rate	Insurance	401k	
3		154	Paige Jones	427 John A. Creighton Boulevard	26	42,900.00	15%	100.00	8%	
4		240	Elijah Ward	888 192nd Street Anytown, USA	26	64,600.00	16%	200.00	7%	
5		319	Elizabeth Marshall	530 Dodge Street Anytown, USA	52	72,300.00	24%	300.00	3%	
6		331	Cooper Smith	271 Dodge Street Anytown, USA	12	99,700.00	20%	300.00	5%	
7		428	Isabella Harris	715 136th Street Anytown, USA :	26	57,600.00	25%	100.00	5%	
8		451	Kaylee Perez	772 North 30th Street Anytown,	12	82,800.00	23%	200.00	7%	
9		527	Kimberly Hall	652 Regency Parkway Drive Any	12	41,700.00	17%	300.00	4%	
10		540	Jesus Clark	803 Fontenelle Boulevard Anytc	52	83,100.00	18%	200.00	5%	
11		665	Kylie Woods	245 Fontenelle Boulevard Anytc	26	70,400.00	21%	100.00	1%	
12		981	Jackson Stephens	827 Harrison Street Anytown, US	52	50,200.00	18%	100.00	8%	
13										
14										

The user will select an employee ID from a data validation list in cell L3. From that piece of data, the employee's name, address, and other information will be pulled into the form. The formulas for the paystub form in Figure 14.2 are shown here:

Employee Name

```
=VLOOKUP($L$3,$B$3:$I$12,2,FALSE)
```

Pay

```
=VLOOKUP($L$3,$B$3:$I$12,5,FALSE)/VLOOKUP($L$3,$B$3:$I$12,4,FALSE)
```

Taxes

```
=(M7-O8-O9)*VLOOKUP($L$3,$B$3:$I$12,6,FALSE)
```

Insurance

```
=VLOOKUP($L$3,$B$3:$I$12,7,FALSE)
```

Retirement

```
=M7*VLOOKUP($L$3,$B$3:$I$12,8,FALSE)
```

Total

```
=SUM(O7:O10)
```

Net Pay

```
=M7-O11
```

The formula to retrieve the employee's name uses the VLOOKUP function. VLOOKUP takes four arguments: lookup value, lookup range, column, and match. VLOOKUP will search down the first column of the lookup range until it finds the lookup value. Once the lookup value is found, VLOOKUP returns the value in the column identified by the column argument. In this case, the column argument is 2, and VLOOKUP returns the employee's name from the second column.

FIGURE 14.2

A simplified paystub form

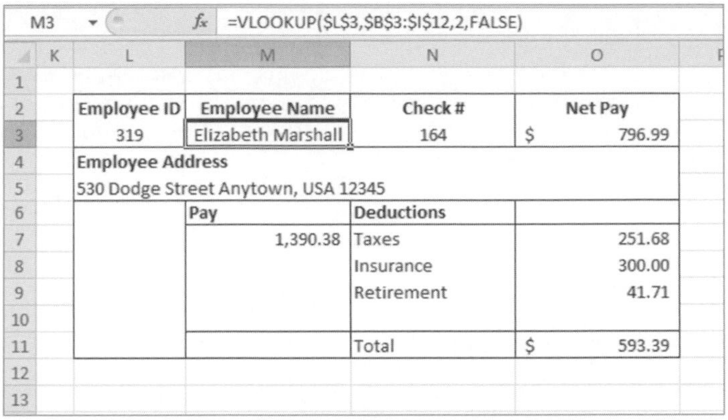

M3	▼	*fx*	=VLOOKUP($L$3,$B$3:$I$12,2,FALSE)

◢	K	L	M	N	O	P
1						
2		Employee ID	Employee Name	Check #	Net Pay	
3		319	Elizabeth Marshall	164	$ 796.99	
4		Employee Address				
5		530 Dodge Street Anytown, USA 12345				
6			Pay	Deductions		
7			1,390.38	Taxes	251.68	
8				Insurance	300.00	
9				Retirement	41.71	
10						
11				Total	$ 593.39	
12						
13						

> **NOTE**
>
> All the VLOOKUP functions in this example have FALSE as the final argument. A FALSE in the match argument tells VLOOKUP to return a value only if it finds an exact match. If it doesn't find an exact match, VLOOKUP returns N/A#. Figure 14.7, later in this chapter, shows an example of using TRUE to get an approximate match.

The other formulas also use VLOOKUP with a few twists. The address and insurance formulas work just like the employee name formula, but they pull from a different column. The pay formula uses two VLOOKUPs; one is divided by the other. The employee's annual pay is pulled from the fifth column, and that is divided by the frequency from the fourth column, resulting in the pay for one paystub.

The retirement formula pulls the percentage from the eighth column and multiplies that by the gross pay to calculate the deduction. Finally, the taxes formula deducts both insurance and retirement from gross pay and multiplies that by the tax rate, found with VLOOKUP pulling from the sixth column.

Of course, payroll calculations are a little more complex than this, but once you understand how VLOOKUP works, you can build ever more complex models.

Looking up an exact value based on any lookup column

Unlike the table used in Figure 14.1, not all tables have the value that you want to look up in the leftmost column. Fortunately, Excel provides some functions for returning values that are to the right of the value you're looking up.

Figure 14.3 shows the locations of our stores by city and state. We want to return the city and store number when the user selects the state from a drop-down list.

```
City:  =INDEX(B3:D25,MATCH(G4,C3:C25,FALSE),1)
Store: =INDEX(B3:D25,MATCH(G4,C3:C25,FALSE),3)
```

FIGURE 14.3

A list of stores with their city and state locations

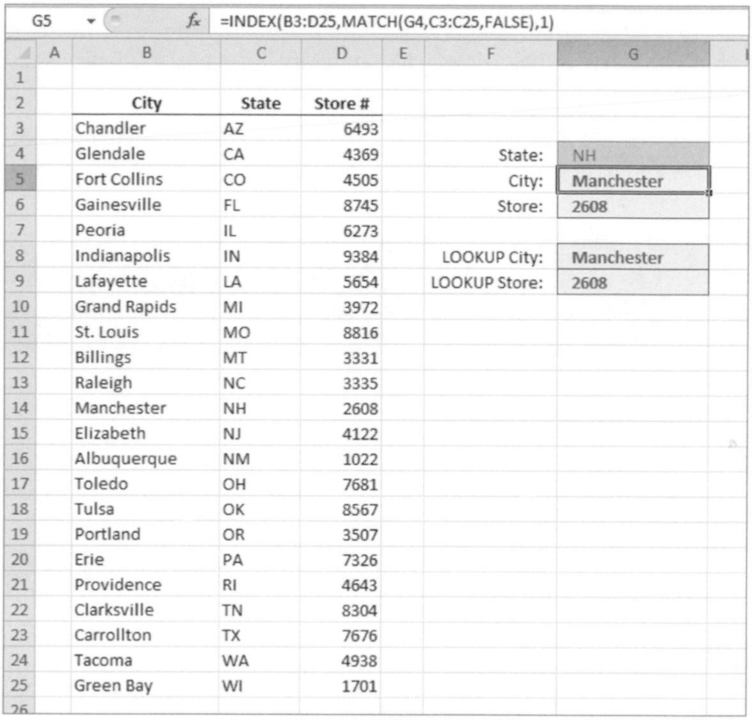

G5 =INDEX(B3:D25,MATCH(G4,C3:C25,FALSE),1)

	A	B	C	D	E	F	G
1							
2		City	State	Store #			
3		Chandler	AZ	6493			
4		Glendale	CA	4369		State:	NH
5		Fort Collins	CO	4505		City:	Manchester
6		Gainesville	FL	8745		Store:	2608
7		Peoria	IL	6273			
8		Indianapolis	IN	9384		LOOKUP City:	Manchester
9		Lafayette	LA	5654		LOOKUP Store:	2608
10		Grand Rapids	MI	3972			
11		St. Louis	MO	8816			
12		Billings	MT	3331			
13		Raleigh	NC	3335			
14		Manchester	NH	2608			
15		Elizabeth	NJ	4122			
16		Albuquerque	NM	1022			
17		Toledo	OH	7681			
18		Tulsa	OK	8567			
19		Portland	OR	3507			
20		Erie	PA	7326			
21		Providence	RI	4643			
22		Clarksville	TN	8304			
23		Carrollton	TX	7676			
24		Tacoma	WA	4938			
25		Green Bay	WI	1701			
26							

The `INDEX` function returns the value from a particular row and column of a range. In this case, we pass it our table of stores, a row argument in the form of a `MATCH` function, and a column number. For the City formula, we want the first column, so the column argument is 1. For the Store formula, we want the third column, so the column argument is 3.

Unless the range you use starts in A1, the row and column will not match the row and column in the spreadsheet. They relate to the top-left cell in the range, not the spreadsheet as a whole. A formula like `=INDEX(G2:P10,2,2)` would return the value in cell H3. The cell H3 is in the second row and the second column of the range G2:P10.

14

TIP

The second argument of the `MATCH` function can only be a range that is one row tall or one column wide. If you send it a range that's a rectangle, `MATCH` returns the `#N/A` error.

To get the correct row, we use a `MATCH` function. The `MATCH` function returns the position in the list in which the lookup value is found. It has three arguments.

Lookup value: The value we want to find

Lookup array: The single column or single row to look in

Match type: For exact matches only, set this argument to FALSE or 0

The value we want to match is the state in cell G4, and we're looking for it in the range C3:C25, our list of states. MATCH looks down the range until it finds NH. It finds it in the 12th position, so 12 is used by INDEX as the row argument.

With MATCH computed, INDEX now has all it needs to return the right value. It goes to the 12th row of the range and gets the value from either the first column (for City) or the third column (for Store #).

> **NOTE**
>
> If you pass INDEX a row number that is more rows than are included in the range or a column number that is more columns than are included in the range, INDEX returns the #REF! error.

Looking up values horizontally

If the data is structured in such a way that your lookup value is in the top row rather than the first column and you want to look down the rows for data rather than across the columns, Excel has a function just for you.

Figure 14.4 shows a table of cities and their temperatures. The user will select a city from a drop-down box, and you will return the temperature to the cell just below it.

=HLOOKUP(C5,C2:L3,2,FALSE)

FIGURE 14.4

A table of cities and temperatures

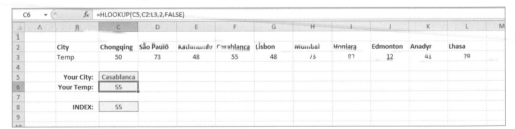

The HLOOKUP function has the same arguments as VLOOKUP. The *H* in HLOOKUP stands for "horizontal," while the *V* in VLOOKUP stands for "vertical." Instead of looking down the first column for the *lookup_value* argument, HLOOKUP looks across the first row. When it finds a match, it returns the value from the second row of the matching column.

Hiding errors returned by lookup functions

So far, we've used FALSE for the last argument of our lookup functions so that we return only exact matches. When we force a lookup function to return an exact match and it can't find one, it returns the #N/A error.

The #N/A error is useful in Excel models because it alerts you when a match cannot be found. But you may be using all or a portion of your model for reporting, and #N/As are ugly. Excel has functions to see those errors and return something different.

Figure 14.5 shows a list of companies and CEOs. The other list shows CEOs and salaries. A VLOOKUP function is used to combine the two tables. But we obviously don't have salary information for all of the CEOs, and we have a lot of #N/A errors.

```
=VLOOKUP(C3,$F$3:$G$11,2,FALSE)
```

FIGURE 14.5

A report of CEO salaries

	A	B	C	D	E	F	G
			D3 fx =VLOOKUP(C3,$F$3:$G$11,2,FALSE)				
1							
2		**Company**	**CEO**	**Salary**		**Name**	**2012 Salary**
3		Activision Blizzard Inc	Robert A. Kotick	#N/A		David M. Cote	33,247,178
4		CBS Corp	Leslie Moonves	62,157,026		Gregory B. Maffei	45,302,040
5		Cheniere Energy Inc	Charif Souki	#N/A		John H. Hammergren	51,744,999
6		Credit Acceptance Corp	Brett A. Roberts	#N/A		Leslie Moonves	62,157,026
7		Discovery Communications Inc	David M. Zaslav	#N/A		Mario J. Gabelli	68,970,486
8		Disney (Walt) Co	Robert A. Iger	#N/A		Marissa A. Mayer	36,615,404
9		Exxon Mobil Corp	R. W. Tillerson	40,266,501		Mark G. Parker	35,212,678
10		Gamco Investors Inc	Mario J. Gabelli	68,970,486		R. W. Tillerson	40,266,501
11		HCA Holdings Inc	Richard M. Bracken	#N/A		Ralph Lauren	36,325,782
12		Honeywell International Inc	David M. Cote	33,247,178			
13		Jefferies Group Llc	Richard B. Handler	#N/A			
14		Level 3 Communications Inc	James Q. Crowe	#N/A			
15		Liberty Interactive Corp	Gregory B. Maffei	45,302,040			
16		Mckesson Corp	John H. Hammergren	51,744,999			
17		Nike Inc	Mark G. Parker	35,212,678			
18		Nuance Communications Inc	Paul A. Ricci	#N/A			
19		Oracle Corp	Lawrence J. Ellison	#N/A			
20		Pall Corp	Lawrence Kingsley	#N/A			
21		Ralph Lauren Corp	Ralph Lauren	36,325,782			
22		Tesla Motors Inc	Elon Musk	#N/A			
23		Viacom Inc	Philippe P. Dauman	#N/A			
24		Yahoo Inc	Marissa A. Mayer	36,615,404			
25							

14

In Figure 14.6, the formula has been changed to use the IFERROR function to return a blank if there's no information available.

FIGURE 14.6

A cleaner report

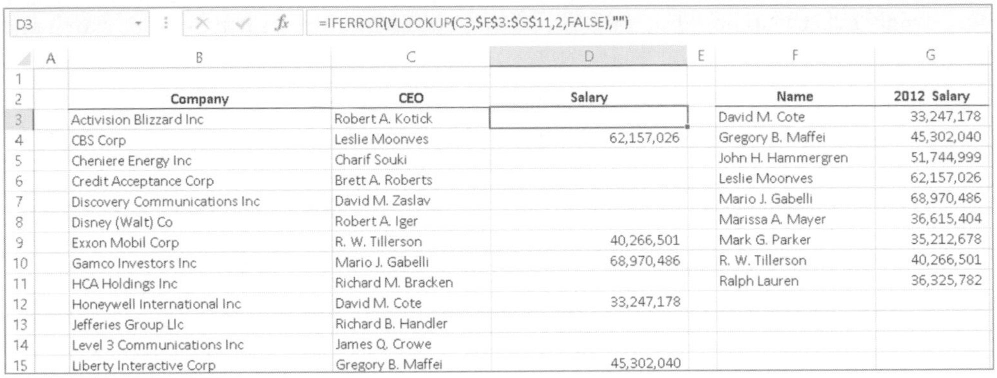

	A	B	C	D	E	F	G
1							
2		Company	CEO	Salary		Name	2012 Salary
3		Activision Blizzard Inc	Robert A. Kotick			David M. Cote	33,247,178
4		CBS Corp	Leslie Moonves	62,157,026		Gregory B. Maffei	45,302,040
5		Cheniere Energy Inc	Charif Souki			John H. Hammergren	51,744,999
6		Credit Acceptance Corp	Brett A. Roberts			Leslie Moonves	62,157,026
7		Discovery Communications Inc	David M. Zaslav			Mario J. Gabelli	68,970,486
8		Disney (Walt) Co	Robert A. Iger			Marissa A. Mayer	36,615,404
9		Exxon Mobil Corp	R. W. Tillerson	40,266,501		Mark G. Parker	35,212,678
10		Gamco Investors Inc	Mario J. Gabelli	68,970,486		R. W. Tillerson	40,266,501
11		HCA Holdings Inc	Richard M. Bracken			Ralph Lauren	36,325,782
12		Honeywell International Inc	David M. Cote	33,247,178			
13		Jefferies Group Llc	Richard B. Handler				
14		Level 3 Communications Inc	James Q. Crowe				
15		Liberty Interactive Corp	Gregory B. Maffei	45,302,040			

Formula bar: `=IFERROR(VLOOKUP(C3,$F$3:$G$11,2,FALSE),"")`

```
=IFERROR(VLOOKUP(C3,$F$3:$G$11,2,FALSE),"")
```

The IFERROR function accepts a value or formula for its first argument and an alternate return value for its second argument. When the first argument returns an error, the second argument is returned. When the first argument is not an error, the results of the first argument are returned.

In this example, we've made our alternate return value an empty string (two double quotes with nothing between them). That keeps the report nice and clean. But you could return anything you want, such as "No info" or zero.

> **TIP**
>
> The IFERROR function checks for every error that Excel can return, including #N/A, #DIV/0!, and #VALUE. Note that you can't restrict which errors IFERROR catches.
>
> Excel provides three other error trapping functions:
>
> - ISERROR returns TRUE if its argument returns any error.
> - ISERR returns TRUE if its argument returns any error except #N/A.
> - ISNA returns TRUE if its argument returns #N/A and returns FALSE for anything else, including other errors.
>
> All of these error-trapping functions return TRUE or FALSE and are most commonly used with an IF function.

Finding the closest match from a list of banded values

The VLOOKUP, HLOOKUP, and MATCH functions allow the data to be sorted in any order. Each of them has a final argument that will force the function to find an exact match or return an error if it cannot.

These functions also work on sorted data for the times when you want only an approximate match. Figure 14.7 shows a method for calculating income tax withholding. The withholding table doesn't have every possible value; rather, it has bands of values. You first determine into which band the employee's pay falls, and then you use the information on that row to compute the withholding in cell D16.

```
=VLOOKUP(D15,B3:E10,3,TRUE)+(D15-
VLOOKUP(D15,B3:E10,1,TRUE))*VLOOKUP(D15,B3:E10,4,TRUE)
```

FIGURE 14.7

Computing income tax withholding

⁄	A	B	C	D	E	F
1						
2		Wages over	But not over	Base amount	Percentage	
3		-	325	-	0.0%	
4		325	1,023	-	10.0%	
5		1,023	3,163	69.80	15.0%	
6		3,163	6,050	390.80	25.0%	
7		6,050	9,050	1,112.56	28.0%	
8		9,050	15,906	195.56	33.0%	
9		15,906	17,925	4,215.03	35.0%	
10		17,925		4,921.68	39.6%	
11						
12		Bi-weekly wage:		2,307.69		
13		Withholding allowances:		2		
14		Allowance:		303.80		
15		Wage less allowance:		2,003.89		
16		Withholding amount:		216.93		
17						
18						

The formula uses three VLOOKUP functions to get three pieces of data from the table. The final argument for each VLOOKUP formula is set to TRUE, indicating that we want only an approximate match.

To get a correct result when using a final argument of TRUE, the data in the lookup column (column B in Figure 14.7) must be sorted lowest to highest. VLOOKUP looks down the first column and stops when the *next* value is higher than the lookup value. In that way, it finds the largest value that is not larger than the lookup value.

CAUTION

Finding an approximate match with a lookup function does not find the *closest* match. Rather, it finds the largest match that's not larger than the lookup value, even if the next highest value is closer to the lookup value.

If the data in the lookup column isn't sorted lowest to highest, you may not get an error, but you will likely get an incorrect result. The lookup functions use a *binary search* to find an approximate match. A binary search basically starts in the middle of the lookup column and determines whether the match will be in the first half or the second half of the values. Then it splits that half in the middle and looks either forward or backward depending on the middle value. That process is repeated until the result is found.

You can see with a binary search that unsorted values could cause the lookup function to choose the wrong half to look in and return bad data.

In the example in Figure 14.7, VLOOKUP stops at row 5 because 1,023 is the largest value in the list that's not larger than our lookup value of 2,003.89. The three sections of the formula work as follows:

- The first VLOOKUP returns the base amount in the third column, or 69.80.
- The second VLOOKUP subtracts the "Wages over" amount (from the first column) from the total wages.
- The last VLOOKUP returns the percentage in the fourth column. This percentage is multiplied by the "excess wages," and the result is added to the base amount.

When all three VLOOKUP functions are evaluated, the formula computes as follows:

```
=69.80 + (2,003.89 - 1,023.00) * 15.0%
```

TIP

The method the lookup functions use to find an approximate match is much faster than an exact match. For an exact match, the function has to look at every single value in the lookup column. If you know your data will always be sorted lowest to highest and will always contain an exact match, you can decrease calculation time by setting the last argument to TRUE. An approximate match lookup will always find an exact match if it exists and the data is sorted.

Finding the closest match with the INDEX and MATCH functions

As with all of our lookup formulas, the INDEX and MATCH combination can be substituted. Like VLOOKUP and HLOOKUP, MATCH also has a final argument to find approximate matches. MATCH has the added advantage of being able to work with data that is sorted highest to lowest (see Figure 14.8).

The VLOOKUP-based formula from Figure 14.7 returns #N/A as shown in cell D16 in Figure 14.8. This is because VLOOKUP looks at the middle of the lookup column, determines that it is higher than the lookup value, and then looks only at values before the middle value. Because our data is sorted in descending order, there are no values before the middle value that are lower than the lookup value.

FIGURE 14.8

The same withholding table as Figure 14.7 except that the data is sorted in descending order

	A	B	C	D	E	F
1						
2		Wages over	But not over	Base amount	Percentage	
3		17,925		4,921.68	39.6%	
4		15,906	17,925	4,215.03	35.0%	
5		9,050	15,906	195.56	33.0%	
6		6,050	9,050	1,112.56	28.0%	
7		3,163	6,050	390.80	25.0%	
8		1,023	3,163	69.80	15.0%	
9		325	1,023	-	10.0%	
10		-	325	-	0.0%	
11						
12		Bi-weekly wage:		2,307.69		
13		Withholding allowances:		2		
14			Allowance:	303.80		
15		Wage less allowance:		2,003.89		
16		Withholding amount:		#N/A		
17						
18		INDEX and MATCH:		216.93		
19						
20						

The INDEX and MATCH formula in cell D18 of Figure 14.8 returns the correct result and is shown here:

```
=INDEX(B3:E10,MATCH(D15,B3:B10,-1)+1,3)+(D15-
INDEX(B3:E10,MATCH(D15,B3:B10,-1)+1,1))*INDEX(B3:E10,MATCH
(D15,B3:B10,-1)+1,4)
```

The final argument of MATCH can be –1, 0, or 1.

- –1 is used for data that is sorted highest to lowest. It finds the smallest value in the lookup column that is larger than the lookup value. There is no equivalent method using VLOOKUP or HLOOKUP.
- 0 is used for unsorted data to find the exact match. It is equivalent to setting the final argument of VLOOKUP or HLOOKUP to FALSE.
- 1 is used for data that is sorted lowest to highest. It finds the largest value in the lookup column that is smaller than the lookup value. It is equivalent to setting the final argument of VLOOKUP or HLOOKUP to TRUE.

With a final argument of –1, MATCH finds a value that is larger than the lookup value, and the formula adds 1 to the result to get the proper row.

Looking up values from multiple tables

Sometimes the data that you want to look up can come from more than one table depending on a choice that the user makes. In Figure 14.9, a withholding calculation similar to

Figure 14.7 is shown. The difference is that the user can select whether the employee is single or married. If the user chooses Single, the data is looked up in the single-person table, and if the user chooses Married, the data is looked up in the married table.

FIGURE 14.9

Computing income tax withholding from two tables

	A	B	C	D	E	F
1						
2		*Married person*				
3		**Wages over**	**But not over**	**Base amount**	**Percentage**	
4		-	325	-	0.0%	
5		325	1,023	-	10.0%	
6		1,023	3,163	69.80	15.0%	
7		3,163	6,050	390.80	25.0%	
8		6,050	9,050	1,112.56	28.0%	
9		9,050	15,906	195.56	33.0%	
10		15,906	17,925	4,215.03	35.0%	
11		17,925		4,921.68	39.6%	
12						
13		*Single person*				
14		**Wages over**	**But not over**	**Base amount**	**Percentage**	
15		-	87	-	0.0%	
16		87	436	-	10.0%	
17		436	1,506	34.90	15.0%	
18		1,506	3,523	195.40	25.0%	
19		3,523	7,254	699.65	28.0%	
20		7,254	15,667	1,744.33	33.0%	
21		15,667	15,731	4,520.62	35.0%	
22		15,731		4,543.02	39.6%	
23						
24						
25		Married or Single:		Single		
26		Bi-Weekly wages		4,038.46		
27		Withholding allowances:		3		
28		Allowance:		455.70		
29		Wage less allowance:		3,582.76		
30		Withholding amount:		716.38		
31						
32						

In Excel, we can use *named ranges* and the INDIRECT function to direct our lookup to the appropriate table. Before we can write our formula, we need to name two ranges: Married for the married-person table and Single for the single-person table. Follow these steps to create the named ranges:

1. **Select the range B4:E11.**
2. **Choose Define Name from the Formulas tab on the Ribbon.** The New Name dialog box shown in Figure 14.10 is displayed.

3. **Change the Name box to Married.**

4. **Click OK.**

5. **Select the range B15:E22.**

6. **Choose Define Name from the Formulas tab on the Ribbon.**

7. **Change the Name box to Single.**

8. **Click OK.**

FIGURE 14.10

The New Name dialog box

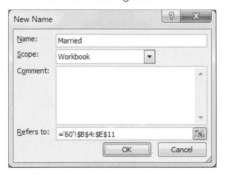

There is a data validation drop-down in cell D25 in Figure 14.9. The drop-down box contains the terms *Married* and *Single*, which are identical to the names that we just created. We'll be using the value in D25 to determine in which table we'll look, so the values must be identical.

The revised formula for computing the withholding follows:

```
=VLOOKUP(D29,INDIRECT(D25),3,TRUE)+(D29-VLOOKUP(D29,INDIRECT(D25),1,
TRUE))*VLOOKUP(D29,INDIRECT(D25),4,TRUE)
```

The formula in this example is strikingly similar to the one shown in Figure 14.7. The only difference is that an INDIRECT function is used in place of the table's location.

INDIRECT takes an argument named *ref_text*. The ref_text argument is a text representation of a cell reference or a named range. In Figure 14.9, cell D25 contains the text *Single*. INDIRECT attempts to convert that into a cell or range reference. If ref_text is not a valid range reference, as in our case, INDIRECT checks the named ranges to see whether there is a match. Had we not already created a range named Single, INDIRECT would return the #REF! error.

INDIRECT has a second optional argument named *a1*. The a1 argument is TRUE if ref_text is in the A1 style of cell references and FALSE if ref_text is in the R1C1 style of cell

14

references. For named ranges, a1 can be either TRUE or FALSE, and INDIRECT will return the correct range.

CAUTION

INDIRECT can also return ranges from other worksheets or even other workbooks. However, if it references another workbook, that workbook must be open. INDIRECT does not work on closed workbooks.

Looking up a value based on a two-way matrix

A two-way matrix is a rectangular range of cells. That is, it's a range with more than one row and more than one column. In other formulas, we've used the INDEX and MATCH combination as an alternative to some of the lookup functions. But INDEX and MATCH were made for two-way matrices.

Figure 14.11 shows a table of sales figures by region and year. Each row represents a region, and each column represents a year. We want the user to select a region and a year and return the sales figure at the intersection of that row and column.

```
=INDEX(C4:F9,MATCH(C13,B4:B9,FALSE),MATCH(C14,C3:F3,FALSE))
```

FIGURE 14.11

Sales data by region and year

	A	B	C	D	E	F	G
			fx	=INDEX(C4:F9,MATCH(C13,B4:B9,FALSE),MATCH(C14,C3:F3,FALSE))			
1							
2		Regional Sales Report					
3		Region	2010	2011	2012	2013	Total
4		South	1,525,017	1,504,678	1,227,847	1,019,616	5,277,158
5		Northeast	2,704,237	2,135,564	1,411,782	716,535	6,968,118
6		North	3,563,687	4,441,886	4,805,431	3,716,674	16,527,678
7		West	4,489,700	2,661,064	796,330	2,898,601	10,835,695
8		Mid-Atlantic	2,167,319	1,357,850	776,850	3,024,542	7,326,561
9		Canada	1,861,239	3,578,280	4,069,389	1,475,301	10,984,209
10		Total	16,311,199	15,669,322	13,087,629	12,851,269	57,919,419
11							
12							
13		Region:	North				
14		Year:	2011				
15		Sales:	4,441,886				
16							

By now you're no doubt familiar with INDEX and MATCH. Unlike other formulas, we're using two MATCH functions within the INDEX function. The second MATCH function returns the column argument of INDEX as opposed to hard-coding a column number.

Recall that MATCH returns the position in a list of the matched value. In Figure 14.11, the North region is matched, so MATCH returns 3 because it's the third item in the list. That becomes the row argument for INDEX. The year 2012 is matched across the header row, and since 2011 is the second item, MATCH returns 2. INDEX then takes the 2 and 3 returned by the MATCH functions to return the proper value.

Using default values for match

Let's add a twist to our sales lookup formula. We'll change the formula to allow the user to select only a region, to select only a year, or to select neither. If one of the selections is omitted, we'll assume that the user wants the total. If neither is selected, we'll return the total for the whole table.

```
=INDEX(C4:G10,IFERROR(MATCH(C13,B4:B10,FALSE),COUNTA(B4:B10)),IFERROR
(MATCH(C14,C3:G3,FALSE),COUNTA(C3:G3)))
```

The overall structure of the formula is the same, but we've changed a few details. The range we're using for INDEX now includes row 10 and column G. Each MATCH function's range is also extended. Finally, both MATCH functions are surrounded by an IFERROR function that will return the Total row or column.

The alternate value for IFERROR is a COUNTA function. COUNTA counts both numbers and text and, in effect, returns the position of the last row or column in our range. We could have hard-coded those values, but if we happen to insert a row or column, COUNTA will adjust to always return the last one.

FIGURE 14.12

Returning totals from the sales data

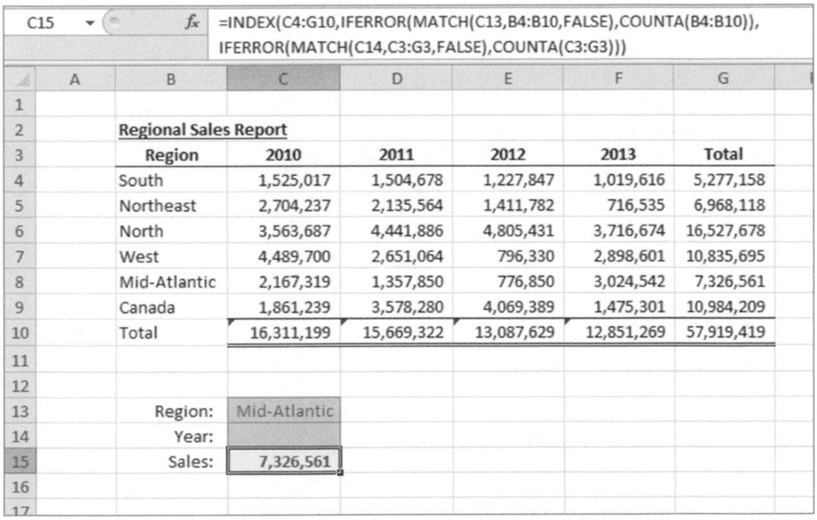

| C15 | fx | =INDEX(C4:G10,IFERROR(MATCH(C13,B4:B10,FALSE),COUNTA(B4:B10)), |
| | | IFERROR(MATCH(C14,C3:G3,FALSE),COUNTA(C3:G3))) |

	A	B	C	D	E	F	G
1							
2		**Regional Sales Report**					
3		Region	2010	2011	2012	2013	Total
4		South	1,525,017	1,504,678	1,227,847	1,019,616	5,277,158
5		Northeast	2,704,237	2,135,564	1,411,782	716,535	6,968,118
6		North	3,563,687	4,441,886	4,805,431	3,716,674	16,527,678
7		West	4,489,700	2,651,064	796,330	2,898,601	10,835,695
8		Mid-Atlantic	2,167,319	1,357,850	776,850	3,024,542	7,326,561
9		Canada	1,861,239	3,578,280	4,069,389	1,475,301	10,984,209
10		Total	16,311,199	15,669,322	13,087,629	12,851,269	57,919,419
11							
12							
13		Region:	Mid-Atlantic				
14		Year:					
15		Sales:	7,326,561				
16							
17							

Figure 14.12 shows the same sales table, but the user has left the Year input blank. Since there are no blanks in the column headers, MATCH returns #N/A. When it encounters that error, IFERROR passes control to the value_if_error argument, and the last column is passed to INDEX.

Finding a value based on multiple criteria

Figure 14.13 shows a table of departmental budgets. When the user selects a region and department, we want a formula to return the budget. We can't use VLOOKUP for this formula because it accepts only one lookup value. You need two values because the regions and departments appear multiple times.

You can use the SUMPRODUCT function to get the row that contains both lookup values as follows:

=SUMPRODUCT(($B$3:$B$45=H5)*($C$3:$C$45=H6)*($E$3:$E$45))

FIGURE 14.13

A table of departmental budgets

	A	B	C	D	E	F	G	H
			fx	=SUMPRODUCT(($B$3:$B$45=H5)*($C$3:$C$45=H6)*($E$3:$E$45))				
1								
2		Region	Department	Manager	Budget			
3		Mid-Atlantic	Legal	Jose Palmer	4,406,018			
4		Canada	Legal	Audrey Washington	2,564,165			
5		North	Logistics	Samantha Allen	1,443,535		Region:	South
6		Mid-Atlantic	Customer Service	Katherine Nichols	2,834,014		Department:	Accounting
7		Pacific Northwest	Quality Asurance	David Gordon	1,119,596		Budget:	697,697
8		Mid-Atlantic	Operational	Lillian Hart	2,949,401		Manager:	Brooke Bailey
9		Mid-Atlantic	Sales	Claire Peterson	2,371,246			
10		East	Inventory	Hannah Porter	3,043,499			
11		Mid-Atlantic	Services	Victoria Gomez	1,621,716			
12		South	Accounting	Brooke Bailey	697,697			
13		Mid-Atlantic	Insurance	Layla Green	1,458,914			
14		North	Sales	Alex Cox	2,922,128			
15		North	Business Development	Genesis Mills	3,699,755			
16		South	Business Development	Isaac Chavez	930,133			
17		Pacific Northwest	Services	Adam Howard	2,609,312			
18		South	Quality Asurance	Evelyn Burns	1,660,933			
19		Mid-Atlantic	Business Development	Jack Black	644,173			
20		Pacific Northwest	Customer Service	Wyatt Harris	4,487,298			
21		Mid-Atlantic	Marketing	Maria Cook	1,391,005			

SUMPRODUCT compares every cell in a range with a value and returns an array of TRUEs and FALSEs depending on the result. When multiplied with another array, TRUE becomes 1, and FALSE becomes 0. The third parenthetical section in the SUMPRODUCT function does not contain a comparison because that range contains the value we want to return.

If either the Region comparison or the Department comparison is FALSE, the total for that line will be 0. A FALSE result is converted to zero, and anything times zero is zero. If both Region and Department match, both comparisons return 1. The two 1s are multiplied with the corresponding row in column E, and that's the value returned.

In the example shown in Figure 14.13, when SUMPRODUCT gets to row 12, it multiplies 1 * 1 * 697,697. That number is summed with the other rows, all of which are zero because they contain at least one FALSE. The resulting SUM is the value 697,697.

Returning text with SUMPRODUCT

SUMPRODUCT works this way only when we want to return a number. If we want to return text, all of the text values would be treated as zero, and SUMPRODUCT would always return zero.

However, we can pair SUMPRODUCT with the INDEX and ROW functions to return text. If we want to return the manager's name, for example, we could use the following formula:

```
=INDEX(D:D,SUMPRODUCT(($B$3:$B$45=H5)*($C$3:$C$45=H6)*(ROW($E$3:$E$45))),1)
```

Instead of including the values from column E, the ROW function is used to include the row numbers in the array. SUMPRODUCT now computes 1 * 1 * 12 when it gets to row 12. The 12 is then used for the row argument in INDEX against the entire column D:D. Because the ROW function returns the row in the worksheet and not the row in our table, INDEX uses the whole column as its range.

Finding the last value in a column

Figure 14.14 shows an unsorted list of invoices. We want to find the last invoice in the list. A simple way to find the last item in the column is to use the INDEX function and count the items in the list to determine the last row.

```
=INDEX(B:B,COUNTA(B:B)+1)
```

FIGURE 14.14

A list of invoices

	A	B	C	D	E	F	G
				F5 ▾ (		fx =INDEX(B:B,COUNTA(B:B)+1)	
1							
2		Invoice #	Item Count	Amount			
3		IN6787	53	555.73			
4		IN4374	160	940.56		Last Invoice	Last Amount
5		IN5061	40	3,026.10		IN6513	3,326.98
6		IN4305	146	4,885.94			
7		IN1477	84	969.46			
8		IN5552	97	2,979.33			
9		IN8685	200	2,950.74			
10		IN1491	40	3,970.50			
11		IN2408	155	3,332.94			
12		IN6513	75	3,326.98			
13							
14							

14

The INDEX function when used on a single column needs only a row argument. The third argument indicates the column isn't necessary. COUNTA is used to count the nonblank cells in column B. That count is increased by 1 because we have a blank cell in the first row. The INDEX function returns the 12th row of column B.

> **CAUTION**
>
> COUNTA counts numbers, text, dates, and anything except blanks. If there are blank rows in your data, COUNTA will not return the desired result.

Finding the last number using LOOKUP

INDEX and COUNTA are great for finding values when there are no blank cells in the range. If you have blanks and the values you're searching for that are numbers, you can use LOOKUP and a really large number. The formula in cell G5 of Figure 14.14 uses this technique.

```
=LOOKUP(9.99E+307,D:D)
```

The lookup value is the largest number that Excel can handle (just under 1 with 308 zeros behind it). Since LOOKUP won't find a value that large, it stops at the last value it does find, and that's the value returned.

> **TIP**
>
> A number like 9.99E+307 is written in *exponential notation*. The number before the *E* has one number to the left of the decimal and two to the right. The number after the *E* is how many places are required to move the decimal point to show the number in regular notation (307 in this case). A positive number means to move the decimal to the right, and a negative number means to move it to the left. A number like 4.32E-02 is equivalent to 0.0432.

This LOOKUP method has the additional advantage of returning the last number, even if there are text, blanks, or errors in the range.

Using Formulas for Financial Analysis

IN THIS CHAPTER

Performing common business calculations

Leveraging Excel's financial functions

Spreadsheets got their start in the accounting and finance departments back when it was all done with paper and pencil. And even though Excel has grown far beyond a simple electronic ledger sheet, it's still a required tool in business.

In this chapter, you'll look at some formulas commonly used in accounting, finance, and other areas of businesses.

Performing Common Business Calculations

This section provides a reference for some of the more common business- and financial-oriented formulas that you may be asked to create when working as a business analyst using Excel.

 This book's website, www.wiley.com/go/excel2019bible, includes a copy of the sample workbook for this chapter. The file is named Financial Analysis.xlsx.

Calculating gross profit margin and gross profit margin percent

Gross margin is the money left over after subtracting the cost of goods sold from the revenue. It's the amount of sales that the business uses to cover overhead and other indirect costs. To compute the gross margin, simply subtract the cost of goods sold from the revenue. For gross margin percent, divide the gross margin by revenue. Figure 15.1 shows the financial statements of a manufacturing company. Gross margin is shown in cell C5, and gross margin percent is shown in cell D5.

```
Gross Margin: =C3-C4
Gross Margin Percent: =C5/$C$3
```

FIGURE 15.1

Financial statement for a manufacturing company

	C5	fx	=C3-C4				
	A	B	C	D	E	F	G
1							
2			2013		2012		
3		Revenue	$55,656	100%	$65,875	100%	
4		Cost of Goods Sold	41,454	74%	47,852	73%	
5		Gross Margin	14,202	26%	18,023	27%	
6							
7		Research Development	2,046	4%	2,466	4%	
8		Selling, General, and Administrative Expenses	6,528	12%	6,404	10%	
9							
10		Operating Margin	5,628	10%	9,153	14%	
11							
12		Interest Expense	465	1%	467	1%	
13		Other Income and Expense	1,368	2%	3,197	5%	
14							
15		Net Profit	$3,795	7%	$5,489	8%	
16							
17							

The gross margin formula simply subtracts cell C4 from cell C3. The gross margin percent divides C5 by C3, but note that the C3 reference is absolute because it has dollar signs. This allows you to copy the formula to other lines on the income statement to see the percentage of revenue, a common analysis performed on income statements.

Calculating markup

Markup is often confused with gross margin percent, but they are different. *Markup* is the percentage added to costs to arrive at a selling price. Figure 15.2 shows the sale of a single product, the markup applied, and the gross margin realized when sold.

FIGURE 15.2

Markup and gross margin percent from a single product

	C4	fx	=(C3/C2)-1		
	A	B	C	D	E
1					
2		Cost of product	465.00		465.00
3		Selling price	614.00		683.82
4		Markup	32%		47%
5					
6		Revenue	614.00		683.82
7		Cost of Goods Sold	465.00		465.00
8		Gross Margin	149.00		218.82
9		Gross Margin Percent	24%		32%
10					
11					

The markup is computed by dividing the selling price by the cost and subtracting 1.

```
=(C3/C2)-1
```

By marking up the cost of the product 32%, you achieve a 24% gross margin. If you want to mark up a product to get a 32% margin (as shown in column E of Figure 15.2), use the following formula:

```
=1/(1-E9)-1
```

Using this formula, you would need to mark up this product 47% if you want your income statement to show a 32% gross margin.

Calculating EBIT and EBITDA

Earnings before interest and taxes (EBIT) and *earnings before interest, taxes, depreciation, and amortization* (EBITDA) are common calculations for evaluating the results of a business. Both are computed by adding back certain expenses to earnings, also known as *net profit*.

Figure 15.3 shows an income statement and the results of the EBIT and EBITDA calculations below it.

EBIT

```
=C18+VLOOKUP("Interest Expense",$B$2:$C$18,2,FALSE)+VLOOKUP("Income
Tax Expense",$B$2:$C$18,2,FALSE)
```

EBITDA

```
=C20+VLOOKUP("Depreciation Expense",$B$2:$C$18,2,FALSE)+VLOOKUP
("Amortization Expense",$B$2:$C$18,2,FALSE)
```

FIGURE 15.3

An income statement with EBIT and EBITDA calculations

C20		f_x	=C18+VLOOKUP("Interest Expense",$B$2:$C$18,2,FALSE)+ VLOOKUP("Income Tax Expense",$B$2:$C$18,2,FALSE)				
	A	B	C	D	E	F	
1							
2		Revenue	65,245				
3		Cost of Goods Sold	39,147				
4		Gross Margin	26,098				
5							
6		Selling Expenses					
7		Adminstrative Expenses	8,213				
8		Depreciation Expense	7,245				
9		Amortization Expense	2,444				
10		Total Operating Expenses	17,902				
11							
12		Operating Income	8,196				
13							
14		Other Expenses	654				
15		Interest Expense	6,215				
16		Income Tax Expense	3,215				
17							
18		Net Income (Loss)	(1,888)				
19							
20		EBIT	7,542				
21		EBITDA	17,231				
22							

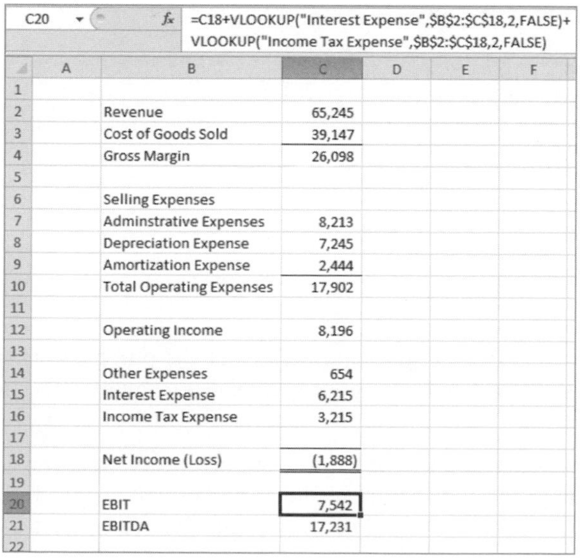

The EBIT formula starts with net loss in C18 and uses two VLOOKUP functions to find the interest expense and income tax expense from the income statement. For EBITDA, the formula starts with the result of the EBIT calculation and uses the same VLOOKUP technique to add back the depreciation expense and amortization expense.

There is a benefit to using VLOOKUP rather than simply using the cell references to those expenses. If the lines on the income statement are moved around, the EBIT and EBITDA formulas won't need to be changed.

 See Chapter 14, "Using Formulas for Matching and Lookups," for more on the VLOOKUP function.

Calculating cost of goods sold

Cost of goods sold is the amount you paid for all the goods you sold. It is a critical component to calculating gross. If you use a perpetual inventory system, you calculate the cost of goods sold for every sale made. For simpler systems, however, you can calculate it based on a physical inventory at the end of the accounting period.

Figure 15.4 shows how to calculate the cost of goods sold with only the beginning and ending inventory counts and the total of all of the inventory purchased in the period.

Goods Available for Sale

    =SUM(C2:C3)

Cost of Goods Sold

    =C4-C5

FIGURE 15.4

Calculating cost of goods sold

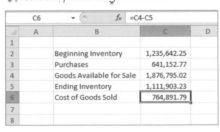

The *goods available for sale* is the beginning inventory plus all of the purchases made. It is an intermediate calculation that shows what your ending inventory would be if you didn't sell anything.

The *cost of goods sold* calculation simply subtracts the ending inventory from the goods available for sale. If you had the goods at the start of the period or you bought them during the period but you don't have them at the end of the period, then they must have been sold.

Calculating return on assets

Return on assets (ROA) is a measure of how efficiently a business is using its assets to generate income. For example, a company with a higher ROA can generate the same profit as one with a lower ROA using fewer or cheaper assets.

To compute ROA, divide the profits for a period of time by the average of the beginning and ending total assets. Figure 15.5 shows a simple balance sheet and income statement and the resulting ROA.

```
=G15/AVERAGE(C12:D12)
```

FIGURE 15.5

A return on assets calculation

	B	C	D	E	F	G
1						
2	**Balance Sheet**				**Income Statement**	
3	Cash	$1,186	$124		Revenue	$55,656
4	Accounts Receivable	3,884	3,026		Cost of Goods Sold	41,454
5	Inventories	8,355	7,651		Gross Margin	14,202
6	Total Current Assets	13,425	10,801			
7					Research Development	2,046
8	Property and Equipment	4,320	4,516		S,G & A Expenses	6,528
9	Other Assets	578	322			
10	Total Long-term Assets	4,898	4,838		Operating Margin	5,628
11						
12	Total Assets	$18,323	$15,639		Interest Expense	465
13					Other Income and Expense	1,368
14	Accounts Payable	$1,670	$2,644			
15	Accrued Expenses	1,334	1,431		Net Profit	$3,795
16	Notes Payable Current	788	761			
17	Total Current Liabilities	3,792	4,836			
18					Return on Assets	22.35%
19	Notes Payable Long Term	3,177	3,244		Return on Equity	40.13%
20	Total Liabilities	6,969	8,080			
21						
22	Common Stock	453	453			
23	Additional Paid-in Capital	4,562	4,562			
24	Retained Earnings	6,339	2,544			
25	Total Equity	11,354	7,559			
26						
27	Total Liabiltiies and Equity	$18,323	$15,639			
28						

The numerator is simply the net profit from the income statement. The denominator uses the AVERAGE function to find the average total assets for the period.

Calculating return on equity

Another common profitability measure is *return on equity* (ROE). An investor may use ROE to determine whether their investment in the business is being put to good use. Like ROA, ROE divides net profit by the average of a balance sheet item over the same period. ROE,

15

however, uses average total equity rather than average total assets. The formula to calculate ROE from Figure 15.5 is as follows:

```
=G15/AVERAGE(C25:D25)
```

Calculating break even

A business may want to determine how much revenue it will need to achieve a net profit of exactly $0. This is called *break even*. The business will estimate its fixed expenses and estimate the percentage of each of its variable expenses. Using those numbers, it can back into a revenue amount that will result in the break even.

Figure 15.6 shows a break-even calculation. Column C shows either an *F* for a fixed expense or a percentage for an expense that varies as revenue changes. For example, research and development will be spent according to a budget and doesn't change if revenue increases or decreases. On the other hand, if the business pays a commission, the selling expenses will rise and fall with revenues.

FIGURE 15.6

A break-even calculation

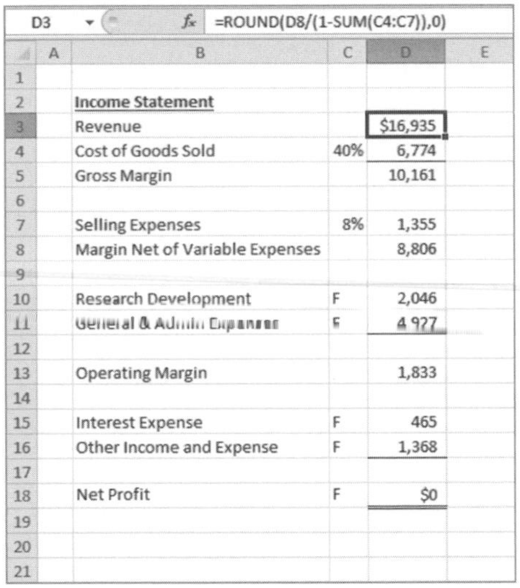

	A	B	C	D	E
1					
2		Income Statement			
3		Revenue		$16,935	
4		Cost of Goods Sold	40%	6,774	
5		Gross Margin		10,161	
6					
7		Selling Expenses	8%	1,355	
8		Margin Net of Variable Expenses		8,806	
9					
10		Research Development	F	2,046	
11		General & Admin Expenses	F	4,927	
12					
13		Operating Margin		1,833	
14					
15		Interest Expense	F	465	
16		Other Income and Expense	F	1,368	
17					
18		Net Profit	F	$0	
19					
20					
21					

The following formulas are used in Figure 15.6:

Operating Margin

```
=SUM(D15:D18)
```

Margin Net of Variable Expenses

```
=SUM(D10:D13)
```

Gross Margin

    =SUM(D7:D8)

Revenue

    =ROUND(D8/(1-SUM(C4:C7)),0)

The two variable expenses shown in Figure 15.6, cost of goods sold and selling expenses, are calculated by multiplying the revenue figure by the percentage. The formulas from Figure 15.6 are shown here:

Cost of Goods Sold

    =ROUND(D3*C4,0)

Selling Expenses

    =ROUND(D3*C7,0)

To build the break-even model in Figure 15.6, follow these steps:

1. **Enter 0 into cell D18 to indicate zero net profit.**

2. **Enter the fixed expense amounts in column D next to their labels in column B.**

3. **Enter the percentage the company pays in commission in cell C7 (8% in this example).**

4. **Enter a percentage equal to 1 minus the expected gross margin in cell C4.** In this example, the company expects a 60% gross margin percent, so 40% is entered in C4.

5. **In cell D13, enter the formula for the operating margin shown earlier.** The operating margin must be the sum of interest expense and other income and expense. As shown in Figure 15.6, if we estimate the interest expense to be $465 and the other income and expense to be $1,368, then the operating margin must be $1,833 for the net profit to be zero.

6. **In cell D8, enter the formula for the margin net of variable expenses shown earlier.** This calculation is operating margin plus the fixed operating expenses. It will drive the revenue calculation.

7. **In cell D7, enter the formula for selling expenses shown earlier.** We haven't entered the revenue formula yet, so this will be zero for now. But once revenue is entered, it will show the correct value.

8. **Enter the formula for cost of goods sold in cell D4.** Like the selling expenses formula, this will return zero until revenue is computed.

9. **Finally, enter the formula for revenue in cell D3.** The revenue calculation divides the margin net of variable expenses by 1 minus the sum of the variable percentages. In Figure 15.6, the two variable expenses will be 48% (40% plus 8%) of revenue. One minus that number, 52%, is divided into the margin net of variable expenses to get the revenue.

15

If this company makes a 60% gross margin, pays 8% in commissions, and has estimated the fixed expenses accurately, it will need to sell $16,935 to break even.

Calculating customer churn

Customer churn is the measure of how many customers you lose in a given period. It's an important metric in subscription-based businesses, although it's applicable to other revenue models as well. If your growth rate (the rate at which you are adding new customers) is higher than your churn rate, then your customer base is growing. If not, you're losing customers faster than you can add them, and something needs to change.

Figure 15.7 shows a churn calculation for a company with recurring monthly revenue. You need to know the number of customers at the beginning and end of the month and the number of new customers in that month.

Subscribers Lost

=C2+C3-C4

Churn Rate

=C6/C2

FIGURE 15.7

Calculating the churn rate

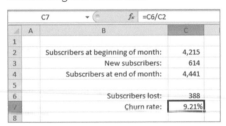

	A	B	C
1			
2		Subscribers at beginning of month:	4,215
3		New subscribers:	614
4		Subscribers at end of month:	4,441
5			
6		Subscribers lost:	388
7		Churn rate:	9.21%
8			

To determine the number of customers lost during the month, the number of new customers is added to the number of customers at the beginning of the month. Next, the number of customers at the end of the month is subtracted from that total. Finally, the number of customers lost during the month is divided by the number of customers at the beginning of the month to get the churn rate.

In this example, the business has a churn rate of 9.21%. It is adding more customers than it is losing, so that churn rate may not be seen as a problem. However, if the churn rate is higher than expected, the company may want to investigate why it's losing customers and change its pricing, product features, or some other aspect of its business.

Calculating annual churn rate

If a business has monthly recurring revenue, it means that customers sign up and pay for one month at a time. For those companies, it makes sense to calculate the churn rate on a monthly basis. Any new customers during the month will not churn in the same month because they've already paid for the month.

A typical magazine, however, signs up subscribers for an annual subscription. A meaningful churn rate calculation for them would be an annual churn rate. If a business wants to calculate a churn rate for a longer period than its recurring revenue model, such as calculating an annual churn for a business with monthly subscribers, the formula changes slightly. Figure 15.8 shows an annual churn rate calculation.

```
Annual churn rate: =C6/AVERAGE(C2,C4)
```

FIGURE 15.8

Annual churn rate of monthly recurring revenue

	A	B	C	D
	C7		fx =C6/AVERAGE(C2,C4)	
1				
2		Subscribers at beginning of year:	4,215	
3		New subscribers:	7,415	
4		Subscribers at end of year:	10,664	
5				
6		Subscribers lost:	966	
7		Annual churn rate:	12.98%	
8				

The number of lost subscribers is divided by the average of beginning and ending subscribers. Because the period of the churn rate is different than the period of the recurring revenue, some of those 7,415 new subscribers canceled their subscriptions within the year, albeit in a later month than they first subscribed.

Calculating average customer lifetime value

Customer lifetime value (CLV) is a calculation that estimates the gross margin contributed by one customer over that customer's life. The churn rate calculated in Figure 15.7 is a component of CLV.

Figure 15.9 shows a calculation of CLV using the churn rate previously calculated. The first step is to calculate the average gross margin per customer.

Gross Margin

```
=F2-F3
```

15

Average Customer Margin

```
=F4/AVERAGE(C4,C10)
```

Customer Lifetime Value

```
=F6/C7
```

FIGURE 15.9

Customer lifetime value calculation

F7	▼	f_x	=F6/C7			
A	B	C	D	E	F	G
1						
2	Subscribers at beginning of month:	4,215		Monthly revenue	564,810	
3	New subscribers:	614		Cost of goods sold	225,924	
4	Subscribers at end of month:	4,441		Gross Margin	338,886	
5						
6	Subscribers lost:	388		Average customer margin	76.31	
7	Churn rate:	9.21%		Customer Lifetime Value	828.97	
8						
9						

To calculate CLV, follow these steps:

1. **Calculate the gross margin.**
2. **Calculate the average customer margin by dividing the gross margin by the average number of customers for the month.** Because the gross margin was earned over the month, you have to divide by the average number of customers instead of either the beginning or ending customer count.
3. **Calculate the CLV by dividing the average customer margin by the churn rate.**

In this example, each customer will contribute an estimated $828.97 over their lifetime.

Calculating employee turnover

Employee turnover is a measure of how well an organization is hiring and retaining talent. A high turnover rate indicates that the organization is not hiring the right people or not retaining people, possibly because of inadequate benefits or below-average pay. Separations commonly include both voluntary and involuntary terminations.

Figure 15.10 shows the employment changes of an organization over a 12-month period. New hires are added to and separations are subtracted from the number of employees at the beginning of the month to get the ending employee count.

Average Monthly Employment

```
=AVERAGE(F3:F14)
```

Separations

```
=SUM(E3:E14)
```

Employee Turnover

```
=F17/F16
```

FIGURE 15.10

Monthly employment changes over one year

	F18		f_x	=F17/F16	
A	B	C	D	E	F
1					
2	Month	Beg. Employees	New Hires	Separations	End. Employees
3	Jan	625	10	7	628
4	Feb	628	2	7	623
5	Mar	623	4	1	626
6	Apr	626	6	3	629
7	May	629	5	1	633
8	Jun	633	5	2	636
9	Jul	636	2	5	633
10	Aug	633	3	5	631
11	Sep	631	2	6	627
12	Oct	627	4	2	629
13	Nov	629	10	5	634
14	Dec	634	8	2	640
15					
16			Average monthly employment		630.75
17				Separations	46.00
18				Employee Turnover	7.29%
19					

Employee turnover is simply the ratio of separations to average monthly employment. The AVERAGE function is used to calculate the average ending count of employees over the months. Separations are summed using SUM and are divided by the average monthly employments.

The result can be compared to industry averages or companies in the same industry. Different industries experience different turnover rates, so comparing them can lead to poor decisions. You don't have to calculate turnover for a 12-month period, but doing so removes seasonal employment variations that can skew results.

Leveraging Excel's Financial Functions

It's a safe bet that the most common use of Excel is to perform calculations involving money. Every day, people make hundreds of thousands of financial decisions based on the numbers that are calculated in a spreadsheet. These decisions range from simple ("Can I afford to buy a new car?") to complex ("Will purchasing XYZ Corporation result in a positive cash flow in the next 18 months?"). This section discusses basic financial calculations that you can perform with the assistance of Excel.

Converting interest rates

Two common methods for quoting interest rates are the *nominal* rate and the *effective* rate.

Nominal Rate   This is the stated rate, and it is usually paired with a compounding period, for example, 3.75% APR compounded monthly. In this example, 3.75% is the nominal rate, APR is short for annual percentage rate (meaning that the rate is applied on an annual basis), and one month is the compounding period.

15

Effective Rate   This is the actual rate paid. If the nominal rate period is the same as the compounding period, the nominal and effective rates are identical. However, as is usually the case, when the interest compounds over a shorter period than the nominal rate period, the effective rate will be higher than the nominal rate.

Figure 15.11 shows 12 compounding periods in the middle of a 30-year loan. The original loan was for $165,000, has a nominal rate of 3.75% APR compounded monthly, and calls for 30 annual payments of $9,169.68 each.

FIGURE 15.11

A partial amortization schedule to compute the effective rate

		F21		f_x	=EFFECT(F20,12)		
	A	B	C	D	E	F	G
1							
2		Date	Payment	Principal	Interest	Balance	
3						152,151.73	
4		1/10/2015	-	(475.47)	475.47	152,627.20	
5		2/10/2015	-	(476.96)	476.96	153,104.16	
6		3/10/2015	-	(478.45)	478.45	153,582.61	
7		4/10/2015	-	(479.95)	479.95	154,062.56	
8		5/10/2015	-	(481.45)	481.45	154,544.01	
9		6/10/2015	-	(482.95)	482.95	155,026.96	
10		7/10/2015	-	(484.46)	484.46	155,511.42	
11		8/10/2015	-	(485.97)	485.97	155,997.39	
12		9/10/2015	-	(487.49)	487.49	156,484.88	
13		10/10/2015	-	(489.02)	489.02	156,973.90	
14		11/10/2015	-	(490.54)	490.54	157,464.44	
15		12/10/2015	9,169.68	8,677.60	492.08	148,786.84	
16							
17				Total interest paid		5,804.79	
18				Effective Rate		3.815%	
19							
20				Given Nominal Rate		3.750%	
21				Compute Effective Rate		3.815%	
22							
23				Given Effective Rate		3.815%	
24				Compute Nominal Rate		3.750%	
25							

In each period that the interest compounds but no payment is made, the balance goes up by the amount of interest. When the payment is made, a little of it goes to the last month's interest, and the rest of it reduces the principal.

Cell F17 sums all of the interest compounded over the year, and cell F18 divides it by the beginning balance to get the effective rate. Fortunately, we don't have to create a whole amortization schedule to convert interest rates. Excel provides the EFFECT and NOMINAL worksheet functions to do that job.

Effective Rate

```
=EFFECT(F20,12)
```

Nominal Rate

```
=NOMINAL(F23,12)
```

Both EFFECT and NOMINAL take two arguments: the rate to be converted and the *npery* argument. The rate to be converted is the effective rate for NOMINAL and the nominal rate for EFFECT. The npery argument is the number of compounding periods in the nominal rate period. In this example, the nominal rate is annual because the term APR was used. There are 12 months in a year, so there are 12 compounding periods in our nominal rate. If, for example, you had a loan with an APR that compounded daily, the npery argument would be 365.

Computing effective rate with FV

The effective rate can also be computed with the FV function. With a handy function such as EFFECT, there's no need to resort to FV, but it can be instructive to understand the relationship between EFFECT and FV.

```
=FV(3.75%/12,12,0,-1)-1
```

This formula computes the future value of a $1 loan at 3.75% compounded monthly for one year, and then it subtracts the original $1. If you were to take this loan, you would pay back $1.03815 after the year was over. This means you'd owe an additional $0.03815 more than you borrowed, or, effectively, 3.815%.

Creating a loan payment calculator

Excel's PMT worksheet function is used to calculate your monthly payment on a loan. You can hard-code the values, such as the loan amount and interest rate, into the function's arguments, but by entering those values in cells and using the cells as the arguments, you can easily change the values to see how the payment changes.

Figure 15.12 shows a simple payment calculator. The user enters values in C2:C4, and the payment is calculated in C6 with the following formula:

```
=PMT(C3/12,C4*12,C2,0,0)
```

FIGURE 15.12

A simple loan payment calculator

The PMT function takes three required arguments and one optional argument:

Rate (required)   The *rate argument* is the annual nominal interest rate divided by the number of compounding periods in a year. In this example, the interest compounds monthly, so the interest rate in C3 is divided by 12.

nper (required) The *nper argument* is the number of payments that will be made over the life of the loan. Since our user input asks for years and our payments are monthly, the number of years in C4 is multiplied by 12.

pv (required) The *pv argument*, or present value, is the amount being borrowed. Excel's loan functions, of which PMT is one, work on a cash flow basis. When you think about present value and payments as cash inflows and outflows, it's easier to understand when the value should be positive or negative. In this example, the bank is loaning us $215,000, which is a cash inflow and thus positive. The result of the PMT function is a negative because the payments will be cash outflows.

> **TIP**
>
> If you want the PMT function to return a positive value, you can change the pv argument to a negative number. That's like calculating the payment from the bank's perspective: The loan is a cash outflow, and the payments are cash inflows.

> **CAUTION**
>
> The most common mistake in financial formulas is a mismatch between compounding periods and payment frequency. In this example, the rate is divided by 12 to make it a monthly rate, and the nper is multiplied by 12 to make it a monthly payment. Both arguments are converted to monthly, so they match, and we get the correct result.
>
> If we forgot to divide our rate by 12, Excel would think that we were entering a monthly rate, and the payment would be way too high. Similarly, if we entered years for our nper and a monthly rate, Excel would think that we were paying only once a year.
>
> Excel doesn't really know whether you enter months, years, or days. It only cares that the rate and nper match.

Creating an amortization schedule

With the payment amount calculated, we can create an amortization schedule that will show how much of each payment is principal and interest and what the loan balance will be after each payment. Figure 15.13 shows a portion of the amortization schedule.

The columns are of the amortization schedule are detailed here:

Pmt No The number of the payment being made. A 1 is entered into D11. The formula =D11+1 is entered into D12 and copied down to D370 (our amortization schedule can handle 360 payments).

Pmt Amt The amount of the PMT calculation rounded to the nearest penny. While Excel can calculate a lot of decimal places, we can write a check only for dollars and cents. This means there will be a small balance at the end of the loan. The formula =-ROUND($C$6,2) is entered in E11 and filled down through E370.

Principal   The amount of each payment applied to the loan balance. The formula =E11-G11 is entered in F11 and filled down through F370.

Interest   The amount of each payment that is interest. The balance after the prior payment is multiplied by the interest rate divided by 12. The total is rounded to two decimal places. The formula =ROUND(H10*$C$3/12,2) is entered in G11 and filled down through G370.

FIGURE 15.13

A partial amortization schedule

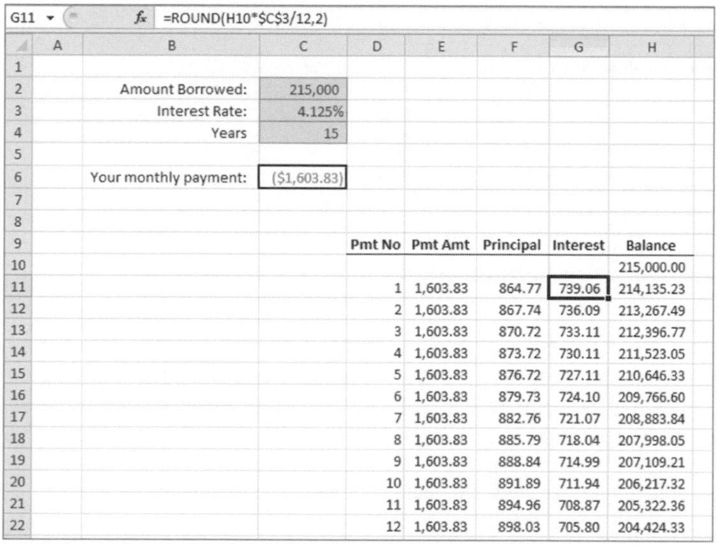

G11 ▾		fx	=ROUND(H10*$C$3/12,2)					
▲	A	B	C	D	E	F	G	H
1								
2		Amount Borrowed:	215,000					
3		Interest Rate:	4.125%					
4		Years	15					
5								
6		Your monthly payment:	($1,603.83)					
7								
8								
9				Pmt No	Pmt Amt	Principal	Interest	Balance
10								215,000.00
11				1	1,603.83	864.77	739.06	214,135.23
12				2	1,603.83	867.74	736.09	213,267.49
13				3	1,603.83	870.72	733.11	212,396.77
14				4	1,603.83	873.72	730.11	211,523.05
15				5	1,603.83	876.72	727.11	210,646.33
16				6	1,603.83	879.73	724.10	209,766.60
17				7	1,603.83	882.76	721.07	208,883.84
18				8	1,603.83	885.79	718.04	207,998.05
19				9	1,603.83	888.84	714.99	207,109.21
20				10	1,603.83	891.89	711.94	206,217.32
21				11	1,603.83	894.96	708.87	205,322.36
22				12	1,603.83	898.03	705.80	204,424.33

Balance   The balance of the loan after the payment. The formula =C2 is entered in H10 representing the original amount of the loan. Starting in C3 and continuing down to C370, the formula =H10-F11 reduces the balance by the principal portion of the payment.

In the example shown in Figure 15.13, the number of years was entered as 15, compared to 30 in Figure 15.12. Reducing the length of the loan increases the amount of the payment.

The final step is to hide rows beyond the loan term. This is done with conditional formatting that changes the font color to white. A white font color against a white background effectively hides the data. The formula for the conditional formatting is shown here and in Figure 15.14.

    =$D12>$C$4*12

15

FIGURE 15.14

Conditional formatting to hide rows

This formula compares the payment number in column D to the number of years in C4 times 12. When the payment number is larger, the formula returns TRUE, and the white font color formatting is applied. When the payment number is less than or equal to the total number of payments, no conditional formatting is applied.

 See Chapter 5, "Formatting Worksheets," for more information on conditional formatting.

Creating a variable-rate mortgage amortization schedule

In Figure 15.13, we created an amortization schedule for a loan with a fixed interest rate. There are also loans where the rate changes at times during the life of the loan. Often, these loans have an interest rate that's tied to a published index, such as the London Interbank Offered Rate (LIBOR), plus a fixed percentage. Those interest rates are usually stated as "LIBOR plus 3%," for example.

Figure 15.15 shows an amortization schedule for a loan with a variable interest rate. A Rate column was added to the amortization schedule so that it will be obvious when the changes occur. A separate table is used to record when the rate changes.

FIGURE 15.15

A variable rate amortization schedule

	G11	▼	f_x	=VLOOKUP(D11,$K$11:$L$23,2,TRUE)									
	A	B	C	D	E	F	G	H	I	J	K	L	M
1													
2		Amount Borrowed:	215,000										
3		Interest Rate:	4.125%										
4		Years	15										
5													
6		Your monthly payment:	($1,603.83)										
7													
8													
9				Pmt No	Pmt Amt	Principal	Rate	Interest	Balance		Interest Changes		
10									215,000.00		Pmt No.	New Rate	
11				1	1,603.83	864.77	4.125%	739.06	214,135.23		1	4.125%	
12				2	1,603.83	867.74	4.125%	736.09	213,267.49		10	3.875%	
13				3	1,603.83	870.72	4.125%	733.11	212,396.77		98	4.000%	
14				4	1,603.83	873.72	4.125%	730.11	211,523.05				
15				5	1,603.83	876.72	4.125%	727.11	210,646.33				
16				6	1,603.83	879.73	4.125%	724.10	209,766.60				
17				7	1,603.83	882.76	4.125%	721.07	208,883.84				
18				8	1,603.83	885.79	4.125%	718.04	207,998.05				
19				9	1,603.83	888.84	4.125%	714.99	207,109.21				
20				10	1,603.83	935.04	3.875%	668.79	206,174.17				
21				11	1,603.83	938.06	3.875%	665.77	205,236.11				
22				12	1,603.83	941.09	3.875%	662.74	204,295.02				
23				13	1,603.83	944.13	3.875%	659.70	203,350.89				
24				14	1,603.83	947.18	3.875%	656.65	202,403.71				
25				15	1,603.83	950.23	3.875%	653.60	201,453.48				

The Rate column contains the following formula to select the proper rate from the rate table:

```
=VLOOKUP(D11,$K$11:$L$23,2,TRUE)
```

The Interest column formula changes to use the rate in column G rather than the rate in C3:

```
=ROUND(I10*G11/12,2)
```

The Rate column uses a VLOOKUP with a fourth argument of TRUE. The fourth argument of TRUE requires that the rate table be sorted in ascending order. Then VLOOKUP looks up the payment number in the rate table. It doesn't require an exact match, but it returns the row where the next payment number is larger than the lookup value. For instance, when the lookup value is 16, VLOOKUP returns the second row of the rate table because the payment number in the next row, 98, is larger than the lookup value.

 See Chapter 14 for more examples of VLOOKUP.

The interest rate column formula is similar to the one used in the example shown in Figure 15.13, except that the absolute reference to $C$3 is replaced by a reference to column G (G11 for the formula in row 11).

15

Using dates instead of payment numbers

The two amortization schedules for this section and the previous one use the payment number to identify each payment. In reality, those payments will be due on the same day of the month. This allows the amortization schedule to be used for loans that start on any date. Figure 15.16 shows an amortization schedule using dates.

FIGURE 15.16

A date-based amortization schedule

To modify the schedule to show the dates, follow these steps:

1. **Enter the first payment date in cell D11.**

2. **Enter the following formula in D12 and fill down:**

   ```
   =DATE(YEAR(D11),MONTH(D11)+1,DAY(D11))
   ```

3. **Change the Pmt No column in the rate table column to the date the rate changed.**

4. **Change the formula in the conditional formatting to the following formula:**

   ```
   =$D12>=DATE(YEAR($D$11),MONTH($D$11)+($C$4*12),DAY($D$11))
   ```

Calculating depreciation

Excel provides a number of depreciation-related worksheet functions including DB, DDB, SLN, and SYD. In this section, we'll look at calculating straight line (SLN) and variable-declining balance (VDB) depreciation.

> **NOTE**
>
> The depreciation for the first and last years of an asset's life is usually different than for the middle year. A *convention* is employed so that a full year's depreciation is not taken for the first year. Common conventions are half-year, mid-month, and mid-quarter. For the half-year convention, the asset is assumed to have been purchased at the halfway point of the year, and consequently one-half of a normal year's depreciation is recorded for that year.

Figure 15.17 shows a depreciation schedule for five assets using the straight-line method and a half-year convention.

FIGURE 15.17

A straight-line depreciation schedule

| 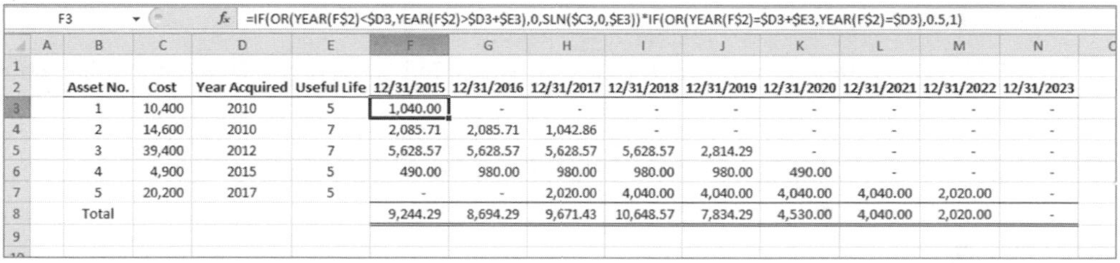 F3 | | fx | =IF(OR(YEAR(F$2)<$D3,YEAR(F$2)>$D3+$E3),0,SLN($C3,0,$E3))*IF(OR(YEAR(F$2)=$D3+$E3,YEAR(F$2)=$D3),0.5,1) |

	A	B	C	D	E	F	G	H	I	J	K	L	M	N
1														
2		Asset No.	Cost	Year Acquired	Useful Life	12/31/2015	12/31/2016	12/31/2017	12/31/2018	12/31/2019	12/31/2020	12/31/2021	12/31/2022	12/31/2023
3		1	10,400	2010	5	1,040.00	-	-	-	-	-	-	-	-
4		2	14,600	2010	7	2,085.71	2,085.71	1,042.86	-	-	-	-	-	-
5		3	39,400	2012	7	5,628.57	5,628.57	5,628.57	5,628.57	2,814.29	-	-	-	-
6		4	4,900	2015	5	490.00	980.00	980.00	980.00	980.00	490.00	-	-	-
7		5	20,200	2017	5	-	-	2,020.00	4,040.00	4,040.00	4,040.00	4,040.00	2,020.00	-
8		Total				9,244.29	8,694.29	9,671.43	10,648.57	7,834.29	4,530.00	4,040.00	2,020.00	-
9														

Columns B:E contain the following user-entered data:

Asset No.   A unique identifier for each asset. It's not necessary for the schedule, but it is handy for keeping track of assets.

Cost   The amount paid to put the asset in service. This includes the price paid for the asset, any taxes associated with purchase, the cost to ship the asset to its place of service, and any costs to install the asset so that it's ready for use. This is also known as *basis* or *cost basis*.

Year Acquired   The year the asset was put into service. This may be different than the year the payment was made to purchase the asset. It determines when depreciation starts.

Useful Life   The number of years you estimate the asset will provide service.

The formula shown in F3:N7 follows:

```
=IF(OR(YEAR(F$2)<$D3,YEAR(F$2)>$D3+$E3),0,SLN($C3,0,$E3))*IF(OR(YEAR
(F$2)=$D3+$E3,YEAR(F$2)=$D3),0.5,1)
```

15

The main part of this formula is SLN($C3,0,$E3). The SLN worksheet function computes the straight-line depreciation for one period. It takes three arguments: cost, salvage, and life. For simplicity, the salvage value for this example is set to zero, meaning that the asset's cost will be fully depreciated at the end of its useful life.

The SLN function is pretty simple. But this is a depreciation schedule, so there's more work to do. The first IF function determines if the column is within the asset's useful life. If the year of the date in F2 is less than the year acquired, then the asset isn't in service yet, and the depreciation is zero. If F2 is greater than the year acquired plus the useful life, the asset is already fully depreciated, and the depreciation is zero. Both of these conditionals are wrapped in an OR function so that if either is true, the whole expression returns TRUE. If both are FALSE, however, the SLN function is returned.

 See Chapter 13, "Using Formulas for Conditional Analysis," for more examples of using IF with OR.

The second part of the formula is also an IF and OR combination. These conditional statements determine whether the year in F2 is either the first year of depreciation or the last year. If either is true, the straight-line result is multiplied by 0.5 representing the half-year convention employed here.

All the cell references in this formula are anchored so that the formula can be copied down and to the right and the cell references change appropriately. References to row 2 are anchored on the row so that we're always evaluating the date in row 2. References to the columns C:E are anchored on the columns, so Cost, Year Acquired, and Useful Life stay the same as the formula is copied.

 See Chapter 9, "Introducing Formulas and Functions," for more information on relative and absolute cell references.

Calculating accelerated depreciation

The straight-line method depreciates an asset equally over all of the years of its useful life. Some organizations use an accelerated method, a method that depreciates at a higher rate at the beginning of an asset's life and a lower rate at the end. The theory is that an asset loses more value when it is first put in service than in its last year of operation.

Excel provides the DDB function (double-declining balance) for accelerated depreciation. DDB computes what the straight-line method would be for the remaining asset value and doubles it. The problem with DDB is that it doesn't depreciate the whole asset within the useful life. The depreciation amount gets smaller and smaller, but it runs out of useful life before it gets to zero.

The most common application of accelerated depreciation is to start with a declining balance method, and once the depreciation falls below the straight-line amount, the method is switched to straight line for the remaining life. Fortunately, Excel provides the VDB function that has that logic built in. Figure 15.18 shows a depreciation schedule using the following VDB-based formula:

```
=IF(OR(YEAR(F$2)<$D3,YEAR(F$2)>$D3+$E3),0,VDB($C3,
0,$E3*2,IF(YEAR(F$2)=$D3,0,IF(YEAR(F$2)=$D3+$E3,$E3*2-1,
(YEAR(F$2)-$D3)*2-1)),IF(YEAR(F$2)=$D3,1,IF(YEAR(F$2)=$D3+$E3,
$E3*2,(YEAR(F$2)-$D3)*2+1)))))
```

FIGURE 15.18

An accelerated depreciation schedule

	A	B	C	D	E	F	G	H	I	J	K	L	M	N
		F3				=IF(OR(YEAR(F$2)<$D3,YEAR(F$2)>$D3+$E3),0,VDB($C3,0,$E3*2,IF(YEAR(F$2)=$D3,0, IF(YEAR(F$2)=$D3+$E3,$E3*2-1,(YEAR(F$2)-$D3)*2-1)), IF(YEAR(F$2)=$D3,1,IF(YEAR(F$2)=$D3+$E3,$E3*2,(YEAR(F$2)-$D3)*2+1)))))							
1														
2		Asset No.	Cost	Year Acquired	Useful Life	12/31/2015	12/31/2016	12/31/2017	12/31/2018	12/31/2019	12/31/2020	12/31/2021	12/31/2022	12/31/2023
3		1	10,400	2010	5	681.57	-	-	-	-	-	-	-	-
4		2	14,600	2010	7	1,417.94	1,417.94	708.97	-	-	-	-	-	-
5		3	39,400	2012	7	4,836.26	3,826.49	3,826.49	3,826.49	1,913.25	-	-	-	-
6		4	4,900	2015	5	980.00	1,411.20	903.17	642.25	642.25	321.13	-	-	-
7		5	20,200	2017	5	-	-	4,040.00	5,817.60	3,723.26	2,647.65	2,647.65	1,323.83	-
8		Total				7,915.77	6,655.63	9,478.63	10,286.34	6,278.76	2,968.78	2,647.65	1,323.83	-
9														

You might have noticed that this formula is a little more complicated than the SLN formula from the previous example. Don't worry, we'll step through it piece by piece so that you understand it:

```
=IF(OR(YEAR(F$2)<$D3,YEAR(F$2)>$D3+$E3),0,VDB(...))))
```

The first part of the formula is identical to the SLN formula shown earlier. If the date in row 2 is not within the useful life, the depreciation is zero. If it is, the VDB function is evaluated:

```
VDB($C3,0,$E3*2,starting_period,ending_period)
```

The first three arguments to VDB are the same as the SLN arguments: cost, salvage value, and life. SLN returns the same value for every period so that we don't have to tell SLN which period to calculate. But VDB returns a different amount depending on the period. The last two arguments of VDB tell it which period to compute. The life in E3 is doubled, which will be explained in the next section.

Starting_period

```
IF(YEAR(F$2)=$D3,0,IF(YEAR(F$2)=$D3+$E3,$E3*2-1,(YEAR(F$2)-$D3)*2-1))
```

None of Excel's depreciation functions take into account the convention. That is, Excel calculates depreciation as if you bought all of your assets on the first day of the year. That's not very practical. In this section, we're assuming a half-year convention so that only half of the depreciation is taken in the first and last years. To accomplish this with VDB, we have to trick Excel into thinking that the asset has twice its useful life.

15

For an asset with a five-year useful life, the period for the first year goes from 0 to 1. For the second year, the periods span 1–3. The third year spans periods 3–5. That continues until the last year, which spans 9–10 (10 is double the five-year life). The starting period portion of the formula evaluates like this:

- If the year to compute is the acquisition year, make the starting period 0.
- If the year to compute is the last year, make the starting period the useful life times 2 and subtract 1.
- For all other years, subtract the acquisition year from the year to compute, multiply by 2, and subtract 1.

The ending period portion of the formula is similar to the starting period portion. For the first year, it ends at period 1. For the last year, it ends at the useful life times 2. For the middle years, it does the same calculation except that it adds one instead of subtracting.

By doubling the useful life, say from 7 periods to 14 periods for a 7-year asset, we can introduce the half-year convention into a declining balance function like VDB.

Calculating present value

The *time value of money* (TVM) is an important concept in accounting and finance. The idea is that a dollar today is worth less than the same dollar tomorrow. The difference in the two values is the income that you can create with that dollar. The income may be interest from a savings account or the return on an investment.

Excel provides several functions for dealing with TVM, such as the PV function for calculating the present value. In its simplest form, PV *discounts* a future value amount by a discount rate to arrive at the present value. If I promise to pay you $10,000 one year from now, how much would you take today instead of waiting? Figure 15.19 shows how you would calculate that amount:

    =PV(C4,C3,0,-C2)

FIGURE 15.19

A present value calculation

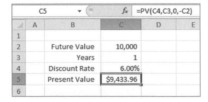

The present value calculator in Figure 15.19 suggests that you would take $9,434 now instead of $10,000 a year from now. If you took the $9,434 and were able to earn 6% over the next year, you would have $10,000 at the end of the year.

The PV function accepts five arguments:

Rate   Also known as the discount rate, the *rate* argument is the return you think you could make on your money over the discount period. It is the biggest factor in determining the present value, and it can also be the hardest to determine. If you're conservative, you might pick a lower rate—something you're sure you can achieve. If you were to use the money to pay off a loan with a fixed rate, the discount rate would be easy to determine.

nper   The *nper* is the period of time to discount the future value. In this example, the nper is 1 year and is entered in cell C3. The rate and the period must be in the same units. That is, if you enter an annual rate, nper must be expressed as years. If you use a monthly rate, nper must be expressed as months.

pmt   The *pmt* argument is the regular payments received over the discount period. When there is only one payment, as in this example, that amount is the future value and the payment amount is zero. The pmt argument must also the match the nper argument. If your nper is 10 and you enter pmt, PV assumes that you'll get that payment amount 10 times over the discount period. The next example shows a present value calculation with payments.

FV   The *future value* amount is the amount you will receive at the end of the discount period. Excel's financial functions work on a cash flow basis. That means the future value and present value have opposite signs. For this example, the future value was made negative so that the formula result would return a positive number.

type   The *type* argument can be 0 if the payments are received at the end of the period or 1 if the payments are received at the beginning of the period. This argument has no effect on this example because our payment amount is 0. The type argument can be omitted in which case it is assumed to be 0.

Calculating the present value of future payments

Another use of PV is to calculate the present value of a series of equal future payments. If, for example, you owed $5,000 of rent for an office over the next 10 years, you can use PV to calculate how much you would be willing to pay to get out of the lease. Figure 15.20 shows the present value calculation for that scenario.

```
=PV(C4,C3,-C2,0,1)
```

If your landlord thought he could make 3% on the money, he might be willing to accept $43,930 instead of ten $5,000 payments over the next 10 years. The type argument is set to 1 in this example because rents are usually made at the beginning of the period.

When used on payments, the PV function is actually taking the present value of each payment individually and adding up all the results. Figure 15.20 shows the calculation broken out by payment. The first payment's present value is the same as the payment amount because it's due now. The Year 2 payment is due one year from now, and it is discounted to $4,854. The last payment, due nine years from now, is discounted to $3,832. All of the present value calculations are added up. Fortunately, PV does all the heavy lifting for you.

15

FIGURE 15.20

The present value of a series of future payments

	C5	▼	f_x	=PV(C4,C3,-C2,0,1)	
◢	A	B	C	D	E
1					
2		Rent	5,000		
3		Years	10		
4		Discount Rate	3.00%		
5		Present Value	43,931		
6					
7		Year	Rent	PV	
8		1	5,000	5,000	
9		2	5,000	4,854	
10		3	5,000	4,713	
11		4	5,000	4,576	
12		5	5,000	4,442	
13		6	5,000	4,313	
14		7	5,000	4,187	
15		8	5,000	4,065	
16		9	5,000	3,947	
17		10	5,000	3,832	
18				43,931	
19					
20					

Calculating net present value

The PV function used in Figure 15.20 can calculate the present value of future cash flows if all the cash flows are the same. But sometimes that's not the case. The NPV (net present value) function is Excel's solution to calculating the present value of uneven future cash flows.

Suppose someone wanted you to invest $30,000 in a new business. In exchange for your investment, you would be entitled to an annual dividend over the next seven years. The estimated amounts of those dividends are shown in the schedule in Figure 15.21. Further suppose that you would like to earn an 8% return on your money.

To determine whether this investment is worth your while, you can use the NPV function shown here to calculate the net present value of that investment:

    =NPV(C2,C5:C11)

NPV discounts each cash flow separately based on the rate, just like PV value does. Unlike PV, however, NPV accepts a range of future cash flows rather than just a single payment amount. NPV doesn't have an nper argument because the number of values in the range determines the number of future cash flows.

Although the payments can be for different amounts, they are still assumed to be at regular intervals (one year in this example). And like the other TVM functions in this chapter, the rate period must be consistent with the payment period. In this example, the 8% return you'd like is an annual return, and the payments are annual, so they match. If you were getting a quarterly dividend, you would have to adjust the rate to a quarterly return.

FIGURE 15.21

The net present value of expected future cash flows

The NPV for these cash flows calculates to $33,068. Since the required investment to get those cash flows, $30,000, is less than the NPV (and assuming the estimates are correct), these would be good investments. In fact, this data shows that you would make something more than the 8% return you wanted.

Calculating positive and negative cash flows

In the previous example, you were asked to make a large up-front investment to get future cash flows. Another scenario where NPV can be used is when you make smaller payments at the beginning of the investment period with the expectation of future cash inflows at the end.

Instead of one $30,000 payment, assume that you would only have to invest $15,000 the first year, $10,000 the second year, and $5,000 the third year. The amount you're required to invest goes down as the business grows and is able to use its own profits to grow. By year 4, no further investment is required, and it's expected that the business will be profitable enough to start paying a dividend.

Figure 15.22 shows a schedule where you pay in for the first three years and get money back the last four. The NPV function is the same as before; only the inputs have changed.

```
=NPV(C2,C5:C11)
```

15

FIGURE 15.22

The net present value of both positive and negative cash flows

	C13	▾	f_x	=NPV(C2,C5:C11)	
⊿	A	B	C	D
1				
2		Desired Return:	8.00%	
3				
4		Date	Expected Future Cash Flow	
5		12/31/2015	(15,000)	
6		12/31/2016	(10,000)	
7		12/31/2017	(5,000)	
8		12/31/2018	7,000	
9		12/31/2019	9,100	
10		12/31/2020	11,830	
11		12/31/2021	15,142	
12				
13		Net Present Value:	1,197	
14				
15				

In the first NPV example, the amount invested was not part of the calculation. We simply took the result of the NPV function and compared it to the investment amount. In this example, a portion of the investment is also in the future, so the invested amounts are shown as negatives (cash outflows), and the eventual dividends are shown as positive amounts (cash inflows).

Instead of comparing the result to an initial investment amount, this NPV calculation is compared to zero. If the NPV is greater than zero, then the series of cash flows returns something greater than 8%. If it's less than zero, the return is less than 8%. Based on the data in Figure 15.22, it's a good investment.

Calculating an internal rate of return

In the previous example, we calculated the net present value of future expected cash flows and compared it to our initial investment amount. Because the net present value was greater than the initial investment, we knew that the rate of return would be greater than our desired rate. But what is the actual rate of return?

Excel's IRR function can be used to calculate the internal rate of return of future cash flows (see Figure 15.23). IRR is closely related to NPV. IRR computes the rate of return that causes the NPV of those same cash flows to be exactly zero.

For IRR, we have to structure our data a little differently. There has to be at least one positive and one negative cash flow in the values range. If you have all positive values, this means you invest nothing and receive only money. That would be a great investment but not very realistic. Typically, the cash outflows are at the beginning of the investment period, and the cash inflows are at the end. But it's not always that way, as long as there is at least one of each.

Note that we have to include the initial investment for IRR to work. The first row was added to show the initial $30,000 investment. The following IRR formula shows that the investment return is 10.53%:

```
=IRR(C3:C10,0.08)
```

FIGURE 15.23

The internal rate of return of a series of future cash flows

	C12	▾	f_x	=IRR(C3:C10,0.08)	
⊿	A	B		C	D
1					
2		Date		Expected Future Cash Flow	
3		12/31/2014		(30,000)	
4		12/31/2015		4,000	
5		12/31/2016		4,760	
6		12/31/2017		5,664	
7		12/31/2018		6,797	
8		12/31/2019		7,477	
9		12/31/2020		8,225	
10		12/31/2021		9,458	
11					
12		Internal Rate of Return:		10.53%	
13					

The first argument for IRR is the range of cash flows. The second argument is a guess of what is the internal rate of return. If you don't supply a guess, Excel uses 10% as the guess. IRR works by calculating the present value of each cash flow based on the guessed rate. If the sum of those is greater than zero, it reduces the rate and tries again. Excel keeps iterating through rates and summing present values until the sum is zero. Once the present values sum to zero, it returns that rate.

Calculating nonperiodic future cash flows

For both the NPV function and the IRR function, the future cash flows are assumed to be at regular intervals. That may not always be the case. For cash flows at irregular intervals, Excel provides the XIRR function.

XIRR requires one more argument than IRR: dates. IRR doesn't need to know the dates because it assumes that the cash flows are the same distance apart. Whether they are one day apart or one year, IRR doesn't care. The rate it returns will be consistent with the cash flows. That is, if the cash flows are annual, the rate will be an annual rate. If the cash flows are quarterly, the rate will be quarterly.

> **TIP**
>
> XIRR has a related function for calculating the net present value of nonperiodic cash flows called XNPV. Like XIRR, XNPV requires a matching range of dates.

15

Figure 15.24 shows a schedule of nonperiodic cash flows. On some days, the investment loses money and requires a cash injection. On other days, the investment makes money and returns it to the investor. Over all the cash flows, the investor makes an annual return of 10.14%. The following formula uses XIRR to calculate the return:

```
=XIRR(C3:C17,B3:B17,0.08)
```

FIGURE 15.24

The internal rate of return of nonperiodic cash flows

	A	B	C	D
			f =XIRR(C3:C17,B3:B17,0.08)	
		C19		
1				
2		Date	Cash Flows	
3		6/1/2015	(6,723)	
4		8/17/2015	(14,856)	
5		11/6/2015	5,856	
6		12/12/2015	(4,171)	
7		1/21/2016	8,039	
8		3/10/2016	(12,384)	
9		5/18/2016	13,860	
10		7/23/2016	(12,894)	
11		8/26/2016	7,196	
12		11/18/2016	14,907	
13		1/9/2017	(6,636)	
14		2/28/2017	3,964	
15		4/25/2017	(13,690)	
16		7/3/2017	6,185	
17		9/22/2017	14,785	
18				
19		Internal Rate of Return:	10.14%	
20				
21				

Internally, XIRR works in much the same way as IRR. It calculates the present value of each cash flow individually, iterating through rate guesses until the sum of the present values is zero. It bases the present value calculations on the number of days between the current cash flow and the one just previous in date order. Then it annualizes the rate of return.

Performing financial forecasting

Forecasting refers to predicting values based on historical values. The values can be financial (for example, sales or income) or any other time-based data (for example, number of employees).

Excel 2019 makes the forecasting process easier than ever.

This workbook is available on this book's website at www.wiley.com/go/excel2019bible. The file is named forecasting example.xlsx.

To create a forecast, start with historical, time-based data—for example, monthly sales. Figure 15.25 shows a simple example. Column B contains monthly sales data from 2012 through 2015. We also created a chart, which shows that sales tend to be cyclical, with lower sales during the summer months. The goal is to forecast the monthly sales for the next two years.

FIGURE 15.25

Four years of monthly sales data

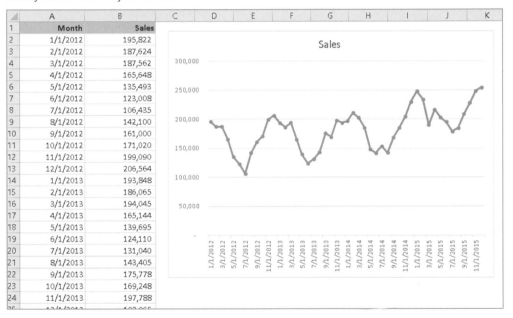

Start by selecting the data. For this example, we selected the range A1:B49. Choose Data ⇨ Forecast ⇨ Forecast Sheet, and Excel displays the Create Forecast Worksheet dialog box shown in Figure 15.26. (Options is clicked to display additional parameters.) The dialog box shows a chart that displays the historical data, the forecasted data, and the confidence limits for the forecast.

15

FIGURE 15.26

The Create Forecast Worksheet dialog box

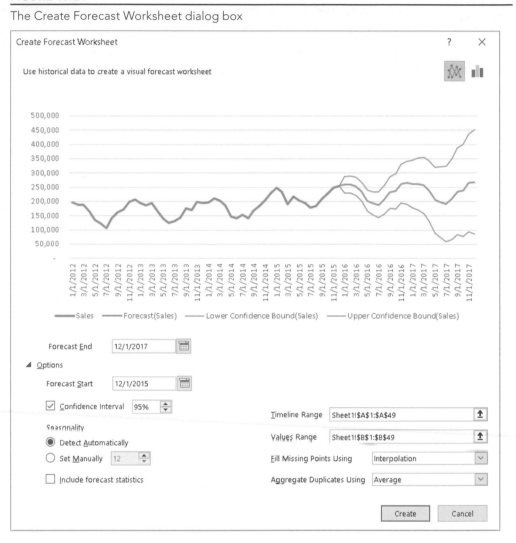

The confidence interval (depicted as thinner lines in the chart) determines the "plus or minus" values for the forecast and indicates the degree of confidence in the forecast. A higher confidence interval results in a wider prediction range. Note that the chart shown in the dialog box adjusts as you change options.

Click Create and Excel inserts a new worksheet that contains a table and a chart. Figure 15.27 shows part of this table. The table displays the forecasted values, along with the lower and upper confidence intervals. These values are generated using the new FORECAST.ETS and FORECAST.ETS.CONFINT functions. These are fairly complex functions, which explains why Excel does all the work.

FIGURE 15.27

The forecast worksheet contains a table and a chart.

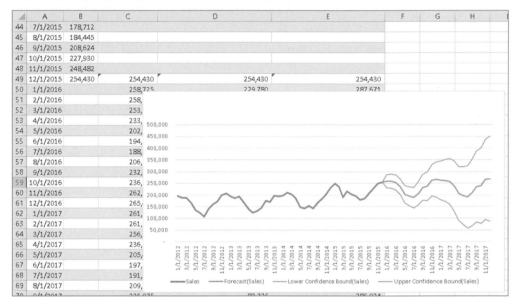

Using Formulas for Statistical Analysis

IN THIS CHAPTER

Working with weighted averages

Smoothing data with moving averages

Creating descriptive statistics

Creating frequency distributions

E xcel is an excellent tool for performing statistical analysis, in part because of the many statistical functions that it provides. In this chapter, you'll look at formulas for performing statistical analyses such as moving averages, descriptive statistics, and frequency distributions.

 This book's website, www.wiley.com/go/excel2019bible, includes a copy of the sample workbook for this chapter. The file is named Statistical Analysis.xlsx.

Working with Weighted Averages

A *weighted average* is used to average values where each value plays a larger or smaller role in the whole set. Figure 16.1 shows an investment portfolio. For each fund in the portfolio, the total value of the investment and the return on that investment are shown. We want to determine the total return on the portfolio. A simple average won't do because each investment contributes a different amount to the whole portfolio.

To compute the weighted average, the percentage that each investment contributes to the total value of the portfolio is multiplied by that investment's rate of return. The SUMPRODUCT function is ideal for multiplying two sets of values and summing each result. SUMPRODUCT takes up to 255 arguments separated by commas, but we need only two arguments for this formula.

    =SUMPRODUCT((C3:C7/$C$8),D3:D7)

The first argument takes each investment's value and divides it by the total value. This results in five percentages that represent the weight of each investment. For the Roboto Bond Fund, the weight is 17%, and it is computed by dividing 72,021.35 by 423,655.02. The second argument is the rate of return.

FIGURE 16.1

An investment portfolio with rates of return

	D8 ▼	f_x =SUMPRODUCT((C3:C7/$C$8),D3:D7)			
◢	A	B	C	D	E
1					
2		Investment	Value	Rate of Return	
3		Roboto Bond Fund	72,021.35	2.500%	
4		Duff Small Cap Fund	25,419.31	7.410%	
5		Ziff Value Investor Fund A	97,440.65	4.400%	
6		Cogswell International Fund	88,967.56	5.100%	
7		Sparkle Growth and Income Fund	139,806.15	10.120%	
8		**Weighted Average Return**	423,655.02	6.292%	
9					
10					
11					

The dollar signs in the $C$8 reference cause that reference to be absolute rather than relative. See Chapter 9 for a discussion of relative and absolute cell references.

SUMPRODUCT multiplies each element of the first argument by the corresponding element in the second argument. The element C3/C8 is multiplied by D3, the element C4/C8 is multiplied by D4, and so on. When all five elements are multiplied, SUMPRODUCT sums the five results.

If we used AVERAGE to find the simple average of the returns, we would get 5.906%. That's lower than our weighted average because investments such as the Sparkle Growth and Income Fund have both a higher return than average and represent a larger proportion of the portfolio.

Alternatively, all of the work that SUMPRODUCT does to compute the weighted average could be done with simpler functions in adjacent cells. Figure 16.2 shows the same calculation, but rather than using SUMPRODUCT in one cell, each investment's weight is calculated in its own cell, the effect of the rate on the whole is calculated, and those values are summed.

FIGURE 16.2

Expanding a weighted average calculation into adjacent cells

	F8			f_x	=SUM(F3:F7)		
	A	B	C	D	E	F	G
1							
2		Investment	Value	Rate of Return	Weight	Contribution	
3		Roboto Bond Fund	72,021.35	2.500%	17%	0.425%	
4		Duff Small Cap Fund	25,419.31	7.410%	6%	0.445%	
5		Ziff Value Investor Fund A	97,440.65	4.400%	23%	1.012%	
6		Cogswell International Fund	88,967.56	5.100%	21%	1.071%	
7		Sparkle Growth and Income Fund	139,806.15	10.120%	33%	3.340%	
8		**Weighted Average Return**	423,655.02			6.292%	
9							
10							
11							

Smoothing Data with Moving Averages

A *moving average* is used to smooth out data to provide a clearer picture of the overall trend of the data. It works particularly well when the individual data points are erratic. Figure 16.3 shows a partial listing of golf scores. Anyone who plays the game knows just how erratic scores can be from one round to the next. Figure 16.4 shows a graph of the scores over time. It's difficult to get a sense of how this golfer's game is changing because of the steep peaks and valleys on the chart.

We want to create a chart that shows how the scores are progressing by smoothing out the highs and lows. To do this, we can calculate the moving average of the scores and plot those values on the chart.

```
=IF(ROW()<12,NA(),AVERAGE(OFFSET(D3,-9,0,10,1)))
```

This formula uses a number of Excel functions to accomplish our task. First, an IF function is used to return the #N/A error for the first few scores. The ROW function with no argument returns the row of the current cells. We don't want to start our moving average calculation until we have enough data, so the formula returns #N/A for the first nine rows.

TIP

Excel charts don't show #N/A errors. The NA function is used for values that you don't want to show on your charts.

For the later scores, the AVERAGE function is used to return the arithmetic mean of the prior ten scores. AVERAGE takes up to 255 arguments, but since our values are a contiguous range, we need to supply only one.

FIGURE 16.3

A partial listing of golf scores

	E3	▾	*fx*	=IF(ROW()<12,NA(),AVERAGE(OFFSET(D3,-9,0,10,1)))		
	A	B	C	D	E	F
1						
2		Date	Course	Score	Moving Avg	
3		5/13/2013	Tiburon Golf Club	98	#N/A	
4		5/20/2013	Colbert Hills	88	#N/A	
5		5/27/2013	Colbert Hills	84	#N/A	
6		6/3/2013	Colbert Hills	94	#N/A	
7		6/10/2013	Tiburon Golf Club	85	#N/A	
8		6/17/2013	Tiburon Golf Club	88	#N/A	
9		6/24/2013	Tiburon Golf Club	89	#N/A	
10		7/1/2013	Iron Horse Golf Club	84	#N/A	
11		7/8/2013	Tiburon Golf Club	84	#N/A	
12		7/15/2013	Tiburon Golf Club	97	89.1	
13		7/22/2013	Tiburon Golf Club	97	89.0	
14		7/29/2013	Tiburon Golf Club	84	88.6	
15		8/5/2013	Iron Horse Golf Club	86	88.8	
16		8/12/2013	Tiburon Golf Club	89	88.3	
17		8/19/2013	Tiburon Golf Club	89	88.7	
18		8/26/2013	Tiburon Golf Club	93	89.2	
19		9/2/2013	Tiburon Golf Club	90	89.3	
20		9/9/2013	Tiburon Golf Club	90	89.9	
21		9/16/2013	Tiburon Golf Club	85	90.0	
22		9/23/2013	Indian Creek Golf Course	90	89.3	
23		9/30/2013	Iron Horse Golf Club	94	89.0	
24		10/7/2013	Indian Creek Golf Course	93	89.9	
25		10/14/2013	Bent Tree	90	90.3	
26		10/21/2013	Indian Creek Golf Course	100	91.4	

FIGURE 16.4

A graph of raw golf scores over time

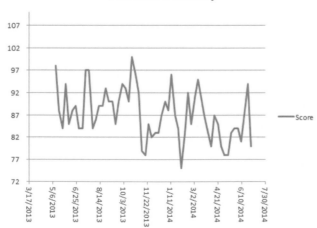

Golf Score History

The OFFSET function is used to return a particular range that's offset from the starting point. The arguments to OFFSET are as follows:

Reference   The cell where the OFFSET function starts.

Rows   The number of rows away from the starting cell where the returned range starts. Negative numbers count up the spreadsheet, while positive numbers count down.

Cols   The number of columns from the starting cell. Negative numbers count to the left, and positive numbers count to the right.

Height   How many rows the returned range should have.

Width   How many columns the returned range should have.

> **TIP**
> The height and width arguments of OFFSET must be positive numbers.

If we make cell D12 the reference argument, that's where OFFSET starts counting. The -9 in the rows argument directs OFFSET to count up nine rows to D3. The 0 (zero) in the cols argument means that OFFSET stays in the same column. After the first two arguments, OFFSET has computed that the start of the returned range will be D3.

The height argument is set to 10, meaning that our range will be ten rows in height, or D3:D12. The width argument of 1 keeps the range at one column wide. The result of OFFSET, and what is passed into AVERAGE, is the range D3:D12. As the formula is copied down, the prior ten scores are averaged.

> **NOTE**
> The number of values to include in a moving average varies depending on the data. You may want to show the previous 12 months, 5 years, or another number that makes sense for your data.

In Figure 16.5, the moving average is added to the chart, and the line for the raw scores is made lighter so that the average line stands out. Showing the average of the last 10 scores provides a clearer picture of where this golfer's game is headed.

Applying exponential smoothing to volatile data

A moving average is a great way to smooth out data. One problem with moving averages is that they give equal weight to each data point in the set. In a six-week moving average, for example, each week's value is given 1/6 weight. With some data sets, more current data points deserve more weight.

Figure 16.6 shows the demand for a product over a 26-week period. The Demand column shows the actual product sold. The Moving Average column attempts to predict the demand based on a simple six-week moving average. The final column uses exponential smoothing to give more weight to recent weeks than past weeks.

```
=(C8*$H$2)+(E8*(1-$H$2))
```

FIGURE 16.5

The moving average is charted over the raw scores.

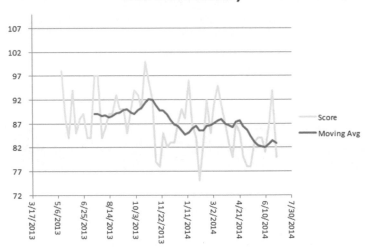

Golf Score History

FIGURE 16.6

The demand of a product over 26 weeks

	A	B	C	D	E	F	G	H
	E9			fx	=(C8*$H$2)+(E8*(1-$H$2))			
1								
2		Week	Demand	Moving Average	Exponential Forecast		Alpha:	0.30
3		1	412		412			
4		2	634		412			
5		3	990		479			
6		4	1,326		632			
7		5	1,485		840			
8		6	1,589		1,034			
9		7	1,780	1,073	1,201			
10		8	2,510	1,301	1,374			
11		9	3,464	1,614	1,715			
12		10	5,057	2,026	2,240			
13		11	4,956	2,648	3,085			
14		12	7,087	3,226	3,646			
15		13	10,985	4,142	4,679			
16		14	14,830	5,677	6,571			
17		15	14,830	7,730	9,049			
18		16	17,945	9,624	10,783			
19		17	17,406	11,772	12,931			
20		18	27,676	13,847	14,274			
21		19	21,310	17,279	18,294			
22		20	19,606	19,000	19,199			
23		21	18,821	19,795	19,321			

The *alpha* value, shown in cell H2 on Figure 16.6, is the weight given to the most recent data point, or 30% in this example. The remaining 70% weight is applied to the rest of the data points. The second most recent is weighted 30% of the remaining 70% (21%), the third most recent is weighted 30% of 70% of 70% (14.7%), and so on.

The prior week's value is multiplied by the alpha value, and that is added to the remaining percentage multiplied by the prior forecast. The prior forecast already has all of the previous calculations built into it.

The further away a demand value gets, the less it impacts the exponential smoothing forecast. In other words, last week's number is more important than the week before last. Figure 16.7 shows a chart of the demand, the moving average, and the exponential forecast. Note how the exponential forecast responds to changes in demand more quickly than the moving average.

FIGURE 16.7

Demand of a product visualized

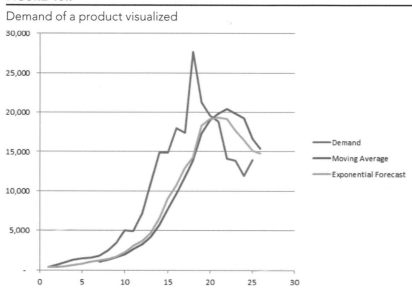

Using Functions to Create Descriptive Statistics

Descriptive statistics allow you to present data in quantitative summaries that are simple to understand. When you sum data, count data, and average data, you're producing descriptive statistics. In this section, we'll take a look at some of the functions that you can use to profile a data set and enable comparisons that can be used in other analyses.

Getting the largest or smallest value

Figure 16.8 shows the average low temperature by month for the city of Marietta, Georgia. We want to determine which months have the highest and lowest average temperature. The first formula will find the maximum average low temperature.

```
=MAX(C3:C14)
```

FIGURE 16.8

Average low temperatures by month

	A	B	C	D	E	F	G
E5			*fx*	=MAX(C3:C14)			
1							
2		Month	Avg Low Temp				
3		JAN	33				
4		FEB	36		Max	Min	
5		MAR	42		70	33	
6		APR	50		Max Month	Min Month	
7		MAY	59		JUL	JAN	
8		JUN	66				
9		JUL	70				
10		AUG	69				
11		SEP	63				
12		OCT	51				
13		NOV	42				
14		DEC	35				
15							

The next formula will return the month that corresponds to the temperature found in the previous formula:

```
=INDEX(B3:B14,MATCH(E5,C3:C14,FALSE),1)
```

Excel provides two functions for finding the largest and smallest values from a range: MAX and MIN. Both formulas accept up to 255 arguments. Our data is in C3:C14, and that is the range passed into MAX and MIN. MAX returns 70, the largest value in the range, and MIN returns 33, the smallest.

 See Chapter 14 for more information on the MATCH and INDEX functions.

To determine to which months those temperatures relate, we start with the INDEX function. The range passed into INDEX is the list of months in B3:B14. The second argument to INDEX is a MATCH function, which returns the position of the lookup value in a list. When we match 70 to our list of temperatures, MATCH returns 7 because 70 is the seventh item in the list. INDEX uses that 7 to return the seventh row of the lists of months, or JUL. The same structure is used for MIN to return JAN, the month with the smallest value.

Both MAX and MIN ignore any text in the range, but if there are errors in the range, they will return an error. If all the errors are text, MAX and MIN return zero.

Getting the Nth largest or smallest value

The MIN and MAX functions are great for finding the largest and smallest values. But sometimes you need to find the second-largest or the fifth-smallest value. Figure 16.9 shows the results of a bowling tournament. The bowlers are sorted alphabetically by name, and that makes it difficult to see who the winners are. We want to identify the first- through third-place bowlers and their scores. This formula returns the third-largest value from the list of scores:

=LARGE($C$3:$C$14,ROW(A3))

FIGURE 16.9

The results of a bowling tournament

	F5	▼	f_x	=LARGE($C$3:$C$14,ROW(A3))				
	A	B	C	D	E	F	G	H
1								
2		Bowler	Score		Position	Score	Bowler	
3		Aidan Knight	352		1st Place	588	Olivia Dunn	
4		Alexa Lee	533		2nd Place	547	Hannah Weaver	
5		Carlos White	389		3rd Place	546	Julian Murray	
6		Dylan Hill	300					
7		Hannah Weaver	547					
8		Jack Price	460					
9		Josiah Stone	511					
10		Julian Murray	546					
11		Justin Mitchell	396					
12		Makayla Simmons	507					
13		Olivia Dunn	588					
14		Vanessa Jackson	384					
15								
16								
17								

The formula to find the bowler's name uses INDEX and MATCH, similar to Figure 16.8.

=INDEX($B$3:$B$14,MATCH(F5,$C$3:$C$14,FALSE),1)

The LARGE and SMALL functions are used to find the Nth largest and smallest values in a list. Like MAX, we pass a range of values into LARGE. But LARGE has another argument for the *N* in the Nth largest value.

> **NOTE**
>
> If two values in the list have the same value, LARGE and SMALL return the same value for the Nth value and the Nth + 1 value. If two competitors had a score of **588**, =LARGE($C$3:$C$14,1) and =LARGE($C$3:$C$14,2) would both return **588**.

In cell F3, we use ROW(A1) to determine N. The ROW function returns the row for the cell passed to it, row 1 in this case. We could simply pass the number 1 to the LARGE function, but by using ROW(A1), we can copy this formula down to increase the row. The A1 reference is relative, and when the formula is copied to cell F4, it becomes ROW(A2). That returns 2, and the LARGE function in F4 then returns the second largest value.

 See Chapter 9 for more information on absolute and relative cell references.

The LARGE function is appropriate here because higher bowling scores are better. If, instead, we had a list of race times, then the SMALL function would be used because lower times are better.

Another way to determine the Nth largest or smallest number is the RANK function. The RANK function takes three arguments: the number to be ranked, the list of all the numbers, and the sort order. Figure 16.10 shows another result of a competition, but this time the lowest time is the winner. It also includes another column to rank each result, and that formula is shown here:

=RANK(C3,$C$3:$C$14,1)

FIGURE 16.10

The results of a race

	A	B	C	D	E	F	G	H	I
				D3		=RANK(C3,$C$3:$C$11,1)			
1									
2		Competitor	Time	Rank		Position	Time	Competitor	
3		Gianna Ruiz	0:20:35	1		1st Place	0:20:35	Gianna Ruiz	
4		Jessica Powell	0:24:22	6		2nd Place	0:21:38	Alexandra Mitchell	
5		Chase Ellis	0:29:26	12		3rd Place	0:21:42	Isaiah Peters	
6		Ayden Taylor	0:27:50	9					
7		Addison West	0:29:13	10					
8		Alexandra Mitchell	0:21:38	2					
9		Natalie Greene	0:29:13	10					
10		Jose Harper	0:24:38	7					
11		Isaiah Peters	0:21:42	3					
12		Carlos Pierce	0:26:56	8					
13		Alexis Coleman	0:23:41	5					
14		Jeremiah Dunn	0:22:50	4					
15									
16									
17									

To determine the rank of Gianna Ruiz, we pass into RANK the time in C3, the total list of times in C3:C14, and the order. The order is 1 in this example, because we want the lowest number to have rank 1. If we want the highest number to be ranked 1, the final argument would be 0.

TIP

When there is a tie, RANK will return the same result for the tied values. If two racers had a time of 20:35, RANK would return 1 for both. The next lowest time would receive a rank of 3. None of the values would rank 2 because the tied values take up both the 1 and 2 ranking.

Excel 2010 introduced two new functions for handling ties with ranking: RANK.AVG and RANK.EQ. The RANK.EQ function mirrors the results of RANK from prior versions. That is, the same value returns the same ranking. The RANK.AVG function works differently. It returns the average ranking for all values that match.

Assume the data in Figure 16.10 showed four racers with a time of 21:38, the second lowest time. RANK.AVG would return 1 for the best time and 3.5 for four matching second-place times. Those four times occupy the ranks 2, 3, 4, and 5. The average of those four rankings is 3.5.

Unlike LARGE and SMALL, which return the actual values, RANK returns the position of the value in the list if the list were sorted according to the last argument. To get the actual values, we need to use INDEX and MATCH just as we did for the names. The formula in cell G3 to return the time of the first-place competitor is shown here:

```
=INDEX($C$3:$C$14,MATCH(ROW(A1),$D$3:$D$14,FALSE),1)
```

 See Chapter 14 for more information on the MATCH and INDEX functions.

Calculating mean, median, and mode

When someone refers to average, they are usually referring to the arithmetic mean: the sum of the values divided by the count of the values. There are two other averages, median and mode, that you can calculate in Excel.

Figure 16.11 shows a list of 20 students and their grade on an assignment. We want to analyze the grades by finding the mean, median, and mode and draw conclusions from the results.

```
=AVERAGE(C3:C22)
=MEDIAN(C3:C22)
=MODE(C3:C22)
```

You can see from Figure 16.11 that the mean is 85.1, the median is 90.5, and the mode is 93.0. The mean is computed using the AVERAGE function, which sums all the values in the range and divides by the number of values. How the median and mode compare to the average may provide some insights into the data.

The median is computed using the aptly named MEDIAN function. If all the grades are listed in order, MEDIAN returns the value that's right in the middle. Because we have an even number of grades, there is not an exact middle value. In that case, MEDIAN returns the mean of the two values closest to the middle. After sorting the grades, Figure 16.12 shows that 90 and 91 are the two grades closest to the middle.

FIGURE 16.11

A list of students and grades

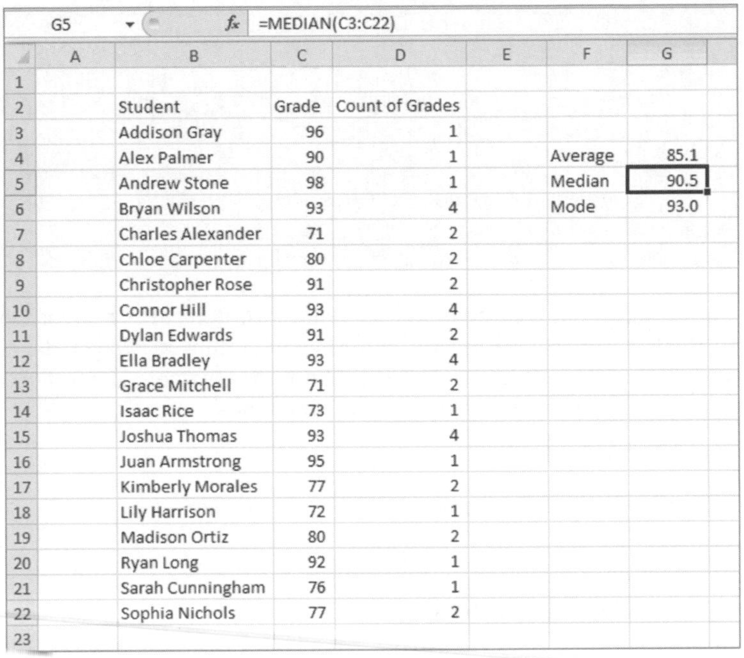

	A	B	C	D	E	F	G
				fx =MEDIAN(C3:C22)			
1							
2		Student	Grade	Count of Grades			
3		Addison Gray	96	1			
4		Alex Palmer	90	1		Average	85.1
5		Andrew Stone	98	1		Median	90.5
6		Bryan Wilson	93	4		Mode	93.0
7		Charles Alexander	71	2			
8		Chloe Carpenter	80	2			
9		Christopher Rose	91	2			
10		Connor Hill	93	4			
11		Dylan Edwards	91	2			
12		Ella Bradley	93	4			
13		Grace Mitchell	71	2			
14		Isaac Rice	73	1			
15		Joshua Thomas	93	4			
16		Juan Armstrong	95	1			
17		Kimberly Morales	77	2			
18		Lily Harrison	72	1			
19		Madison Ortiz	80	2			
20		Ryan Long	92	1			
21		Sarah Cunningham	76	1			
22		Sophia Nichols	77	2			
23							

A big difference between AVERAGE and MEDIAN indicates that the grades are not evenly distributed through the population. In our case, there appears to be large gap between the higher-scoring students and the lower-scoring students. In other cases, it may just be one unusually large or small number that affects the AVERAGE but not the MEDIAN.

The mode is calculated using the MODE function. MODE returns the grade that appears most frequently. Figure 16.11 shows a count of each grade next to the grade. From this, you can see that 93 occurs four times—the most of any grade. If all of the values appear an equal number of times, MODE returns #N/A. If more than one grade appears the same number of times, MODE returns the first one it finds.

FIGURE 16.12

The grades listing sorted by grade

	A	B	C	D	E	F	G	H
						K13 ▼ fx		
1								
2		Student	Grade	Count of Grades				
3		Andrew Stone	98	1				
4		Addison Gray	96	1		Average	85.1	
5		Juan Armstrong	95	1		Median	90.5	
6		Bryan Wilson	93	4		Mode	93.0	
7		Connor Hill	93	4				
8		Ella Bradley	93	4				
9		Joshua Thomas	93	4				
10		Ryan Long	92	1				
11		Christopher Rose	91	2				
12		Dylan Edwards	91	2			90.5	
13		Alex Palmer	90	1				
14		Chloe Carpenter	80	2				
15		Madison Ortiz	80	2				
16		Kimberly Morales	77	2				
17		Sophia Nichols	77	2				
18		Sarah Cunningham	76	1				
19		Isaac Rice	73	1				
20		Lily Harrison	72	1				
21		Charles Alexander	71	2				
22		Grace Mitchell	71	2				
23								
24								
25								

Bucketing Data into Percentiles

Separating data into buckets or bins provides insight into how each value compares to the whole. Figure 16.13 shows a partial list of employees who process a product and the number of defects per 1,000 products that were identified by the quality assurance department. We want to bucket this data into four bins to identify top performers and those employees who may need more training. Excel provides the QUARTILE function to calculate the demarcation line between each quartile. A quartile is a bucket that holds 25% of the data.

```
=QUARTILE($C$3:$C$32,5-ROW(A1))
```

FIGURE 16.13

Identifying quartiles for product defects

	A	B	C	D	E	F	G	H
			fx	=QUARTILE($C$3:$C$32,5-ROW(A1))			G3	

	A	B	C	D	E	F	G	H
1								
2		Employee	Defects per 1000	Quartile				
3		Adam Jordan	47	1		Maximum	50.0	
4		Alex Cox	31	3		75th percentile	44.5	
5		Alexa Gonzalez	50	1		50th percentile	31.0	
6		Alyssa Cook	41	2		25th percentile	23.0	
7		Amelia Rivera	30	3				
8		Anna Garcia	30	3				
9		Audrey Cox	23	4				
10		Chloe Marshall	27	3				
11		Eli Green	34	2				
12		Eric Greene	48	1				
13		Evan Stone	17	4				
14		Evelyn Harris	22	4				
15		Gabriel Webb	43	2				
16		Gabriella Davis	45	1				
17		Genesis Bailey	23	4				
18		Isabella Marshall	49	1				
19		Jaden Hart	50	1				
20		Jeremiah Palmer	19	4				
21		Joseph Morgan	17	4				
22		Katelyn Howard	31	3				
23		Kyle Washington	19	4				
24		Lauren Allen	47	1				
25		Layla Gardner	47	1				
26		Lillian Matthews	27	3				
27		Mason Marshall	41	2				
28		Nathaniel Griffin	42	2				
29		Samuel Chavez	21	4				
30		Sean Gomez	39	2				
31		Victoria Freeman	20	4				
32		William Cox	27	3				
33								

The QUARTILE function provides the demarcation lines. The MATCH formula in cell D3 in Figure 16.13 identifies which quartile the value in cell C3 falls into. That formula is then copied down for all the values.

```
=MATCH(C3,$G$3:$G$6,-1)
```

The QUARTILE function takes a range of values and an integer representing which quartile to return (the *quart* argument). Acceptable values for the *quart* argument are 0 for the minimum value, 1 for the 25th percentile, 2 for the 50th percentile, 3 for the 75th percentile, and 4 for the maximum values. If the *quart* argument is not in the range 0–4, QUARTILE returns an error. If the *quart* argument has a decimal, the value is truncated, and only the integer portion is used.

The *quart* argument in our QUARTILE function uses the expression 5-ROW(A1). This allows the *quart* argument to decrease by 1 as the formula is copied down. For cell G3, the expression returns 4 for the maximum value in the range. When the formula is copied down to G4, the A1 reference changes to A2, and the expression returns 5-2 or 3 for the 75th percentile.

> **NOTE**
>
> The QUARTILE function applies a percentage to one less than the count of values to find the two values that surround the demarcation line. Then it interpolates between those two values to find the result.
>
> For the 75th percentile, QUARTILE computes .75*(30-1) for the 30 values in Figure 16.14 to get 21.75. Then it sorts the data from lowest to highest and counts down 21 rows from the lowest value. Since the result of the first calculation is not a whole number, it interpolates between the two values. In this case, counting down 21 rows is the value 43, and the next value is 45. The interpolation uses the decimal portion of 21.75 to find the value that is 75% of the way between 43 and 45 or 43+((45-43)*.75), which is 44.5.
>
> Similarly, for the 50th percentile, QUARTILE computes .5*(30-1) to get 14.5. Counting down from the lowest values, the 50th percentile falls between Alex Cox's 31 and Katelyn Howard's 31. Since both values are the same, the interpolation is easy and returns 31. Figure 16.14 shows the same employee and defect data sorted with the demarcation lines identified.

To find into which quartile each value falls, the MATCH function is used against the range of QUARTILE calculations. Because our quartile data is in descending order, the last argument of MATCH is -1— *Greater than*. MATCH returns the position in the list where the value is found but stops when the next value is less than the lookup value. When attempting to match the value 47, MATCH sees that the second value (44.5) is less than the lookup value and stops at the first position.

Identifying Statistical Outliers with an Interquartile Range

In the preceding formula, we used the QUARTILE function to group data into buckets. While the QUARTILE function is handy when you require relatively symmetrical quartiles, this function shrinks the distance between the upper and lower quartiles (making it more difficult to identify true statistical outliers).

Excel offers another function called QUARTILE.EXC. QUARTILE.EXC excludes the median (middle number) from the population. This function results in quartiles that are further from the center of the whole. This gives us a better estimate of actual population and a potentially more accurate view of what values should be considered outliers.

Figure 16.15 shows a set of employees and the number of defects per 1,000 products. This data set has a wider spread of values. We want to determine which employees are outside a reasonable range (outliers) for further investigation.

FIGURE 16.14

Sorted data and demarcation lines

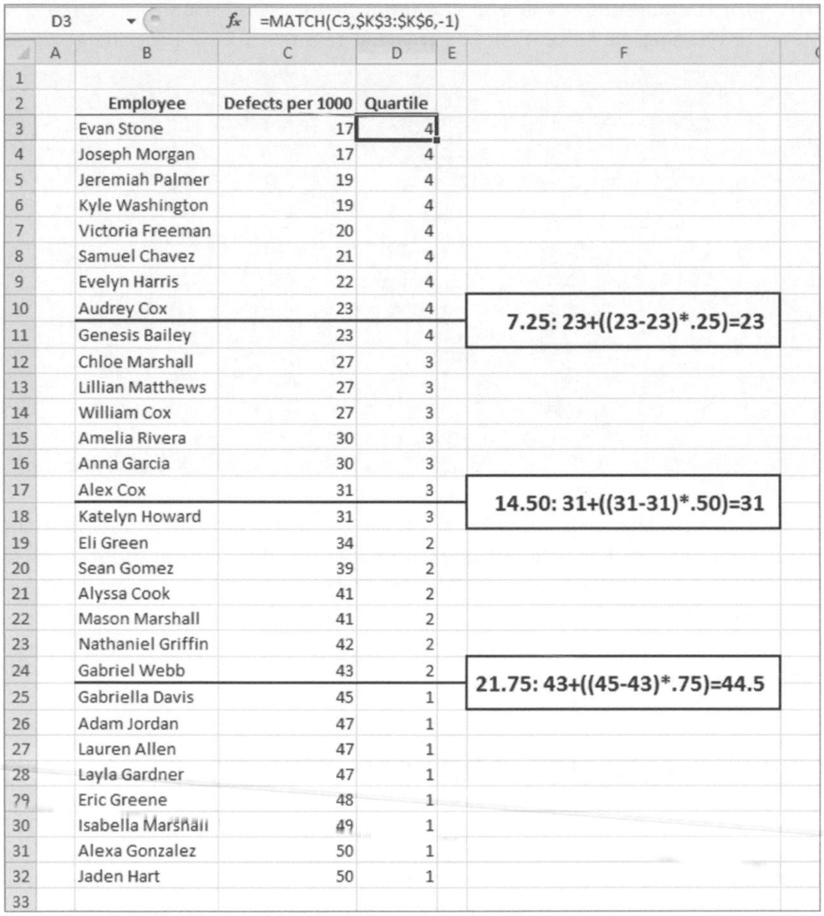

	A	B	C	D	E	F
	D3	▼	f_x =MATCH(C3,$K$3:$K$6,-1)			
1						
2		Employee	Defects per 1000	Quartile		
3		Evan Stone	17	4		
4		Joseph Morgan	17	4		
5		Jeremiah Palmer	19	4		
6		Kyle Washington	19	4		
7		Victoria Freeman	20	4		
8		Samuel Chavez	21	4		
9		Evelyn Harris	22	4		
10		Audrey Cox	23	4		7.25: 23+((23-23)*.25)=23
11		Genesis Bailey	23	4		
12		Chloe Marshall	27	3		
13		Lillian Matthews	27	3		
14		William Cox	27	3		
15		Amelia Rivera	30	3		
16		Anna Garcia	30	3		
17		Alex Cox	31	3		14.50: 31+((31-31)*.50)=31
18		Katelyn Howard	31	3		
19		Eli Green	34	2		
20		Sean Gomez	39	2		
21		Alyssa Cook	41	2		
22		Mason Marshall	41	2		
23		Nathaniel Griffin	42	2		
24		Gabriel Webb	43	2		21.75: 43+((45-43)*.75)=44.5
25		Gabriella Davis	45	1		
26		Adam Jordan	47	1		
27		Lauren Allen	47	1		
28		Layla Gardner	47	1		
29		Eric Greene	48	1		
30		Isabella Marshall	49	1		
31		Alexa Gonzalez	50	1		
32		Jaden Hart	50	1		
33						

To identify outliers, we'll use a method called a *leveraged interquartile range*. An interquartile range is simply the data that lies in the middle 50% (between the 75th percentile and the 25th percentile). The "leveraged" part means that we expand that middle range by a factor and establish fences. Any data outside the fence is considered an outlier.

The formulas used in Figure 16.15 are shown here:

```
75th percentile: =QUARTILE.EXC($C$3:$C$22,3)
25th percentile: =QUARTILE.EXC($C$3:$C$22,1)
Interquartile Range: =G4-G5
```

```
Fence Factor: 1.5
Upper Fence: =G4+(G6*G8)
Lower Fence: =G5-(G6*G8)

Outliers: =IF(C3<$G$10,"Low",IF(C3>$G$9,"High",""))
```

16

FIGURE 16.15

Identifying outliers using a leveraged interquartile range

	A	B	C	D	E	F	G
	D3		▾	fx	=IF(C3<$G$10,"Low",IF(C3>$G$9,"High",""))		
1							
2		Employee	Defects per 1000	Outliers			
3		Alex Cox	64				
4		Alyssa Cook	104	High		75th percentile	65.5
5		Amelia Rivera	44			25th percentile	42.5
6		Anna Garcia	56			Interquartile Range	23.0
7		Audrey Cox	46				
8		Chloe Marshall	46			Fence Factor	1.5
9		Eli Green	66			Upper Fence	100.00
10		Evan Stone	6	Low		Lower Fence	8.00
11		Evelyn Harris	47				
12		Genesis Bailey	52				
13		Jeremiah Palmer	10				
14		Joseph Morgan	5	Low			
15		Katelyn Howard	46				
16		Kyle Washington	7	Low			
17		Lillian Matthews	46				
18		Mason Marshall	110	High			
19		Samuel Chavez	90				
20		Sean Gomez	101	High			
21		Victoria Freeman	42				
22		William Cox	52				
23							

The QUARTILE.EXC function is used to determine the 75th percentile and 25th percentile using arguments of 3 and 1, respectively. The interquartile range is the difference between these two.

In a nonleveraged interquartile range, you would simply subtract the interquartile range from the 25th percentile to get a lower fence and add it to the 75th percentile to get an upper fence. This method can result in too many outliers. By multiplying the interquartile range by a factor (1.5 in this example), we expand the fences to isolate the truly extreme values. Figure 16.16 shows the same data sorted by defects and the demarcation lines of the quartiles, interquartile range, and the upper and lower fences.

FIGURE 16.16

Leveraged interquartile ranges expand the fences outward.

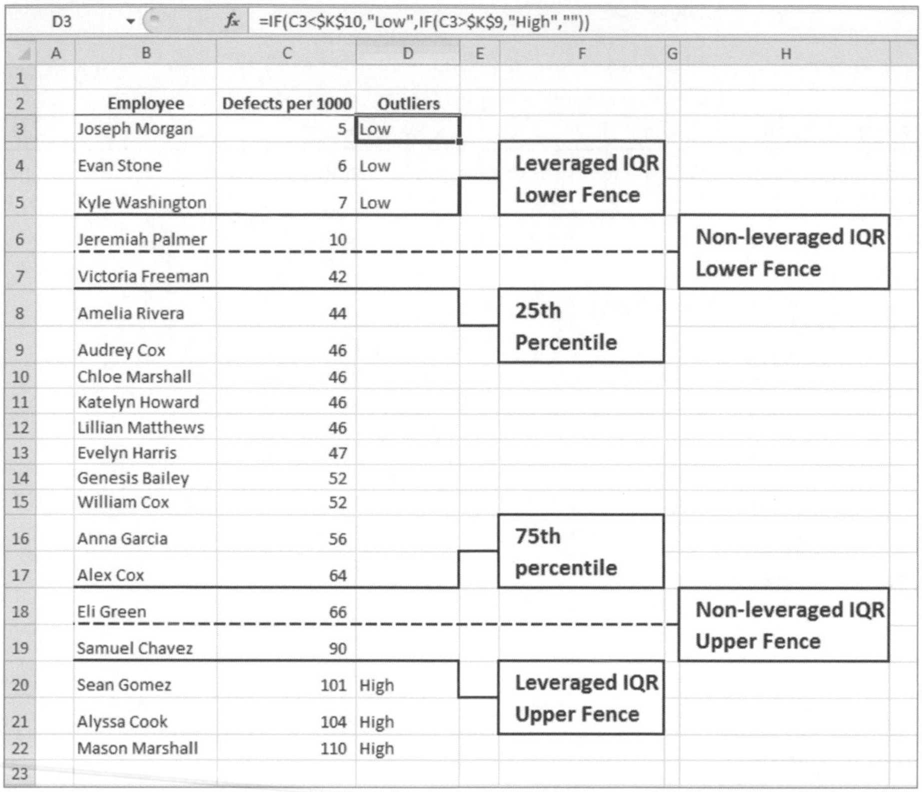

	D3	▼ (	f_x	=IF(C3<$K$10,"Low",IF(C3>$K$9,"High",""))				
▲	A	B	C	D	E	F	G	H
1								
2		Employee	Defects per 1000	Outliers				
3		Joseph Morgan	5	Low				
4		Evan Stone	6	Low		Leveraged IQR Lower Fence		
5		Kyle Washington	7	Low				
6		Jeremiah Palmer	10					Non-leveraged IQR Lower Fence
7		Victoria Freeman	42					
8		Amelia Rivera	44			25th Percentile		
9		Audrey Cox	46					
10		Chloe Marshall	46					
11		Katelyn Howard	46					
12		Lillian Matthews	46					
13		Evelyn Harris	47					
14		Genesis Bailey	52					
15		William Cox	52					
16		Anna Garcia	56			75th percentile		
17		Alex Cox	64					
18		Eli Green	66					Non-leveraged IQR Upper Fence
19		Samuel Chavez	90					
20		Sean Gomez	101	High		Leveraged IQR Upper Fence		
21		Alyssa Cook	104	High				
22		Mason Marshall	110	High				
23								

To determine the upper fence, we multiply the fence factor by the interquartile range and add the result to the 75th percentile. The same result is subtracted from the 25th percentile to establish the lower fence.

> **TIP**
> You may find that fence factor of 1.5 excludes values that you consider outliers or includes values that you consider normal. There's nothing magic about 1.5. Simply adjust the factor up or down if it doesn't fit your data.

With our fences established, we use a nested IF formula to determine whether each value is greater than the upper fence or less than the lower fence. The text "High" or "Low" is returned by the nested IF formula for the outliers, and an empty string ("") is returned for those that are inside the fences.

Creating a Frequency Distribution

Quartiles are a popular way to group data into bins, which is why Excel has a dedicated QUARTILE function. Sometimes, however, you may want to group your data into bins that you define. Figure 16.17 shows a partial list of 50 invoices and the total amount sold on each invoice. We want to determine how common it is for our customers to make purchases between $1 and $100, $101 and $200, and so on.

FIGURE 16.17

Calculating the frequency with custom bins

	G3	▾	f_x {=FREQUENCY(C3:C52,F3:F12)}					
	A	B	C	D	E	F	G	H
1								
2		Invoice #	Total Sale			Bins	Frequency	
3		IN1288	263.66		-	100	4	
4		IN1388	273.37		100	200	2	
5		IN1395	232.24		200	300	20	
6		IN1518	725.03		300	400	3	
7		IN1793	969.66		400	500	2	
8		IN1860	264.95		500	600	2	
9		IN2239	204.54		600	700	3	
10		IN2379	246.78		700	800	4	
11		IN2782	202.64		800	900	4	
12		IN2887	376.77		900	1,000	6	
13		IN2917	243.42					
14		IN3243	277.74					
15		IN3321	689.93					
16		IN3476	795.39					
17		IN3534	716.55					
18		IN3942	41.68					
19		IN4024	249.15					
20		IN4139	631.67					
21		IN4154	982.17					
22		IN4271	802.17					

Excel's FREQUENCY function will count all the invoices that fall within the bins we define.

    =FREQUENCY(C3:C52,F3:F12)

The FREQUENCY function is an array function. This means that instead of pressing Enter to commit the formula, you must press Ctrl+Shift+Enter. Excel will insert curly braces ({ }) around the formula to indicate that it has been array-entered.

 We explore array functions in detail in Chapter 18.

FREQUENCY takes two arguments: a range of data to be grouped into bins and a range of numbers that represent the highest amount for that bin. First, enter the bin values in column F. Column E does not affect the formula; it's just there to show the lower bound of each bin.

To enter FREQUENCY into column G, first select the range G3:G12 and then type the formula. While you'll only be entering the formula into G3, committing the formula with Ctrl+Shift+Enter will fill the formula in the entire range selected.

The results of the FREQUENCY formula show that a large number of customers purchase between $200 to $300 per visit.

An alternative to the FREQUENCY function

If you attempt to delete one of the cells in the FREQUENCY formula range, Excel will tell you that "You cannot change part of an array." Excel treats FREQUENCY, and all array functions, as one unit. You can change the whole array, just not individual cells within it. If you want to change the bins, you have to delete and re-enter the array.

The COUNTIFS function can also be used to create a frequency distribution. Since COUNTIFS is not an array formula, it's easier to change the bins or expand or contract the range. For the data in Figure 16.18, the COUNTIFS function is shown here:

```
=COUNTIFS($C$3:$C$52,">"&E3,$C$3:$C$52,"<="&F3)
```

FIGURE 16.18

Using the COUNTIFS function to create a frequency distribution

G3			×	✓	fx	=COUNTIFS($C$3:$C$52,">"&E3,$C$3:$C$52,"<="&F3)		
	A	B	C	D	E	F	G	H	I
1									
2		Invoice #	Total Sale		Bins		Frequency		
3		IN1288	263.66		-	100	4		
4		IN1388	273.37		100	200	2		
5		IN1395	232.24		200	300	20		
6		IN1518	725.03		300	400	3		
7		IN1793	969.66		400	500	2		
8		IN1860	264.95		500	600	2		
9		IN2239	204.54		600	700	3		
10		IN2379	246.78		700	800	4		
11		IN2782	202.64		800	900	4		
12		IN2887	376.77		900	1,000	6		
13		IN2917	243.42						

Unlike FREQUENCY, COUNTIFS needs the lower bound of the bin (column E). It counts all of the values that are greater than the lower bound and less than or equal to the upper bound. Rather than array entering this formula, it's simply copied down for as many bins as we've defined.

 Feel free to revisit Chapter 13 for a more detailed look at the COUNTIFS function.

Using Formulas with Tables and Conditional Formatting

IN THIS CHAPTER

Highlighting cells that meet certain criteria

Highlighting differences between data sets

Conditional formatting based on dates

*C*onditional formatting is the term given to the functionality where Excel dynamically changes the formatting of a value, cell, or range of cells based on a set of conditions that you define. Conditional formatting allows you to look at your Excel reports and make split-second determinations on which values are "good" and which are "bad," all based on formatting.

In this chapter, we'll give you a few examples of how the conditional formatting feature in Excel can be used in conjunction with formulas to add an extra layer of visualizations to your analyses.

 This book's website, www.wiley.com/go/excel2019bible, includes a copy of the sample workbook for this chapter. The file is named Using Functions with Conditional Formatting.xlsx.

NOTE
Feel free to revisit Chapter 5 for a refresher on conditional formatting.

Highlighting Cells That Meet Certain Criteria

One of the more basic conditional formatting rules that you can create is the highlighting of cells that meet some business criteria. This first example demonstrates the formatting of cells with values that are lower than a hard-coded value of 4000 (see Figure 17.1).

FIGURE 17.1

The cells in this table are conditionally formatted to show a red background for values less than 4000.

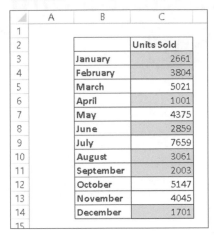

To build this basic formatting rule, follow these steps:

1. **Select the data cells in your target range (cells C3:C14 in this example).**

2. **Click the Home tab of the Excel Ribbon and then select Conditional Formatting ⇨ New Rule New Rule.** This will open the New Formatting Rule dialog box shown in Figure 17.2.

FIGURE 17.2

Configure the New Formatting Rule dialog box to apply the needed formula rule.

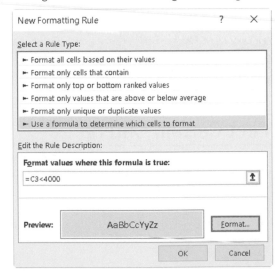

3. **In the list box at the top of the dialog box, click the option called Use a formula to determine which cells to format.** This selection evaluates values based on a formula you specify. If a particular value evaluates to true, then the conditional formatting is applied to that cell.

4. **In the formula input box, enter the formula shown here.** Note that we are simply referencing the first cell in our target range. There is no need to reference the entire range.

   =C3<4000

CAUTION

Note in the formula that we exclude the absolute reference dollar symbols ($) for the target cell (C3). If you click cell C3 with your mouse instead of typing it in, Excel will automatically make your cell reference absolute. It's important that you don't include the absolute reference dollar symbols in your target cell, as you need Excel to apply this formatting rule based on each cell's own value.

---

5. **Click the Format button and choose your desired formatting.** This will open the Format Cells dialog box where you'll have a full set of options for formatting the font, border, and fill for your target cell.

6. **Click the OK button once you've completed choosing your formatting options.**

7. **Click the OK button twice to confirm your formatting rule back on the New Formatting Rule dialog box.**

TIP

If you need to edit your conditional formatting rule, simply place your cursor in any of the data cells within your formatted range and then go to the Home tab and select Conditional Formatting ➪ Manage Rules. This will open the Conditional Formatting Rules Manager dialog box. Click the rule that you want to edit and then click the Edit Rule button.

Highlighting cells based on the value of another cell

In many cases, the formatting rule for your cells will be based on how they compare to the value of another cell. Take the example illustrated in Figure 17.3. Here the cells are conditionally highlighted if their respective values fall below the Prior Year Average value shown in cell B3.

FIGURE 17.3

The cells in this table are conditionally formatted to show a red background for values falling below the Prior Year Average value.

	A	B	C	D	E
1					
2		Prior Year Average		Month	Units Sold
3		3500		January	2661
4				February	3804
5				March	5021
6				April	1001
7				May	4375
8				June	2859
9				July	7659
10				August	3061
11				September	2003
12				October	5147
13				November	4045
14				December	1701

To build this basic formatting rule, follow these steps:

1. **Select the data cells in your target range (cells E3:E14 in this example).**

2. **Click the Home tab of the Excel Ribbon and then select Conditional Formatting ⇨ New Rule New Rule.** This will open the New Formatting Rule dialog box shown in Figure 17.4.

FIGURE 17.4

Configure the New Formatting Rule dialog box to apply the needed formula rule.

3. **In the list box at the top of the dialog box, click the option called Use a formula to determine which cells to format.** This selection evaluates values based on a formula you specify. If a particular value evaluates to true, then the conditional formatting is applied to that cell.

4. **In the formula input box, enter the formula shown here.** Note that we are simply comparing our target cell (E3) with the value in the comparison cell ($B$3). As with standard formulas, you'll need to ensure that you use absolute references so that each value in your range is compared to the appropriate comparison cell.

    =E3<$B$3

5. **Click the Format button and choose your desired formatting.** This will open the Format Cells dialog box where you'll have a full set of options for formatting the font, border, and fill for your target cell.

6. **Click the OK button once you've completed choosing your formatting options.**

7. **Click the OK button twice to confirm your formatting rule back on the New Formatting Rule dialog box.**

Highlighting Values That Exist in List1 but Not List2

You'll often be asked to compare two lists and pick out the values that are in one list but not the other. Conditional formatting is an ideal way to present your findings. Figure 17.5 illustrates a conditional formatting exercise that compares customers from 2018 and 2019, highlighting those customers in 2019 that are new customers, that is, those customers who did not exist in 2018.

FIGURE 17.5

You can conditionally format the values that exist in one list but not the other.

	A	B	C	D	E	F
1						
2		2018			2019	
3		Customer_Name	Revenue		Customer_Name	Revenue
4		GKNEAS Corp.	$2,333.60		JAMSEA Corp.	$2,324.36
5		JAMSEA Corp.	$2,324.36		JAMWUS Corp.	$2,328.53
6		JAMWUS Corp.	$2,328.53		JAYKA Corp.	$2,328.53
7		JAYKA Corp.	$2,328.53		JUSDAN Corp.	$3,801.86
8		MAKUTE Corp.	$2,334.01		MAKUTE Corp.	$2,334.01
9		MOSUNC Corp.	$2,311.70		MALEBO Corp.	$3,099.45
10		NCUANT Corp.	$2,311.79		MOSUNC Corp.	$2,311.70
11		OSADUL Corp.	$2,311.50		NCUANT Corp.	$2,311.79
12		RRCAR Corp.	$2,315.14		OSADUL Corp.	$2,311.50
13		RULLAN Corp.	$2,332.94		PUNSKE Corp.	$7,220.80
14		SMATHE Corp.	$2,336.59		REBUST Corp.	$14,224.84
15		SOFANU Corp.	$2,333.60		RRCAR Corp.	$2,315.14
16		SUMTUK Corp.	$2,321.61		RULLAN Corp.	$2,332.94
17		TULUSS Corp.	$2,311.96		RUTANS Corp.	$4,175.75
18		UDGUWU Corp.	$2,328.58		SCHOUL Corp.	$5,931.46

To build this basic formatting rule, follow these steps:

1. **Select the data cells in your target range (cells E4:E28 in this example).**

2. **Click the Home tab of the Excel Ribbon and then select Conditional Formatting ⇨ New Rule New Rule.** This will open the New Formatting Rule dialog box shown in Figure 17.6.

FIGURE 17.6

Configure the New Formatting Rule dialog box to apply the needed formula rule.

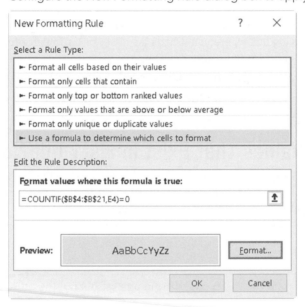

3. **In the list box at the top of the dialog box, click the option called Use a formula to determine which cells to format.** This selection evaluates values based on a formula you specify. If a particular value evaluates to true, then the conditional formatting is applied to that cell.

4. **In the formula input box, enter the formula shown here.** Note we're using the COUNTIF function to evaluate whether the value in the target cell (E4) is found in our comparison range ($B$4:$B$21). If the value is not found, the COUNTIF function will return a 0, thus triggering the conditional formatting. As with standard formulas, you'll need to ensure that you use absolute references so that each value in your range is compared to the appropriate comparison cell.

   =COUNTIF($B$4:$B$21,E4)=0

5. **Click the Format button and choose your desired formatting.** This will open the Format Cells dialog box, where you'll have a full set of options for formatting the font, border, and fill for your target cell.

6. **Click the OK button once you've completed choosing your formatting options.**

7. **Click the OK button twice to confirm your formatting rule back on the New Formatting Rule dialog box.**

 For more detail on the `COUNTIF` function, see Chapter 13.

Highlighting Values That Exist in List1 and List2

Sometimes, you'll need to compare two lists and pick out only the values that exist in *both* lists. Again, conditional formatting is an ideal way to present your findings. Figure 17.7 illustrates a conditional formatting exercise that compares customers from 2018 and 2019, highlighting those customers in 2019 who are in both lists.

FIGURE 17.7

You can conditionally format the values that exist in both lists.

	A	B	C	D	E	F
1						
2		**2018**			**2019**	
3		Customer_Name	Revenue		Customer_Name	Revenue
4		GKNEAS Corp.	$2,333.60		JAMSEA Corp.	$2,324.36
5		JAMSEA Corp.	$2,324.36		JAMWUS Corp.	$2,328.53
6		JAMWUS Corp.	$2,328.53		JAYKA Corp.	$2,328.53
7		JAYKA Corp.	$2,328.53		JUSDAN Corp.	$3,801.86
8		MAKUTE Corp.	$2,334.01		MAKUTE Corp.	$2,334.01
9		MOSUNC Corp.	$2,311.70		MALEBO Corp.	$3,099.45
10		NCUANT Corp.	$2,311.79		MOSUNC Corp.	$2,311.70
11		OSADUL Corp.	$2,311.50		NCUANT Corp.	$2,311.79
12		RRCAR Corp.	$2,315.14		OSADUL Corp.	$2,311.50
13		RULLAN Corp.	$2,332.94		PUNSKE Corp.	$7,220.80
14		SMATHE Corp.	$2,336.59		REBUST Corp.	$14,224.84
15		SOFANU Corp.	$2,333.60		RRCAR Corp.	$2,315.14
16		SUMTUK Corp.	$2,321.61		RULLAN Corp.	$2,332.94

To build this basic formatting rule, follow these steps:

1. **Select the data cells in your target range (cells E4:E28 in this example).**

2. **Click the Home tab of the Excel Ribbon and then select Conditional Formatting ⇨ New Rule New Rule.** This will open the New Formatting Rule dialog box shown in Figure 17.8.

FIGURE 17.8

Configure the New Formatting Rule dialog box to apply the needed formula rule.

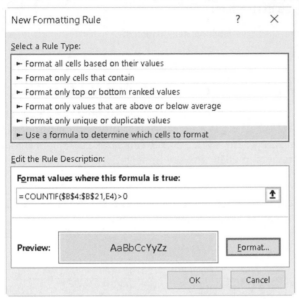

3. **In the list box at the top of the dialog box, click the option called Use a formula to determine which cells to format.** This selection evaluates values based on a formula you specify. If a particular value evaluates to true, then the conditional formatting is applied to that cell.

4. **In the formula input box, enter the formula shown here.** Note we're using the COUNTIF function to evaluate whether the value in the target cell (E4) is found in our comparison range ($B$4:$B$21). If the value is found, the COUNTIF function will return a number greater than 0, thus triggering the conditional formatting. As with standard formulas, you'll need to ensure that you use absolute references so that each value in your range is compared to the appropriate comparison cell.

   `=COUNTIF($B$4:$B$21,E4)>0`

5. **Click the Format button and choose your desired formatting.** This will open the Format Cells dialog box, where you'll have a full set of options for formatting the font, border, and fill for your target cell.

6. **Click the OK button once you've completed choosing your formatting options.**

7. **Click the OK button twice to confirm your formatting rule back on the New Formatting Rule dialog box.**

Highlighting Based on Dates

You may find it useful to indicate visually when certain dates trigger a certain scenario. For instance, when working with timecards and scheduling, it is often beneficial to be able to pinpoint easily any dates that fall on weekends. The conditional formatting rule illustrated in Figure 17.9 highlights all of the weekend dates in the list of values.

FIGURE 17.9

You can conditionally format any weekend dates in a list of dates.

	A	B
1		
2		Highlight Weekends
3		1/23/2012
4		12/28/2009
5		9/26/2010
6		12/8/2014
7		4/25/2010
8		11/7/2012
9		7/31/2014
10		11/24/2014
11		12/28/2010
12		7/28/2011
13		12/17/2014
14		8/3/2014
15		5/1/2011
16		4/2/2011
17		7/17/2009
18		8/12/2009

To build this basic formatting rule, follow these steps:

1. **Select the data cells in your target range (cells B3:B18 in this example)**
2. **Click the Home tab of the Excel Ribbon and then select Conditional Formatting ⇨ New Rule New Rule.** This will open the New Formatting Rule dialog box shown in Figure 17.10.

FIGURE 17.10

Configure the New Formatting Rule dialog box to apply the needed formula rule.

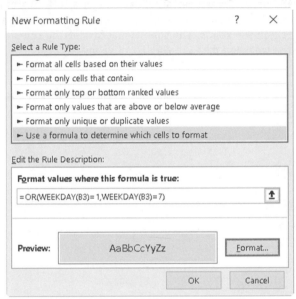

3. **In the list box at the top of the dialog box, click the option called Use a formula to determine which cells to format.** This selection evaluates values based on a formula you specify. If a particular value evaluates to true, then the conditional formatting is applied to that cell.

4. **In the formula input box, enter the formula shown here. Note we're using the** WEEKDAY **function to evaluate the weekday number of the target cell (B3).** If the target cell returns as weekday 1 or 7, it means that the date in B3 is a weekend date. In this case, the conditional formatting will be applied.

   =OR(WEEKDAY(B3)=1,WEEKDAY(B3)=7)

5. **Click the Format button and choose your desired formatting.** This will open the Format Cells dialog box, where you'll have a full set of options for formatting the font, border, and fill for your target cell.

6. **Click the OK button once you've completed choosing your formatting options.**

7. **Click the OK button twice to confirm your formatting rule back on the New Formatting Rule dialog box.**

Highlighting days between two dates

Some analysis requires the identification of dates that fall within a certain time period. Figure 17.11 demonstrates how you can apply conditional formatting that highlights dates based on a start date and end date. As the start and end dates are adjusted, the conditional formatting adjusts with them.

FIGURE 17.11

You can conditionally format dates that fall between a start and end date.

	A	B	C	D	E
1					
2		Start	End		Highlight Days within 2010 and 2012
3		1/1/2010	12/31/2012		1/23/2012
4					12/28/2009
5					9/26/2010
6					12/8/2014
7					4/25/2010
8					11/7/2012
9					7/31/2014
10					11/24/2014
11					12/28/2010
12					7/28/2011
13					12/17/2014
14					8/3/2014
15					5/1/2011
16					4/2/2011
17					7/17/2009
18					8/12/2009

To build this basic formatting rule, follow these steps:

1. **Select the data cells in your target range (cells E3:E18 in this example), click the Home tab of the Excel Ribbon, and then select Conditional Formatting ⇨ New Rule New Rule.** This will open the New Formatting Rule dialog box shown in Figure 17.12.

FIGURE 17.12

Configure the New Formatting Rule dialog box to apply the needed formula rule.

2. **In the list box at the top of the dialog box, click the option called Use a formula to determine which cells to format.** This selection evaluates values based on a formula you specify. If a particular value evaluates to true, then the conditional formatting is applied to that cell.

3. **In the formula input box, enter the formula shown here.** Note we're using the AND function to compare the date in our target cell (E3) to both the start and end dates found in cells $B$3 and $C$3, respectively. If the target cell falls within the start and end dates, the formula will evaluate to TRUE, thus triggering the conditional formatting.

   =AND(E3>=$B$3,E3<=$C$3)

4. **Click the Format button and choose your desired formatting.** This will open the Format Cells dialog box, where you'll have a full set of options for formatting the font, border, and fill for your target cell.

5. **Click the OK button once you've completed choosing your formatting options.**

6. **Click the OK button twice to confirm your formatting rule back on the New Formatting Rule dialog box.**

Highlighting dates based on a due date

The example shown in Figure 17.13 demonstrates that you can conditionally format dates that are past due by a given number of days. In this scenario, the dates that are over 90 days overdue are highlighted with a red background.

FIGURE 17.13

You can conditionally format dates based on due date.

	A	B	C
1			
2			
3			Due Date
4			04/25/18
5			05/04/18
6			05/04/18
7			03/28/18
8			04/22/18
9			03/31/18

To build this basic formatting rule, follow these steps:

1. **Select the data cells in your target range (cells C4:C9 in this example), click the Home tab of the Excel Ribbon, and then select Conditional Formatting ⇨ New Rule New Rule.** This will open the New Formatting Rule dialog box shown in Figure 17.14.

FIGURE 17.14

Configure the New Formatting Rule dialog box to apply the needed formula rule.

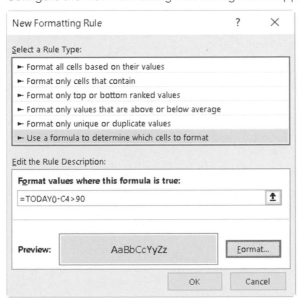

New Formatting Rule   ?   ✕

Select a Rule Type:

► Format all cells based on their values
► Format only cells that contain
► Format only top or bottom ranked values
► Format only values that are above or below average
► Format only unique or duplicate values
► Use a formula to determine which cells to format

Edit the Rule Description:

Format values where this formula is true:

=TODAY()-C4>90

Preview: AaBbCcYyZz   Format...

                        OK   Cancel

2. **In the list box at the top of the dialog box, click the option called Use a formula to determine which cells to format.** This selection evaluates values based on a formula you specify. If a particular value evaluates to true, then the conditional formatting is applied to that cell.

3. **In the formula input box, enter the formula shown here**. In this formula, we're evaluating whether today's date is greater than 90 days past the date in our target cell (C4). If so, the conditional formatting will be applied.

   `=TODAY()-C4>90`

4. **Click the Format button and choose your desired formatting.** This will open the Format Cells dialog box, where you'll have a full set of options for formatting the font, border, and fill for your target cell.

5. **Click the OK button once you've completed choosing your formatting options.**

6. **Click the OK button twice to confirm your formatting rule back on the New Formatting Rule dialog box.**

Understanding and Using Array Formulas

O ne of Excel's most interesting (and most powerful) features is its ability to work with arrays in formulas. When you understand this concept, you'll be able to create elegant formulas that appear to perform spreadsheet magic.

This chapter introduces the concept of arrays, and it is required reading for anyone who wants to become a master of Excel formulas.

 Most of the examples in this chapter are available on this book's website at www.wiley.com/go/ excel2019bible. The filename is Array Formulas.xlsx.

Understanding Array Formulas

If you do any computer programming, you've probably been exposed to the concept of an array. An *array* is a collection of items operated on collectively or individually. In Excel, an array can be one-dimensional or two-dimensional. These dimensions correspond to rows and columns. For example, a one-dimensional array can be stored in a range that consists of one row (a horizontal array) or one column (a vertical array). A two-dimensional array can be stored in a rectangular range of cells. Excel doesn't support three-dimensional arrays (but its VBA programming language does).

As you'll see, arrays don't have to be stored in cells. You can also work with arrays that exist only in Excel's memory. Then you can use an array formula to manipulate this information and return a result. Excel supports two types of array formulas:

Single-cell array formulas Work with arrays stored in ranges or in memory and produce a result displayed in a single cell.

Multicell array formulas Work with arrays stored in ranges or in memory and produce an array as a result. Because a cell can hold only one value, a multicell array formula is entered into a range of cells.

This section presents two array formula examples: one that occupies multiple cells and another that occupies only one cell.

A multicell array formula

Figure 18.1 shows a simple worksheet set up to calculate product sales. Normally, you'd calculate the value in column D (total sales per product) with a formula such as the one that follows, and then you'd copy this formula down the column.

```
=B2*C2
```

FIGURE 18.1

Column D contains formulas to calculate the total for each product.

	A	B	C	
1	Product	Units Sold	Unit Price	
2	AR-998	3	$50	
3	BZ-011	10	$100	
4	MR-919	5	$20	
5	TR-811	9	$10	
6	TS-333	3	$60	
7	ZL-001	1	$200	
8				

After you copy the formula, the worksheet contains six formulas in column D.

An alternative method uses a single formula (a *multicell array formula*) to calculate all six values in D2:D7. This single formula occupies six cells and returns an array of six values.

To create a multicell array formula to perform the calculations, follow these steps:

1. Select a range to hold the results. In this case, the range is D2:D7. Because you can't display more than one value in a single cell, you select six cells to make this array work.

2. Type the following formula:

```
=B2:B7*C2:C7
```

3. Press Ctrl+Shift+Enter to enter the formula. Normally, you press Enter to enter a formula. Because this is an array formula, however, press Ctrl+Shift+Enter.

The formula is entered into all six selected cells. If you examine the Formula bar, you see the following:

```
{=B2:B7*C2:C7}
```

Excel places curly brackets around the formula to indicate that it's an array formula.

This formula performs its calculations and returns a six-item array. The array formula actually works with two other arrays, both of which happen to be stored in ranges. The values for the first array are stored in B2:B7, and the values for the second array are stored in C2:C7.

This multicell array formula returns the same values as these six normal formulas entered into individual cells in D2:D7:

```
=B2*C2
=B3*C3
=B4*C4
=B5*C5
=B6*C6
=B7*C7
```

Using a multicell array formula rather than individual formulas does offer a few advantages:

- It's a good way to ensure that all formulas in a range are identical.
- Using a multicell array formula makes it less likely that you'll overwrite a formula accidentally. You can't change or delete just one cell in a multicell array formula. Excel displays an error message if you attempt to do so.
- Using a multicell array formula will almost certainly prevent novices from tampering with your formulas.

Using a multicell array formula as described in the preceding list also has some potential disadvantages:

- Inserting a new row into the range is impossible. But in some cases, the inability to insert a row is a positive feature. For example, you might not want users to add rows because it would affect other parts of the worksheet.
- If you add new data to the bottom of the range, you need to modify the array formula to accommodate the new data.

A single-cell array formula

Now it's time to take a look at a *single-cell array formula*. Check out Figure 18.2, which is similar to Figure 18.1. Notice, however, that the formulas in column D have been deleted.

The goal is to calculate the sum of the total product sales without using the individual calculations that were in column D.

FIGURE 18.2

The array formula in cell C9 calculates the total sales without using intermediate formulas.

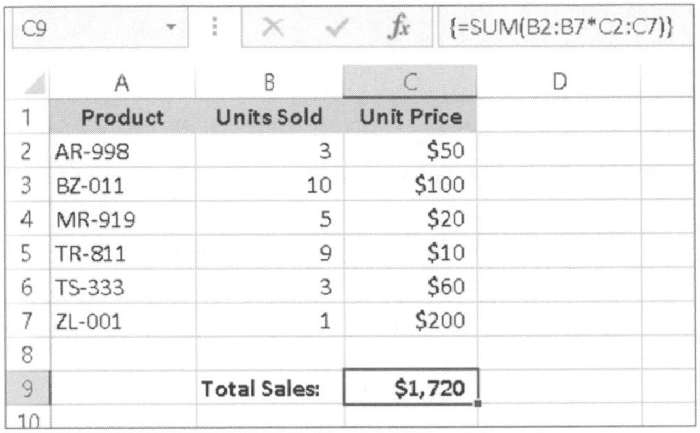

	A	B	C	D
C9			f_x {=SUM(B2:B7*C2:C7)}	
	A	B	C	D
1	Product	Units Sold	Unit Price	
2	AR-998	3	$50	
3	BZ-011	10	$100	
4	MR-919	5	$20	
5	TR-811	9	$10	
6	TS-333	3	$60	
7	ZL-001	1	$200	
8				
9		Total Sales:	$1,720	
10				

The following array formula is in cell C9:

```
{=SUM(B2:B7*C2:C7)}
```

When you enter this formula, make sure that you press Ctrl+Shift+Enter (and don't type the curly brackets because Excel automatically adds them for you).

This formula works with two arrays, both of which are stored in cells. The first array is stored in B2:B7, and the second array is stored in C2:C7. The formula multiplies the corresponding values in these two arrays and creates a new array (that exists only in memory). The new array consists of six values, which can be represented like this (the reason for using semicolons is explained a bit later):

```
{150;1000;100;90;180;200}
```

The SUM function then operates on this new array and returns the sum of its values.

> **NOTE**
> In this case, you can use the SUMPRODUCT function to obtain the same result without using an array formula:
> =SUMPRODUCT(B2:B7,C2:C7)

As you can see, however, array formulas allow many other types of calculations that are otherwise not possible.

Creating an Array Constant

The examples in the preceding section used arrays stored in worksheet ranges. The examples in this section demonstrate an important concept: an array doesn't have to be stored in a range of cells. This type of array, which is stored in memory, is referred to as an array constant.

To create an array constant, list its items and surround them with curly brackets. Here's an example of a five-item horizontal array constant:

    {1,0,1,0,1}

The following formula uses the SUM function, with the preceding array constant as its argument. The formula returns the sum of the values in the array (which is 3):

    =SUM({1,0,1,0,1})

Notice that this formula uses an array, but the formula itself isn't an array formula. Therefore, you don't press Ctrl+Shift+Enter to enter the formula—although entering it as an array formula will still produce the same result.

> **NOTE**
> When you specify an array directly (as shown previously), you must provide the curly brackets around the array elements. When you enter an array formula, on the other hand, you do not supply the curly brackets.

At this point, you probably don't see any advantage to using an array constant. The following formula, for example, returns the same result as the previous formula. The advantages, however, will become apparent:

    =SUM(1,0,1,0,1)

Here's a formula that uses two array constants:

    =SUM({1,2,3,4}*{5,6,7,8})

The formula creates a new array (in memory) that consists of the product of the corresponding elements in the two arrays. The new array is as follows:

    {5,12,21,32}

This new array is then used as an argument for the SUM function, which returns the result (70). The formula is equivalent to the following formula, which doesn't use arrays:

    =SUM(1*5,2*6,3*7,4*8)

Alternatively, you can use the SUMPRODUCT function. The formula that follows is not an array formula, but it uses two array constants as its arguments:

    =SUMPRODUCT({1,2,3,4},{5,6,7,8})

18

A formula can work with both an array constant and an array stored in a range. The following formula, for example, returns the sum of the values in A1:D1, each multiplied by the corresponding element in the array constant:

```
=SUM((A1:D1*{1,2,3,4}))
```

This formula is equivalent to the following:

```
=SUM(A1*1,B1*2,C1*3,D1*4)
```

An array constant can contain numbers, text, logical values (TRUE or FALSE), and even error values, such as #N/A. Numbers can be in integer, decimal, or scientific format. You must enclose text in double quotation marks. You can use different types of values in the same array constant, as in this example:

```
{1,2,3,TRUE,FALSE,TRUE,"Moe","Larry","Curly"}
```

An array constant can't contain formulas, functions, or other arrays. Numeric values can't contain dollar signs, commas, parentheses, or percent signs. For example, the following is an invalid array constant:

```
{SQRT(32),$56.32,12.5%}
```

Understanding the Dimensions of an Array

As stated previously, an array can be one-dimensional or two-dimensional. A one-dimensional array's orientation can be horizontal (corresponding to a single row) or vertical (corresponding to a single column).

One-dimensional horizontal arrays

Each element in a *one-dimensional horizontal array* is separated by a comma, and the array can be displayed in a row of cells. If you use a non-English-language version of Excel, your list separator character may be a semicolon.

The following example is a one-dimensional horizontal array constant:

```
{1,2,3,4,5}
```

Displaying this array in a range requires five consecutive cells in a row. To enter this array into a range, select a range of cells that consists of one row and five columns. Then enter the following formula and press Ctrl+Shift+Enter:

```
={1,2,3,4,5}
```

NOTE

If you enter this array into a *horizontal* range that consists of more than five cells, the extra cells will contain #N/A (which denotes unavailable values). If you enter this array into a vertical range of cells, only the first item (1) will appear in each cell.

The following example is another horizontal array; it has seven elements and is made up of text strings:

```
{"Sun","Mon","Tue","Wed","Thu","Fri","Sat"}
```

To enter this array, select seven cells in a row and type the following (and then press Ctrl+Shift+Enter):

```
={"Sun","Mon","Tue","Wed","Thu","Fri","Sat"}
```

One-dimensional vertical arrays

The elements in a *one-dimensional vertical array* are separated by semicolons, and the array can be displayed in a column of cells. The following is a six-element vertical array constant:

```
{10;20;30;40;50;60}
```

Displaying this array in a range requires six cells in a column. To enter this array into a range, select a range of cells that consists of six rows and one column. Then enter the following formula, followed by Ctrl+Shift+Enter:

```
={10;20;30;40;50;60}
```

The following is another example of a vertical array; this one has four elements:

```
{"Widgets";"Sprockets";"Doodads";"Thingamajigs"}
```

Two-dimensional arrays

A *two-dimensional array* uses commas to separate its horizontal elements and semicolons to separate its vertical elements. If you use a non-English-language version of Excel, the item-separator character may be a semicolon (for horizontal elements) and a backslash (for vertical elements). If you are not sure, open the example file for this chapter and examine a two-dimensional array. The item-separator characters are translated automatically to your language version.

The following example shows a 3 × 4 array constant:

```
{1,2,3,4;5,6,7,8;9,10,11,12}
```

Displaying this array in a range requires 12 cells. To enter this array into a range, select a range of cells that consists of three rows and four columns. Then type the following formula, and press Ctrl+Shift+Enter:

```
={1,2,3,4;5,6,7,8;9,10,11,12}
```

Figure 18.3 shows how this array appears when entered into a range (in this case, B3:E5).

FIGURE 18.3

A 3 × 4 array entered into a range of cells

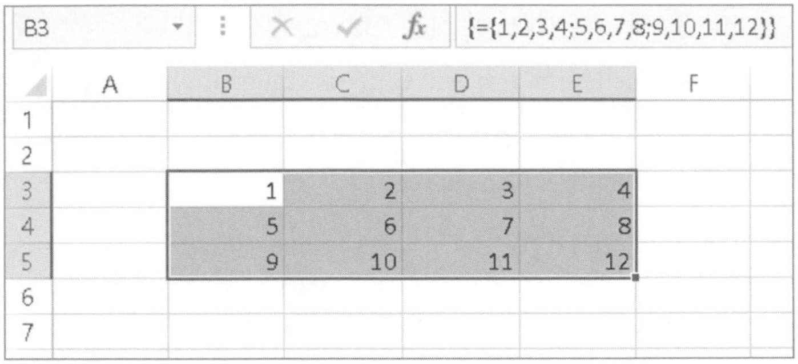

If you enter an array into a range that has more cells than array elements, Excel displays #N/A in the extra cells. Figure 18.4 shows a 3 × 4 array entered into a 10 × 5 cell range.

FIGURE 18.4

A 3 × 4 array entered into a 10 × 5 cell range

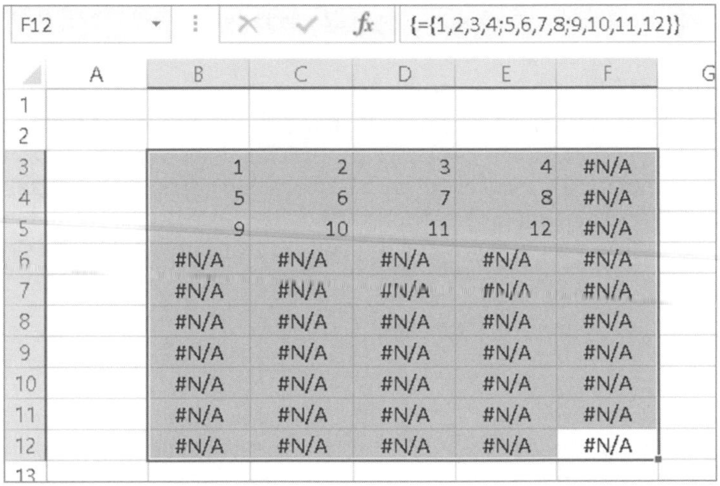

Each row of a two-dimensional array must contain the same number of items. The array that follows, for example, isn't valid, because the third row contains only three items:

```
{1,2,3,4;5,6,7,8;9,10,11}
```

Excel doesn't allow you to enter a formula that contains an invalid array.

Naming Array Constants

You can create an array constant, give it a name, and then use this named array in a formula. Technically, a *named array* is a named formula.

 Chapter 4, "Working with Excel Ranges and Tables," and Chapter 9, "Introducing Formulas and Functions," cover the topic of names and named formulas.

Figure 18.5 shows a named array being created from the New Name dialog box. (Access this dialog box by choosing Formulas ➪ Defined Names ➪ Define Name.) The name of the array is DayNames, and it refers to the following array constant:

{"Sun","Mon","Tue","Wed","Thu","Fri","Sat"}

FIGURE 18.5

Creating a named array constant

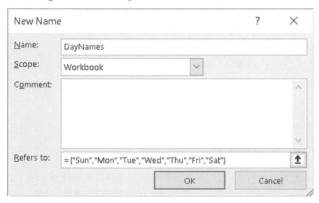

Notice that in the New Name dialog box, the array is defined (in the Refers To field) using a leading equal sign (=). Without this equal sign, the array is interpreted as a text string rather than an array. Also, you must type the curly brackets when defining a named array constant; Excel doesn't enter them for you.

After creating this named array, you can use it in a formula. Figure 18.6 shows a worksheet that contains a multicell array formula entered into the range B2:H2. The formula is as follows:

{=DayNames}

FIGURE 18.6

Using a named array constant in an array formula

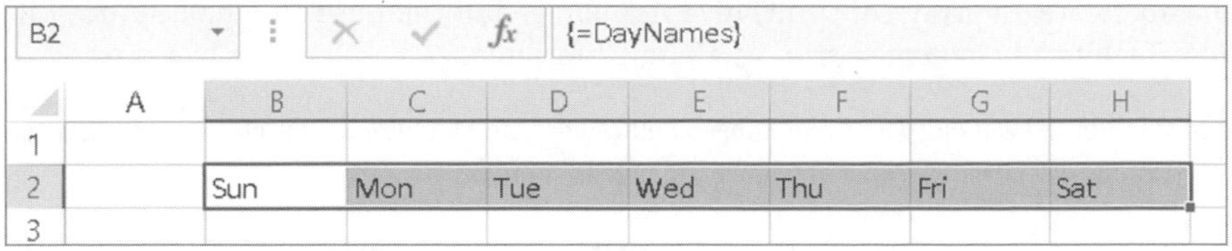

B2	▼	:	✕	✓	*fx*	{=DayNames}	

◢	A	B	C	D	E	F	G	H
1								
2		Sun	Mon	Tue	Wed	Thu	Fri	Sat
3								

To enter this formula, select seven cells in a row, type **=DayNames**, and press Ctrl+Shift+Enter.

Because commas separate the array elements, the array has a horizontal orientation. Use semicolons to create a vertical array, or you can use the Excel TRANSPOSE function to insert a horizontal array into a vertical range of cells. (See "Transposing an array" later in this chapter.) The following array formula, which is entered into a seven-cell vertical range, uses the TRANSPOSE function:

```
{=TRANSPOSE(DayNames)}
```

You also can access individual elements from the array by using the Excel INDEX function. The following formula, for example, returns Wed, the fourth item in the DayNames array:

```
=INDEX(DayNames,4)
```

Working with Array Formulas

This section deals with the mechanics of selecting cells that contain arrays and entering and editing array formulas. These procedures differ a bit from working with ordinary ranges and formulas.

Entering an array formula

When you enter an array formula into a cell or range, you must follow a special procedure so that Excel knows you want an array formula rather than a normal formula. You enter a normal formula into a cell by pressing Enter. You enter an array formula into one or more cells by pressing Ctrl+Shift+Enter.

Don't enter the curly brackets when you create an array formula; Excel inserts them for you. If the result of an array formula consists of more than one value, you must select all of the cells in the results range before you enter the formula. If you fail to do so, only the first element of the result is returned.

Selecting an array formula range

You can manually select the cells that contain a multicell array formula by using the normal cell selection procedures, or you can use either of the following methods:

- **Activate any cell in the array formula range.** Choose Home ⇨ Editing ⇨ Find & Select ⇨ Go To, or just press F5. The Go To dialog box appears. In the Go To dialog box, click the Special button and then choose the Current Array option. Click OK to close the dialog box.
- **Activate any cell in the array formula range, and press Ctrl+/ (forward slash) to select the cells that make up the array.**

Editing an array formula

If an array formula occupies multiple cells, you must edit the entire range as though it were a single cell. The key point to remember is that you can't change just one element of a multicell array formula. If you attempt to do so, Excel displays the message shown in Figure 18.7.

FIGURE 18.7

Excel's warning message reminds you that you can't edit just one cell of a multicell array formula.

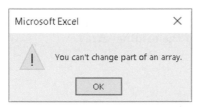

To edit an array formula, select all the cells in the array range and activate the Formula bar as usual. (Click it or press F2.) Excel removes the curly brackets from the formula while you edit it. Edit the formula and then press Ctrl+Shift+Enter to enter the changes. All of the cells in the array now reflect your editing changes (and the curly brackets reappear).

The following rules apply to multicell array formulas. If you try to do any of these things, Excel lets you know about it:

- You can't change the contents of any individual cell that makes up an array formula.
- You can't move cells that make up part of an array formula (but you can move an entire array formula).
- You can't delete cells that form part of an array formula (but you can delete an entire array).
- You can't insert new cells into an array range. This rule includes inserting rows or columns that would add new cells to an array range.
- You can't use multicell array formulas inside a table that was created by choosing Insert ⇨ Tables ⇨ Table. Similarly, you can't convert a range to a table if the range contains a multicell array formula.

Although you can't change any individual cell that makes up a multicell array formula, you can apply formatting to the entire array or only to parts of it.

Expanding or contracting a multicell array formula

Often, you may need to expand a multicell array formula (to include more cells) or contract it (to include fewer cells). Doing so requires these steps:

1. **Select the entire range that contains the array formula.**
2. **Press F2 to enter Edit mode.**
3. **Press Ctrl+Enter.** This step enters an identical (nonarray) formula into each selected cell.
4. **Change your range selection to include additional or fewer cells, but make sure that the active cell is a cell that's part of the original array.**
5. **Press F2 to re-enter Edit mode.**
6. **Press Ctrl+Shift+Enter.**

Array Formulas: The Downside

If you've followed along in this chapter, you probably understand some of the advantages of using array formulas. The main advantage, of course, is that an array formula enables you to perform otherwise impossible calculations. As you gain more experience with arrays, however, you undoubtedly will also discover some disadvantages.

Array formulas are one of the least understood features of Excel. Consequently, if you plan to share a workbook with someone who may need to make modifications, you should probably avoid using array formulas. Encountering an array formula when you don't know what it is can be confusing.

You can easily forget to enter an array formula by pressing Ctrl+Shift+Enter. (Also, if you edit an existing array, you must remember to use this key combination to complete the edits.) Except for logical errors, this is probably the most common problem that users have with array formulas. If you press Enter by mistake after editing an array formula, just press F2 to get back into Edit mode and then press Ctrl+Shift+Enter.

Another potential problem with array formulas is that they can sometimes slow your worksheet's recalculations, especially if you use very large arrays. On a faster system, this delay in speed may not be a problem. But, conversely, using an array formula is almost always faster than using a custom VBA function. See Chapter 43, "Creating Custom Worksheet Functions," for more information about creating custom VBA functions.

Using Multicell Array Formulas

This section contains examples that demonstrate additional features of multicell array formulas (array formulas that are entered into a range of cells). These features include creating arrays from values, performing operations, using functions, transposing arrays, and generating consecutive integers.

Creating an array from values in a range

The following array formula creates an array from a range of cells. Figure 18.8 shows a workbook with some data entered into A1:C4. The range D8:F11 contains a single array formula:

{=A1:C4}

FIGURE 18.8

Creating an array from a range

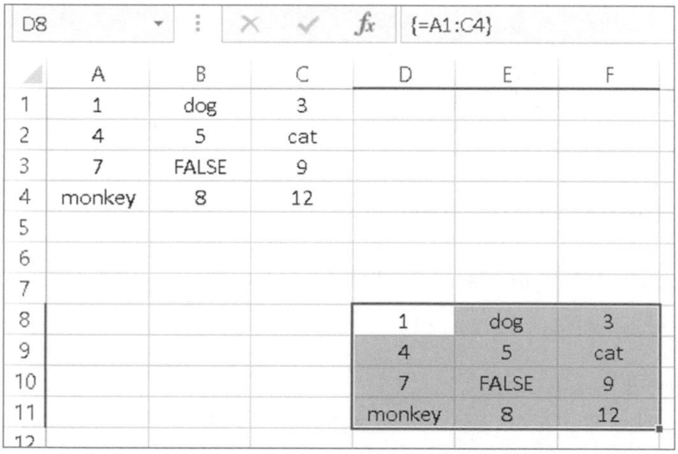

The array in D8:F11 is linked to the range A1:C4. Change any value in A1:C4, and the corresponding cell in D8:F11 reflects that change. It's a one-way link, of course. You can't change a value in D8:F11.

Creating an array constant from values in a range

In the preceding example, the array formula in D8:F11 essentially created a link to the cells in A1:C4. It's possible to sever this link and create an array constant made up of the values in A1:C4:

1. **Select the cells that contain the array formula (the range D8:F11, in this example).**

2. **Press F2 to edit the array formula.**

3. **Press F9 to convert the cell references to values.**

4. **Press Ctrl+Shift+Enter to re-enter the array formula (which now uses an array constant).**

The array constant is as follows:

{1,"dog",3;4,5,"cat";7,False,9;"monkey",8,12}

Figure 18.9 shows how this looks in the Formula bar.

FIGURE 18.9

After you press F9, the Formula bar displays the array constant.

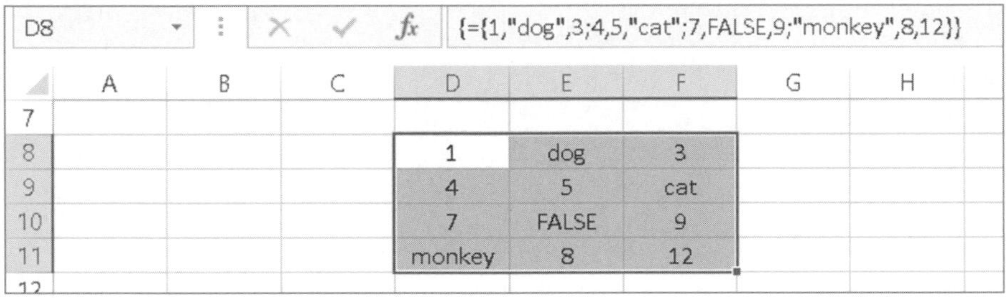

Performing operations on an array

So far, most of the examples in this chapter simply entered arrays into ranges. The following array formula creates a rectangular array and multiplies each array element by 2:

{={1,2,3,4;5,6,7,8;9,10,11,12}*2}

Figure 18.10 shows the result when you enter this formula into a range.

The following array formula multiplies each array element by itself:

{={1,2,3,4;5,6,7,8;9,10,11,12}*{1,2,3,4;5,6,7,8;9,10,11,12}}

The following array formula is a simpler way of obtaining the same result. Figure 18.11 shows the result when you enter this formula into a range:

{={1,2,3,4;5,6,7,8;9,10,11,12}^2}

If the array is stored in a range (such as B8:E10), the array formula returns the square of each value in the range as follows:

{=B8:E10^2}

FIGURE 18.10

Performing a mathematical operation on an array

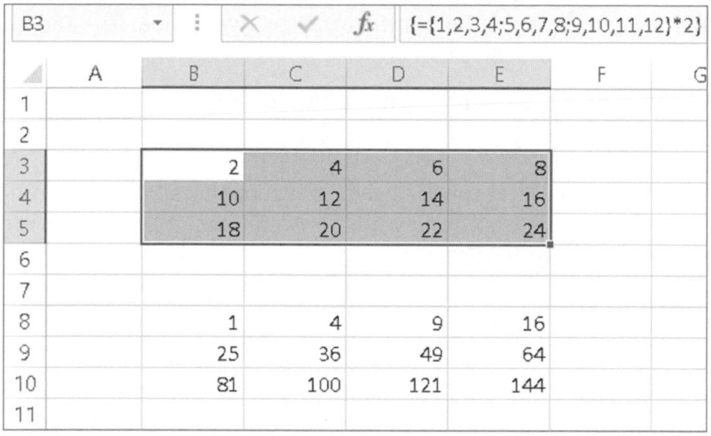

FIGURE 18.11

Multiplying each array element by itself

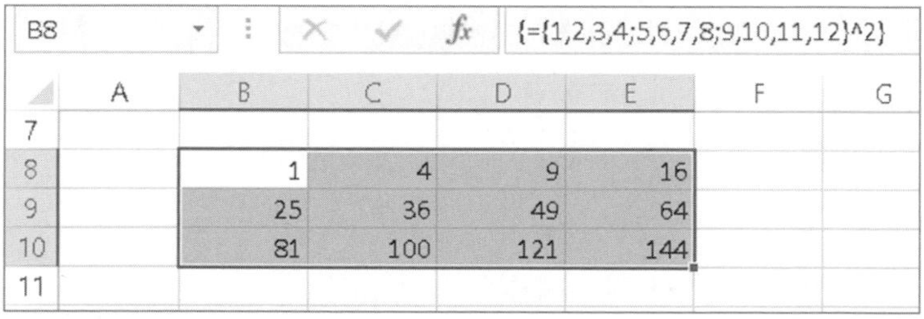

Using functions with an array

As you may expect, you can also use worksheet functions with an array. The following array formula, which you can enter into a ten-cell vertical range, calculates the square root of each array element in the array constant:

```
{=SQRT({1;2;3;4;5;6;7;8;9;10})}
```

If the array is stored in a range, a multicell array formula such as the one that follows returns the square root of each value in the range:

```
{=SQRT(A1:A10)}
```

Transposing an array

When you transpose an array, you essentially convert rows to columns and columns to rows. In other words, you can convert a horizontal array to a vertical array (and vice versa). Use the TRANSPOSE function to transpose an array.

Consider the following one-dimensional horizontal array constant:

    {1,2,3,4,5}

You can enter this array into a vertical range of cells by using the TRANSPOSE function. To do so, select a range of five cells that occupy five rows and one column. Then enter the following formula and press Ctrl+Shift+Enter:

    =TRANSPOSE({1,2,3,4,5})

The horizontal array is transposed, and the array elements appear in the vertical range.

Transposing a two-dimensional array works in a similar manner. Figure 18.12 shows a two-dimensional array entered into a range normally and entered into a range by using the TRANSPOSE function. The formula in A1:D3 is as follows:

    {={1,2,3,4;5,6,7,8;9,10,11,12}}

FIGURE 18.12

Using the TRANSPOSE function to transpose a rectangular array

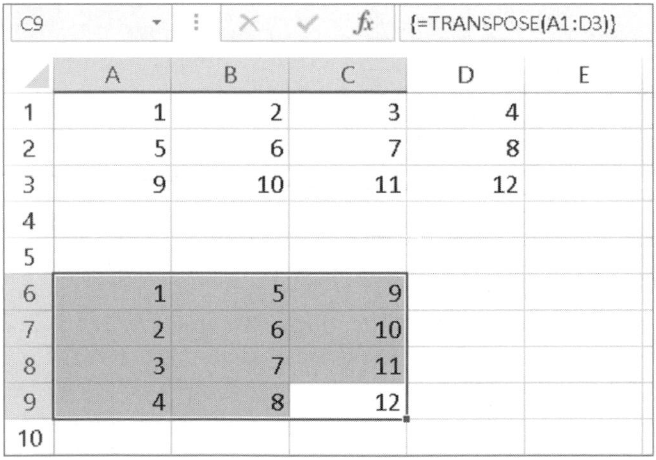

The formula in A6:C9 is as follows:

    {=TRANSPOSE({1,2,3,4;5,6,7,8;9,10,11,12})}

You can, of course, use the TRANSPOSE function to transpose an array stored in a range. The following formula, for example, uses an array stored in A1:D3 (three rows, four columns). You can enter this array formula into a range that consists of three rows and four columns:

{=TRANSPOSE(A1:C4)}

Generating an array of consecutive integers

Generating an array of consecutive integers for use in a complex array formula is often useful. The ROW function, which returns a row number, is ideal for this. Consider the array formula shown here, entered into a vertical range of 12 cells:

{=ROW(1:12)}

This formula generates a 12-element array that contains integers from 1 to 12. To demonstrate, select a range that consists of 12 rows and 1 column and enter the array formula into the range. You'll find that the range is filled with 12 consecutive integers (as shown in Figure 18.13).

FIGURE 18.13

Using an array formula to generate consecutive integers

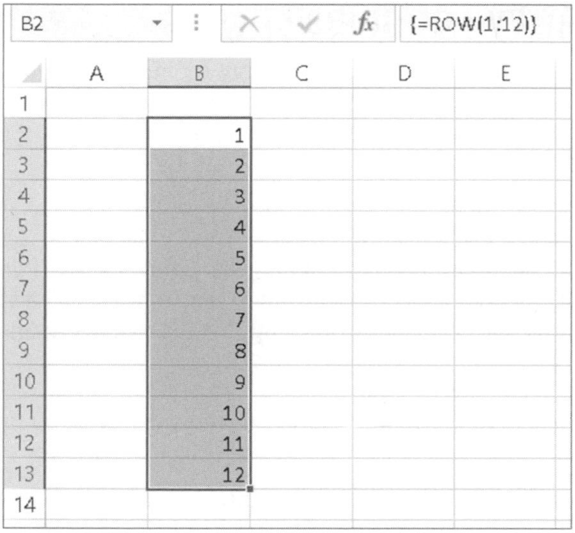

If you want to generate an array of consecutive integers, a formula like the one shown previously is good—but not perfect. To see the problem, insert a new row above the range that contains the array formula. Excel adjusts the row references so that the array formula now reads as follows:

{=ROW(2:13)}

The formula that originally generated integers from 1 to 12 now generates integers from 2 to 13.

For a better solution, use this formula:

```
{=ROW(INDIRECT("1:12"))}
```

This formula uses the INDIRECT function, which takes a text string as its argument. Excel does not adjust the references contained in the argument for the INDIRECT function. Therefore, this array formula always returns integers from 1 to 12.

Worksheet Functions That Return an Array

Several of the Excel worksheet functions use arrays; you must enter into multiple cells a formula that uses one of these functions as an array formula. These functions include FORECAST, FREQUENCY, GROWTH, LINEST, LOGEST, MINVERSE, MMULT, and TREND. Consult the Excel Help system for more information.

Using Single-Cell Array Formulas

The examples in the preceding section all used a multicell array formula—a single array formula that's entered into a range of cells. The real power of using arrays becomes apparent when you use single-cell array formulas. This section contains examples of array formulas that occupy a single cell.

Counting characters in a range

Suppose you have a range of cells that contains text entries (see Figure 18.14). If you need to get a count of the total number of characters in that range, the "traditional" method involves creating a formula like the one that follows and copying it down the column:

```
=LEN(A1)
```

Then you use a SUM formula to calculate the sum of the values returned by these intermediate formulas.

The following array formula does the job without using any intermediate formulas:

```
{=SUM(LEN(A1:A14))}
```

The array formula uses the LEN function to create a new array (in memory) that consists of the number of characters in each cell of the range. In this case, the new array is as follows:

```
{10,9,8,5,6,5,5,10,11,14,6,8,8,7}
```

The array formula is then reduced to the following:

```
=SUM({10,9,8,5,6,5,5,10,11,14,6,8,8,7})
```

FIGURE 18.14

The goal is to count the number of characters in a range of text.

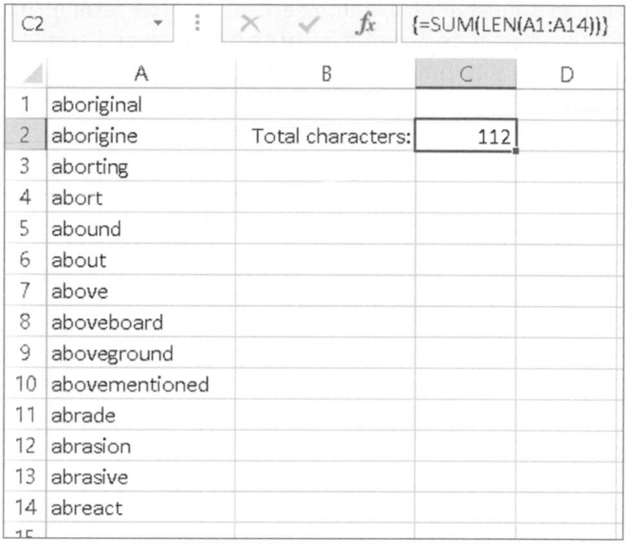

| C2 | ▼ | ⋮ | ✕ | ✓ | *fx* | {=SUM(LEN(A1:A14))} |

◢	A	B	C	D
1	aboriginal			
2	aborigine	Total characters:	112	
3	aborting			
4	abort			
5	abound			
6	about			
7	above			
8	aboveboard			
9	aboveground			
10	abovementioned			
11	abrade			
12	abrasion			
13	abrasive			
14	abreact			
1₅				

The formula returns the sum of the array elements: 112.

Summing the three smallest values in a range

If you have values in a range named Data, you can determine the smallest value by using the SMALL function:

```
=SMALL(Data,1)
```

You can determine the second smallest and third smallest values by using these formulas:

```
=SMALL(Data,2)
=SMALL(Data,3)
```

To add the three smallest values, you can use a formula like this:

```
=SUM(SMALL(Data,1),SMALL(Data,2),SMALL(Data,3))
```

This formula works fine, but using an array formula is more efficient. The following array formula returns the sum of the three smallest values in a range named Data:

```
{=SUM(SMALL(Data,{1,2,3}))}
```

The formula uses an array constant as the second argument for the SMALL function. This generates a new array, which consists of the three smallest values in the range. This array is then passed to the SUM function, which returns the sum of the values in the new array.

18

Figure 18.15 shows an example in which the range A1:A10 is named Data. The SMALL function is evaluated three times, each time with a different second argument. The first time, the SMALL function has a second argument of 1, and it returns –5. The second time, the second argument for the SMALL function is 2, and it returns 0 (the second smallest value in the range). The third time, the SMALL function has a second argument of 3, and it returns the third smallest value of 2.

FIGURE 18.15

An array formula returns the sum of the three smallest values in A1:A10.

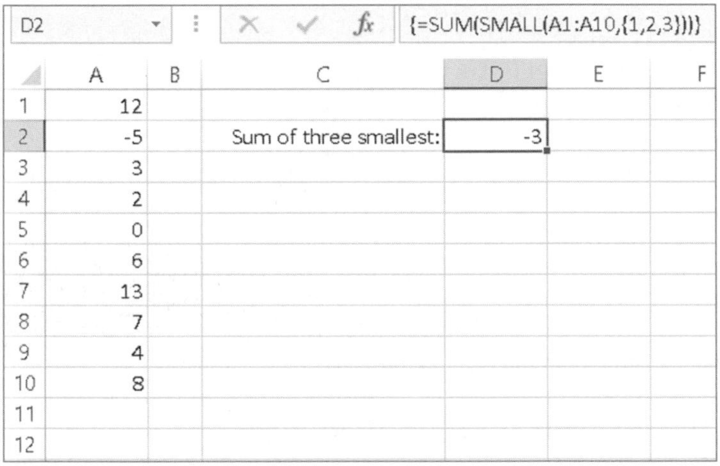

| D2 | ▼ | ⋮ | ✕ | ✓ | *fx* | {=SUM(SMALL(A1:A10,{1,2,3}))} |

◢	A	B	C	D	E	F
1	12					
2	-5		Sum of three smallest:	-3		
3	3					
4	2					
5	0					
6	6					
7	13					
8	7					
9	4					
10	8					
11						
12						

Therefore, the array that's passed to the SUM function is as follows:

```
{-5,0,2}
```

The formula returns the sum of the array (–3).

Counting text cells in a range

Suppose you need to count the number of text cells in a range. The COUNTIF function seems like it might be useful for this task—but it's not. COUNTIF is useful only if you need to count values in a range that meets some criterion (for example, values greater than 12).

To count the number of text cells in a range, you need an array formula. The following array formula uses the IF function to examine each cell in a range. It then creates a new array (of the same size and dimensions as the original range) that consists of 1s and 0s, depending on whether the cell contains text. This new array is then passed to the SUM function, which returns the sum of the items in the array. The result is a count of the number of text cells in the range:

```
{=SUM(IF(ISTEXT(A1:D5),1,0))}
```

This general array formula type (that is, an IF function nested in a SUM function) is useful for counting. See Chapter 13, "Using Formulas for Conditional Analysis," for additional examples of IF and SUM functions.

Figure 18.16 shows an example of the preceding formula in cell C7. The array created by this formula is as follows:

$$\{0,1,1,1;1,0,0,0;1,0,0,0;1,0,0,0;1,0,0,0\}$$

FIGURE 18.16

An array formula returns the number of text cells in the range.

C7			✕ ✓	fx	{=SUM(IF(ISTEXT(A1:D5),1,0))}		
	A	B	C	D	E	F	
1		Jan	Feb	Mar			
2	Region 1	7	4	9			
3	Region 2	8	2	8			
4	Region 3	12	1	9			
5	Region 4	14	6	10			
6							
7	No. of text cells:		7				
8							

Notice that this array contains five rows of four elements (the same dimensions as the range).

Here is a slightly more efficient variation on this formula:

```
{=SUM(ISTEXT(A1:D5)*1)}
```

This formula eliminates the need for the IF function and takes advantage of the fact that

```
TRUE * 1 = 1
```

and

```
FALSE * 1 = 0
```

Eliminating intermediate formulas

One key benefit of using an array formula is that you can often eliminate intermediate formulas in your worksheet, which makes your worksheet more compact and eliminates the need to display irrelevant calculations. Figure 18.17 shows a worksheet that contains pre-test and post-test scores for students. Column D contains formulas that calculate the changes between the pre-test and the post-test scores.

419

FIGURE 18.17

Without an array formula, calculating the average change requires intermediate formulas in column D.

	A	B	C	D	E	F
D17			fx	{=AVERAGE(C2:C15-B2:B15)}		
1	Student	Pre-Test	Post-Test	Change		
2	Andy	56	67	11		
3	Beth	59	74	15		
4	Cindy	98	92	-6		
5	Duane	78	79	1		
6	Eddy	81	100	19		
7	Francis	92	94	2		
8	Georgia	100	100	0		
9	Hilda	92	99	7		
10	Isabel	54	69	15		
11	Jack	91	92	1		
12	Kent	80	88	8		
13	Linda	45	68	23		
14	Michelle	71	92	21		
15	Nancy	94	83	-11		
16						
17		**Average Change:**		7.57		

With an array formula (see Figure 18.7), you can eliminate column D. The following array formula calculates the average of the changes but does not require the formulas in column D:

```
{=AVERAGE(C2:C15-B2:B15)}
```

How does it work? The formula uses two arrays, the values of which are stored in two ranges (B2:B15 and C2:C15). The formula creates a new array that consists of the differences between each corresponding element in the other arrays. This new array is stored in Excel's memory, not in a range. The AVERAGE function then uses this new array as its argument and returns the result.

The new array, calculated from the two ranges, consists of the following elements:

```
{11,15,-6,1,19,2,0,7,15,1,8,23,21,-11}
```

The formula, therefore, is equivalent to this:

```
=AVERAGE({11,15,-6,1,19,2,0,7,15,1,8,23,21,-11})
```

Excel evaluates the function and displays the results, 7.57.

You can use additional array formulas to calculate other measures for the data in this example. For instance, the following array formula returns the largest change (that is, the greatest improvement). This formula returns 23, which represents Linda's test scores.

    {=MAX(C2:C15-B2:B15)}

The following array formula returns the smallest value in the Change column. This formula returns –11, which represents Nancy's test scores:

    {=MIN(C2:C15-B2:B15)}

Using an array instead of a range reference

If your formula uses a function that requires a range reference, you may be able to replace that range reference with an array constant. This is useful in situations in which the values in the referenced range do not change.

> **NOTE**
>
> A notable exception to using an array constant in place of a range reference in a function is with the database functions that use a reference to a criteria range (for example, DSUM). Unfortunately, using an array constant instead of a reference to a criteria range does not work.

Figure 18.18 shows a worksheet that uses a lookup table to display a word that corresponds to an integer. For example, looking up a value of 9 returns Nine from the lookup table in D1:E10. The formula in cell C1 is as follows:

    =VLOOKUP(B1,D1:E10,2,FALSE)

FIGURE 18.18

You can replace the lookup table in D1:E10 with an array constant.

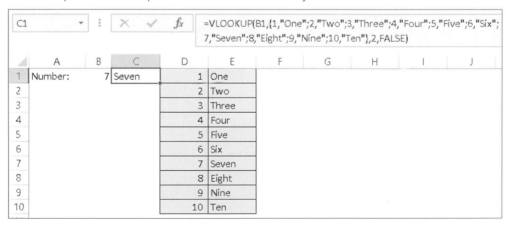

18

For information about lookup formulas, see Chapter 14, "Using Formulas for Matching and Lookups."

You can use a two-dimensional array in place of the lookup range. The following formula returns the same result as the previous formula, but it does not require the lookup range in D1:E10:

```
=VLOOKUP(B1,{1,"One";2,"Two";3,"Three";4,"Four";5,"Five";6,"Six";7,"S
even";8,"Eight";9,"Nine";10,"Ten"},2,FALSE)
```

Making Your Formulas Error-Free

IN THIS CHAPTER

Identifying and correcting common formula errors

Using Excel auditing tools

Using formula AutoCorrect

Tracing cell relationships

Checking spelling and related features

I
t goes without saying that you want your Excel worksheets to produce accurate results. Unfortunately, it's not always easy to be certain that the results are correct, especially if you deal with large, complex worksheets. This chapter introduces the tools and techniques available to help identify, correct, and prevent errors.

Finding and Correcting Formula Errors

Making a change in a worksheet—even a relatively minor change—may produce a ripple effect that introduces errors in other cells. For example, accidentally entering a value into a cell that previously held a formula is all too easy to do. This simple error can have a major impact on other formulas, and you may not discover the problem until long after you make the change—if you discover the problem at all.

Formula errors tend to fall into one of the following general categories:

Syntax errors   You have a problem with the syntax of a formula. For example, a formula may have mismatched parentheses, or a function may not have the correct number of arguments.

Logical errors   A formula doesn't return an error, but it contains a logical flaw that causes it to return an incorrect result.

Incorrect reference errors   The logic of the formula is correct, but the formula uses an incorrect cell reference. As a simple example, the range reference in a SUM formula may not include all of the data that you want to sum.

Semantic errors   An example is a function name that is spelled incorrectly. Excel will attempt to interpret it as a name and will display the #NAME? error.

Circular references   A circular reference occurs when a formula refers to its own cell, either directly or indirectly. Circular references are useful in a few cases, but most of the time, a circular reference indicates a problem.

Array formula entry error   When entering (or editing) an array formula, you must press Ctrl+Shift+Enter to enter the formula. If you fail to do so, Excel doesn't recognize the formula as an array formula, and you may get an error or incorrect results.

Incomplete calculation errors   The formulas simply aren't calculated fully. To ensure that your formulas are fully calculated, press Ctrl+Alt+Shift+F9.

 Refer to Chapter 18, "Understanding and Using Array Formulas," for an introduction to array formulas.

Syntax errors are usually the easiest to identify and correct. In most cases, you'll know when your formula contains a syntax error. For example, Excel won't permit you to enter a formula with mismatched parentheses. Other syntax errors also usually result in an error display in the cell.

The following sections describe common formula problems and offer advice on identifying and correcting them.

Mismatched parentheses

In a formula, every left parenthesis must have a corresponding right parenthesis. If your formula has mismatched parentheses, Excel usually won't permit you to enter it. An exception to this rule involves a simple formula that uses a function. For example, if you enter the following formula (which is missing a closing parenthesis), Excel accepts the formula and provides the missing parenthesis:

```
=SUM(A1:A500
```

A formula may have an equal number of left and right parentheses, but the parentheses may not match properly. For example, consider the following formula, which converts a text string such that the first character is uppercase and the remaining characters are lowercase. This formula has five pairs of parentheses, and they match properly:

```
=UPPER(LEFT(A1))&RIGHT(LOWER(A1),LEN(A1)-1)
```

The following formula also has five pairs of parentheses, but they're mismatched. The result displays a syntactically correct formula that simply returns the wrong result:

```
=UPPER(LEFT(A1)&RIGHT(LOWER(A1),LEN(A1)-1))
```

Often, parentheses that are in the wrong location will result in a *syntax error,* which is usually a message that tells you that you entered too many or too few arguments for a function.

TIP
Excel can help you with mismatched parentheses. When you're editing a formula and you move the cursor over a parenthesis, Excel displays it (and its matching parenthesis) in bold for about one-half second. In addition, Excel color-codes pairs of nested parentheses while you're editing a formula.

Using Formula AutoCorrect

When you enter a formula that has a syntax error, Excel attempts to determine the problem and offers a suggested correction.

Be careful when accepting corrections for your formulas from Excel because it doesn't always guess correctly. For example, imagine that you entered the following formula (which has mismatched parentheses):

```
=AVERAGE(SUM(A1:A12,SUM(B1:B12))
```

Excel then proposes the following correction to the formula:

```
=AVERAGE(SUM(A1:A12,SUM(B1:B12)))
```

You may be tempted to accept the suggestion without even thinking. In this case, the proposed formula is syntactically correct, but it's not what you intended. The correct formula is as follows:

```
=AVERAGE(SUM(A1:A12),SUM(B1:B12))
```

Cells are filled with hash marks

A cell is filled with a series of hash marks (#) for one of two reasons:

- **The column is not wide enough to accommodate the formatted numeric value.** To correct it, you can make the column wider or use a different number format. (See Chapter 23, "Visualizing with Custom Number Formats and Shapes.")
- **The cell contains a formula that returns an invalid date or time.** For example, Excel doesn't support dates prior to 1900 or the use of negative time values. A formula that returns either of these values results in a cell filled with hash marks. Widening the column won't fix it.

Blank cells are not blank

Some Excel users have discovered that by pressing the spacebar, the contents of a cell seem to erase. Actually, pressing the spacebar inserts an invisible space character, which isn't the same as erasing the cell.

For example, the following formula returns the number of nonempty cells in range A1:A10. If you "erase" any of these cells by using the spacebar, these cells are included in the count, and the formula returns an incorrect result:

```
=COUNTA(A1:A10)
```

19

If your formula doesn't ignore blank cells the way that it should, check to make sure that the blank cells are really blank. Here's how to search for cells that contain only blank characters:

1. **Press Ctrl+F.** The Find and Replace dialog box appears.

2. **Click the Options button to expand the dialog box so that it displays additional options.**

3. **In the Find What box, enter * *.** That's an asterisk, followed by a space, followed by another asterisk.

4. **Make sure that the Match Entire Cell Contents check box is selected.**

5. **Click Find All.** If any cells that contain only space characters are found, Excel lists the cell address at the bottom of the Find and Replace dialog box.

Extra space characters

If you have formulas or use procedures that rely on comparing text, be careful that your text doesn't contain additional space characters. Adding an extra space character is particularly common when data has been imported from another source.

Excel automatically removes trailing spaces from values that you enter, but trailing spaces in text entries are not deleted. It's impossible to tell just by looking at a cell whether it contains one or more trailing space characters.

You can leverage the TRIM function to identify values that contain leading spaces, trailing spaces, and multiple spaces within a text string. For instance, this formula will return FALSE if the text in cell A1 contains leading spaces, trailing spaces, or multiple spaces.

```
=TRIM(A1)=A1
```

Formulas returning an error

A formula may return any of the following error values:

- #DIV/0!
- #N/A
- #NAME?
- #NULL!
- #NUM!
- #REF!
- #VALUE!

The following sections summarize possible problems that may cause these errors.

TIP

Excel allows you to choose the way error values are printed. To access this feature, display the Page Setup dialog box and select the Sheet tab. You can choose to print error values as displayed (the default) or as blank cells, dashes, or #N/A. To display the Page Setup dialog box, click the dialog box launcher of the Page Layout ➪ Page Setup group.

Tracing Error Values

Often, an error in one cell is the result of an error in a precedent cell. For help in identifying the cell causing an error value to appear, activate the cell that contains the error and then choose Formulas ➪ Formula Auditing ➪ Error Checking ➪ Trace Error. Excel draws arrows to indicate which cell is the source of the error.

After you identify the error, choose Formulas ➪ Formula Auditing ➪ Remove Arrows to get rid of the arrow display.

#DIV/0! errors

Division by zero is not a valid operation. If you create a formula that attempts to divide by zero, Excel displays its familiar #DIV/0! error value.

Because Excel considers a blank cell to be zero, you also get this error if your formula divides by a missing value.

To avoid the error display, you can use an IF function to check for a blank cell. For instance, this formula will display an empty string if cell B4 is blank or contains 0; otherwise, it displays the calculated value:

```
=IF(B4=0,"",C4/B4)
```

Another approach is to use an IFERROR function to check for *any* error condition. The following formula, for example, displays an empty string if the formula results in any type of error:

```
=IFERROR(C4/B4,"")
```

NOTE

The IFERROR function was introduced in Excel 2007. For compatibility with previous versions of Excel, use this formula:

```
=IF(ISERROR(C4/B4),"",C4/B4)
```

19

#N/A errors

The #N/A error occurs if any cell referenced by a formula displays #N/A.

The #N/A error also occurs when a LOOKUP function (HLOOKUP, LOOKUP, MATCH, or VLOOKUP) can't find a match.

If you would like to display an empty string instead of #N/A, use the IFNA function in a formula like this:

```
=IFNA(VLOOKUP(A1,C1:F50,4,FALSE),"")
```

NOTE

The IFNA function was introduced in Excel 2013. For compatibility with previous versions, use a formula like this:
=IF(ISNA(VLOOKUP(A1,C1:F50,4,FALSE)),"",VLOOKUP(A1,C1:F50,4,FALSE))

#NAME? errors

The #NAME? error occurs under these conditions:

- The formula contains an undefined range or cell name.
- The formula contains text that Excel *interprets* as an undefined name. A misspelled function name, for example, generates a #NAME? error.
- The formula contains text that isn't enclosed in quotation marks.
- The formula contains a range reference that omits the colon between the cell addresses.
- The formula uses a worksheet function that's defined in an add-in, and the add-in is not installed.

CAUTION

Excel has a bit of a problem with range names. If you delete a name for a cell or a range and the name is used in a formula, the formula continues to use the name, even though it's no longer defined. As a result, the formula displays #NAME?. You might expect Excel automatically to convert the names to their corresponding cell references, but this doesn't happen.

#NULL! errors

A #NULL! error occurs when a formula attempts to use an intersection of two ranges that don't actually intersect. Excel's intersection operator is a space. The following formula, for example, returns #NULL! because the two ranges don't intersect:

```
=SUM(B5:B14 A16:F16)
```

The following formula doesn't return #NULL! but displays the contents of cell B9, which represents the intersection of the two ranges:

```
=SUM(B5:B14 A9:F9)
```

You also see a #NULL! error if you accidentally omit an operator in a formula. For example, this formula is missing the second operator:

```
= A1+A2 A3
```

#NUM! errors

A formula returns a #NUM! error if any of the following occurs:

- You pass a nonnumeric argument to a function when a numeric argument is expected (for example, $1,000 instead of 1000).
- You pass an invalid argument to a function, such as attempting to calculate the square root of a negative number. This formula returns #NUM!:

```
=SQRT(-12)
```

- A function that uses iteration can't calculate a result. Examples of functions that use iteration are IRR and RATE.
- A formula returns a value that is too large or too small. Excel supports values between –1E-307 and 1E+307.

#REF! errors

A #REF! error occurs when a formula uses an invalid cell reference. This error can occur in the following situations:

- You delete the row column of a cell that is referenced by the formula. For example, the following formula displays a #REF! error if row 1, column A, or column B is deleted:

```
=A1/B1
```

- You delete the worksheet of a cell that is referenced by the formula. For example, the following formula displays a #REF! error if Sheet2 is deleted:

```
=Sheet2!A1
```

- You copy a formula to a location that invalidates the relative cell references. For example, if you copy the following formula from cell A2 to cell A1, the formula returns #REF! because it attempts to refer to a nonexistent cell:

```
=A1-1
```

- You cut a cell (choose Home ➪ Clipboard ➪ Cut) and then paste it to a cell that's referenced by a formula. The formula will display #REF!.

19

#VALUE! errors

A #VALUE! error is common and can occur under the following conditions:

- An argument for a function is of an incorrect data type, or the formula attempts to perform an operation using incorrect data. For example, a formula that adds a value to a text string returns the #VALUE! error.
- A function's argument is a range when it should be a single value.
- A custom worksheet function is not calculated. You can press Ctrl+Alt+F9 to force a recalculation.
- A custom worksheet function attempts to perform an operation that is not valid. For example, custom functions can't modify the Excel environment or make changes to other cells.
- You forget to press Ctrl+Shift+Enter when entering an Array formula.

Pay Attention to the Colors

When you edit a cell that contains a formula, Excel color-codes the cell and range references in the formula. Excel also outlines the cells and ranges used in the formula by using corresponding colors. Therefore, you can see at a glance the cells that are used in the formula.

You also can manipulate the colored outline to change the cell or range reference. To change the references used in a formula, drag the outline's border or fill handle (at the lower right of the outline). This technique is often easier than editing the formula.

Operator precedence problems

As noted in Chapter 9, Excel has some straightforward rules about the order in which mathematical operations are performed. When in doubt (or when you simply need to clarify your intentions), you should use parentheses to ensure that operations are performed in the correct order. For example, the following formula multiplies A1 by A2 and then adds 1 to the result. The multiplication is performed first because it has a higher order of precedence:

```
=1+A1*A2
```

The following is a clearer version of this formula. The parentheses aren't necessary, but in this case, the order of operations is perfectly obvious:

```
=1+(A1*A2)
```

Notice that the negation operator symbol is the same as the subtraction operator symbol. This, as you may expect, can cause some confusion. Consider these two formulas:

```
=-3^2
=0-3^2
```

The first formula, as expected, returns 9. The second formula, however, returns −9. Squaring a number always produces a positive result, so how is it that Excel can return the −9 result?

In the first formula, the minus sign is a *negation* operator and has the highest precedence. However, in the second formula, the minus sign is a *subtraction* operator, which has a lower precedence than the exponentiation operator. Therefore, the value 3 is squared, and then the result is subtracted from 0 (zero), which produces a negative result.

Using parentheses, as shown in the following formula, causes Excel to interpret the operator as a minus sign rather than a negation operator. This formula returns −9:

```
=-(3^2)
```

Formulas are not calculated

If you use custom worksheet functions written in VBA, you may find that the formulas that use these functions fail to be recalculated and may display incorrect results. For example, assume that you wrote a VBA function that returns the number format of a referenced cell. If you change the number format, the function will continue to display the previous number format. That's because changing a number format doesn't trigger a recalculation.

To force a single formula to be recalculated, select the cell, press F2, and then press Enter. To force a recalculation of all formulas, press Ctrl+Alt+F9.

Problems with decimal precision

By their nature, computers don't have infinite precision. Excel stores numbers in binary format by using 8 bytes, which can handle numbers with 15-digit accuracy. Some numbers can't be expressed precisely by using 8 bytes, so the number is stored as an approximation.

To demonstrate how this lack of precision may cause problems, enter the following formula into cell A1:

```
=(5.1-5.2)+1
```

The result should be 0.9. However, if you format the cell to display 15 decimal places, you discover that Excel calculates the formula with a result of 0.899999999999999. This result occurs because the operation in parentheses is performed first, and this intermediate result stores in binary format by using an approximation. The formula then adds 1 to this value, and the approximation error is propagated to the final result.

In many cases, this type of error doesn't present a problem. However, if you need to test the result of that formula by using a logical operator, it *may* present a problem. For example, the following formula (which assumes that the previous formula is in cell A1) returns FALSE:

```
=A1=.9
```

19

One solution to this type of error is to use the ROUND function. The following formula, for example, returns TRUE because the comparison is made by using the value in A1 rounded to one decimal place:

```
=ROUND(A1,1)=0.9
```

Here's another example of a "precision" problem. Try entering the following formula:

```
=(1.333-1.233)-(1.334-1.234)
```

This formula should return 0, but it actually returns -2.22045E-16 (a number very close to zero).

If that formula is in cell A1, the following formula returns Not Zero:

```
=IF(A1=0,"Zero","Not Zero")
```

One way to handle these "very close to zero" rounding errors is to use a formula like this:

```
=IF(ABS(A1)<1E-6,"Zero","Not Zero")
```

This formula uses the less-than operator (<) to compare the absolute value of the number with a very small number. This formula returns Zero.

"Phantom link" errors

You may open a workbook and see a message asking whether you want to update links in a workbook. This message sometimes appears even when a workbook contains no linked formulas. Often, these phantom links are created when you copy a worksheet that contains names.

First, try choosing File ➪ Info ➪ Edit Links to Files to display the Edit Links dialog box. Then select each link and click Break Link. If that doesn't solve the problem, this phantom link may be caused by an erroneous name. Choose Formulas ➪ Defined Names ➪ Name Manager and scroll through the list of names in the Name Manager dialog box. If you see a name that refers to #REF!, delete the name. The Name Manager dialog box has a Filter button that lets you filter the names. For example, you can filter the lists to display only the names with errors.

Using Excel Auditing Tools

Excel includes a number of tools that can help you track down formula errors. This section describes the auditing tools built into Excel.

Identifying cells of a particular type

The Go to Special dialog box is a handy tool that enables you to locate cells of a particular type. To display this dialog box, choose Home ➪ Editing ➪ Find & Select ➪ Go to Special.

You can use the Go to Special dialog box to select cells of a certain type, which can often help you identify errors. For example, if you choose the Formulas option, Excel selects all of the cells that contain a formula. If you zoom the worksheet out to a small size, you can get a good idea of the worksheet's organization.

To zoom a worksheet, use the zoom controls on the right side of the status bar or press Ctrl while you move the scroll wheel on your mouse.

Viewing formulas

You can become familiar with an unfamiliar workbook by displaying the formulas rather than the results of the formulas. To toggle the display of formulas, choose Formulas ➪ Formula Auditing ➪ Show Formulas.

You may want to create a second window for the workbook before issuing this command. This way, you can see the formulas in one window and the results of the formula in the other window. Choose View ➪ Window ➪ New Window to open a new window.

 See Chapter 4, "Working with Excel Ranges and Tables," for more information about this command.

Tracing cell relationships

To understand how to trace cell relationships, you need to familiarize yourself with the following two concepts:

Cell precedents   Applicable only to cells that contain a formula, a formula cell's precedents are all of the cells that contribute to the formula's result. A *direct precedent* is a cell that you use directly in the formula. An *indirect precedent* is a cell that isn't used directly in the formula but is used by a cell that you refer to in the formula.

Cell dependents These formula cells depend upon a particular cell. A cell's dependents consist of all formula cells that use the cell. Again, the formula cell can be a direct dependent or an indirect dependent.

For example, consider this simple formula entered into cell A4:

```
=SUM(A1:A3)
```

Cell A4 has three precedent cells (A1, A2, and A3), which are all direct precedents. Cells A1, A2, and A3 all have at least one dependent cell (cell A4).

Identifying cell precedents for a formula cell often sheds light on why the formula isn't working correctly. Conversely, knowing which formula cells depend on a particular cell is also helpful. For example, if you're about to delete a formula, you may want to check whether it has any dependents.

Identifying precedents

You can identify cells used by a formula in the active cell in a number of ways:

- **Press F2.** The cells that are used directly by the formula are outlined in color, and the color corresponds to the cell reference in the formula. This technique is limited to identifying cells on the same sheet as the formula.
- **Choose Home ➪ Editing ➪ Find & Select ➪ Go to Special to display the Go to Special dialog box.** Select the Precedents option and then select either Direct Only (for direct precedents only) or All Levels (for direct and indirect precedents). Click OK and Excel selects the precedent cells for the formula. This technique is limited to identifying cells on the same sheet as the formula.
- **Press Ctrl+[.** This selects all direct precedent cells on the active sheet.
- **Press Ctrl+Shift+{.** This selects all precedent cells (direct and indirect) on the active sheet.
- **Choose Formulas ➪ Formula Auditing ➪ Trace Precedents.** Excel will draw arrows to indicate the cell's precedents. Click this button multiple times to see additional levels of precedents.
- **Choose Formulas ➪ Formula Auditing ➪ Remove Arrows to hide the arrows.**

Identifying dependents

You can identify formula cells that use a particular cell in a number of ways:

- **Choose Home ➪ Editing ➪ Find & Select ➪ Go to Special to display the Go to Special dialog box.** Select the Dependents option and then select either Direct Only (for direct dependents only) or All Levels (for direct and indirect dependents). Click OK. Excel selects the cells that depend on the active cell. This technique is limited to identifying cells on the active sheet only.
- **Press Ctrl+].** This selects all direct dependent cells on the active sheet.
- **Press Ctrl+Shift+}.** This selects all dependent cells (direct and indirect) on the active sheet.

■ **Choose Formulas ⇨ Formula Auditing ⇨ Trace Dependents.** Excel will draw arrows to indicate the cell's dependents. Click this button multiple times to see additional levels of dependents. Choose Formulas ⇨ Formula Auditing ⇨ Remove Arrows to hide the arrows.

Tracing error values

If a formula displays an error value, Excel can help you identify the cell that is causing that error value. An error in one cell is often the result of an error in a precedent cell. Activate a cell that contains an error value and then choose Formulas ⇨ Formula Auditing ⇨ Error Checking ⇨ Trace Error. Excel draws arrows to indicate the error source.

Fixing circular reference errors

If you accidentally create a circular reference formula, Excel displays a warning message—`Circular Reference`—with the cell address in the status bar. It also draws arrows on the worksheet to help you identify the problem. If you can't figure out the source of the problem, choose Formulas ⇨ Formula Auditing ⇨ Error Checking ⇨ Circular References. This command displays a list of all cells that are involved in the circular references. Start by selecting the first cell listed and then work your way down the list until you figure out the problem.

Using the background error-checking feature

Some people may find it helpful to take advantage of the Excel automatic error-checking feature. This feature is enabled or disabled via the Enable Background Error Checking check box, found on the Formulas tab of the Excel Options dialog box, shown in Figure 19.1. In addition, you can use the check boxes in the Error Checking Rules section to specify which types of errors to check.

When error checking is turned on, Excel continually evaluates the formulas in your worksheet. If a potential error is identified, Excel places a small triangle in the upper-left corner of the cell. When the cell is activated, a drop-down control appears. Clicking this drop-down control provides you with options. The options vary, depending on the type of error.

In many cases, you'll choose to ignore an error by selecting the Ignore Error option. Selecting this option eliminates the cell from subsequent error checks. However, all previously ignored errors can be reset so that they appear again. (Use the Reset Ignored Errors button on the Formulas tab of the Excel Options dialog box.)

You can choose Formulas ⇨ Formula Auditing ⇨ Error Checking to display a dialog box that describes each potential error cell in sequence, much like using a spell-checking command.

> **CAUTION**
>
> The error-checking feature isn't perfect. In fact, it's not even close to perfect. In other words, you can't assume that you have an error-free worksheet simply because Excel doesn't identify potential errors! Also, be aware that this error-checking feature won't catch a common type of error, namely, overwriting a formula cell with a value.

19

FIGURE 19.1

Excel can check your formulas for potential errors.

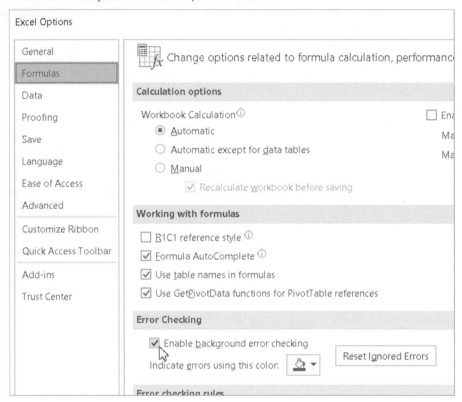

Using Formula Evaluator

Formula Evaluator lets you see the various parts of a nested formula evaluated in the order in which the formula is calculated. To use Formula Evaluator, select the cell that contains the formula and then choose Formulas ⇨ Formula Auditing ⇨ Evaluate Formula to display the Evaluate Formula dialog box (see Figure 19.2).

FIGURE 19.2

The Evaluate Formula dialog box shows a formula being calculated one step at a time.

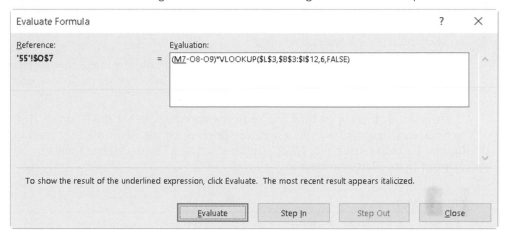

Click the Evaluate button to show the result of calculating the expressions within the formula. Each click of the button performs another calculation. This feature may seem a bit complicated at first, but if you spend some time working with it, you'll understand how it works and see the value.

Excel provides another way to evaluate a part of a formula:

1. **Select the cell that contains the formula.**
2. **Press F2 to get into Cell Edit mode.**
3. **Use your mouse to highlight the portion of the formula you want to evaluate, or press Shift and use the navigation keys.**
4. **Press F9.**

The highlighted portion of the formula displays the calculated result. You can evaluate other parts of the formula or press Esc to cancel and return your formula to its previous state.

CAUTION

Be careful when using this technique because if you press Enter (rather than Esc), the formula will be modified to use the calculated values.

Searching and Replacing

Excel has a powerful search-and-replace feature that makes it easy to locate information in a worksheet or across multiple worksheets in a workbook. As an option, you can also search for text and replace it with other text.

To access the Find and Replace dialog box, start by selecting the range that you want to search. If you select any single cell, Excel searches the entire sheet. Choose Home ⇨ Editing ⇨ Find & Select ⇨ Find (or press Ctrl+F).

If you're simply looking for information in the worksheet, select the Find tab. If you want to replace existing text with new text, use the Replace tab. Also note that you can use the Options button to display (or hide) additional options. The dialog box shown in Figure 19.3 displays these additional options.

FIGURE 19.3

Use the Find and Replace dialog box to locate information in a worksheet or workbook.

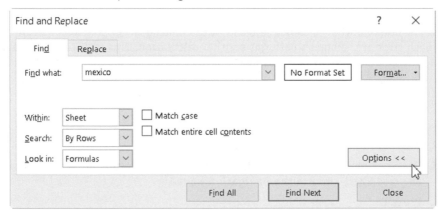

Searching for information

Enter the information to search for in the Find What text box and then specify any of the following options:

Within drop-down list   Specify where to search (the current sheet or the entire workbook).

Search drop-down list   Specify the direction (by rows or by columns).

Look In drop-down list   Specify what cell parts to search (formulas, values, or comments).

Match Case check box   Specify whether the search should be case sensitive.

Match Entire Cell Contents check box   Specify whether the entire cell contents must be matched.

Format button   Click to search for cells that have a particular formatting. (See the upcoming "Searching for formatting" section.)

Click Find Next to locate the matching cells one at a time or click Find All to locate all matches. If you use the Find All button, the Find and Replace dialog box expands to display the addresses of all matching cells in a list. When you select an entry in this list, Excel scrolls the worksheet so that you can view it in context.

> **TIP**
>
> After using Find All, press Ctrl+A to select all the found cells in the worksheet.

> **NOTE**
>
> Because the Find and Replace dialog box is modeless, you can access the worksheet and make changes without the need to dismiss the dialog box.

Replacing information

To replace text with other text, use the Replace tab in the Find and Replace dialog box. Enter the text to be replaced in the Find What field and then enter the new text in the Replace With field. Specify other options as described in the previous section.

Click Find Next to locate the first matching item and then click Replace to do the replacement. When you click the Replace button, Excel locates the next matching item. To override the replacement, click Find Next. To replace all items without verification, click Replace All. If the replacement didn't occur as you planned, you can use the Undo button on the Quick Access toolbar (or press Ctrl+Z).

> **TIP**
>
> To delete information, enter the text to be deleted in the Find What field, but leave the Replace With field empty.

Searching for formatting

From the Find and Replace dialog box, you can also locate cells that contain a particular type of formatting. As an option, you can replace that formatting with another type of formatting. For example, assume that you want to locate all cells that are formatted as bold and then change that formatting to bold and italic. Follow these steps:

1. **Choose Home ➪ Editing ➪ Find & Select ➪ Replace or press Ctrl+H.** The Find and Replace dialog box appears.
2. **Make sure that the Replace tab is displayed.** If necessary, click the Options button to expand the dialog box.
3. **If the Find What and Replace With fields are not empty, delete their contents.**

19

4. **Click the top Format button.** The Find Format dialog box appears. This dialog box resembles the standard Format Cells dialog box.

5. **Select the Font tab.**

6. **Select Bold in the Font Style list and then click OK.**

7. **Click the bottom Format button.** The Replace Format dialog box appears.

8. **Select the Font tab.**

9. **Select Bold Italic from the Font Style list and then click OK.**

10. **In the Find and Replace dialog box, click Replace All.** Excel locates all cells that have bold formatting and changes the formatting to bold italic.

You can also find formatting based on a particular cell. In the Find Format dialog box, click the Choose Format from Cell button and then click the cell that contains the formatting you're looking for.

> **CAUTION**
> The Find and Replace dialog box can't find background color formatting in tables that was applied using table styles or formatting that is applied based on conditional formatting.

Spell-checking your worksheets

If you use a word-processing program, you probably take advantage of its spell-checker feature. Spelling mistakes can be just as embarrassing when they appear in a spreadsheet. Fortunately, Microsoft includes a spell-checker with Excel.

To access the spell-checker, choose Review ⇨ Proofing ⇨ Spelling, or press F7. To check the spelling in just a particular range, select the range before you activate the spell-checker.

> **NOTE**
> The spell-checker checks cell contents, text in graphics objects and charts, and page headers and footers. Even the contents of hidden rows and columns are checked.

The Spelling dialog box works similarly to other spell-checkers with which you may be familiar. If Excel encounters a word that isn't in the current dictionary or that is misspelled, it offers a list of suggestions. You can respond by clicking one of these buttons:

Ignore Once Ignore the word and continue the spell-check.

Ignore All Ignore the word and all subsequent occurrences of it.

Add to Dictionary Add the word to the dictionary.

Change Change the word to the selected word in the Suggestions list.

Change All Change the word to the selected word in the Suggestions list and change all subsequent occurrences of it without asking.

AutoCorrect   Add the misspelled word and its correct spelling (which you select from the list) to the AutoCorrect list.

Using AutoCorrect

AutoCorrect is a handy feature that automatically corrects common typing mistakes. You can also add words to the list that Excel corrects automatically. The AutoCorrect dialog box appears in Figure 19.4. To access this feature, choose File ⇨ Options. In the Excel Options dialog box, select the Proofing tab and then click the AutoCorrect Options button.

FIGURE 19.4

Use the AutoCorrect dialog box to control the spelling corrections Excel makes automatically.

This dialog box has several options:

Correct TWo INitial CApitals   Automatically corrects words with two initial uppercase letters. For example, BUdget is converted to Budget. This mistake is common among fast typists. You can click the Exceptions button to specify a list of exceptions to this rule.

Capitalize First Letter of Sentences   Capitalizes the first letter in a sentence. All other letters are unchanged.

Capitalize Names of Days   Capitalizes the days of the week. If you enter monday, Excel converts it to Monday.

Correct Accidental Use of cAPS LOCK key   Corrects errors caused if you accidentally pressed the CapsLock key while typing.

Replace Text as You Type   AutoCorrect automatically changes incorrect words as you type them.

Excel includes a long list of AutoCorrect entries for commonly misspelled words. In addition, it has AutoCorrect entries for some symbols. For example, (c) is replaced with ©, and (r) is replaced with ®. You can also add your own AutoCorrect entries. For example, if you find that you frequently misspell the word *January* as *Janruary*, you can create an AutoCorrect entry so that it's changed automatically. To create a new AutoCorrect entry, enter the misspelled word in the Replace box and the correctly spelled word in the With field. You can also delete entries that you no longer need.

> **TIP**
>
> You can use the AutoCorrect feature to create shortcuts for commonly used words or phrases. For example, if you work for a company named Consolidated Data Processing Corporation, you can create an AutoCorrect entry for an abbreviation, such as *cdp*. Then, whenever you type cdp, Excel automatically changes it to Consolidated Data Processing Corporation. Just make sure that you don't use a combination of characters that might normally appear in your text and be replaced erroneously.

> **NOTE**
>
> In some cases, you may want to override the AutoCorrect feature. For example, you may literally need to enter **(c)** rather than a copyright symbol. Just click the Undo button on the Quick Access toolbar or press Ctrl+Z.

You can use the AutoFormat as You Type tab of the AutoCorrect dialog box to control a few other automatic settings in Excel.

The Actions tab enables what were formerly known as *Smart Tags* for certain types of data in your worksheets. The types of actions that Excel recognizes vary depending on the types of software that are installed on your system. For example, if you enable the Financial Symbol action, you can right-click a cell that contains a financial symbol (such as MSFT, for Microsoft) and choose Additional Cell Actions, and you'll be presented with a list of options. For example, you can insert a refreshable stock price in your worksheet.

Part III

Creating Charts and Other Visualizations

The five chapters in this part deal with charts and visualizations. You'll discover how to use Excel's graphics capabilities to display your data in a chart or as Sparkline graphics. In addition, you'll learn to use Excel's other drawing and graphics tools to enhance your worksheets with meaningful visualizations of your data.

Getting Started with Excel Charts

IN THIS CHAPTER

How Excel handles charts

The parts of a chart

The basic steps for creating a chart

Working with charts

Looking at examples of chart types

C harts offer a visual representation of numeric values; they are at-a-glance views that allow you to specify relationships between data values, point out differences, and observe business trends. Few mechanisms allow you to absorb data faster than a chart, which can be a key component in your dashboard.

While most people think of a spreadsheet product such as Excel, they think of crunching rows and columns of numbers. But Excel is no slouch when it comes to presenting data visually in the form of a chart. In this chapter, we present an overview of Excel's charting capabilities and show you how to create and customize your own charts using Excel.

 Most of the examples in this chapter are available on this book's website at `www.wiley.com/go/ excel2019bible`. **The filename is** `Intro to Charts.xlsx`.

What Is a Chart?

Let's start with the basics. A *chart* is a visual representation of numeric values. Charts (also known as *graphs*) have been an integral part of spreadsheets since the early days of Lotus 1-2-3. Charts generated by early spreadsheet products were extremely crude by today's standards. Over the years, however, the quality and flexibility have improved significantly. You'll find that Excel provides you with the tools to create a wide variety of highly customizable charts that can help you effectively communicate your message.

Displaying data in a well-conceived chart can make your numbers more understandable. Because a chart presents a picture, charts are particularly useful for summarizing a series of numbers and their interrelationships. Making a chart can often help you spot trends and patterns that might otherwise go unnoticed.

Figure 20.1 shows a worksheet that contains a simple column chart that depicts a company's sales volume by month. Viewing the chart makes it apparent that sales were off in the summer months (June through August), but they increased steadily during the final four months of the year. You could, of course, arrive at this same conclusion simply by studying the numbers. But viewing the chart makes the point much more quickly.

FIGURE 20.1

A simple column chart depicts the sales volume for each month.

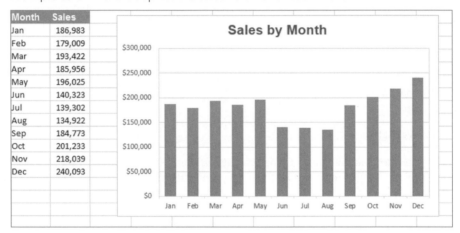

Month	Sales
Jan	186,983
Feb	179,009
Mar	193,422
Apr	185,956
May	196,025
Jun	140,323
Jul	139,302
Aug	134,922
Sep	184,773
Oct	201,233
Nov	218,039
Dec	240,093

A column chart is just one of many different types of charts that you can create with Excel. By the way, creating this chart is simple: select the data in A1:B13, and press Alt+F1.

How Excel handles charts

Before you can create a chart, you must have some numbers (data). The data, of course, is stored in the cells in a worksheet. Normally, the data that is used by a chart resides in a single worksheet, but that's not a strict requirement. A chart can use data that's stored in any number of worksheets, and the worksheets can even be in different workbooks. The decision to use data from one sheet or multiple sheets really depends on your data model, the nature of your data sources, and the interactivity that you want to give your dashboard.

A chart is essentially an "object" that Excel creates upon request. This object consists of one or more *data series*, displayed graphically. The appearance of the data series depends on the selected *chart type*. For example, if you create a line chart that uses two data series, the chart contains two lines, and each line represents one data series. The data for each series is stored in a separate row or column. Each point on the line is determined by the value in a single cell and is represented by a marker. You can distinguish the lines by their thickness, line style, color, or data markers.

Figure 20.2 shows a line chart that plots two data series across a nine-year period. The series are identified by using different data markers (squares versus circles), shown in the *legend* at the bottom of the chart. The lines also use different colors, which is not apparent in the grayscale figure.

FIGURE 20.2

This line chart displays two data series.

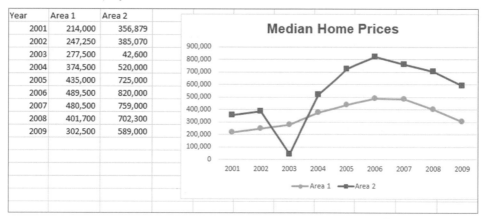

Year	Area 1	Area 2
2001	214,000	356,879
2002	247,250	385,070
2003	277,500	42,600
2004	374,500	520,000
2005	435,000	725,000
2006	489,500	820,000
2007	480,500	759,000
2008	401,700	702,300
2009	302,500	589,000

A key point to keep in mind is that charts are dynamic. In other words, a chart series is linked to the data in your worksheet. If the data changes, the chart is updated automatically to reflect those changes so that your dashboard can show the most current information.

After you've created a chart, you can always change its type, change the formatting, add new data series to it, or change an existing data series so that it uses data in a different range.

Charts can reside in either of two locations in a workbook:

- On a worksheet (an embedded chart)
- On a separate chart sheet

Embedded charts

An *embedded chart* basically floats on top of a worksheet, on the worksheet's drawing layer. The charts shown previously in this chapter are both embedded charts.

As with other drawing objects (such as a text box or a shape), you can move an embedded chart, resize it, change its proportions, adjust its borders, and add effects such as a

20

shadow. Using embedded charts enables you to view the chart next to the data that it uses. Alternatively, you can place several embedded charts together so that they print on a single page.

When you create a chart, it always starts off as an embedded chart. The exception to this rule is when you select a range of data and press F11 to create a default chart. Such a chart is created on a chart sheet.

To make any changes to the actual chart in an embedded chart object, you must click it to *activate* the chart. When a chart is activated, Excel displays the two Chart Tools contextual tabs shown in Figure 20.3: Chart Tools Design and Chart Tools Format.

FIGURE 20.3

Activating a chart displays additional tabs on the Excel Ribbon.

Chart sheets

You can move an embedded chart to its own chart sheet so that you can view it by clicking a sheet tab. When you move a chart to a chart sheet, the chart occupies the entire sheet. If you plan to print a chart on a page by itself, using a chart sheet is often your better choice. If you have many charts to create, you may want to put each one on a separate chart sheet to avoid cluttering your worksheet. This technique also makes locating a particular chart easier because you can change the names of the chart sheets' tabs to provide a description of the chart that it contains. Although chart sheets are not typically used in traditional dashboards, they can come in handy when producing reports that will be viewed in a multitab workbook.

Figure 20.4 shows a chart on a chart sheet. When a chart sheet is activated, Excel displays the Chart Tools contextual tabs, as described in the previous section.

FIGURE 20.4

A chart on a chart sheet

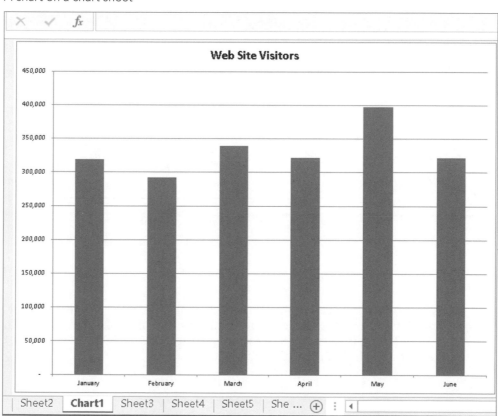

Parts of a chart

A chart is made up of many different elements, and all of these elements are optional. Yes, you can create a chart that contains no chart elements—an empty chart. It's not very useful, but Excel allows it.

Refer to the chart in Figure 20.5 as you read the following description of the chart's elements.

FIGURE 20.5

Parts of a chart

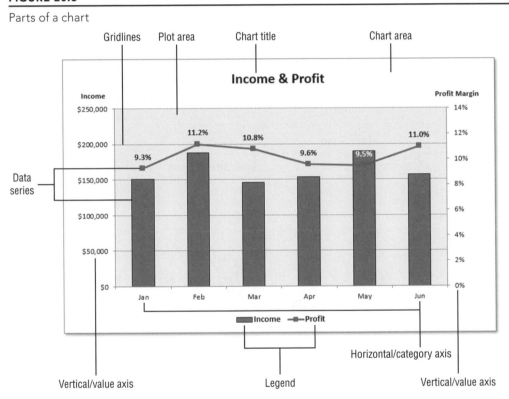

This particular chart is a combination chart that displays both columns and a line. The chart has two *data series:* Income and Profit Margin. Income is plotted as vertical columns, and Profit Margin is plotted as a line with square markers. Each bar (or marker on the line) represents a single *data point* (the value in a cell).

The chart has a horizontal axis, known as the *category axis*. This axis represents the category for each data point (January, February, and so on). This axis doesn't have a label because the category units are obvious.

Notice that this chart has two vertical axes. These are known as *value axes*, and each one has a different scale. The axis on the left is for the column series (Income), and the axis on the right is for the line series (Profit Margin).

The value axes also display scale values. The axis on the left displays scale values from 0 to 250,000, in major unit increments of 50,000. The value axis on the right uses a different scale: 0 percent to 14 percent, in increments of 2 percent. For a value axis, you can control the minimum and maximum values, as well as the increment value.

A chart with two value axes is appropriate because the two data series vary dramatically in scale. If the Profit Margin data was plotted using the left axis, the line would not even be visible.

If a chart has more than one data series, you'll usually need a way to identify the data series or data points. A *legend*, for example, is often used to identify the various series in a chart. In this example, the legend appears at the bottom of the chart. Some charts also display *data labels* to identify specific data points. The example chart displays data labels for the Profit Margin series, but not for the Income series. In addition, most charts (including the example chart) contain a *chart title* and additional labels to identify the axes or categories.

The example chart also contains horizontal *gridlines* (which correspond to the values on the left axis). Gridlines are basically extensions of the value axis scale, which makes it easier for the viewer to determine the magnitude of the data points.

In addition, all charts have a *chart area* (the entire background area of the chart) and a *plot area* (the part that shows the actual chart, including the plotted data, the axes, and the axis labels).

Charts can have additional parts or fewer parts, depending on the chart type. For example, a pie chart (see Figure 20.6) has "slices" and no axes. A 3-D chart may have *walls* and a *floor* (see Figure 20.7).

Several other types of items can be added to a chart. For example, you can add a *trend line* or display *error bars*.

20

FIGURE 20.6

A pie chart

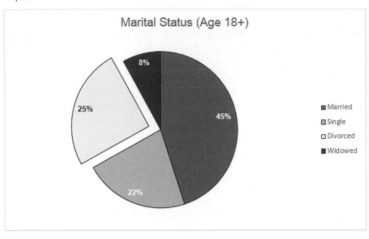

Chart limitations

As with most features in Excel, charts do have limits on the amount of data that they can handle and present. Table 20.1 lists the limitations of Excel charts.

TABLE 20.1   Limitations of Excel Charts

Item	Limitation
Charts in a worksheet	Limited by available memory
Worksheets referred to by a chart	255
Data series in a chart	255
Data points in a data series	32,000
Data points in a data series (3-D charts)	4,000
Total data points in a chart	256,000

FIGURE 20.7

FIGURE 20.7

A 3-D column chart

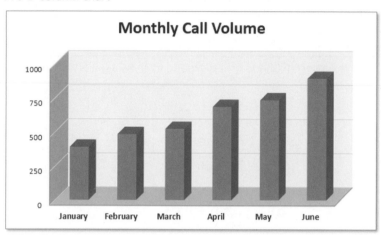

Basic Steps for Creating a Chart

Creating a chart is relatively easy. The following sections describe how to create and then customize a basic chart to best communicate your business goals.

Creating the chart

Follow these general steps to create a chart using the data in Figure 20.8:

1. **Select the data you want to use in the chart.** Make sure you select the column headers if the data has them (in this example, you would select A1:C4). Another option is to select a single cell within a range of data. Excel then uses the entire data range for the chart.

FIGURE 20.8

This data would make a good chart.

	A	B	C
1		Projected	Actual
2	Jan	2,000	1,895
3	Feb	2,500	2,643
4	Mar	3,500	3,648
5			

20

2. **Click the Insert tab and then click a Chart icon in the Charts group.** The icon expands into a gallery list that shows chart subtypes for the selected chart type (see Figure 20.9).

FIGURE 20.9

The icons in the Insert ➪ Charts group expand to show a gallery of chart subtypes.

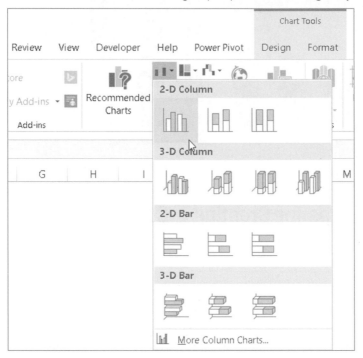

3. **Click a Chart subtype, and Excel then creates the chart of the specified type.** Figure 20.10 shows a column chart created from the data.

> **TIP**
> To create a default chart quickly, select the data and press Alt+F1 to create an embedded chart, or press F11 to create a chart on a chart sheet.

Switching the row and column orientation

When Excel creates a chart, it uses an algorithm to determine whether the data is arranged in columns or in rows. Most of the time Excel guesses correctly, but if it creates the chart using the wrong orientation, you can quickly change it by selecting the chart and choosing Chart Tools Design ➪ Data ➪ Switch Row/Column. This command is a toggle, so if changing the data orientation doesn't improve the chart, just choose the command again (or click the Undo button found on the Quick Access toolbar).

FIGURE 20.10

A column chart with two data series

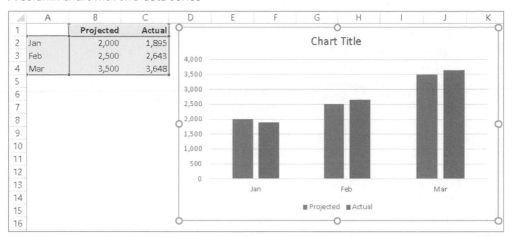

The orientation of the data has a drastic effect on the look (and, perhaps, understand-ability) of your chart. Figure 20.11 shows the column chart in Figure 20.10 after changing the orientation. Notice that the chart now has three data series, one for each month. If the goal of your dashboard is to compare actual with projected values for each month, this version of the chart is much more difficult to interpret because the relevant columns are not adjacent.

FIGURE 20.11

The column chart, after swapping the row/column orientation

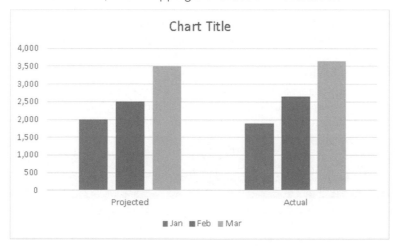

20

Changing the chart type

After you've created a chart, you can easily change the chart type. Although a column chart may work well for a particular data set, there's no harm in checking out some other chart types. You can choose Chart Tools Design ➪ Type ➪ Change Chart Type to display the Change Chart Type dialog box and experiment with other chart types. Figure 20.12 shows the Change Chart Type dialog box.

NOTE

If your chart uses more than one data series, make sure that a chart element other than a data series is selected when you choose the Chart Tools Design ➪ Type ➪ Change Chart Type command. If you select a series, the command changes the chart type of the selected series only.

In the Change Chart Type dialog box, the main categories are listed on the left, and the subtypes are shown as icons. Select an icon and click OK, and Excel displays the chart using the new chart type. If you don't like the result, click the Undo button.

TIP

If the chart is an embedded chart, you can also change a chart's type by using the icons in the Insert ➪ Charts group. In fact, this method is more efficient because it doesn't involve a dialog box.

Applying a chart layout

Each chart type has a number of prebuilt layouts that you can apply with a single mouse click. A layout contains additional chart elements, such as a title, data labels, axes, and so on. This step is optional, but one of the prebuilt designs might be just what you need. Even if the layout isn't exactly what you want, it may be close enough that you need to make only a few adjustments.

To apply a layout, select the chart and use the Chart Tools Design ➪ Chart Layouts ➪ Quick Layout gallery. Figure 20.13 shows how a column chart would look using various layouts.

Applying a chart style

The Chart Tools Design ➪ Chart Styles gallery contains quite a few styles that you can apply to your chart. The styles consist of various color choices and some special effects. Again, this step is optional.

TIP

The styles displayed in the gallery depend on the workbook's theme. When you choose Page Layout ➪ Themes to apply a different theme, you'll see a new selection of chart styles designed for the selected theme.

FIGURE 20.12

The Change Chart Type dialog box

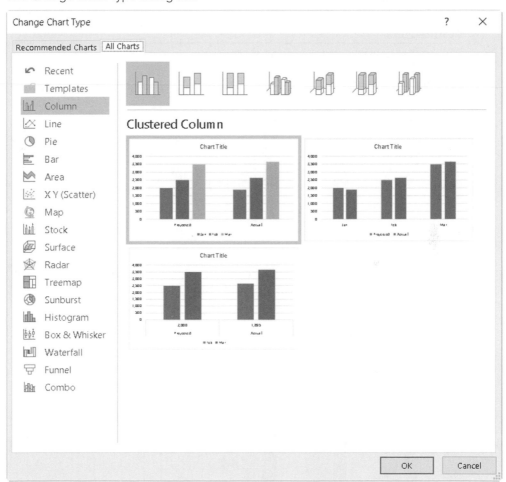

Adding and deleting chart elements

In some cases, applying a chart layout or chart style (as described previously) gives you a chart with all of the elements that you need. Most of the time, however, you'll need to add or remove some chart elements and fine-tune the layout. You do this using the controls on the Chart Tools ⇨Design and Chart Tools ⇨ Format tabs.

For example, to give a chart a title, choose Chart Tools ⇨ Design Add Chart Element ⇨ Chart Title. The control displays some options that determine where the title is placed.

20

Excel inserts a title with the text "Chart Title." Click the text and replace it with your actual chart title.

FIGURE 20.13

One-click design variations of a column chart

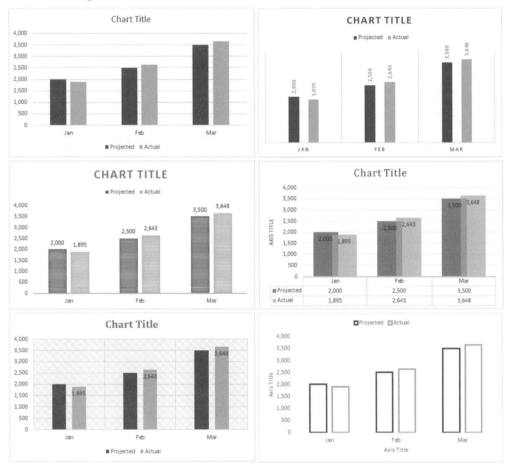

Formatting chart elements

Every element in a chart can be formatted and customized in many ways. Many users are content with charts that are created using the steps described earlier in this chapter. Because you're reading this book, however, you probably want to find out how to customize charts for maximum impact.

 Chapter 21 provides a detailed look into formatting and customizing charts.

Excel provides two ways to format and customize individual chart elements. Each of the following methods require that you select the chart element first:

- Use the Ribbon controls on the Chart Tools Format tab.
- Press Ctrl+1 to display the Format task pane that's specific to the selected chart element.

You can also double-click a chart element to display the Format task pane for the element.

For example, assume that you'd like to change the color of the columns for one of the series in the chart. Click any column in the series (which selects the entire series). Then choose Chart Tools Format ⇨ Shape Styles ⇨ Shape Fill, and choose a color from the displayed list.

To change the properties of the outline around the columns, use the Chart Tools Format ⇨ Shape Styles ⇨ Shape Outline control.

To change the effects used in the columns (for example, to add a shadow), use the Chart Tools Format ⇨ Shape Styles ⇨ Shape Effects control.

Alternatively, you can select a series in the chart, press Ctrl+1, and use the Format Data Series task pane, as shown in Figure 20.14. Note that this is a tabbed pane. Click a tab or icon along the top and then expand a section on the left side to view additional controls. It's also a docked pane, so you can click another element in the chart. In other words, you don't have to close the task pane to see the changes you specify.

FIGURE 20.14

Using the Format Data Series task pane

Modifying and Customizing Charts

The sections that follow cover common chart modifications.

> **NOTE**
>
> Before you can modify a chart, you must activate it. To activate an embedded chart, click it. Doing so activates the chart and also selects the element that you click. To activate a chart on a chart sheet, just click its sheet tab.

Moving and resizing a chart

If your chart is an embedded chart, you can freely move and resize it with your mouse. Click the chart's border and then drag the border to move the chart. Drag any of the eight "handles" to resize the chart. The handles consist of white circles that appear on the chart's corners and edges when you click the chart's border. When the mouse pointer turns into a double arrow, click and drag to resize the chart.

When a chart is selected, you can use the Chart Tools Format ➪ Size controls to adjust the height and width of the chart. Use the spinners, or type the dimensions directly into the Height and Width controls. Oddly, Excel does not provide similar controls to specify the top and left positions of the chart.

To move an embedded chart, just click its border at any location except one of the eight resizing handles. Then drag the chart to its new location. You also can use standard cut-and-paste techniques to move an embedded chart. Select the chart and choose Home ➪ Clipboard ➪ Cut (or press Ctrl+X). Then activate a cell near the desired location and choose Home ➪ Clipboard ➪ Paste (or press Ctrl+V). The new location can be in a different worksheet or even in a different workbook. If you paste the chart to a different workbook, it will be linked to the data in the original workbook. Another way to move a chart to a different location is to choose Chart Tools Design ➪ Location ➪ Move Chart. This command displays the Move Chart dialog box, which lets you specify a new sheet for the chart (either a chart sheet or a worksheet).

Converting an embedded chart to a chart sheet

When you create a chart using the icons in the Insert ➪ Charts group, the result is always an embedded chart. If you'd prefer that your chart be located on a chart sheet, you can easily move it.

To convert an embedded chart to a chart on a chart sheet, select the chart and choose Chart Tools Design ➪ Location ➪ Move Chart to display the Move Chart dialog box shown in Figure 20.15. Select the New Sheet option and (optionally) provide a different name for the chart sheet.

To convert a chart on a chart sheet to an embedded chart, activate the chart sheet and then choose Chart Tools Design ➪ Location ➪ Move Chart to display the Move Chart dialog box. Select the Object In option and specify the sheet by using the drop-down control.

FIGURE 20.15

Use the Move Chart dialog box to move an embedded chart to a chart sheet (or vice versa).

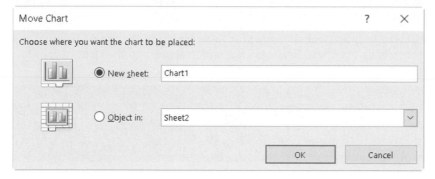

Copying a chart

To make an exact copy of an embedded chart, select the chart and choose Home ➪ Clipboard ➪ Copy (or press Ctrl+C). Then activate a cell near the desired location and choose Home ➪ Clipboard ➪ Paste (or press Ctrl+V). The new location can be in a different worksheet or even in a different workbook. If you paste the chart to a different workbook, it will be linked to the data in the original workbook.

To copy a chart on a chart sheet, press Ctrl while you drag the sheet tab to a new location in the tab list.

Deleting a chart

To delete an embedded chart, simply click the chart and then press Delete. When the Ctrl key is pressed, you can select multiple charts and then delete them all with a single press of the Delete key.

To delete a chart sheet, right-click its sheet tab and choose Delete from the shortcut menu. To delete multiple chart sheets, select them by pressing Ctrl while you click the sheet tabs.

Adding chart elements

To add new elements to a chart (such as a title, legend, data labels, or gridlines), activate the chart and use the controls in the Chart Elements + icon, which appears to the right of the chart. Note that each item expands to display additional options.

You can also use the Add Chart Element control on the Chart Tools Design tab, in the Chart Layouts group.

20

Moving and deleting chart elements

Some elements within a chart can be moved: titles, legend, and data labels. To move a chart element, simply click it to select it and then drag its border.

The easiest way to delete a chart element is to select it and then press Delete. You can also use the controls on the Chart Elements icon, which appears to the right of the chart, to reposition chart elements.

> **NOTE**
>
> A few chart elements consist of multiple objects. For example, the data labels element consists of one label for each data point. To move or delete one data label, click once to select the entire element and then click a second time to select the specific data label. You can then move or delete the single data label.

Formatting chart elements

Many users are content to stick with the predefined chart styles and layouts. For more precise customizations, Excel allows you to work with individual chart elements and apply additional formatting. You can use the Ribbon commands for some modifications, but the easiest way to format chart elements is to right-click the element and choose Format *<Element>* from the shortcut menu. The exact command depends on the element that you select. For example, if you right-click the chart's title, the shortcut menu command is Format Chart Title.

The Format command displays a task pane with options for the selected element. Changes that you make are displayed immediately in the chart. When you select a new chart element, the task pane changes to display the properties for the newly selected element. You can keep this task pane displayed while you work on the chart. It can be docked alongside the left or right part of the window or made free-floating and sizable.

> **TIP**
>
> If the Format task pane isn't displayed, you can double-click a chart element to display it.

Refer to the "Exploring the Format Task Pane" sidebar for an explanation of how the Format task panes work.

> **TIP**
>
> If you apply formatting to a chart element and decide that it wasn't such a good idea, you can revert to the original formatting for the particular chart style. Right-click the chart element and choose Reset to Match Style from the shortcut menu. To reset the entire chart, select the chart area when you issue the command.

Exploring the Format Task Pane

The Format task pane can be a bit deceiving. It contains many options that aren't visible, and you sometimes have to do quite a bit of clicking to find the formatting option you want.

The name of a given Format task pane depends on which chart element is selected. For instance, Figure 20.14 shows the task pane for a data series. The options available on the Format task pane will vary quite a bit, depending on which chart element you selected.

Regardless of the element that you select, however, the Format task pane will present you with icons at the top. Each icon has its own set of controls, which can be expanded to expose a set of formatting and customization options.

At first, the Format task pane will seem complicated and confusing. But as you get better acquainted with it, using the task pane gets much easier.

 You will dive deep into customizing and formatting charts in Chapter 21.

Copying a chart's formatting

If you create a nicely formatted chart and realize that you need to create several more charts that have the same formatting, you have these three choices:

- **Make a copy of the original chart and then change the data used in the copied chart.** One way to change the data used in a chart is to choose the Chart Tools Design ⇨ Data ⇨ Select Data command and make the changes in the Select Data Source dialog box.

- **Create the other charts, but don't apply any formatting.** Then activate the original chart and press Ctrl+C. Select one of the other charts, and choose Home ⇨ Clipboard ⇨ Paste ⇨ Paste Special. In the Paste Special dialog box, click the Formats option and then click OK. Repeat for each additional chart.

- **Create a chart template and then use the template as the basis for the new charts, or you can apply the new template to existing charts.** See Chapter 21 for more information about chart templates.

Renaming a chart

When you activate an embedded chart, its name appears in the Name box (located to the left of the Formula bar). To change the name of an embedded chart, simply select the chart and then enter the desired name in the Name box.

20

Why rename a chart? If a worksheet has many charts, you may prefer to activate a particular chart by name. Just type the chart's name in the Name box and press Enter. It's much easier to remember a chart named Monthly Sales as opposed to a chart named Chart 9.

NOTE

When you rename a chart, Excel allows you to use a name that already exists for another chart. Normally, it doesn't matter if multiple charts have the same name, but it can cause problems if you use VBA macros that select a chart by name.

Printing charts

Printing embedded charts is nothing special; you print them the same way that you print a worksheet. As long as you include the embedded chart in the range that you want to print, Excel prints the chart as it appears on-screen. When printing a sheet that contains embedded charts, it's a good idea to preview first (or use Page Layout view) to ensure that your charts don't span multiple pages. If you created the chart on a chart sheet, Excel always prints the chart on a page by itself.

TIP

If you select an embedded chart and choose File ➪ Print, Excel prints the chart on a page by itself and does *not* print the worksheet data.

If you don't want a particular embedded chart to appear on your printout, access the Format Chart Area task pane and select the Size & Properties icon. Then expand the Properties section and clear the Print Object check box.

Understanding Chart Types

People who create charts usually do so to make a point or to communicate a specific message. Often, the message is explicitly stated in the chart's title or in a text box within the chart. The chart itself provides visual support.

Choosing the correct chart type is often a key factor in the effectiveness of the message. Therefore, it's often well worth your time to experiment with various chart types to determine which one conveys your message best.

In almost every case, the underlying message in a chart is some type of comparison. Examples of some general types of comparisons include the following:

- **Comparing an item to other items:** A chart may compare sales in each of a company's sales regions.
- **Comparing data over time:** A chart may display sales by month and indicate trends over time.

- **Making relative comparisons:** A common pie chart can depict relative proportions in terms of pie "slices."
- **Comparing data relationships:** An XY chart is ideal for this comparison. For example, you might show the relationship between monthly marketing expenditures and sales.
- **Comparing frequency:** You can use a common histogram, for example, to display the number (or percentage) of students who scored within a particular grade range.
- **Identifying outliers or unusual situations:** If you have thousands of data points, creating a chart may help identify data that isn't representative.

Choosing a chart type

A common question among Excel users is "How do I know which chart type to use for my data?" Unfortunately, this question has no cut-and-dried answer. Perhaps the best answer is a vague one: use the chart type that gets your message across in the simplest way. A good starting point is Excel's recommended charts. Select your data and choose Insert ⇨ Charts ⇨ Recommended Charts to see the chart types that Excel suggests. Remember that these suggestions are not always the best choices.

> **NOTE**
>
> In the Ribbon, the Charts group of the Insert tab shows the Recommended Charts button, plus nine other drop-down buttons. All of these drop-down buttons display multiple chart types. For example, column and bar charts are all available from a single drop-down button. Similarly, scatter charts and bubble charts share a single button. Probably the easiest way to choose a particular chart type is to select Insert ⇨ Charts ⇨ Recommended Charts, which displays the Insert Chart dialog box with the Recommended Charts tab displayed. Select the All Charts tab, and you'll have a concise list of all chart and subchart types.

Figure 20.16 shows the same set of data plotted by using six different chart types. Although all six charts represent the same information (monthly website visitors), they look quite different from one another.

The column chart (upper left) is probably the best choice for this particular set of data because it clearly shows the information for each month in discrete units. The bar chart (upper right) is similar to a column chart, but the axes are swapped. Most people are more accustomed to seeing time-based information extend from left to right rather than from top to bottom, so this isn't the optimal choice.

The line chart (middle left) may not be the best choice because it can imply that the data is continuous—that points exist in between the 12 actual data points. This same argument may be made against using an area chart (middle right).

The pie chart (lower left) is simply too confusing and does nothing to convey the time-based nature of the data. Pie charts are most appropriate for a data series in which you want to emphasize proportions among a relatively small number of data points. If you have too many data points, a pie chart can be impossible to interpret.

20

FIGURE 20.16

The same data, plotted by using six chart types

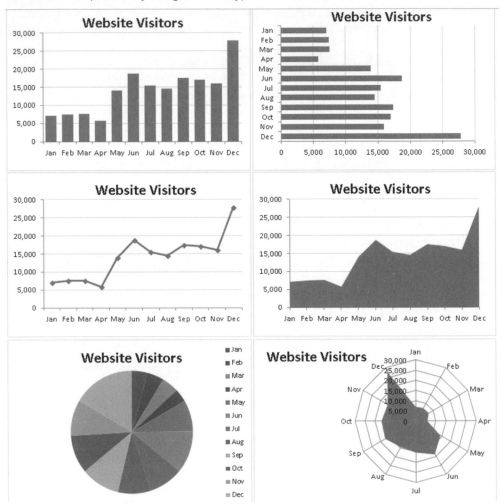

The radar chart (lower right) is clearly inappropriate for this data. People aren't accustomed to viewing time-based information in a circular direction!

Fortunately, changing a chart's type is easy, so you can experiment with various chart types until you find the one that represents your data accurately, clearly, and as simply as possible.

The remainder of this chapter contains more information about the various Excel chart types. The examples and discussion may give you a better handle on determining the most appropriate chart type for your data.

Column charts

Probably the most common chart type is the *column chart*, which displays each data point as a vertical column, the height of which corresponds to the value. The value scale is displayed on the vertical axis, which is usually on the left side of the chart. You can specify any number of data series, and the corresponding data points from each series can be stacked on top of each other. Typically, each data series is depicted in a different color or pattern.

Column charts are often used to compare discrete items, and they can depict the differences between items in a series or items across multiple series. Excel offers seven column-chart subtypes.

Figure 20.17 shows an example of a clustered column chart that depicts monthly sales for two products. From this chart, it's clear that Sprocket sales have always exceeded Widget sales. In addition, Widget sales have been declining over the five-month period, whereas Sprocket sales are increasing.

The same data, in the form of a stacked column chart, is shown in Figure 20.18. This chart has the added advantage of depicting the combined sales over time. It shows that total sales have remained fairly steady each month, but the relative proportions of the two products have changed.

FIGURE 20.17

This clustered column chart compares monthly sales for two products.

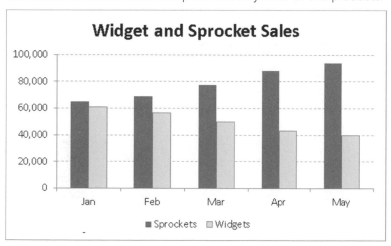

20

FIGURE 20.18

This stacked column chart displays sales by product and depicts the total sales.

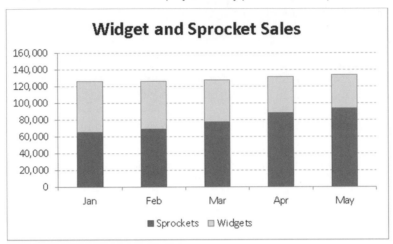

Figure 20.19 shows the same sales data plotted as a 100% stacked column chart. This chart type shows the relative contribution of each product by month. Notice that the vertical axis displays percentage values, not sales amounts. This chart provides no information about the actual sales volumes, but such information could be provided using data labels. This type of chart is often a good alternative to using several pie charts. Instead of using a pie to show the relative sales volume in each year, the chart uses a column for each year.

FIGURE 20.19

This 100% stacked column chart displays monthly sales as a percentage.

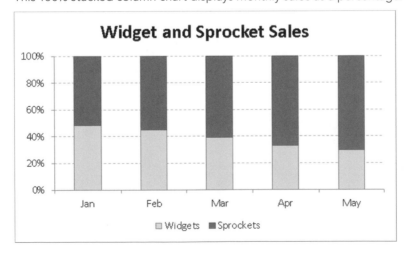

Figure 20.20 shows the same data plotted with a 3-D clustered column chart (on the left). The name is a bit deceptive because the chart uses only two dimensions, not three. Many people use this type of chart because it has more visual pizzazz.

FIGURE 20.20

3-D column charts.

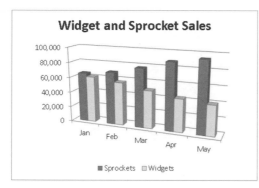 

Compare this chart with the chart on the right. This is a "true" 3-D column chart (which has a second category axis). This type of chart may be appealing visually, but precise comparisons are difficult because of the distorted perspective view.

Bar charts

A *bar chart* is essentially a column chart that has been rotated 90 degrees clockwise. One distinct advantage to using a bar chart is that the category labels may be easier to read. Figure 20.21 shows a bar chart that displays a value for each of ten survey items. The category labels are lengthy, and displaying them legibly with a column chart would be difficult. Excel offers six bar chart subtypes.

> **NOTE**
>
> Unlike a column chart, no subtype displays multiple series along a third axis. (That is, Excel does not provide a 3-D Bar Chart subtype.) You can add a 3-D look to a bar chart, but it will be limited to two axes.

You can include any number of data series in a bar chart. In addition, the bars can be "stacked" from left to right.

Line charts

Line charts are often used to plot continuous data and are useful for identifying trends. For example, plotting daily sales as a line chart may enable you to identify sales fluctuations over time. Normally, the category axis for a line chart displays equal intervals. Excel supports seven line chart subtypes.

20

See Figure 20.22 for an example of a line chart that depicts monthly data (676 data points). Although the data varies quite a bit on a monthly basis, the chart clearly depicts the cycles.

FIGURE 20.21

If you have lengthy category labels, a bar chart may be a good choice.

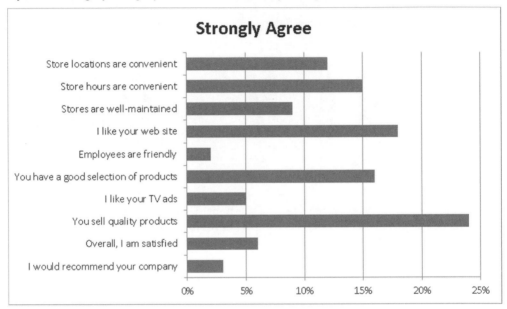

A line chart can use any number of data series, and you distinguish the lines by using different colors, line styles, or markers. Figure 20.23 shows a line chart that has three series. The series are distinguished by markers (circles, squares, and triangles) and different line colors. When the chart is printed on a noncolor printer, the markers are the only way to identify the lines.

The final line chart example, shown in Figure 20.24, is a 3-D line chart. Although it has a nice visual appeal, it's certainly not the clearest way to present the data. In fact, it's fairly worthless.

FIGURE 20.22

A line chart often can help you spot trends in your data.

Pie charts

A *pie chart* is useful when you want to show relative proportions or contributions to a whole. A pie chart uses only one data series. Pie charts are most effective with a small number of data points. Generally, a pie chart should use no more than five or six data points (or slices). A pie chart with too many data points can be difficult to interpret.

CAUTION

All of the values in a pie chart must be positive numbers. If you create a pie chart that uses one or more negative values, the negative values will be converted to positive values, which is probably not what you intended.

20

FIGURE 20.23

This line chart displays three series.

FIGURE 20.24

This 3-D line chart does not present the data very well.

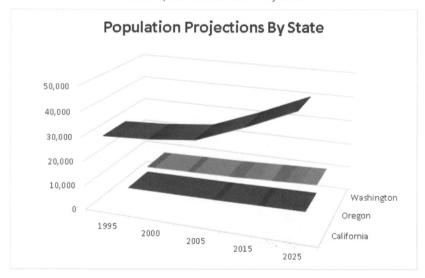

You can "explode" one or more slices of a pie chart for emphasis (see Figure 20.25). Activate the chart and click any pie slice to select the entire pie. Then click the slice that you want to explode and drag it away from the center.

FIGURE 20.25

A pie chart with one slice exploded

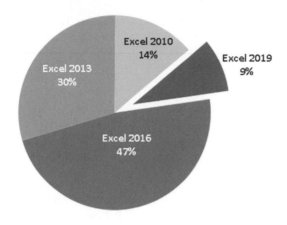

Excel Usage At XYZ Corporation

The "pie of pie" and "bar of pie" chart subtypes enable you to display a secondary chart that provides more detail for one of the pie slices. Figure 20.26 shows an example of a bar of pie chart. The pie chart shows the breakdown of four expense categories: Rent, Supplies, Utilities, and Salary. The secondary bar chart provides an additional regional breakdown of the Salary category.

FIGURE 20.26

A bar of pie chart that shows detail for one of the pie slices

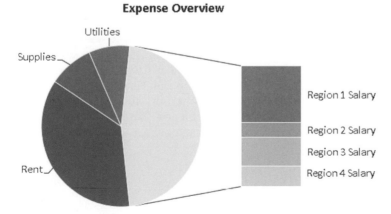

20

The data used in the chart resides in A2:B8. When the chart was created, Excel made a guess as to which categories belong to the secondary chart. In this case, the guess was to use the last three data points for the secondary chart—and the guess was incorrect.

To correct the chart, right-click any of the pie slices and choose Format Data Series. In the Format Data Series task pane, select the Series Options icon and make the changes. In this example, we chose Split Series by Position and specified that the second plot contains four values in the series.

Another pie chart subtype is called a *doughnut chart*. It's basically a pie chart with a hole in the middle. Unlike a pie chart, however, a doughnut chart can display multiple series.

XY (scatter) charts

Another common chart type is an *XY chart* (also known as scatter grams or scatter plots). An XY chart differs from most other chart types in that both axes display values. (An XY chart has no category axis.)

This type of chart often is used to show the relationship between two variables. Figure 20.27 shows an example of an XY chart that plots the relationship between sales calls made (horizontal axis) and sales (vertical axis). Each point in the chart represents one month. The chart shows that these two variables are positively related: months in which more calls were made typically had higher sales volumes.

> **NOTE**
> Although these data points correspond to time, the chart doesn't convey any time-related information. In other words, the data points are plotted based only on their two values.

Area charts

Think of an *area chart* as a line chart in which the area below the line has been colored in. Figure 20.28 shows an example of a stacked area chart. Stacking the data series enables you to see the total clearly, plus the contribution by each series.

Figure 20.29 shows the same data, plotted as a 3-D area chart. As you can see, it's not an example of an effective chart. The data for products B and C is partially obscured. In some cases, the problem can be resolved by rotating the chart or using transparency. But usually the best way to salvage a chart like this is to select a new chart type.

FIGURE 20.27

An XY chart shows the relationship between two variables.

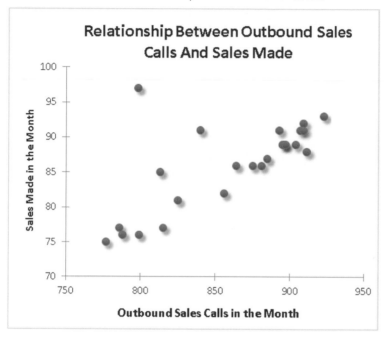

FIGURE 20.28

A stacked area chart

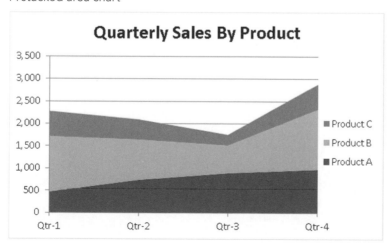

20

FIGURE 20.29

This 3-D area chart is not a good choice.

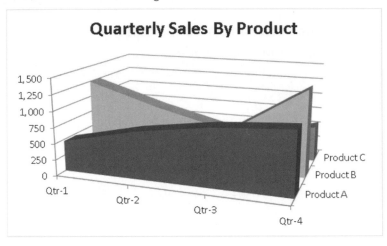

Radar charts

You may not be familiar with this type of chart. A *radar chart* is a specialized chart that has a separate axis for each category, and the axes extend outward from the center of the chart. The value of each data point is plotted on the corresponding axis.

Figure 20.30 shows an example of a radar chart on the left. This chart plots two data series across 12 categories (months) and shows the seasonal demand for snow skis versus water skis. Note that the water-ski series partially obscures the snow-ski series.

FIGURE 20.30

Plotting ski sales using a radar chart with 12 categories and two series

Using a radar chart to show seasonal sales may be an interesting approach, but it's certainly not the best chart type. As you can see, the stacked bar chart on the right shows the information much more clearly.

Surface charts

Surface charts display two or more data series on a surface. As Figure 20.31 shows, these charts can be quite interesting. Unlike other charts, Excel uses color to distinguish values, not to distinguish the data series. The number of colors used is determined by the major unit scale setting for the value axis. Each color corresponds to one major unit.

> **NOTE**
>
> A surface chart does not plot 3-D data points. The series axis for a surface chart, as with all other 3-D charts, is a category axis—not a value axis. In other words, if you have data that is represented by x, y, and z coordinates, it can't be plotted accurately on a surface chart unless the x and y values are equally spaced.

Bubble charts

Think of a *bubble chart* as an XY chart that can display an additional data series, which is represented by the size of the bubbles. As with an XY chart, both axes are value axes. (There is no category axis.)

Figure 20.32 shows an example of a bubble chart that depicts the results of a weight-loss program. The horizontal value axis represents the original weight, the vertical value axis shows the number of weeks in the program, and the size of the bubbles represents the amount of weight lost.

Stock charts

Stock charts are most useful for displaying stock-market information. These charts require three to five data series, depending on the subtype.

Figure 20.33 shows an example of each of the four stock chart types. The two charts on the bottom display the trade volume and use two value axes. The daily volume, represented by columns, uses the axis on the left. The *up-bars*, sometimes referred to as *candlesticks*, are the vertical lines that depict the difference between the opening and closing price. A black up-bar indicates that the closing price was lower than the opening price.

Stock charts aren't just for stock price data. Figure 20.34 shows a stock chart that depicts the high, low, and average temperatures for each day in May. This is a high-low-close chart.

20

FIGURE 20.31

A surface chart

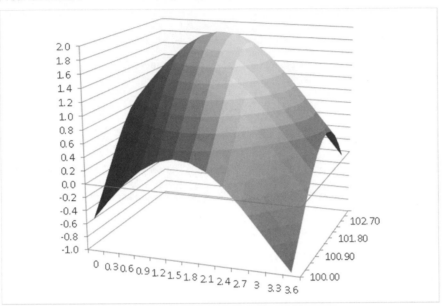

FIGURE 20.32

A bubble chart

Participant	Original Weight	Weeks in Program	Weight Loss
Ray	285	12	31
Pat	442	3	16
Jill	240	5	28
George	275	18	34
Kevin	290	2	4
Joe	380	18	15
Cindy	188	13	13
Terry	301	7	32

Weight Loss as a Function of Weeks in Program and Original Weight

FIGURE 20.33

The four stock chart subtypes

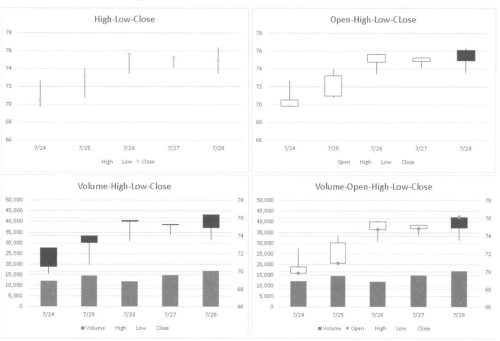

FIGURE 20.34

Plotting temperature data with a stock chart

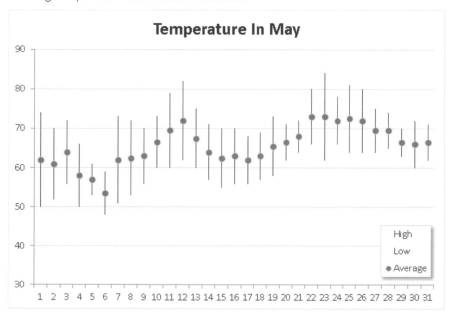

New Chart Types for Excel

Starting with Excel 2016, Microsoft started introducing new chart types to its collection of visualizations. This section presents an example of each new chart type, along with an explanation of the type of data required.

Histogram charts

Histogram charts were introduced with Excel 2016. A histogram displays the count of data items in each of several discrete bins. With a bit of effort, you can create a histogram by using a standard column chart or by using the Analysis ToolPak (see Chapter 33, "Analyzing Data with the Analysis ToolPak"). But using the new histogram chart type makes it easier.

Figure 20.35 shows a histogram created from 105 student test scores. The bins are displayed as category labels. You control the number of bins by using the Axis Options section of the Format Axis task pane. In this example, we specified eight bins, and Excel took care of all of the details.

FIGURE 20.35

Displaying a student grade distribution using a histogram chart

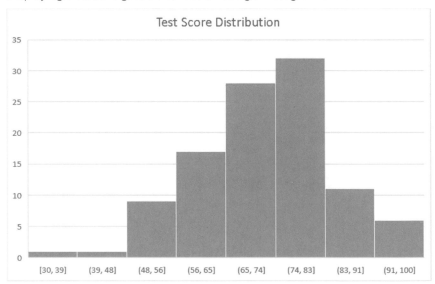

Pareto charts

The *Pareto chart* (introduced with Excel 2016) is a combination chart in which columns are displayed in descending order, and the columns use the left axis. The line shows the cumulative percentage and uses the right axis.

Figure 20.36 shows a Pareto chart created from the data in range A2:B14. Notice that Excel sorted the items in the chart. The line shows, for example, that approximately 50 percent of all complaints are in the top three categories.

FIGURE 20.36

A Pareto chart displays the number of complaints graphically.

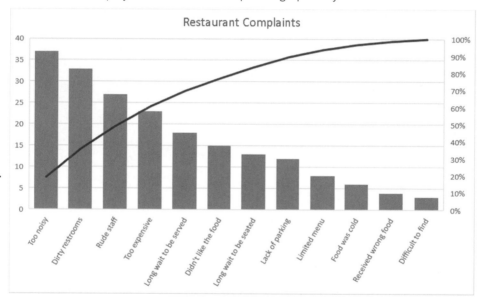

Waterfall charts

A *waterfall chart* is used to show the cumulative effect of a series of numbers, usually both positive and negative numbers. The result is a staircase-like display. Waterfall charts were introduced in Excel 2016.

Figure 20.37 shows a waterfall chart that uses the data in column D. Waterfall charts typically display the ending total as the last bar, with its origin at zero. To display the total column correctly, select the column, right-click, and choose Set as Total from the shortcut menu.

FIGURE 20.37

A waterfall chart showing positive and negative net cash flows

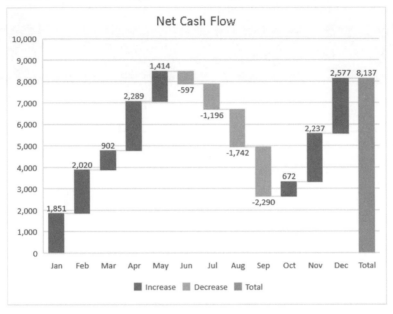

Box & whisker charts

A *box & whisker chart* (introduced as a chart type in Excel 2016) is often used to summarize data visually. In the past, it was possible to create such charts using Excel, but it required quite a bit of setup work. Now, it's simple.

Figure 20.38 shows a box & whisker chart created for four groups of subjects. The data is in a two-column table. In the chart, the vertical lines extending from the box represent the numerical range of the data (minimum and maximum values). The "boxes" represent the 25th through the 75th percentile. The horizontal line inside the box is the median value (or 50th percentile), and the X is the average. This type of chart enables the viewer to make quick comparisons among groups of data.

FIGURE 20.38

A box & whisker chart that summarizes data for four groups

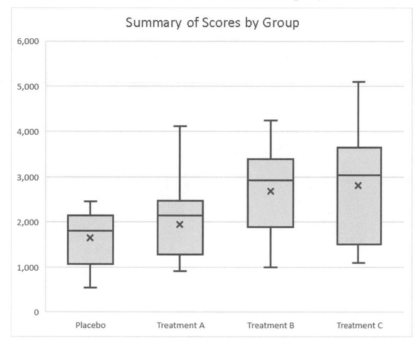

The Series Options section of the Format Data Series task pane contains some options for this chart type.

Sunburst charts

Sunburst charts were introduced with Excel 2016. A sunburst chart is like a pie chart with multiple concentric layers. This chart type is most useful for data that's organized hierarchically. Figure 20.39 shows an example of a sunburst chart that depicts a music collection. It shows the number of tracks by genre and subgenre. Note that some genres have no subgenres.

A sunburst chart that depicts a music collection by genre and subgenre

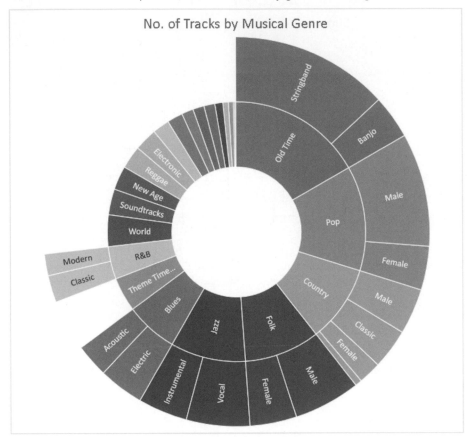

A potential problem with the chart type is that some slices are so small that the data labels can't be displayed.

Treemap charts

With the release of Excel 2016, *treemap charts* were included as a chart type. Like a sunburst chart, a treemap chart is suited for hierarchical data. The data, however, is represented as rectangles. Figure 20.40 shows the data from the previous example, plotted as a treemap chart.

Funnel charts

Funnel charts are new with Excel 2019. Funnel charts are ideal for representing the relative values in each stage of a process. These charts are typically used to visualize sales pipelines (see Figure 20.41).

FIGURE 20.40

A treemap chart that depicts a music collection by genre and subgenre

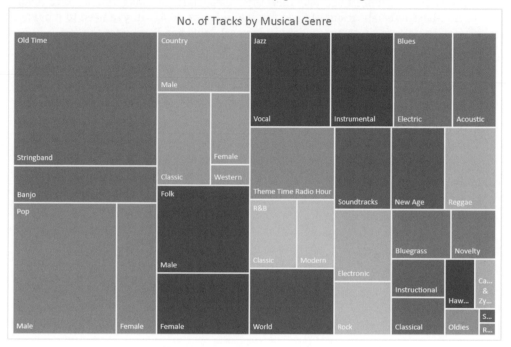

FIGURE 20.41

A Funnel chart visualizing the value in each stage of a sales pipeline

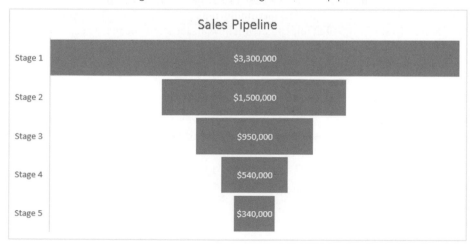

Map charts

Excel 2019 includes a new *map chart* type. Map charts leverage Bing maps to render location-based visualizations. As you can see in Figure 20.42, all you need to provide are location indicators (in this case, country names), and then Excel does the rest.

Map charts are remarkably flexible, allowing you create a chart based on province names, county names, cities, and even ZIP codes. As long as Bing can recognize the values that you are using to identify geography, your chart will render seamlessly.

FIGURE 20.42

Map charts are ideal for visualizing location-based data.

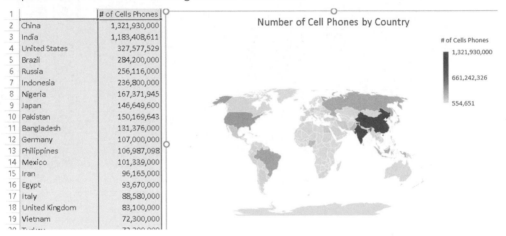

Double-clicking the map will active the Format Data Series task pane (see Figure 20.43), exposing a handful of unique formatting options. These options allow you to change the projection (flat or curved map), the area (show all locations or just those that have data), and the series color (apply color banding based on values).

FIGURE 20.43

Map charts come with unique customization options.

Using Advanced Charting Techniques

Excel makes creating a basic chart easy. Select your data, choose a chart type, and you're finished. You may take a few extra seconds and select one of the prebuilt chart styles and maybe even select one of the chart layouts. But if your goal is to create the most effective chart possible, you probably want to take advantage of the additional customization techniques available in Excel.

Customizing a chart involves changing its appearance, as well as possibly adding new elements to it. These changes can be purely cosmetic (such as changing colors, modifying line widths, or adding a shadow) or quite substantial (say, changing the axis scales or adding a second value axis). Chart elements that you might add include such features as a data table, a trend line, or error bars.

The preceding chapter introduced charting in Excel and described how to create basic charts. This chapter takes the topic to the next level. You learn how to customize your charts to the maximum so that they look exactly like you want. You also pick up some slick charting tricks that will make your charts even more impressive.

Selecting Chart Elements

Modifying a chart is similar to everything else you do in Excel: first you make a selection (in this case, select a chart element), and then you issue a command to do something with your selection.

You can select only one chart element (or one group of chart elements) at a time. For example, if you want to change the font for two axis labels, you must work on each set of axis labels separately.

Excel provides three ways, described in the following sections, to select a particular chart element:

- Mouse
- Keyboard
- Chart Elements control

Selecting with the mouse

To select a chart element with your mouse, just click the element. The chart element appears with small circles at the corners.

> **TIP**
>
> Some chart elements can be a bit tricky to select. To ensure that you select the chart element that you intended to select, view the Chart Elements control, located in the Chart Tools ⇨ Format ⇨ Current Selection group of the Ribbon (see Figure 21.1). Or, if the Format task pane is displayed, you can identify the selected chart element by the title of the task pane. Press Ctrl+1 to display the Format task pane.

FIGURE 21.1

The Chart Elements control (in the upper-left corner) displays the name of the selected chart element. In this example, the "chart title" is selected.

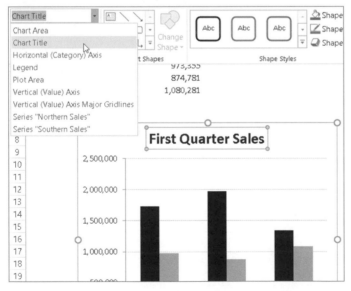

When you move the mouse over a chart, a small *chart tip* displays the name of the chart element under the mouse pointer. When the mouse pointer is over a data point, the chart tip also displays the value of the data point.

> **TIP**
>
> If you find these chart tips annoying, you can turn them off. Choose File ⇨ Options, and select the Advanced tab in the Excel Options dialog box. Locate the Chart section, and clear either or both the Show Chart Element Names on Hover or the Show Data Point Values on Hover check boxes.

Some chart elements (such as a series, a legend, and data labels) consist of multiple items. For example, a chart series element is made up of individual data points. To select a particular data point, click twice: first click the series to select it, and then click the specific element within the series (for example, a column or a line chart marker). Selecting the element enables you to apply formatting to only a particular data point in a series.

You may find that some chart elements are difficult to select with the mouse. If you rely on the mouse for selecting a chart element, you may have to click it several times before the desired element is actually selected. Fortunately, Excel provides other ways to select a chart element, and it's worth your while to be familiar with them. Keep reading to see how.

Selecting with the keyboard

When a chart is active, you can use the up-arrow and down-arrow navigation keys on your keyboard to cycle among the chart's elements. Again, keep your eye on the Chart Elements control to ensure that the selected chart element is what you think it is.

- **When a chart series is selected:** Use the left-arrow and right-arrow keys to select an individual item within the series.
- **When a set of data labels is selected:** You can select a specific data label by using the left-arrow or right-arrow key.
- **When a legend is selected:** Select individual elements within the legend by using the left-arrow or right-arrow key.

Selecting with the Chart Elements control

The Chart Elements control is located in the Chart Tools ⇨ Format ⇨ Current Selection group. This control displays the name of the currently selected chart element. It's a dropdown control, and you can use it to select a particular element in the active chart.

The Chart Elements control also appears in the Mini toolbar, which is displayed when you right-click a chart element (see Figure 21.2).

FIGURE 21.2

Using the Chart Elements control in the Mini toolbar

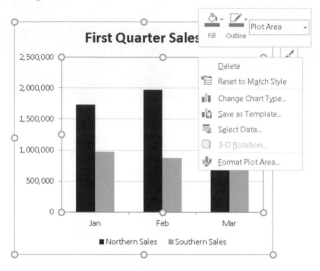

The Chart Elements control enables you to select only the top-level elements in the chart. To select an individual data point within a series, for example, you need to select the series and then use the navigation keys (or your mouse) to select the desired data point.

> **NOTE**
>
> When a single data point is selected, the Chart Elements control *will* display the name of the selected element even though it's not actually available for selection from the drop-down list.

> **TIP**
>
> If you do a lot of work with charts, you may want to add the Chart Elements control to your Quick Access toolbar. That way, it will always be visible regardless of which Ribbon tab is showing. To add the control to your Quick Access toolbar, right-click the down arrow in the Chart Elements control in the Ribbon and choose Add to Quick Access Toolbar.

Exploring the User Interface Choices for Modifying Chart Elements

You have four main ways of working with chart elements: the Format task pane, the icons that display to the right of the chart, the Ribbon, and the Mini toolbar.

Using the Format task pane

When a chart element is selected, use the element's Format task pane to format or set options for the element. Each chart element has a unique Format task pane that contains controls specific to the element (although many Format task panes have controls in common). To access the Format task pane, use any of these methods:

- Double-click the chart element.
- Right-click the chart element and then choose Format *xxxx* from the shortcut menu (where *xxxx* is the name of the element).
- Select a chart element and then choose Chart Tools ➪ Format ➪ Current Selection ➪ Format Selection.
- Select a chart element and press Ctrl+1.

Any of these actions displays the Format task pane from which you can make many changes to the selected chart element. For example, Figure 21.3 shows the task pane that appears when a chart's value axis is selected. The task pane is free-floating, not docked. Note that a scrollbar is displayed, which means that all of the options can't fit in the vertical space for the task pane.

FIGURE 21.3

Use the Format task pane to set the properties of a selected chart element—in this case, the chart's value axis.

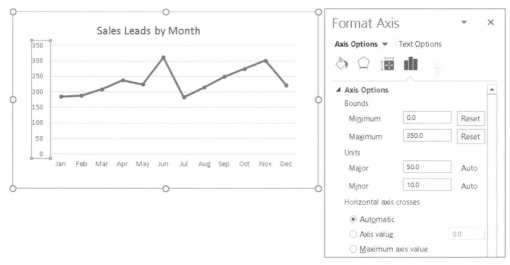

> **TIP**
>
> Normally, the Format task pane is docked on the right side of the window. But you can click the title and drag it anywhere that you like and resize it. To redock the task pane, maximize the Excel window, and then drag the task pane to the right side of the window. If you select a different chart element, the Format task pane changes to display the options appropriate for the new element.

Using the chart customization buttons

When a chart is selected, three buttons appear to the right of the chart (see Figure 21.4). These buttons, when clicked, expand to show various options. The icons are as follows:

Chart Elements   Use these tools to hide or display specific elements in the chart. Note that each item can be expanded to show additional options. To expand an item in the Chart Elements list, hover your mouse over the item and click the arrow that appears.

Chart Styles   Use this icon to select from prebuilt chart styles or change the color scheme of the chart.

Chart Filters   Use this icon to hide or display data series and specific points in a data series or hide and display categories. Some chart types do not display the Chart Filters button.

FIGURE 21.4

Chart customization buttons

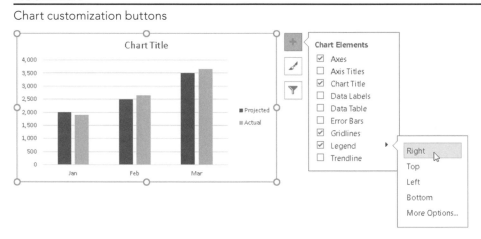

Using the Ribbon

The controls in the Chart Tools ➪ Format tab are used to change the appearance of the selected chart element. Although the commands found on the Ribbon do *not* comprise a comprehensive set of tools for chart elements, you can modify the Shape Fill, Shape Outline, and Shape Effects settings for most elements in a chart.

Here are a few formatting actions that you can take right from the Ribbon (after you have selected your chart element):

Change the Fill Color: Choose Chart Tools ➪ Format ➪ Shape Styles ➪ Shape Fill, and select a color.

Change the Border or Outline Color: Choose Chart Tools ➪ Format ➪ Shape Styles ➪ Shape Outline, and select a color.

Change the width and style of lines: Choose Chart Tools ➪ Format ➪ Shape Styles ➪ Shape Effects, and add one or more effects.

Change font color: Choose Home ➪ Font ➪ Font Color

Using the Mini toolbar

When you right-click an element in a chart, Excel displays a shortcut menu and the Mini toolbar. The Mini toolbar contains icons (Style, Fill, Outline) that, when clicked, display formatting options. For some chart elements, the Style icon isn't relevant, so the Mini toolbar displays the Chart Elements control (which you can use to select another chart element).

Modifying the Chart Area

The *Chart Area* is an object that contains all other elements in the chart. You can think of it as a chart's master background or container.

The only modifications that you can make to the Chart Area are cosmetic. You can change its fill color, outline, or effects such as shadows and soft edges.

> **NOTE**
>
> If you set the Chart Area of an embedded chart to use No Fill, the chart becomes transparent and the underlying cells are visible. Figure 21.5 shows a chart that uses No Fill and No Outline in its Chart Area. The Plot Area, Legend, and Chart Title *do* use a fill color. Adding a shadow to these other elements makes them appear to be floating above the worksheet.

The Chart Area element also controls all of the fonts used in the chart. For example, if you want to change every font in the chart, you don't need to format each text element separately. Just select the Chart Area and then make the change from the options of the Home ➪ Font group or the Format Chart Area task pane.

FIGURE 21.5

The Chart Area element uses No Fill, so the underlying cells are visible.

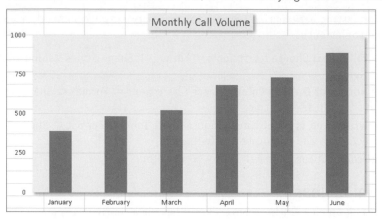

Resetting Chart Element Formatting

If you go overboard formatting a chart element, you can always reset it to its original state. Just select the element and choose Chart Tools ➪ Format ➪ Current Selection ➪ Reset to Match Style. Or right-click the chart element and choose Reset to Match Style from the shortcut menu.

To reset all formatting changes in the entire chart, select the Chart Area before you issue the Reset to Match Style command.

Modifying the Plot Area

The *Plot Area* is the part of the chart that contains the actual chart. More specifically, the Plot Area is a container for the chart series.

TIP

If you set the Shape Fill property to No Fill, the Plot Area will be transparent. Therefore, the fill color applied to the Chart Area will show through.

You can move and resize the Plot Area. Select the Plot Area and then drag a border to move it. To change the size of the Plot Area, drag one of the corner handles.

Different chart types vary in the way that they respond to changes in the Plot Area dimensions. For example, you can't change the relative dimensions of the Plot Area of a pie chart or a radar chart. The Plot Area of these charts is always square. With other chart types, though, you can change the aspect ratio of the Plot Area by changing either the height or the width.

Figure 21.6 shows a chart in which the Plot Area was resized to make room for an inserted shape that contains text.

FIGURE 21.6

Reducing the size of the Plot Area makes room for the shape.

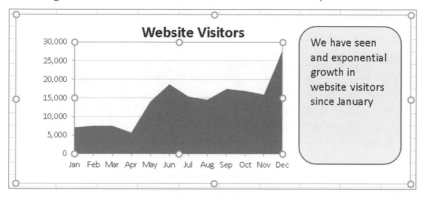

In some cases, the size of the Plot Area changes automatically when you adjust other elements of your chart. For example, if you add a legend to a chart, the size of the Plot Area may be reduced to accommodate the legend.

TIP

Changing the size and position of the Plot Area can have a dramatic effect on the overall look of your chart. When you're fine-tuning a chart, you'll probably want to experiment with various sizes and positions for the Plot Area.

Working with Titles in a Chart

A chart can have several different types of titles:

- Chart title
- Category axis title
- Value axis title
- Secondary category axis title
- Secondary value axis title
- Depth axis title (for true 3-D charts)

The number of titles that you can use depends on the chart type. For example, a pie chart supports only a chart title because it has no axes.

The easiest way to add a chart title is to use the Chart Elements button (the plus sign), which appears to the right of the chart. Activate the chart, click the Chart Elements button, and enable the Chart Title item. To specify a location, move the mouse over the Chart Title item and click the arrow. You can then specify the location for the Chart Title. Click More Options to display the Format Chart Title task pane.

The same basic procedure applies to axis titles. You have additional options to specify which axis titles you want.

After you add a title, you can replace the default text and drag the title to a different position. However, you can't change the size of a title by dragging its borders. The only way to change the size of a title is to change the font size.

> **TIP**
>
> The chart title or any of the axis titles can also use a cell reference. For example, you can create a link so the chart always displays the text contained in cell A1 as its title. To create a link, select the title, type an equal sign (=), point to the cell, and press Enter. After you create the link, the Formula bar displays the cell reference when you select the title.

Adding Free-Floating Text to a Chart

Text in a chart is not limited to titles. In fact, you can add free-floating text anywhere you want. To do so, activate the chart and choose Insert ➪ Text ➪ Text Box. Click in the chart to create the text box and enter the text. You can resize the text box, move it, change its formatting, and so on. You can also add a shape to the chart and then add text to the shape (if the shape is one that accepts text). Refer to Figure 21.6 for an example of an inserted shape with text.

Working with a Legend

A chart's *legend* consists of text and keys that identify the data series in the chart. A *key* is a small graphic that corresponds to the chart's series (one key for each series).

To add a legend to your chart, activate the chart and click the Chart Elements icon to the right of the chart. Place a check mark next to Legend. To specify a location for the legend, click the arrow next to the Legend item and choose a location (Right, Top, Left, or Bottom). After you add a legend, you can drag it to move it anywhere you like.

The quickest way to remove a legend is to select it and then press Delete.

You can select individual items within a legend and format them separately. For example, you may want to make the text bold to draw attention to a particular data series. To select an element in the legend, first select the legend and then click the desired element.

If you didn't include legend text when you originally selected the cells to create the chart, Excel displays Series 1, Series 2, and so on, in the legend. To add series names, choose Chart Tools ⇨ Design ⇨ Data ⇨ Select Data to display the Select Data Source dialog box (see Figure 21.7). Select the series name, and click the Edit button. In the Edit Series dialog box, type the series name or enter a cell reference that contains the series name. Repeat for each series that needs to be named.

FIGURE 21.7

Use the Select Data Source dialog box to change the name of a data series.

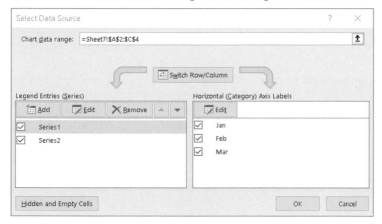

In some cases, you may prefer to omit the legend and use callouts to identify the data series. Figure 21.8 shows a chart with no legend. Instead, it uses shapes to identify each series. These shapes are from the Callouts section of the Chart Tools ⇨ Format ⇨ Insert Shapes gallery.

FIGURE 21.8

Using shapes as callouts in lieu of a legend

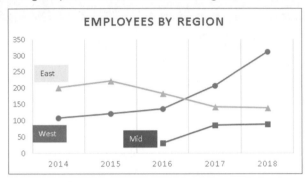

Copying Chart Formatting

You created a killer chart and spent hours customizing it. Now you need to create another one just like it but with a different set of data. What are your options? You have several choices:

Copy the formatting   Create your new chart with the default formatting. Then select your original chart and choose Home ⇨ Clipboard ⇨ Copy (or press Ctrl+C). Click your new chart and choose Home ⇨ Clipboard ⇨ Paste ⇨ Paste Special. In the Paste Special dialog box, select the Formats option.

Copy the chart and change the data sources   Press Ctrl while you click the original chart and drag. This creates an exact copy of your chart. Then choose Chart Tools ⇨ Design ⇨ Data ⇨ Select Data. In the Select Data Source dialog box, specify the data for the new chart in the Chart Data Range field.

Create a chart template   Select your chart, right-click the Chart Area, and choose Save as Template from the shortcut menu. Excel prompts you for a name. When you create your next chart, use this template as the chart type. For more information about using chart templates, see "Creating Chart Templates" later in this chapter.

Working with Gridlines

Gridlines can help the viewer determine what the chart series represents numerically. Gridlines simply extend the tick marks on an axis. Some charts look better with gridlines, while others appear more cluttered. Sometimes horizontal gridlines alone are enough, although XY charts often benefit from both horizontal and vertical gridlines.

To add or remove gridlines, activate the chart and click the Chart Elements button to the right of the chart. Place a check mark next to Gridlines. To specify the type of gridlines, click the arrow to the right of the Gridlines item.

To modify the color or thickness of a set of gridlines, click one of the gridlines and use the commands from the Chart Tools ⇨ Format ⇨ Shape Styles group. Or, use the controls in the Format Major (or Format Minor) Gridlines task pane.

If gridlines seem too overpowering, consider changing them to a lighter color or use one of the dashed line options.

Modifying the Axes

Charts vary in the number of axes they use. Pie, doughnut, sunburst, and treemap charts have no axes. All 2-D charts have two axes but can have three (if you use a secondary value axis) or four (if you use a secondary category axis in an XY chart). True 3-D charts have three axes.

Excel gives you a great deal of control over these axes via the Format Axis task pane. The content of this task pane varies depending on the type of axis selected.

Modifying the value axis

To change a value axis, right-click it and choose Format Axis. Figure 21.9 shows one panel (Axis Options) of the Format Axis task pane for a value axis. In this case, the Axis Options section is expanded, and the other three sections are contracted. The other icons along the top of this task pane deal with cosmetic and number formatting for the axis.

By default, Excel determines the minimum and maximum axis values automatically, based on the numerical range of the data. To override this automatic axis scaling, enter your own minimum and maximum values in the Bounds section. If you change these values, the word *Auto* changes to a Reset button. Click Reset to revert to automatic axis scaling.

Excel also adjusts the major and minor axis units automatically. Again, you can override Excel's choice and specify different units.

Adjusting the bounds of a value axis can affect the chart's appearance. In some cases, manipulating the scale can present a false picture of the data. Figure 21.10 shows two line charts that depict the same data. The chart on the right uses Excel's default (Auto) axis bounds values. In the chart on the left, the Minimum bound value was set to 10,000, and the Maximum bound value was set to 500,000. The first chart makes the differences in the data seem more prominent. The second chart gives the impression that there isn't much change over time.

FIGURE 21.9

The Format Axis task pane for a value axis

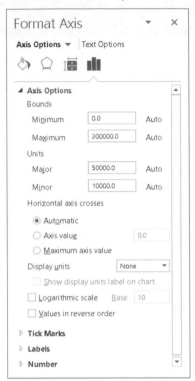

FIGURE 21.10

These two charts show the same data but use different value axis bounds.

The actual scale you use depends on the situation. There are no hard-and-fast rules regarding setting scale values, except that you shouldn't misrepresent data by manipulating the chart to prove a point that doesn't exist.

> **TIP**
>
> If you're preparing several charts that use similarly scaled data, keeping the bounds the same is a good idea so that the charts can be compared more easily.

Another option in the Format Axis task pane is Values in Reverse Order. The left chart in Figure 21.11 uses default axis settings. The right chart uses the Values in Reverse Order option, which reverses the scale's direction. Notice that the category axis is at the top. If you would prefer that it remain at the bottom of the chart, select the Maximum Axis Value option for the Horizontal Axis Crosses setting.

FIGURE 21.11

The right chart uses the Values in Reverse Order option

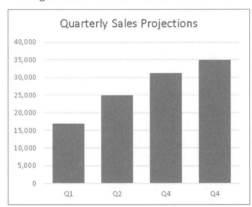 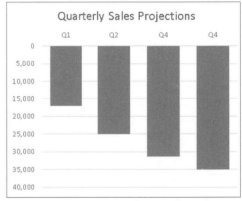

If the values to be plotted cover a large numerical range, you may want to use a logarithmic scale for the value axis. A log scale is most often used for scientific applications. Figure 21.12 shows two charts. The top chart uses a standard scale, and the bottom chart uses a logarithmic scale.

> **NOTE**
>
> For a logarithmic scale, the Base setting is 10, so each scale value in the chart is 10 times greater than the one below it. Increasing the major unit to 100 results in a scale in which each tick mark value is 100 times greater than the one below it. You can specify a base value between 2 and 1,000.

 This workbook, `log scale.xlsx`, is available on this book's website at www.wiley.com/go/excel2019bible.

FIGURE 21.12

These charts display the same data, but the bottom chart uses a logarithmic scale.

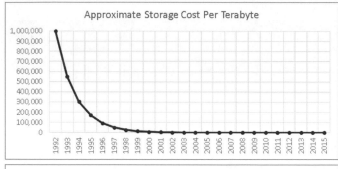

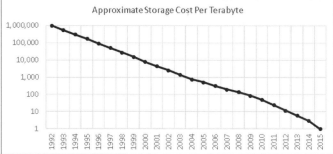

If your chart uses large numbers, you may want to change the Display Units settings. Figure 21.13 shows a chart (left) that uses large numbers. The chart on the right uses the Display Units as Thousands settings, with the option Show Display Units Labels on Chart. We added "of Miles" to the label.

FIGURE 21.13

The chart on the right uses display units of thousands.

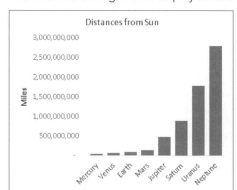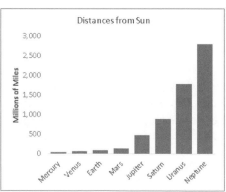

To adjust the tick marks displayed on an axis, click the Tick Marks section of the Format Axis dialog box to expand that section. The Major and Minor Tick Mark options control the way the tick marks are displayed. *Major tick marks* are the axis tick marks that normally have labels next to them. *Minor tick marks* fall between the major tick marks.

If you expand the Labels section, you can position the axis labels at three distinct locations: Next to Axis, High, and Low.

Refer to Figure 21.14. When you combine these settings with the Axis Crosses At option, you have a great deal of flexibility.

FIGURE 21.14

Excel offers a great deal of flexibility in how you can display axis labels and crossing points.

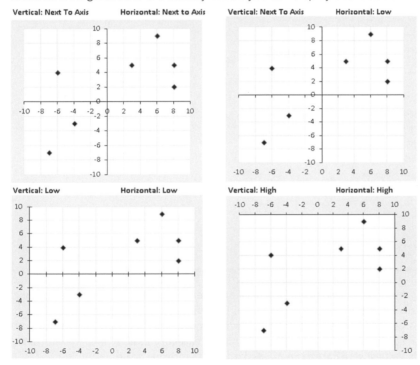

The last section of the task pane, Number, lets you specify the number formatting for the value axis. Normally, the number formatting is linked to the source data, but you can override that.

Modifying the category axis

Figure 21.15 shows part of the Axis Options section of the Format Axis task pane when a category axis is selected. Some options are the same as those for a value axis.

FIGURE 21.15

Some of the options available for a category axis

An important setting is Axis Type: Text or Date. When you create a chart, Excel recognizes whether your category axis contains date or time values. If it does, it uses a Date category axis. Figure 21.16 shows a simple example. Column A contains dates, and column B contains the values plotted in the column chart. The data consists of values for only 10 dates, yet Excel created the chart with 30 intervals on the category axis. It recognized that the category axis values were dates and created an equal-interval scale.

You can override Excel's decision to use a Date category axis by choosing the Text Axis option for Axis Type. Figure 21.17 shows the chart after making this change. In this case, using a time-based category axis (as shown in Figure 21.16) presents a much truer picture of the data.

Excel chooses the way to orient the category labels, but you can override its choice. Figure 21.18 shows a column chart with month labels. Because of the lengthy category labels, Excel displays the text at an angle. If you make the chart wider, the labels will then appear horizontally. You can also adjust the labels using the Alignment controls in the Size & Properties section of the Format Axis task pane.

FIGURE 21.16

Excel recognizes dates and creates a time-based category axis.

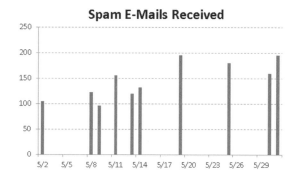

FIGURE 21.17

Overriding the Excel time-based category axis

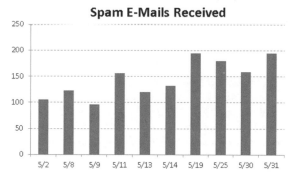

Keep in mind that category axis labels can consist of more than one column. Figure 21.19 shows a chart that displays three columns of text for the category axis. We selected the range A1:E10 and created a column chart, and Excel figured out the category axis.

FIGURE 21.18

Excel determines the way to display category axis labels.

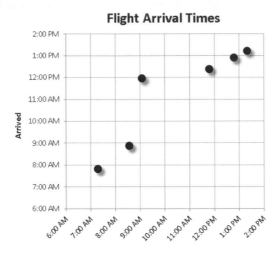

Don't Be Afraid to Experiment (But on a Copy)

We'll let you in on a secret: the key to mastering charts in Excel is experimentation, otherwise known as *trial and error*. Excel's charting options can be overwhelming, even to experienced users. This book doesn't even pretend to cover all of the charting features and options. Your job, as a potential charting master, is to dig deep and try the various options in your charts. With a bit of creativity, you can create original-looking charts.

After you create a basic chart, make a copy of the chart for your experimentation. That way, if you mess it up, you can always revert to the original and start again. To make a copy of an embedded chart, click the chart and press Ctrl+C. Then activate a cell and press Ctrl+V. To make a copy of a chart sheet, press Ctrl while you click the sheet tab and then drag it to a new location among the other tabs.

FIGURE 21.19

This chart uses three columns of text for the category axis labels.

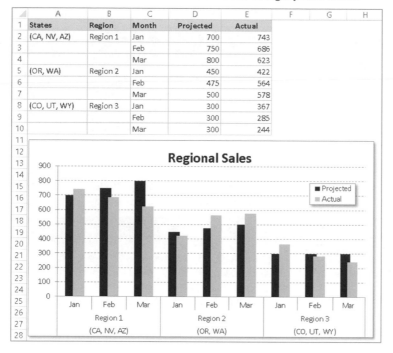

Working with Data Series

Every chart consists of one or more data series. This data translates into chart columns, bars, lines, pie slices, and so on. This section discusses some common operations that involve a chart's data series.

When you select a data series in a chart, Excel does the following:

- Displays the series name in the Chart Elements control (located in the Chart Tools ⇨ Format ⇨ Current Selection group
- Displays the Series formula in the Formula bar
- Highlights the cells used for the selected series by outlining them in color

You can make changes to a data series by using the options on the Ribbon or from the Format Data Series task pane. This task pane varies depending on the type of data series on which you're working (column, line, pie, and so on).

CAUTION

If the Format task pane isn't already displayed, the easiest way to display the Format Data Series task pane is to double-click the chart series. Be careful, however: if a data series is already selected, double-clicking brings up the Format Data Point task pane. Changes that you make affect only one point in the data series. To edit the *entire series*, make sure that a chart element other than the data series is selected before you double-click the data series. Or, just press Ctrl+1 to display the task pane.

Deleting or hiding a data series

To delete a data series in a chart, select the data series and press Delete. The data series disappears from the chart. The data in the worksheet, of course, remains intact.

NOTE

You can delete all data series from a chart. If you do so, the chart appears empty. It retains its settings, however. Therefore, you can add a data series to an empty chart, and it again looks like a chart.

To hide a data series temporarily, activate a chart and click the Chart Filters button on the right. Remove the check mark from the data series that you want to hide, click Apply, and that data series is hidden—but it's still associated with the chart, so you can unhide it later. You can't hide all the series, though. At least one must be visible. The Chart Filters button also lets you hide individual points in a series. Note that the new chart types introduced in Excel 2016 and Excel 2019 do not display a Chart Filters button.

Adding a new data series to a chart

If you want to add another data series to an existing chart, one approach is to re-create the chart and include the new data series. However, adding the data to the existing chart is usually easier, and your chart retains any customization that you've made.

Excel provides three ways to add a new data series to a chart:

- **Use the Select Data Source dialog box:** Activate the chart and choose Chart Tools ➪ Design ➪ Data ➪ Select Data. In the Select Data Source dialog box, click the Add button and Excel displays the Edit Series dialog box. Specify the series name (as a cell reference or text) and the range that contains the series values. The Select Data Source dialog box is also accessible from the shortcut menu displayed by right-clicking many elements in a chart.
- **Drag the range outline:** If the data series to be added is contiguous with other data in the chart, you can click the Chart Area in the chart. Excel highlights and

outlines the data in the worksheet. Click one of the corners of the outline and drag to highlight the new data. This method works only for embedded charts.

■ **Copy and paste:** Select the range to add and press Ctrl+C to copy it to the Clipboard. Then activate the chart and press Ctrl+V to paste the data into the chart.

TIP

If the chart was originally made from data in a table (created via Insert ⇨ Tables ⇨ Table), the chart is updated automatically when you add new rows or columns to the table (or remove rows or columns). If you have a chart that is updated frequently with new data, you can save time and effort by creating the chart from data in a table.

Changing data used by a series

You may find that you need to modify the range that defines a data series. For example, say you need to add new data points or remove old ones from the data set. The following sections describe several ways to change the range used by a data series.

Changing the data range by dragging the range outline

If you have an embedded chart, the easiest way to change the data range for a data series is to drag the range outline. When you select a series in a chart, Excel outlines the data range used by that series. You can drag the small dot in the lower-right corner of the range outline to extend or contract the data series. In Figure 21.20, the range outline will be dragged to include two additional data points.

FIGURE 21.20

Changing a chart's data series by dragging the range outline

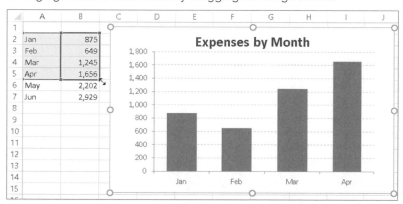

You can also click and drag one of the sides of the outline to move the outline to a different range of cells.

In some cases, you'll also need to adjust the range that contains the category labels. The labels are also outlined, and you can drag the outline to expand or contract the range of labels used in the chart.

If your chart is on a chart sheet, you need to use one of the two methods described next. These methods also work with embedded charts.

Using the Edit Series dialog box

Another way to update the chart to reflect a different data range is to use the Edit Series dialog box. A quick way to display this dialog box is to right-click the series in the chart and then choose Select Data from the shortcut menu. The Select Source Data dialog box appears. Select the data series in the list, and click Edit to display the Edit Series dialog box, as shown in Figure 21.21.

FIGURE 21.21

The Edit Series dialog box

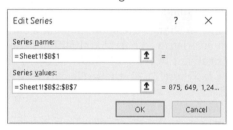

You can change the entire data range used by the chart by adjusting the range references in the Chart Data Range field. Or, you can select a series from the list and click Edit to modify the selected series.

Editing the Series formula

Every data series in a chart has an associated SERIES formula, which appears in the Formula bar when you select a data series in a chart. If you understand the way a SERIES formula is constructed, you can edit the range references in the SERIES formula directly to change the data used by the chart.

> **NOTE**
>
> The SERIES formula is not a real formula. In other words, you can't use it in a cell, and you can't use worksheet functions within the SERIES formula. You can, however, edit the arguments in the SERIES formula.

A SERIES formula has the following syntax:

```
=SERIES(series_name, category_labels, values, order, sizes)
```

The arguments that you can use in the SERIES formula include the following:

- series_name (optional): A reference to the cell that contains the series name used in the legend. If the chart has only one series, the name argument is used as the title. This argument can also consist of text in quotation marks. If omitted, Excel creates a default series name (for example, Series 1).

- category_labels (optional): A reference to the range that contains the labels for the category axis. If omitted, Excel uses consecutive integers beginning with 1. For XY charts, this argument specifies the X values. A noncontiguous range reference is also valid. The ranges' addresses are separated by commas and enclosed in parentheses. The argument could also consist of an array of comma-separated values (or text in quotation marks) enclosed in curly brackets.

- values (required): A reference to the range that contains the values for the series. For XY charts, this argument specifies the Y values. A noncontiguous range reference is also valid. The range addresses are separated by a comma and enclosed in parentheses. The argument could also consist of an array of comma-separated values enclosed in curly brackets.

- order (required): An integer that specifies the plotting order of the series. This argument is relevant only if the chart has more than one series. Using a reference to a cell is not allowed.

- sizes (only for bubble charts): A reference to the range that contains the values for the size of the bubbles in a bubble chart. A noncontiguous range reference is also valid. The range addresses are separated by commas and enclosed in parentheses. The argument can also consist of an array of values enclosed in curly brackets.

Range references in a SERIES formula are always absolute (contain two dollar signs), and they always include the sheet name. For example, note the following:

```
=SERIES(Sheet1!$B$1,,Sheet1!$B$2:$B$7,1)
```

> **TIP**
>
> You can substitute range names for the range references. If you do so, Excel changes the reference in the SERIES formula to include the workbook name (if it's a workbook-level name) or to include the worksheet name (if it's a sheet-level name). For example, if you use a workbook-level range named MyData (in a workbook named budget.xlsx), the SERIES formula looks like this:
>
> ```
> =SERIES(Sheet1!$B$1,,budget.xlsx!MyData,1)
> ```

 For more information about named ranges, see Chapter 4, "Working with Excel Ranges and Tables."

Displaying data labels in a chart

Sometimes, you may want your chart to display the actual numerical value for each data point. To add labels to data series in a chart, select the series and click the Add Elements button on the right side of the chart. Place a check mark next to Data Labels. Click the arrow next to the Data Labels item to specify the position for the labels.

To add data labels for all series, use the same procedure, but start by selecting something other than a data series.

Figure 21.22 shows three minimalist charts with data labels.

FIGURE 21.22

These charts use data labels and don't display axes.

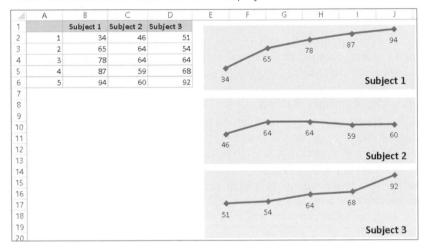

To change the type of information that appears in data labels, select the data labels for a series and use the Format Data Labels task pane. (If the task pane isn't visible, press Ctrl+1.) Then use the Label Options section to customize the data labels. For example, you can include the series name and the category name along with the value.

The data labels are linked to the worksheet, so if your data changes, the labels also change. If you want to override the data label with other text, select the label and enter the new text.

In some situations, you may need to use other data labels for a series. In the Format Data Labels task pane, select Value from Cells (in the Label Options section) and click Select Range to specify the range that contains the data point labels.

Figure 21.23 shows an XY chart that uses data labels stored in a range. In versions prior to Excel 2013, adding these data labels had to be done manually or with the assistance of a macro. Because it's a new feature (introduced in Excel 2013), data labels applied using this method will not be displayed in Excel 2007 or earlier.

FIGURE 21.23

Data labels linked to text in an arbitrary range

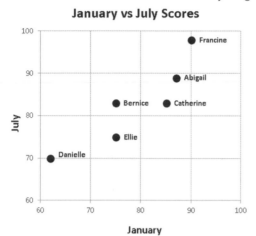

> **TIP**
>
> Often, the data labels aren't positioned properly. For example, a label may be obscured by another data point or another label. If you select an individual data label, you can drag the label to a better location. To select an individual data label, click once to select them all and then click the single data label.

Handling missing data

Sometimes, data that you're charting may be missing one or more data points. As shown in Figure 21.24, Excel offers three ways to handle the missing data:

Gaps   Missing data is simply ignored, and the data series will have a gap. This is the default.

Zero   Missing data is treated as zero.

Connect Data Points with Line   Missing data is interpolated, calculated by using data on either side of the missing point(s). This option is available for line charts, area charts, and XY charts only.

To specify how to deal with missing data for a chart, choose Chart Tools ➪ Design ➪ Data ➪ Select Data. In the Select Data Source dialog box, click the Hidden and Empty Cells button. Excel displays its Hidden and Empty Cell Settings dialog box. Make your choice in the dialog box. The option that you choose applies to the entire chart, and you can't set a different option for different series in the same chart.

FIGURE 21.24

Three options for dealing with missing data

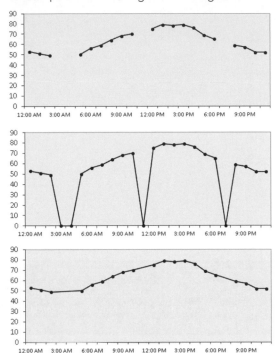

> **TIP**
>
> Normally, a chart doesn't display data that's in a hidden row or column. You can use the Hidden and Empty Cell Settings dialog box to force a chart to use hidden data, though.

Adding error bars

Some chart types support error bars. *Error bars* often are used to indicate "plus or minus" information that reflects uncertainty in the data. Error bars are appropriate for area, bar, column, line, and XY charts only.

To add error bars, select a data series and then click the Add Elements icon to the right of the chart. Add a check mark next to Error Bars. Click the arrow next to the Error Bars item to specify the type of error bars. If necessary, you can fine-tune the error bar settings from the Format Error Bars task pane. The types of error bars are as follows:

Fixed value   The error bars are fixed by an amount that you specify.

Percentage   The error bars are a percentage of each value.

Standard deviation(s)   The error bars are in the number of standard deviation units that you specify. (Excel calculates the standard deviation of the data series.)

Standard error   The error bars are one standard error unit. (Excel calculates the standard error of the data series.)

Custom   You set the error bar units for the upper or lower error bars. You can enter either a value or a range reference that holds the error values that you want to plot as error bars.

The chart shown in Figure 21.25 displays error bars based on percentage.

FIGURE 21.25

This line chart series displays error bars based on percentage.

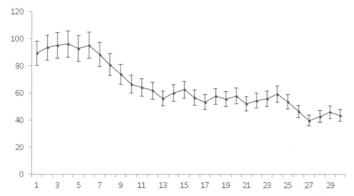

TIP

A data series in an XY chart can have error bars for both the X values and the Y values.

 A workbook with several other error bar examples is available on this book's website at www.wiley .com/go/excel2019bible. **The filename is** error bars example.xlsx.

Adding a trendline

When you're plotting data over time, you may want to display a trendline that describes the data. A *trendline* points out general trends in your data. In some cases, you can forecast future data with trendlines.

To add a trendline, select the data series and click the Add Elements button to the right of the chart. Place a check mark next to Trendline.

To specify the type of trendline, click the arrow to the right of the Trendline item. The type of trendline that you choose depends on your data. Linear trends (see Figure 21.26) are most commonly used and the easiest to apply.

FIGURE 21.26

Applying a trend line

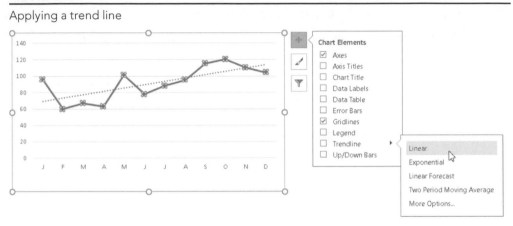

For more control over a trendline, select More Options from the trendline choices shown in Figure 21.26.

This will activate the Format Trendline task pane illustrated in Figure 21.27. Here you can apply more advanced trendlines such as logarithmic, exponential, and moving average trendlines.

Creating combination charts

A *combination chart* is a single chart that consists of series that use different chart types. A combination chart may also include a second value axis. For example, you may have a chart that shows both columns and lines, with two value axes. The value axis for the columns is on the left, and the value axis for the line is on the right. A combination chart requires at least two data series.

Figure 21.28 shows a column chart with two data series. The values for the Precipitation series are so low that they're barely visible on the Value Axis scale. This is a good candidate for a combination chart.

FIGURE 21.27

The trendline depicts the relationship between height and weight.

FIGURE 21.28

The Precipitation series is barely visible.

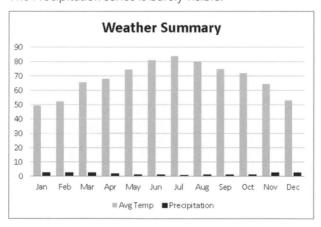

The following steps describe how to convert this chart into a combination chart (column and line) that uses a second value axis:

1. **Activate the chart, and choose Chart Tools ⇨ Design ⇨ Type ⇨ Change Chart type.** The Change Chart Type dialog box appears.

2. **Select the All Charts tab.**

3. **In the list of chart types, click Combo.**

4. **For the Avg Temp series, specify Clustered Column as the chart type.**

5. **For the Precipitation series, specify Line as the chart type and click the Secondary Axis check box.**

6. **Click OK to insert the chart.**

Figure 21.29 shows the Change Chart dialog box after specifying the parameters for each series.

FIGURE 21.29

Using the Change Chart dialog box to convert a chart into a combination chart

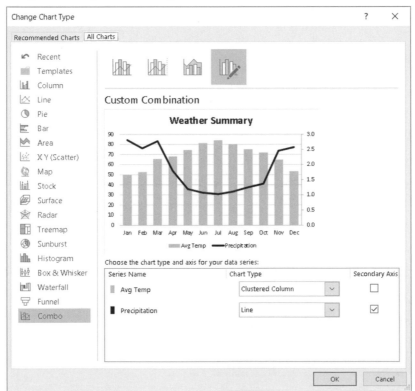

This workbook is available on this book's website at `www.wiley.com/go/excel2019bible`. The filename is `weather combination chart.xlsx`.

21

Displaying a data table

There may be situations where it's valuable to show all of the data values along with the plotted data points. However, adding data labels can inundate your audience with a bevy of numbers that muddle the chart.

Instead of using data labels, you can attach a data table to your Excel chart. A data table allows you to see the data values for each plotted data point beneath the chart, showing the data without overcrowding the chart itself.

To add a data table to a chart, activate the chart and click the Add Element button to the right of the chart. Place a check mark next to Data Table. Click the arrow to the right of the Data Table item for a few options. Figure 21.30 shows a combination chart that includes a data table.

FIGURE 21.30

This combination chart includes a data table that displays the values of the data points.

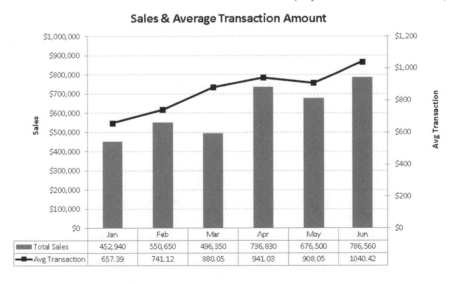

Not all chart types support data tables. If the Data Table option isn't available, this means the chart doesn't support this feature.

> **TIP**
>
> Using a data table is probably best suited for charts on chart sheets. If you need to show the data used in an embedded chart, you can do so using data in cells, which gives you more formatting flexibility.

Creating Chart Templates

This section describes how to create custom chart templates. A template includes customized chart formatting and settings. When you create a new chart, you can choose to use your template rather than a built-in chart type.

If you find that you're continually customizing your charts in the same way, you can probably save some time by creating a template. Or, if you create lots of combination charts, you can create a combination chart template and avoid making the manual adjustments required for a combination chart.

To create a chart template, follow these steps:

1. **Create a chart to serve as the basis for your template.** The data you use for this chart isn't critical, but for best results it should be typical of the data that you'll eventually be plotting with your custom chart type.
2. **Apply any formatting and customizations that you like.** This step determines the appearance of the charts created from the template.
3. **Activate the chart, right-click the Chart Area or the Plot Area, and choose Save as Template from the shortcut menu.** The Save Chart Template dialog box appears.
4. **Provide a name for the template and click Save.** Make sure you don't change the proposed directory for the file.

To create a chart based on a template, follow these steps:

1. **Select the data to be used in the chart.**
2. **Choose Insert ⇨ Charts ⇨ Recommended Charts.** The Insert Chart dialog box appears.
3. **Select the All Charts tab.**
4. **From the left side of the Insert Chart dialog box, select Templates.** Excel displays a thumbnail for each custom template that has been created.
5. **Click the thumbnail that represents the template you want to use and then click OK.** Excel creates the chart based on the template you selected.

> **NOTE**
>
> You can also apply a template to an existing chart. Select the chart and choose Chart Tools ⇨ Design ⇨ Type ⇨ Change Chart Type to display the Change Chart Type dialog box, which is identical to the Insert Chart dialog box.

Creating Sparkline Graphics

IN THIS CHAPTER

Introducing the Sparkline graphics feature

Adding Sparklines to a worksheet

Customizing Sparklines

Making a Sparkline display only the most recent data

A Sparkline is a small chart that's displayed in a single cell. A Sparkline allows you to spot time-based trends or variations quickly in data. Because they're so compact, Sparklines are almost always used in a group.

Although Sparklines look like miniature charts (and can sometimes take the place of a chart), this feature is completely separate from the charting feature. For example, charts are placed on a worksheet's draw layer, and a single chart can display several series of data. A Sparkline is displayed inside a cell and displays only one series of data.

 See Chapter 20, "Getting Started with Excel Charts," and Chapter 21, "Advanced Charting Features," for information about *real* charts.

This chapter introduces Sparklines and presents examples that demonstrate how to use them in your worksheets.

> **NOTE**
> Sparklines were introduced in Excel 2010. If you create a workbook that uses Sparklines and that workbook is opened using Excel 2007 or earlier, the Sparkline cells will be empty.

 All examples in this chapter are available on this book's website at www.wiley.com/go/excel2019bible. The filename is sparkline examples.xlsx.

Sparkline Types

Excel supports three types of Sparklines. Figure 22.1 shows examples of each, displayed in column H. Each Sparkline depicts the six data points to the left.

FIGURE 22.1

Three groups of Sparklines

◢	A	B	C	D	E	F	G	H
1	Line Sparklines							
2								
3	Fund Number	Jan	Feb	Mar	Apr	May	Jun	Sparklines
4	A-13	103.98	98.92	88.12	86.34	75.58	71.2	
5	C-09	212.74	218.7	202.18	198.56	190.12	181.74	
6	K-88	75.74	73.68	69.86	60.34	64.92	59.46	
7	W-91	91.78	95.44	98.1	99.46	98.68	105.86	
8	M-03	324.48	309.14	313.1	287.82	276.24	260.9	
9								
10	Column Sparklines							
11								
12	Fund Number	Jan	Feb	Mar	Apr	May	Jun	Sparklines
13	A-13	103.98	98.92	88.12	86.34	75.58	71.2	
14	C-09	212.74	218.7	202.18	198.56	190.12	181.74	
15	K-88	75.74	73.68	69.86	60.34	64.92	59.46	
16	W-91	91.78	95.44	98.1	99.46	98.68	105.86	
17	M-03	324.48	309.14	313.1	287.82	276.24	260.9	
18								
19	Win/Loss Sparklines							
20								
21	Fund Number	Jan	Feb	Mar	Apr	May	Jun	Sparklines
22	A-13	#N/A	-5.06	10.8	1.78	-10.76	-4.38	
23	C-09	#N/A	5.96	-16.52	-3.62	-8.44	-8.38	
24	K-88	#N/A	-2.06	-3.82	-9.52	4.58	-5.46	
25	W-91	#N/A	3.66	2.66	1.36	-0.78	7.18	
26	M-03	#N/A	-15.34	3.96	-25.28	-11.58	-15.34	

Line Similar to a line chart. As an option, the line can display with a marker for each data point. The first group in Figure 22.1 shows line Sparklines with markers. A quick glance reveals that, with the exception of Fund Number W-91, the funds have been losing value over the six-month period.

Column Similar to a column chart. The second group in Figure 22.1 shows the same data displayed with column Sparklines.

Win/Loss A "binary" type chart that displays each data point as a high block or a low block. The third group shows win/loss Sparklines. Notice that the data is different. Each cell displays the change from the previous month. In the Sparkline, each data point is depicted as a high block (win) or a low block (loss). In this example, a positive change from the previous month is a win, and a negative change from the previous month is a loss.

Why Sparklines?

If the term *Sparkline* seems odd, don't blame Microsoft. Edward Tufte coined the term *sparkline*, and in his book, *Beautiful Evidence* (Graphics Press, 2006), he describes it as follows:

> *Sparklines*: Intense, simple, word-sized graphics

In the case of Excel, Sparklines are cell-sized graphics. As you see in this chapter, Sparklines aren't limited to lines.

Creating Sparklines

Figure 22.2 shows some data to be summarized with Sparklines.

FIGURE 22.2

Data to be summarized with Sparklines

▲	A	B	C	D	E	F	G	H	I	J	K	L	M
1	Average Monthly Precipitation (Inches)												
2													
3		Jan	Feb	Mar	Apr	May	Jun	Jul	Aug	Sep	Oct	Nov	Dec
4	ASHEVILLE, NC	4.06	3.83	4.59	3.5	4.41	4.38	3.87	4.3	3.72	3.17	3.82	3.39
5	BAKERSFIELD, CA	1.18	1.21	1.41	0.45	0.24	0.12	0	0.08	0.15	0.3	0.59	0.76
6	BATON ROUGE, LA	6.19	5.1	5.07	5.56	5.34	5.33	5.96	5.86	4.84	3.81	4.76	5.26
7	BILLINGS, MT	0.81	0.57	1.12	1.74	2.48	1.89	1.28	0.85	1.34	1.26	0.75	0.67
8	DAYTONA BEACH, FL	3.13	2.74	3.84	2.54	3.26	5.69	5.17	6.09	6.61	4.48	3.03	2.71
9	EUGENE, OR	7.65	6.35	5.8	3.66	2.66	1.53	0.64	0.99	1.54	3.35	8.44	8.29
10	HONOLULU,HI	2.73	2.35	1.89	1.11	0.78	0.43	0.5	0.46	0.74	2.18	2.26	2.85
11	ST. LOUIS, MO	2.14	2.28	3.6	3.69	4.11	3.76	3.9	2.98	2.96	2.76	3.71	2.86
12	TUCSON, AZ	0.99	0.88	0.81	0.28	0.24	0.24	2.07	2.3	1.45	1.21	0.67	1.03

To create Sparkline graphics, follow these steps:

1. **Select the data that will be depicted (data only, not column or row headings); if you're creating multiple Sparklines, select all the data.** In this example, start by selecting B4:M12.

2. **With the data selected, choose Insert ➪ Sparklines, and click one of the three Sparkline types: Line, Column, or Win/Loss.** The Create Sparklines dialog box, shown in Figure 22.3, appears.

FIGURE 22.3

Use the Create Sparklines dialog box to specify the data range and the location for the Sparkline graphics.

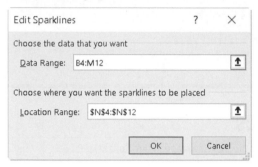

3. **Specify the location for the Sparklines.** Typically, you'll put the Sparklines next to the data, but that's not a requirement. Most of the time, you'll use an empty range to hold the Sparklines. However, Excel doesn't prevent you from inserting Sparklines into cells that already contain data. The Sparkline location that you specify must match the source data in terms of number of rows or number of columns. For this example, specify N4:N12 as the location range.

4. **Click OK.** Excel creates the Sparkline graphics of the type you specified.

The Sparklines are linked to the data, so if you change any of the values in the data range, the Sparkline graphic will update. Often, you'll want to increase the column width or row height to improve the readability of the Sparklines.

> **TIP**
>
> Most of the time, you'll create Sparklines on the same sheet that contains the data. If you want to create Sparklines on a different sheet, start by activating the sheet where the Sparklines will be displayed. Then, in the Create Sparklines dialog box, specify the source data either by pointing or by typing the complete sheet reference (for example, Sheet1!A1:C12). The Create Sparklines dialog box lets you specify a different sheet for the Data Range but not for the Location Range. Or, you can just create the Sparklines on the same sheet as the data and then cut and paste the cells to a different worksheet.

Figure 22.4 shows column Sparklines for the precipitation data.

FIGURE 22.4

Column Sparklines summarize the precipitation data for nine cities.

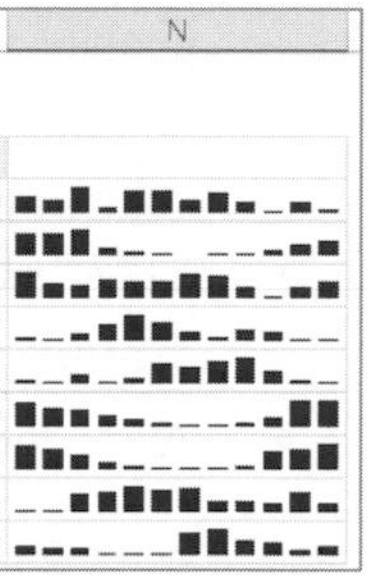

	A	B	C	D	E	F	G	H	I	J	K	L	M	N
1	Average Monthly Precipitation (Inches)													
2														
3		Jan	Feb	Mar	Apr	May	Jun	Jul	Aug	Sep	Oct	Nov	Dec	
4	ASHEVILLE, NC	4.06	3.83	4.59	3.5	4.41	4.38	3.87	4.3	3.72	3.17	3.82	3.39	
5	BAKERSFIELD, CA	1.18	1.21	1.41	0.45	0.24	0.12	0	0.08	0.15	0.3	0.59	0.76	
6	BATON ROUGE, LA	6.19	5.1	5.07	5.56	5.34	5.33	5.96	5.86	4.84	3.81	4.76	5.26	
7	BILLINGS, MT	0.81	0.57	1.12	1.74	2.48	1.89	1.28	0.85	1.34	1.26	0.75	0.67	
8	DAYTONA BEACH, FL	3.13	2.74	3.84	2.54	3.26	5.69	5.17	6.09	6.61	4.48	3.03	2.71	
9	EUGENE, OR	7.65	6.35	5.8	3.66	2.66	1.53	0.64	0.99	1.54	3.35	8.44	8.29	
10	HONOLULU,HI	2.73	2.35	1.89	1.11	0.78	0.43	0.5	0.46	0.74	2.18	2.26	2.85	
11	ST. LOUIS, MO	2.14	2.28	3.6	3.69	4.11	3.76	3.9	2.98	2.96	2.76	3.71	2.86	
12	TUCSON, AZ	0.99	0.88	0.81	0.28	0.24	0.24	2.07	2.3	1.45	1.21	0.67	1.03	

Understanding Sparkline Groups

In most situations, you'll probably create a *group* of Sparklines—one for each row or column of data. A worksheet can hold any number of Sparkline groups. Excel remembers each group, and you can work with the group as a single unit. For example, you can select one Sparkline in a group and then modify the formatting of all Sparklines in the group. When you select one Sparkline cell, Excel displays an outline of all of the other Sparklines in the group.

You can, however, perform some operations on an individual Sparkline in a group:

- Change the Sparkline's data source. Select the Sparkline cell and choose Sparkline Tools Design ➪ Sparkline ➪ Edit Data ➪ Edit Single Sparkline's Data. Excel displays a dialog box that lets you change the data source for the selected Sparkline.

- Delete the Sparkline. Select the Sparkline cell and choose Sparkline Tools Design ➪ Group ➪ Clear ➪ Clear Selected Sparklines.

Both operations are available from the shortcut menu that appears when you right-click a Sparkline cell.

You can also ungroup a set of Sparklines by selecting any Sparkline in the group and choosing Sparkline Tools Design ➪ Group ➪ Ungroup. After you ungroup a set of Sparklines, you can work with each Sparkline individually.

Note that you can also delete an entire Sparkline group (should you want to start from scratch). Simply select Sparkline Tools Design ➪ Group ➪ Clear ➪ Clear Selected Sparkline Groups.

Customizing Sparklines

When you activate a cell that contains a Sparkline, Excel displays an outline around all of the Sparklines in its group. You can then use the commands on the Sparkline Tools Design tab to customize the group of Sparklines.

Sizing Sparkline cells

When you change the width or height of a cell that contains a Sparkline, the Sparkline adjusts accordingly. In addition, you can insert a Sparkline into merged cells.

Figure 22.5 shows the same Sparkline, displayed at four sizes resulting from changing the column width or row height and merging cells. As you can see, the size and proportions of the cell (or merged cells) make a big difference in the appearance.

FIGURE 22.5

A Sparkline at various sizes

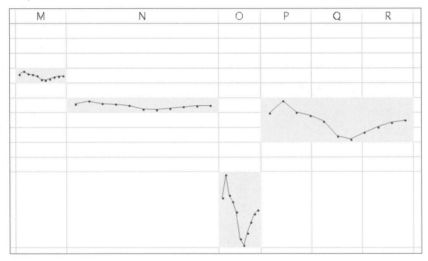

Handling hidden or missing data

By default, if you hide rows or columns that are used in a Sparkline graphic, the hidden data does not appear in the Sparkline. Also, missing data (an empty cell) is displayed as a gap in the graphic.

To change these settings, choose Sparkline Tools Design ➪ Sparkline ➪ Edit Data ➪ Hidden and Empty Cells. In the Hidden and Empty Cell Settings dialog box that appears (see Figure 22.6), specify how to handle hidden data and empty cells.

FIGURE 22.6

The Hidden and Empty Cell Settings dialog box

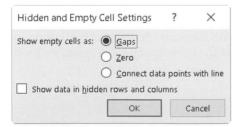

Changing the Sparkline type

As mentioned earlier, Excel supports three Sparkline types: Line, Column, and Win/Loss. After you create a Sparkline or group of Sparklines, you can easily change the type by selecting the Sparkline and clicking one of the three icons in the Sparkline Tools Design ⇨ Type group. If the selected Sparkline is part of a group, all Sparklines in the group are changed to the new type.

> **TIP**
>
> If you've customized the appearance, Excel remembers your customization settings for each type if you switch among Sparkline types.

Changing Sparkline colors and line width

After you've created a Sparkline, changing the color is easy. Use the controls in the Sparkline Tools Design ⇨ Style group.

> **NOTE**
>
> Colors used in Sparkline graphics are tied to the document theme. Therefore, if you change the theme (by choosing Page Layout ⇨ Themes ⇨ Themes), the Sparkline colors will change to the new theme colors.

 See Chapter 5, "Formatting Worksheets," for more information about document themes.

For Line Sparklines, you can also specify the line width. Choose Sparkline Tools Design ⇨ Style ⇨ Sparkline Color ⇨ Weight.

Highlighting certain data points

Use the commands in the Sparkline Tools Design ⇨ Show group to customize the Sparklines to highlight certain aspects of the data. The options are as follows:

High Point   Apply a different color to the highest data point in the Sparkline.

Low Point   Apply a different color to the lowest data point in the Sparkline.

Negative Points   Apply a different color to negative values in the Sparkline.

First Point   Apply a different color to the first data point in the Sparkline.

Last Point   Apply a different color to the last data point in the Sparkline.

Markers   Show data markers in the Sparkline. This option is available only for Line Sparklines.

You control the color of the highlighting by using the Marker Color control in the Sparkline Tools Design ⇨ Style group. Unfortunately, you can't change the size of the markers in Line Sparklines.

Figure 22.7 shows some Line Sparklines with various types of highlighting applied.

FIGURE 22.7

Highlighting options for Line Sparklines

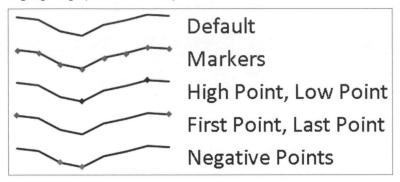

Adjusting Sparkline axis scaling

When you create one or more Sparklines, they all use (by default) automatic axis scaling. In other words, the minimum and maximum vertical axis values are determined automatically for each Sparkline in the group, based on the numeric range of the data used by the Sparkline.

The Sparkline Tools Design ➪ Group ➪ Axis command lets you override this automatic behavior and control the minimum and maximum value for each Sparkline or for a group of Sparklines. For even more control, you can use the Custom Value option and specify the minimum and maximum for the Sparkline group.

> **NOTE**
> Sparklines don't actually display a vertical axis, so you're essentially adjusting an invisible axis.

Figure 22.8 shows two groups of Sparklines. The group at the top uses the default axis settings (Automatic for Each Sparkline). Each Sparkline shows the six-month trend for the product, but there is no indication of the magnitude of the values.

FIGURE 22.8

The bottom group of Sparklines shows the effect of using the same axis minimum and maximum values for all Sparklines in a group.

For the Sparkline group at the bottom (which uses the same data), we changed the vertical axis minimum and maximum to use the Same for All Sparklines setting. With these settings in effect, the magnitude of the values across the products is apparent, but the trend across the months within a product is not.

The axis scaling option that you choose depends upon what aspect of the data you want to emphasize.

Faking a reference line

One useful feature that's missing in the Excel implementation of Sparklines is a reference line. For example, it might be useful to show performance relative to a goal. If the goal is displayed as a reference line in a Sparkline, the viewer can quickly see whether the performance for a period exceeded the goal.

You can, however, transform the data and then use a Sparkline axis as a fake reference line. Figure 22.9 shows an example. Students have a monthly reading goal of 500 pages. The range of data shows the actual pages read, with Sparklines in column H. The Sparklines show the six-month page data, but it's impossible to tell who exceeded the goal and when they did it.

FIGURE 22.9

Sparklines display the number of pages read per month.

	A	B	C	D	E	F	G	H
3								
4				Pages Read				
5		Jan	Feb	Mar	Apr	May	Jun	
6	Ann	450	412	632	663	702	512	
7	Bob	309	215	194	189	678	256	
8	Chuck	608	783	765	832	483	763	
9	Dave	409	415	522	598	421	433	
10	Ellen	790	893	577	802	874	763	
11	Frank	211	59	0	0	185	230	
12	Giselle	785	764	701	784	214	185	
13	Henry	350	367	560	583	784	663	
14								

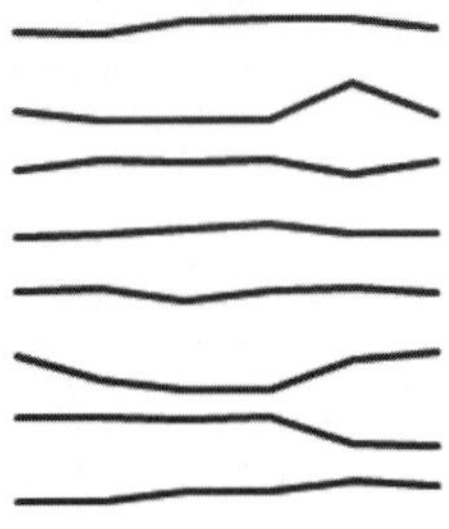

Figure 22.10 shows another approach: transforming the data such that meeting the goal is expressed as a 1 and failing to meet the goal is expressed as a –1. We used the following formula (in cell B18) to transform the original data:

```
=IF(B6>$C$2,1,-1)
```

FIGURE 22.10

Using Win/Loss Sparklines to display goal achievement

	A	B	C	D	E	F	G	H
15								
16				Pages Read (Did or Did Not Meet Goal)				
17		Jan	Feb	Mar	Apr	May	Jun	
18	Ann	-1	-1	1	1	1	1	
19	Bob	-1	-1	-1	-1	1	-1	
20	Chuck	1	1	1	1	-1	1	
21	Dave	-1	-1	1	1	-1	-1	
22	Ellen	1	1	1	1	1	1	
23	Frank	-1	-1	-1	-1	-1	-1	
24	Giselle	1	1	1	1	-1	-1	
25	Henry	-1	-1	1	1	1	1	
26								

We copied this formula to the other cells in the B18:G25 range.

Using the transformed data, we created Win/Loss Sparklines to visualize the results. This approach is better than the original, but it doesn't convey any magnitude differences. For example, you can't tell whether the student missed the goal by 1 page or by 500 pages.

Figure 22.11 shows a better approach. Here, we transformed the original data by subtracting the goal from the pages read. The formula in cell B31 is as follows:

```
=B6-$C$2
```

FIGURE 22.11

The axis in the Sparklines represents the goal.

	A	B	C	D	E	F	G	H
28								
29				Pages Read (Relative to Goal)				
30		Jan	Feb	Mar	Apr	May	Jun	
31	Ann	-50	-88	132	163	202	12	
32	Bob	-191	-285	-306	-311	178	-244	
33	Chuck	108	283	265	332	-17	263	
34	Dave	-91	-85	22	98	-79	-67	
35	Ellen	290	393	77	302	374	263	
36	Frank	-289	-441	-500	-500	-315	-270	
37	Giselle	285	264	201	284	-286	-315	
38	Henry	-150	-133	60	83	284	163	
39								
40								

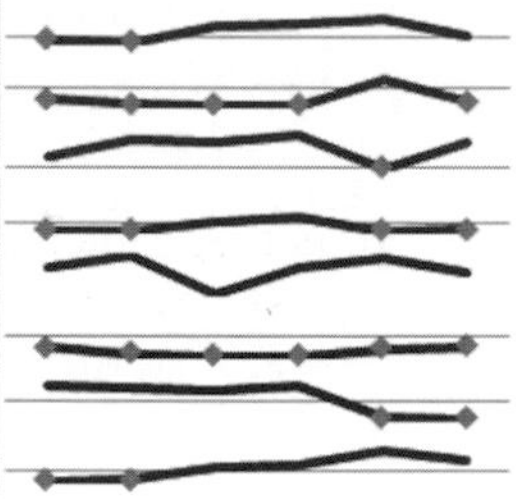

We copied this formula to the other cells in the B31:G38 range and created a group of Line Sparklines with the axis turned on. We also enabled the Negative Points option so that negative values (failure to meet the goal) clearly stand out.

Specifying a Date Axis

Normally, data displayed in a Sparkline is assumed to be at equal intervals. For example, a Sparkline might display a daily account balance, sales by month, or profits by year. But what if the data isn't at equal intervals?

Figure 22.12 shows data, by date, along with a Sparklines graphic created from column B. Notice that some dates are missing, but the Sparkline shows the columns as if the values were spaced at equal intervals.

FIGURE 22.12

The Sparkline displays the values as if they are at equal time intervals.

	A	B	C	D
1	Date	Amount		
2	1/1/2019	154		
3	1/2/2019	201		
4	1/3/2019	245		
5	1/4/2019	176		
6	1/11/2019	267		
7	1/12/2019	289		
8	1/13/2019	331		
9	1/14/2019	365		
10	1/18/2019	298		
11	1/19/2019	424		
12				

To better depict the data, the solution is to specify a date axis. Select the Sparkline and choose Sparkline Tools Design ⇨ Group ⇨ Axis ⇨ Date Axis Type. Excel displays a dialog box, asking for the range that contains the dates. In this example, specify range A2:A11. Click OK, and the Sparkline displays gaps for the missing dates (see Figure 22.13).

FIGURE 22.13

After specifying a date axis, the Sparkline shows the values accurately.

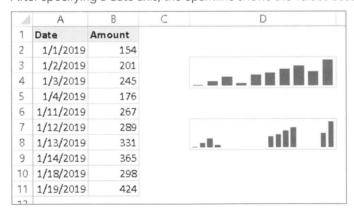

	A	B	C	D
1	Date	Amount		
2	1/1/2019	154		
3	1/2/2019	201		
4	1/3/2019	245		
5	1/4/2019	176		
6	1/11/2019	267		
7	1/12/2019	289		
8	1/13/2019	331		
9	1/14/2019	365		
10	1/18/2019	298		
11	1/19/2019	424		

Auto-Updating Sparklines

If a Sparkline uses data in a normal range of cells, adding new data to the beginning or end of the range does not force the Sparkline to use the new data. You need to use the Edit Sparklines dialog box to update the data range. (Choose Sparkline Tools Design ⇨ Sparkline ⇨ Edit Data.) But if the Sparkline data is in a column within a table (created by choosing Insert ⇨ Tables ⇨ Table), the Sparkline will use new data that's added to the end of the table.

Figure 22.14 shows an example. The Sparkline was created using the data in the Rate column of the table. When you add the new rate for September, the Sparkline will automatically update its Data Range.

FIGURE 22.14

Creating a Sparkline from data in a table

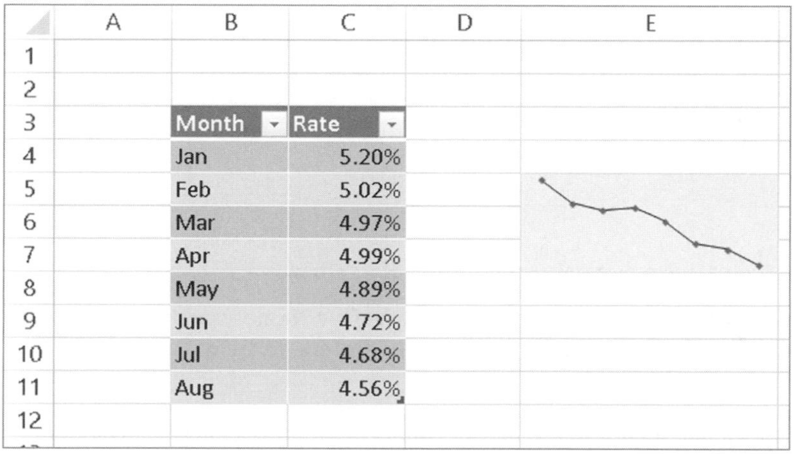

Displaying a Sparkline for a Dynamic Range

The example in this section describes how to create a Sparkline that displays only the most recent data points in a range. Figure 22.15 shows a worksheet that tracks daily sales. The Sparkline, in merged cells E4:E5, displays only the seven most recent data points in column B. When new data is added to column B, the Sparkline will adjust to show only the most recent seven days of sales.

FIGURE 22.15

Using a dynamic range name to display only the last seven data points in a Sparkline

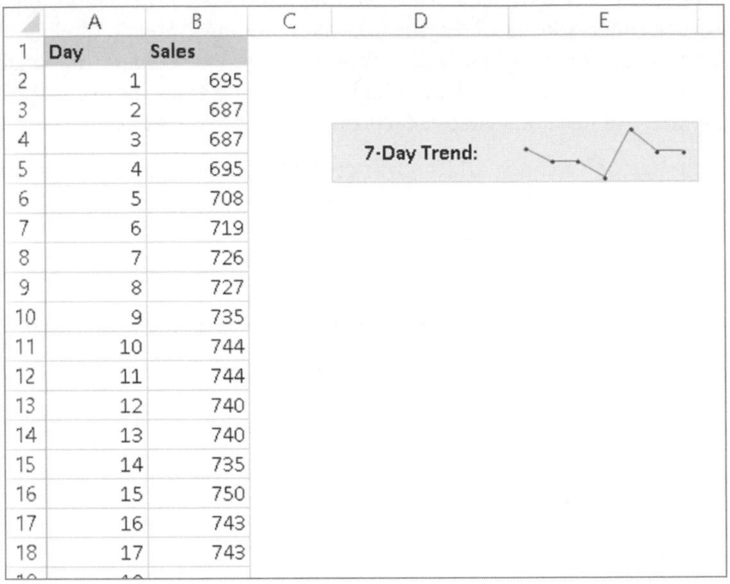

	A	B	C	D	E
1	Day	Sales			
2	1	695			
3	2	687			
4	3	687		7-Day Trend:	
5	4	695			
6	5	708			
7	6	719			
8	7	726			
9	8	727			
10	9	735			
11	10	744			
12	11	744			
13	12	740			
14	13	740			
15	14	735			
16	15	750			
17	16	743			
18	17	743			

We started by creating a dynamic range name. Here's how:

1. **Choose Formulas ⇨ Defined Names ⇨ Define Name, specify `Last7` as the Name, and enter the following formula in the Refers To field:**

   `=OFFSET($B$2,COUNTA($B:$B)-7-1,0,7,1)`

   This formula calculates a range by using the `OFFSET` function. The first argument is the first cell in the range (B2). The second argument is the number of cells in the column (minus the number to be returned and minus 1 to accommodate the label in B1). The name always refers to the last seven nonempty cells in column B. To display a different number of data points, change both instances of 7 to a different value.

2. **Chose Insert ⇨ Sparklines ⇨ Line.** The Create Sparklines dialog box appears.

3. **In the Data Range field, type `Last7` (the dynamic range name); specify cell E4 as the Location Range.** The Sparkline shows the data in range B11:B17.

4. **Add new data to column B.** The Sparkline adjusts to display only the last seven data points.

Visualizing with Custom Number Formats and Shapes

IN THIS CHAPTER

Custom formatting numbers

Creating visualizations with shapes and icons

Creating your own infographic elements

An overview of Excel's other graphics tools

Visualization is the presentation of abstract concepts or data in visual terms through some sort of graphical imagery. A traffic light, for example, is a visualization of the abstract concepts of stop and go.

In the business world, visualizations help us to communicate and process the meaning of data faster than simple tables of numbers. Excel offers business analysts a wide array of features that can be used to add visualizations to dashboards and reports.

In this chapter, you explore some of the formatting techniques that you can leverage to add layers of visualizations and turn your data into meaningful views.

 All of the examples in this chapter are available on this book's website at `www.wiley.com/go/ excel2019bible`. The filename is `Visualizations.xlsx`.

Visualizing with Number Formatting

When you enter a number into a cell, you can display that number in a variety of different formats. Excel has quite a few built-in number formats, but sometimes there are none that are exactly what you need.

This chapter describes how to create custom number formats, and it provides many examples that you can use as is or adapt to your needs.

Doing basic number formatting

The Number group on the Home tab of the Ribbon contains several controls for applying common number formats quickly. The Number Format drop-down control gives you quick access to 11 common number formats. In addition, the Number group contains some buttons. When you click one of these buttons, the selected cells take on the specified number format. Table 23.1 summarizes the formats that these buttons perform in the U.S. English version of Excel.

TABLE 23.1   Number-Formatting Buttons on the Ribbon

Button Name	Formatting Applied
Accounting Number Format	Adds a dollar sign to the left, separates thousands with a comma, and displays the value with two digits to the right of the decimal point. This is a drop-down control, so you can select other common currency symbols.
Percent Style	Displays the value as a percentage, with no decimal places. This button applies a style to the cell.
Comma Style	Separates thousands with a comma and displays the value with two digits to the right of the decimal place. It's like the Accounting number format but without the currency symbol. This button applies a style to the cell.
Increase Decimal	Increases the number of digits to the right of the decimal point by one.
Decrease Decimal	Decreases the number of digits to the right of the decimal point by one.

NOTE

Some of these buttons actually apply predefined styles to the selected cells. You can access Excel's styles by using the Style gallery in the Styles group on the Home tab. You can modify the styles by right-clicking the style name and choosing Modify from the shortcut menu. See Chapter 5, "Formatting Worksheets," for details.

Using shortcut keys to format numbers

Another way to apply number formatting is to use shortcut keys. Table 23.2 summarizes the shortcut key combinations that you can use to apply common number formatting to the selected cells or range. Notice that these are the shifted versions of the number keys along the top of a typical keyboard.

TABLE 23.2   Number-Formatting Keyboard Shortcuts

Key Combination	Formatting Applied
Ctrl+Shift+~	General number format (that is, unformatted values).
Ctrl+Shift+!	Two decimal places, thousands separator, and a hyphen for negative values.
Ctrl+Shift+@	Time format with the hour, minute, and AM or PM.
Ctrl+Shift+#	Date format with the day, month, and year.

Key Combination	Formatting Applied
Ctrl+Shift+$	Currency format with two decimal places. (Negative numbers appear in parentheses.)
Ctrl+Shift+%	Percentage format with no decimal places.
Ctrl+Shift+^	Scientific notation number format with two decimal places.

Using the Format Cells dialog box to format numbers

For maximum control of number formatting, you can use the Number tab in the Format Cells dialog box. You can access this dialog box in any of several ways:

- **Click the dialog box launcher at the bottom right of the Home ⇨ Number group.**
- **Choose Home ⇨ Number ⇨ Number Format ⇨ More Number Formats.**
- **Press Ctrl+1.**
- **Right-click a range of cells and select Format Cells command.**

The Number tab in the Format Cells dialog box contains 12 categories of number formats from which to choose. When you select a category from the list box, the right side of the dialog box changes to display appropriate options.

Here are the number format categories, along with some general comments:

General   The default format; it displays numbers as integers, as decimals, or in scientific notation if the value is too wide to fit into the cell.

Number   Specify the number of decimal places, whether to use your system's thousands separator (for example, a comma) to separate thousands, and how to display negative numbers.

Currency   Specify the number of decimal places, choose a currency symbol, and display negative numbers. This format always uses the system thousands separator symbol (for example, a comma) to separate thousands.

Accounting   Differs from the Currency format in that the currency symbols always line up vertically, regardless of the number of digits displayed in the value.

Date   Choose from a variety of date formats, and select the locale for your date formats.

Time   Choose from a number of time formats and select the locale for your time formats.

Percentage   Choose the number of decimal places; always displays a percent sign.

Fraction   Choose from among nine fraction formats.

Scientific   Displays numbers in exponential notation (with an E): $2.00E+05 = 200,000$. You can choose the number of decimal places to display to the left of E.

Text   When applied to a value, causes Excel to treat the value as text (even if it looks like a value). This feature is useful for such items as numerical part numbers and credit card numbers.

Special   Contains additional number formats. The list varies, depending on the locale you choose. For the English (United States) locale, the formatting options are Zip Code, Zip Code +4, Phone Number, and Social Security Number.

Custom   Define custom number formats not included in any of the other categories.

Getting fancy with custom number formatting

You may not know it, but when you apply number formatting, you are actually giving Excel instructions using a number format string. A number format string is a code that tells Excel how you want the values a given range to appear cosmetically.

To see this code, follow these steps to apply basic number formatting:

1. **Right-click a range of cells, and select Format Cells.** The Format Cells dialog box appears.

2. **Open the Number tab; then choose the Number category, select the Use 1000 Separator check box, 0 decimal places, and enclose negative numbers in parentheses.**

3. **Click the Custom category as shown in Figure 23.1.** Excel takes you to a screen that exposes the syntax that makes up the format you selected.

FIGURE 23.1

The Type input box allows you to customize the syntax for the number format.

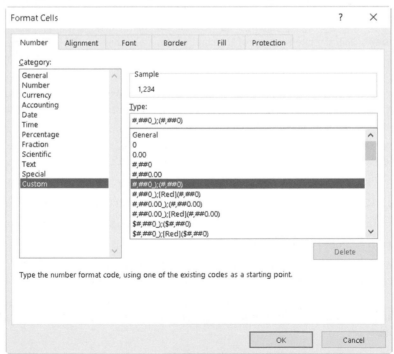

Number formatting strings consist of different individual number formats separated by semicolons. In this case, you see two different formats: the format to the left of the semicolon and the format to the right of the semicolon.

```
#,##0_);(#,##0)
```

By default, any formatting to the left of the first semicolon is applied to positive numbers, and any formatting to the right of the first semicolon is applied to negative numbers. So, with this choice, negative numbers will be formatted with parentheses, whereas positive numbers will be formatted as a simple number, like the following:

```
(1,890)
```

```
1,982
```

> **NOTE**
>
> Note that the syntax for the positive formatting in the previous example ends with _). This tells Excel to leave a space the width of a parenthesis character at the end of positive numbers. This ensures that positive and negative numbers align nicely when negative numbers are wrapped in parentheses.

You can edit the syntax in the Type input box so that the numbers are formatted differently. For example, try changing the syntax to the following:

```
+#,##0;-#,##0
```

When this syntax is applied, positive numbers will start with the + symbol, and negative numbers will start with a – symbol, like so:

```
+1,200
```

```
-15,000
```

This comes in handy when formatting percentages. For instance, you can apply a custom percent format by entering the following syntax into the Type input box:

```
+0%;-0%
```

This syntax gives you percentages that look like the following:

```
+43%
```

```
-54%
```

You can get fancy and wrap your negative percentages with parentheses with the following syntax:

```
0%_);(0%)
```

This syntax gives you percentages that look like the following:

```
43%
```

```
(54%)
```

23

NOTE

If you include only one format syntax, meaning that you don't add a second formatting option with the use of a semi-colon separator, that one format will be applied to all numbers, negative or positive.

Formatting numbers in thousands and millions

Formatting numbers to appear in thousands or millions is a way to present value without inundating your audience with overlarge numbers. To show your numbers in thousands, highlight them, right-click, and select Format Cells.

After the Format Cells dialog box opens, click the Custom category to get to the screen shown in Figure 23.1. In the Type input box, enter the following syntax:

    #,##0,

After you confirm your changes, your numbers will automatically appear in the thousands place.

The beautiful thing here is that this technique doesn't change or truncate your numeric values in any way. Excel is simply applying a cosmetic effect to the number. To see what this means, take a look at Figure 23.2.

FIGURE 23.2

Formatting numbers applies only a cosmetic look. Look in the formula bar to see the real, unformatted number.

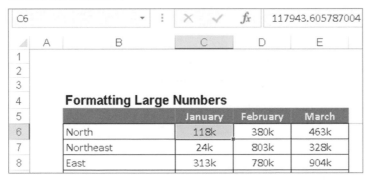

The selected cell has been formatted to show in thousands. You see 118k. But if you look in the formula bar above it, you'll see the real unformatted number (117943.605787004). The 118k you are seeing in the cell is a cosmetically formatted version of the real number shown in the formula bar.

> **NOTE**
>
> Custom number formatting has obvious advantages over using other techniques to format numbers to thousands. For instance, many beginning analysts would convert numbers to thousands by dividing them by 1,000 in a formula. But that changes the integrity of the number dramatically. When you perform a mathematical operation in a cell, you are literally changing the value represented in that cell. This forces you to carefully keep track of and maintain the formulas you introduced simply to achieve a cosmetic effect. Using custom number formatting avoids that by changing only how the number looks, keeping the actual number intact.

If needed, you can even indicate that the number is in thousands by adding "k" to the number syntax.

```
#,##0,"k"
```

This would show your numbers like this:

```
118k
```

```
318k
```

You can use this technique on both positive and negative numbers.

```
#,##0,"k"; (#,##0,"k")
```

After applying this syntax, your negative numbers also appear in thousands.

```
118k
```

```
(318k)
```

Need to show numbers in millions? Easy. Simply add two commas to the number format syntax in the Type input box.

```
#,##0.00,, "m"
```

Note the use of the extra decimal places (.00). When converting numbers to millions, it's often useful to show additional precision points, as in the following example:

```
24.65 m
```

Hiding and suppressing zeros

In addition to formatting positive and negative numbers, Excel allows you to provide a format for zeros. You do this by adding another semicolon to your custom number syntax. By default, any format syntax placed after the second semicolon is applied to any number that evaluates to zero.

For example, the following syntax applies a format that shows n/a for any cells that contain zeros:

```
#,##0_);(#,##0);"n/a"
```

You can also use this to suppress zeros entirely. If you add the second semicolon but don't follow it with any syntax, cells containing zeroes will appear blank.

```
#,##0_);(#,##0);
```

Again, custom number formatting affects only the cosmetic look of the cell. The actual data in the cell is not affected. Figure 23.3 demonstrates this. The selected cell is formatted so that zeros appear as n/a, but if you look at the Formula bar, you can see the actual unformatted cell contents.

FIGURE 23.3

Custom number formatting that shows zeros as n/a

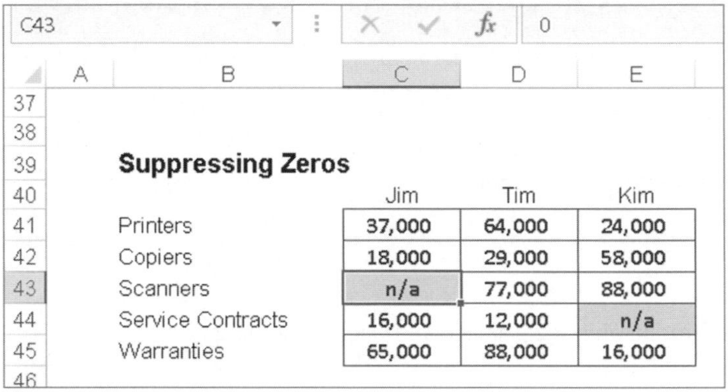

Applying custom format colors

In addition to controlling the look of your numbers with custom number formatting, you can also control their color. For instance, to format percentages so that positive percentages appear blue with a + symbol, while negative percentages appear red with a − symbol, enter this syntax in the Type input box:

```
[Blue]+0%;[Red]-0%
```

Notice that all it takes to apply a color is to enter the color name wrapped in square brackets: [ ].

There are only certain colors (the eight Visual Basic colors) you can call out by name, as shown here. These colors make up the first eight colors of Excel's legacy palette (the standard 56 colors that were the default in versions pre-2007).

```
[Black]
[Blue]
[Cyan]
[Green]
[Magenta]
[Red]
[White]
[Yellow]
```

Although you would typically specify a custom color by name, not all the Visual Basic colors are pleasing. Visual Basic Green is notoriously difficult to look at (bright neon green). See for yourself by entering the following code into the Type input box:

    [Green]+0%;[Red]-0%

The good news is that there are 56 colors defined in the standard color palette by number. Every color in the standard 56-color palette is represented by a number. To call up a color by number, you would use [ColorN], where N represents a number from 1 to 56.

In this example, you can use [Color10] to present a much more acceptable green.

    [Color10]+0%;[Red]-0%

Formatting dates and times

Custom number formatting isn't just for numbers. You can also format dates and times. As Figure 23.4 illustrates, you use the same dialog box to apply date and time formats using the Type input box.

FIGURE 23.4

Dates and times can also be formatted using the Format Cells dialog box.

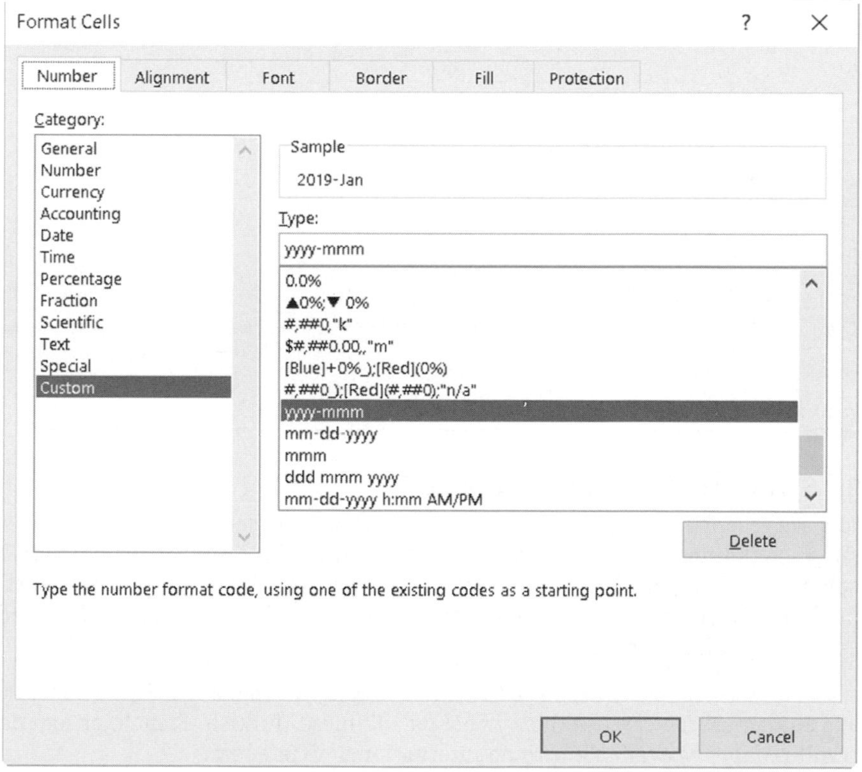

The code used for date and time formatting is fairly intuitive. For example, ddd is the syntax for the three-letter day, mmm is the syntax for the three-letter month, and yyyy is the syntax for the four-digit year.

There are several variations on the format for days, months, years, hours, and minutes. It's worthwhile to take some time and experiment with different combinations of syntax strings.

Table 23.3 lists some common date and time format codes that you can use as starter syntax for your reports and dashboards.

TABLE 23.3   Common Date and Time Format Codes

Format Code	1/31/2019 7:42:53 PM Displays As
M	1
Mm	01
mmm	Jan
mmmm	January
mmmmm	J
dd	31
ddd	Thu
dddd	Thursday
Yy	19
yyyy	2019
mmm-yy	Jan-19
dd/mm/yyyy	31/01/2019
dddd mmm yyyy	Thursday Jan 2019
mm-dd-yyyy h:mm AM/PM	01-31-2019 7:42 PM
h AM/PM	7 PM
h:mm AM/PM	7:42 PM
h:mm:ss AM/PM	7:42:53 PM

Using symbols to enhance reporting

Symbols are essentially tiny graphics, not unlike those you see when you use the Wingdings, Webdings, or other fancy fonts. However, symbols are not really fonts. They're Unicode characters. *Unicode characters* are a set of industry-standard text elements designed to provide a reliable character set that remains viable on any platform regardless of international font differences.

One example of a commonly used symbol is the copyright symbol (©). This symbol is a Unicode character. You can use this symbol on a Chinese, Turkish, French, or American PC, and it will reliably be available with no international differences.

In terms of Excel presentations, Unicode characters (or symbols) can be used in places where conditional formatting cannot. For instance, in the chart labels that you see in Figure 23.5, the x-axis shows some trending arrows that allow for an extra layer of analysis. This couldn't be done with conditional formatting.

FIGURE 23.5

Use symbols to add an extra layer of analysis to charts.

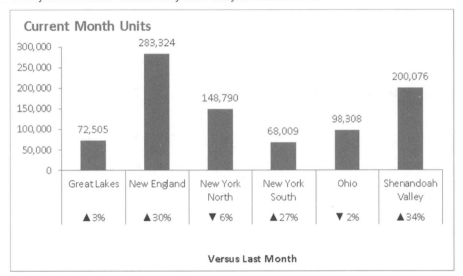

Let's take some time to review the steps that led to the chart in Figure 23.5.

Start with the data shown in Figure 23.6. Note that you have a designated cell to hold any symbols that you're going to use (C1 in this case). This cell isn't really all that important. It's just a holding cell for the symbols that you'll insert.

FIGURE 23.6

Our starting data with a holding cell for our symbols

	A	B	C	D
1		Symbols>>		
2				
3		vs. Prior Month	Market	Current Month
4		3%	Great Lakes	72,505
5		30%	New England	283,324
6		-6%	New York North	148,790
7		27%	New York South	68,009
8		-2%	Ohio	98,308
9		34%	Shenandoah Valley	200,076

Now, follow these steps:

1. **Click in C1 and then select the Symbol command on the Insert tab.** The Symbol dialog box shown in Figure 23.7 opens.

FIGURE 23.7

Use the Symbol dialog box to insert the desired symbols into your holding cell.

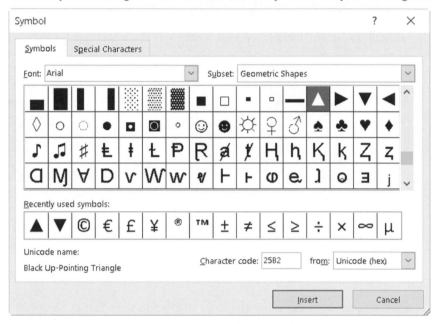

2. **Find and select your desired symbols by clicking the Insert button after each symbol.** In this scenario, select the upward-pointing triangle and click Insert. Then click the downward-pointing triangle and click Insert. Close the dialog box when you're done. At this point, you have the up triangle and down triangle symbols in cell C1, as shown in Figure 23.8.

FIGURE 23.8

Copy the newly inserted symbols to the Clipboard.

	A	B	C	D
1		Symbols>>	▲▼	
2				
3		vs. Prior Month	Market	Current Month
4		3%	Great Lakes	72,505
5		30%	New England	283,324
6		-6%	New York North	148,790
7		27%	New York South	68,009
8		-2%	Ohio	98,308
9		34%	Shenandoah Valley	200,076

3. **Click the C1 cell, go to the Formula bar, and copy the two symbols by highlighting them and pressing Ctrl+C on your keyboard.**

4. **Go to your data table, right-click the percentages, and then select Format Cells.**

5. **In the Format Cells dialog box, create a new custom format by pasting the up- and down-triangle symbols into the appropriate syntax parts (see Figure 23.9).** In this case, any positive percentage will be preceded with the up-triangle symbol, and any negative percentage will be preceded with the down-triangle symbol.

FIGURE 23.9

Create a custom number format using the symbols.

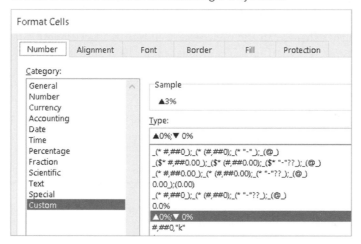

6. **Click OK.** The symbols are now part of your number formatting.

Figure 23.10 illustrates what your percentages look like. Change any number from positive to negative (or vice versa), and Excel automatically applies the appropriate symbol.

FIGURE 23.10

Your symbols are now part of your number formatting.

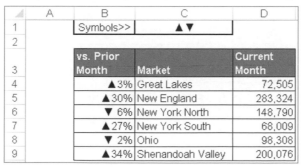

Because charts automatically adopt number formatting, a chart created from this data will show the symbols as part of the labels. Simply use this data as the source for the chart.

This is just one way to use symbols in your reporting. With this basic technique, you can insert symbols to add visual appeal to tables, pivot tables, formulas, or any other object you can think of.

Using Shapes and Icons as Visual Elements

Microsoft Office, including Excel, provides access to a variety of customizable graphics images known as *shapes*. You might want to insert shapes to create simple diagrams, display text, or just add some visual appeal to a worksheet.

Keep in mind that shapes can add unnecessary clutter to a worksheet. Perhaps the best advice is to use shapes sparingly. Ideally, shapes can help draw attention to some aspect of your worksheet. They shouldn't be the main attraction.

Inserting a shape

You can add a shape to a worksheet by choosing Insert ➪ Shapes from the Illustrations group. The Shapes gallery, shown in Figure 23.11, opens to show you the choices.

FIGURE 23.11

The Shapes gallery

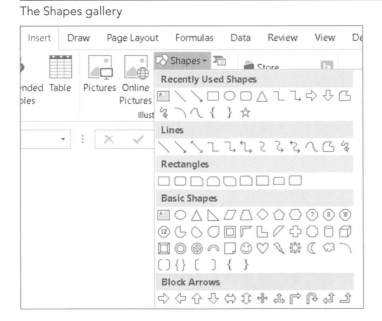

Shapes are organized into categories, and the category at the top displays the shapes that you've used most recently. To insert a shape into a worksheet, you can do one of the following:

- **Click the shape in the Shapes gallery and then click in the worksheet.** A default-sized shape is added to your worksheet.
- **Click the shape and then drag in the worksheet.** This allows you to create a larger or a smaller shape or a shape with different proportions than the default.

Here are a few tips to keep in mind when creating shapes:

- Every shape has a name. Some have generic names like Shape 1 and Shape 2, but others are given more descriptive names (for example, Rectangle 1). To change the name of a shape, select it, type a new name in the Name box, and press Enter.
- To select a specific shape on a worksheet, just click it.
- When you create a shape by dragging, hold down the Shift key to maintain the object's default proportions.
- You can control the way objects appear on-screen in the Advanced tab of the Excel Options dialog box. (Choose File ⇨ Options.) This setting appears in the Display Options for This Workbook section. Normally, the All option is selected under For Objects Show. You can hide all objects by choosing Nothing (Hide Objects). Hiding objects may speed things up if your worksheet contains complex objects that take a long time to redraw.

Inserting SVG icon graphics

Excel 2019 includes a new icon library that offers free Scalable Vector Graphics (SVG) icons. SVG graphics can be sized and formatted without losing image quality. These icon graphics are essentially a modern set of graphic files that can be used to add visual elements to your Excel dashboards, infographics, and reporting solutions.

To add an icon to your worksheet, select Insert ⇨ Icons from the Illustrations group. This activates the Insert Icons dialog box (see Figure 23.12). Here you can browse by category and then double-click the graphic you want to use. Excel will insert it into your workbook.

23

FIGURE 23.12

The Microsoft Office Icons Library

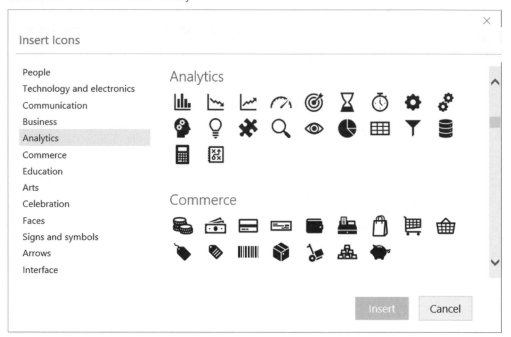

Selecting and Hiding Shape Objects

An easy way to select an object is to use the Selection task pane. Just select any shape and then choose Drawing Tools ➪ Format ➪ Arrange ➪ Selection Pane. Or, if a shape isn't selected, you can choose Home ➪ Editing ➪ Find & Select ➪ Selection Pane.

Each object on the active worksheet is listed in the Selection task pane. Just click the object's name to select it. To select multiple objects, press Ctrl while you click the names.

To hide an object, click the "eye" icon to the right of its name. Use the buttons at the top of the task pane to hide (or show) all items quickly.

Formatting shapes and icons

Although icons feel and behave like standard shapes, they have different contextual menus (see Figure 23.13).

FIGURE 23.13

Shapes and icons have different contextual tabs.

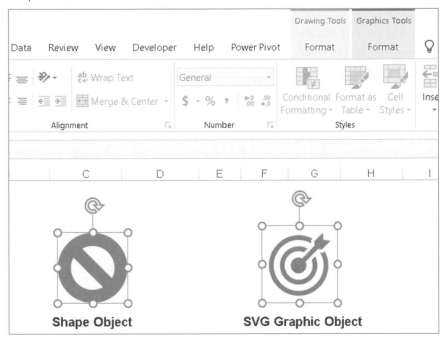

When you select a shape, the Drawing Tools ➪ Format contextual tab is available, with the following groups of commands:

Insert Shapes   Insert new shapes; change a shape to a different shape.

Shape Styles   Change the overall style of a shape; modify the shape's fill, outline, or effects.

WordArt Styles   Modify the appearance of the text within a shape.

Arrange   Adjust the "stack order" of shapes, align shapes, group multiple shapes, and rotate shapes.

Size   Change the size of a shape by typing dimensions.

When you select an icon, the Graphics Tools ➪ Format contextual tab is available with the following groups of commands:

Change Graphic   Replace an existing graphic with a new graphic from a file, the Microsoft icons gallery, or an online source.

Graphics Styles   Change the overall style of the selected graphic; modify the shape's fill, outline, or effects.

Accessibility   Provide alternate text for the seeing impaired.

Arrange   Adjust the "stack order" of shapes, align shapes, group multiple shapes, and rotate shapes.

Size   Change the size of a shape by typing dimensions.

As an alternative to the Ribbon, you can use the Format Shape and Format Graphic task panes, respectively. Right-click the shape or icon and choose the Format option. The task pane contains some additional formatting options that aren't on the Ribbon. Changes appear immediately, and you can keep the Format Shape task pane open while you work.

You could read 20 pages about formatting shapes and icons, but it wouldn't be a very efficient way of learning. The best way, by far, to learn about formatting shapes and icons is to experiment. The formatting commands are intuitive, and you can always use Undo if a command doesn't do what you expected it to do.

Enhancing Excel reports with shapes

Most of us think of Excel shapes as mildly useful objects that can be added to a worksheet if we need to show a square, some arrows, a circle, and so forth. But if you use your imagination, you can leverage Excel shapes to create stylized interfaces that can really enhance your dashboards. Here are a few examples how Excel shapes can spice up your dashboards and reports.

Creating visually appealing containers with shapes

A *peekaboo tab* lets you tag a section of your dashboard with a label that looks like it's wrapping around your dashboard components. In the example illustrated in Figure 23.14, a peekaboo tab is used to label this group of components as belonging to the North region.

FIGURE 23.14

Peekaboo tab

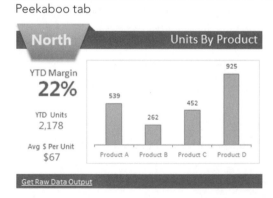

As you can see in Figure 23.15, there is no real magic here. It's just a set of shapes and text boxes that are cleverly arranged to give the impression that a label is wrapping around to show the region name.

FIGURE 23.15

Deconstructed view of the peekaboo tab

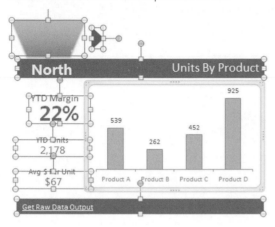

Want to draw attention to handful of key metrics? Try wrapping your key metrics with a peekaboo banner. The banner shown in Figure 23.16 goes beyond boring text labels, allowing you to create the feeling that a banner is wrapping around your numbers. Again, this effect is achieved by layering a few Excel shapes so that they fall nicely on top of each other, creating a cohesive effect.

FIGURE 23.16

A visual banner made with shapes

Layering shapes to save space

Here's an idea to get the most out of your dashboard real estate. You can layer pie charts with column charts to create a unique set of views (see Figure 23.17).

FIGURE 23.17

Combine shapes with a chart to save dashboard real estate.

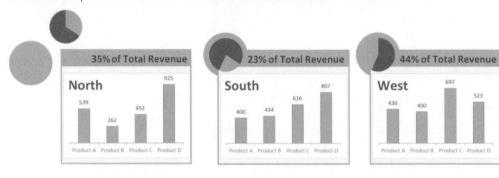

Each pie chart represents the percent of total revenue and a column chart showing some level of detail for the region. Simply layer your pie chart on top of a circle shape and a column chart.

Constructing your own infographic widgets with shapes

Excel offers a way to alter shapes by editing their anchor points. This opens up the possibility of creating your own infographic widgets. Right-click a shape and select Edit Points. This places little points all around the shape (see Figure 23.18). You can then drag the points to reconfigure the shape.

FIGURE 23.18

Use the Edit Points feature to construct your own shape.

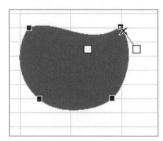

Constructed shapes can be combined with other shapes to create interesting infographic elements that can be used in your Excel dashboards. In Figure 23.19, a newly constructed shape is combined with a standard oval and text box to create nifty infographic widgets.

FIGURE 23.19

Using a newly constructed shape to create custom infographic elements

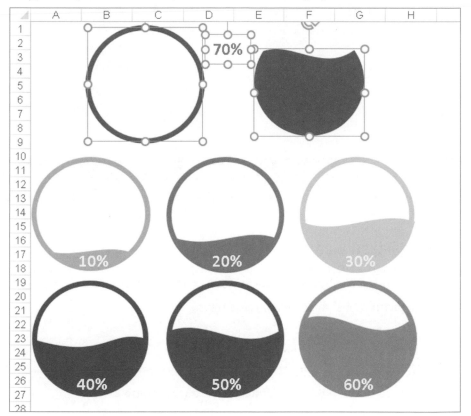

Creating dynamic labels

Dynamic labeling is less a function in Excel than it is a concept. *Dynamic labels* are labels that change to correspond to the data you're viewing.

Figure 23.20 illustrates one example of this concept. The selected Text Box shape is linked to cell C3 (note the formula in the Formula bar). As the value in cell C3 changes, the text box displays the updated value.

FIGURE 23.20

Text Box shapes can be linked to cells.

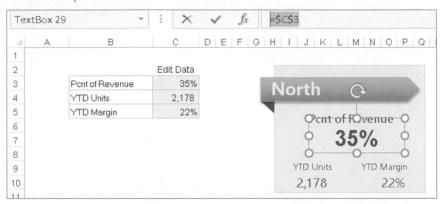

> **NOTE**
> Be aware that Text Box shape objects cannot display more than 255 characters.

Creating linked pictures

A *linked picture* is a special kind of shape that displays a live picture of everything in a given range. Think of a linked picture as a camera that monitors a range of cells.

To "take a picture" of a range, follow these steps:

1. **Select the range.**
2. **Press Ctrl+C to copy the range.**
3. **Activate another cell.**
4. **Choose Home ⇨ Paste ⇨ Linked Picture (see Figure 23.21).**

The result is a live picture of the range you selected in step 1.

FIGURE 23.21

Pasting a linked picture

Linked pictures give you the freedom to test different layouts and chart sizes without the need to work around column widths, hidden rows, or other such nonsense. In addition, linked pictures have access to the Picture Tools formatting options. When you click on a linked picture, you can go to the Picture Tools contextual tab and play around with the picture styles there.

Figure 23.22 illustrates two linked pictures displaying the contents of the ranges on the left. As those ranges change, the linked pictures on the right will update. These can be moved, resized, and even placed on a completely different sheet.

23

FIGURE 23.22

Using linked pictures to enhance visualizations

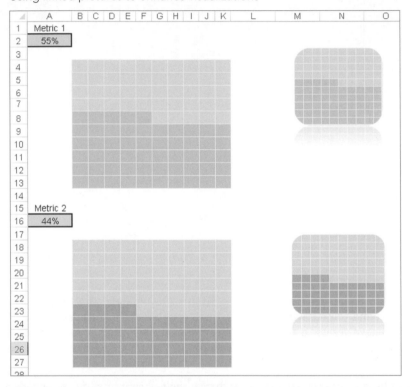

TIP

The Excel Camera tool provides an easier way to create a linked picture. Unfortunately, it's not on the Ribbon interface, so it's not that easy to find. If you use this feature frequently, you can save some time by adding the Excel Camera tool to your Quick Access toolbar as follows:

1. Right-click the Quick Access toolbar, and choose Customize Quick Access Toolbar from the shortcut menu that appears. The Excel Options dialog box appears, with the Quick Access Toolbar tab selected.

2. Select Command Not in the Ribbon from the drop-down list on the left.

3. Select Camera from the list and click Add.

4. Click OK to close the Excel Options dialog box.

After you add the Camera tool to your Quick Access toolbar, you can select a range of cells and click the Camera tool to take a "picture" of the range. Then click in the worksheet, and Excel places a live picture of the selected range on the worksheet's draw layer. If you make changes to the original ranges, the changes are shown in the picture of the range.

Using SmartArt and WordArt

Using *SmartArt*, you can insert a variety of highly customizable diagrams into a worksheet, and you can change the overall look of the diagram with a few mouse clicks. This feature was introduced in Office 2007, and it is probably most useful for PowerPoint users. But many Excel users will be able to make good use of SmartArt.

SmartArt basics

To insert SmartArt into a worksheet, choose the SmartArt command found under Insert ⇨ Illustrations. Excel displays the dialog box shown in Figure 23.23. The diagrams are arranged in categories along the left. When you find one that looks appropriate, click it for a larger view in the panel on the right, which also provides some usage tips. Then click OK to insert the graphic.

FIGURE 23.23

Inserting a SmartArt graphic

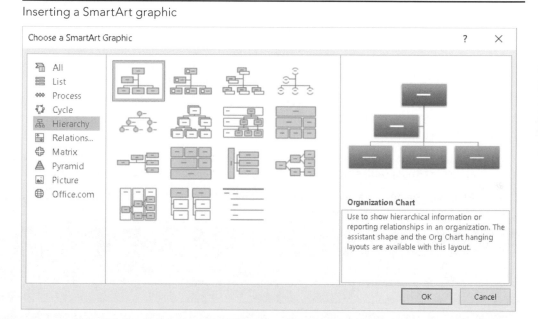

23

When you insert or select a SmartArt diagram, Excel displays the Type Your Text Here window that guides you through entering text (see Figure 23.24)

FIGURE 23.24

Entering text for an organizational chart

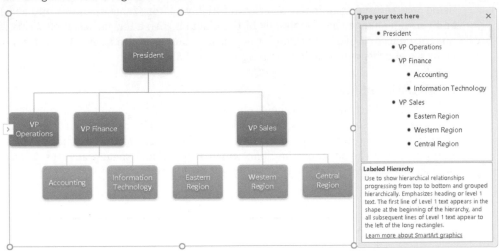

To add an element to the SmartArt graphic, choose SmartArt Tools ⇨ Design ⇨ Create Graphic ⇨ Add Shape. Or, you can just select an item and press Enter.

When working with SmartArt, keep in mind that you can move, resize, or format individually any element within the graphic. Select the element and then use the tools on the SmartArt Tools ⇨ Format tab.

You can easily change the layout of a SmartArt diagram. Select the object and then choose SmartArt Tools ⇨ Design ⇨ Layouts. Any text that you've entered remains intact.

After you decide on a layout, you may want to consider other styles or colors available in the SmartArt Tools ⇨ Design ⇨ SmartArt Styles group.

TIP

SmartArt styles available vary depending on the document theme assigned to the workbook. To change a workbook's theme, choose Page Layout ⇨ Themes ⇨ Themes. Switching to a different theme can have a dramatic impact on the appearance of SmartArt diagrams.

WordArt basics

You can use *WordArt* to create graphical effects in text.

To insert a WordArt graphic on a worksheet, choose Insert ⇨ Text ⇨ WordArt and then select a style from the gallery. Excel inserts an object with the placeholder text Your text here. Replace that text with your own, resize it, and apply other formatting if you like.

When you select a WordArt image, Excel displays its Drawing Tools contextual menu. Use the controls to vary the look of your WordArt. Or, right-click and choose Format Shape to use the task pane.

Word Art consists of two components: the text and the shape that contains the text. The Format Shape task pane has two headings (Shape Options and Text Options). The Ribbon controls in the Drawing Tools ⇨ Format ⇨ Shape Styles group operate on the shape that contains the text—not the text. To apply text formatting, use the controls in the Drawing Tools ⇨ Format ⇨ WordArt Styles group. You can also use some of the standard formatting controls on the Home tab or the Mini toolbar.

Working with Other Graphics Types

Excel can import a variety of graphics into a worksheet. You have several choices:

Inserting an image from your computer If the graphics image that you want to insert is available in a file, you can easily import the file into your worksheet. Choose Insert ⇨ Illustrations ⇨ Pictures. The Insert Picture dialog box appears, allowing you to browse for the file. Oddly, you can't drag and drop an image into a worksheet, but you can drag an image from your web browser and drop it into a worksheet.

Inserting an image from an online source Choose Insert ⇨ Illustrations ⇨ Online Pictures. The Insert Pictures window appears, allowing you to search for an image.

Copying and pasting If an image is on the Windows Clipboard, you can paste it into a worksheet by choosing Home ⇨ Clipboard ⇨ Paste (or by pressing Ctrl+V).

About graphics files

Graphics files come in two main categories:

Bitmap Bitmap images are made up of discrete dots. They usually look pretty good at their original size but often lose clarity if you increase the size. Examples of common bitmap file formats include BMP, PNG, JPEG, TIFF, and GIF.

Vector Vector-based images, on the other hand, are composed of points and paths that are represented by mathematical equations, so they retain their crispness regardless of their size. Examples of common vector file formats include CGM, WMF, and EPS.

You can find millions of graphics files free for the taking on the Internet. Be aware, however, that some graphics files have copyright restrictions.

CAUTION
Using bitmap graphics in a worksheet can dramatically increase the size of your workbook.

23

When you insert a picture on a worksheet, you can modify the picture in a number of ways from the Picture Tools ⇨ Format contextual tab, which becomes available when you select a picture object. For example, you can adjust the color, contrast, and brightness. In addition, you can add borders, shadows, reflections, and so on—similar to the operations available for shapes.

In addition, you can right-click and choose Format Picture to use the controls in the Format Picture task pane.

An interesting feature is *Artistic Effects*. This command can apply a number of Photoshop-like effects to an image. To access this feature, select an image and choose Picture Tools ⇨ Format ⇨ Adjust ⇨ Artistic Effects. Each effect is somewhat customizable, so if you're not happy with the default effect, try adjusting some options.

You might be surprised by some of the image enhancements that are available, including the ability to remove the background from photos. The best way to learn about these features is to dig in and experiment. Even if you have no need for image enhancement, you might find that it's a fun diversion when you need a break from working with numbers.

Inserting screenshots

Excel can also capture and insert a screenshot of any program currently running on your computer (including another Excel window). To use the screenshot feature, follow these steps:

1. **Make sure the window you want to use displays the content you want.**
2. **Choose Insert ⇨ Illustrations ⇨ Screenshot.** You'll see a gallery that contains thumbnails of all windows open on your computer (except the current Excel window).
3. **Click the image you want.** Excel inserts it into your worksheet.

You can use any of the normal picture tools to work with screenshots.

If you don't want to capture a complete window, choose Screen Clipping in step 2. Then click and drag your mouse to select the area of the screen to capture.

Displaying a worksheet background image

If you want to use a graphics image for a worksheet's background (similar to wallpaper on the Windows Desktop), choose Page Layout ⇨ Page Setup ⇨ Background and select a graphics file. The selected graphics file is tiled on the worksheet.

Unfortunately, worksheet background images are for on-screen display only. These images do not appear when the worksheet is printed.

Using the Equation Editor

The final section in this chapter deals with the Equation Editor. Use this feature to insert a nicely formatted mathematical equation as a graphics object.

Figure 23.25 shows an example of an equation in a worksheet. Keep in mind that these equations do not perform calculations; they're for display purposes only.

FIGURE 23.25

An equation created by the Equation Editor

$$x = \frac{-b \pm \sqrt{b^2 - 4ac}}{2a}$$

The best way to become familiar with the Equation Editor is to insert one of the premade equations. Choose Insert ⇨ Symbols ⇨ Equation, and choose one of equations from the gallery. The equation is inserted into your worksheet.

When you select an Equation object, you have access to two contextual tabs:

Drawing Tools   Used to format the container object

Equation Tools   Used to edit the equation

The Equation Tools ⇨ Design tab contains three groups of controls:

Tools   Used to insert a new equation or control how the equation is displayed. Click the dialog box launcher in the bottom-right corner of the Tools group to display the Equation Options dialog box, where you can specify the way the equation is copied and define keyboard shortcuts (click Math AutoCorrect).

Symbols   Contains common mathematical symbols and operators that you can use in your equations.

Structures   Contains templates for various structures that are used in equations.

Describing how to use the Equation tools is more difficult than actually using them. Generally, you add a structure and then edit the various parts by adding text or symbols. You can put structures inside structures, and there is no limit to the complexity of the equations. It might be a bit tricky at first, but it doesn't take long before you understand how it works.

Implementing Excel Dashboarding Best Practices

IN THIS CHAPTER

Preparing for a dashboard project

Dashboard modeling best practices

Dashboard design best practices

A *dashboard* is a visual interface that provides at-a-glance views into key measures relevant to a particular objective or business process. Dashboards have three main attributes:

- Dashboards are typically graphical in nature, providing visualizations that help focus attention on key trends, comparisons, and exceptions.
- Dashboards often display data that is relevant only to the goal of the dashboard.
- Because dashboards are designed with a specific purpose or goal, they inherently contain predefined conclusions that relieve end users from performing their own analysis.

Maybe you've been hit with dashboard fever. Or, your manager might be hounding you with dashboard fever. Whatever the case, if you're being asked to create dashboard solutions in Excel, it's tempting to start pulling a few charts together to create the dashboards you need.

Before you go into the world ready to use the charting techniques you've gathered here, however, it's valuable to understand some of the best practices for designing and creating dashboards.

This chapter is not about the mechanics of Excel. It is a look at some of the best practices and design principles to keep in mind as you develop your own reporting solutions.

Preparing for a Dashboard Project

Imagine that your manager asks you to create a dashboard that provides everything there is to know about monthly service subscriptions. Do you jump to action and slap together whatever comes to mind? Do you take a guess at what your manager wants to see and hope that it's useful? These questions sound ridiculous, but such situations happen more than you think.

To approach a dashboarding project, you truly have to get into the dashboard state of mind. Dashboarding requires far more preparation than standard Excel analyses. It calls for closer communication with business leaders and a deeper understanding of user requirements.

Consider how many times a manager has asked you for an analysis and then said, "No, I meant this." Or, "Now that I see it, I realize that I need this." As frustrating as this can be for a single analysis, imagine running into it again and again during the creation of a complex dashboard with several data integration processes. The question is, would you rather spend your time on the front end gathering user requirements or spend time on the back end painstakingly redesigning the dashboard because it doesn't meet expectations?

The process of gathering user requirements doesn't have to be an overly complicated or formal one. Here are some simple things you can do to ensure that you have a solid idea of the purpose of the dashboard.

Establishing the audience and purpose for the dashboard

Chances are that your manager has been asked to create the reporting mechanism and has passed the task to you. Don't be afraid to ask about the source of the initial request. Talk to the requestors about what they're really asking for. Discuss the purpose of the dashboard and the triggers that caused them to ask for a dashboard in the first place. You may find that after discussing the matter, a simple Excel report meets their needs, forgoing the need for a full-on dashboard.

If a dashboard is indeed warranted, talk about who are the end users. Take some time to meet with a few of the end users to talk about how they'd use the dashboard. Will the dashboard be used as a performance tool for regional managers? Will the dashboard be used to share data with external customers? Talking through these fundamental questions with the right people will help to align your thoughts and avoid the creation of a dashboard that doesn't fulfill the necessary requirements.

Delineating the measures for the dashboard

Most dashboards are designed around a set of measures, or *key performance indicators* (KPIs). A KPI is an indicator of the performance of a task deemed to be essential to daily operations or processes. The idea is that a KPI reveals performance that is outside the normal range for a particular measure, so therefore it often signals the need for attention and intervention. Although the measures you place into your dashboards may not officially be called KPIs, they undoubtedly serve the same purpose, that is, to draw attention to problem areas.

The measures used on a dashboard should absolutely support the initial purpose of that dashboard. For example, if you're creating a dashboard focused on supply chain processes, it may not make sense to have human resources' headcount data incorporated. It's generally a good practice to avoid nice-to-know data in your dashboards simply to fill white space or because the data is available. If the data doesn't support the core purpose of the dashboard, leave it out.

Cataloging the required data sources

When you have the list of measures that need to be included on the dashboard, it's important to take a tally of the available systems to determine whether the data required to produce those measures are available. Ask yourself the following questions:

- Do you have access to the necessary data sources?
- How often are those data sources refreshed?
- Who owns and maintains those data sources?
- What are the processes to get the data from those resources?
- Does the data even exist?

These are all questions that you need answered when negotiating dashboard development time, data refresh intervals, and change management.

Defining the dimensions and filters for the dashboard

In the context of reporting, a *dimension* is a data category used to organize business data. Examples of dimensions are Region, Market, Branch, Manager, or Employee. When you define a dimension in the user requirements stage of development, you're determining how the measures should be grouped or distributed. For example, if your dashboard should report data by employee, you need to ensure that your data collection and aggregation processes include employee detail. As you can imagine, adding a new dimension after the dashboard is built can get complicated, especially when your processes require many aggregations across multiple data sources. The bottom line is that locking down the dimensions for a dashboard early in the process definitely saves you headaches.

Along those same lines, you want to get a clear sense of the types of filters that are required. In the context of dashboards, *filters* are mechanisms that allow you to narrow the scope of the data to a single dimension. For example, you can filter on Year, Employee, or Region. Again, if you don't account for a particular filter while building your dashboarding process, you'll likely be forced into an unpleasant redesign of both your data collection processes and your dashboard.

If you're confused by the difference between dimensions and filters, think about a simple Excel table. A dimension is like a column of data (such as a column containing employee names) in an Excel table. A filter, then, is the mechanism that allows you to narrow your table to show only the data for a particular employee. For example, if you apply Excel's AutoFilter to the employee column, you are building a filter mechanism into your table.

Determining the need for drill-down features

Many dashboards provide *drill-down features* that allow users to "drill" into the details of a specific measure. You want to get a clear understanding of the types of drill-downs your users have in mind.

To most users, a drill-down feature means the ability to get a raw data table supporting the measures shown on the dashboard. Although getting raw data isn't always practical

24

or possible, discussing these requests will, at a minimum, allow you to talk to your users about additional reporting, links to other data sources, and other solutions that may help them get the data they need.

Establishing the refresh schedule

A *refresh schedule* refers to the schedule by which a dashboard is updated to show the latest information available. Because you're the one responsible for building and maintaining the dashboard, you should have a say in the refresh schedules, as your manager may not know what it takes to refresh the dashboard in question.

While you're determining the refresh schedule, keep in mind the refresh rates of the different data sources whose measures you need to retrieve. You can't refresh your dashboard any faster than your data sources. Also, negotiate enough development time to build macros that aid in automation of redundant and time-consuming refresh tasks.

Implementing Dashboard Modeling Best Practices

Most people spend very little time thinking about the supporting data model behind a reporting process. If they think about it at all, they usually start by imagining a mock-up of the finished dashboard and work backward from there.

Instead of seeing just the finished dashboard in your head, try to think of the end-to-end process. Where will you get the data? How should the data be structured? What analysis will need to be performed? How will the data be fed to the dashboard? How will the dashboard be refreshed?

Obviously, the answers to these questions are highly situation specific. However, some data modeling best practices will guide you to a new way of thinking about your reporting process. These are discussed in the next few sections.

Separating data, analysis, and presentation

One of the most important concepts in a data model is the separation of data, analysis, and presentation. The fundamental idea is that you don't want your data to become too tied into any one particular way of presenting that data.

To get your mind around this concept, think about an invoice. When you receive an invoice, you don't assume that the financial data on that invoice is the true source of your data. It's merely a presentation of data that's actually stored in some database. That data can be analyzed and presented to you in many other manners: in charts, in tables, or even on websites. This sounds obvious, but Excel users often fuse data, analysis, and presentation together.

For instance, we've seen Excel workbooks that contain 12 tabs, each representing a month. On each tab, data for that month is listed along with formulas, pivot tables, and summaries. Now what happens when you're asked to provide summary by quarter? Do you add more formulas and tabs to consolidate the data on each of the month tabs? The fundamental problem in this scenario is that the tabs actually represent data values that are fused into the presentation of your analysis.

A best practice for avoiding these kinds of scalability issues is to build three layers into your data model: a data layer, an analysis layer, and a presentation layer.

You can think of these layers as three different spreadsheets in an Excel workbook: one sheet to hold the raw data that feeds your report, one sheet to serve as a staging area where the data is analyzed and shaped, and one sheet to serve as the presentation layer.

The analysis layer consists primarily of formulas that analyze and pull data from the data layer into formatted tables commonly referred to as *staging tables*. These staging tables ultimately feed the reporting components in your presentation layer (such as charts, conditional formatting, and other visualizations). In short, the sheet that contains the analysis layer becomes the staging area where data is summarized and shaped to feed your dashboard components.

There are a couple of benefits to this setup. First, the entire reporting model can be refreshed easily simply by replacing the raw data with an updated data set. The formulas in the analysis tab continue to work with the latest data. Second, any additional analysis can easily be created by using different combinations of formulas on the analysis tab. If you need data that doesn't exist in the data sheet, you can easily append a column to the end of the raw data set without disturbing the analysis or presentation sheets.

Note that you don't necessarily have to place your data, analysis, and presentation layers on different spreadsheets. In small data models, you may find it easier to place your data in one area of a spreadsheet while building your staging tables in another area of the same spreadsheet.

Along those same lines, remember that you're not limited to just three spreadsheets either. That is to say, you can have several sheets that provide the raw data, several sheets that analyze, and several sheets that serve as the presentation layer.

Wherever you choose to place the different layers, keep in mind that the idea remains the same—the analysis layer should primarily consist of formulas that pull data from the data sheets into staging tables used to feed your presentation.

Starting with appropriately structured data

Not all data sets are created equal. Although some data sets work in a standard Excel environment, they may not work for data modeling purposes. Before building your data model, you will want to be sure that your source data is appropriately structured for dashboarding purposes.

Spreadsheet reports make for ineffective data models

Spreadsheet reports display highly formatted, summarized data, and they are often designed as presentation tools for management or executive users. A typical spreadsheet report makes judicious use of empty space for formatting, repeats data for aesthetic purposes, and presents only high-level analysis.

Although a spreadsheet report may look nice, it doesn't make for an effective data model. Why? The primary reason is that these reports offer no separation of data, analysis, and presentation. You're essentially locked into one analysis.

Flat data files lend themselves nicely to data models

The next type of file format is a flat file. *Flat files* are data repositories organized by row and column. Each row corresponds to a set of data elements, or a *record*. Each column is a *field*. A field corresponds to a unique data element in a record. Furthermore, there's no extra spacing, and each row (or record) corresponds to a unique set of information.

Flat files lend themselves nicely to data modeling in Excel because they can be detailed enough to hold the data you need and still be conducive to a wide array of analysis with simple formulas: SUM, AVERAGE, VLOOKUP, and SUMIF, just to name a few.

Avoiding turning your data model into a database

In an effort to have as much data as possible at their fingertips, many Excel users bring into their spreadsheets every piece of data on which they can lay their hands. You can spot these people by the 40-megabyte files they send through e-mail. You've seen these spreadsheets: two tabs that contain the presentation and six hidden tabs that contain thousands of rows of data (most of which isn't used). They essentially build a database in their spreadsheet.

What's wrong with utilizing as much data as possible? Well, here are a few issues:

- **Aggregating data within Excel increases the number of formulas.** If you're bringing in all raw data, you have to aggregate that data in Excel. This inevitably causes you to increase exponentially the number of formulas that you have to employ and maintain. Remember that your data model is a vehicle for presenting analyses, not processing raw data. The data that works best in reporting mechanisms is what's already been aggregated and summarized into useful views that can be navigated and fed to dashboard components. Importing data that's already been aggregated as much as possible is far better. For example, if you need to report on Revenue by Region and Month, there's no need to import sales transactions into your data model. Instead, use an aggregated table consisting of Region, Month, and Sum of Revenue.

- **Your data model will be distributed with your dashboard.** In other words, because your dashboard is fed by your data model, you need to maintain the model behind the scenes (likely in hidden tabs) when distributing the dashboard. Besides the fact that it causes the file size to be unwieldy, including too much data in your data model can actually degrade the performance of your dashboard. Why? When you open an Excel file, the entire file is loaded into memory or RAM to ensure quick data processing and access. The drawback to this behavior is that Excel requires a great deal of RAM to process even the smallest change in your spreadsheet. You may have noticed that when you try to perform an action on a large formula-intensive data set, Excel is slow to respond, giving you a "Calculating" indicator in the status bar. The larger your data set is, the less efficient the data crunching in Excel will be.

■ **Large data sets can cause difficulty in scalability.** Imagine that you're working in a small company and you're using monthly transactions in your data model. Each month holds 80,000 rows of data. As time goes on, you build a robust process complete with all of the formulas, pivot tables, and macros that you need to analyze the data that's stored in your neatly maintained tab. Now what happens after one year? Do you start a new tab? How do you analyze two data sets on two different tabs as one entity? Are your formulas still good? Do you have to write new macros?

These are all issues that can be avoided by importing only aggregated and summarized data that's useful to the core purpose of your reporting needs.

Documenting and organizing your data model

Wanting to keep your data model limited to one worksheet tab is natural. Most users would think that keeping track of one tab is much simpler than using different tabs. However, limiting your data model to one tab has its drawbacks, including the following:

■ **Using one tab typically places limits on your analysis.** Because only so many data sets can fit on a tab, using one tab limits the number of analyses that can be represented in your data model. This in turn limits the analysis your dashboard can offer. Consider adding tabs to your data model to provide additional data and analysis that may not fit on just one tab.

■ **Too much on one tab makes for a confusing data model.** When working with large data sets, you need plenty of staging tables to aggregate and shape the raw data so that it can be fed to your reporting components. If you use only one tab, you're forced to position these staging tables below or to the right of your data sets. Although this may provide all of the elements needed to feed your presentation layer, a good deal of scrolling is necessary to view all of the elements positioned in a wide range of areas. This makes the data model difficult to understand and maintain. Use separate tabs to hold your analysis and staging tables, particularly in data models that contain large data sets occupying a lot of real estate.

■ **Using one tab limits the amount of documentation that you can include.** You'll find that your data models easily become a complex system of intertwining links among components, input ranges, output ranges, and formulas. Sure, it all makes sense while you're building your data model, but try coming back to it after a few months. You'll find that you've forgotten what each data range does and how each range interacts with the final presentation layer. To avoid this problem, consider adding a model map tab to your data model. The *model map* tab essentially summarizes the key ranges in the data model and allows you to document how each range interacts with the reporting components in the final presentation layer.

24

You can include any information that you think is appropriate in your model map. The idea is to give yourself a handy reference tool that guides you or others through the elements in your data model.

Implementing Dashboard Design Best Practices

When collecting user requirements for your dashboarding project, there's a heavy focus on the data aspects of the dashboard: the types of data needed, the dimensions of data required, the data sources to be used, and so on. This is a good thing—without solid data processes, your dashboards won't be effective or maintainable. That being said, here's another aspect to your dashboarding project that calls for the same fervor in preparation: the *design aspect*.

Excel users live in a world of numbers and tables, not visualization and design. Your typical Excel analysts have no background in visual design and are often left to rely on their own visual instincts to design their dashboards. As a result, most Excel-based dashboards have little thought given to effective visual design, often resulting in overly cluttered and ineffective user interfaces.

The good news is that dashboarding has been around for such a long time that there's a vast knowledge base of prescribed visualization and dashboard design principles. Many of these principles seem like common sense; even so, these are concepts that Excel users don't often find themselves thinking about. Because this chapter is about getting into the dashboard state of mind, we'll break that trend and review a few dashboard design principles that improve the look and feel of your Excel dashboards.

Keep it simple

Dashboard design expert Stephen Few has the mantra "Simplify, simplify, simplify." The basic idea is that dashboards cluttered with too many measures or too much eye candy can dilute the significant information that you're trying to present. How many times has someone told you that your reports look "busy"? In essence, this complaint means that too much is going on in the page or on-screen, making it hard to see the actual data.

Here are a few steps that you can take to ensure simpler and more effective dashboard designs.

Don't turn your dashboard into a data repository

Admit it. You include as much information on a report as possible, primarily to avoid being asked for additional information. We all do it. But in the dashboard state of mind, you have to fight the urge to force every piece of data available onto your dashboards.

Overwhelming users with too much data can cause them to lose sight of the primary goal of the dashboard and focus on inconsequential data. The measures used on a dashboard should support the initial purpose of that dashboard. Avoid the urge to fill white space for the sake of symmetry and appearances. Don't include nice-to-know data just because the data is available. If the data doesn't support the core purpose of the dashboard, leave it out.

Avoid the fancy formatting

The key to communicating effectively with your dashboards is to present your data as simply as possible. There's no need to wrap it in eye candy to make it more interesting. It's okay to have a dashboard with little to no color or formatting. You'll find that the lack of fancy formatting only serves to call attention to the actual data. Focus on the data and not the shiny, happy graphics. Here are a few guidelines:

- **Avoid using colors or background fills to partition your dashboards.** Colors, in general, should be used sparingly, reserved for providing information about key data points. For example, assigning the colors red, yellow, and green to measures traditionally indicates performance level. Adding these colors to other sections of your dashboard only serves to distract your audience.
- **De-emphasize borders, backgrounds, and other elements that define dashboard areas.** Try to use the natural white space between your components to partition your dashboard. If borders are necessary, format them to hues lighter than the ones you've used for your data. Light grays are typically ideal for borders. The idea is to indicate sections without distracting from the information displayed.
- **Avoid applying fancy effects such as gradients, pattern fills, shadows, glows, soft edges, and other formatting.** Excel makes it easy to apply effects that make everything look shiny, glittery, and generally happy. Although these formatting features make for great marketing tools, they don't do your reporting mechanisms any favors.
- **Don't try to enhance your dashboards with clip art or pictures.** Not only do they do nothing to further data presentation, they often just look tacky.

Limit each dashboard to one printable page

Dashboards, in general, should provide at-a-glance views into key measures relevant to particular objectives or business processes. This implies that all of the data is immediately viewable on the one page. Although including all of your data on one page isn't always the easiest thing to do, there's much benefit to being able to see everything on one page or screen. You can compare sections more easily, you can process cause-and-effect relationships more effectively, and you rely less on short-term memory. When a user has to scroll left, right, or down, these benefits are diminished. Furthermore, users tend to believe that when information is placed out of normal view (areas that require scrolling), it's somehow less important.

But what if you can't fit all of the data on one sheet? First, review the measures on your dashboard and determine whether they really need to be there. Next, format your dashboard to use less space (format fonts, reduce white space, and adjust column widths and row heights). Finally, try adding interactivity to your dashboard, allowing users to change views dynamically to show only those measures that are relevant to them.

24

Format numbers effectively

There will undoubtedly be lots of numbers on your dashboards. Some of them will be in charts, and others will be in tables. Remember that every piece of information on your dashboard should have a reason for being there. It's important that you format your numbers effectively to allow your users to understand the information they represent without confusion or hindrance. Here are some guidelines to keep in mind when formatting the numbers on your dashboards and reports:

- **Always use commas to make numbers easier to read.** For example, instead of 2345, show 2,345.
- **Use decimal places only if that level of precision is required.** For instance, there's rarely a benefit for showing the decimal places in a dollar amount, such as $123.45. In most cases, the $123 will suffice. Likewise in percentages, use only the minimum number of decimals required to represent the data effectively. For example, instead of 43.21%, you may be able to get away with 43%.
- **Use the dollar symbol only when you need to clarify that you're referring to monetary values.** If you have a chart or table that contains all revenue values and there's a label clearly stating this, you can save room and pixels by leaving out the dollar symbol.
- **Format large numbers to the thousands or millions place.** For instance, instead of displaying 16,906,714, you can format the number to read 17M.

Use titles and labels effectively

It's common sense, but many people often fail to label items on dashboards effectively. If your manager looks at your dashboard and asks you, "What is this telling me?" you likely have labeling issues. Here are a few guidelines for effective labeling on your dashboards and reports:

- **Always include a timestamp on your reporting mechanisms.** This minimizes confusion when distributing the same dashboard or report in monthly or weekly installments.
- **Always include some text indicating when the data for the measures was retrieved.** In many cases, the timing of the data is a critical piece of information when analyzing a measure.
- **Use descriptive titles for each component on your dashboard.** This allows users to identify clearly what they're looking at. Be sure to avoid cryptic titles with lots of acronyms and symbols.
- **Although it may seem counterintuitive, it's generally good practice to de-emphasize labels by formatting them to hues lighter than the ones used for your data.** Lightly colored labels give your users the information they need without distracting them from the information displayed. Ideal colors for labels are those commonly found in nature: soft grays, browns, blues, and greens.

Part IV

Managing and Analyzing Data

Excel is a superb data-analysis tool—if you know how to extract the information that you really need. In this part, you'll learn how to obtain, clean up, and analyze data in Excel. As you'll see, many of the data-analysis capabilities in Excel are both surprisingly powerful and easy to use.

Importing and Cleaning Data

IN THIS CHAPTER

- Importing data into Excel
- Manipulating and cleaning data
- Using Flash Fill to extract and concatenate data
- Reviewing a checklist for data cleaning
- Exporting data to other formats

Data is everywhere. For example, if you run a website, you're collecting data continually, and you may not even know it. Every visit to your site generates information that is stored in a file on your server. This file contains lots of useful information, if you take the time to examine it.

That's just one example of data collection. Virtually every automated system collects data and stores it. Most of the time, the system that collects the data is also equipped to verify and analyze the data—but not always. And, of course, data is also collected manually. A nonautomated telephone survey is a good example.

Excel is a good tool for analyzing data, and it's often used to summarize the information and display it in the form of tables and charts. But often, the data that's collected isn't perfect. For one reason or another, it needs to be cleaned up before it can be analyzed.

One common use for Excel is as a tool to clean up data. Cleaning up data involves getting raw data into a worksheet and then manipulating it so that it conforms to various requirements. In the process, the data will be made consistent so that it can be properly analyzed.

This chapter describes the various ways to get data into a worksheet, and it provides some tips to help you clean it up.

Importing Data

Before you can do anything with data, you must get it into a worksheet. Excel is able to import most common text file formats, and it can retrieve data from websites.

Importing from a file

This section describes the file types that Excel can open directly, using the File ⇨ Open command. Figure 25.1 shows the list of file filter options that you can specify in the Open dialog box.

FIGURE 25.1

Filtering by file extension in the Open dialog box

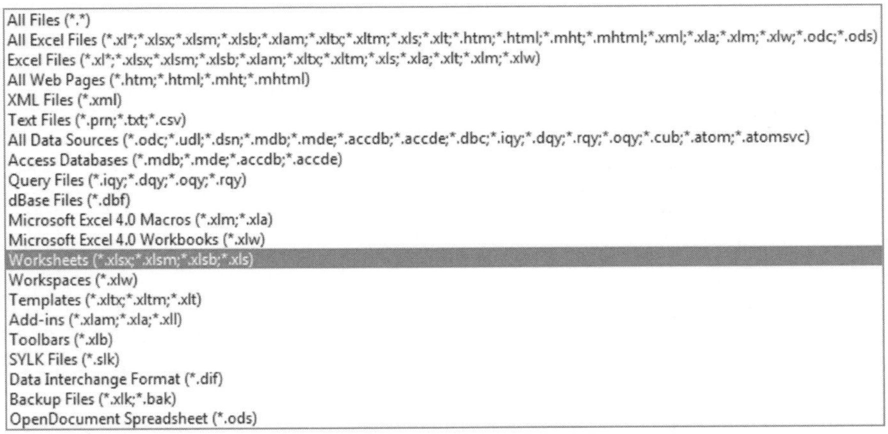

All Files (*.*)
All Excel Files (*.xl*;*.xlsx;*.xlsm;*.xlsb;*.xlam;*.xltx;*.xltm;*.xls;*.xlt;*.htm;*.html;*.mht;*.mhtml;*.xml;*.xla;*.xlm;*.xlw;*.odc;*.ods)
Excel Files (*.xl*;*.xlsx;*.xlsm;*.xlsb;*.xlam;*.xltx;*.xltm;*.xls;*.xla;*.xlt;*.xlm;*.xlw)
All Web Pages (*.htm;*.html;*.mht;*.mhtml)
XML Files (*.xml)
Text Files (*.prn;*.txt;*.csv)
All Data Sources (*.odc;*.udl;*.dsn;*.mdb;*.mde;*.accdb;*.accde;*.dbc;*.iqy;*.dqy;*.rqy;*.oqy;*.cub;*.atom;*.atomsvc)
Access Databases (*.mdb;*.mde;*.accdb;*.accde)
Query Files (*.iqy;*.dqy;*.oqy;*.rqy)
dBase Files (*.dbf)
Microsoft Excel 4.0 Macros (*.xlm;*.xla)
Microsoft Excel 4.0 Workbooks (*.xlw)
Worksheets (*.xlsx;*.xlsm;*.xlsb;*.xls)
Workspaces (*.xlw)
Templates (*.xltx;*.xltm;*.xlt)
Add-ins (*.xlam;*.xla;*.xll)
Toolbars (*.xlb)
SYLK Files (*.slk)
Data Interchange Format (*.dif)
Backup Files (*.xlk;*.bak)
OpenDocument Spreadsheet (*.ods)

Spreadsheet file formats

In addition to the current file formats (XLSX, XLSM, XLSB, XLTX, XLTM, and XLAM), Excel 2019 can open workbook files from all previous versions of Excel:

- **XLS:** Binary files created by Excel 4, Excel 95, Excel 97, Excel 2000, Excel 2002, and Excel 2003
- **XLM:** Binary files that contain Excel 4 macros (no data)
- **XLT:** Binary files for an Excel template
- **XLA:** Binary files for an Excel add-in

Excel can also open ODS files, the OpenDocument spreadsheet format, created by other spreadsheet products. ODS files are produced by a variety of "open" software programs, including Google Sheets, Apache OpenOffice, LibreOffice, and several others.

Database file formats

Excel 2019 can open the following database file formats:

Access files: These files have various extensions, including `.mdb` and `.accdb`.

dBase files: These files are produced by dBase III and dBase IV. Excel does not support dBase II files.

When you try to open database files using File ⇨ Open, Excel doesn't actually open the file. Instead, it creates an external data connection to the table in the database that you select. Excel supports various types of database connections that enable you to access data selectively. For example, instead of "opening" a database and selecting a table, you can perform a query on a table to retrieve only the records that you need (rather than the entire table).

Text file formats

A text file contains raw characters, with no formatting. Excel can open most types of text files:

CSV: This stands for "comma-separated values." Columns are delimited with a comma, and rows are delimited with a carriage return.

TXT: Columns are delimited with a tab, and rows are delimited with a carriage return.

PRN: Columns are delimited with multiple space characters, and rows are delimited with a carriage return. Excel imports this type of file into a single column.

DIF: This file format was originally used by the VisiCalc spreadsheet. This is rarely used.

SYLK: This file format was originally used by Multiplan. This is rarely used.

Most of these text file types have variants. For example, text files produced on a Mac have different end-of-row characters. Excel can usually handle the variants without a problem.

When you attempt to open a text file in Excel, the Text Import Wizard might kick in to help you specify how you want the data to be retrieved.

TIP

To bypass the Text Import Wizard, press Shift while you click the Open button in the Open dialog box.

When Excel Can't Open a File

If Excel doesn't support a particular file format, don't be too quick to give up. It's likely that others have had the same problem as you. Try searching the Web for the file extension, plus the word *Excel*. It's possible that a file converter is available, or maybe someone has figured out how to use an intermediary program to open the file and export it into a format that Excel recognizes.

25

HTML files

Excel can open most HTML files, which can be stored on your local drive or on a web server. The way that the HTML code renders in Excel varies considerably. Sometimes, the HTML file may look exactly as it does in a browser. At other times, it may bear little resemblance, especially if the HTML file uses Cascading Style Sheets (CSS) for its layout.

In some cases, you can access data on the Web by using Power Query. We discuss this topic in Part V, "Understanding Power Pivot and Power Query."

XML files

Extensible Markup Language (XML) is a text file format suitable for structured data. Data is enclosed in tags, which also serve to describe the data.

Excel can open XML files, and simple files will display with little or no effort. Complex XML files will require some work, however. A discussion of this topic is beyond the scope of this book. You'll find information about getting data from XML files in Excel's Help system and online.

Importing vs. opening

When you use File ➪ Open to open a file that's not in a traditional Excel format, you may be opening the file, or you may be importing it, depending on the file type. As mentioned, database files aren't opened. Rather, a table from inside the database file is imported.

XML files are another example of a format that may not open directly. When you open an XML file, you have the choice of opening it as a read-only workbook or importing it into a table.

Text files are opened directly. Excel understands CSV files, so it doesn't have to ask you any questions when you open them. For tab-delimited or fixed-width files, the Text Import Wizard will guide you in identifying where the data begins and ends.

When a file is opened directly, the Excel title bar will show the file's name. Figure 25.2 shows the Excel title bar after a file named `reunion.txt` was opened. When the File ➪ Open process actually imports the data, it's imported into a new workbook. In that case, the title bar will have a generic new workbook name, like `Book1`.

FIGURE 25.2

Excel's title bar displays the opened file's name.

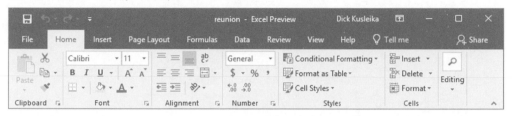

Importing a text file

One of the advantages of importing a text file instead of opening it is that you can put the data into a specific range in a worksheet rather than starting in cell A1. In this example, we'll show you how to import a text file to a specific range, and we'll walk through the steps of the Text Import Wizard.

Beginning with Excel 2019, importing text files is done through Get & Transform rather than the legacy Text Import Wizard. Get & Transform is a powerful feature, and we discuss it at length in Part V, "Understanding Power Pivot and Power Query." For this example, however, we're going to use the legacy wizard. With all of Get & Transform's power, it took away some flexibility like not having a header row. It's valuable to know both ways of importing text files.

Before we begin, we have to enable the legacy wizard. To do that, choose File ➪ Options ➪ Data and check From Text (Legacy), as shown in Figure 25.3. This will add the necessary menu item for the next step.

Figure 25.4 shows a small CSV file. The following instructions describe how to import this file, named `monthly.csv`, beginning at cell C3.

25

FIGURE 25.3

Enabling the legacy import wizard

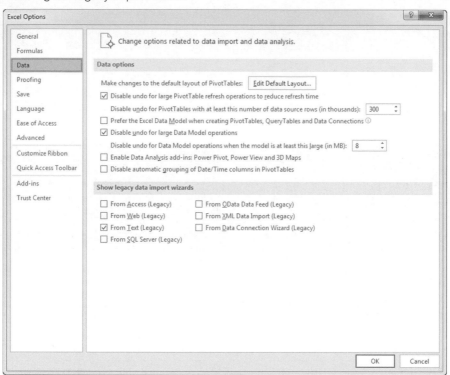

FIGURE 25.4

This CSV file will be imported.

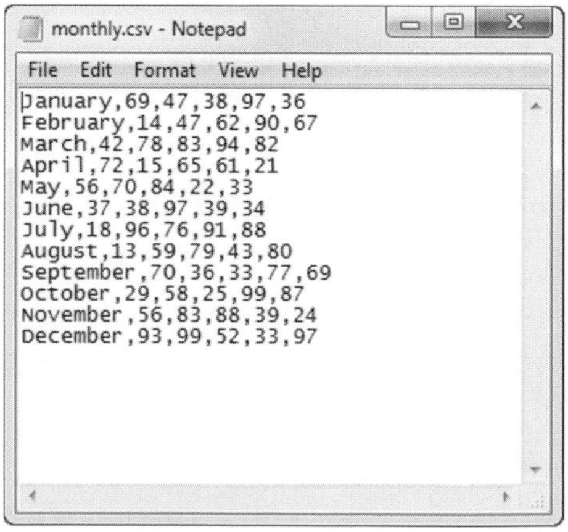

1. **Choose Data ⇨ Get & Transform Data ⇨ Get Data ⇨ Legacy Wizards ⇨ From Text (Legacy).** The Import Text File dialog box appears.

2. **Navigate to the folder that contains the text file.**

3. **Select the file from the list and then click the Import button.** The Text Import Wizard appears, as shown in Figure 25.5.

FIGURE 25.5

Step 1 of the Text Import Wizard

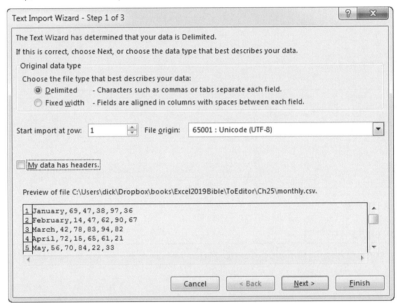

4. **Select Delimited and make sure that the My Data Has Headers check box is unchecked. Click Next to go to step 2.**

5. **Choose Comma as the delimiter (see Figure 25.6).**

6. **Click the Finish button.** The Import Data dialog box appears, as shown in Figure 25.7.

7. **In the Import Data dialog box, specify the location for the imported data.** It can be a cell in an existing worksheet or a new worksheet.

8. **Click OK, and Excel imports the data (see Figure 25.8).**

25

FIGURE 25.6

Select the delimiter in step 2 of the Text Import Wizard.

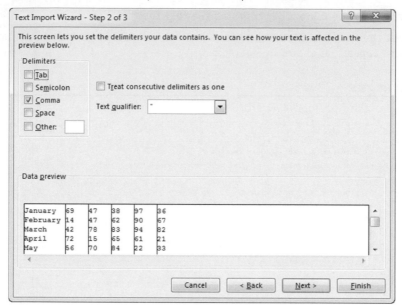

FIGURE 25.7

Using the Import Data dialog box to import a CSV file

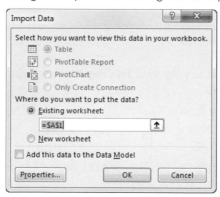

FIGURE 25.8

This range contains data imported directly from a CSV file.

▲	A	B	C	D	E	F	G
1	January	69	47	38	97	36	
2	February	14	47	62	90	67	
3	March	42	78	83	94	82	
4	April	72	15	65	61	21	
5	May	56	70	84	22	33	
6	June	37	38	97	39	34	
7	July	18	96	76	91	88	
8	August	13	59	79	43	80	
9	September	70	36	33	77	69	
10	October	29	58	25	99	87	
11	November	56	83	88	39	24	
12	December	93	99	52	33	97	
13							
14							

Copying and pasting data

If all else fails, you can try standard copy-and-paste techniques. If you can copy data from an application (for example, a word-processing program or a document displayed in a PDF viewer), there's a good chance that you can paste it into an Excel workbook. For the best results, try pasting using the Home ⇨ Clipboard ⇨ Paste ⇨ Paste Special command, and try the various paste options listed. Usually, pasted data will require some cleanup.

Cleaning Up Data

This section discusses a variety of techniques that you can use to clean up data in a worksheet.

 Chapter 11, "Using Formulas to Manipulate Text," contains additional examples of text-related formulas that may be helpful when cleaning data.

Removing duplicate rows

If data is compiled from multiple sources, it may contain duplicate rows. Most of the time, you will want to eliminate the duplicates. In the past, removing duplicate data was essentially a manual task—although it could be automated by using a confusing advanced filter technique. But now removing duplicate rows is easy, thanks to Excel's Remove Duplicates command (introduced in Excel 2007).

25

Start by moving the cell cursor to any cell within your data range. Choose Data ⇨ Data Tools ⇨ Remove Duplicates, and the Remove Duplicates dialog box, shown in Figure 25.9, appears.

FIGURE 25.9

Use the Remove Duplicates dialog box to delete duplicate rows.

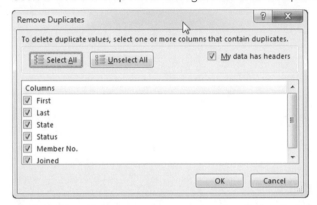

The Remove Duplicates dialog box lists all of the columns in your data range or table. Place a check mark next to the columns that you want to be included in the duplicate search. Most of the time, you'll want to select all of the columns, which is the default. Click OK, and Excel weeds out the duplicate rows and displays a message that tells you how many duplicates it removed. If Excel deleted too many rows, you can undo the procedure by clicking Undo (or by pressing Ctrl+Z).

When you select all columns in the Remove Duplicates dialog box, Excel will delete a row only if the content of every column is duplicated. In some situations, you may not care about matching some columns, so you would deselect those columns in the Remove Duplicates dialog box. For example, if each row has a unique ID code, Excel would never find any duplicate rows. So, you'd want to uncheck that column in the Remove Duplicates dialog box.

When duplicate rows are found, the first row is kept, and subsequent duplicate rows are deleted.

Identifying duplicate rows

If you would like to identify duplicate rows so that you can examine them without automatically deleting them, here's another method. Unlike the technique described in the previous section, this method looks at actual values, not formatted values.

Create a formula to the right of your data that concatenates each of the cells to the left. The formulas that follow assume that the data is in columns A:F.

Enter this formula into cell G2:

```
=CONCAT(A2:F2)
```

Add another formula in cell H2. This formula displays the number of times a value in column G occurs:

```
=COUNTIF(G:G,G2)
```

Copy these formulas down the column for each row of your data.

Column H displays the number of occurrences of that row. Unduplicated rows will display 1. Duplicated rows will display a number that corresponds to the number of times that row appears.

Figure 25.10 shows a simple example. If you don't care about a particular column, just omit it from the formula in column G. For example, if you want to find duplicates regardless of the Status column, change the formula in G2 to the following:

```
=CONCAT(A2:C2,E2:F2)
```

Splitting text

When importing data, you might find that multiple values are imported into a single column. Figure 25.11 shows an example of this type of import problem.

TIP

The data in Figure 25.11 is displayed in a fixed-width font (Courier New). With the default font, it was not apparent that the data lined up nicely in fixed-width columns.

FIGURE 25.10

Using formulas to identify duplicate rows

	A	B	C	D	E	F	G	H	I
						H4 ▼ : × ✓ fx =COUNTIF(G:G,G4)			
1	First	Last	State	Status	Member No.	Joined			
2	Joshua	Elliott	NJ	Active	99-3325	12/21/1909 JoshuaElliottNJ99-33253643		1	
3	Brian	Dunn	MA	Inactive	25-7251	3/22/2007 BrianDunnMAInactive25-725139163		1	
4	Sara	Diaz	MA	Inactive	62-6451	2/22/1976 SaraDiazMAInactive62-645127812		2	
5	Adrian	Cunningham	MS	Active	72-1993	3/18/1939 AdrianCunninghamMSActive72-199314322		1	
6	Zoey	Watkins	WA	Inactive	19-3615	12/30/1968 ZoeyWatkinsWAInactive19-361525202		1	
7	Hayden	Nichols	AR	Inactive	50-7290	5/31/1980 HaydenNicholsARInactive50-729029372		2	
8	Julia	Walker	LA	Active	37-3660	2/25/1913 JuliaWalkerLAActive37-36604805		1	
9	Cole	Carpenter	MN	Active	82-3786	8/18/1914 ColeCarpenterMNActive82-37865344		1	
10	Brooklyn	Stone	MT	Active	43-4609	2/15/1967 BrooklynStoneMTActive43-460924518		1	
11	Adrian	Warren	NY	Inactive	85-4686	6/5/1941 AdrianWarrenNYInactive85-468615132		1	
12	Adam	Ross	AK	Inactive	75-6928	6/22/1951 AdamRossAKInactive75-692818801		1	
13	Brian	Jones	NM	Inactive	46-9552	7/14/1961 BrianJonesNMInactive46-955222476		1	
14	Autumn	Scott	TX	Active	68-5644	7/20/1984 AutumnScottTXActive68-564430883		1	
15	Benjamin	Hill	KS	Active	30-6244	6/15/1955 BenjaminHillKSActive30-624420255		1	
16	Lauren	Myers	CO	Active	77-5108	3/17/1942 LaurenMyersCOActive77-510815417		1	

If the text is all the same length (as in the example), you might be able to write a series of formulas that extract the information to separate columns. The LEFT, RIGHT, and MID functions are useful for this task.

FIGURE 25.11

The imported data was put in one column rather than multiple columns.

	A	B
1	January 80 224 243 74 170 22 250 40 242 132	
2	February 193 99 226 244 106 85 217 239 55 239	
3	March 64 95 32 22 68 238 199 217 139 102	
4	April 62 112 201 225 178 126 54 155 20 138	
5	May 143 96 159 41 182 121 128 100 239 243	
6	June 185 76 76 245 218 206 44 204 132 183	
7	July 203 21 53 136 123 152 225 37 175 203	
8	August 93 83 139 69 114 28 53 198 143 43	
9	September 164 123 193 92 226 169 133 132 121 180	
10	October 120 164 73 48 40 136 202 145 75 213	
11	November 222 30 98 248 165 164 240 121 50 25	
12	December 46 27 177 143 180 136 230 204 155 169	
13		
14		
15		

See Chapter 11 for examples of formulas that extract characters from text.

You should also be aware that Excel offers two nonformula methods to assist in splitting data so that it occupies multiple columns: Text to Columns and Flash Fill.

Using Text to Columns

The Text to Columns command can parse strings into their component parts.

First, make sure the column that contains the data to be split up has enough empty columns to the right to accommodate the extracted data. Then select the data to be parsed and choose Data ➪ Data Tools ➪ Text to Columns. Excel displays the Convert Text to Columns Wizard, which consists of a series of dialog boxes that walk you through the steps to convert a single column of data into multiple columns. Figure 25.12 shows the initial step, in which you choose the type of data:

Delimited   The data to be split is separated by delimiters such as commas, spaces, slashes, or other characters.

Fixed Width   Each component occupies the same number of characters.

FIGURE 25.12

The first dialog box in the Convert Text to Columns Wizard

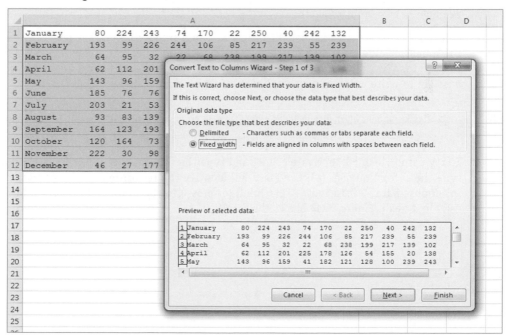

Make your choice and click Next to move on to step 2, which depends on the choice you made in step 1.

If you're working with delimited data, specify the delimiting character. You'll see a preview of the result. If you're working with fixed-width data, specify the column breaks directly in the preview window.

When you're satisfied with the column breaks, click Next to move to step 3. In this step, you can click a column in the preview window and specify formatting for the column. For example, if you have data that looks like a number but is really text, you can format the column as Text so that you preserve any leading zeros. Click Finish, and Excel splits the data as specified.

Using Flash Fill

The Text to Columns Wizard works well for many types of data. But sometimes you'll encounter data that can't be parsed by that wizard. For example, the Text to Columns Wizard is useless if you have variable-width data that doesn't have delimiters. In such a case, the Flash Fill feature might save the day. But keep in mind that Flash Fill works successfully only when the data is consistent.

Flash Fill uses pattern recognition to extract data (and also concatenate data). Just enter a few examples in a column that's adjacent to the data and choose Data ⇨ Data Tools ⇨ Flash Fill (or press Ctrl+E). Excel analyzes the examples and attempts to fill in the remaining cells. If Excel didn't recognize the pattern you had in mind, press Ctrl+Z, add another example or two, and try again.

Figure 25.13 shows a worksheet with some text in a single column. The goal is to extract the numeric value from each text string and put the number into a separate cell. The Text to Columns Wizard can't do it because the space delimiters aren't consistent. It might be possible to write an array formula, but it would be complicated.

 This workbook, which also includes other Flash Fill examples, is available on this book's website at www.wiley.com/go/excel2019bible. The filename is `flash fill demo.xlsx`.

To try using Flash Fill, activate cell B1 and type the first number (**20**). Move to B2, and type the second number (**6**). Can Flash Fill identify the remaining numbers and fill them in? Choose Data ⇨ Data Tools ⇨ Flash Fill (or press Ctrl+E), and Excel fills in the remaining cells in a flash. Figure 25.14 shows the result.

FIGURE 25.13

The goal is to extract the numbers in column A.

	A	B	C
1	The box weighed 20 pounds.		
2	Bob is 6 feet tall.		
3	She drove for 9.5 hours straight.		
4	Pi is 3.14159		
5	He drank 5 cups of coffee.		
6	The sales tax was $3.12 for that item.		
7	15 people showed up for jury duty		
8	He was in 7th heaven.		
9	The square root of 16 is four.		
10	Where is the 90210 zip code?		
11			
12			
13			

FIGURE 25.14

Using manually entered examples in B1 and B2, Excel's Flash Fill feature makes some incorrect guesses.

	A	B	C
1	The box weighed 20 pounds.	20	
2	Bob is 6 feet tall.	6	
3	She drove for 9.5 hours straight.	5	
4	Pi is 3.14159	14159	
5	He drank 5 cups of coffee.	5	
6	The sales tax was $3.12 for that item.	12	
7	15 people showed up for jury duty	15	
8	He was in 7th heaven.	7	
9	The square root of 16 is four.	16	
10	Where is the 90210 zip code?	90210	
11			
12			
13			
14			

As you can see, Excel identified most of the values. Accuracy increases if you provide more examples. For example, provide an example of a decimal number. Delete the suggested values in Column B, enter `3.12` in cell B6, and press Ctrl+E. This time, Flash Fill gets all of them correct (see Figure 25.15).

25

FIGURE 25.15

After you enter an example of a decimal number, Excel gets all of the values correct.

⊿	A	B	C
1	The box weighed 20 pounds.	20	
2	Bob is 6 feet tall.	6	
3	She drove for 9.5 hours straight.	9.5	
4	Pi is 3.14159	3.14159	
5	He drank 5 cups of coffee.	5	
6	The sales tax was $3.12 for that item.	3.12	
7	15 people showed up for jury duty	15	
8	He was in 7th heaven.	7	
9	The square root of 16 is four.	16	
10	Where is the 90210 zip code?	90210	
11			
12			
13			
14			
15			
16			

This simple example demonstrates two important points:

- You must examine your data carefully after using Flash Fill. Just because the first few rows are correct, you can't assume that Flash Fill worked correctly for all rows.
- Flash Fill accuracy increases when you provide more examples.

Figure 25.16 shows another example: names in column A. The goal is to extract the first, last, and middle names (if it has one). In column B, Flash Fill successfully gets all of the first names using only two examples (Mark and Tim). Plus, it successfully extracted all of the last names (column C) using Russell and Colman. Extracting the middle names or initials (column D) didn't work until examples that included a space on either side of the middle name were included.

To summarize, Excel's Flash Fill is an interesting idea, but it works reliably only if the data is consistent. Even when you think it worked correctly, make sure that you examine the results carefully. And think twice before trusting it with important data because there's no way to document the way the data was extracted. But the main limitation is that (unlike formulas) Flash Fill is not a dynamic technique. If your data changes, the flash-filled column does not update.

> **NOTE**
>
> You can also use the Flash Fill feature to create new data from multiple columns. Just provide a few examples of the way that you want the data to be combined, and Excel will figure out the pattern and fill in the column. Using Flash Fill to create data seems to work much better than using it to extract data. But then again, it's also easier to create formulas that create data from existing columns.

FIGURE 25.16

Using Flash Fill to split names

	A	B	C	D	E
1	Mark Russell	Mark	Russell		
2	Tim Colman	Tim	Colman		
3	Sam Daniel Bains	Sam	Bains	Daniel	
4	Fred James Foster	Fred	Foster	James	
5	James J. Wehr	James	Wehr	J.	
6	Mitch Nicholls	Mitch	Nicholls		
7	Neal McCaslin	Neal	McCaslin		
8	Ned Poulakis	Ned	Poulakis		
9	Paul T. Wingfield	Paul	Wingfield	T.	
10	Peter Gans	Peter	Gans		
11	Ron E. Hoffman	Ron	Hoffman	E.	
12	Julia Hayes	Julia	Hayes		
13	Richard P Light	Richard	Light	P	
14	Ray Walker	Ray	Walker		
15	Robert F. Mahaney	Robert	Mahaney	F.	
16	Robert Fist	Robert	Fist		
17					
18					

Changing the case of text

Often, you'll want to make text in a column consistent in terms of case. Excel provides no direct way to change the case of text, but it's easy to do with formulas. (See the sidebar "Transforming Data with Formulas.")

The three relevant functions are as follows:

UPPER: This converts the text to ALL UPPERCASE.

LOWER: This converts the text to all lowercase.

PROPER: This converts the text to Proper Case. (The first letter in each word is capital-ized, as in a proper name.)

These functions are quite straightforward. They operate only on alphabetic characters and just ignore all other characters and return them unchanged.

If you use the PROPER function, you'll probably need to do some additional cleanup to handle exceptions. The following are examples of transformations that you probably would consider incorrect:

- The letter following an apostrophe is always capitalized (for example, Don'T). This is done, apparently, to handle names like O'Reilly.

25

- The PROPER function doesn't handle names with an embedded capital letter, such as McDonald.
- "Minor" words such as *and* and *the* are always capitalized. For example, some people would prefer that the third word in United States Of America not be capitalized.

You can correct some of these problems by using Find and Replace.

Transforming Data with Formulas

Many of the data cleanup examples in this chapter describe how to use formulas and functions to transform data in some way. For example, you can use the UPPER function to transform text into uppercase. When the data is transformed, you'll have two columns: the original data and the transformed data. Almost always, you'll want to replace the original data with the transformed data. Here's how to do it:

1. **Insert a new temporary column for formulas to transform the original data.**
2. **Create your formulas in the temporary column, and make sure that the formulas do what they were intended to do.**
3. **Select the formula cells.**
4. **Choose Home ⇨ Clipboard ⇨ Copy (or press Ctrl+C).**
5. **Select the original data cells.**
6. **Choose Home ⇨ Clipboard ⇨ Paste ⇨ Values (V).**

This procedure replaces the original data with the transformed data. Then you can delete the temporary column that holds the formulas.

Removing extra spaces

It's usually a good idea to ensure that data doesn't have extra spaces. It's difficult to spot a space character at the end of a text string. Extra spaces can cause lots of problems, especially when you need to compare text strings. The text *July* is not the same as the text *July* with a space appended to the end. The first is four characters long, and the second is five characters long.

The TRIM function removes all leading and trailing spaces and replaces interior multiple spaces with a single space. This formula uses the TRIM function. The formula returns Fourth Quarter Earnings (with no excess spaces):

    =TRIM("   Fourth   Quarter   Earnings   ")

Data that is imported from a web page often contains a different type of space: a nonbreaking space, indicated by   in HTML code. In Excel, this character can be generated by this formula:

    =CHAR(160)

You can use a formula like this to replace those spaces with normal spaces:

```
=SUBSTITUTE(A2,CHAR(160)," ")
```

Or you can use this formula to replace the nonbreaking space character with normal spaces and to remove excess spaces:

```
=TRIM(SUBSTITUTE(A2,CHAR(160)," "))
```

Removing strange characters

Often, data imported into an Excel worksheet contains strange (sometimes unprintable) characters. You can use the CLEAN function to remove all nonprinting characters from a string. If the data is in cell A2, this formula will do the job:

```
=CLEAN(A2)
```

> **NOTE**
>
> The CLEAN function can miss some nonprinting Unicode characters. It's programmed to remove the first 32 non-printing characters in the 7-bit ASCII code. Consult the Excel Help system for information on how to remove the non-printing Unicode characters. (Search Help for the CLEAN function.)

Converting values

In some cases, you may need to convert values from one system to another. For example, you may import a file that has values in fluid ounces, and they need to be expressed in milliliters. Excel's handy CONVERT function can perform that and many other conversions.

If cell A2 contains a value in ounces, the following formula converts it to milliliters:

```
=CONVERT(A2,"oz","ml")
```

This function is extremely versatile and can handle most common measurement units in the following categories: weight and mass, distance, time, pressure, force, energy, power, magnetism, temperature, volume, liquid, area, bits and bytes, and speed.

Excel can also convert between number bases. You may import a file that contains hexadecimal values, and you need to convert them to decimal. Use the HEX2DEC function to perform this conversion. For example, the following formula returns 1,279, the decimal equivalent of its hex argument:

```
=HEX2DEC("4FF")
```

Excel can also convert from binary to decimal (BIN2DEC) and from octal to decimal (OCT2DEC).

Functions that convert from decimal to another number base are DEC2HEX, DEC2BIN, and DEC2OCT.

Excel 2013 introduced a new function, BASE, that converts a decimal number to any number base. Note that there is not a function that works in the opposite direction. Excel does

25

not provide a function that converts any number base to decimal. You're limited to binary, octal, and hexadecimal.

Classifying values

Often, you may have values that need to be classified into a group. For example, if you have ages of people, you might want to classify them into groups such as 17 or younger, 18–24, 25–34, and so on.

The easiest way to perform this classification is with a lookup table. Figure 25.17 shows ages in column A and classifications in column B. Column B uses the lookup table in D2:E9. The formula in cell B2 is as follows:

```
=VLOOKUP(A2,$D$2:$E$9,2)
```

FIGURE 25.17

Using a lookup table to classify ages into age ranges

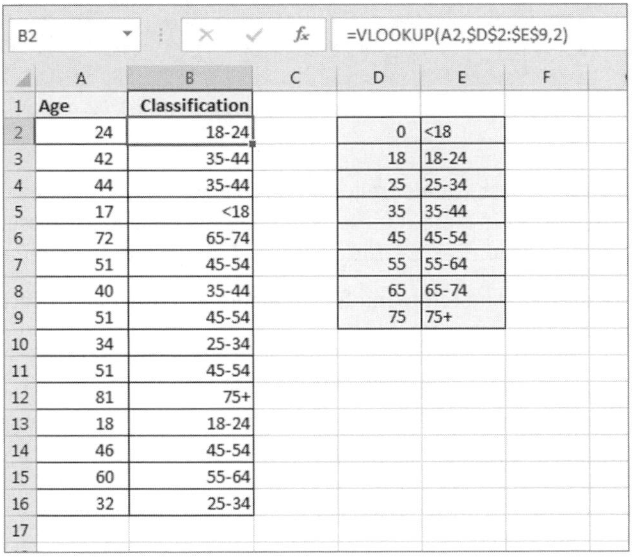

	A	B	C	D	E	F
	Age	Classification				
1	Age	Classification				
2	24	18-24		0	<18	
3	42	35-44		18	18-24	
4	44	35-44		25	25-34	
5	17	<18		35	35-44	
6	72	65-74		45	45-54	
7	51	45-54		55	55-64	
8	40	35-44		65	65-74	
9	51	45-54		75	75+	
10	34	25-34				
11	51	45-54				
12	81	75+				
13	18	18-24				
14	46	45-54				
15	60	55-64				
16	32	25-34				
17						

Formula bar: B2 =VLOOKUP(A2,$D$2:$E$9,2)

This formula was copied to the cells below.

You can also use a lookup table for nonnumeric data. Figure 25.18 shows a lookup table that is used to assign a region to a state.

FIGURE 25.18

Using a lookup table to assign a region for a state

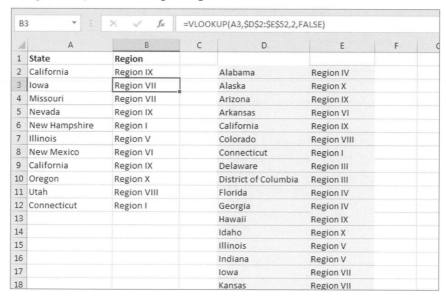

The two-column lookup table is in the range D2:E52. The formula in cell B2, which was copied to the cells below, is as follows:

```
=VLOOKUP(A2,$D$2:$E$52,2,FALSE)
```

 A workbook that contains the examples in this section is available on this book's website at www .wiley.com/go/excel2019bible. **The filename is** `classifying data.xlsx`.

> **TIP**
>
> A side benefit is that the VLOOKUP function will return #N/A if an exact match is not found—a good way to spot misspelled states, in this example. Using FALSE as the last argument in the function indicates that an exact match is required.

Joining columns

To combine data in two more columns, you can use the CONCAT function in a formula. For example, the following formula combines the contents of cells A1, B1, and C1:

```
=CONCAT(A1:C1)
```

Often, you'll need to insert spaces, or some other delimiter, between the cells—for example, if the columns contain a title, first name, and last name. Concatenating using the previous formulas would produce something like Mr.ThomasJones. To add spaces (to produce Mr. Thomas Jones), use the TEXTJOIN function:

```
=TEXTJOIN(" ",TRUE,A1:C1)
```

The first argument of TEXTJOIN is the delimiter that you want to insert between the cell values. The second argument is TRUE to ignore empty cells. If you set the second argument to FALSE and there are empty cells, you'll end up with two delimiters right next to each other.

Figure 25.19 shows three examples of TEXTJOIN. In the first example, there are no empty cells, so the second argument doesn't matter. In the second and third examples, the second argument is set to FALSE and TRUE, respectively, and the delimiter is changed from a space to a comma (so it's easier to see the duplication). Where empty cells are not ignored, two commas are shown together.

FIGURE 25.19

The TEXTJOIN function inserts delimiters between cell values.

	A	B	C	D	E	F	G
1	Title	First	Last	Ignore Empty?	Joined		
2	Mr	Thomas	Jones		Mr Thomas Jones	=TEXTJOIN(" ",TRUE,A2:C2)	
3	Mr		Jones	FALSE	Mr,,Jones	=TEXTJOIN(",",D3,A3:C3)	
4	Mr		Jones	TRUE	Mr,Jones	=TEXTJOIN(",",D4,A4:C4)	
5							
6							
7							

You can also use the Flash Fill feature (discussed earlier in this chapter) to join columns without using formulas. Just provide an example or two in an adjacent column and press Ctrl+E. Excel will perform the concatenation for the other rows.

Rearranging columns

If you need to rearrange the columns in a worksheet, you could insert a blank column and then drag another column into the new blank column. But the moved column leaves a gap, which you need to delete.

Here's an easier way:

1. **Click the column header of the column you want to move.**
2. **Choose Home ⇨ Clipboard ⇨ Cut.**

3. **Click the column header to the right of where you want the column to go.**

4. **Right-click and choose Insert Cut Cells from the shortcut menu.**

Repeat these steps until the columns are in the order you want.

Randomizing the rows

If you need to arrange the rows in random order, here's a quick way to do it. In the column to the right of the data, insert this formula into the first cell and copy it down:

```
=RAND()
```

Then sort the data using this column as the sort key. The rows will be in random order, and you can delete the column.

Extracting a filename from a URL

In some cases, you may have a list of URLs and need to extract only the filename. The following formula returns the filename from a URL. Assume that cell A2 contains this URL:

```
http://example.com/assets/images/horse.jpg
```

The following formula returns `horse.jpg`:

```
=RIGHT(A2,LEN(A2)-FIND("*",SUBSTITUTE(A2,"/","*",LEN(A2)-
LEN(SUBSTITUTE(A2,"/","")))))
```

This formula returns all text that follows the last slash character. If cell A2 doesn't contain a slash character, the formula returns an error.

To extract the URL without the filename, use this formula:

```
=LEFT(A2,FIND("*",SUBSTITUTE(A2,"/","*",LEN(A2)-
LEN(SUBSTITUTE(A2,"/","")))))
```

> **NOTE**
> This type of extraction is a good use for the Flash Fill feature. (See "Splitting text" earlier in this chapter.)

Matching text in a list

You may have some data that you need to check against another list. For example, you may want to identify the data rows in which data in a particular column appears in a different list. Figure 25.20 shows a simple example. The data is in columns A:C. The goal is to identify the rows in which the Member Num appears in the Resigned Members list in column F. These rows can then be deleted.

FIGURE 25.20

The goal is to identify member numbers that are in the Resigned Members list in column F.

	A	B	C	D	E	F	G
	D7 ▾ : × ✓ *fx*	=IF(COUNTIF($F$2:$F$22,B7)>0,"Resigned","")					
1	Name	Member Num	State			Resigned Members	
2	Alice Jones	39-5954	AZ			11-6587	
3	Jennifer Green	46-2010	UT			16-4523	
4	Rhoda Davis	93-1595	AZ			16-8075	
5	Rita Morris	35-5121	WA			21-5865	
6	Debra Hopkins	91-2687	UT			23-5078	
7	Marcela Garcia	93-4652	AZ	Resigned		36-9582	
8	Viola Jenkins	74-4701	CA			39-2953	
9	Charlotte Baker	21-5865	CA	Resigned		40-8172	
10	Angela Gonzalez	79-8010	AZ			42-6818	
11	Michelle Young	93-7380	WA			45-8343	
12	Linda Johnson	16-6377	AZ			58-2363	
13	Annette Williamson	94-2032	CA			58-8192	
14	Ruth Mckinney	58-8192	WA	Resigned		65-3095	
15	Mary Gibson	27-3637	CO			67-5960	
16	Christine Warren	81-8640	AZ			78-4209	
17	Stacey Martin	82-8709	CO			78-8201	
18	Shirley Clarke	99-6607	AZ			81-1158	
19	Rosemary Ross	16-8075	CO	Resigned		86-7291	
20	Waltraud Adams	55-5367	AZ			87-2700	
21	Nancy Martinez	82-4869	CA			93-4652	
22	Dominique Jackson	28-9592	AZ			97-2586	
23	Deanne Elliott	14-3518	WA				
24	Vanessa Hill	31-8125	UT				
25	Claire Jones	74-6730	CO				

 This workbook, named `match names.xlsx`, is available on this book's website at `www.wiley.com/go/excel2019bible`.

Here's a formula, entered into cell D2 and copied down, that will do the job:

```
=IF(COUNTIF($F$2:$F$22,B2)>0,"Resigned","" )
```

This formula displays the word *Resigned* if the member number in column B is found in the Resigned Members list. If the member number is not found, it returns an empty string. If the list is sorted by column D, the rows for all resigned members will appear together and can be quickly deleted.

This technique can be adapted to other types of list-matching tasks.

Changing vertical data to horizontal data

Figure 25.21 shows a common type of data layout that you might see when importing a file. Each record consists of three consecutive cells in a single column: Name, Department, and Location. The goal is to convert this data so that each record appears in three columns.

FIGURE 25.21

Vertical data that needs to be converted to three columns

	A	B
1	Lori Howard	
2	Accounting	
3	Main Office	
4	Jacqueline Espinoza	
5	Sales	
6	West Branch	
7	Jose Collins	
8	Accounting	
9	Main Office	
10	Bernice Ryan	
11	Sales	
12	East Branch	
13	Diana Brown	
14	Accounting	
15	West Branch	
16	Jay J. Davis	
17	Research	
18	Main Office	
19	Shandi Johnson	
20	Accounting	
21	Main Office	
22		
23		

There are several ways to convert this type of data, but here's a method that's fairly easy. It requires a small amount of setup, but the work is done with a single formula, which is copied to a range.

Start by creating some numeric vertical and horizontal "headers," as shown in Figure 25.22. Column C contains numbers that correspond to the first row of each data item (in this case, the name). In this example, we put the following values in column C: 1, 4, 7, 10, 13, 16, and 19. You can use a simple formula to generate this series of numbers.

25

FIGURE 25.22

Headers that are used to convert the vertical data into rows

	A	B	C	D	E	F	G
1	Lori Howard			1	2	3	
2	Accounting		1				
3	Main Office		4				
4	Jacqueline Espinoza		7				
5	Sales		10				
6	West Branch		13				
7	Jose Collins		16				
8	Accounting		19				
9	Main Office						
10	Bernice Ryan						
11	Sales						
12	East Branch						
13	Diana Brown						
14	Accounting						
15	West Branch						
16	Jay J. Davis						
17	Research						
18	Main Office						
19	Shandi Johnson						
20	Accounting						
21	Main Office						
22							

The horizontal range of headers consists of consecutive integers, starting with 1. In this example, each record contains three cells of data, so the horizontal header contains 1, 2, and 3.

This workbook, named `vertical data.xlsx`, is available on this book's website at www.wiley.com/go/excel2019bible.

Here's the formula that goes into cell D2:

```
=OFFSET($A$1,$C2+D$1-2,0)
```

Copy this formula across to the next two columns and down to the next six rows. The result is shown in Figure 25.23.

FIGURE 25.23

A single formula transforms the vertical data into rows.

| E4 | ▾ | : | × | ✓ | f_x | =OFFSET($A$1,$C4+E$1-2,0) |

	A	B	C	D	E	F	G
1	Lori Howard			1	2	3	
2	Accounting		1	Lori Howard	Accounting	Main Office	
3	Main Office		4	Jacqueline Espinoza	Sales	West Branch	
4	Jacqueline Espinoza		7	Jose Collins	Accounting	Main Office	
5	Sales		10	Bernice Ryan	Sales	East Branch	
6	West Branch		13	Diana Brown	Accounting	West Branch	
7	Jose Collins		16	Jay J. Davis	Research	Main Office	
8	Accounting		19	Shandi Johnson	Accounting	Main Office	
9	Main Office						
10	Bernice Ryan						
11	Sales						
12	East Branch						
13	Diana Brown						
14	Accounting						
15	West Branch						
16	Jay J. Davis						
17	Research						
18	Main Office						
19	Shandi Johnson						
20	Accounting						
21	Main Office						
22							
23							

You can easily adapt this technique to work with vertical data that contains a different number of rows. For example, if each record contained ten rows of data, the column C header values would be 1, 11, 21, 31, and so on. The horizontal headers would consist of values 1 through 10 rather than 1 through 3.

Notice that the formula uses an absolute reference to cell A1. That reference won't change when the formula is copied, so all of the formulas use cell A1 as the base. If the data begins in a different cell, change $A$1 to the address of the first cell.

The formula also uses "mixed" referencing in the second argument of the OFFSET function. The C2 reference has a dollar sign in front of C, so column C is the absolute part of the reference. In the D1 reference, the dollar sign is before the 1, so row 1 is the absolute part of the reference.

 See Chapter 9, "Introducing Formulas and Functions," for more about using mixed references in formulas.

25

Filling gaps in an imported report

When you import data, you can sometimes end up with a worksheet that looks something like the one shown in Figure 25.24. This type of report formatting is common. As you can see, an entry in column A applies to several rows of data. If you sort this type of list, the missing data messes things up, and you can no longer tell who sold what when.

FIGURE 25.24

This report contains gaps in the Sales Rep column.

	A	B	C	D	E
1					
2	Sales Rep	Month	Units Sold	Amount	
3	Jane	Jan	182	$15,101	
4		Feb	3350	$34,230	
5		Mar	114	$9,033	
6	George	Jan	135	$8,054	
7		Feb	401	$9,322	
8		Mar	357	$32,143	
9	Beth	Jan	509	$29,239	
10		Feb	414	$38,993	
11		Mar	53	$309	
12	Dan	Jan	323	$9,092	
13		Feb	283	$12,332	
14		Mar	401	$32,933	
15					
16					

If the report is small, you can enter the missing cell values manually or by using a series of Home ➪ Editing ➪ Fill ➪ Down commands (or the Ctrl+D shortcut). But if you have a large list that's in this format, here's a better way:

1. **Select the range that has the gaps (A3:A14, in this example).**
2. **Choose Home ➪ Editing ➪ Find & Select ➪ Go to Special.** The Go to Special dialog box appears.
3. **Select the Blanks option and click OK.** This action selects the blank cells in the original selection.
4. **In the formula bar, type an equal sign (=) followed by the address of the first cell with an entry in the column (=A3, in this example) and press Ctrl+Enter.**
5. **Reselect the original range and press Ctrl+C to copy the selection.**
6. **Choose Home ➪ Clipboard ➪ Paste ➪ Paste Values to convert the formulas to values.**

After you complete these steps, the gaps are filled in with the correct information, and your worksheet looks similar to the one shown in Figure 25.25.

FIGURE 25.25

The gaps are gone, and this list can now be sorted.

	A	B	C	D	E
2	Sales Rep	Month	Units Sold	Amount	
3	Jane	Jan	182	$15,101	
4	Jane	Feb	3350	$34,230	
5	Jane	Mar	114	$9,033	
6	George	Jan	135	$8,054	
7	George	Feb	401	$9,322	
8	George	Mar	357	$32,143	
9	Beth	Jan	509	$29,239	
10	Beth	Feb	414	$38,993	
11	Beth	Mar	53	$309	
12	Dan	Jan	323	$9,092	
13	Dan	Feb	283	$12,332	
14	Dan	Mar	401	$32,933	
15					
16					

 This workbook, named `fill in gaps.xlsx`, is available on this book's website at `www.wiley.com/go/excel2019bible`.

Checking spelling

If you use a word-processing program, you probably take advantage of its spell-checker feature. Spelling mistakes can be embarrassing when they appear in a text document, but they can cause serious problems when they occur within your data. For example, if you tabulate data by month, a misspelled month name will make it appear that a year has 13 months.

To access the Excel spell-checker, choose Review ➪ Proofing ➪ Spelling, or press F7. To check the spelling in just a particular range, select the range before you activate the spell-checker.

If the spell-checker finds any words it doesn't recognize as correct, it displays the Spelling dialog box. The options are fairly self-explanatory.

 See Chapter 19, "Making Your Formulas Error-Free," for more about the Spelling dialog box.

Replacing or removing text in cells

You may need to replace (or remove) certain characters systematically in a column of data. For example, you may need to replace all backslash characters with forward slash characters. In many cases, you can use Excel's Find and Replace dialog box to accomplish this task. To remove text using the Find and Replace dialog box, just leave the Replace With field empty.

25

In other situations, you may need a formula-based solution. Consider the data shown in Figure 25.26. The goal is to replace the second hyphen character with a colon for the part numbers in Column A. Using Find and Replace wouldn't work because there isn't a way to specify that only the second hyphen should be replaced.

FIGURE 25.26

To replace only the second hyphen in these cells, Find and Replace is not an option.

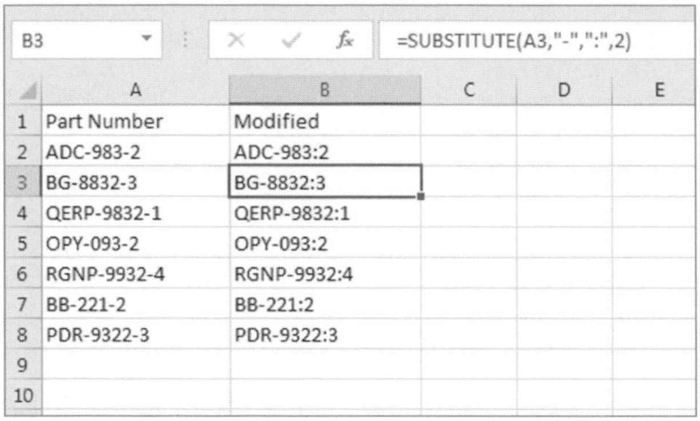

	A	B	C	D	E
	B3 ▼ : × ✓ fx =SUBSTITUTE(A3,"-",":",2)				
1	Part Number	Modified			
2	ADC-983-2	ADC-983:2			
3	BG-8832-3	BG-8832:3			
4	QERP-9832-1	QERP-9832:1			
5	OPY-093-2	OPY-093:2			
6	RGNP-9932-4	RGNP-9932:4			
7	BB-221-2	BB-221:2			
8	PDR-9322-3	PDR-9322:3			
9					
10					

In this case, the solution is a fairly simple formula that replaces the second occurrence of a hyphen with a colon:

```
=SUBSTITUTE(A2,"-",":",2)
```

To remove the second occurrence of a hyphen, just omit the third argument for the SUBSTITUTE function:

```
=SUBSTITUTE(A2,"-",,2)
```

This is another example where Flash Fill can also do the job.

> **NOTE**
>
> If you've worked with programming languages, you may be familiar with the concept of regular expressions. A regular expression is a way to match strings of text using concise (and often confusing) codes. Excel doesn't support regular expressions, but if you search the Web, you'll find ways to incorporate regular expressions in VBA, plus a few add-ins that provide this feature in the workbook environment.

Adding text to cells

If you need to add text to a cell, one solution is to use a new column of formulas. Here are some examples:

- The following formula adds ID: and a space to the beginning of a cell:
```
="ID: "&A2
```

- The following formula adds .mp3 to the end of a cell:

  =A2&".mp3"

- The following formula inserts a hyphen after the third character in a cell:

  =LEFT(A2,3)&"-"&RIGHT(A2,LEN(A2)-3)

You can also use the Flash Fill feature to add text to cells.

Fixing trailing minus signs

Imported data sometimes displays negative values with a trailing minus sign. For example, a negative value may appear as 3,498– rather than the more common –3,498. Excel does not convert these values. In fact, it considers them to be nonnumeric text.

The solution is so simple it may even surprise you:

1. **Select the data that has the trailing minus signs.** The selection can also include positive values.
2. **Choose Data ➪ Data Tools ➪ Text to Columns.** The Text to Columns dialog box appears.
3. **Click Finish.**

This procedure works because of a default setting in the Advanced Text Import Settings dialog box (which you don't even see normally). To display this dialog box, which is shown in Figure 25.27, go to step 3 in the Text to Columns Wizard dialog box and click Advanced.

FIGURE 25.27

The Trailing Minus for Negative Numbers option makes it easy to fix trailing minus signs in a range of data.

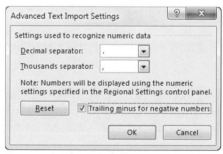

Following a data cleaning checklist

This section contains a list of items that could cause problems with data. Not all of these are relevant to every set of data.

- Does each column have a unique and descriptive header?
- Is each column of data formatted consistently?

25

- Did you check for duplicate or missing rows?
- For text data, are the words consistent in terms of case?
- Did you check for spelling errors?
- Does the data contain any extra spaces?
- Are the columns arranged in the proper (or logical) order?
- Are there any cells blank that shouldn't be blank?
- Did you correct any trailing minus signs?
- Are the columns wide enough to display all data?

Exporting Data

This chapter began with a section on importing data, so it's only appropriate to end it with a discussion of exporting data to a file that's not a standard Excel file.

Exporting to a text file

When you choose File ⇨ Save As, the Save As dialog box lets you choose from a variety of file formats. The three text file types are as follows:

CSV: Comma-separated value files

TXT: Tab-delimited files

PRN: Formatted text

We discuss these file types in the sections that follow.

CSV files

When you export a worksheet to a CSV file, the data is saved as displayed. In other words, if a cell contains 12.8312344 but is formatted to display with two decimal places, the value will be saved as 12.83.

Cells are delimited with a comma character, and rows are delimited with a carriage return and line feed.

> **NOTE**
>
> If you export a file using the Mac variant, rows are delimited with a carriage return only (no line feed character).

Note that if a cell contains a comma, the cell value is saved within quotation marks. If a cell contains a quotation mark character, that character appears twice.

TXT files

Exporting a workbook to a TXT file is almost identical to the CSV file format described earlier. The only difference is that cells are separated by a tab character rather than a comma.

If your worksheet contains any Unicode characters, you should export the file using the Unicode variant. Otherwise, Unicode characters will be saved as question mark characters.

PRN files

A PRN file is very much like a printed image of the worksheet. The cells are separated by multiple space characters. Also, a line is limited to 240 characters. If a line exceeds that limit, the remainder appears on the next line. PRN files are rarely used.

Exporting to other file formats

Excel also lets you save your work in several other formats:

Data Interchange Format   These files have a `.dif` extension. These are not used very often.

Symbolic Link   These files have an `.sylk` extension. These are not used very often.

Portable Document Format   These files have a `.pdf` extension. This is a common "read-only" file format.

XML Paper Specification Document   These files have an `.xps` extension. This is Microsoft's alternative to PDF files. It is not used very often.

Web Page   These files have an `.htm` extension. Often, saving a file as a webpage will generate a directory of ancillary files required to render the page accurately.

OpenDocument Spreadsheet   These files have an `.ods` extension. They're compatible with various open-source spreadsheet programs.

25

Using Data Validation

IN THIS CHAPTER

Getting an overview of Excel's data validation feature

Looking at practical examples of using data validation formulas

This chapter explores a useful Excel feature: data validation. Data validation enables you to add rules for what's acceptable in specific cells, and it allows you to add dynamic elements to your worksheet without using any macro programming.

About Data Validation

The Excel data validation feature allows you to set up rules that determine what can be entered into a cell. For example, you may want to limit data entry in a particular cell to whole numbers between 1 and 12. If the user makes an invalid entry, you can display a custom message, such as the one shown in Figure 26.1.

FIGURE 26.1

Displaying a message when the user makes an invalid entry

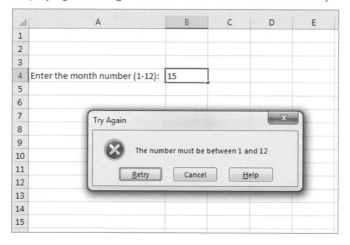

Excel makes it easy to specify the validation criteria. You can also use a formula for more complex criteria.

> **CAUTION**
>
> The Excel data validation feature suffers from a potentially serious problem: if the user copies a cell that does not use data validation and pastes it into a cell that does use data validation, the data validation rules are deleted. In other words, the cell then accepts any type of data. This has always been a problem, and Microsoft still hasn't fixed it in Excel 2019.

Specifying Validation Criteria

To specify the type of data allowable in a cell or range, follow these steps:

1. **Select the cell or range of cells.**
2. **Choose Data ➪ Data Tools ➪ Data Validation. The Data Validation dialog box appears, as shown in Figure 26.2.**

FIGURE 26.2

The three tabs of the Data Validation dialog box

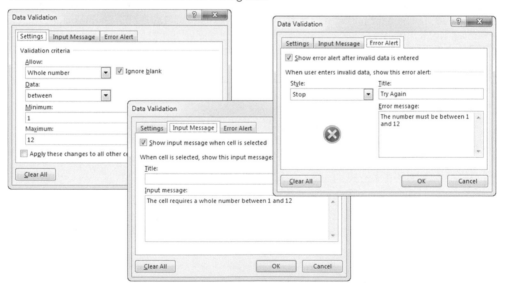

3. **Select the Settings tab.**

4. **Choose an option from the Allow drop-down list.** The contents of the Data Validation dialog box change, displaying controls based on your choice. For example, to specify a formula, select Custom.

5. **Specify the conditions by using the displayed controls.** Your selection in step 4 determines the other controls that you can access.

6. **(Optional) Select the Input Message tab, and specify which message to display when a user selects the cell.** You can use this optional step to tell the user what type of data is expected. If this step is omitted, no message will appear when the user selects the cell.

7. **(Optional) Select the Error Alert tab and specify which error message to display when a user makes an invalid entry.** The selection for Style determines what choices users have when they make invalid entries. For example, choose Stop to prevent an invalid entry. If this step is omitted, a standard message will appear if the user makes an invalid entry.

> **CAUTION**
>
> Even with data validation in effect, a user can enter invalid data. If the Style setting on the Error Alert tab of the Data Validation dialog box is set to Warning or Information, invalid data can be entered. You can identify invalid entries by having Excel circle them (explained in the next section).

8. **Click OK.** The cell or range contains the validation criteria you specified.

Types of Validation Criteria You Can Apply

From the Settings tab of the Data Validation dialog box, you can specify a variety of data validation criteria. The following options are available from the Allow drop-down list. Keep in mind that the other controls on the Settings tab vary, depending on your choice from the Allow drop-down list.

Any Value Selecting this option removes any existing data validation. Note, however, that the input message, if any, still displays if the box is checked on the Input Message tab.

Whole Number The user must enter a whole number. You specify a valid range of whole numbers by using the Data drop-down list. For example, you can specify that the entry must be a whole number greater than or equal to 100.

Decimal The user must enter a number. You specify a valid range of numbers by refining the criteria from choices in the Data drop-down list. For example, you can specify that the entry must be between 0 and 1.

List   The user must choose from a list of entries that you provide. Type a comma-separated list of values in the Source text box. This option is useful, and we discuss it in detail later in this chapter. (See "Creating a Drop-Down List.")

Date   The user must enter a date. You specify a valid date range from the choices in the Data drop-down list. For example, you can specify that the data entered must be greater than or equal to January 1, 2019.

Time   The user must enter a time. You specify a valid time range from choices in the Data drop-down list. For example, you can specify that the data entered must be greater than 12 p.m.

Text Length   The length of the data (number of characters) is limited. You specify a valid length by using the Data drop-down list and the Length text box. For example, you can specify that the length of the data entered be 1 (a single alphanumeric character).

Custom   To use this option, you must supply a logical formula that determines the validity of the user's entry. (A logical formula returns either TRUE or FALSE.) You can enter the formula directly into the Formula control (which appears when you select the Custom option), or you can specify a cell reference that contains a formula. This chapter contains examples of useful formulas.

The Settings tab of the Data Validation dialog box contains these other check boxes:

Ignore Blank   If selected, blank entries are allowed.

In-cell Dropdown   If you select List in the Allow drop-down list, you can choose to show or hide a drop-down arrow in the cell to aid the user in the selecting a valid value.

Apply These Changes to All Other Cells with the Same Settings   If selected, the changes that you make apply to all other cells that contain the original data validation criteria.

> **TIP**
>
> The Data ⇨ Data Tools ⇨ Data Validation drop-down list contains an item named Circle Invalid Data. When you select this item, circles appear around cells that contain incorrect entries. If you correct an invalid entry, the circle disappears. To get rid of the circles, choose Data ⇨ Data Tools ⇨ Data Validation ⇨ Clear Validation Circles. In Figure 26.3, valid entries are defined as values between 1 and 105. Values that are not within this numerical range are circled.

FIGURE 26.3

Excel can draw circles around invalid entries (in this case, cells that contain values greater than 105).

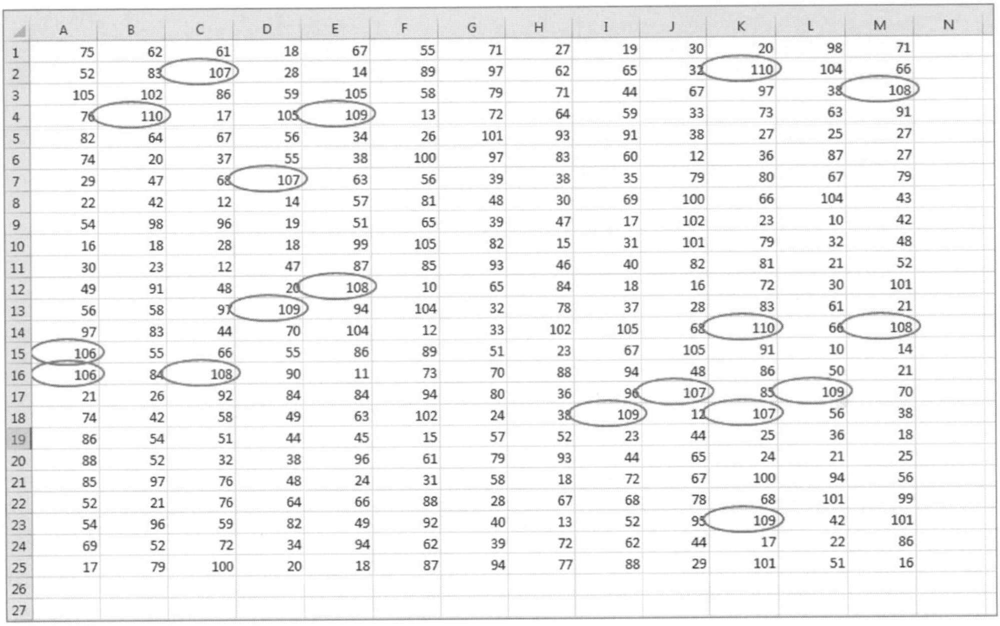

	A	B	C	D	E	F	G	H	I	J	K	L	M	N
1	75	62	61	18	67	55	71	27	19	30	20	98	71	
2	52	83	107	28	14	89	97	62	65	31	110	104	66	
3	105	102	86	59	105	58	79	71	44	67	97	38	108	
4	76	110	17	105	109	13	72	64	59	33	73	63	91	
5	82	64	67	56	34	26	101	93	91	38	27	25	27	
6	74	20	37	55	38	100	97	83	60	12	36	87	27	
7	29	47	68	107	63	56	39	38	35	79	80	67	79	
8	22	42	12	14	57	81	48	30	69	100	66	104	43	
9	54	98	96	19	51	65	39	47	17	102	23	10	42	
10	16	18	28	18	99	105	82	15	31	101	79	32	48	
11	30	23	12	47	87	85	93	46	40	82	81	21	52	
12	49	91	48	20	108	10	65	84	18	16	72	30	101	
13	56	58	97	109	94	104	32	78	37	28	83	61	21	
14	97	83	44	70	104	12	33	102	105	68	110	66	108	
15	106	55	66	55	86	89	51	23	67	105	91	10	14	
16	106	84	108	90	11	73	70	88	94	48	86	50	21	
17	21	26	92	84	84	94	80	36	96	107	85	109	70	
18	74	42	58	49	63	102	24	38	109	11	107	56	38	
19	86	54	51	44	45	15	57	52	23	44	25	36	18	
20	88	52	32	38	96	61	79	93	44	65	24	21	25	
21	85	97	76	48	24	31	58	18	72	67	100	94	56	
22	52	21	76	64	66	88	28	67	68	78	68	101	99	
23	54	96	59	82	49	92	40	13	52	93	109	42	101	
24	69	52	72	34	94	62	39	72	62	44	17	22	86	
25	17	79	100	20	18	87	94	77	88	29	101	51	16	
26														
27														

Creating a Drop-Down List

One of the most common uses of data validation is to create a drop-down list in a cell. Figure 26.4 shows an example that uses the month names in cells A1:A12 as the list source.

To create a drop-down list in a cell, follow these steps:

1. **Enter the list items into a single-row or single-column range.** These items will appear in the drop-down list.

2. **Select the cell that will contain the drop-down list and then choose Data ⇨ Data Tools ⇨ Data Validation.** The Data Validation dialog box appears.

3. **From the Settings tab, select the List option (from the Allow drop-down list) and specify the range that contains the list, using the Source control.** The range can be in a different worksheet, but it must be in the same workbook.

FIGURE 26.4

This drop-down list (with an Input Message) was created using data validation.

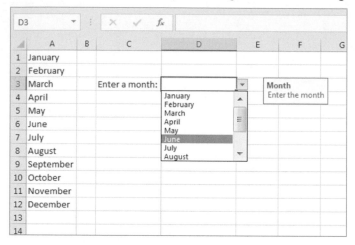

> **TIP**
>
> If you will be adding new items to the list, put the items in a single-column table that was created by using Insert ⇨ Tables ⇨ Table. Excel will then update the list of options when you add or remove items from the table column.

4. **Make sure that the In-Cell Dropdown check box is selected.**

5. **Set any other Data Validation options as desired.**

6. **Click OK.** The cell displays an input message (if specified), and a drop-down arrow when it's activated.

7. **Click the arrow and choose an item from the list that appears.**

> **TIP**
>
> If you have a short list, you can enter the items directly into the Source control on the Settings tab of the Data Validation dialog box. (This control appears when you choose the List option in the Allow drop-down list.) Just separate each item with list separators specified in your regional settings (a comma if you use the U.S. regional settings).

Unfortunately, you cannot control the font size used in drop-down lists. If the cell that displays the drop-down is formatted to show large text, the drop-down list does not use that formatting. If you zoom out on a worksheet, it may be difficult to read the items.

Using Formulas for Data Validation Rules

For simple data validation, the data validation feature is quite straightforward and easy to use. The real power of this feature, though, becomes apparent when you use the Custom option and supply a formula.

The formula that you specify must be a logical formula that returns either TRUE or FALSE. If the formula evaluates to TRUE, the data is considered valid and remains in the cell. If the formula evaluates to FALSE, a message box appears that displays the message that you specify on the Error Alert tab of the Data Validation dialog box.

Specify a formula in the Data Validation dialog box by selecting the Custom option from the Allow drop-down list of the Settings tab. Enter the formula directly into the Formula control, or enter a reference to a cell that contains a formula. The Formula control appears on the Settings tab of the Data Validation dialog box when the Custom option is selected.

We present several examples of formulas used for data validation in the section "Data Validation Formula Examples" later in this chapter.

Understanding Cell References

If the formula that you enter into the Data Validation dialog box contains a cell reference, that reference is considered a relative reference, based on the upper-left cell in the selected range.

The following example clarifies this concept. Suppose you want to allow only an odd number to be entered into the range B2:B10. None of the Excel data validation rules can limit entry to odd numbers, so a formula is required.

Follow these steps:

1. **Select the range (B2:B10 in this example) and make sure that cell B2 is the active cell.**
2. **Choose Data ⇨ Data Tools ⇨ Data Validation.** The Data Validation dialog box appears.
3. **Select the Settings tab, and select the Custom option (from the Allow drop-down list).**
4. **Enter the following formula in the Formula field, as shown in Figure 26.5:**

   `=ISODD(B2)`

   This formula uses the ISODD function, which returns TRUE if its numeric argument is an odd number. Notice that the formula refers to the active cell, which is cell B2.

FIGURE 26.5

Entering a data validation formula

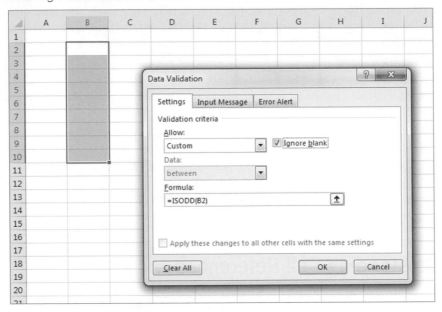

5. **On the Error Alert tab, choose Stop for the Style and then type** `An odd number is required here` **in the Error Message field.**

6. **Click OK to close the Data Validation dialog box.**

Notice that the formula entered contains a reference to the upper-left cell in the selected range. This data validation formula was applied to a range of cells, so you might expect that each cell would contain the same data validation formula. Because you entered a relative cell reference as the argument for the ISODD function, Excel adjusts the formula for the other cells in the B2:B10 range. To demonstrate that the reference is relative, select cell B5 and examine its formula displayed in the Data Validation dialog box. You'll see that the formula for this cell is

`=ISODD(B5)`

> **NOTE**
> An alternative method is to enter the logical formula into a cell and then enter a cell reference in the Formula field in the Data Validation dialog box. For this example, cell C2 would contain `=ISODD(B2)`, and that formula would be copied down the column to cell C10. Then the Formula field in the Data Validation dialog box would have this formula: `=C2`. Most of the time, entering the formula into the Formula field is easier and more efficient.

Generally, when entering a data validation formula for a range of cells, you use a reference to the active cell, which is normally the upper-left cell in the selected range. An exception is when you need to refer to a specific cell. For example, suppose that you select range A1:B10, and you want your data validation to allow only values that are greater than the value in cell C1. You would use this formula:

```
=A1>$C$1
```

In this case, the reference to cell C1 is an absolute reference; it will not be adjusted for the cells in the selected range, which is just what you want. The data validation formula for cell A2 looks like this:

```
=A2>$C$1
```

The relative cell reference is adjusted, but the absolute cell reference is not.

Data Validation Formula Examples

The following sections contain a few data validation examples that use a formula entered directly into the Formula control on the Settings tab of the Data Validation dialog box. These examples help you understand how to create your own data validation formulas.

> **CAUTION**
>
> All the examples in this section are available at this book's website at www.wiley.com/go/excel2019bible. The file is named data validation examples.xlsx.

Accepting text only

Excel has a data validation option to limit the length of text entered into a cell, but it doesn't have an option to force text (rather than a number) into a cell. To force a cell or range to accept only text (no values), use the following data validation formula:

```
=ISTEXT(A1)
```

This formula assumes that the active cell in the selected range is cell A1.

Accepting a larger value than the previous cell

The following data validation formula enables the user to enter a value only if it's greater than the value in the cell directly above it:

```
=A2>A1
```

This formula assumes that A2 is the active cell in the selected range. Note that you can't use this formula for a cell in row 1.

Accepting nonduplicate entries only

The following data validation formula does not permit the user to make a duplicate entry in the range A1:C20:

```
=COUNTIF($A$1:$C$20,A1)=1
```

This is a logical formula that returns TRUE if the value in the cell occurs only one time in the A1:C20 range. Otherwise, it returns FALSE, and the Duplicate Entry dialog box is displayed.

This formula assumes that A1 is the active cell in the selected range. Note that the first argument for COUNTIF is an absolute reference. The second argument is a relative reference, and it adjusts for each cell in the validation range. Figure 26.6 shows this validation criterion in effect using a custom error alert message. The user is attempting to enter 17 into cell B5.

FIGURE 26.6

Using data validation to prevent duplicate entries in a range

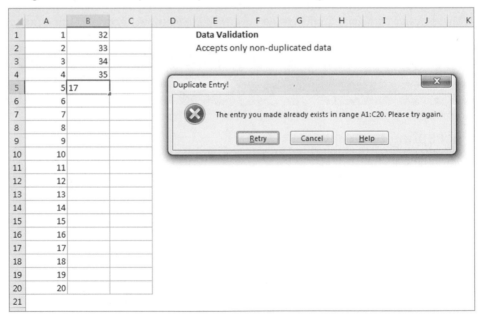

Accepting text that begins with a specific character

The following data validation formula demonstrates how to check for a specific character. In this case, the formula ensures that the user's entry is a text string that begins with the letter *A* (uppercase or lowercase):

```
=LEFT(A1)="a"
```

This is a logical formula that returns TRUE if the first character in the cell is the letter *A*. Otherwise, it returns FALSE. This formula assumes that the active cell in the selected range is cell A1.

The following formula is a variation of this validation formula. It uses wildcard characters in the second argument of the COUNTIF function. In this case, the formula ensures that the entry begins with the letter *A* and contains exactly five characters:

```
=COUNTIF(A1,"A????")=1
```

Accepting dates by the day of the week

The following data validation formula assumes that the cell entry is a date, and it ensures that the date is a Monday:

```
=WEEKDAY(A1)=2
```

This formula assumes that the active cell in the selected range is cell A1. It uses the WEEKDAY function, which returns 1 for Sunday, 2 for Monday, and so on. Note that the WEEKDAY function accepts any nonnegative value as an argument (not just dates).

Accepting only values that don't exceed a total

Figure 26.7 shows a simple budget worksheet, with the budget item amounts in the range B1:B6. The planned budget is in cell E5, and the user is attempting to enter a value in cell B4 that would cause the total (cell E6) to exceed the budget. The following data validation formula ensures that the sum of the budget items does not exceed the budget:

```
=SUM($B$1:$B$6)<=$E$5
```

Creating a dependent list

As we described previously, you can use data validation to create a drop-down list in a cell (see "Creating a Drop-Down List" earlier in this chapter). This section explains how to use a drop-down list to control the entries that appear in a second drop-down list. In other words, the second drop-down list is dependent upon the value selected in the first drop-down list.

FIGURE 26.7

Using data validation to ensure that the sum of a range does not exceed a certain value

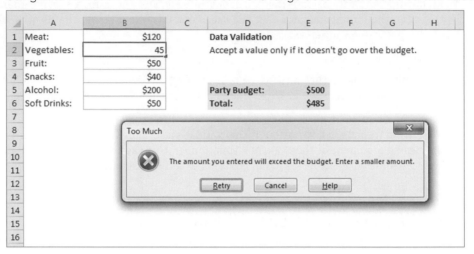

Figure 26.8 shows a simple example of a dependent list created by using data validation. Cell E2 contains data validation that displays a three-item list from the range A1:C1 (Vegetables, Fruits, and Meats). When the user chooses an item from the list, the second list (in cell F2) displays the appropriate items.

FIGURE 26.8

The items displayed in the list in cell F2 depend on the list item selected in cell E2.

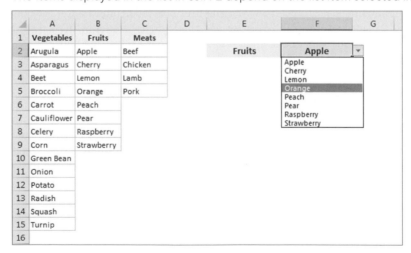

This worksheet uses three named ranges:

> Vegetables: A2:A15
> Fruits: B2:B9
> Meats: C2:C5

Cell F2 contains data validation that uses this formula:

```
=INDIRECT($E$2)
```

Therefore, the drop-down list displayed in F2 depends on the value displayed in cell E2.

Using Data Validation without Restricting Entry

The most common use of data validation is to prevent a user from entering invalid data. But data validation can also be used as a component of your spreadsheet's user interface without actually preventing the user's entry. The two examples of showing an input message and making suggestions would require quite a bit of VBA programming to accomplish, but it can be accomplished easily with data validation.

Showing an input message

Data validation provides a way to display a message when the user selects a cell. Normally, this message would tell the user what would be considered invalid data for that cell to prevent them from getting the error message (when they actually enter invalid data). But you can use this message for anything.

Figure 26.9 shows an input message reminding the user to complete a previous step. The Allow drop-down list is set to Any Value, so the user is not prevented from entering anything into this cell. It's just a reminder set to a cell that the user will likely use early in the process of completing this workbook.

FIGURE 26.9

Data validation can be used to show messages to the user.

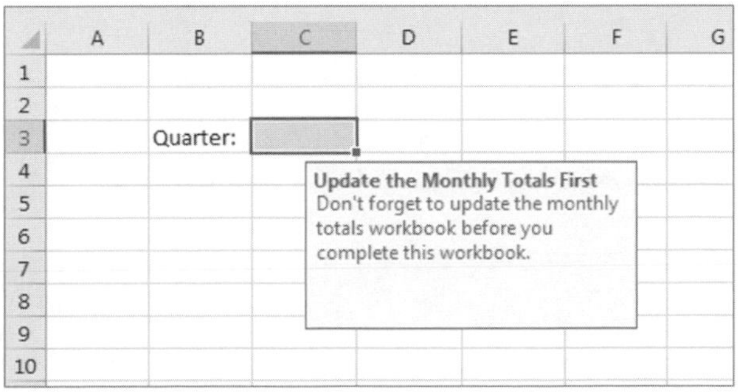

Making suggested entries

The default Style value on the Error Alert tab of the Data Validation dialog box is Stop. This not only displays a message, but it also prevents the user from completing the entry of invalid data. There are two other options, Warning and Information, which will allow the user to enter data. You can also deselect the check box and Excel will not show any message.

Suppose that you have a field where the user is to enter the name of a fruit. To help the user, you provide a list of common fruits, but you want the user to be able to enter fruits that aren't on the list. The list is merely there to save the user some typing if they need to enter a common fruit.

To set up this scenario, select List and point to the list of fruits, as shown in Figure 26.10. Then deselect the Show Error Alert After Invalid Data is Entered check box on the Error Alert tab. Now the user can select from the list or type in a fruit that's not on the list. Of course, you can't prevent the user from typing in nonsense.

FIGURE 26.10

Data Validation dialog box

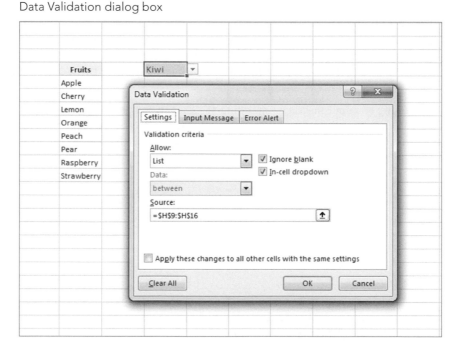

Creating and Using Worksheet Outlines

IN THIS CHAPTER

Introducing worksheet outlines

Creating an outline

Working with outlines

I f you use a word processor, you may be familiar with the concept of an outline. Most word processors (including Microsoft Word) have an outline mode that lets you view only the headings and subheadings in your document. You can easily expand a heading to show the text below it. Using an outline makes visualizing the structure of your document easy.

Excel also is capable of using outlines. Understanding this feature can make working with certain types of worksheets much easier for you.

Introducing Worksheet Outlines

You'll find that some worksheets are more suitable for outlines than others. You can use outlines to create summary reports that don't show all of the details. If your worksheet uses hierarchical data with subtotals, it's probably a good candidate for an outline.

The best way to understand how worksheet outlining works is to look at an example. Figure 27.1 shows a simple sales summary sheet without an outline. Formulas are used to calculate subtotals by region and by quarter.

Figure 27.2 shows the same worksheet after the outline was created by selecting only the rows and using Data ⇨ Outline ⇨ Group ⇨ Auto Outline. Notice that Excel adds a new section to the left of the screen. This section contains outline controls that enable you to determine which level to view. This particular outline has three levels: States, Regions (each region consists of states grouped into categories such as West, East, and Central), and Grand Total (the sum of each region's subtotal).

FIGURE 27.1

A simple sales summary with subtotals

	A	B	C	D	E	F	G	H	I	J	K
1	State	Jan	Feb	Mar	Qtr-1	Apr	May	Jun	Qtr-2	Total	
2	California	1,118	1,960	1,252	4,330	1,271	1,557	1,679	4,507	8,837	
3	Washington	1,247	1,238	1,028	3,513	1,345	1,784	1,574	4,703	8,216	
4	Oregon	1,460	1,954	1,726	5,140	1,461	1,764	1,144	4,369	9,509	
5	Arizona	1,345	1,375	1,075	3,795	1,736	1,555	1,372	4,663	8,458	
6	West Total	5,170	6,527	5,081	16,778	5,813	6,660	5,769	18,242	35,020	
7	New York	1,429	1,316	1,993	4,738	1,832	1,740	1,191	4,763	9,501	
8	New Jersey	1,735	1,406	1,224	4,365	1,706	1,320	1,290	4,316	8,681	
9	Massachusetts	1,099	1,233	1,110	3,442	1,637	1,512	1,006	4,155	7,597	
10	Florida	1,705	1,792	1,225	4,722	1,946	1,327	1,357	4,630	9,352	
11	East Total	5,968	5,747	5,552	17,267	7,121	5,899	4,844	17,864	35,131	
12	Kentucky	1,109	1,078	1,155	3,342	1,993	1,082	1,551	4,626	7,968	
13	Oklahoma	1,309	1,045	1,641	3,995	1,924	1,499	1,941	5,364	9,359	
14	Missouri	1,511	1,744	1,414	4,669	1,243	1,493	1,820	4,556	9,225	
15	Illinois	1,539	1,493	1,211	4,243	1,165	1,013	1,445	3,623	7,866	
16	Kansas	1,973	1,560	1,243	4,776	1,495	1,125	1,387	4,007	8,783	
17	Central Total	7,441	6,920	6,664	21,025	7,820	6,212	8,144	22,176	43,201	
18	Grand Total	18,579	19,194	17,297	55,070	20,754	18,771	18,757	58,282	113,352	
19											

FIGURE 27.2

The worksheet after creating an outline

1 2 3		A	B	C	D	E	F	G	H	I	J	K
	1	State	Jan	Feb	Mar	Qtr-1	Apr	May	Jun	Qtr-2	Total	
	2	California	1,118	1,960	1,252	4,330	1,271	1,557	1,679	4,507	8,837	
	3	Washington	1,247	1,238	1,028	3,513	1,345	1,784	1,574	4,703	8,216	
	4	Oregon	1,460	1,954	1,726	5,140	1,461	1,764	1,144	4,369	9,509	
	5	Arizona	1,345	1,375	1,075	3,795	1,736	1,555	1,372	4,663	8,458	
	6	West Total	5,170	6,527	5,081	16,778	5,813	6,660	5,769	18,242	35,020	
	7	New York	1,429	1,316	1,993	4,738	1,832	1,740	1,191	4,763	9,501	
	8	New Jersey	1,735	1,406	1,224	4,365	1,706	1,320	1,290	4,316	8,681	
	9	Massachusetts	1,099	1,233	1,110	3,442	1,637	1,512	1,006	4,155	7,597	
	10	Florida	1,705	1,792	1,225	4,722	1,946	1,327	1,357	4,630	9,352	
	11	East Total	5,968	5,747	5,552	17,267	7,121	5,899	4,844	17,864	35,131	
	12	Kentucky	1,109	1,078	1,155	3,342	1,993	1,082	1,551	4,626	7,968	
	13	Oklahoma	1,309	1,045	1,641	3,995	1,924	1,499	1,941	5,364	9,359	
	14	Missouri	1,511	1,744	1,414	4,669	1,243	1,493	1,820	4,556	9,225	
	15	Illinois	1,539	1,493	1,211	4,243	1,165	1,013	1,445	3,623	7,866	
	16	Kansas	1,973	1,560	1,243	4,776	1,495	1,125	1,387	4,007	8,783	
	17	Central Total	7,441	6,920	6,664	21,025	7,820	6,212	8,144	22,176	43,201	
	18	Grand Total	18,579	19,194	17,297	55,070	20,754	18,771	18,757	58,282	113,352	
	19											
	20											
	21											

Figure 27.3 depicts the outline after clicking the 2 header, which collapses everything below the second level of details. Now the outline shows only the totals for the regions. You

can partially expand the outline to show the detail for a particular region by clicking one of the plus-sign buttons. Collapsing the outline to level 1 shows only the headers and the Grand Total row.

FIGURE 27.3

The worksheet after collapsing the outline to the second level

	A	B	C	D	E	F	G	H	I	J	K
1	State	Jan	Feb	Mar	Qtr-1	Apr	May	Jun	Qtr-2	Total	
6	West Total	5,170	6,527	5,081	16,778	5,813	6,660	5,769	18,242	35,020	
11	East Total	5,968	5,747	5,552	17,267	7,121	5,899	4,844	17,864	35,131	
17	Central Total	7,441	6,920	6,664	21,025	7,820	6,212	8,144	22,176	43,201	
18	Grand Total	18,579	19,194	17,297	55,070	20,754	18,771	18,757	58,282	113,352	

Excel can create outlines in both directions. In the preceding examples, the outline is a row (vertical) outline. Figure 27.4 shows the same model after a column (horizontal) outline was added by selecting the columns and using Data ⇨ Outline ⇨ Group ⇨ Auto Outline. When both outlines are in effect, Excel also displays outline controls at the top.

FIGURE 27.4

The worksheet after adding a column outline

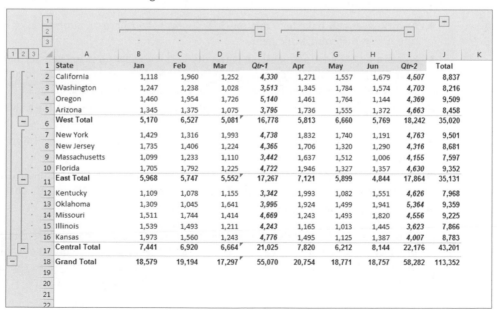

	A	B	C	D	E	F	G	H	I	J	K
1	State	Jan	Feb	Mar	Qtr-1	Apr	May	Jun	Qtr-2	Total	
2	California	1,118	1,960	1,252	4,330	1,271	1,557	1,679	4,507	8,837	
3	Washington	1,247	1,238	1,028	3,513	1,345	1,784	1,574	4,703	8,216	
4	Oregon	1,460	1,954	1,726	5,140	1,461	1,764	1,144	4,369	9,509	
5	Arizona	1,345	1,375	1,075	3,795	1,736	1,555	1,372	4,663	8,458	
6	West Total	5,170	6,527	5,081	16,778	5,813	6,660	5,769	18,242	35,020	
7	New York	1,429	1,316	1,993	4,738	1,832	1,740	1,191	4,763	9,501	
8	New Jersey	1,735	1,406	1,224	4,365	1,706	1,320	1,290	4,316	8,681	
9	Massachusetts	1,099	1,233	1,110	3,442	1,637	1,512	1,006	4,155	7,597	
10	Florida	1,705	1,792	1,225	4,722	1,946	1,327	1,357	4,630	9,352	
11	East Total	5,968	5,747	5,552	17,267	7,121	5,899	4,844	17,864	35,131	
12	Kentucky	1,109	1,078	1,155	3,342	1,993	1,082	1,551	4,626	7,968	
13	Oklahoma	1,309	1,045	1,641	3,995	1,924	1,499	1,941	5,364	9,359	
14	Missouri	1,511	1,744	1,414	4,669	1,243	1,493	1,820	4,556	9,225	
15	Illinois	1,539	1,493	1,211	4,243	1,165	1,013	1,445	3,623	7,866	
16	Kansas	1,973	1,560	1,243	4,776	1,495	1,125	1,387	4,007	8,783	
17	Central Total	7,441	6,920	6,664	21,025	7,820	6,212	8,144	22,176	43,201	
18	Grand Total	18,579	19,194	17,297	55,070	20,754	18,771	18,757	58,282	113,352	

If you create both a row outline and a column outline in a worksheet, you can work with each outline independently of the other. For example, you can show the row outline at the second level and the column outline at the first level. Figure 27.5 shows the model with both outlines collapsed at the second level. The result is a high-level summary table that displays regional totals by quarter.

FIGURE 27.5

The worksheet with both outlines collapsed at the second level

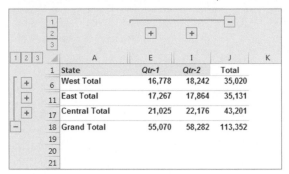

 You can find the workbook used in the preceding examples on this book's website at www.wiley.com/go/excel2019bible. **The file is named** outline example.xlsx.

Keep in mind the following points about worksheet outlines:

- A worksheet can have only one outline. If you need to create more than one outline, use a different worksheet.
- You can either create an outline manually or have Excel do it for you automatically. If you choose the latter option, you may need to do some preparation to get the worksheet in the proper format. (The next section covers both methods.)
- You can create an outline either for all data on a worksheet or just for a selected data range.
- You can remove an outline with a single command: Data ⇨ Outline ⇨ Ungroup ⇨ Clear Outline. See "Removing an outline" later in this chapter.
- You can hide the outline symbols (to free screen space) but retain the outline. We show you how in the "Hiding the outline symbols" section later in this chapter.
- An outline can have up to eight nested levels.

Worksheet outlines can be quite useful. If your main objective is to summarize a large amount of data, though, you may be better off using a PivotTable. A PivotTable is much more flexible and doesn't require that you create the subtotal formulas; it does the summarizing for you automatically. The ultimate solution depends on your data source. If you're entering data from scratch, the most flexible approach is to enter it in a normalized table format and create a PivotTable.

 We discuss PivotTables (and normalized data) in Chapter 29, "Introducing PivotTables," and Chapter 30, "Analyzing Data with PivotTables."

Creating an Outline

This section describes the two ways to create an outline: automatically and manually. Before you create an outline, you need to ensure that data is appropriate for an outline and that the formulas are set up properly.

Preparing the data

What type of data is appropriate for an outline? Generally, the data should be arranged in a hierarchy, such as a budget that consists of an arrangement similar to the following:

Company
    Division
        Department
            Budget Category
                Budget Item

In this case, each budget item (for example, airfare and hotel expenses) is part of a budget category (for example, travel expenses). Each department has its own budget, and the departments are rolled up into divisions. The divisions make up the company. This type of arrangement is well suited for a row outline.

The data arrangement suitable for an outline is essentially a summary table of your data. In some situations, your data will be "normalized" data—one data point per row. You can easily create a PivotTable to summarize such data; a PivotTable is much more flexible than an outline.

 See Chapter 29, "Introducing PivotTables," and Chapter 30, "Analyzing Data with PivotTables," for more information about PivotTables.

After you create such an outline, you can view the information at any level of detail that you want by clicking the outline controls. When you need to create reports for different levels of management, consider using an outline. For example, upper management may want to see only the division totals, division managers may want to see totals by department, and department managers will want to see the full details for their departments.

Keep in mind that using an outline isn't a security feature. The data that's hidden when an outline is collapsed can easily be revealed when the outline is expanded.

You can include time-based information that is rolled up into larger units (such as months and quarters) in a column outline. Column outlines work just like row outlines, however, and the levels don't have to be time based.

Before you create an outline, you need to make sure that all of the summary formulas are entered correctly and consistently. In this context, *consistently* means that the formulas are in the same relative location. Generally, formulas that compute summary formulas (such as subtotals) are entered below the data to which they refer. In some cases, however, the summary formulas are entered above the referenced cells. Excel can handle either method, but you must be consistent throughout the range that you outline. If the summary formulas aren't consistent, automatic outlining won't produce the results you want.

> **NOTE**
> If your summary formulas aren't consistent (that is, some are above and some are below the data), you still can create an outline, but you must do it manually.

Creating an outline automatically

Excel can create an outline for you automatically in a few seconds, whereas it may take you ten minutes or more to do the same thing manually.

> **NOTE**
> If you've created a table for your data (by choosing Insert ⇨ Tables ⇨ Table), Excel can't create an outline automatically. You can create an outline from a table, but you must do so manually.

To have Excel create an outline, move the cell pointer anywhere within the range of data that you're outlining. Then choose Data ⇨ Outline ⇨ Group ⇨ Auto Outline. Excel analyzes the formulas in the range and creates the outline. Depending on the formulas that you have, Excel creates a row outline, a column outline, or both.

If the worksheet already has an outline, Excel asks whether you want to modify the existing outline. Click Yes to force Excel to remove the old outline and create a new one.

> **NOTE**
> Excel automatically creates an outline when you choose Data ⇨ Outline ⇨ Subtotal, which inserts subtotal formulas automatically.

Creating an outline manually

Usually, letting Excel create the outline is the best approach. It's much faster and less error prone. If the outline that Excel creates isn't what you have in mind, however, you can create one manually.

When Excel creates a row outline, the summary rows must be all below the data or all above the data; they can't be mixed. Similarly, for a column outline, the summary columns must be all to the right of the data or all to the left of the data. If your worksheet doesn't meet these requirements, you have two choices:

- Rearrange the worksheet so that it does meet the requirements.
- Create the outline manually.

You also need to create an outline manually if the range doesn't contain formulas. You may have imported a file and want to use an outline to display it better. Because Excel uses the positioning of the formulas to determine how to create the outline, it can't make an outline without formulas.

Creating an outline manually consists of creating groups of rows (for row outlines) or groups of columns (for column outlines). To create a group of rows, follow these steps:

1. **Select the rows that you want to include in the group.** One way to do this is to click a row number and then drag to select other adjacent rows.

> **CAUTION**
>
> Don't select the row that has the summary formulas. You don't want these rows to be included in the group.

2. **Choose Data ⇨ Outline ⇨ Group ⇨ Group.** Excel displays outline symbols for the group.
3. **Repeat this process for each group that you want to create.** When you collapse the outline, Excel hides rows in the group, but the summary row, which isn't in the group, remains in view.

> **CAUTION**
>
> If you select a range of cells (rather than entire rows or columns) before you create a group, Excel displays a dialog box asking what you want to group. It then groups entire rows or columns based on the option you select.

You can also select groups of groups to create multilevel outlines. When you create multi-level outlines, always start with the innermost groupings and then work your way out. If you realize that you grouped the wrong rows, you can ungroup the group by selecting the rows and choosing Data ⇨ Outline ⇨ Ungroup ⇨ Ungroup.

Here are keyboard shortcuts that you can use that speed up grouping and ungrouping:

Alt+Shift+right arrow: Groups selected rows or columns

Alt+Shift+left arrow: Ungroups selected rows or columns

Creating outlines manually can be confusing at first, but if you stick with it, you'll become a pro in no time.

27

Figure 27.6 shows a worksheet with a three-level outline of this book. We had to create it manually because it has no formulas, just text.

FIGURE 27.6

An outline of this book, created manually

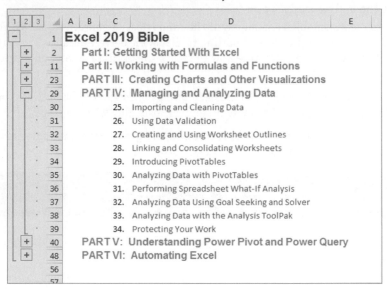

 This workbook is available on this book's website at www.wiley.com/go/excel2019bible. The file is named book outline.xlsx.

Working with Outlines

This section discusses the basic operations that you can perform with a worksheet outline.

Displaying levels

To display various outline levels, click the appropriate outline symbol. These symbols consist of headers with numbers on them (1, 2, and so on) or a plus sign (+) or minus sign (−). Refer to Figure 27.5, which shows these symbols for a row and column outline.

Clicking the 1 header collapses the outline so that it displays no detail (just the highest summary level of information), clicking the 2 header expands the outline to show one level, and so on. The number of headers depends on the number of outline levels. Choosing a level number displays the detail for that level, plus any levels with lower numbers. To display all levels (the most detail), click the highest-level number.

You can expand a particular section by clicking its plus-sign button, or you can collapse a particular section by clicking its minus-sign button. In short, you have complete control over the details that Excel exposes or hides in an outline.

If you prefer, you can use the Hide Detail and Show Detail commands on the Data ⇨ Outline group to hide and show details, respectively.

> **TIP**
>
> If you constantly adjust the outline to show different reports, consider using the Custom Views feature to save a particular view and give it a name. Then you can quickly switch among the named views. Choose View ⇨ Workbook Views ⇨ Custom Views.

Adding data to an outline

You may need to add additional rows or columns to an outline. In some cases, you may be able to insert new rows or columns without disturbing the outline, and the new rows or columns become part of the outline. In other cases, you'll find that the new row or column is not part of the outline. If you create the outline automatically, choose Data ⇨ Outline ⇨ Group ⇨ Auto Outline. Excel makes you verify that you want to modify the existing outline. If you create the outline manually, you need to make the adjustments manually as well.

Removing an outline

After you no longer need an outline, you can remove it by choosing Data ⇨ Outline ⇨ Ungroup ⇨ Clear Outline. Excel fully expands the outline by displaying all hidden rows and columns, and the outline symbols disappear. Be careful before you remove an outline, however. You can't make it reappear by clicking the Undo button; you must re-create the outline from scratch.

Adjusting the outline symbols

When you create a manual outline, Excel puts the outline symbols below the summary rows. This can be unintuitive because you need to click the symbol in the row below the section that you want to expand.

If you prefer that the outline symbols appear in the same row as the summary row, click the dialog box launcher in the lower right of the Data ⇨ Outline group. Excel displays the dialog box shown in Figure 27.7. Remove the check mark from the Summary Rows Below Detail option and click OK. The outline will now display the outline symbols in a more logical position.

FIGURE 27.7

Use the Settings dialog box to adjust the position of the outline symbols.

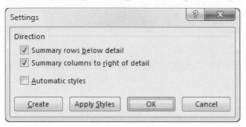

Hiding the outline symbols

The outline symbols that Excel displays when an outline is present take up quite a bit of space. (The exact amount depends on the number of levels.) If you want to see as much as possible on-screen, you can temporarily hide these symbols without removing the outline. Press Ctrl+8 to toggle the outline symbols on and off. When the outline symbols are hidden, you can't expand or collapse the outline.

> **NOTE**
>
> When you hide the outline symbols, the outline still is in effect, and the worksheet displays the data at the current outline level. (That is, some rows or columns may be hidden.)

The Custom Views feature, which saves named views of your outline, also saves the status of the outline symbols as part of the view, enabling you to name some views with the outline symbols and other views without them.

Linking and Consolidating Worksheets

IN THIS CHAPTER

Using various methods to link workbooks

Consolidating multiple worksheets

I n this chapter, we discuss two procedures for using data from other workbooks or worksheets: linking and consolidating. *Linking* is the process of using references to cells in external workbooks to get data into your worksheet. *Consolidating* involves combining or summarizing information from two or more worksheets (which can be in multiple workbooks).

Linking Workbooks

Excel allows you to create formulas that contain references to other workbook files. With such formulas, the workbooks are linked in such a way that one depends on the other. The workbook that contains the external reference formulas is the dependent workbook (because it contains formulas that depend on another workbook). The workbook that contains the information used in the external reference formula is the source workbook (because it's the source of the information).

When you consider linking workbooks, you may ask yourself the following question: if Workbook A needs to access data that's in Workbook B, why not just enter the data into Workbook A in the first place? In some cases, you can. But the real value of linking becomes apparent when the source workbook is being continually updated by another person or group. Creating a link in Workbook A to Workbook B means that in Workbook A, you always have access to the most recent information in Workbook B because Workbook A is updated whenever Workbook B changes.

Linking workbooks also can be helpful if you need to consolidate different files. For example, each regional sales manager may store data in a separate workbook. You can create a summary workbook that first uses link formulas to retrieve specific data from each manager's workbook and then calculates totals across all regions.

Linking also is useful as a way to break up a large workbook into smaller files. You can create smaller workbooks that are linked with a few key external references.

Linking has its downside, however. External reference formulas are somewhat fragile, and accidentally severing the links that you create is relatively easy. You can prevent this mistake if you understand how linking works. Later in the chapter, we discuss some problems that may arise and how to avoid them. (See "Avoiding Potential Problems with External Reference Formulas.")

 The website for this book at `www.wiley.com/go/excel2019bible` contains two linked files that you can use to get a feel for the way linking works. The files are named `source.xlsx` and `dependent.xlsx`. As long as these files remain in the same folder, the links will be maintained.

Creating External Reference Formulas

You can create an external reference formula by using several different techniques:

Type the cell references manually   These references may be lengthy because they include workbook and sheet names and possibly even drive and path information. These references can also point to workbooks stored on the Internet. The advantage of manually typing the cell references is that the source workbook doesn't have to be open. The disadvantage is that it's error prone. Mistyping a single character makes the formula return an error (or possibly return a wrong value from the workbook).

Point to the cell references   If the source workbook is open, you can use the standard pointing techniques to create formulas that use external references.

Paste the links   Copy your data to the Clipboard. Then, with the source workbook open, choose Home ⇨ Clipboard ⇨ Paste ⇨ Paste Link (N). Excel pastes the copied data as external reference formulas.

Choose Data ⇨ Data Tools ⇨ Consolidate   For more on this method, see the section "Consolidating worksheets by using the Consolidate dialog box" later in this chapter.

Understanding link formula syntax

Ideally, you won't have to enter too many external links manually. But it's good to know the structure of links in case you have to troubleshoot a problem. The general syntax for an external reference formula is as follows:

```
=[WorkbookName]SheetName!CellAddress
```

Precede the cell address with the workbook name (in brackets), followed by the worksheet name and an exclamation point. Here's an example of a formula that uses cell A1 in the Sheet1 worksheet of a workbook named Budget.xlsx:

```
=[Budget.xlsx]Sheet1!A1
```

If the workbook name or the sheet name in the reference includes one or more spaces, you must enclose the text in single quotation marks. For example, here's a formula that refers to cell A1 on `Sheet1` in a workbook named `Annual Budget.xlsx`:

```
='[Annual Budget.xlsx]Sheet1'!A1
```

When a formula links to a different workbook, you don't need to open the other workbook. However, if the workbook is closed and not in the current folder, you must add the complete path to the reference. Here's an example:

```
='C:\Data\Excel\Budget\[Annual Budget.xlsx]Sheet1'!A1
```

If the workbook is stored on the Internet, the formula will also include the URL. Here's an example:

```
='https://d.docs.live.net/86a6d7c1f41bd208/Documents/[Annual Budget
.xlsx]Sheet1'!A1
```

> **NOTE**
> Single quotes are always required when the link includes a path or a URL, even if the path or URL includes no spaces.

Creating a link formula by pointing

Entering external reference formulas manually usually isn't the best approach because you can easily make an error. Instead, have Excel build the formula for you, as follows:

1. **Open the source workbook.**
2. **Select the cell in the dependent workbook that will hold the formula.**
3. **Type an equal sign (=).**
4. **Activate the source workbook, select the source worksheet, and then select the cell or range and press Enter.** The dependent workbook is reactivated.

When you point to the cell or range, Excel automatically takes care of the details and creates a syntactically correct external reference. When you're using this method, the cell reference is always an absolute reference (such as $A$1). If you plan to copy the formula to create additional link formulas, you need to change the absolute reference to a relative reference by removing the dollar signs for the cell address.

As long as the source workbook remains open, the external reference doesn't include the path (or URL) to the workbook. If you close the source workbook, however, the external reference formulas change to include the full path (or URL).

Externally linked cells can also be an argument to a function, like SUM or VLOOKUP. Anywhere you would point to a cell on the same workbook as the function, you can point to a cell in another workbook. A SUM function with an external link looks like this:

```
=SUM([source.xlsx]Sheet1!$B$3:$B$5)
```

Pasting links

Pasting links provides another way to create external reference formulas. This method is applicable when you want to create formulas that simply reference other cells rather than use links as part of a larger formula. Follow these steps:

1. **Open the source workbook.**

2. **Select the cell or range that you want to link, and then copy it to the Clipboard.** Ctrl+C is the quickest way.

3. **Activate the dependent workbook, and select the cell in which you want the link formula to appear.** If you're pasting a copied range, just select the upper-left cell.

4. **Choose Home ⇨ Clipboard ⇨ Paste ⇨ Paste Link (N).**

Working with External Reference Formulas

This section discusses some key points that you need to know when working with links. Understanding these details can help prevent some common errors.

Creating links to unsaved workbooks

Excel enables you to create link formulas to unsaved workbooks (and even to nonexistent workbooks). Assume that you have two workbooks open (Book1 and Book2) and you haven't saved either of them. If you create a link formula to Book1 in Book2 and then save Book2, Excel displays a confirmation dialog box like the one shown in Figure 28.1.

FIGURE 28.1

This confirmation message indicates that the workbook you're saving contains references to a workbook that you haven't yet saved.

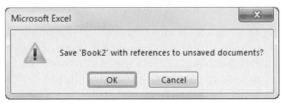

Typically, you don't want to save a workbook that has links to an unsaved document. To avoid this prompt, save the source workbook first.

You can also create links to documents that don't exist. You may want to do so if you'll be using a source workbook from a colleague but the file hasn't yet arrived. When you enter an external reference formula that refers to a nonexistent workbook, Excel displays its Update

Values dialog box, which resembles the Open dialog box. If you click Cancel, the formula retains the workbook name that you entered, but it returns a #REF! error.

When the source workbook becomes available, you can choose Data ⇨ Queries & Connections ⇨ Edit Links to update the link. (See "Updating links" later in this chapter.) After doing so, the error goes away, and the formula displays its proper value.

Opening a workbook with external reference formulas

When you open a workbook that contains links, Excel displays a dialog box (shown in Figure 28.2) that asks you what to do. Your options are as follows:

Update   The links are updated with the current information in the source file(s).

Don't Update   The links are not updated, and the workbook displays the previous values returned by the link formulas.

Help   The Excel Help screen displays so that you can read about links.

TIP

To prevent Excel from displaying the dialog box shown in Figure 28.2, open the Excel Options dialog box, select the Advanced tab, and in the General section, remove the check mark from Ask to Update Automated Links. That disables the dialog box for all workbooks.

FIGURE 28.2

Excel displays this dialog box when you open a workbook that contains links to other files.

What if you choose to update the links but the source workbook is no longer available? If Excel can't locate a source workbook that's referred to in a link formula, it displays a dialog box with two choices:

Continue   Open the workbook, but don't update the links.

Edit Links   Display the Edit Links dialog box, shown in Figure 28.3. Click the Change Source button to specify a different workbook, or click the Break Link button to destroy the link and keep the current values.

FIGURE 28.3

The Edit Links dialog box

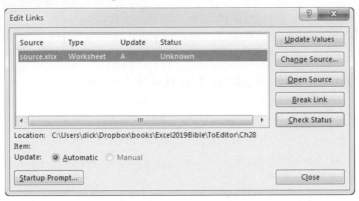

You can also access the Edit Links dialog box by choosing Data ➪ Queries & Connections ➪ Edit Links. The Edit Links dialog box lists all source workbooks plus other types of links to other documents.

Changing the startup prompt

When you open a workbook that contains one or more external reference formulas, by default Excel displays the dialog box that asks how you want to handle the links (refer to Figure 28.2). You can eliminate this prompt by changing a setting in the Startup Prompt dialog box (see Figure 28.4).

FIGURE 28.4

Use the Startup Prompt dialog box to specify how Excel handles links when the workbook is opened.

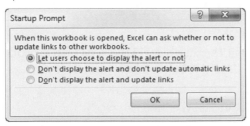

To display the Startup Prompt dialog box, choose Data ➪ Queries & Connections ➪ Edit Links. The Edit Links dialog box (refer to Figure 28.3) appears. In the Edit Links dialog box, click the Startup Prompt button and then select the option that describes how you want to handle the links.

Updating links

If you want to ensure that your link formulas have the latest values from their source workbooks, you can force an update. For example, say that you just discovered that someone made changes to the source workbook and saved the latest version to your network server. In such a case, you may want to update the links to display the current data.

To update linked formulas with their current value, open the Edit Links dialog box (Data ⇨ Queries & Connections ⇨ Edit Links), choose the appropriate source workbook in the list, and then click the Update Values button (refer to Figure 28.3). Excel updates the link formulas with the latest version of the source workbook.

> **NOTE**
> Excel always sets worksheet links to the Automatic Update option in the Edit Links dialog box, and you can't change them to Manual, which means that Excel updates the links only when you open the workbook. Excel doesn't automatically update links when the source file changes (unless the source workbook is open).

Changing the link source

In some cases, you may need to change the source workbook for your external references. For example, say that you have a worksheet that has links to a file named `Preliminary Budget`, but you later receive a finalized version named `Final Budget`.

You can change the link source using the Edit Links dialog box (choose Data ⇨ Queries & Connections ⇨ Edit Links). Select the source workbook that you want to change, and click the Change Source button (refer to Figure 28.3). Excel displays the Change Source dialog box from which you can select a new source file. After you select the file, all external reference formulas that referred to the old file are updated.

Severing links

If you have external references in a workbook and then decide that you no longer need the links, you can convert the external reference formulas to values, thereby severing the links. To do so, access the Edit Links dialog box (choose Data ⇨ Queries & Connections ⇨ Edit Links), select the linked file in the list, and then click Break Link (refer to Figure 28.3).

> **CAUTION**
> Excel prompts you to verify your intentions because you can't undo this operation.

Avoiding Potential Problems with External Reference Formulas

Using external reference formulas can be quite useful, but the links may be unintentionally severed. As long as the source file hasn't been deleted, you can almost always reestablish lost links. If you open the workbook and Excel can't locate the file, you see a dialog box that enables you to specify the workbook and re-create the links. You also can change the source file by clicking the Change Source button in the Edit Links dialog box (choose Data ⇨ Queries & Connections ⇨ Edit Links). The following sections discuss some pointers that you must remember when you use external reference formulas.

Renaming or moving a source workbook

If you or someone else renames the source document or moves it to a different folder, Excel won't be able to update the links. You need to use the Edit Links dialog box and specify the new source document. (See "Changing the link source" earlier in this chapter.)

> **NOTE**
>
> If the source and dependent files reside in the same folder, you can move both of the files to a different folder. In such a case, the links remain intact.

Using the Save As command

If both the source workbook and the dependent workbook are open, Excel doesn't display the full path to the source file in the external reference formulas. If you use the File ⇨ Save As command to give the source workbook a new name, Excel modifies the external references to use the new workbook name. In some cases, this change may be what you want. But in other cases, it may not.

Here's an example of how using File ⇨ Save As can cause a problem. You finished working on a source workbook and save the file. Then you decide to be safe and make a backup copy on a different drive, using File ⇨ Save As. The formulas in the dependent workbook now refer to the backup copy, not the original source file. This is not what you want.

Bottom line? Be careful when you choose File ⇨ Save As with a workbook that is the source of a link in another open workbook.

Modifying a source workbook

If you open a workbook that is the source for a link, be extremely careful if the workbook that contains the link isn't open. For example, if you add a new row to the source workbook, all of the cells move down one row. When you open the dependent workbook, it continues to use the old cell references, which is probably not what you want.

> **NOTE**
>
> It's easy to determine the source workbooks for a particular dependent workbook: just examine the files listed in the Edit Links dialog box (choose Data ⇨ Queries & Connections ⇨ Edit Links). However, it's not possible to determine whether a particular workbook is used as the source for another workbook.

You can avoid this problem by doing the following:

- **Always opening the dependent workbook(s) when you modify the source workbook:** If you do so, Excel adjusts the external references in the dependent workbook when you make changes to the source workbook.
- **Using names rather than cell references in your link formula:** This approach is the safest.
- **Using a formula to refer to a cell:** Your source workbook may not be structured to allow this method.

The following link formula refers to cell C21 on Sheet1 in the budget.xlsx workbook:

```
=[budget.xlsx]Sheet1!$C$21
```

If cell C21 is named Total, you can write the formula using that name:

```
=budget.xlsx!Total
```

Using a name ensures that the link retrieves the correct value, even if you add or delete rows or columns from the source workbook.

By the way, notice that the filename isn't enclosed in brackets. That's because Total is assumed to be a workbook-level name and doesn't need to be qualified with a sheet name. If Total were a sheet-level name (defined on Sheet1), the formula would be as follows:

```
=[budget.xlsx]Sheet1!Total
```

 See Chapter 4, "Working with Excel Ranges and Tables," for more information about creating names for cells and ranges.

If your source workbook contains a list of months and values and you want to return the July value, you can use a formula such as the following:

```
=VLOOKUP("July",source.xlsx!MonthValues,2,FALSE)
```

The source workbook has a workbook-level name MonthValues. If you used a normal cell reference, you would still have a problem if rows were inserted into the source workbook. However, by naming the entire range, you don't have to make a named range for each month separately.

Using Intermediary links

Excel doesn't place many limitations on the complexity of your network of external references. For example, Workbook A can contain external references that refer to Workbook B, which can contain an external reference that refers to Workbook C. In this case, a value in Workbook A can ultimately depend on a value in Workbook C. Workbook B is an intermediary link.

We don't recommend using intermediary links, but if you must use them, be aware that Excel doesn't update external reference formulas if the dependent workbook isn't open. In the preceding example, assume that Workbooks A and C are open. If you change a value in Workbook C, Workbook A won't reflect the change because you didn't open Workbook B (the intermediary link).

Consolidating Worksheets

The term *consolidation*, in the context of worksheets, refers to several operations that involve multiple worksheets or multiple workbook files. In some cases, consolidation involves creating link formulas. Here are two common examples of consolidation:

- The budget for each department in your company is stored in a single workbook, with a separate worksheet for each department. You need to consolidate the data and create a company-wide budget on a single sheet.
- Each department head submits a budget to you in a separate workbook file. Your job is to consolidate these files into a company-wide budget.

These types of tasks can be difficult or quite easy. The task is easy if the information is laid out in the same way in each worksheet. If the worksheets aren't laid out identically, they may be similar enough. In the second example, some budget files submitted to you may be missing categories that aren't used by a particular department. In this case, you can use a handy feature in Excel that matches data by using row and column titles. We discuss this feature in "Consolidating worksheets by using the Consolidate dialog box" later in this chapter.

If the worksheets bear little or no resemblance to each other, your best option may be to edit the sheets so that they correspond to one another. Or return the files to the department heads and ask that they submit them using a standardized format. Better yet, redesign your workflow to use normalized tables that can be used as the source for PivotTables.

You can use any of the following techniques to consolidate information from multiple workbooks:

- Use external reference formulas.
- Copy the data and choose Home ➪ Clipboard ➪ Paste ➪ Paste Link (N).
- Use the Consolidate dialog box, which you get to by choosing Data ➪ Data Tools ➪ Consolidate.

Time to Rethink Your Consolidation Strategy?

If you're reading this chapter, there's a good chance that you're looking for a way to combine data from multiple sources. The consolidation methods we describe can work, but they may not be the most efficient way to approach the problem.

A typical budget is actually a summary. It's usually much easier to work with "normalized" data, which consists of one row per data item. Then you can use Excel's most sophisticated tool (a PivotTable) to consolidate and summarize the information.

For example, a budget for Region 1 might show a value for training expenses for the IT department for January. Instead of just entering this number into a grid, you gain a lot of flexibility by putting it into a table with multiple columns that describe the number. For example, this single item can be represented as a row in a normalized table with these six headings: Region, Department, Expense Description, Month, Year, and Budget Amount.

If each regional manager submitted his budget information in this format, it would be a simple matter to combine the data in a single worksheet and then create a PivotTable that displays a summary in just about any layout you want.

Consolidating worksheets by using formulas

Consolidating with formulas simply involves creating formulas that use references to other worksheets or other workbooks. Here are the primary advantages to using this method of consolidation:

- If the values in the source worksheets change, the formulas are updated automatically.
- The source workbooks don't need to be open when you create the consolidation formulas.

If you're consolidating the worksheets in the same workbook and all the worksheets are laid out identically, the consolidation task is simple. You can just use standard formulas to create the consolidations. For example, to compute the total for cell A1 in worksheets named `Sheet2` through `Sheet10`, enter the following formula:

```
=SUM(Sheet2:Sheet10!A1)
```

You can enter this formula manually or use the multisheet selection technique. You can then copy this formula to create summary formulas for other cells.

 See Chapter 4, "Working with Excel Ranges and Tables," for more on multisheet selection.

If the consolidation involves other workbooks, you can use external reference formulas to perform your consolidation. For example, if you want to add the values in cell B2 from `Sheet1` in two workbooks (named `Region1` and `Region2`), you can use the following formula:

```
=[Region1.xlsx]Sheet1!B2+[Region2.xlsx]Sheet1!B2
```

You can include any number of external references in this formula, up to the 8,000-character limit for a formula. However, if you use many external references, such a formula can be quite lengthy and confusing if you need to edit it.

If the worksheets that you're consolidating aren't laid out in the same way, you can still use formulas, but you need to ensure that each formula refers to the correct cell—a task that is both tedious and error prone.

Consolidating worksheets by using Paste Special

Another method of consolidating information is to use the Paste Special dialog box. This technique takes advantage of the fact that the Paste Special dialog box can perform a mathematical operation when it pastes data from the Clipboard. For example, you can use the Add option to add the copied data to the selected range. Figure 28.5 shows the Paste Special dialog box.

FIGURE 28.5

Choosing the Add operation in the Paste Special dialog box

This method is applicable only when all the worksheets that you're consolidating are open. The disadvantage is that the consolidation isn't dynamic. In other words, it doesn't generate formulas that refer to the original source data. So, if any data that was consolidated changes, the consolidation is no longer accurate.

Here's how to use this method:

1. **Copy the data from the first source range.**

2. **Activate the dependent workbook and select a location for the consolidated data.** A single cell is sufficient.

3. **Choose Home ⇨ Clipboard ⇨ Paste ⇨ Paste Special.** The Paste Special dialog box appears.

4. **Choose the Values option and the Add operation and then click OK.**

Repeat these steps for each source range that you want to consolidate. Make sure that the consolidation location in step 2 is the same for each paste operation.

CAUTION

This method is probably the worst way of consolidating data. It can be rather error prone, and the lack of formulas means that there is no "trail." If an error is discovered, it may be difficult or impossible to determine the source of the error.

Consolidating worksheets by using the Consolidate dialog box

For the ultimate in data consolidation, use the Consolidate dialog box. This method is flexible, and in some cases it even works if the source worksheets aren't laid out identically. This technique can create consolidations that are static (no link formulas) or dynamic (with link formulas). The data consolidation feature supports the following methods of consolidation:

By position   This method is accurate only if the worksheets are laid out identically.

By category   Excel uses row and column labels to match data in the source worksheets. Use this option if the data is laid out differently in the source worksheets or if some source worksheets are missing rows or columns.

Figure 28.6 shows the Consolidate dialog box, which appears when you choose Data ⇨ Data Tools ⇨ Consolidate.

FIGURE 28.6

The Consolidate dialog box enables you to specify ranges to consolidate.

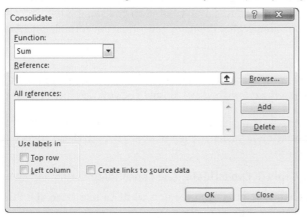

28

The following is a description of the controls in this dialog box:

Function drop-down list   Specify the type of consolidation. Sum is the most commonly used consolidation function, but you can also select from 10 other options.

Reference box   Specify a range from a source file that you want to consolidate. You can enter the range reference manually or use any standard pointing technique (if the workbook is open). Named ranges are also acceptable. After you enter the range in this box, click Add to add it to the All References list. If you consolidate by position, don't include labels in the range; if you consolidate by category, do include labels in the range.

All References list box   This contains the list of references that you've added with the Add button.

Use Labels In check boxes   Use this to instruct Excel to perform the consolidation by examining the labels in the top row, the left column, or both positions. Use these options when you consolidate by category.

Create Links to Source Data check box   When you select this option, Excel adds summary formulas for each label and creates an outline. If you don't select this option, the consolidation doesn't use formulas, and an outline isn't created.

Browse button   Click to display a dialog box that enables you to select a workbook to open. It inserts the filename in the Reference box, but you have to supply the range reference. You'll find that your job is much easier if all the workbooks to be consolidated are open.

Add button   Click to add the reference in the Reference box to the All References list. Make sure that you click this button after you specify each range.

Delete button   Click to delete the selected reference from the All References list.

Viewing a workbook consolidation example

The simple example in this section demonstrates the power of the data consolidation feature. Figure 28.7 shows three single-sheet workbooks that will be consolidated. These worksheets report three months of product sales. Notice, however, that all don't report on the same products. In addition, the products aren't listed in the same order. In other words, these worksheets aren't laid out identically. Creating consolidation formulas manually would be a tedious task.

 These workbooks are available on this book's website at www.wiley.com/go/excel2019bible. The files are named region1.xlsx, region2.xlsx, and region3.xlsx.

To consolidate this information, start with a new workbook. You don't need to open the source workbooks, but consolidation is easier if they're open. Follow these steps to consolidate the workbooks:

1. **Choose Data ⇨ Data Tools ⇨ Consolidate.** The Consolidate dialog box appears.
2. **Select the type of consolidation summary you want to use from the Function drop-down list.** Use Sum for this example.

FIGURE 28.7

Three worksheets to be consolidated

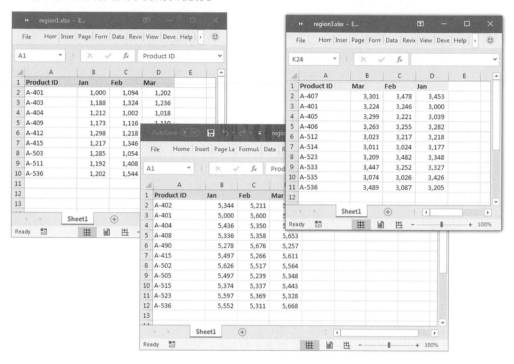

3. **Enter the reference for the first worksheet to consolidate.** If the workbook is open, you can point to the reference; if it isn't open, click the Browse button to locate the file on disk. The reference must include a range. You can use a range that includes complete columns, such as A:K. This range is larger than the actual range to consolidate, but using this range ensures that the consolidation will still work if new rows and columns are added to the source file.

4. **When the reference in the Reference box is correct, click Add to add it to the All References list.**

5. **Enter the reference for the second worksheet.** You can point to the range in the Region2 workbook, or you can simply edit the existing reference by changing Region1 to Region2 and then clicking Add. This reference is added to the All References list.

6. **Enter the reference for the third worksheet.** Again, you can edit the existing reference by changing Region2 to Region3 and then clicking Add. This final reference is added to the All References list.

7. **Because the worksheets aren't laid out in the same way, select the Left Column and the Top Row check boxes to force Excel to match the data by using the labels.**

8. **Select the Create Links to Source Data check box to make Excel create an outline with external references.**

9. **Click OK to begin the consolidation.**

Excel creates the consolidation, beginning at the active cell. Notice that Excel created an outline, which is collapsed to show only the subtotals for each product. If you expand the outline (by clicking the number 2 or the plus-sign symbols in the outline), you can see the details. Examine it further, and you discover that each detail cell is an external reference formula that uses the appropriate cell in the source file. Therefore, the consolidated results are updated automatically when values are changed in any of the source workbooks.

Figure 28.8 shows the result of the consolidation, and Figure 28.9 shows the detail information (with the outline expanded).

FIGURE 28.8

The result of consolidating the information in three workbooks

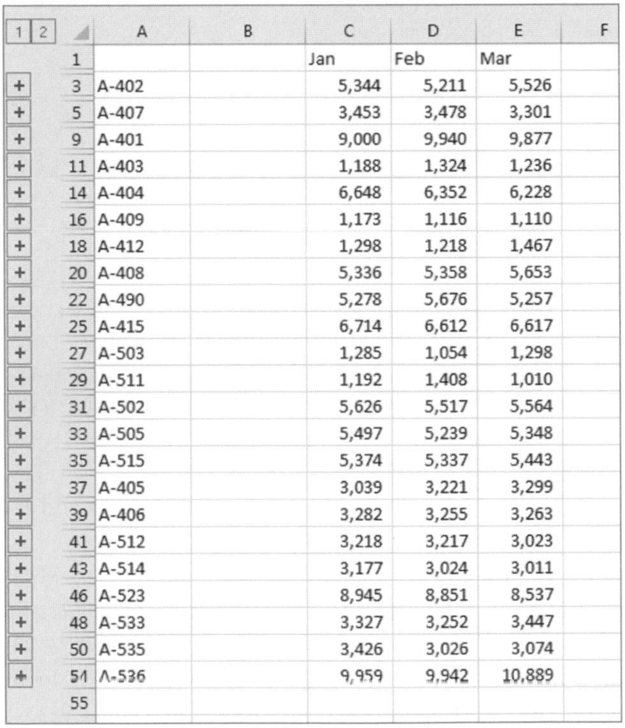

	A	B	C (Jan)	D (Feb)	E (Mar)	F
3	A-402		5,344	5,211	5,526	
5	A-407		3,453	3,478	3,301	
9	A-401		9,000	9,940	9,877	
11	A-403		1,188	1,324	1,236	
14	A-404		6,648	6,352	6,228	
16	A-409		1,173	1,116	1,110	
18	A-412		1,298	1,218	1,467	
20	A-408		5,336	5,358	5,653	
22	A-490		5,278	5,676	5,257	
25	A-415		6,714	6,612	6,617	
27	A-503		1,285	1,054	1,298	
29	A-511		1,192	1,408	1,010	
31	A-502		5,626	5,517	5,564	
33	A-505		5,497	5,239	5,348	
35	A-515		5,374	5,337	5,443	
37	A-405		3,039	3,221	3,299	
39	A-406		3,282	3,255	3,263	
41	A-512		3,218	3,217	3,023	
43	A-514		3,177	3,024	3,011	
46	A-523		8,945	8,851	8,537	
48	A-533		3,327	3,252	3,447	
50	A-535		3,426	3,026	3,074	
54	A-536		9,959	9,942	10,889	

FIGURE 28.9

Expanding the outline to show more details

	A	B	C	D	E	F
1			Jan	Feb	Mar	
2		Region2	5,344	5,211	5,526	
3	A-402		5,344	5,211	5,526	
4		Region3	3,453	3,478	3,301	
5	A-407		3,453	3,478	3,301	
6		Region1	1,000	1,094	1,202	
7		Region2	5,000	5,600	5,451	
8		Region3	3,000	3,246	3,224	
9	A-401		9,000	9,940	9,877	
10		Region1	1,188	1,324	1,236	
11	A-403		1,188	1,324	1,236	
12		Region1	1,212	1,002	1,018	
13		Region2	5,436	5,350	5,210	
14	A-404		6,648	6,352	6,228	
15		Region1	1,173	1,116	1,110	
16	A-409		1,173	1,116	1,110	
17		Region1	1,298	1,218	1,467	
18	A-412		1,298	1,218	1,467	
19		Region2	5,336	5,358	5,653	
20	A-408		5,336	5,358	5,653	
21		Region2	5,278	5,676	5,257	
22	A-490		5,278	5,676	5,257	
23		Region1	1,217	1,346	1,006	
24		Region2	5,497	5,266	5,611	
25	A-415		6,714	6,612	6,617	
26		Region1	1,285	1,054	1,298	
27	A-503		1,285	1,054	1,298	
28		Region1	1,192	1,408	1,010	

 For more information on Excel outlines, see Chapter 27, "Creating and Using Worksheet Outlines."

Refreshing a consolidation

When you choose the option to create formulas, the external references in the consolidation workbook are created only for data that exists at the time of the consolidation. Therefore, if new rows are added to any of the original workbooks, the consolidation must be redone. Fortunately, the consolidation parameters are stored with the workbook, so it's a simple matter to rerun the consolidation if necessary. That's why specifying complete columns and including extra columns (step 3 in the preceding section) is a good idea.

Excel remembers the references that you entered in the Consolidate dialog box and saves them with the workbook. That way, if you want to refresh a consolidation, you won't have to reenter the references. Just display the Consolidate dialog box, verify that the ranges are correct, and then click OK.

> **CAUTION**
>
> When Excel has an outline applied, like after you consolidate, rerunning the consolidation can be unpredictable. The sure-fire way to rerun a consolidation is to clear the outline, delete the cell contents, display the consolidation dialog, and click OK.

Learning more about consolidation

Excel is flexible regarding the sources that you can consolidate. You can consolidate data from the following:

- Open workbooks.
- Closed workbooks. You need to enter the reference manually, but you can use the Browse button to get the filename part of the reference.
- The same workbook in which you're creating the consolidation.

And, of course, you can mix and match any of the preceding choices in a single consolidation.

If you perform the consolidation by matching labels, be aware that the matches must be exact. For example, Jan doesn't match January. The matching is not case sensitive, however, so April does match APRIL. In addition, the labels can be in any order, and they don't need to be in the same order in all of the source ranges.

If you don't select the Create Links to Source Data check box, Excel generates a static consolidation. (It doesn't create formulas.) Therefore, if the data on any of the source worksheets changes, the consolidation won't update automatically. To update the summary information, you need to choose Data ➪ Data Tools ➪ Consolidate again.

 If you do select the Create Links to Source Data check box, Excel creates a standard worksheet outline that you can manipulate by using the techniques described in Chapter 27.

Introducing PivotTables

The PivotTable feature is perhaps the most technologically sophisticated component in Excel. With only a few mouse clicks, you can slice and dice data in dozens of different ways and produce just about any type of summary you can imagine.

If you haven't yet discovered the power of PivotTables, this chapter provides an introduction, and Chapter 30, "Analyzing Data with PivotTables," continues with many examples that demonstrate how easy it is to create powerful data summaries using PivotTables.

About PivotTables

A *PivotTable* is essentially a dynamic summary report generated from a database. The database can reside in a worksheet (in the form of a table) or in an external data file. A PivotTable can help transform endless rows and columns of numbers into a meaningful presentation of the data—and do it so quickly you'll be amazed.

Perhaps the most powerful aspect of a PivotTable is its interactivity. After you create a PivotTable, you can rearrange the information in almost any way imaginable and even insert special formulas that perform new calculations. You even can create post hoc groupings of summary items (for example, combine Northern Region totals with Western Region totals). With a few mouse clicks, you can apply formatting to a PivotTable to convert it into an report, albeit with a few limitations.

One minor drawback to using a PivotTable is that, unlike a formula-based summary report, a PivotTable does not update automatically when you change information in the source data. This drawback doesn't pose a serious problem, however, because a single click of the Refresh button forces a PivotTable to update itself with the latest data.

PivotTables were introduced in Excel 97, and this feature improves with every new version of Excel. Unfortunately, many users avoid this feature because they think it's too complicated. After reading this chapter, you'll see that PivotTables are both powerful and easy to master.

A PivotTable example

The best way to understand the concept of a PivotTable is to see one. Start with Figure 29.1, which shows a portion of the data used in creating the PivotTable in this chapter. This range happens to be in a table (created by using Insert ⇨ Tables ⇨ Table), but that's not a requirement for creating a PivotTable.

FIGURE 29.1

This table is used to create a PivotTable.

	A	B	C	D	E	F	G
1	Date	Weekday	Amount	AcctType	OpenedBy	Branch	Customer
2	4/1/2019	Friday	5,000	IRA	New Accts	Central	Existing
3	4/1/2019	Friday	10,000	CD	Teller	North County	Existing
4	4/1/2019	Friday	500	Checking	New Accts	Central	Existing
5	4/1/2019	Friday	11,779	CD	Teller	Central	New
6	4/1/2019	Friday	4,623	Savings	New Accts	North County	Existing
7	4/1/2019	Friday	8,721	Savings	New Accts	Westside	New
8	4/1/2019	Friday	15,276	Savings	New Accts	North County	Existing
9	4/1/2019	Friday	5,000	Savings	New Accts	Westside	Existing
10	4/1/2019	Friday	12,000	CD	New Accts	Westside	Existing
11	4/1/2019	Friday	13,636	CD	New Accts	North County	Existing
12	4/1/2019	Friday	7,177	Savings	Teller	North County	Existing
13	4/1/2019	Friday	6,837	Savings	New Accts	Westside	Existing
14	4/1/2019	Friday	3,171	Checking	New Accts	Westside	Existing
15	4/1/2019	Friday	50,000	Savings	New Accts	Central	Existing
16	4/1/2019	Friday	4,690	Checking	New Accts	North County	New
17	4/1/2019	Friday	12,438	Checking	New Accts	Central	Existing
18	4/1/2019	Friday	5,000	Checking	New Accts	North County	Existing
19	4/1/2019	Friday	7,000	Savings	New Accts	North County	New
20	4/1/2019	Friday	11,957	Checking	New Accts	Central	Existing
21	4/1/2019	Friday	14,571	CD	Teller	Central	New
22	4/1/2019	Friday	15,000	CD	New Accts	Central	Existing
23	4/1/2019	Friday	5,879	Checking	New Accts	Central	Existing
24	4/1/2019	Friday	4,000	Savings	New Accts	Central	Existing
25	4/1/2019	Friday	15,759	CD	Teller	Westside	Existing
26	4/1/2019	Friday	7,427	Checking	New Accts	North County	Existing
27	4/1/2019	Friday	4,500	Checking	New Accts	North County	New
28	4/1/2019	Friday	12,962	Checking	Teller	Central	Existing
29	4/1/2019	Friday	500	Checking	New Accts	Central	New
30	4/1/2019	Friday	5,364	Checking	Teller	Central	New
31	4/1/2019	Friday	16,000	CD	New Accts	Central	New
32	4/1/2019	Friday	14,867	Checking	Teller	North County	Existing

This table consists of a month's worth of new account information for a three-branch bank. The table contains 712 rows, and each row represents a new account opened at the bank. The table has the following columns:

- The date the account was opened
- The day of the week the account was opened
- The opening deposit amount
- The account type (CD, checking, savings, or IRA)
- Who opened the account (a teller or a new-account representative)
- The branch at which it was opened (Central, Westside, or North County)
- The type of customer (an existing customer or a new customer)

 This workbook, named `bank accounts.xlsx`, is available on this book's website at `www.wiley.com/go/excel2019bible`.

The bank accounts database contains quite a bit of information. In its current form, though, the data doesn't reveal much. To make the data more useful, you need to summarize it. Summarizing a database is essentially the process of arranging the data differently in order to answer questions about it. The following are a few of the questions that may be of interest to the bank's management:

- What is the daily total new deposit amount for each branch?
- Which day of the week accounts for the most deposits?
- How many accounts were opened at each branch, broken down by account type?
- How much money was used to open accounts?
- What types of accounts do tellers open most often?
- In which branch do tellers open the most checking accounts for new customers?

You can, of course, spend time sorting the data and creating formulas to answer these questions. But almost always, a PivotTable is a better choice. Creating a PivotTable takes only a few seconds and doesn't require a single formula. In addition, PivotTables are much less prone to error than creating formulas.

Later in this chapter, you'll see several PivotTables that answer the preceding questions.

Figure 29.2 shows a PivotTable created from the bank data. This PivotTable shows the amount of new deposits, broken down by branch and account type. This particular summary is one of dozens of summaries that you can produce from this data.

Figure 29.3 shows another PivotTable generated from the bank data. This PivotTable uses a drop-down Report Filter for the Customer item (in row 2). In the figure, the PivotTable displays the data only for existing customers. (The user can also select New or All from the drop-down control.)

29

FIGURE 29.2

A simple PivotTable

	A	B	C	D	E	F	G
1							
2							
3	Sum of Amount	Column l ▼					
4	Row Labels ▼	CD	Checking	IRA	Savings	Grand Total	
5	Central	1,361,885	802,403	68,380	885,757	3,118,425	
6	North County	1,209,910	392,516	134,374	467,414	2,204,214	
7	Westside	650,237	292,995	10,000	336,088	1,289,320	
8	Grand Total	3,222,032	1,487,914	212,754	1,689,259	6,611,959	
9							
10							
11							

FIGURE 29.3

A PivotTable that uses a report filter

	A	B	C	D	E
1					
2	Customer	Existing ▼			
3					
4	Sum of Amount	Column Labels ▼			
5	Row Labels ▼	Central	North County	Westside	Grand Total
6	CD	974,112	845,522	356,079	2,175,713
7	Checking	505,822	208,375	144,391	858,588
8	IRA	68,380	125,374	10,000	203,754
9	Savings	548,198	286,891	291,728	1,126,817
10	Grand Total	2,096,512	1,466,162	802,198	4,364,872
11					
12					

Notice the change in the orientation of the table? For this PivotTable, branches appear as column labels, and account types appear as row labels. This change, which took about five seconds to make, is another example of the flexibility of a PivotTable.

Why *Pivot*?

Are you curious about the term *pivot*?

Pivot, as a verb, means to rotate or revolve. If you think of your data as a physical object, a PivotTable lets you rotate the data summary and look at it from different angles or perspectives. A PivotTable allows you to move fields around easily, nest fields within each other, and even create ad hoc groups of items.

If you were handed a strange object and asked to identify it, you'd probably look at it from several different angles in an attempt to figure it out. Working with a PivotTable is similar to investigating a strange object. In this case, the object happens to be your data. A PivotTable invites experimentation, so feel free to rotate and manipulate the PivotTable until you're satisfied. You may be surprised at what you discover.

Data appropriate for a PivotTable

A PivotTable requires that your data be in the form of a rectangular table. You can store the database in either a worksheet range (which can be a table or just a normal range) or an external database file. And although Excel can generate a PivotTable from any database, not all databases benefit.

Generally speaking, fields in a table consist of two types of information:

Data Contains a value or data to be summarized. For the bank account example, the Amount field is a data field.

Category Describes the data. For the bank account data, the Date, Weekday, AcctType, OpenedBy, Branch, and Customer fields are category fields because they describe the data in the Amount field.

NOTE
A database table that's appropriate for a PivotTable is said to be "normalized." In other words, each record (or row) contains information that describes the data.

A single table can have any number of data fields and category fields. When you create a PivotTable, you usually want to summarize one or more of the data fields. Conversely, the values in the category fields appear in the PivotTable as rows, columns, or filters.

Exceptions exist, however, and you may find the Excel PivotTable feature useful even for databases that don't contain actual numerical data fields.

 Chapter 30 has an example of a PivotTable created from non-numeric data.

Figure 29.4 shows an example of an Excel range that is not appropriate for a PivotTable. You might recognize this data from the outline example in Chapter 27, "Creating and

Using Worksheet Outlines." Although the range contains descriptive information about each value, it does not consist of normalized data. In fact, this range actually resembles a PivotTable summary, but it's much less flexible.

FIGURE 29.4

This range is not appropriate for a PivotTable.

	A	B	C	D	E	F	G	H	I	J	K
1	State	Jan	Feb	Mar	Qtr-1	Apr	May	Jun	Qtr-2	Total	
2	California	1,118	1,960	1,252	4,330	1,271	1,557	1,679	4,507	8,837	
3	Washington	1,247	1,238	1,028	3,513	1,345	1,784	1,574	4,703	8,216	
4	Oregon	1,460	1,954	1,726	5,140	1,461	1,764	1,144	4,369	9,509	
5	Arizona	1,345	1,375	1,075	3,795	1,736	1,555	1,372	4,663	8,458	
6	West Total	5,170	6,527	5,081	16,778	5,813	6,660	5,769	18,242	35,020	
7	New York	1,429	1,316	1,993	4,738	1,832	1,740	1,191	4,763	9,501	
8	New Jersey	1,735	1,406	1,224	4,365	1,706	1,320	1,290	4,316	8,681	
9	Massachusetts	1,099	1,233	1,110	3,442	1,637	1,512	1,006	4,155	7,597	
10	Florida	1,705	1,792	1,225	4,722	1,946	1,327	1,357	4,630	9,352	
11	East Total	5,968	5,747	5,552	17,267	7,121	5,899	4,844	17,864	35,131	
12	Kentucky	1,109	1,078	1,155	3,342	1,993	1,082	1,551	4,626	7,968	
13	Oklahoma	1,309	1,045	1,641	3,995	1,924	1,499	1,941	5,364	9,359	
14	Missouri	1,511	1,744	1,414	4,669	1,243	1,493	1,820	4,556	9,225	
15	Illinois	1,539	1,493	1,211	4,243	1,165	1,013	1,445	3,623	7,866	
16	Kansas	1,973	1,560	1,243	4,776	1,495	1,125	1,387	4,007	8,783	
17	Central Total	7,441	6,920	6,664	21,025	7,820	6,212	8,144	22,176	43,201	
18	Grand Total	18,579	19,194	17,297	55,070	20,754	18,771	18,757	58,282	113,352	
19											

Figure 29.5 shows the same data but normalized. This range contains 78 rows of data—one for each of the six monthly sales values for the 13 states. Notice that each row contains category information for the sales value. This table is an ideal candidate for a PivotTable, and it contains all the information necessary to summarize the information by region or quarter.

Figure 29.6 shows a PivotTable created from the normalized data. As you can see, it's similar to the nonnormalized data shown in Figure 29.4. Working with normalized data provides ultimate flexibility in designing reports.

FIGURE 29.5

This range contains normalized data and is appropriate for a PivotTable.

	A	B	C	D	E	F
1	State	Region	Month	Qtr	Sales	
2	California	West	Jan	Qtr-1	1,118	
3	California	West	Feb	Qtr-1	1,960	
4	California	West	Mar	Qtr-1	1,252	
5	California	West	Apr	Qtr-2	1,271	
6	California	West	May	Qtr-2	1,557	
7	California	West	Jun	Qtr-2	1,679	
8	Washington	West	Jan	Qtr-1	1,247	
9	Washington	West	Feb	Qtr-1	1,238	
10	Washington	West	Mar	Qtr-1	1,028	
11	Washington	West	Apr	Qtr-2	1,345	
12	Washington	West	May	Qtr-2	1,784	
13	Washington	West	Jun	Qtr-2	1,574	
14	Oregon	West	Jan	Qtr-1	1,460	
15	Oregon	West	Feb	Qtr-1	1,954	
16	Oregon	West	Mar	Qtr-1	1,726	
17	Oregon	West	Apr	Qtr-2	1,461	
18	Oregon	West	May	Qtr-2	1,764	
19	Oregon	West	Jun	Qtr-2	1,144	
20	Arizona	West	Jan	Qtr-1	1,345	
21	Arizona	West	Feb	Qtr-1	1,375	
22	Arizona	West	Mar	Qtr-1	1,075	

FIGURE 29.6

A PivotTable created from normalized data

	A	B	C	D	E	F	G	H	I	J
1										
2	Sum of Sales	Col								
3		⊟Qtr-1			Qtr-1 Total	⊟Qtr-2			Qtr-2 Total	Grand Total
4	Row Labels	Jan	Feb	Mar		Apr	May	Jun		
5	⊟Central									
6	Illinois	1,539	1,493	1,211	4,243	1,165	1,013	1,445	3,623	7,866
7	Kansas	1,973	1,560	1,243	4,776	1,495	1,125	1,387	4,007	8,783
8	Kentucky	1,109	1,078	1,155	3,342	1,993	1,082	1,551	4,626	7,968
9	Missouri	1,511	1,744	1,414	4,669	1,243	1,493	1,820	4,556	9,225
10	Oklahoma	1,309	1,045	1,641	3,995	1,924	1,499	1,941	5,364	9,359
11	Central Total	7,441	6,920	6,664	21,025	7,820	6,212	8,144	22,176	43,201
12										
13	⊟East									
14	Florida	1,705	1,792	1,225	4,722	1,946	1,327	1,357	4,630	9,352
15	Massachusetts	1,099	1,233	1,110	3,442	1,637	1,512	1,006	4,155	7,597
16	New Jersey	1,735	1,406	1,224	4,365	1,706	1,320	1,290	4,316	8,681
17	New York	1,429	1,316	1,993	4,738	1,832	1,740	1,191	4,763	9,501
18	East Total	5,968	5,747	5,552	17,267	7,121	5,899	4,844	17,864	35,131
19										
20	⊟West									
21	Arizona	1,345	1,375	1,075	3,795	1,736	1,555	1,372	4,663	8,458
22	California	1,118	1,960	1,252	4,330	1,271	1,557	1,679	4,507	8,837
23	Oregon	1,460	1,954	1,726	5,140	1,461	1,764	1,144	4,369	9,509
24	Washington	1,247	1,238	1,028	3,513	1,345	1,784	1,574	4,703	8,216
25	West Total	5,170	6,527	5,081	16,778	5,813	6,660	5,769	18,242	35,020
26										
27	Grand Total	18,579	19,194	17,297	55,070	20,754	18,771	18,757	58,282	113,352

29

This workbook, named `normalized data.xlsx`, is available on this book's website at www .wiley.com/go/excel2019bible.

Creating a PivotTable Automatically

How easy is it to create a PivotTable? This task requires practically no effort if your data is appropriately structured and you choose a Recommended PivotTable.

If your data is in a worksheet, select any cell within the data range and choose Insert ⇨ Tables ⇨ Recommended PivotTables. Excel quickly scans your data, and the Recommended PivotTables dialog box presents thumbnails that depict some PivotTables from which you can choose. Figure 29.7 shows the Recommended PivotTables dialog box for the bank account data.

FIGURE 29.7

Selecting a Recommended PivotTable

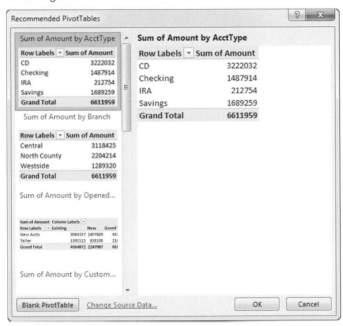

The PivotTable thumbnails use your actual data, and there's a good chance that one of them will be exactly what you're looking for—or at least close to what you're looking for. Select a thumbnail, click OK, and Excel creates the PivotTable on a new worksheet.

When any cell in a PivotTable is selected, Excel displays the PivotTable Fields task pane. You can use this task pane to make changes to the layout of the PivotTable.

If none of the Recommended PivotTables is suitable, you have two choices:

- Create a PivotTable that's close to what you want and then use the PivotTable Fields task pane to modify it.
- Click the Blank PivotTable button (at the bottom of the Recommended PivotTables dialog box) and create a PivotTable manually.

Creating a PivotTable Manually

In this section, we describe the basic steps required to create a PivotTable using the bank account data described earlier in this chapter. Creating a PivotTable is an interactive process. It's not at all uncommon to experiment with various layouts until you find one with which you're satisfied. If you're unfamiliar with the elements of a PivotTable, see the sidebar "PivotTable Terminology."

Specifying the data

If your data is in a worksheet range, select any cell in that range and then choose Insert ⇨ Tables ⇨ PivotTable. The Create PivotTable dialog box, shown in Figure 29.8, appears.

FIGURE 29.8

In the Create PivotTable dialog box, you tell Excel where the data is and where you want the PivotTable.

Excel attempts to guess the range, based on the location of the active cell. If you're creating a PivotTable from an external data source, you need to select that option and then click Choose Connection to specify the data source.

> **TIP**
>
> If you're creating a PivotTable from data in a worksheet, it's a good idea first to create a table for the range. (Choose Insert ⇨ Tables ⇨ Table.) Then, if you expand the table by adding new rows of data, the PivotTable will automatically adjust to cover the whole table without the need to indicate the new data range manually.

Specifying the location for the PivotTable

Use the bottom section of the Create PivotTable dialog box to indicate the location for your PivotTable. The default location is on a new worksheet, but you can specify any range on any worksheet, including the worksheet that contains the data.

Click OK, and Excel creates an empty PivotTable and displays a PivotTable Fields task pane, as shown in Figure 29.9.

> **TIP**
>
> The PivotTable Fields task pane is typically docked on the right side of the Excel window. Drag its title bar to move it anywhere you like. Also, if you click a cell outside the PivotTable, the task pane is temporarily hidden.

Laying out the PivotTable

Next, set up the actual layout of the PivotTable. You can do so by using of the following techniques:

- Drag the field names (at the top of the PivotTable Fields task pane) to one of the four boxes at the bottom of the task pane.
- Place a check mark next to the item at the top of the PivotTable Fields task pane. Excel places the field into one of the four boxes at the bottom. You can drag it to a different box, if necessary.
- Right-click a field name at the top of the PivotTable Fields task pane, and choose its location from the shortcut menu (for example, Add to Row Labels).

The following steps create the PivotTable presented earlier in this chapter (see "A PivotTable example"). For this example, drag the items from the top of the PivotTable Fields task pane to the areas in the bottom of the PivotTable Fields task pane.

1. **Drag the Amount field into the Values area.** At this point, the PivotTable displays the total of all the values in the Amount column.
2. **Drag the AcctType field into the Rows area.** Now the PivotTable shows the total amount for each of the account types.

FIGURE 29.9

Use the PivotTable Fields task pane to build the PivotTable.

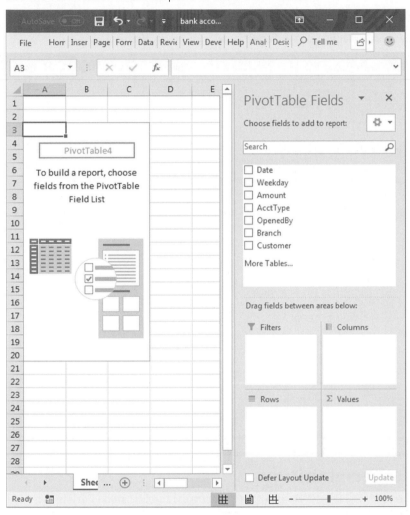

3. **Drag the Branch field into the Columns area.** The PivotTable shows the amount for each account type, cross-tabulated by branch. The PivotTable updates itself automatically with every change you make in the PivotTable Fields task pane.

4. **Right-click any cell in the PivotTable and choose Number Format.** Excel displays the Number tab of the Format Cells dialog box.

5. **Select a number format and click OK.** Excel applies the format to all numeric cells in the PivotTable.

Figure 29.10 shows the completed PivotTable.

FIGURE 29.10

After a few simple steps, the PivotTable shows a summary of the data.

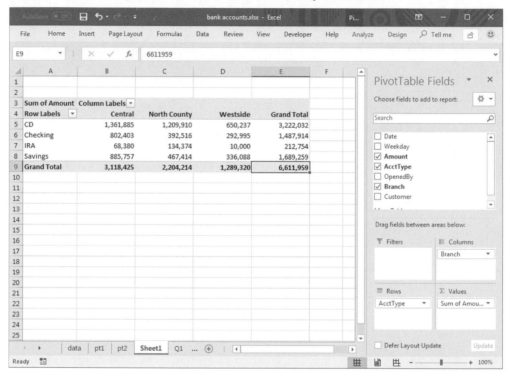

PivotTable Terminology

Understanding the terminology associated with PivotTables is the first step in mastering this feature. Refer to the accompanying figure to get your bearings.

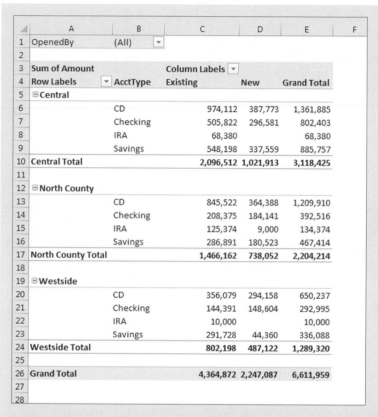

	A	B	C	D	E	F
1	OpenedBy	(All)				
2						
3	Sum of Amount		Column Labels			
4	Row Labels	AcctType	Existing	New	Grand Total	
5	⊟Central					
6		CD	974,112	387,773	1,361,885	
7		Checking	505,822	296,581	802,403	
8		IRA	68,380		68,380	
9		Savings	548,198	337,559	885,757	
10	Central Total		2,096,512	1,021,913	3,118,425	
11						
12	⊟North County					
13		CD	845,522	364,388	1,209,910	
14		Checking	208,375	184,141	392,516	
15		IRA	125,374	9,000	134,374	
16		Savings	286,891	180,523	467,414	
17	North County Total		1,466,162	738,052	2,204,214	
18						
19	⊟Westside					
20		CD	356,079	294,158	650,237	
21		Checking	144,391	148,604	292,995	
22		IRA	10,000		10,000	
23		Savings	291,728	44,360	336,088	
24	Westside Total		802,198	487,122	1,289,320	
25						
26	Grand Total		4,364,872	2,247,087	6,611,959	
27						
28						

Column labels   A field that has a column orientation in the PivotTable. Each item in the field occupies a column. In the figure, Customer represents a column field that contains two items (Existing and New). You can have nested column fields.

Grand totals   A row or column that displays totals for all cells in a row or column in a PivotTable. You can specify that grand totals be calculated for rows, columns, both, or neither. The PivotTable in the figure shows grand totals for both rows and columns.

Group   A collection of items treated as a single item. You can group items manually or automatically (group dates into months, for example). The PivotTable in the figure does not have defined groups.

Item   An element in a field that appears as a row or column header in a PivotTable. In the figure, Existing and New are items for the Customer field. The Branch field has three items: Central, North County, and Westside. AcctType has four items: CD, Checking, IRA, and Savings.

Refresh   Recalculates the PivotTable after making changes to the source data.

Row labels   A field that has a row orientation in the PivotTable. Each item in the field occupies a row. You can have nested row fields. In the figure, both Branch and AcctType represent row fields.

Continues

29

continued

Source data   The data used to create a PivotTable. It can reside in a worksheet or an external database.

Subtotals   A row or column that displays subtotals for detail cells in a row or column in a PivotTable. The PivotTable in the figure displays subtotals for each branch, below the data. You can also display subtotals above the data or hide subtotals. The label for a subtotal is the Item name that's being totaled and the word *Total*.

Table Filter   A field that has a page orientation in the PivotTable, which is used to limit what data is summarized. You can display one item, multiple items, or all items in a page field at one time. In the figure, OpenedBy represents a page field that displays All (that is, not filtered).

Values area   The cells in a PivotTable that contain the summary data. Excel offers several ways to summarize the data (sum, average, count, and so on).

NEW FEATURE

If you find that you're making the same layout changes to PivotTables every time you create one, you can now save certain layout options as your default. Choose File ➪ Options ➪ Data and click Edit Default Layout to show the Edit Default Layout dialog box.

Here you can set certain options that all new PivotTables will inherit. Even easier, use the Import button to set all the options automatically based on the PivotTable you specify.

Formatting the PivotTable

By default, PivotTables use General number formatting. To change the number format for all data, right-click any value and choose Number Format from the shortcut menu. Then use the Format Cells dialog box to change the number format for the displayed data.

You can apply any of several built-in styles to a PivotTable. Select any cell in the PivotTable and then choose PivotTable Tools ➪ Design ➪ PivotTable Styles to select a style. Fine-tune the display by using the controls in the PivotTable Tools ⇨ Design ⇨ PivotTable Style Options group.

You can also use the controls from the PivotTable ⇨ Design ⇨ Layout group to control various elements in the PivotTable. You can adjust any of the following elements:

Subtotals   Hide subtotal, or choose where to display them (above or below the data).

Grand Totals   Choose which types, if any, to display.

Report Layout   Choose from three different layout styles (compact, outline, or tabular). You can also choose to hide repeating labels.

Blank Row   Add a blank row between items to improve readability.

The PivotTable Tools ⇨ Analyze ⇨ Show group contains additional options that affect the appearance of your PivotTable. For example, you use the Show Field Headers button to toggle the display of the field headings.

Still more PivotTable options are available from the PivotTable Options dialog box. To display this dialog box, choose PivotTable Tools ⇨ Analyze ⇨ PivotTable ⇨ Options, or right-click any cell in the PivotTable and choose PivotTable Options from the shortcut menu.

The best way to become familiar with all of these layout and formatting options is to experiment.

PivotTable Calculations

PivotTable data is most frequently summarized using a sum. However, you can display your data using a number of different summary techniques, specified in the Value Field Settings dialog box. The quickest way to display this dialog box is to right-click any value in the PivotTable and choose Value Field Settings from the shortcut menu. This dialog box has two tabs: Summarize Values By and Show Values As.

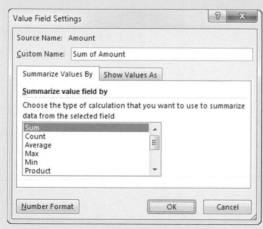

Continues

continued

Use the Summarize Values By tab to select a different summary function. Your choices are Sum, Count, Average, Max, Min, Product, Count Numbers, StdDev, StdDevp, Var, and Varp.

To display your values in a different form, use the drop-down control on the Show Values As tab. You have many options from which to choose, including as a percentage of the total or subtotal.

This dialog box also provides a way to apply a number format to the values. Just click the button and choose your number format.

Modifying the PivotTable

After you create a PivotTable, changing it is easy. For example, you can add further summary information by using the PivotTable Fields task pane. Figure 29.11 shows our PivotTable after we dragged a second field (OpenedBy) to the Rows section in the PivotTable Fields task pane.

FIGURE 29.11

Two fields are used for row labels.

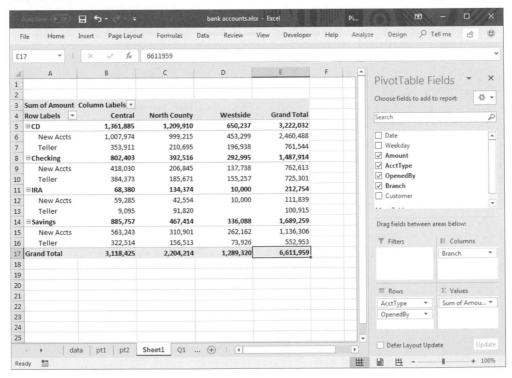

Here are some tips on other PivotTable modifications you can make:

- To remove a field from the PivotTable, select it in the bottom part of the PivotTable Fields task pane and then drag it away.
- If an area has more than one field, you can change the order in which the fields are listed by dragging the field names. Doing so determines how nesting occurs, and it affects the appearance of the PivotTable.
- To remove a field temporarily from the PivotTable, remove the check mark from the field name in the top part of the PivotTable Fields task pane. The PivotTable is redisplayed without that field. Place the check mark back on the field name, and it appears in its previous section.
- If you add a field to the Filters section, the field items appear in a drop-down list, which allows you to filter the displayed data by one or more items. Figure 29.12 shows an example. The Date field was put into the Filters area. The PivotTable is now showing the data only for a single day (once it was selected from the drop-down list in cell B1).

FIGURE 29.12

The PivotTable is filtered by date.

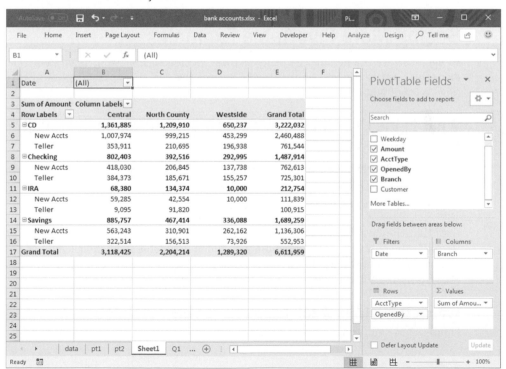

Copying a PivotTable's Content

A PivotTable is flexible, but it does have some limitations. For example, you can't add new rows or columns, change any of the calculated values, or enter formulas within the PivotTable. If you want to manipulate a PivotTable in ways not normally permitted, make a copy of it so that it's no longer linked to its data source.

To copy a PivotTable, select the entire table and choose Home ➪ Clipboard ➪ Copy (or press Ctrl+C). Then activate a new worksheet and choose Home Clipboard ➪ Paste ➪ Paste Values. The PivotTable formatting is not copied—even if you repeat the operation and use the Formats option in the Paste Special dialog box.

To copy the PivotTable and its formatting, use the Office Clipboard to paste. If the Office Clipboard is not displayed, click the dialog box launcher in the bottom right of the Home ➪ Clipboard group.

The contents of the PivotTable are copied to the new location so that you can do whatever you like to them.

Note that the copied information is not a PivotTable, and it is no longer linked to the source data. If the source data changes, your copied PivotTable will not reflect these changes.

Seeing More PivotTable Examples

To demonstrate the flexibility of this feature, we created some additional PivotTables. The examples use the bank account data and answer the questions posed earlier in this chapter. (See "A PivotTable example.")

What is the daily total new deposit amount for each branch?

Figure 29.13 shows the PivotTable that answers this question.

- The Branch field is in the Columns section.
- The Date field is in the Rows section.
- The Amount field is in the Values section and is summarized by Sum.

Note that the PivotTable can also be sorted by any column. For example, you can sort the Grand Total column in descending order to find out which day of the month had the largest amount of new funds. To sort, just right-click any cell in the column to sort and choose Sort from the shortcut menu.

Which day of the week accounts for the most deposits?

Figure 29.14 shows the PivotTable that answers this question.

FIGURE 29.13

This PivotTable shows daily totals for each branch.

	A	B	C	D	E	F
1						
2	Sum of Amount	Branch ▾				
3	Row Labels ▾	Central	North County	Westside	Grand Total	
4	4/1/2019	179,011	139,196	51,488	369,695	
5	4/2/2019	72,256	27,805	7,188	107,249	
6	4/4/2019	146,290	164,305	122,828	433,423	
7	4/5/2019	101,480	50,294	97,415	249,189	
8	4/6/2019	188,018	91,724	52,738	332,480	
9	4/7/2019	271,227	196,188	53,525	520,940	
10	4/8/2019	105,087	77,674	92,013	274,774	
11	4/11/2019	172,920	43,953	89,258	306,131	
12	4/12/2019	70,300	44,621	39,797	154,718	
13	4/13/2019	143,921	176,698	29,075	349,694	
14	4/14/2019	117,800	114,418	36,064	268,282	
15	4/15/2019	191,611	62,787	85,015	339,413	
16	4/18/2019	79,394	72,262	48,337	199,993	
17	4/19/2019	209,916	213,728	53,721	477,365	
18	4/20/2019	125,276	140,739	56,444	322,459	
19	4/21/2019	79,355	35,753	3,419	118,527	
20	4/22/2019	188,509	236,269	97,210	521,988	
21	4/25/2019	218,889	137,025	85,828	441,742	
22	4/26/2019	150,139	29,040	95,998	275,177	
23	4/27/2019	56,379	72,948	43,472	172,799	
24	4/28/2019	62,192	43,217	12,128	117,537	
25	4/29/2019	170,279	22,570	19,429	212,278	
26	4/30/2019	18,176	11,000	16,930	46,106	
27	Grand Total	3,118,425	2,204,214	1,289,320	6,611,959	
28						

FIGURE 29.14

This PivotTable shows new account totals by day of the week.

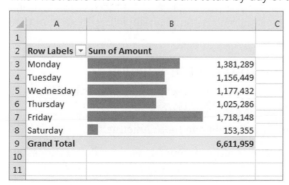

	A	B	C
1			
2	Row Labels ▾	Sum of Amount	
3	Monday		1,381,289
4	Tuesday		1,156,449
5	Wednesday		1,177,432
6	Thursday		1,025,286
7	Friday		1,718,148
8	Saturday		153,355
9	Grand Total		6,611,959
10			
11			

- The Weekday field is in the Rows section.
- The Amount field is in the Values section and is summarized by Sum.

We added conditional formatting data bars to make it easier to see how the days compare. As you see, the largest deposit days are Fridays.

 See Chapter 17, "Using Formulas with Tables and Conditional Formatting," for more information about conditional formatting.

How many accounts were opened at each branch, broken down by account type?

Figure 29.15 shows a PivotTable that answers this question.

FIGURE 29.15

This PivotTable uses the Count function to summarize the data.

⬛	A	B	C	D	E	F	G
1							
2	Count of Amount	AcctType ▾					
3	Row Labels ▾	CD	Checking	IRA	Savings	Grand Total	
4	Central	97	158	8	99	362	
5	North County	60	61	15	61	197	
6	Westside	54	59	5	35	153	
7	Grand Total	211	278	28	195	712	
8							
9							

- The AcctType field is in the Columns section.
- The Branch field is in the Rows section.
- The Amount field is in the Values section and is summarized by Count.

So far, all of the PivotTable examples have used the Sum summary function. In this case, we changed the summary function to Count. To change the summary function to Count, right-click any cell in the Values area and choose Summarize Values By ➪ Count from the shortcut menu.

How much money was used to open the accounts?

Figure 29.16 shows a PivotTable that answers this question. For example, 253 (or 35.53%) of the new accounts were for an amount of $5,000 or less.

This PivotTable is unusual because it uses only one field: Amount.

- The Amount field is in the Rows section (grouped, to show dollar ranges).
- The Amount field is also in the Values section and is summarized by Count.
- A third instance of the Amount field is the Values section, summarized by Count and displayed as Percent of Column Total.

FIGURE 29.16

This PivotTable counts the number of accounts that fall into each value range.

	A	B	C	D
1				
2	Row Labels ▼	Count	Pct	
3	1-5000	253	35.53%	
4	5001-10000	192	26.97%	
5	10001-15000	222	31.18%	
6	15001-20000	19	2.67%	
7	20001-25000	3	0.42%	
8	25001-30000	1	0.14%	
9	30001-35000	3	0.42%	
10	40001-45000	3	0.42%	
11	45001-50000	5	0.70%	
12	60001-65000	2	0.28%	
13	70001-75000	5	0.70%	
14	75001-80000	1	0.14%	
15	85001-90000	3	0.42%	
16	**Grand Total**	**712**	**100.00%**	
17				
18				

When you initially add the Amount field to the Rows section, the PivotTable will show one row for each unique dollar amount. To group the values, right-click one of the row items and choose Group from the shortcut menu. Then use the Grouping dialog box to set up bins of $5,000 increments. Note that the Grouping dialog box does not appear if you select more than one row label.

The second instance of the Amount field (in the Values section) is summarized by Count. To change from the default Sum, right-click any value and choose Summarize Data By ⇨ Count from the shortcut menu.

Add another instance of Amount to the Values section, and set it up to display as a percentage. Right-click a value in column C and choose Show Values As ⇨ % of Column Total. This option is also available in the Show Values As tab of the Value Field Settings dialog box.

What types of accounts do tellers open most often?

The PivotTable in Figure 29.17 shows that the most common account opened by tellers is a checking account.

- The AcctType field is in the Rows section.
- The OpenedBy field is in the Filters section.
- The Amount field is in the Values section (summarized by Count).
- A second instance of the Amount field is in the Values section (shown as % of Column Total).

29

FIGURE 29.17

This PivotTable uses a filter to show only the teller data.

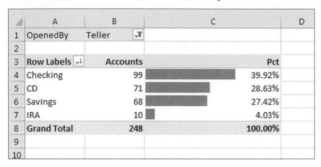

This PivotTable uses the OpenedBy field as a filter and is showing the data only for tellers. Sort the rows so that the largest value is at the top by right-clicking any of the values, choosing Sort, and choosing Sort Largest to Smallest. To display the data bars, use conditional formatting.

 See Chapter 17 for more information about conditional formatting.

In which branch do tellers open the most checking accounts for new customers?

Figure 29.18 shows a PivotTable that answers this question. At the Central branch, tellers opened 23 checking accounts for new customers.

FIGURE 29.18

This PivotTable uses three filters.

	A	B	C
1	Customer	New .T	
2	OpenedBy	Teller .T	
3	AcctType	Checking .T	
4			
5	Row Labels ▾	Accounts	
6	Central	23	
7	North County	10	
8	Westside	10	
9	Grand Total	43	
10			
11			

- The Customer field is in the Filters section.
- The OpenedBy field is in the Filters section.
- The AcctType field is in the Filters section.
- The Branch field is in the Rows section.
- The Amount field is in the Values section, summarized by Count.

This PivotTable uses three report filters. The Customer field is filtered to show only New, the OpenedBy field is filtered to show only Teller, and the AcctType field is filtered to show only Checking.

Learning More

The examples in this chapter should give you an appreciation for the power and flexibility of Excel PivotTables. The next chapter drills down a bit deeper and covers some advanced features of PivotTables—with lots of examples.

29

Analyzing Data with PivotTables

IN THIS CHAPTER

Creating a PivotTable from non-numeric data

Grouping items in a PivotTable

Creating a calculated field or a calculated item in a PivotTable

Understanding the data model feature

The previous chapter introduced PivotTables. There we presented several examples to demonstrate the types of PivotTable summaries that you can generate from a set of data.

This chapter continues the discussion and explores the details of creating effective PivotTables. Creating a basic PivotTable is easy, and the examples in this chapter demonstrate additional PivotTable features that you may find helpful. We urge you to try these techniques with your own data. If you don't have suitable data, use the files available on this book's website.

Working with Non-numeric Data

Most PivotTables are created from numeric data, but PivotTables are also useful with some types of non-numeric data. Because you can't sum non-numbers, this technique involves counting.

Figure 30.1 shows a table and a PivotTable generated from the table. The table consists of a list of 400 employees, along with their location and gender. As you can see, the table has no numeric values, but you can create a useful PivotTable that counts the items rather than sums them. The PivotTable (in range E2:H10) cross-tabulates the Location field by the Gender field for the 400 employees, and it shows the count for each combination of location and gender.

FIGURE 30.1

This table doesn't have any numeric fields, but you can use it to generate the PivotTable shown next to it.

	A	B	C	D	E	F	G	H
1	Employee	Location	Gender					
2	Al Grubbs	California	Male		Count			
3	Sarah Parks	New York	Female			Female	Male	Total
4	Cheryl Cory	California	Female		Arizona	5	15	20
5	Gregory Steiger	California	Male		California	44	64	108
6	Sheila Wigfall	California	Female		Massachusetts	43	47	90
7	Pedro H. Nicholson	Arizona	Male		New York	51	40	91
8	Howard Keach	California	Male		Pennsylvania	17	29	46
9	Heather Lichtenstein	Washington	Female		Washington	16	29	45
10	Janet Woodson	Arizona	Female		Total	176	224	400
11	Hosea Pierson	New York	Male					
12	Nadine Blankenship	New York	Female					
13	Roy Greene	New York	Male					
14	William N. Campbell	New York	Male					
15	Stephen Foster	New York	Male					
16	Charles S. Billings	Pennsylvania	Male					
17	Margaret Sirois	California	Female					
18	PhyllisTodd	Massachusetts	Female					
19	Mary Brinkmann	New York	Female					
20	Janie Little	Massachusetts	Female					
21	Bob Hunsberger	Pennsylvania	Male					

A workbook that demonstrates the pivot table created from non-numeric data is available on this book's website at www.wiley.com/go/excel2019bible. The file is named employee list.xlsx.

Here are the PivotTable Fields task pane settings we used for this PivotTable:

- The Gender field is used for the Columns.
- The Location field is used for the Rows.
- Location is also used for the Values, and it is summarized by Count.
- The PivotTable has the field headers turned off by using the Field Headers toggle control in the PivotTable Tools Analyze ⇨ Show group.

> **NOTE**
>
> The Employee field is not used. This example uses the Location field for the Values section, but you can actually use any of the three fields because the PivotTable is displaying a count.

Figure 30.2 shows the PivotTable after making some additional changes.

- To show percentages, add a second instance of the Location field to the Values section. Then right-click a value in that column and choose Show Values As ➪ % of Column Total.
- Change the field names in the PivotTable to `Ct` and `Pct` by simply selecting those cells and typing the new name.
- Select a PivotTable style that makes it easier to distinguish the columns.

FIGURE 30.2

Changing the PivotTable to show counts and percentages

	Female		Male		Total Ct	Total Pct
	Ct	Pct	Ct	Pct		
Arizona	5	2.8%	15	6.7%	20	5.0%
California	44	25.0%	64	28.6%	108	27.0%
Massachusetts	43	24.4%	47	21.0%	90	22.5%
New York	51	29.0%	40	17.9%	91	22.8%
Pennsylvania	17	9.7%	29	12.9%	46	11.5%
Washington	16	9.1%	29	12.9%	45	11.3%
Total	176	100.0%	224	100.0%	400	100.0%

Grouping PivotTable Items

One of the most useful features of a PivotTable is the ability to combine items into groups. You can group items that appear in the Rows or Columns section in the PivotTable Fields task pane. Excel offers two ways to group items:

Manually After creating the PivotTable, select the items to be grouped and then choose PivotTable Tools Analyze ➪ Group ➪ Group Selection, or you can select the items, right-click, and choose Group from the shortcut menu.

Automatically If the items are numeric (or dates), use the Grouping dialog box to specify how you would like to group the items. Select any single item and then choose PivotTable Tools Analyze ➪ Group ➪ Group Field, or right-click a single item and choose Group from the shortcut menu. In either case, the Grouping dialog box appears. Use this dialog box to specify how to group the items.

NOTE

If you plan on creating multiple PivotTables that use different groupings, make sure you read the sidebar "Multiple Groups from the Same Data Source."

30

A manual grouping example

Figure 30.3 shows the PivotTable example from the previous sections, with two groups created from the Row Labels. To create the first group, hold down the Ctrl key and select

Arizona, California, and Washington in the PivotTable. Then right-click the selected cells and choose Group from the shortcut menu. Select the three other states in the same manner and create a second group. Replace the default group names (Group 1 and Group 2) with more meaningful names (Western Region and Eastern Region).

FIGURE 30.3

A PivotTable with two groups

Count			
	Female	Male	Total
⊟Western Region			
Arizona	5	15	20
California	44	64	108
Washington	16	29	45
⊟Eastern Region			
Massachusetts	43	47	90
New York	51	40	91
Pennsylvania	17	29	46
Total	176	224	400

You can create any number of groups and even create groups of groups.

Excel provides a number of layout options for displaying a PivotTable. You may want to experiment with these options when you use groups. These commands are on the PivotTable Tools Design tab of the Ribbon. There are no rules for choosing a particular option. The key is to try a few and see which makes your PivotTable look the best. In addition, try various style options in the PivotTable Tools Design tab. Often, the style that you choose can greatly enhance readability.

Figure 30.4 shows PivotTables using various options for displaying subtotals, grand totals, and styles.

 A workbook that contains these grouping examples is available on this book's website at www .wiley.com/go/excel2019bible. The file is named grouping examples.xlsx.

FIGURE 30.4

PivotTables with options for subtotals and grand totals

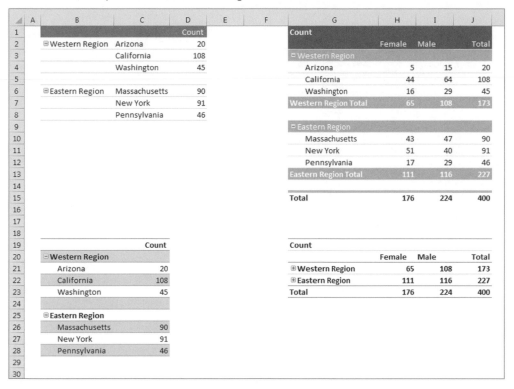

Automatic grouping examples

When a field contains numbers, dates, or times, Excel can create groups automatically. The two examples in this section demonstrate automatic grouping.

Grouping by date

Figure 30.5 shows a portion of a simple table with two fields: Date and Sales. This table has 731 rows and covers the dates between January 1, 2019, and December 31, 2020. The goal is to summarize the sales information by month.

FIGURE 30.5

You can use a PivotTable to summarize the sales data by month.

▲	A	B	
1	Date	Sales	
2	1/1/2019	3,830	
3	1/2/2019	3,763	
4	1/3/2019	4,362	
5	1/4/2019	3,669	
6	1/5/2019	3,942	
7	1/6/2019	4,488	
8	1/7/2019	4,416	
9	1/8/2019	3,371	
10	1/9/2019	3,628	
11	1/10/2019	4,548	
12	1/11/2019	5,493	
13	1/12/2019	5,706	
14	1/13/2019	6,579	
15	1/14/2019	6,333	
16	1/15/2019	6,101	
17	1/16/2019	5,289	
18	1/17/2019	5,349	
19	1/18/2019	5,814	
20	1/19/2019	6,501	
21	1/20/2019	6,513	

 A workbook demonstrating how to group pivot table items by date is available on this book's website at www.wiley.com/go/excel2019bible. The file is grouping sales by date.xlsx.

Figure 30.6 shows a PivotTable (in Columns D:E) created from the data. The Date field is in the Rows section, and the Sales field is in the Values section. When you add a date field to a PivotTable, Excel automatically groups the dates and adds the grouped fields to your PivotTable. If you prefer to not have your dates grouped, you can click Undo immediately after you add the date field to the PivotTable. You can also modify the grouping manually.

To group the items by month, select either of the years and choose PivotTable Tools Analyze ⇨ Group ⇨ Group Field (or right-click and choose Group from the shortcut menu). The Grouping dialog box, shown in Figure 30.7, appears. Excel supplies values for the Starting At and Ending At fields. The values cover the entire range of data, and you can change them if you like.

FIGURE 30.6

The PivotTable with Excel's automatic grouping

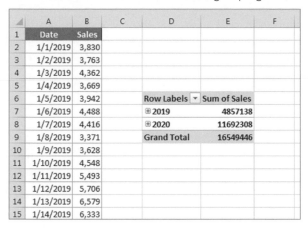

FIGURE 30.7

Use the Grouping dialog box to group PivotTable items by dates.

In the By list box, select only Months and Years and deselect any other groupings Excel may have automatically created (such as Quarters). Verify that the starting and ending dates are correct for your data. Click OK. The Date items in the PivotTable are grouped by years and by months, as shown in Figure 30.8.

30

FIGURE 30.8

The PivotTable, after grouping by month and year

Row Labels	Sum of Sales
⊟2019	4,857,138
Jan	167,624
Feb	137,825
Mar	214,896
Apr	100,872
May	158,005
Jun	117,649
Jul	295,248
Aug	518,966
Sep	612,673
Oct	699,854
Nov	863,085
Dec	970,441
⊟2020	11,692,308
Jan	974,625
Feb	1,004,760
Mar	1,077,642
Apr	986,495
May	1,042,915
Jun	926,014
Jul	965,328
Aug	939,093
Sep	970,203
Oct	951,452
Nov	950,802
Dec	902,979
Grand Total	16,549,446

> **NOTE**
>
> If you select only Months in the By list box in the Grouping dialog box, months in different years combine. For example, the January item would display the sum of sales for 2019 and 2020.

Figure 30.9 shows another view of the data, grouped by quarter and by year.

FIGURE 30.9

This PivotTable shows sales by quarter and by year.

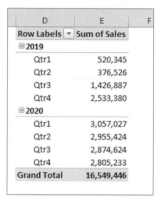

Row Labels	Sum of Sales
⊟ **2019**	
Qtr1	520,345
Qtr2	376,526
Qtr3	1,426,887
Qtr4	2,533,380
⊟ **2020**	
Qtr1	3,057,027
Qtr2	2,955,424
Qtr3	2,874,624
Qtr4	2,805,233
Grand Total	**16,549,446**

Multiple Groups from the Same Data Source

If you create multiple PivotTables from the same data source, you may have noticed that grouping a field in one PivotTable affects the other PivotTables. Specifically, all of the other PivotTables automatically use the same grouping. Sometimes, this is exactly what you want. At other times, it's not at all what you want. For example, you might like to see two PivotTable reports: one that summarizes data by month and year and another that summarizes the data by quarter and year.

Grouping affects other PivotTables because all of the PivotTables are using the same PivotTable "cache." Unfortunately, there is no direct way to force a PivotTable to use a new cache. But there is a way to trick Excel into using a new cache. The trick involves giving multiple range names to the source data.

For example, name your source range `Table1` and then give the same range a second name: `Table2`. The easiest way to name a range is to use the Name box to the left of the Formula bar. Select the range, type a name in the Name box, and press Enter. Then, with the range still selected, type a different name and press Enter. Excel will display only the first name, but you can verify that both names exist by choosing Formulas ➪ Defined Names ➪ Name Manager.

When you create the first PivotTable, specify `Table1` as the Table/Range. When you create the second PivotTable, specify `Table2` as the Table/Range. Each PivotTable will use a separate cache, and you can create groups in one PivotTable, independent of the other PivotTable.

You can use this trick with existing PivotTables. Make sure you give the data source a different name. Then select the PivotTable and choose PivotTable Tools Analyze ➪ Data ➪ Change Data Source. In the Change PivotTable Data Source dialog box, type the new name that you gave to the range. This will cause Excel to create a new PivotCache for the PivotTable.

30

Grouping by time

Figure 30.10 shows a set of data in columns A:B. Each row is a reading from a measurement instrument, taken at one-minute intervals throughout an entire day. The table has 1,440 rows, each representing one minute. The PivotTable (in columns D:G) summarizes the data by hour.

FIGURE 30.10

This PivotTable is grouped by hours.

	A	B	C	D	E	F	G
1	Time	Reading			Average	Minimum	Maximum
2	6/15/2019 0:00	105.32		12 AM	110.50	104.37	116.21
3	6/15/2019 0:01	105.35		1 AM	118.57	112.72	127.14
4	6/15/2019 0:02	104.37		2 AM	124.39	115.75	130.36
5	6/15/2019 0:03	106.40		3 AM	122.74	112.85	132.90
6	6/15/2019 0:04	106.42		4 AM	129.29	123.99	133.52
7	6/15/2019 0:05	105.45		5 AM	132.91	125.88	141.04
8	6/15/2019 0:06	107.46		6 AM	139.67	132.69	146.06
9	6/15/2019 0:07	109.49		7 AM	128.18	117.53	139.65
10	6/15/2019 0:08	110.54		8 AM	119.24	112.10	129.38
11	6/15/2019 0:09	110.54		9 AM	134.36	129.11	142.79
12	6/15/2019 0:10	110.55		10 AM	136.16	130.91	142.89
13	6/15/2019 0:11	109.56		11 AM	122.79	108.63	138.10
14	6/15/2019 0:12	107.60		12 PM	111.76	106.43	116.71
15	6/15/2019 0:13	107.68		1 PM	104.91	98.48	111.86
16	6/15/2019 0:14	109.69		2 PM	119.71	110.37	130.55
17	6/15/2019 0:15	107.76		3 PM	131.83	121.92	139.65
18	6/15/2019 0:16	107.81		4 PM	131.05	123.36	137.94
19	6/15/2019 0:17	108.83		5 PM	138.90	133.05	145.06
20	6/15/2019 0:18	109.85		6 PM	134.71	129.29	139.89
21	6/15/2019 0:19	111.94		7 PM	123.09	113.97	135.23
22	6/15/2019 0:20	114.04		8 PM	118.13	112.64	125.65
23	6/15/2019 0:21	112.12		9 PM	112.64	108.09	117.72
24	6/15/2019 0:22	112.21		10 PM	103.19	96.13	110.49
25	6/15/2019 0:23	112.25		11 PM	106.01	100.03	111.76
26	6/15/2019 0:24	113.34		Grand Total	123.11	96.13	146.06
27	6/15/2019 0:25	112.41					
28	6/15/2019 0:26	112.42					

 This **workbook, named** `time-based grouping.xlsx`, **is available on this book's website at** www`.wiley.com/go/excel2019bible`.

Here are the settings to use for this PivotTable:

- The Values area has three instances of the Reading field, and each instance displays a different summary method (Average, Minimum, and Maximum). To change the summary method for a column, right-click any cell in the column and choose the Summarize Values By and then appropriate option.

■ The Time field is in the Rows section. Use the Grouping dialog box to group by hours.

Using a PivotTable to Create a Frequency Distribution

Excel provides a number of ways to create a frequency distribution, but none of these methods is easier than using a PivotTable. Figure 30.11 shows part of a table of 221 students and the test score for each. The goal is to determine how many students are in each ten-point range (1–10, 11–20, and so on).

FIGURE 30.11

Creating a frequency distribution for these test scores is simple.

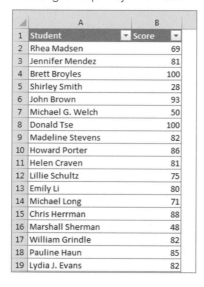

	A	B
1	Student	Score
2	Rhea Madsen	69
3	Jennifer Mendez	81
4	Brett Broyles	100
5	Shirley Smith	28
6	John Brown	93
7	Michael G. Welch	50
8	Donald Tse	100
9	Madeline Stevens	82
10	Howard Porter	86
11	Helen Craven	81
12	Lillie Schultz	75
13	Emily Li	80
14	Michael Long	71
15	Chris Herrman	88
16	Marshall Sherman	48
17	William Grindle	82
18	Pauline Haun	85
19	Lydia J. Evans	82

 This workbook, named `frequency distribution.xlsx`, **is available on this book's website at** `www.wiley.com/go/excel2019bible`.

The PivotTable is simple.

■ The Score field is in the Rows section (grouped).
■ Another instance of the Score field is in the Values section (summarized by Count).

The Grouping dialog box that generated the bins specified that the groups start at 1, end at 100, and are incremented by 10.

Figure 30.12 shows the frequency distribution of the test scores, along with a PivotChart. (See "Creating PivotCharts" later in this chapter.) The Scores are filtered so that the PivotTable (and chart) do not show the <1 category and the >101 category.

FIGURE 30.12

The PivotTable and PivotChart show the frequency distribution for the test scores.

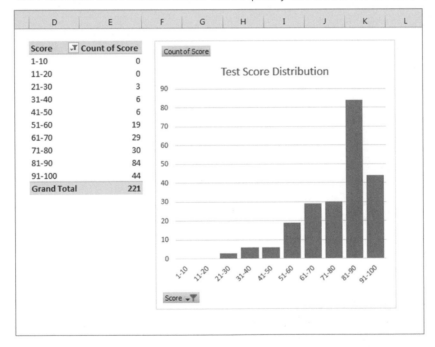

Creating a Calculated Field or Calculated Item

Perhaps the most confusing aspect of PivotTables is calculated fields versus calculated items. Many PivotTable users simply avoid dealing with calculated fields and items. However, these features can be useful, and they really aren't that complicated once you understand the way they work.

First, here are some basic definitions:

Calculated field A new field created from other fields in the PivotTable. If your PivotTable source is a worksheet table, an alternative to using a calculated field is to add a new column to the table and create a formula to perform the desired calculation. A calculated field must reside in the Values area of the PivotTable. You can't use a calculated field in the Columns area, in the Rows area, or in the Filter area.

Calculated item Uses the contents of other items within a field of the PivotTable. If your PivotTable source is a worksheet table, an alternative to using a calculated item is to insert one or more rows and write formulas that use values in other rows. A calculated item must reside in the Columns area, Rows area, or Filters area of a PivotTable. You can't use a calculated item in the Values area.

The formulas used to create calculated fields and calculated items aren't standard Excel formulas. In other words, you don't enter the formulas into cells. Rather, you enter these formulas into a dialog box, and they're stored along with the PivotTable data.

The examples in this section use the worksheet table shown in Figure 30.13. The table consists of 5 columns and 48 rows. Each row describes monthly sales information for a particular sales representative. For example, Amy is a sales rep for the North region, and she sold 239 units in January for total sales of $23,040.

Figure 30.14 shows a PivotTable created from the data. This PivotTable shows Sales (Values area), cross-tabulated by Month (Rows area) and by SalesRep (Columns area).

30

FIGURE 30.13

This data demonstrates calculated fields and calculated items.

	A	B	C	D	E
1	SalesRep	Region	Month	Sales	Units Sold
2	Amy	North	Jan	$23,040	239
3	Amy	North	Feb	$24,131	79
4	Amy	North	Mar	$24,646	71
5	Amy	North	Apr	$22,047	71
6	Amy	North	May	$24,971	157
7	Amy	North	Jun	$24,218	92
8	Amy	North	Jul	$25,735	175
9	Amy	North	Aug	$23,638	87
10	Amy	North	Sep	$25,749	557
11	Amy	North	Oct	$24,437	95
12	Amy	North	Nov	$25,355	706
13	Amy	North	Dec	$25,899	180
14	Bob	North	Jan	$20,024	103
15	Bob	North	Feb	$23,822	267
16	Bob	North	Mar	$24,854	96
17	Bob	North	Apr	$22,838	74
18	Bob	North	May	$25,320	231
19	Bob	North	Jun	$24,733	164
20	Bob	North	Jul	$21,184	68
21	Bob	North	Aug	$23,174	114
22	Bob	North	Sep	$25,999	84
23	Bob	North	Oct	$22,639	260

FIGURE 30.14

This PivotTable was created from the sales data.

	G	H	I	J	K
Sum of Sales		Column Labe ▼			
Row Labels ▼		Amy	Bob	Chuck	Doug
Jan		23,040	20,024	19,886	26,264
Feb		24,131	23,822	23,494	29,953
Mar		24,646	24,854	21,824	25,041
Apr		22,047	22,838	22,058	29,338
May		24,971	25,320	20,280	25,150
Jun		24,218	24,733	23,965	27,371
Jul		25,735	21,184	23,032	25,044
Aug		23,638	23,174	21,273	29,506
Sep		25,749	25,999	21,584	29,061
Oct		24,437	22,639	19,625	27,113
Nov		25,355	23,949	19,832	25,953
Dec		25,899	23,179	20,583	28,670
Grand Total		293,866	281,715	257,436	328,464

The examples that follow create

- A calculated field, to compute average sales per unit
- Four calculated items, to compute the quarterly sales commission

Creating a calculated field

Because a PivotTable is a special type of range, you can't insert new rows or columns within the PivotTable, which means you can't insert formulas to perform calculations with the data in a PivotTable. However, you can create calculated fields for a PivotTable. A calculated field consists of a calculation that can involve other fields.

A calculated field is basically a way to display new information (derived from other fields) in a PivotTable. It's an alternative to creating a new column in your source data. In many cases, you may find it easier to insert a new column in the source range with a formula that performs the desired calculation. A calculated field is most useful when the data comes from a source that you can't easily manipulate, such as an external database.

In the sales example, suppose you want to calculate the average sales amount per unit. You can compute this value by dividing the Sales field by the Units Sold field. The result shows a new field (a calculated field) for the PivotTable.

Use the following procedure to create a calculated field that consists of the Sales field divided by the Units Sold field:

1. **Select any cell within the PivotTable.**
2. **Choose PivotTable Tools Analyze ⇨ Calculations ⇨ Fields, Items, & Sets ⇨ Calculated Field.** The Insert Calculated Field dialog box appears.
3. **Enter a descriptive name in the Name box, and specify the formula in the Formula box (see Figure 30.15).** The formula can use worksheet functions and other fields from the data source. For this example, the calculated field name is Average Unit Price, and the formula is as follows:

   ```
   =Sales/'Units Sold'
   ```

4. **Click Add to add this new field.**
5. **Click OK to close the Insert Calculated Field dialog box.**

> **NOTE**
>
> You can create the formula manually by typing it or by double-clicking items in the Fields list box. Double-clicking an item transfers it to the Formula field. Because the Units Sold field contains a space, Excel adds single quotes around the field name.

After you create the calculated field, Excel adds it to the Values area of the PivotTable. (It also appears in the PivotTable Fields task pane.) You can treat it just like any other field, with one exception: you can't move it to the Rows, Columns, or Filters areas. It must remain in the Values area.

30

FIGURE 30.15

The Insert Calculated Field dialog box

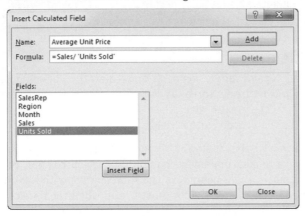

Figure 30.16 shows the PivotTable after adding the calculated field. The new field displayed Sum of Average Unit Price, but the label was shortened to Avg Price.

FIGURE 30.16

This PivotTable uses a calculated field.

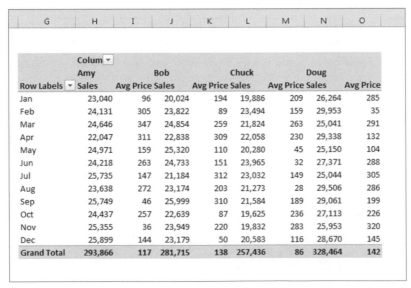

Row Labels	Amy Sales	Avg Price	Bob Sales	Avg Price	Chuck Sales	Avg Price	Doug Sales	Avg Price
Jan	23,040	96	20,024	194	19,886	209	26,264	285
Feb	24,131	305	23,822	89	23,494	159	29,953	35
Mar	24,646	347	24,854	259	21,824	263	25,041	291
Apr	22,047	311	22,838	309	22,058	230	29,338	132
May	24,971	159	25,320	110	20,280	45	25,150	104
Jun	24,218	263	24,733	151	23,965	32	27,371	288
Jul	25,735	147	21,184	312	23,032	149	25,044	305
Aug	23,638	272	23,174	203	21,273	28	29,506	286
Sep	25,749	46	25,999	310	21,584	189	29,061	199
Oct	24,437	257	22,639	87	19,625	236	27,113	226
Nov	25,355	36	23,949	220	19,832	283	25,953	320
Dec	25,899	144	23,179	50	20,583	116	28,670	145
Grand Total	293,866	117	281,715	138	257,436	86	328,464	142

Inserting a calculated item

The preceding section describes how to create a calculated field. Excel also enables you to create a calculated item for a PivotTable field. Keep in mind that a calculated field can be an alternative to adding a new field (column) to your data source. A calculated item, on the other hand, is an alternative to adding a new row to the data source—a row that contains a formula that refers to other rows.

In this example, you create four calculated items. Each item represents the commission earned on the quarter's sales, according to the following schedule:

Quarter 1: 10% of January, February, and March sales

Quarter 2: 11% of April, May, and June sales

Quarter 3: 12% of July, August, and September sales

Quarter 4: 12.5% of October, November, and December sales

To create a calculated item to compute the commission for January, February, and March, follow these steps:

1. **Select any cell in the Row Labels or Column Labels area of the PivotTable and choose PivotTable Tools Analyze ⇨ Calculations ⇨ Fields, Items, & Sets ⇨ Calculated Item.** The Insert Calculated Item dialog box appears.

2. **Enter a name for the new item in the Name field, and specify the formula in the Formula field (see Figure 30.17).** The formula can use items in other fields, but it can't use worksheet functions. For this example, the new item is named Qtr1 Commission, and the formula appears as follows:

   `= (Jan+Feb+Mar)*10%`

3. **Click Add.**

4. **Repeat steps 2 and 3 to create three additional calculated items:**

   Qtr2 Commission: `= (Apr+May+Jun)*11%`

   Qtr3 Commission: `= (Jul+Aug+Sep)*12%`

   Qtr4 Commission: `= (Oct+Nov+Dec)*12.5%`

5. **Click OK to close the dialog box.**

FIGURE 30.17

The Insert Calculated Item dialog box

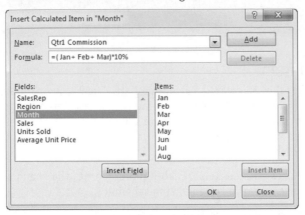

> **NOTE**
> A calculated item, unlike a calculated field, does not appear in the PivotTable Fields task pane. Only fields appear in the field list.

> **CAUTION**
> If you use a calculated item in your PivotTable, you may need to turn off the Grand Total display for columns to avoid double counting. In this example, the Grand Total includes the calculated items, so the commission amounts are included with the sales amounts. To turn off Grand Totals, choose PivotTable Tools Design ⇨ Layout ⇨ Grand Totals ⇨ Off for Rows and Columns.

After you create the calculated items, they appear in the PivotTable. Figure 30.18 shows the PivotTable after adding the four calculated items. Notice that the calculated items are added to the end of the Month items. You can rearrange the items by selecting the cell and dragging its border. Another option is to create two groups (manually): one for the sales numbers and one for the commission calculations. Figure 30.19 shows the PivotTable after creating the two groups and adding subtotals.

FIGURE 30.18

This PivotTable uses calculated items for quarterly totals.

Row Labels	Amy Sales	Avg Price	Bob Sales	Avg Price	Chuck Sales	Avg Price	Doug Sales	Avg Price
Jan	23,040	96	20,024	194	19,886	209	26,264	285
Feb	24,131	305	23,822	89	23,494	159	29,953	35
Mar	24,646	347	24,854	259	21,824	263	25,041	291
Apr	22,047	311	22,838	309	22,058	230	29,338	132
May	24,971	159	25,320	110	20,280	45	25,150	104
Jun	24,218	263	24,733	151	23,965	32	27,371	288
Jul	25,735	147	21,184	312	23,032	149	25,044	305
Aug	23,638	272	23,174	203	21,273	28	29,506	286
Sep	25,749	46	25,999	310	21,584	189	29,061	199
Oct	24,437	257	22,639	87	19,625	236	27,113	226
Nov	25,355	36	23,949	220	19,832	283	25,953	320
Dec	25,899	144	23,179	50	20,583	116	28,670	145
Qtr1 Commission	7,182	185	6,870	147	6,520	200	8,126	79
Qtr2 Commission	7,836	223	8,018	155	7,293	51	9,004	146
Qtr3 Commission	9,015	92	8,443	265	7,907	63	10,033	253
Qtr4 Commission	9,461	77	8,721	84	7,505	181	10,217	205
Grand Total	**327,360**	**117**	**313,767**	**138**	**286,661**	**86**	**365,845**	**142**

FIGURE 30.19

The PivotTable, after creating two groups and adding subtotals

Row Labels	Amy Sales	Avg Price	Bob Sales	Avg Price	Chuck Sales	Avg Price	Doug Sales	Avg Price
⊟ **Monthly Sales**								
Jan	23,040	96	20,024	194	19,886	209	26,264	285
Feb	24,131	305	23,822	89	23,494	159	29,953	35
Mar	24,646	347	24,854	259	21,824	263	25,041	291
Apr	22,047	311	22,838	309	22,058	230	29,338	132
May	24,971	159	25,320	110	20,280	45	25,150	104
Jun	24,218	263	24,733	151	23,965	32	27,371	288
Jul	25,735	147	21,184	312	23,032	149	25,044	305
Aug	23,638	272	23,174	203	21,273	28	29,506	286
Sep	25,749	46	25,999	310	21,584	189	29,061	199
Oct	24,437	257	22,639	87	19,625	236	27,113	226
Nov	25,355	36	23,949	220	19,832	283	25,953	320
Dec	25,899	144	23,179	50	20,583	116	28,670	145
Monthly Sales Total	**293,866**	**117**	**281,715**	**138**	**257,436**	**86**	**328,464**	**142**
⊟ **Quarterly Commissions**								
Qtr1 Commission	7,182	185	6,870	147	6,520	200	8,126	79
Qtr2 Commission	7,836	223	8,018	155	7,293	51	9,004	146
Qtr3 Commission	9,015	92	8,443	265	7,907	63	10,033	253
Qtr4 Commission	9,461	77	8,721	84	7,505	181	10,217	205
Quarterly Commissions Total	**33,494**	**114**	**32,052**	**137**	**29,225**	**85**	**37,381**	**147**

30

A Reverse PivotTable

The Excel PivotTable feature creates a summary table from a list. But what if you want to perform the opposite operation? Often, you may have a two-way summary table, and it would be convenient if the data were in the form of a normalized list.

In the accompanying figure, range A1:E13 contains a summary table with 48 data points. Notice that this summary table is similar to a PivotTable. Column G:I shows part of a 48-row table that was derived from the summary table. In other words, every value in the original summary table is converted to a row, which also contains the region name and month. This type of table is useful because it can be sorted and manipulated in other ways. And you can create a PivotTable from this transformed table.

▲	A	B	C	D	E	F	G	H	I	J
1		North	South	East	West		Col1	Col2	Col3	
2	Jan	132	233	314	441		Jan	North	132	
3	Feb	143	251	314	447		Jan	South	233	
4	Mar	172	252	345	450		Jan	East	314	
5	Apr	184	290	365	452		Jan	West	441	
6	May	212	299	401	453		Feb	North	143	
7	Jun	239	317	413	457		Feb	South	251	
8	Jul	249	350	427	460		Feb	East	314	
9	Aug	263	354	448	468		Feb	West	447	
10	Sep	291	373	367	472		Mar	North	172	
11	Oct	294	401	392	479		Mar	South	252	
12	Nov	302	437	495	484		Mar	East	345	
13	Dec	305	466	504	490		Mar	West	450	
14							Apr	North	184	
15	Select a cell in the summary table above, then click the						Apr	South	290	
16	button to create a table with one row per data point.						Apr	East	365	
17	Replace the column headings to describe the fields.						Apr	West	452	
18	This macro can be used with any 2-way table						May	North	212	
19							May	South	299	
20			Convert				May	East	401	
21							May	West	453	
22							Jun	North	239	
23							Jun	South	317	
24							Jun	East	413	

The companion website contains a workbook, `reverse pivot.xlsm`, which has a VBA macro that will convert any two-way summary table into a three-column normalized table.

Another way to perform this type of transformation is to use Get & Transform. See Chapter 39, "Transforming Data with Power Query," for an example.

Filtering PivotTables with Slicers

A slicer is an interactive control that makes it easy to filter data in a PivotTable. Figure 30.20 shows a PivotTable with three slicers, each representing a particular field. In this case, the PivotTable is displaying data for new and existing customers, opened by tellers at the North County branch.

FIGURE 30.20

FIGURE 30.20

Using slicers to filter the data displayed in a PivotTable

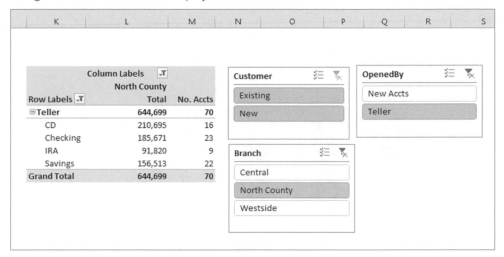

The same type of filtering can be accomplished by using the field labels in the PivotTable, but slicers are intended for those who might not understand how to filter data in a PivotTable. Slicers can also be used to create an attractive and easy-to-use interactive "dashboard."

To add one or more slicers to a worksheet, start by selecting any cell in a PivotTable. Then choose Insert ⇨ Filters ⇨ Slicer. The Insert Slicers dialog box appears, with a list of all fields in the PivotTable. Place a check mark next to the slicers you want and then click OK.

Slicers can be moved and resized, and you can change the look. To remove the effects of filtering by a particular slicer, click the "clear filter" icon in the slicer's upper-right corner.

To use a slicer to filter data in a PivotTable, just click a button. To display multiple values, press Ctrl while you click the buttons in a slicer or click the Multi-Select icon at the top right of the slicer window. Press Shift and click to select a series of consecutive buttons.

Figure 30.21 shows a PivotTable and a PivotChart. Two slicers are used to filter the data (by state and by month). In this case, the PivotTable and PivotChart show only the data for Kansas, Missouri, and New York for the months of January through March. Slicers provide a quick and easy way to create an interactive chart.

30

FIGURE 30.21

Using slicers to filter a PivotTable by state and by month

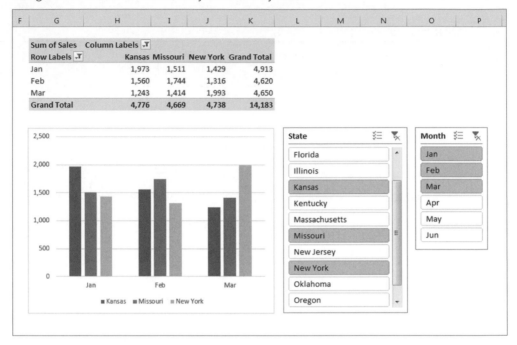

 This workbook, named `pivot table slicers.xlsx`, is available on this book's website at www
.wiley.com/go/excel2019bible.

Filtering PivotTables with a Timeline

A timeline is conceptually similar to a slicer, but this control is designed to simplify time-based filtering in a PivotTable.

A timeline is relevant only if your PivotTable has a field that's formatted as a date. This feature does not work with times. To add a timeline, select a cell in a PivotTable and choose Insert ⇨ Filters ⇨ Timeline. A dialog box appears listing all date-based fields. If your PivotTable doesn't have a field formatted as a date, Excel displays an error.

Figure 30.22 shows a PivotTable created from the data in columns A:E. This PivotTable uses a timeline set to allow date filtering by quarters. Click a button that corresponds to the quarter that you want to view, and the PivotTable is updated immediately. To select a range of quarters, drag the edges of an already-selected quarter forward or backward. Other filtering options (selectable from the drop-down in the upper-right corner) are Years, Months, and Days. In the figure, the PivotTable displays data from the last two quarters of 2019.

FIGURE 30.22

Using a timeline to filter a PivotTable by date

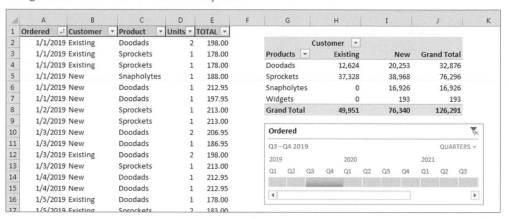

A workbook that uses a timeline is available on this book's website at www.wiley.com/go/
excel2019bible. The filename is pivot table timeline.xlsx.

You can, of course, use both slicers and a timeline for a PivotTable. A timeline has the same
type of formatting options as slicers, so you can create an attractive interactive dashboard
that simplifies PivotTable filtering.

Referencing Cells within a PivotTable

After you create a PivotTable, you may want to create formulas that reference one or more
cells within it. Figure 30.23 shows a simple PivotTable that displays income and expense
information for three years. In this PivotTable, the Month field is hidden, so the PivotTable
shows the year totals.

FIGURE 30.23

The formulas in column F reference cells in the PivotTable.

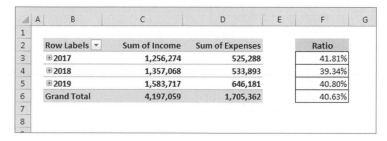

This workbook, named `pivot table referencing.xlsx`, is available on this book's website at www.wiley.com/go/excel2019bible.

Column F contains formulas, and this column is not part of the PivotTable. These formulas calculate the expense-to-income ratio for each year. You can create these formulas by pointing to the cells in the PivotTable. You may expect to see this formula in cell F3:

```
=D3/C3
```

In fact, the formula in cell F3 is

```
=GETPIVOTDATA("Sum of Expenses",$B$2,"Year",2017)/GETPIVOTDATA("Sum
of Income",$B$2,"Year",2017)
```

When you use the pointing technique to create a formula that references a cell in a PivotTable, Excel replaces those simple cell references with a much more complicated `GETPIVOTDATA` function. If you type the cell references manually (instead of pointing to them), Excel doesn't use the `GETPIVOTDATA` function. Why use the `GETPIVOTDATA` function? Using the `GETPIVOTDATA` function helps to ensure that the formula will continue to reference the intended cells if the PivotTable layout is changed.

Figure 30.24 shows the PivotTable after expanding the years to show the month detail. As you can see, the formulas in column F still show the correct result even though the referenced cells are in a different location. Had we used simple cell references, the formula would return incorrect results after expanding the years.

FIGURE 30.24

After expanding the PivotTable, formulas that use the `GETPIVOTDATA` function continue to display the correct result.

Row Labels	Sum of Income	Sum of Expenses		Ratio
⊟ 2017	1,256,274	525,288		41.81%
Jan	98,085	42,874		39.34%
Feb	98,698	44,167		40.80%
Mar	102,403	43,349		40.63%
Apr	106,044	43,102		
May	105,361	45,005		
Jun	105,729	44,216		
Jul	105,557	43,835		
Aug	109,669	41,952		
Sep	107,233	44,071		
Oct	105,048	43,185		
Nov	107,446	44,403		
Dec	105,001	45,129		
⊟ 2018	1,357,068	533,893		
Jan	109,699	46,245		

Creating PivotCharts

A PivotChart is a graphical representation of a data summary displayed in a PivotTable. If you're familiar with creating charts in Excel, you'll have no problem creating and customizing PivotCharts. All Excel charting features are available in a PivotChart.

 See Chapter 20, "Getting Started with Excel Charts," and Chapter 21, "Advanced Charting Techniques," to learn more about charting in Excel.

Excel provides several ways to create a PivotChart:

- Select any cell in an existing PivotTable and then choose PivotTable Tools Analyze ⇨ Tools ⇨ PivotChart.
- Select any cell in an existing PivotTable and then choose Insert ⇨ Charts ⇨ PivotChart.
- Choose Insert ⇨ Charts ⇨ PivotChart ⇨ PivotChart. If the active cell is not within a PivotTable, Excel prompts you for the data source and creates a PivotChart.
- Choose Insert ⇨ Charts ⇨ PivotChart ⇨ PivotChart & PivotTable. Excel prompts you for the data source and creates a PivotTable and a PivotChart. This command is available only when the active cell is not within a PivotTable.

A PivotChart example

Figure 30.25 shows part of a table that tracks daily sales by region. The Date field contains dates for the entire year (excluding weekends), the Region field contains the region name (Eastern, Southern, or Western), and the Sales field contains the sales amount.

 This workbook, named `sales by region pivot chart.xlsx`, is available on this book's website at `www.wiley.com/go/excel2019bible`.

30

FIGURE 30.25

This data will be used to create a PivotChart.

	A	B	C	D
1	Date	Region	Sales	
2	1/1/2019	Eastern	10,909	
3	1/2/2019	Eastern	11,126	
4	1/5/2019	Eastern	11,224	
5	1/6/2019	Eastern	11,299	
6	1/7/2019	Eastern	11,265	
7	1/8/2019	Eastern	11,328	
8	1/9/2019	Eastern	11,494	
9	1/12/2019	Eastern	11,328	
10	1/13/2019	Eastern	11,598	
11	1/14/2019	Eastern	11,868	
12	1/15/2019	Eastern	11,702	
13	1/16/2019	Eastern	11,846	
14	1/19/2019	Eastern	11,898	
15	1/20/2019	Eastern	11,871	
16	1/21/2019	Eastern	12,053	
17	1/22/2019	Eastern	12,073	
18	1/23/2019	Eastern	12,153	
19	1/26/2019	Eastern	12,226	
20	1/27/2019	Eastern	12,413	

Figure 30.26 shows a PivotTable created from this data. The Date field is in the Rows area, and the daily dates have been grouped into months. The Region field is in the Columns area. The Sales field is in the Values area.

FIGURE 30.26

This PivotTable summarizes sales by region and by month.

	A	B	C	D
3	Sum of Sales	Column Label		
4	Row Labels	Eastern	Southern	Western
5	Jan	259,416	170,991	100,708
6	Feb	255,487	134,812	99,740
7	Mar	284,294	140,918	103,848
8	Apr	273,772	144,346	124,772
9	May	268,057	119,220	131,716
10	Jun	282,089	122,156	133,071
11	Jul	289,019	120,989	162,555
12	Aug	258,844	97,790	162,644
13	Sep	264,537	106,315	193,012
14	Oct	273,592	104,383	213,761
15	Nov	279,259	93,118	223,203
16	Dec	309,802	104,962	260,102
17	Grand Total	3,298,168	1,460,000	1,909,132

The PivotTable is certainly easier to interpret than the raw data, but the trends would be easier to spot in a chart.

To create a PivotChart, select any cell in the PivotTable and choose PivotTable Tools Analyze ⇨ Tools ⇨ PivotChart. The Insert Chart dialog box appears, from which you can choose a chart type. For this example, select a Line chart and then click OK. Excel creates the PivotChart shown in Figure 30.27. The chart makes it easy to see an upward sales trend for the Western division, a downward trend for the Southern division, and relatively flat sales for the Eastern division.

FIGURE 30.27

The PivotChart uses the data displayed in the PivotTable.

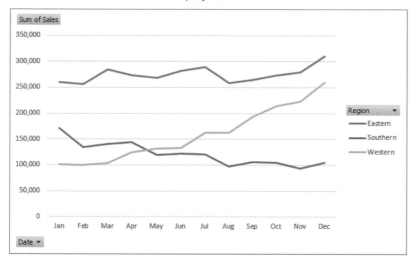

A PivotChart includes field buttons that let you filter the chart's data. To remove some or all of the field buttons, select the PivotChart and use the Field Buttons control in the PivotChart Tools Analyze ⇨ Show/Hide group.

When you select a PivotChart, the Ribbon displays a new contextual tab: PivotChart Tools. The commands in the Design and Format tabs are virtually identical to those for a standard Excel chart, so you can manipulate the PivotChart any way you like. The Analyze tab contains selected commands from the PivotTable Tools Analyze tab, such as Refresh and Insert Slicer.

If you modify the underlying PivotTable, the chart adjusts automatically to display the new summary data. Figure 30.28 shows the PivotChart after the Date grouping is changed to quarters.

30

FIGURE 30.28

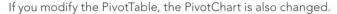

If you modify the PivotTable, the PivotChart is also changed.

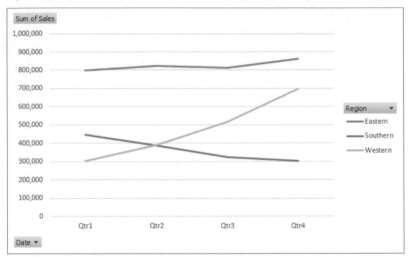

More about PivotCharts

Keep in mind these points when using PivotCharts:

- **A PivotTable and a PivotChart are joined in a two-way link.** If you make structural or filtering changes to one, the other is also changed.
- **When you activate a PivotChart, the PivotTable Fields task pane changes to the PivotChart Fields task pane.** In this task pane, Legend (Series) replaces the Columns area, and Axis (Category) replaces the Rows area.
- **The field buttons in a PivotChart contain the same controls as the PivotChart's field headers.** These controls allow you to filter the data that's displayed in the PivotTable and PivotChart. If you make changes to the PivotChart using these buttons, those changes are also reflected in the PivotTable.
- **If you have a PivotChart linked to a PivotTable and you delete the underlying PivotTable, the PivotChart remains.** The PivotChart's Series formulas contain the original data, stored in arrays.
- **By default, PivotCharts are embedded in the sheet that contains the PivotTable.** To move the PivotChart to a different worksheet (or to a Chart sheet), choose PivotChart Tools Analyze ➪ Actions ➪ Move Chart.
- **You can create multiple PivotCharts from a PivotTable, and you can manipulate and format the charts separately.** However, all of the charts display the same data.
- **A normal chart, when selected, displays the icons to the right: Chart Elements, Chart Styles, and Chart Filters.** A PivotChart does not display the Chart Filters icon.

- **Slicers and timelines also work with PivotCharts.** See the examples earlier in this chapter.
- **Don't forget about themes.** You can choose Page Layout ⇨ Themes ⇨ Themes to change the workbook theme, and your PivotTable and PivotChart will both reflect the new theme.

Using the Data Model

So far, this chapter has focused exclusively on PivotTables that are created from a single table of data. A feature called the *data model* brings significantly more power to PivotTables. With the data model, you can use multiple tables of data in a single PivotTable. You'll need to create one or more "table relationships" so that the data can be tied together.

A workbook can have only one data model. Any data model set up in a particular workbook applies to all PivotTables that use the data model. You can't have one model for one PivotTable and another model for another PivotTable within the same workbook.

> **NOTE**
> The data model was introduced in Excel 2013, so workbooks that use this feature are not compatible with previous versions.

 Part V, "Understanding Power Pivot and Power Query," contains more information on the data model.

Figure 30.29 shows parts of three tables that are in a single workbook. (Each table is in its own worksheet and is shown in a separate window.) The tables are named Orders, Customers, and Regions. The Orders table contains information about product orders. The Customers table contains information about the company's customers. The Regions table contains a region identifier for each state.

Notice that the Orders and Customers tables have a CustomerID column in common, and the Customers and Regions tables have a State column in common. The common columns will be used to form relationships among the tables.

These relationships are "one-to-many." For every row in the Orders table, there is exactly one corresponding row in the Customers table, and that row is determined by the CustomerID column. For any row in the Customers table, there can be many rows in the Orders table. The Orders table is the many, and the Customers table is the one in the one-to-many relationship. Similarly, for every row in the Customers table, there is exactly one corresponding row in the Regions table, and that row is determined by the State column. And for any row in Regions, there can be many matching rows in Customers.

30

FIGURE 30.29

These three tables will be used for a PivotTable, using the data model.

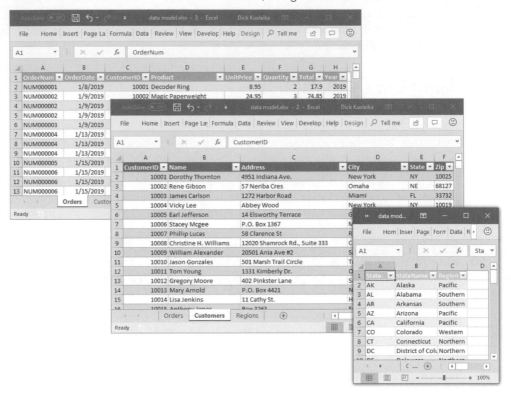

 The example in this section is available on this book's website at `www.wiley.com/go/excel 2019bible`. You can use the workbook named `data model.xlsx` to follow along with the example. The workbook named `data model complete.xlsx` shows the final PivotTable.

> **NOTE**
> A PivotTable created using the data model has some restrictions, as opposed to a PivotTable created from a single table. Most notably, you can't group items or create calculated fields or calculated items.

For this example, the goal is to summarize sales by state, by region, and by year. Notice that the sales and date information is in the Orders table, the state information is in the Customers table, and the region names are in the Regions table. Therefore, all three tables will be used to generate this PivotTable.

Start by creating a PivotTable (in a new worksheet) from the Orders table. Follow these steps:

1. **Select any cell within the Orders table and choose Insert ➪ Tables ➪ PivotTable.** The Create PivotTable dialog box appears.

2. **Select the Add This Data to the Data Model check box and click OK.** Notice that the PivotTable Fields task pane is a bit different when you're working with the data model. The task pane contains two tabs: Active and All. The Active tab lists only the Orders table. The All tab lists all of the tables in the workbook.

   Figure 30.30 shows the All tab of the PivotTable Fields task pane, with all three tables expanded to show their column headers. To change the layout of the task pane, click the drop-down Tools control and choose Fields Section and Areas Section Side-by-Side.

FIGURE 30.30

The PivotTable Fields task pane for a data model

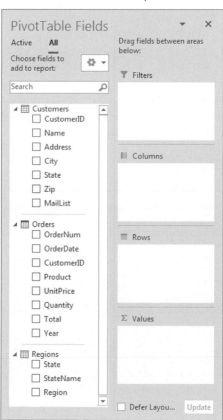

The icon next to the Orders table is slightly different than the icons for the other two tables (see Figure 30.30). You made the Orders table part of the data model when you checked the box creating the PivotTable. The other two tables are not currently part of the data model.

3. **Choose Data ⇨ Data Tools ⇨ Relationships and click the New button.** This shows the Manage Relationships dialog box. It's empty because we haven't set up our relationships yet. Figure 30.31 shows the Create Relationships dialog box that appears when you click the New button.

FIGURE 30.31

The Create Relationships dialog box

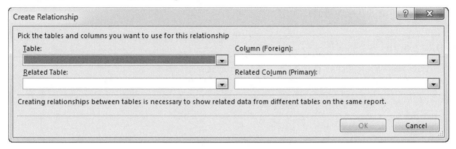

4. **Relate the Orders table to the Customers table.** Select Data Model Table: Orders and CustomerID in the top section and Worksheet Table: Customers and CustomerID in the bottom section. Compare your Create Relationship dialog box to Figure 30.32 and click OK.

FIGURE 30.32

Relating the Orders table to the Customers table

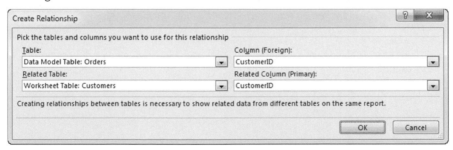

5. **Relate the Customers table to the Regions table.** Click the New button in the Manage Relationships dialog box and create a relationship similar to how you did it in the previous step (see Figure 30.33). Notice how the Customers table is now identified as being part of the data model. When you created the relationship in the previous step, you added the Customers table to the data model.

FIGURE 30.33

Relating the Customers and Regions tables by state

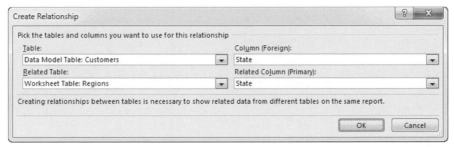

6. **Build the PivotTable.** After you've closed the Manage Relationships dialog box, you're ready to build the PivotTable. Move the Region and StateName fields to the Rows area, move the Year field to the Columns area, and move the Total field to the Values area. Figure 30.34 shows the PivotTable after this step. (Some of the data in Figure 30.34 was collapsed so that more of the PivotTable can be seen.)

The PivotTable based on three tables is complete. All that remains is some formatting. You can format your PivotTable to suit your taste. To make your PivotTable look like the one in data model complete.xlsx, follow this steps:

1. **Add the slicers.** Choose PivotTable Tools Analyze ➪ Filter ➪ Insert Slicer, select the All tab, and select Product and MailList.

2. **Format the slicers.** Right-click the MailList slicer and choose Size and Properties. In the Position and Layout section of the Format Slicer pane, change the Number of Columns property to 2.

3. **Format the values.** Right-click any value in the PivotTable and choose Number Format. Choose Number, set Decimal Places to 2, and select the Use 1000 Separator check box.

4. **Add region subtotals.** Right-click any Region item (such as Central) and choose Field Settings. On the Subtotals and Filters tab, choose Automatic.

30

FIGURE 30.34

A PivotTable based on the data model

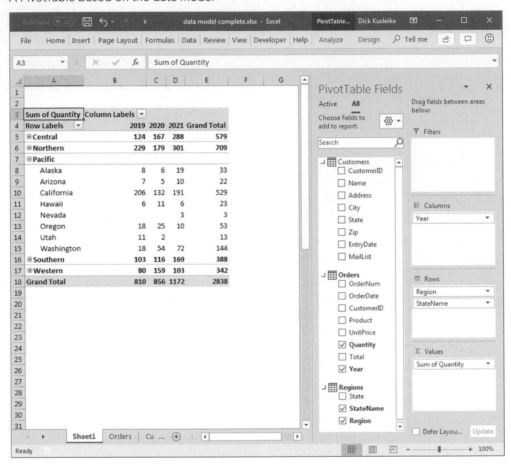

5. **Add a blank line between regions.** On the Layout & Print tab of the Field Settings dialog box, check the Insert Blank Line after Each Item Label check box.

Figure 30.35 shows the final, formatted PivotTable.

FIGURE 30.35

Formatting applied to the data model PivotTable

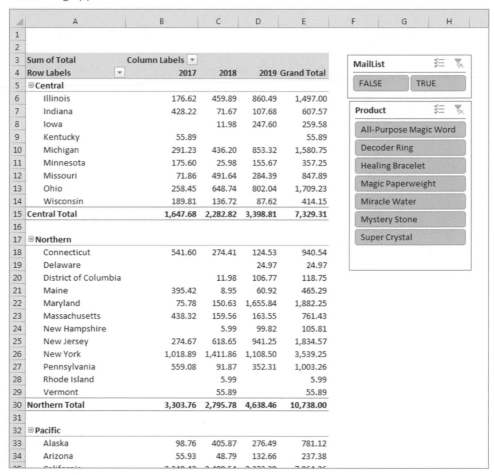

Performing Spreadsheet What-If Analysis

One of the most appealing aspects of Excel is its ability to create dynamic models. A dynamic model uses formulas that instantly recalculate when you change values in cells that are used by the formulas. When you change values in cells in a systematic manner and observe the effects on specific formula cells, you're performing a type of what-if analysis.

What-if analysis is the process of asking such questions as "What happens if the interest rate on the loan changes to 7.5 percent?" and "What occurs if we raise our product prices by 5 percent?"

If you set up your worksheet properly, answering such questions is simply a matter of plugging in new values and observing the results of the recalculation. Excel provides useful tools to assist you in your what-if endeavors.

Looking at a What-If Example

Figure 31.1 shows a simple worksheet model that calculates information pertaining to a mortgage loan. The worksheet is divided into two sections: the input cells and the result cells (which contain formulas).

FIGURE 31.1

This simple worksheet model uses four input cells to produce the results.

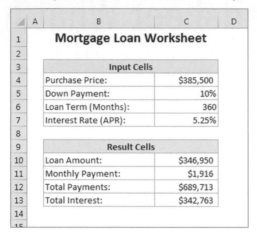

 This workbook is available on this book's website at www.wiley.com/go/excel2019bible. The filename is mortgage loan.xlsx.

With this worksheet, you can easily answer the following what-if questions:

- What if I can negotiate a lower purchase price on the property?
- What if the lender requires a 20 percent down payment?
- What if I can get a 40-year mortgage?
- What if the interest rate increases to 5.50 percent?

You can answer these questions by simply changing the values in the cells in range C4:C7 and observing the effects in the dependent cells (C10:C13). You can, of course, vary any number of input cells simultaneously.

Avoid Hard-Coding Values in a Formula

The mortgage calculation example, simple as it is, demonstrates an important point about spreadsheet design: You should always set up your worksheet so that you have maximum flexibility to make changes. Perhaps the most fundamental rule of spreadsheet design is the following:

Do not hard-code values in a formula. Instead, store the values in separate cells and use cell references in the formula.

The term *hard-code* refers to the use of actual values, or constants, in a formula. In the mortgage loan example, all of the formulas use references to cells, not actual values.

You could use the value 360, for example, for the loan term argument of the PMT function in cell C11 of Figure 31.1. Using a cell reference has two advantages. First, you'll have no doubt about the values that the formula uses. (They aren't buried in the formula.) Second, you can easily change the value—typing a new value in the cell is easier than editing the formula.

Using values in formulas may not seem like much of an issue when only one formula is involved, but just imagine what would happen if this value were hard-coded into several hundred formulas that were scattered throughout a worksheet.

Exploring Types of What-If Analyses

Not surprisingly, Excel can handle much more sophisticated models than the preceding example. To perform a what-if analysis using Excel, you have three basic options:

Manual what-if analysis   Plug in new values and observe the effects on formula cells.

Data tables   Create a special type of table that displays the results of selected formula cells as you systematically change one or two input cells.

Scenario Manager   Create named scenarios and generate reports that use outlines or PivotTables.

We discuss each of these types of what-if analysis in the rest of this chapter.

Performing manual what-if analysis

A manual what-if analysis doesn't require too much explanation. In fact, the example that opens this chapter demonstrates how it's done. Manual what-if analysis is based on the idea that you have one or more input cells that affect one or more key formula cells. You change the value in the input cells and observe the formula calculations. You may want to print the results or save each scenario to a new workbook. The term *scenario* refers to a specific set of values in one or more input cells.

Manual what-if analysis is common. People often use this technique without even realizing that they're doing a what-if analysis. This method of performing what-if analysis certainly has nothing wrong with it, but you should be aware of some other techniques.

 If your input cells are not located near the formula cells, consider using a Watch Window to monitor the formula results in a movable window. We discuss this feature in Chapter 3, "Performing Basic Worksheet Operations."

Creating data tables

This section describes one of Excel's most underutilized features: data tables. A *data table* is a dynamic range that summarizes formula cells for varying input cells. You can create a data table fairly easily, but data tables have some limitations. In particular, a data table can deal with only one or two input cells at a time. This limitation becomes clear as you view the examples.

> **NOTE**
>
> Scenario Manager, discussed later in this chapter (see "Using Scenario Manager"), can produce a report that summarizes any number of input cells and result cells.

Don't confuse a data table with a standard table (created by choosing Insert ➪ Tables ➪ Table). These two features are completely independent.

Creating a one-input data table

A one-input data table displays the results of one or more formulas for various values of a single input cell. Figure 31.2 shows the general layout for a one-input data table. You need to set up the table manually yourself. This is not something that Excel will do for you.

FIGURE 31.2

How a one-input data table is set up

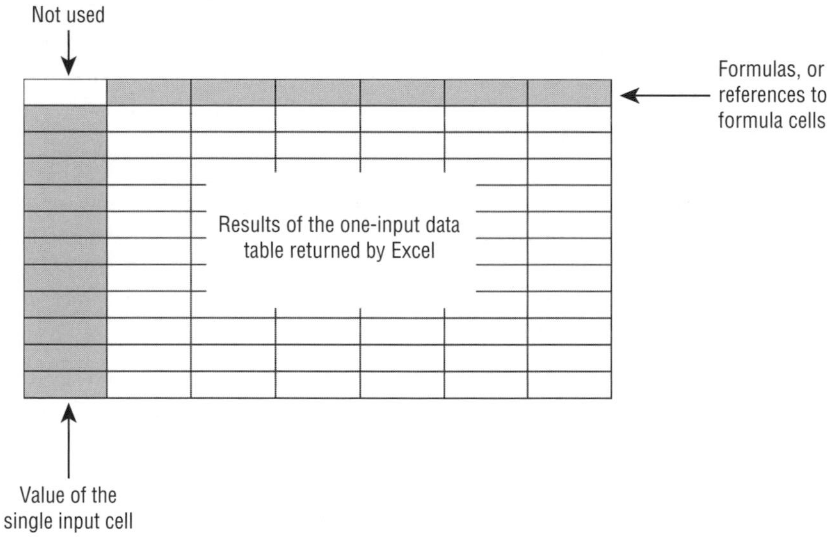

You can place the data table anywhere in a worksheet. The left column contains various values for the single input cell. The top row contains references to formulas located elsewhere in the worksheet. You can use a single formula reference or any number of formula references. The upper-left cell of the table remains empty. Excel calculates the values that result from each value of the input cell and places them under each formula reference.

This example uses the mortgage loan worksheet from earlier in the chapter (see "Looking at a What-If Example"). The goal of this exercise is to create a data table that shows the values of the four formula cells (loan amount, monthly payment, total payments, and total interest) for various interest rates ranging from 4.5% to 6.5%, in 0.25% increments.

This workbook is available on this book's website at www.wiley.com/go/excel2019bible. The file is named mortgage loan data table.xlsx.

Figure 31.3 shows the setup for the data table area. Row 3 consists of references to the formulas in the worksheet. For example, cell F3 contains the formula =C10, and cell G3 contains the formula =C11. Row 2 and column D contain optional descriptive labels that are not actually part of the data table. Column E contains the values of the single input cell (interest rate) that Excel will use in the table.

FIGURE 31.3

Preparing to create a one-input data table

	A	B	C	D	E	F	G	H	I	J
1		Mortgage Loan Worksheet								
2						Loan Amt	Mo Pmt	Total Pmts	Total Int	
3		Input Cells				$346,950	$1,916	$689,713	$342,763	
4		Purchase Price:	$385,500		4.50%					
5		Down Payment:	10%		4.75%					
6		Loan Term:	360		5.00%					
7		Interest Rate (Months):	5.25%		5.25%					
8					5.50%					
9		Result Cells			5.75%					
10		Loan Amount:	$346,950		6.00%					
11		Monthly Payment:	$1,916		6.25%					
12		Total Payments:	$689,713		6.50%					
13		Total Interest:	$342,763							
14										
15										

To create the table, select the entire data table range (in this case, E3:I12) and then choose Data ⇨ Forecast ⇨ What-If Analysis ⇨ Data Table. The Data Table dialog box, shown in Figure 31.4, appears.

You must specify the worksheet cell that contains the input value. Because variables for the input cell appear in the left column in the data table, you place this cell reference in the Column Input Cell field. Enter **C7** or point to the cell in the worksheet. Leave the Row Input Cell field blank. Click OK, and Excel fills in the table with the calculated results (see Figure 31.5).

FIGURE 31.4

The Data Table dialog box

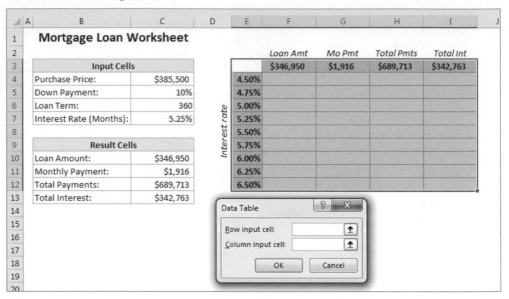

FIGURE 31.5

The result of the one-input data table

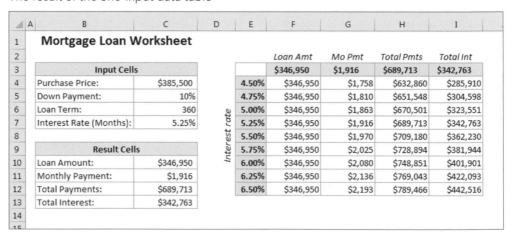

31

CAUTION

Using the Data Table command wipes out Excel's undo stack. Operations that you perform prior to using this command cannot be undone.

Using this table, you can now see the calculated loan values for varying interest rates. Notice that the Loan Amt column (column F) doesn't vary. That's because the formula in cell C10 doesn't depend on the interest rate.

If you examine the contents of the cells that Excel entered as a result of this command, you'll see that the data is generated with a multicell array formula:

```
{=TABLE(,C7)}
```

A multicell array formula is a single formula that can produce results in multiple cells (see Chapter 18, "Understanding and Using Array Formulas"). Because the table uses formulas, Excel updates the table that you produce if you change the cell references in the first row or plug in different interest rates in the first column.

NOTE

You can arrange a one-input table vertically (as in this example) or horizontally. If you place the values of the input cell in a row, you enter the input cell reference in the Row Input Cell field of the Data Table dialog box.

Creating a two-input data table

As the name implies, a two-input data table lets you vary two input cells. You can see the setup for this type of table in Figure 31.6. Although it looks similar to a one-input table, the two-input table has one critical difference: it can show the results of only one formula at a time. With a one-input table, you can place any number of formulas, or references to formulas, across the top row of the table. In a two-input table, this top row holds the values for the second input cell. The upper-left cell of the table contains a reference to the single result formula.

Using the mortgage loan worksheet, you could create a two-input data table that shows the results of a formula (say, monthly payment) for various combinations of two input cells (such as interest rate and down-payment percent). To see the effects on other formulas, you simply create multiple data tables—one for each formula cell that you want to summarize.

The example in this section uses the worksheet shown in Figure 31.7 to demonstrate a two-input data table. In this example, a company wants to conduct a direct-mail promotion to sell its product. The worksheet calculates the net profit from the promotion.

FIGURE 31.6

The setup for a two-input data table

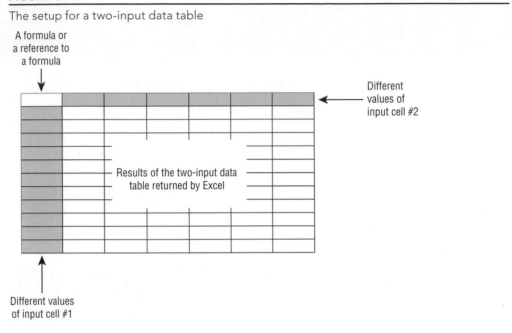

A formula or
a reference to
a formula

Different
values of
input cell #2

Results of the two-input data
table returned by Excel

Different values
of input cell #1

FIGURE 31.7

This worksheet calculates the net profit from a direct-mail promotion.

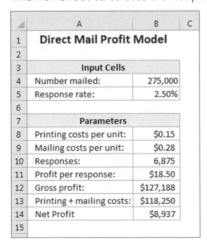

	A	B	C
1	**Direct Mail Profit Model**		
2			
3	**Input Cells**		
4	Number mailed:	275,000	
5	Response rate:	2.50%	
6			
7	**Parameters**		
8	Printing costs per unit:	$0.15	
9	Mailing costs per unit:	$0.28	
10	Responses:	6,875	
11	Profit per response:	$18.50	
12	Gross profit:	$127,188	
13	Printing + mailing costs:	$118,250	
14	Net Profit	$8,937	
15			

This workbook, named `direct mail data table.xlsx`, **is on this book's website at** `www.wiley.com/go/excel2019bible`.

This model uses two input cells: the number of promotional pieces mailed and the antici-pated response rate. The following items appear in the Parameters area:

Printing costs per unit The cost to print a single mailer. The unit cost varies with the quantity: $0.20 each for quantities less than 200,000; $0.15 each for quantities of 200,001 through 300,000; and $0.10 each for quantities of more than 300,000. The following formula is used:

```
=IF(B4<200000,0.2,IF(B4<300000,0.15,0.1))
```

Mailing costs per unit A fixed cost, $0.28 per unit mailed.

Responses The number of responses, calculated from the response rate and the number mailed. The formula in this cell is as follows:

```
=B4*B5
```

Profit per response A fixed value. The company knows that it will realize an average profit of $18.50 per order.

Gross profit This is a simple formula that multiplies the profit-per-response by the num-ber of responses:

```
=B10*B11
```

Print + mailing costs This formula calculates the total cost of the promotion:

```
=B4*(B8+B9)
```

Net Profit This formula calculates the bottom line—the gross profit minus the printing and mailing costs.

If you enter values for the two input cells, you see that the net profit varies quite a bit, often going negative to produce a net loss.

Figure 31.8 shows the setup of a two-input data table that summarizes the net profit at various combinations of quantity and response rate; the table appears in the range E4:M14. Cell E4 contains a formula that references the Net Profit cell:

```
=B14
```

To create the data table, follow these steps:

1. **Enter the response rate values in F4:M4.**
2. **Enter the number mailed values in E5:E14.**
3. **Select the range E4:M14, and choose Data ⇨ Forecast ⇨ What-If Analysis ⇨ Data Table.** The Data Table dialog box appears.

FIGURE 31.8

Preparing to create a two-input data table

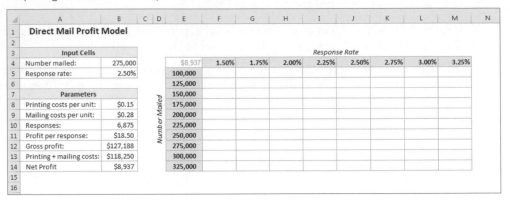

4. **Specify B5 as the Row input cell (the response rate) and B4 as the Column input (the number mailed).**

5. **Click OK.** Excel fills in the data table.

Figure 31.9 shows the result. As you can see, quite a few of the combinations of response rate and quantity mailed result in a loss rather than a profit.

FIGURE 31.9

The result of the two-input data table

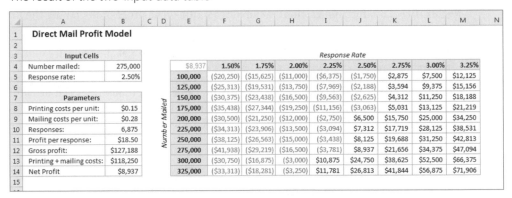

As with the one-input data table, this data table is dynamic. You can change the formula in cell E4 to refer to another cell (such as gross profit), or you can enter some different values for Response Rate and Number Mailed.

Using Scenario Manager

Data tables are useful, but they have a few limitations:

- You can vary only one or two input cells at a time.
- Setting up a data table is not intuitive.
- A two-input table shows the results of only one formula cell (although you can create additional tables for more formulas).
- In many situations, you're interested in a few select combinations, not an entire table that shows all possible combinations of two input cells.

The Scenario Manager is a fairly easy way to automate some aspects of your what-if models. You can store different sets of input values (called *changing cells* in the terminology of Scenario Manager) for any number of variables and give a name to each set. You can then select a set of values by name, and Excel displays the worksheet by using those values. You can also generate a summary report that shows the effect of various combinations of values on any number of result cells. These summary reports can be an outline or a PivotTable.

For example, your annual sales forecast may depend on several factors. Consequently, you can define three scenarios: best case, worst case, and most likely case. You then can switch to any of these scenarios by selecting the named scenario from a list. Excel substitutes the appropriate input values in your worksheet and recalculates the formulas.

Defining scenarios

To introduce you to Scenario Manager, this section starts with an example that uses a simplified production model, as shown in Figure 31.10.

FIGURE 31.10

A simple production model to demonstrate Scenario Manager

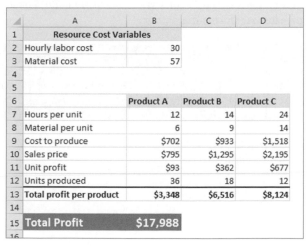

	A	B	C	D
1	**Resource Cost Variables**			
2	Hourly labor cost	30		
3	Material cost	57		
4				
5				
6		**Product A**	**Product B**	**Product C**
7	Hours per unit	12	14	24
8	Material per unit	6	9	14
9	Cost to produce	$702	$933	$1,518
10	Sales price	$795	$1,295	$2,195
11	Unit profit	$93	$362	$677
12	Units produced	36	18	12
13	**Total profit per product**	**$3,348**	**$6,516**	**$8,124**
14				
15	**Total Profit**	**$17,988**		
16				

This workbook, named `production model scenarios.xlsx`, **is available on this book's website at** `www.wiley.com/go/excel2019bible`.

This worksheet contains two input cells: the hourly labor cost (cell B2) and the unit cost for materials (cell B3). The company produces three products, and each product requires a different number of hours and a different amount of materials to produce.

Formulas calculate the total profit per product (row 13) and the total combined profit (cell B15). Management—trying to predict the total profit but uncertain what the hourly labor cost and material costs will be—has identified three scenarios, which are listed in Table 31.1.

TABLE 31.1 Three Scenarios for the Production Model

Scenario	Hourly Cost	Materials Cost
Best Case	30	57
Worst Case	38	62
Most Likely	34	59

The Best Case scenario has the lowest hourly cost and the lowest materials cost. The Worst Case scenario has high values for both the hourly cost and the materials cost. The third scenario, Most Likely, has intermediate values for both of these input cells. The managers need to be prepared for the worst case, however, and they're interested in what would happen under the Best Case scenario.

Choose Data ⇨ Forecast ⇨ What-If Analysis ⇨ Scenario Manager to display the Scenario Manager dialog box. When you first open this dialog box, it tells you that no scenarios are defined, which is not too surprising because you're just starting. As you add named scenarios, they appear in the Scenarios list in this dialog box.

TIP

It's a good idea to create names for the changing cells and all of the result cells that you want to examine. Excel uses these names in the dialog boxes and in the reports that it generates. If you use names, keeping track of what's going on is much easier; names also make your reports more readable.

To add a scenario, click the Add button in the Scenario Manager dialog box. Excel displays its Add Scenario dialog box, shown in Figure 31.11.

FIGURE 31.11

Use the Add Scenario dialog box to create a named scenario.

This dialog box consists of four parts:

Scenario Name   You can give the scenario any name you like.

Changing Cells   These are the input cells for the scenario. You can enter the cell addresses directly or point to them. If you've created a name for the cells, type the name. Nonadjacent cells are allowed; if pointing to multiple cells, press Ctrl while you click the cells. Each named scenario can use the same set of changing cells or different changing cells. The number of changing cells for a scenario is limited to 32.

Comment   By default, Excel displays the name of the person who created the scenario and the date it was created. You can change this text, add new text to it, or delete it. If you name the scenario well, you may not need much of a comment. However, some scenarios are so complex that more information will be useful both to you and to others who use your workbook.

Protection   The two Protection options (preventing changes and hiding a scenario) are in effect only when you protect the worksheet and choose the Scenario option in the Protect Sheet dialog box. Protecting a scenario prevents anyone from modifying it; a hidden scenario doesn't appear in the Scenario Manager dialog box.

In this example, define the three scenarios that are listed in Table 31.1. The changing cells are Hourly cost (B2) and Materials cost (B3).

After you enter the information in the Add Scenario dialog box, click OK. Excel then displays the Scenario Values dialog box, shown in Figure 31.12. This dialog box displays one field for each changing cell that you specified in the previous dialog box. Enter the values for each cell in the scenario. If you click OK, you return to the Scenario Manager dialog box, which then displays your named scenario in its list. If you have more scenarios to create, click the Add button to return to the Add Scenario dialog box.

FIGURE 31.12

You enter the values for the scenario in the Scenario Values dialog box.

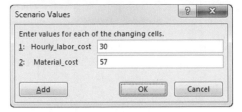

Displaying scenarios

After you define all the scenarios and return to the Scenario Manager dialog box, the dialog box displays the names of your defined scenarios. Select one of the scenarios and then click the Show button (or double-click the Scenario name). Excel inserts the corresponding values into the changing cells and calculates the worksheet to show the results for that scenario. Figure 31.13 shows an example of selecting a scenario.

FIGURE 31.13

Selecting a scenario to display

Using the Scenarios Drop-Down List

The Scenarios drop-down list shows all the defined scenarios and enables you to display a scenario quickly. Oddly, this useful tool doesn't appear on the Ribbon. But if you use Scenario Manager, you can add the Scenarios control to your Quick Access toolbar. Here's how to do it:

1. **Right-click the Quick Access toolbar, and choose Customize Quick Access Toolbar from the shortcut menu.** The Excel Options dialog box appears with the Quick Access Toolbar tab selected.
2. **From the Choose Commands From drop-down list, select Commands Not in the Ribbon.**
3. **Scroll down the list and select Scenario.**
4. **Click the Add button.**
5. **Click OK to close the Excel Options dialog box.**

Alternatively, you can add the Scenarios control to the Ribbon. See Chapter 8, "Customizing the Excel User Interface," for additional details on customizing the Quick Access toolbar and the Ribbon.

Modifying scenarios

After you've created scenarios, you may need to change them. To do so, follow these steps:

1. **Click the Edit button in the Scenario Manager dialog box to change one or more of the values for the changing cells of a scenario.**
2. **From the Scenarios list, select the scenario that you want to change and then click the Edit button.** The Edit Scenario dialog box appears.
3. **Click OK.** The Scenario Values dialog box appears.
4. **Make your changes and then click OK to return to the Scenario Manager dialog box.** Notice that Excel automatically updates the Comments box with new text that indicates when the scenario was modified.

Merging scenarios

In workgroup situations, you may have several people working on a spreadsheet model, and several people may have defined various scenarios. The marketing department, for example, may have its opinion of what the input cells should be, the finance department may have another opinion, and your CEO may have yet another opinion.

Excel makes it easy to merge these various scenarios into a single workbook. Before you merge scenarios, make sure that the workbook from which you're merging is open:

1. **Click the Merge button in the Scenario Manager dialog box.**
2. **From the Merge Scenarios dialog box that appears, choose the workbook that contains the scenarios you're merging in the Book drop-down list.**

3. **Choose the sheet that contains the scenarios you want to merge from the Sheet list box and click Add.** Notice that the dialog box displays the number of scenarios in each sheet as you scroll through the Sheet list box.

4. **Click OK.** You return to the previous dialog box, which now displays the scenario names that you merged from the other workbook.

Generating a scenario report

If you've created multiple scenarios, you may want to document your work by creating a scenario summary report. When you click the Summary button in the Scenario Manager dialog box, Excel displays the Scenario Summary dialog box.

You have a choice of report types:

Scenario Summary   The summary report appears in the form of a worksheet outline.

Scenario PivotTable   The summary report appears in the form of a PivotTable.

 See Chapter 27, "Creating and Using Worksheet Outlines," for more information about outlines, and see Chapter 29, "Introducing PivotTables," for an introduction to PivotTables.

For simple cases of scenario management, a standard Scenario Summary report is usually sufficient. If you have many scenarios defined with multiple result cells, however, you may find that a Scenario PivotTable provides more flexibility.

The Scenario Summary dialog box also asks you to specify the result cells (the cells that contain the formulas in which you're interested). For this example, select B13:D13 and B15 (a multiple selection) to make the report show the profit for each product plus the total profit.

> **NOTE**
>
> As you work with Scenario Manager, you may discover its main limitation, namely, that a scenario can use no more than 32 changing cells. If you attempt to use more cells, you get an error message.

Excel creates a new worksheet to store the summary table. Figure 31.14 shows the Scenario Summary form of the report. If you gave names to the changing cells and result cells, the table uses these names; otherwise, it lists the cell references.

FIGURE 31.14

A Scenario Summary report produced by Scenario Manager

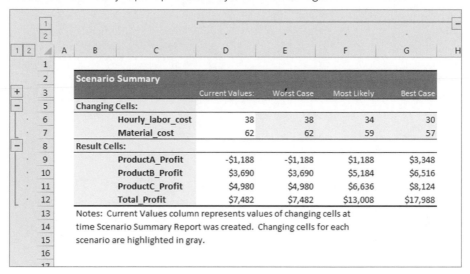

Scenario Summary		Current Values:	Worst Case	Most Likely	Best Case
Changing Cells:					
	Hourly_labor_cost	38	38	34	30
	Material_cost	62	62	59	57
Result Cells:					
	ProductA_Profit	-$1,188	-$1,188	$1,188	$3,348
	ProductB_Profit	$3,690	$3,690	$5,184	$6,516
	ProductC_Profit	$4,980	$4,980	$6,636	$8,124
	Total_Profit	$7,482	$7,482	$13,008	$17,988

Notes: Current Values column represents values of changing cells at
time Scenario Summary Report was created. Changing cells for each
scenario are highlighted in gray.

Analyzing Data Using Goal Seeking and Solver

The preceding chapter discussed what-if analysis—the process of changing input cells to observe the results on other dependent cells. This chapter looks at that process from the opposite perspective: finding the value of one or more input cells that produce a desired result in a formula cell.

Exploring What-If Analysis, in Reverse

Consider the following what-if question: "What is the total profit if sales increase by 20 percent?" If you set up your worksheet model properly, you can change the value in one or more cells to see what happens to the profit cell. The examples in this chapter take the opposite approach. If you know what a formula result should be, Excel can tell you the values that you need to enter in one or more input cells to produce that result. In other words, you can ask a question such as "How much do sales need to increase to produce a profit of $1.2 million?" Excel provides two tools to accomplish this:

Goal Seek Determines the value that you need to enter in a single input cell to produce a result that you want in a dependent (formula) cell.

Solver Determines the values that you need to enter in multiple input cells to produce a result that you want. Moreover, because you can specify additional constraints to the problem, you gain significant problem-solving ability.

Using Single-Cell Goal Seeking

Single-cell goal seeking is a rather simple concept. Excel determines what value in an input cell produces a desired result in a formula cell. The following example shows you how single-cell goal seeking works.

Looking at a goal-seeking example

Figure 32.1 shows the mortgage loan worksheet used in the preceding chapter. This worksheet has four input cells (C4:C7) and four formula cells (C10:C13). Originally, this worksheet was used for a what-if analysis example. This example demonstrates the opposite approach. Rather than supply different input cell values to look at the calculated formulas, this example lets Excel determine one of the input values that will produce the desired result.

FIGURE 32.1

A mortgage calculator with input cells and formula cells

	A	B	C	D
1		Mortgage Loan Worksheet		
2				
3		**Input Cells**		
4		Purchase Price:	$409,000	
5		Down Payment:	20%	
6		Loan Term (Months):	360	
7		Interest Rate (APR):	6.50%	
8				
9		**Result Cells**		
10		Loan Amount:	$327,200	
11		Monthly Payment:	$2,068	
12		Total Payments:	$744,526	
13		Total Interest:	$417,326	
14				
15				

 This workbook is available on this book's website at www.wiley.com/go/excel2019bible. The file is named mortgage loan.xlsx.

Assume that you're in the market for a new home, and you know that you can afford a $1,800 monthly mortgage payment. You also know that a lender can issue a 30-year fixed-rate mortgage loan for 6.50%, based on a 20% down payment. The question is, "What is the maximum purchase price I can afford?" In other words, what value in cell C4 (purchase price) causes the formula in cell C11 (monthly payment) to result in $1,800? In this simple example, you could plug values into cell C4 until C11 displays $1,800. With more complex models, Excel can usually determine the answer much more efficiently.

To answer the question posed in the preceding paragraph, first set up the input cells to match what you already know. Specifically:

1. Enter **20%** into cell C5 (the down payment percent).
2. Enter **360** into cell C6 (the loan term, in months).
3. Enter **6.5%** into cell C7 (the annual interest rate).

Next, choose Data ⇨ Forecast ⇨ What-If Analysis ⇨ Goal Seek. The Goal Seek dialog box appears. Completing this dialog box is similar to forming a sentence. You want to set cell C11 to 1800 by changing cell C4. Enter this information in the dialog box either by typing the cell references or by pointing with the mouse (see Figure 32.2). Click OK to begin the goal-seeking process.

32

FIGURE 32.2

The Goal Seek dialog box

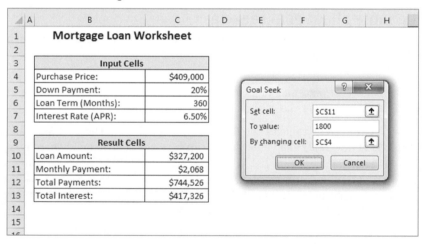

In less than a second, Excel displays the Goal Seek Status box, shown in Figure 32.3. This shows the target value and the value that Excel calculated. In this case, Excel found an exact value. The worksheet now displays the found value in cell C4 ($355,974). As a result of this value, the monthly payment amount is $1,800. At this point, you have two options:

- Click OK to replace the original value with the found value. After doing so, you can use Undo to return to the original value.
- Click Cancel to restore your worksheet to the form that it had before you chose Goal Seek.

FIGURE 32.3

Goal Seek has found a solution.

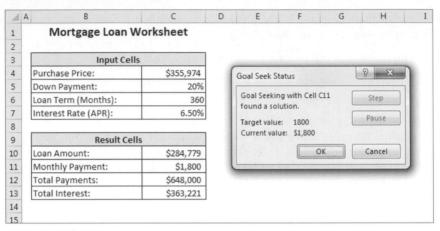

Learning more about goal seeking

Excel can't always find a value that produces the result that you're seeking. Sometimes a solution simply doesn't exist. In such a case, the Goal Seek Status box informs you of that fact.

At other times, however, Excel may report that it can't find a solution, but you're pretty sure that one exists. If that's the case, you can try the following options:

- Change the current value of the By Changing Cell field in the Goal Seek dialog box (refer to Figure 32.2) to a value that is closer to the solution and then reissue the command.

- Adjust the Maximum iterations setting on the Formulas tab of the Excel Options dialog box (choose File ➪ Options). Increasing the number of iterations (or calculations) makes Excel try more possible solutions.

- Double-check your logic and make sure that the formula cell does, indeed, depend on the specified changing cell.

> **NOTE**
>
> Like all computer programs, Excel has limited precision. To demonstrate this limitation, enter =A1^2 into cell A2. Then use the Goal Seek dialog box to find the value in cell A1 (which is empty) that makes the formula return 16. Excel comes up with a value of 4.00002269, which is close to the square root of 16 but certainly not exact. You can adjust the precision for goal seeking on the Formulas tab of the Excel Options dialog box. (Make the Maximum Change value smaller.)

> **NOTE**
>
> In some cases, multiple values of the input cell produce the same desired result. For example, the formula =A1^2 returns 16 if cell A1 contains either –4 or +4. If you use goal seeking when multiple solutions are possible, Excel gives you the solution that is closest to the current value.

Introducing Solver

The Excel Goal Seek feature is a useful tool, but it clearly has limitations. It can solve for only one adjustable cell, and it returns only a single solution. Excel's powerful Solver tool extends this concept by enabling you to do the following:

- Specify multiple adjustable cells.
- Specify constraints on the values that the adjustable cells can have.
- Generate a solution that maximizes or minimizes a particular worksheet cell.
- Generate multiple solutions to a problem.

Although goal seeking is a relatively simple operation, using Solver can be much more complicated. In fact, Solver is probably one of the most difficult (and potentially frustrating) features in Excel, and it isn't for everyone. In fact, most Excel users have no use for this feature. However, many users find that having this much power is worth spending the extra time to learn about it.

Looking at appropriate problems for Solver

Problems that are appropriate for Solver fall into a relatively narrow range. They typically involve situations that meet the following criteria:

- A target cell depends on other cells and formulas. Typically, you want to maximize or minimize this target cell or set it equal to some value.
- The target cell depends on a group of cells (called *changing cells*) that Solver can adjust to affect the target cell.
- The solution must adhere to certain limitations, or constraints.

After you set up your worksheet appropriately, you can use Solver to adjust the changing cells and produce the result that you want in your target cell, while simultaneously meeting all of the constraints that you defined.

No Solver Command?

You access Solver by choosing Data ⇨ Analyze ⇨ Solver. If this command isn't available, you need to install the Solver add-in. It's a simple process:

1. **Choose File ⇨ Options**. The Excel Options dialog box appears.

2. **Select the Add-Ins tab.**

3. **At the bottom of the dialog box, select Excel Add-Ins from the Manage drop-down list and then click Go.** The Add-Ins dialog box appears.

4. **Place a check mark next to Solver Add-In and then click OK.**

After you perform these steps, the Solver add-in loads whenever you start Excel.

Seeing a simple Solver example

We start with a simple example to introduce Solver and then present some increasingly complex examples to demonstrate what this feature can do.

Figure 32.4 shows a worksheet that is set up to calculate the profit for three products. Column B shows the number of units of each product, Column C shows the profit per unit for each product, and Column D contains formulas that calculate the total profit for each product by multiplying the units by the profit per unit.

FIGURE 32.4

Use Solver to determine the number of units to maximize the total profit.

	A	B	C	D	E
1					
2		Units	Profit/Unit	Profit	
3	Product A	25	$13	$325	
4	Product B	25	$18	$450	
5	Product C	25	$22	$550	
6	Total	75		$1,325	
7					

 This workbook, named three products.xlsx, is available on this book's website at www.wiley.com/go/excel2019bible.

You don't need an MBA to realize that the greatest profit comes from Product C. Therefore, to maximize total profit, the logical solution is to produce only Product C. If things were really this simple, you wouldn't need tools such as Solver. As in most situations, this company has some constraints that must be met:

- The combined production capacity is 300 total units.
- The company needs 50 units of Product A to fill an existing order.
- The company needs 40 units of Product B to fill an anticipated order.
- Because the market for Product C is relatively limited, the company doesn't want to produce more than 40 units of this product.

These four constraints make the problem more realistic and a bit more challenging. In fact, it's a perfect problem for Solver.

Here are the basic steps for using Solver:

1. **Set up the worksheet with values and formulas.** Make sure you format cells logically; for example, if you can't produce partial units of your products, format those cells to contain numbers with no decimal values.
2. **Choose Data ⇨ Analyze ⇨ Solver.** The Solver Parameters dialog box appears.
3. **Specify the target cell (also known as the objective).**
4. **Specify the range that contains the changing cells.**
5. **Specify the constraints.**
6. **Change the Solver options, if necessary.**
7. **Click Solve, and let Solver go to work.**

To start Solver to tackle this example, choose Data ⇨ Analyze ⇨ Solver. The Solver Parameters dialog box appears. Figure 32.5 shows this dialog box, set up to solve the problem.

In this example, the target cell is D6—the cell that calculates the total profit for three products.

1. **Enter D6 into the Set Objective field of the Solver Parameters dialog box.**
2. **Because the objective is to maximize this cell, select the Max option button.**
3. **Specify the changing cells (which are in the range B3:B5) in the By Changing Variable Cells field.** The next step is to specify the constraints on the problem. The constraints are added one at a time and appear in the Subject to the Constraints list.
4. **To add a constraint, click the Add button.** The Add Constraint dialog box, shown in Figure 32.6, appears. This dialog box has three parts: a Cell Reference value, an operator, and a Constraint value.

FIGURE 32.5

The Solver Parameters dialog box

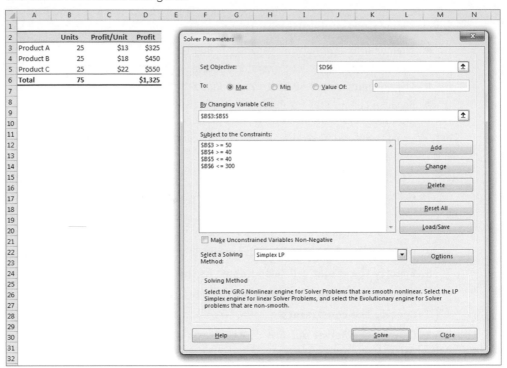

FIGURE 32.6

The Add Constraint dialog box

5. **To set the first constraint (that the total production capacity is 300 units), enter B6 as the Cell Reference value, choose less than or equal to (<=) from the drop-down list of operators, and enter 300 as the Constraint value.**

6. **Click Add, and enter the remaining constraints.** Table 32.1 summarizes the constraints for this problem.

TABLE 32.1 **Constraints Summary**

Constraint	Expressed As
Capacity is 300 units	B6<=300
At least 50 units of Product A	B3>=50
At least 40 units of Product B	B4>=40
No more than 40 units of Product C	B5<=40

7. **After you enter the last constraint, click OK to return to the Solver Parameters dialog box, which now lists the four constraints.**

8. **For the Solving Method, use Simplex LP.**

9. **Click the Solve button to start the solution process.** You can watch the progress on-screen, and Excel soon announces that it has found a solution. The Solver Results dialog box is shown in Figure 32.7.

FIGURE 32.7

Solver displays this dialog box when it finds a solution to the problem.

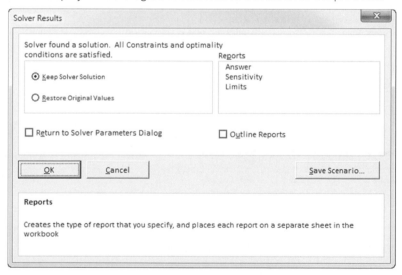

At this point, you have the following options:

- Keep the solution that Solver found.
- Restore the original changing cell values.
- Create any or all of the three reports that describe what Solver did.
- Click the Save Scenario button to save the solution as a scenario so that Scenario Manager can use it.

See Chapter 31, "Performing Spreadsheet What-If Analysis," for more on Scenario Manager.

The Reports section of the Solver Results dialog box lets you select any or all of three optional reports. If you specify any report options, Excel creates each report on a new worksheet, with an appropriate name. Figure 32.8 shows an Answer Report. In the Constraints section of the report, three of the four constraints are binding, which means that these constraints were satisfied at their limit with no more room to change.

FIGURE 32.8

One of three reports that Solver can produce

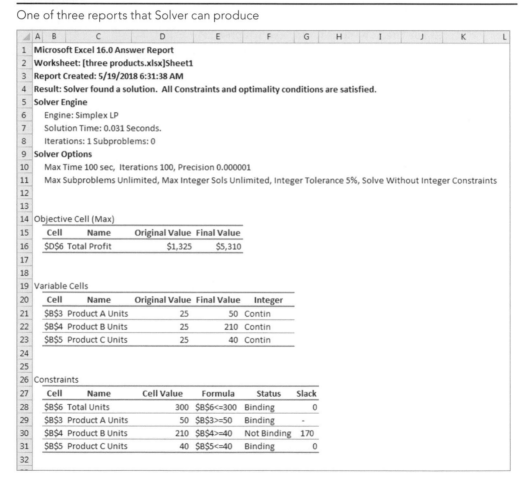

This simple example illustrates the way Solver works. The fact is, you could probably solve this particular problem manually by trial and error. That, of course, isn't always the case.

> **CAUTION**
>
> When you close the Solver Results dialog box (by clicking either OK or Cancel), the Undo stack is cleared. In other words, you can't undo any changes that Solver makes to your workbook.

Exploring Solver options

Before presenting more complex examples, this section discusses the Solver Options dialog box. From this dialog box, you control many aspects of the solution process, as well as load and save model specifications in a worksheet range.

Usually, you want to save a model only when you're using more than one set of Solver parameters with your worksheet. This is because Excel saves the first Solver model automatically with your worksheet (using hidden names). If you save additional models, Excel stores the information in the form of formulas that correspond to the specifications. (The last cell in the saved range is an array formula that holds the options settings.)

It's not unusual for Solver to report that it can't find a solution, even when you know that one should exist. Often, you can change one or more of the Solver options and try again. When you click the Options button in the Solver Parameters dialog box, the Solver Options dialog box, shown in Figure 32.9, appears.

This list describes Solver's options:

Constraint Precision   Specify how close the Cell Reference and Constraint formulas must be to satisfy a constraint. Excel may solve the problem more quickly if you specify less precision.

Use Automatic Scaling   Use when the problem involves large differences in magnitude— when you attempt to maximize a percentage, for example, by varying cells that are very large.

Show Iteration Results   Instruct Solver to pause and display the results after each iteration by selecting this check box.

Ignore Integer Constraints   When this check box is selected, Solver ignores constraints that specify that a particular cell must be an integer. Using this option may allow Solver to find a solution that can't be found otherwise.

Max Time   Specify the maximum amount of time (in seconds) that you want Solver to spend on a problem. If Solver reports that it exceeded the time limit, you can increase the amount of time that it spends searching for a solution.

Iterations   Enter the maximum number of trial solutions that you want Solver to perform.

Max Subproblems   Use this for complex problems. Specify the maximum number of sub-problems that may be explored by the Evolutionary algorithm.

FIGURE 32.9

You can control many aspects of the way Solver solves a problem.

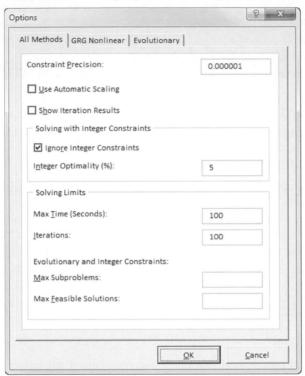

Max Feasible Solutions Use this for complex problems. Specify the maximum number of feasible solutions that may be explored by the Evolutionary algorithm.

> **NOTE**
> The other two tabs in the Options dialog box contain additional options used by the GRG Nonlinear and Evolutionary algorithms.

Seeing Some Solver Examples

The remainder of this chapter consists of examples of using Solver for various types of problems.

Solving simultaneous linear equations

This example describes how to solve a set of three linear equations with three variables. Here's an example of a set of linear equations:

$$4x + y - 2z = 0$$
$$2x - 3y + 3z = 9$$
$$-6x - 2y + z = 0$$

The question that Solver will answer is this: What values of *x*, *y*, and *z* satisfy all three equations?

Figure 32.10 shows a workbook set up to solve this problem. This workbook has three named cells, which makes the formulas more readable:

x: C11
y: C12
z: C13

FIGURE 32.10

Solver will attempt to solve this series of linear equations.

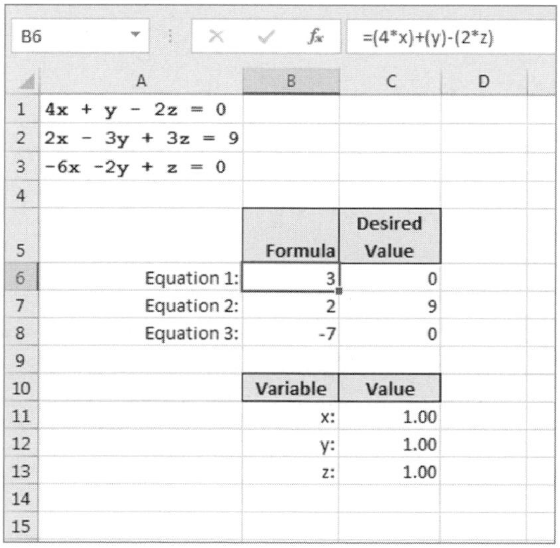
B6 =(4*x)+(y)-(2*z)

	A	B	C	D
1	4x + y - 2z = 0			
2	2x - 3y + 3z = 9			
3	-6x -2y + z = 0			
4				
5		Formula	Desired Value	
6	Equation 1:	3	0	
7	Equation 2:	2	9	
8	Equation 3:	-7	0	
9				
10		Variable	Value	
11		x:	1.00	
12		y:	1.00	
13		z:	1.00	
14				
15				

All three named cells are initialized to 1.0 (which certainly doesn't solve the equations).

This workbook, named `linear equations.xlsx`**, is available on this book's website at** `www.wiley.com/go/excel2019bible`.

The three equations are represented by formulas in the range B6:B8:

B6: `=(4*x)+(y)-(2*z)`

B7: `=(2*x)-(3*y)+(3*z)`

B8: `=-(6*x)-(2*y)+(z)`

These formulas use the values in the x, y, and z named cells. The range C6:C8 contains the desired result for these three formulas.

Solver will adjust the values in x, y, and z—that is, the changing cells in C11:C13—subject to these constraints:

```
B6=C6
B7=C7
B8=C8
```

NOTE

This problem doesn't have a target cell because it's not trying to maximize or minimize anything. However, the Solver Parameters dialog box insists that you specify a formula for the Set Objective field. Therefore, just enter a reference to any cell that has a formula.

Figure 32.11 shows the solution. The x (0.75), y (-2.0), and z (0.5) values satisfy all three equations.

FIGURE 32.11

Solver finds a solution to the linear equations.

	A	B	C	D
1	4x + y - 2z =0			
2	2x - 3y + 3z =9			
3	-6x -2y + z = 0			
4				
5		Formula	Desired Value	
6	Equation 1:	0	0	
7	Equation 2:	9	9	
8	Equation 3:	0	0	
9				
10		Variable	Value	
11		x:	0.75	
12		y:	-2.00	
13		z:	0.50	
14				
15				

> **NOTE**
> A set of linear equations may have one solution, no solution, or an infinite number of solutions.

Minimizing shipping costs

This example involves finding alternative options for shipping materials, while keeping total shipping costs at a minimum (see Figure 32.12). A company has warehouses in Los Angeles, St. Louis, and Boston. Retail outlets throughout the United States place orders, which the company then ships from one of the warehouses. The company wants to meet the product needs of all six retail outlets from available inventory and keep total shipping charges as low as possible.

FIGURE 32.12

This worksheet determines the least expensive way to ship products from warehouses to retail outlets.

Shipping Costs Table

	L.A.	St. Louis	Boston
Denver	$58	$47	$108
Houston	$87	$46	$100
Atlanta	$121	$30	$57
Miami	$149	$66	$83
Seattle	$62	$115	$164
Detroit	$128	$28	$38

Store	Number Needed	No. to ship from... L.A.	St. Louis	Boston	No. to be Shipped
Denver	150	25	25	25	75
Houston	225	25	25	25	75
Atlanta	100	25	25	25	75
Miami	250	25	25	25	75
Seattle	120	25	25	25	75
Detroit	150	25	25	25	75
Total	**995**	**150**	**150**	**150**	**450**

Warehouse Inventory

Starting Inventory:	400	350	500
No. Remaining:	250	200	350

Shipping Costs:	$ 15,125	$ 8,300	$ 13,750	**$37,175**

This workbook, named `shipping costs.xlsx`, is available on this book's website at www. wiley.com/go/excel2019bible.

The following is an explanation of each part of this somewhat complicated workbook:

Shipping Costs Table   This table, in range B2:E8, is a matrix that contains per-unit shipping costs from each warehouse to each retail outlet. The cost to ship a unit from Los Angeles to Denver, for example, is $58.

Product needs of each retail store   This information appears in C12:C17. For example, Denver needs 150 units, Houston needs 225, and so on. C18 contains a formula that calculates the total needed.

Number to ship from   Range D12:F17 holds the adjustable cells that Solver will change. All of these cells are initialized with a value of 25 to give Solver a starting value. Column G contains formulas that sum the number of units the company needs to ship to each retail outlet.

Warehouse inventory   Row 21 contains the amount of inventory at each warehouse, and row 22 contains formulas that subtract the amount shipped (row 18) from the inventory.

Calculated shipping costs   Row 24 contains formulas that calculate the shipping costs. Cell D24 contains the following formula, which is copied to the two cells to the right of cell D24:

```
=SUMPRODUCT(C3:C8,D12:D17)
```

Cell G24 is the total shipping costs for all orders.

Solver fills in values in the range D12:F17 in such a way that minimizes shipping costs while still supplying each retail outlet with the desired number of units. In other words, the solution minimizes the value in cell G24 by adjusting the cells in D12:F17, subject to the following constraints:

- **The number of units needed by each retail outlet must equal the number shipped.** (In other words, all of the orders are filled.) These constraints are represented by the following specifications:

    ```
    C12=G12    C14=G14    C16=G16
    C13=G13    C15=G15    C17=G17
    ```

- **The number of units remaining in each warehouse's inventory must not be negative.** (In other words, they can't ship more than what's available.) This is represented by the following constraint specifications:

    ```
    D22>=0    E22>=0    F22>=0
    ```

- **The adjustable cells can't be negative because shipping a negative number of units makes no sense.** The Solver Parameters dialog box has a handy option: Make Unconstrained Variables Non-Negative. Make sure that this check box is selected.

> **NOTE**
>
> Before you solve this problem with Solver, you may want to attempt to solve this problem manually by entering values in D12:F17 that minimize the shipping costs. And, of course, you need to make sure that all the constraints are met. Doing so may help you better appreciate Solver.

Setting up the problem is the difficult part. For example, you must enter nine constraints. When you have specified all of the necessary information, click the Solve button to put Solver to work. Solver displays the solution shown in Figure 32.13.

FIGURE 32.13

The solution that was created by Solver

	Shipping Costs Table			
		L.A.	St. Louis	Boston
Denver		$58	$47	$108
Houston		$87	$46	$100
Atlanta		$121	$30	$57
Miami		$149	$66	$83
Seattle		$62	$115	$164
Detroit		$128	$28	$38

Store	Number Needed	No. to ship from... L.A.	St. Louis	Boston	No. to be Shipped
Denver	150	150	0	0	150
Houston	225	0	225	0	225
Atlanta	100	0	100	0	100
Miami	250	0	25	225	250
Seattle	120	120	0	0	120
Detroit	150	0	0	150	150
Total	995	270	350	375	995

Warehouse Inventory

Starting Inventory:	400	350	500
No. Remaining:	130	0	125

Shipping Costs: $16,140 $15,000 $24,375 **$55,515**

The total shipping cost is $55,515, and all of the constraints are met. Notice that shipments to Miami come from both St. Louis and Boston and that St. Louis is now out of inventory. As you can imagine, you would never want to run a warehouse completely out of inventory.

If that were the case, you could change the constraints for cells D22:F22 to be greater than some minimum acceptable quantity.

Learning More about Solver

Solver is a complex tool, and this chapter barely scratches the surface. If you'd like to learn more about Solver, visit the website for Frontline Systems (www.solver.com). Frontline Systems is the company that developed Solver for Excel. Its website has several tutorials and lots of helpful information, including a detailed manual that you can download. You can also find additional Solver products for Excel that can handle much more complex problems.

Allocating resources

The example in this section is a common type of problem that's ideal for Solver. Essentially, problems of this sort involve optimizing the volumes of individual production units that use varying amounts of fixed resources. Figure 32.14 shows a simplified example for a toy company.

FIGURE 32.14

Using Solver to maximize profit when resources are limited

	A	B	C	D	E	F	G	H	I	J
1				XYZ Toys Inc.						
2				Materials Needed						
3	Material	Toy A	Toy B	Toy C	Toy D	Toy E	Amt. Avail.	Amt. Used	Amt. Left	
4	Red Paint	0	1	0	1	3	625	250	375	
5	Blue Paint	3	1	0	1	0	640	250	390	
6	White Paint	2	1	2	0	2	1,100	350	750	
7	Plastic	1	5	2	2	1	875	550	325	
8	Wood	3	0	3	5	5	2,200	800	1,400	
9	Glue	1	2	3	2	3	1,500	550	950	
10	Unit Profit	$15	$30	$20	$25	$25				
11	No. to Make	50	50	50	50	50				
12	Profit	$750	$1,500	$1,000	$1,250	$1,250				
13	Total Profit	$5,750								
14										

 This workbook is available on this book's website at www.wiley.com/go/excel2019bible. The file is named allocating resources.xlsx.

This company makes five different toys that use six different materials in varying amounts. For example, Toy A requires 3 units of blue paint, 2 units of white paint, 1 unit of plastic, 3 units of wood, and 1 unit of glue. Column G shows the current inventory of each type of material. Row 10 shows the unit profit for each toy.

The number of toys to make is shown in the range B11:F11. These are the values that Solver determines (the changing cells). The goal of this example is to determine how to allocate the resources to maximize the total profit (B13). In other words, Solver determines how many units of each toy to make. The constraints in this example are relatively simple:

- **Ensure that production doesn't use more resources than are available.** This can be accomplished by specifying that each cell in column I is greater than or equal to zero.
- **Ensure that the quantities produced aren't negative.** This can be accomplished by specifying the Make Unconstrained Variables Non-Negative option.

Figure 32.15 shows the results that are produced by Solver. It shows the product mix that generates $12,365 in profit and uses all resources in their entirety, except for glue.

FIGURE 32.15

Solver determined how to use the resources to maximize the total profit.

	A	B	C	D	E	F	G	H	I	J
1				XYZ Toys Inc.						
2				Materials Needed						
3	Material	Toy A	Toy B	Toy C	Toy D	Toy E	Amt. Avail.	Amt. Used	Amt. Left	
4	Red Paint	0	1	0	1	3	625	625	0	
5	Blue Paint	3	1	0	1	0	640	640	0	
6	White Paint	2	1	2	0	2	1,100	1,100	0	
7	Plastic	1	5	2	2	1	875	875	0	
8	Wood	3	0	3	5	5	2,200	2,200	0	
9	Glue	1	2	3	2	3	1,500	1,353	147	
10	Unit Profit	$15	$30	$20	$25	$25				
11	No. to Make	194	19	158	40	189				
12	Profit	$2,903	$573	$3,168	$1,008	$4,713				
13	Total Profit	$12,365								
14										

Optimizing an investment portfolio

This example demonstrates how to use Solver to help maximize the return on an investment portfolio. A portfolio consists of several investments, each of which has a different yield. In addition, you may have some constraints that involve reducing risk and diversification goals. Without such constraints, a portfolio problem becomes a no-brainer: put all your money in the investment with the highest yield.

This example involves a credit union (a financial institution that takes members' deposits and invests them in loans to other members, bank CDs, and other types of investments). The credit union distributes part of the return on these investments to the members in the form of dividends, or interest on their deposits.

This hypothetical credit union must adhere to some regulations regarding its investments, and the board of directors has imposed some other restrictions. These regulations and restrictions comprise the problem's constraints. Figure 32.16 shows a workbook set up for this problem.

FIGURE 32.16

This worksheet is set up to maximize a credit union's investments, given some constraints.

	A	B	C	D	E
1	Portfolio Amount:	$5,000,000			
2					
3					
4	Investment	Pct Yield	Amount Invested	Yield	Pct. of Portfolio
5	New Car Loans	6.90%	1,000,000	69,000	20.00%
6	Used Car Loans	8.25%	1,000,000	82,500	20.00%
7	Real Estate Loans	8.90%	1,000,000	89,000	20.00%
8	Unsecured Loans	13.00%	1,000,000	130,000	20.00%
9	Bank CDs	4.60%	1,000,000	46,000	20.00%
10	TOTAL		$5,000,000	$416,500	100.00%
11					
12			Total Yield:	8.33%	
13					
14			Auto Loans	40.00%	

 This workbook is available on this book's website at www.wiley.com/go/excel2019bible. The file is named investment portfolio.xlsx.

Allocating the $5 million portfolio is subject to these constraints:

- **The amount that the credit union invests in new-car loans must be at least three times the amount that the credit union invests in used-car loans.** (Used-car loans are riskier investments.) This constraint is represented as

  C5>=C6*3

- **Car loans should make up at least 15% of the portfolio.** This constraint is represented as

  D14>=.15

- **Unsecured loans should make up no more than 25% of the portfolio.** This constraint is represented as

  `E8<=.25`

- **At least 10% of the portfolio should be in bank CDs.** This constraint is represented as

  `E9>=.10`

- **The total amount invested is $5,000,000.**
- **All investments should be positive or zero.**

The changing cells are C5:C9, and the goal is to maximize the total yield in cell D12. Starting values of 1,000,000 have been entered in the changing cells. When you run Solver with these parameters, it produces the solution shown in Figure 32.17, which has a total yield of 9.25%.

FIGURE 32.17

The results of the portfolio optimization

	A	B	C	D	E
1	Portfolio Amount:	$5,000,000			
2					
3					
4	Investment	Pct Yield	Amount Invested	Yield	Pct. of Portfolio
5	New Car Loans	6.90%	562,500	38,813	11.25%
6	Used Car Loans	8.25%	187,500	15,469	3.75%
7	Real Estate Loans	8.90%	2,500,000	222,500	50.00%
8	Unsecured Loans	13.00%	1,250,000	162,500	25.00%
9	Bank CDs	4.60%	500,000	23,000	10.00%
10	TOTAL		$5,000,000	$462,281	100.00%
11					
12			Total Yield:	9.25%	
13					
14			Auto Loans	15.00%	
15					

Analyzing Data with the Analysis ToolPak

Although Excel was designed primarily for business users, people in other disciplines, including education, research, statistics, and engineering, also use the software. One way Excel addresses these nonbusiness users is with its Analysis ToolPak add-in. However, many features in the Analysis ToolPak are valuable for business applications as well.

The Analysis ToolPak: An Overview

The Analysis ToolPak is an add-in that provides analytical capability that normally isn't available in Excel.

These analysis tools offer many features that may be useful to those in the scientific, engineering, and educational communities—not to mention business users whose needs extend beyond the normal spreadsheet fare.

This section provides a quick overview of the types of analyses that you can perform with the Analysis ToolPak. This chapter covers each of the following tools:

- Analysis of variance (three types)
- Correlation
- Covariance
- Descriptive statistics
- Exponential smoothing
- F-test
- Fourier analysis
- Histogram

- Moving average
- Random number generation
- Rank and percentile
- Regression
- Sampling
- T-test (three types)
- Z-test

As you can see, the Analysis ToolPak add-in brings a great deal of additional functionality to Excel. These procedures have limitations, however. In some cases, you may prefer to create your own formulas to do some calculations.

Installing the Analysis ToolPak Add-In

The Analysis ToolPak is implemented as an add-in. Before you can use it, though, you need to make sure that the add-in is installed. Select the Data tab. If you see an Analyze group, showing a Data Analysis button, the Analysis ToolPak is installed. If you can't access Data ⇨ Analyze ⇨ Data Analysis, install the add-in by following these steps:

1. **Choose File ⇨ Options.** The Excel Options dialog box appears.

2. **Select the Add-Ins tab.**

3. **At the bottom of the dialog box, select Excel Add-Ins from the Manage dropdown list and then click Go.** The Add-Ins dialog box appears.

4. **Place a check mark next to Analysis ToolPak.** There is no need to check the add-in named Analysis ToolPak – VBA.

5. **Click OK to close the Add-Ins dialog box.**

Using the Analysis Tools

Using the procedures in the Analysis ToolPak add-in is relatively straightforward as long as you're familiar with the particular analysis type. To use any of these tools, choose Data ⇨ Analyze ⇨ Data Analysis, and the Data Analysis dialog box appears, as shown in Figure 33.1. Scroll through the list until you find the analysis tool that you want to use and then click OK. A dialog box specific to the procedure that you select appears.

Usually, you need to specify one or more input ranges, plus an output range. (Specifying the top-left cell of the output range is sufficient.) Alternatively, you can choose to place the results on a new worksheet or in a new workbook. The procedures vary in the amount of additional information required. In many dialog boxes, you may be able to indicate whether your data range includes labels. If so, you can specify the entire range, including the labels, and indicate to Excel that the first column (or row) contains labels. Excel then uses these labels in the tables that it produces. Most tools also provide different output options that you can select, based on your needs.

FIGURE 33.1

Select your tool from the Data Analysis dialog box.

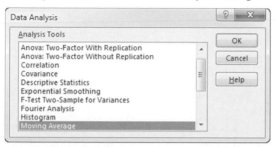

CAUTION

The Analysis ToolPak isn't consistent in the way that it generates its output. In some cases, the procedures use formulas, so you can change your data, and the results update automatically. For other procedures, Excel stores the results as values, so if you change your data, the results don't reflect your changes.

Introducing the Analysis ToolPak Tools

This section describes each tool in the Analysis ToolPak and provides an example. We don't describe every available option in these procedures. If you need to use the advanced analysis tools, you probably already know how to use most of the options not covered here.

Before you use any of these tools, read the appropriate section in Excel's Help system.

 This book's website at www.wiley.com/go/excel2019bible contains a workbook that shows output from all of the tools discussed in this section. The file is named atp examples.xlsx. This workbook also contains some alternative formula-based solutions that are sometimes better than using the Analysis ToolPak.

Analysis of variance

Analysis of variance (sometimes abbreviated as *anova*) is a statistical test that determines whether two or more samples were drawn from the same population. Using tools in the Analysis ToolPak, you can perform three types of analysis of variance:

Single-factor A one-way analysis of variance, with only one sample for each group of data

Two-factor with replication   A two-way analysis of variance, with multiple samples (or replications) for each group of data

Two-factor without replication   A two-way analysis of variance, with a single sample (or replication) for each group of data

Figure 33.2 shows the dialog box for a single-factor analysis of variance. Alpha represents the statistical confidence level for the test.

FIGURE 33.2

Specifying parameters for a single-factor analysis of variance

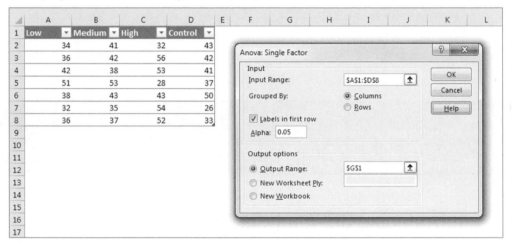

The output for this test consists of the means and variances for each of the samples, the value of F, the critical value of F, and the significance of F (P-value).

Correlation

Correlation is a widely used statistic that measures the degree to which two sets of values vary together. For example, if higher values in one data set are typically associated with higher values in the second data set, the two data sets have a positive correlation. The degree of correlation is expressed as a coefficient that ranges from –1.0 (a perfect negative correlation) to +1.0 (a perfect positive correlation). A correlation coefficient of 0 indicates that the two variables aren't correlated.

Figure 33.3 shows the Correlation dialog box. Specify the input range, which can include any number of variables, arranged in rows or columns.

The output consists of a correlation matrix that shows the correlation coefficient for each variable paired with every other variable.

FIGURE 33.3

The Correlation dialog box

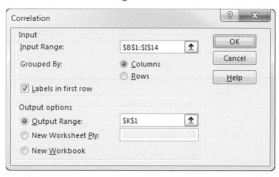

Covariance

The covariance tool produces a matrix that is similar to the one generated by the correlation tool. *Covariance*, like correlation, measures the degree to which two variables vary together. Specifically, covariance is the average of the product of the deviations of each data point pair from their respective means.

Because the covariance tool does not generate formulas, you may prefer to calculate a covariance matrix using the COVAR function.

Descriptive statistics

The *descriptive statistics* tool produces a table that describes your data with some standard statistics. Figure 33.4 shows some sample output.

Because the output for this procedure consists of values (not formulas), you should use this procedure only when you're certain that your data isn't going to change; otherwise, you'll need to re-execute the procedure. You can generate all of these statistics by using formulas.

Exponential smoothing

Exponential smoothing is a technique for predicting data that is based on the previous data point and the previously predicted data point. You can specify the damping factor (also known as a *smoothing constant*), which can range from 0 to 1. This factor determines the relative weighting of the previous data point and the previously predicted data point. You also can request standard errors and a chart.

FIGURE 33.4

Descriptive statistics output

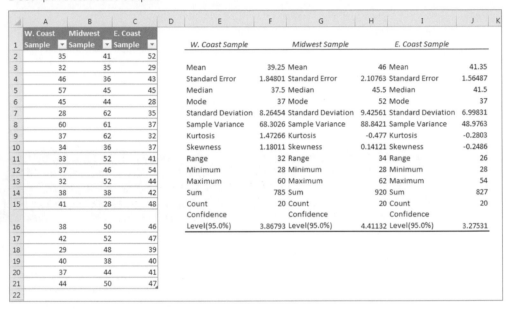

The exponential smoothing procedure generates formulas that use the damping factor you specify. Therefore, if the data changes, Excel updates the formulas.

F-test (two-sample test for variance)

An *F-test* is a commonly used statistical test that enables you to compare two population variances. Figure 33.5 shows a small data set and F-test output.

The output for this test consists of the means and variances for each of the two samples, the value of F, the critical value of F, and the significance of F.

Fourier analysis

Fourier analysis performs a "fast Fourier" transformation of a range of data. Using the Fourier analysis tool, you can transform a range limited to the following sizes: 1, 2, 4, 8, 16, 32, 64, 128, 256, 512, or 1,024 data points. This procedure accepts and generates complex numbers, which are represented as a text string (not numerical values).

FIGURE 33.5

Output from the F-test tool

	A	B	C	D	E	F
1	Group 1 ▼	Group 2 ▼		F-Test Two-Sample for Variances		
2	96	39				
3	78	53			Group 1	Group 2
4	72	51		Mean	75.44444	46.66667
5	78	48		Variance	109.5278	25
6	65	51		Observations	9	9
7	66	42		df	8	8
8	69	44		F	4.381111	
9	87	42		P(F<=f) one-tail	0.025855	
10	68	50		F Critical one-tail	3.438103	
11						

Histogram

The *histogram* tool is useful for producing data distributions and histogram charts. It accepts an Input range and a Bin range. A Bin range is a range of values that specifies the limits for each column of the histogram. If you omit the Bin range, Excel creates 10 equal-interval bins for you. The size of each bin is determined by the following formula:

```
=(MAX(input_range)- MIN(input_range))/10
```

Figure 33.6 shows output from the histogram tool. As an option, you can specify that the resulting histogram be sorted by frequency of occurrence in each bin.

If you specify the Pareto (Sorted Histogram) option, the Bin range must contain values and can't contain formulas. If formulas appear in the Bin range, Excel doesn't sort properly and your worksheet displays error values. The histogram tool doesn't use formulas, so if you change any of the input data, you need to repeat the histogram procedure to update the results.

For other ways of generating frequency distributions, see Chapter 30, "Analyzing Data with PivotTables." Excel 2019 also supports two chart types: Histogram and Pareto. These work with a range of data and do not require a separate bin range. For an example, see Chapter 20, "Getting Started with Excel Charts."

Moving average

The *moving average* tool helps you smooth out a data series that has a lot of variability. This procedure is often used in conjunction with a chart. Excel does the smoothing by computing a moving average of a specified number of values. In many cases, a moving average enables you to spot trends that otherwise would be obscured by noise in the data.

FIGURE 33.6

Use the histogram tool to generate distributions and graphical output.

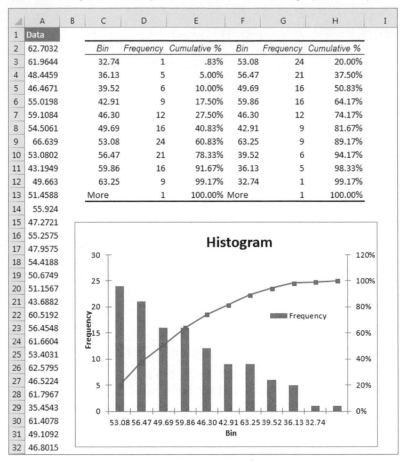

	A	B	C	D	E	F	G	H	I
1	Data								
2	62.7032		Bin	Frequency	Cumulative %	Bin	Frequency	Cumulative %	
3	61.9644		32.74	1	.83%	53.08	24	20.00%	
4	48.4459		36.13	5	5.00%	56.47	21	37.50%	
5	46.4671		39.52	6	10.00%	49.69	16	50.83%	
6	55.0198		42.91	9	17.50%	59.86	16	64.17%	
7	59.1084		46.30	12	27.50%	46.30	12	74.17%	
8	54.5061		49.69	16	40.83%	42.91	9	81.67%	
9	66.639		53.08	24	60.83%	63.25	9	89.17%	
10	53.0802		56.47	21	78.33%	39.52	6	94.17%	
11	43.1949		59.86	16	91.67%	36.13	5	98.33%	
12	49.663		63.25	9	99.17%	32.74	1	99.17%	
13	51.4588		More	1	100.00%	More	1	100.00%	
14	55.924								
15	47.2721								
16	55.2575								
17	47.9575								
18	54.4188								
19	50.6749								
20	51.1567								
21	43.6882								
22	60.5192								
23	56.4548								
24	61.6604								
25	53.4031								
26	62.5795								
27	46.5224								
28	61.7967								
29	35.4543								
30	61.4078								
31	49.1092								
32	46.8015								

Figure 33.7 shows a chart generated by the moving average tool. You can, of course, specify the number of values that you want Excel to use for each average. If you select the Standard Errors check box in the Moving Average dialog box, Excel calculates standard errors and places formulas for these calculations next to the moving average formulas. The standard error values indicate the degree of variability between the actual values and the calculated moving averages.

FIGURE 33.7

A chart produced from data generated by the moving average tool

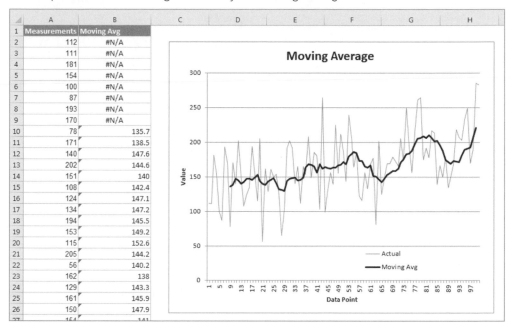

The first few cells in the output are #N/A because too few data points exist to calculate the average for these initial values.

Random number generation

Although Excel contains built-in functions to calculate random numbers, the *random number generation* tool is much more flexible because you can specify what type of distribution you want the random numbers to have. Figure 33.8 shows the Random Number Generation dialog box. The Parameters section varies, depending on the type of distribution that you select.

Number of Variables refers to the number of columns that you want, and Number of Random Numbers refers to the number of rows that you want. For example, if you want 200 random numbers arranged in 10 columns of 20 rows, you specify 10 and 20, respectively, in these fields.

FIGURE 33.8

This dialog box enables you to generate a wide variety of random numbers.

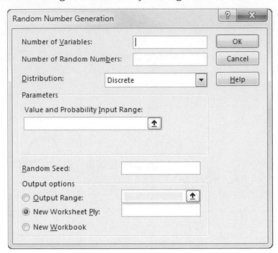

In the Random Seed field, you can specify the starting value that Excel uses in its random-number-generating algorithm. Usually, you leave this field blank. If you want to generate the same random number sequence, however, you can specify a seed between 1 and 32,767 (integer values only). You can create the following types of distributions via the Distribution drop-down list in the Random Number Generation dialog box:

Uniform Every random number has an equal chance of being selected. You specify the upper and lower limits.

Normal The random numbers correspond to a normal distribution. You specify the mean and standard deviation of the distribution.

Bernoulli The random numbers are either 0 or 1, determined by the probability of success that you specify.

Binomial This option returns random numbers based on a Bernoulli distribution over a specific number of trials, given a probability of success that you specify.

Poisson This option generates values in a Poisson distribution. A Poisson distribution is characterized by discrete events that occur in an interval, where the probability of a single occurrence is proportional to the size of the interval. The lambda parameter is the expected number of occurrences in an interval. In a Poisson distribution, lambda is equal to the mean, which also is equal to the variance.

Patterned This option doesn't generate random numbers. Rather, it repeats a series of numbers in steps that you specify.

Discrete   This option enables you to specify the probability that specific values are chosen. It requires a two-column input range; the first column holds the values, and the second column holds the probability of each value being chosen. The sum of the probabilities in the second column must equal 100 percent.

Rank and percentile

The *rank and percentile* tool creates a table that shows the ordinal and percentile ranking for each value in a range. You can also generate ranks and percentiles by using Excel functions (those that begin with RANK and PERCENTILE).

Regression

Use the *regression* tool (see Figure 33.9) to calculate a regression analysis from worksheet data. You can use regression to analyze trends, forecast the future, build predictive models, and, often, make sense out of a series of seemingly unrelated numbers.

FIGURE 33.9

The Regression dialog box

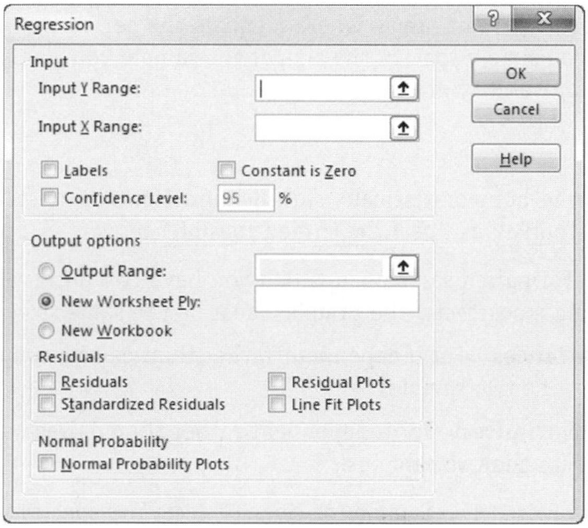

Regression analysis enables you to determine the extent to which one range of data (the dependent variable) varies as a function of the values of one or more other ranges of data (the independent variables). This relationship is expressed mathematically, using values that Excel calculates. You can use these calculations to create a mathematical model of the data and predict the dependent variable by using different values of one or more independent variables. This tool can perform simple and multiple linear regressions and calculate and standardize residuals automatically.

As you can see, the Regression dialog box offers many options:

Input Y Range The range that contains the dependent variable.

Input X Range One or more ranges that contain independent variables.

Constant Is Zero If selected, forces the regression to have a constant of 0 (which means that the regression line passes through the origin; when the X values are 0, the predicted Y value is 0).

Confidence Level The confidence level for the regression.

Residuals The four options in this section of the dialog box enable you to specify whether to include residuals in the output. Residuals are the differences between observed and predicted values.

Normal Probability Generates a chart for normal probability plots.

Sampling

The *sampling* tool generates a random sample from a range of input values. The sampling tool can help you work with a large database by creating a subset of it.

This procedure has two options: periodic and random. If you choose a periodic sample, Excel selects every nth value from the Input range, where n equals the period that you specify. With a random sample, you simply specify the size of the sample you want Excel to select; every value has an equal probability of being chosen.

T-test

Use the *T-test* tool to determine whether a statistically significant difference exists between two small samples. The Analysis ToolPak can perform three types of T-tests:

Paired two-sample for means For paired samples in which you have two observations on each subject (such as a pretest and a posttest). The samples must be the same size.

Two-sample assuming equal variances For independent rather than paired samples. Excel assumes equal variances for the two samples.

Two-sample assuming unequal variances For independent rather than paired samples. Excel assumes unequal variances for the two samples.

Figure 33.10 shows output for the Paired Two Sample for Means T-test. You specify the significance level (alpha) and the hypothesized difference between the two means (that is, the null hypothesis).

FIGURE 33.10

Output from the paired T-test dialog box

	A	B	C	D	E	F	G
1	Student#	Pretest	Posttest		t-Test: Paired Two Sample for Means		
2	1	71	69				
3	2	63	61			Pretest	Posttest
4	3	68	70		Mean	69.619048	71.09524
5	4	67	68		Variance	16.647619	48.79048
6	5	66	61		Observations	21	21
7	6	63	60		Pearson Correlation	0.962743	
8	7	76	83		Hypothesized Mean Difference	0	
9	8	70	72		df	20	
10	9	69	71		t Stat	-2.081522	
11	10	73	77		P(T<=t) one-tail	0.0252224	
12	11	71	72		t Critical one-tail	1.724718	
13	12	66	66		P(T<=t) two-tail	0.0504448	
14	13	70	71		t Critical two-tail	2.0859625	
15	14	78	86				
16	15	68	70				
17	16	75	78				
18	17	65	63				
19	18	67	68				
20	19	71	77				
21	20	74	78				
22	21	71	72				
23							

Z-test (two-sample test for means)

The T-test tool is used for small samples; the *Z-test* tool is used for larger samples or populations. You must know the variances for both input ranges. Generally, use a T-test when your sample size is less than 30 and you don't know the standard deviation of the population. Otherwise, use the Z-test.

Protecting Your Work

IN THIS CHAPTER

Protecting worksheets

Protecting workbooks

Protecting Visual Basic Projects

Creating PDFs and checking documents

The concept of "protection" gets a lot of attention in the Excel forums. It seems that many users want to learn how to protect various workbook elements from being overwritten or copied. Excel has several protection-related features, and those features are covered in this chapter.

Types of Protection

Excel's protection-related features fall into three categories:

Worksheet protection Protecting all or part of a worksheet from being modified or restricting the modifications to certain users

Workbook protection Protecting a workbook from having sheets inserted or deleted and requiring the use of a password to open the workbook

Visual Basic (VB) protection Using a password to prevent others from viewing or modifying your VBA code

> **CAUTION**
>
> Before we discuss these features, you should understand the limitations of security. Using a password to protect some aspect of your work doesn't guarantee that it's secure. Password-cracking utilities (and some simple tricks) have been around for a long time. Using passwords works in the majority of cases, but if unscrupulous individuals are truly intent on getting to your data, they can usually find a way. If security is critical, perhaps Excel isn't the proper tool.

Protecting a Worksheet

You may want to protect a worksheet for a variety of reasons. One common reason is to prevent yourself or others from accidentally deleting formulas or other critical data. A typical scenario is to protect a worksheet so that the data can be changed, but the formulas can't be.

To protect a worksheet, activate the worksheet and choose Review ⇨ Protect ⇨ Protect Sheet. Excel displays the Protect Sheet dialog box, as shown in Figure 34.1. Providing a password is optional. If you enter a password, that password will be required to unprotect the worksheet. If you accept the default options in the Protect Sheet dialog box (and if you haven't unlocked any cells), none of the cells on the worksheet can be modified.

FIGURE 34.1

Use the Protect Sheet dialog box to protect a worksheet.

To unprotect a protected sheet, choose Review ⇨ Protect ⇨ Unprotect Sheet. If the sheet was protected with a password, you're prompted to enter that password.

Unlocking cells

In many cases, you'll want to allow some cells to be changed when the worksheet is protected. For example, your worksheet may have some input cells that are used by formula cells. In such a case, you would want the user to be able to change the input cells but not the formula cells. Every cell has a Locked attribute, and that attribute determines whether the cell can be changed when the sheet is protected.

By default, all cells are locked, and worksheets are unprotected. To change the Locked attribute, select the cell or range, right-click, and choose Format Cells from the shortcut menu (or press Ctrl+1). Select the Protection tab of the Format Cells dialog box (see Figure 34.2), clear the Locked check box, and then click OK.

FIGURE 34.2

Use the Protection tab in the Format Cells dialog box to change the Locked attribute of a cell or range.

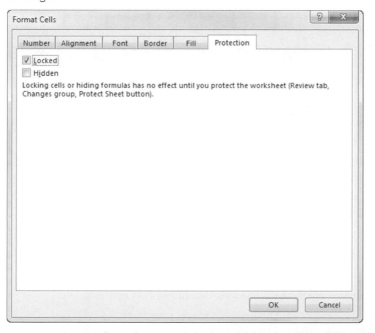

NOTE

The Protection tab of the Format Cells dialog box has another attribute: Hidden. If this check box is selected, the contents of the cell don't appear in the Formula bar when the sheet is protected. The cell isn't hidden in the worksheet. You may want to set the Hidden attribute for formula cells to prevent users from seeing the formula when the cell is selected.

After you unlock the desired cells, choose Review ⇨ Protect ⇨ Protect Sheet to protect the sheet. Then you can change the unlocked cells, but if you attempt to change a locked cell, Excel displays the message shown in Figure 34.3.

FIGURE 34.3

Excel warns you if you attempt to change a locked cell.

> **NOTE**
> The Locked attribute matters only when the worksheet is protected. On an unprotected worksheet, locked and unlocked cells behave the same way.

Sheet protection options

The Protect Sheet dialog box (refer to Figure 34.1) has several options, which determine what the user can do when the worksheet is protected:

Select Locked Cells If this is checked, the user can select locked cells using the mouse or the keyboard. This setting is enabled by default.

Select Unlocked Cells If this is checked, the user can select unlocked cells using the mouse or the keyboard. This setting is enabled by default.

Format Cells If this is checked, the user can apply formatting to locked cells.

Format Columns If this is checked, the user can hide or change the width of columns.

Format Rows If this is checked, the user can hide or change the height of rows.

Insert Columns If this is checked, the user can insert new columns.

Insert Rows If this is checked, the user can insert new rows.

Insert Hyperlinks If this is checked, the user can insert hyperlinks (even in locked cells).

Delete Columns If this is checked, the user can delete columns.

Delete Rows If this is checked, the user can delete rows.

Sort If this is checked, the user can sort data in a range as long as the range doesn't contain locked cells.

Use AutoFilter If this is checked, the user can use existing autofiltering.

Use PivotTable & PivotChart If this is checked, the user can change the layout of PivotTables or create new PivotTables. This setting also applies to PivotCharts.

Edit Objects If this is checked, the user can make changes to objects (such as shapes) and charts, as well as insert or delete comments.

Edit Scenarios If this is checked, the user can use scenario management features.

See Chapter 31, "Performing Spreadsheet What-If Analysis," for more on creating and using scenarios.

TIP

When the worksheet is protected and the Select Unlocked Cells option is selected, pressing Tab moves to the next unlocked cell (and skips locked cells), making data entry much easier.

Assigning user permissions

Excel also offers the ability to assign user-level permissions to different areas on a protected worksheet. You can specify which users can edit a particular range while the worksheet is protected. As an option, you can require a password to make changes.

This feature is rarely used, and the setup procedure is rather complicated. But if you need this level of protection, setting it up might be worth the effort.

1. **Unprotect the worksheet if it's protected.**
2. **Choose Review ⇨ Protect ⇨ Allow Edit Ranges.** The Allow Users to Edit Ranges dialog box appears, as shown in Figure 34.4.

FIGURE 34.4

The Allow Users to Edit Ranges dialog box

3. **Click the New button to show the New Range dialog.**
4. **Fill out the Title, Refers to cells, and Range password fields, and then click the Permissions button.**
5. **Click the Add button to display the Select Users or Groups dialog.**
6. **Type the Windows or domain username and click OK.**
7. **Accept the default Allow setting or change it to Deny and click OK.**

8. **Dismiss the remaining dialog boxes by clicking OK.**

9. **Protect the sheet.** You can click the Protect Sheet button on the Allow Users to Edit Ranges dialog before you dismiss it or use the Protect Sheet command on the Review Ribbon.

Protecting a Workbook

Excel provides two ways to protect a workbook:

- Require a password to open the workbook
- Prevent users from inserting sheets, deleting sheets, hiding sheets, and unhiding sheets

These are not mutually exclusive, so both methods can be applied to a workbook. We discuss each of these methods in the sections that follow.

Requiring a password to open a workbook

Excel lets you save a workbook with a password. After you do so, whoever tries to open the workbook must enter the password.

To add a password to a workbook, follow these steps:

1. **Choose File ➪ Info ➪ Protect Workbook ➪ Encrypt with Password.** The Encrypt Document dialog box, shown in Figure 34.5, appears.

FIGURE 34.5

Specify a workbook password in the Encrypt Document dialog box.

2. **Type a password and click OK.**

3. **Type the password again and click OK.**

4. **Save the workbook.**

To remove a password from a workbook, repeat the same procedure. In step 2, however, delete the existing password symbols from the Encrypt Document dialog box, click OK, and save your workbook.

Figure 34.6 shows the Password dialog box that appears when you try to open a file saved with a password.

FIGURE 34.6

Opening this workbook requires a password.

Excel provides another way to add a password to a document:

1. **Choose File ⇨ Save As and click Browse. The Save As dialog box appears.**
2. **Click the Tools drop-down and choose General Options.** The General Options dialog box appears.
3. **Enter a password in the Password to Open field.**
4. **Click OK.** You're asked to reenter the password before you return to the Save As dialog box.
5. **In the Save As dialog box, make sure that the filename, location, and type are correct; then click Save.**

34

Protecting a workbook's structure

To prevent others (or yourself) from performing certain actions in a workbook, you can protect the workbook's structure. When a workbook's structure is protected, the user may not do the following:

- Insert a sheet
- Delete a sheet
- Hide a sheet
- Unhide a sheet
- Rename a sheet
- Move a sheet

To protect a workbook's structure, follow these steps:

1. **Choose Review ⇨ Protect ⇨ Protect Workbook.** The Protect Structure and Windows dialog box appears, as shown in Figure 34.7.

FIGURE 34.7

The Protect Structure and Windows dialog box

2. **Select the Structure check box.**
3. **(Optional) Enter a password.**
4. **Click OK.**

The Protect Workbook Ribbon tool changes color to indicate that you enabled workbook protection. To unprotect the workbook's structure, choose Review ⇨ Protect ⇨ Protect Workbook again. Workbook protection will be turned off, and the Ribbon tool will change back to its normal color. If the workbook's structure was protected with a password, you're prompted to enter the password.

Protecting a VBA Project

If your workbook contains VBA macros, you may want to protect the VBA Project to prevent others from viewing or modifying your macros. To protect a VBA Project, follow these steps:

1. Press Alt+F11 to activate the VB Editor.

2. Select your project in the Projects window.

3. Choose Tools ⇨ <Project Name> Properties (where <Project Name> corresponds to your Project name). The Project Properties dialog box appears.

4. Select the Protection tab (see Figure 34.8).

FIGURE 34.8

Protecting a VBA Project with a password

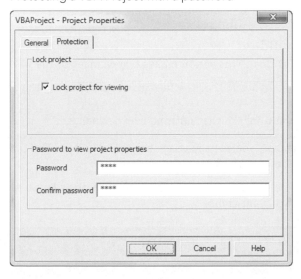

5. Select the Lock Project for Viewing check box.

6. Enter a password (twice).

7. Click OK and then save your file. When the file is closed and then reopened, a password will be required to view or modify the VBA code.

 Part VI, "Automating Excel," discusses VBA macros.

Related Topics

This section covers additional topics related to protecting and distributing your work.

Saving a worksheet as a PDF file

The Portable Document Format (PDF) file format is widely used as a way to present information in a read-only manner with precise control over the layout. Software to display PDF files is available from a number of sources. Excel can create PDF files, but it can't open them.

XPS is another "electronic paper" format, developed by Microsoft as an alternative to the PDF format. At this time, there is little third-party support for the XPS format.

Save a worksheet in PDF or XPS format by choosing File ⇨ Export ⇨ Create PDF/XPS Document ⇨ Create PDF/XPS. The Publish as PDF or XPS dialog box appears; here, you can specify a filename and location and set some other options.

Marking a workbook as final

Excel lets you mark a workbook as final. This action makes two changes to the workbook:

- It makes the workbook read-only so that the file can't be saved using the same name.
- It makes the workbook view-only so that nothing may be changed.

When you open a finalized document, you see a message below the Ribbon. You can override its final status by clicking the Edit Anyway button.

To finalize a workbook, choose File ⇨ Info ⇨ Protect Workbook ⇨ Mark as Final. A dialog box appears, where you can confirm your choice.

> **CAUTION**
>
> Marking a document as final is not a security measure. Anyone who opens the workbook can cancel the mark-as-final designation. Therefore, this method doesn't guarantee that others will not change the workbook.

Inspecting a workbook

If you plan to distribute a workbook to others, you may want to have Excel check the file for hidden data and personal information. This tool can locate hidden information about you, your organization, or the workbook. In some situations, you may not want to share this information with others.

To inspect a workbook, choose File ➪ Info ➪ Check for Issues ➪ Inspect Document. The Document Inspector dialog box appears, as shown in Figure 34.9. Click Inspect, and Excel displays the results of the inspection and gives you the opportunity to remove the items it finds.

FIGURE 34.9

The Document Inspector dialog box identifies hidden and personal information in a workbook.

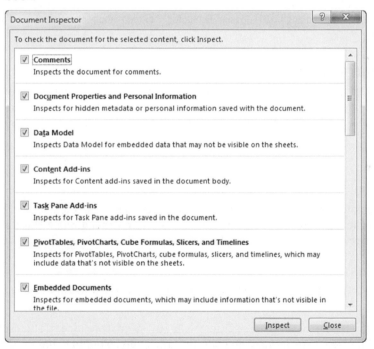

> **CAUTION**
>
> If Excel identifies items in the Document Inspector, it doesn't necessarily mean that they should be removed. In other words, you shouldn't blindly use the Remove All buttons to remove the items that Excel locates. For example, you may have a hidden sheet that serves a critical purpose. Excel will identify that hidden sheet and make it easy for you to delete it. To be on the safe side, always make a backup copy of your workbook before running the Document Inspector.

Two other commands are available in the File ➪ Info ➪ Check for Issues menu:

Check Accessibility   Checks the workbook for content that people with disabilities might find difficult to read

Check Compatibility   Checks the workbook for the presence of features that may not work in previous versions of Excel

 See Chapter 6, "Understanding Excel Files and Templates," for more about checking file compatibility.

Using a digital signature

Excel lets you add a digital signature to a workbook. Using a digital signature is somewhat analogous to signing a paper document. A digital signature helps to ensure the authenticity of the workbook and ensure that the content hasn't been modified since it was signed.

After you sign a workbook, the signature is valid until you make changes and resave the file.

Getting a digital ID

To sign a workbook digitally, you must obtain a certificate from a certified authority that is able to verify the authenticity of your signature. Prices vary, depending on the certificate-granting company.

Signing a workbook

Excel supports two types of digital signatures: a visible signature and an invisible signature.

To add a visible digital signature, choose Insert ➪ Text ➪ Signature Line ➪ Microsoft Office Signature Line. The Signature Setup dialog box appears, and you're prompted for the information for the signature. After you add the signature box, double-click it, and the Sign dialog box appears; here you actually sign the document either by typing your name or by uploading a scanned image of your signature. After signing the document, it will be marked as final. Any change to the file will invalidate the signature.

To add an invisible digital signature, choose File ➪ Info ➪ Protect Workbook ➪ Add a Digital Signature. If the signed workbook is changed in any way, the digital signature is invalidated.

Part V

Understanding Power Pivot and Power Query

Part V introduces to the world of Power Pivot and Power Query. Here, you'll discover how to develop powerful reporting with external data and the Power Pivot data model. You'll also explore how the rich set of tools Power Query offers can help you save time, automate data clean-up, and substantially enhance your data analysis and reporting capabilities.

Introducing Power Pivot

R ecognizing the importance of the business intelligence (BI) revolution and the place Excel holds within it, Microsoft has made substantial investments in improving Excel's BI capabilities, specifically focusing on Excel's self-service BI capabilities and its ability to manage and analyze information better from the increasing number of available data sources.

The key product of this endeavor is Power Pivot. With Power Pivot comes the ability to set up relationships between large, disparate data sources and to merge data sources with hundreds of thousands of rows into one analytical engine within Excel.

Starting with the release of Excel 2013, Microsoft has incorporated Power Pivot directly into Excel. This means the powerful capabilities of Power Pivot are available to you right out of the box!

In this chapter, you'll get an overview of those capabilities, exploring the key features, benefits, and capabilities of Power Pivot.

Understanding the Power Pivot Internal Data Model

At its core, Power Pivot is essentially a SQL Server Analysis Services engine made available through an in-memory process that runs directly within Excel. The technical name for this engine is the *xVelocity analytics engine*. However, in Excel, it's referred to as the internal *data model*.

Every Excel workbook contains an internal data model, which is a single instance of the Power Pivot in-memory engine. This section outlines how to leverage the Power Pivot internal data model to import and integrate disparate data sources.

Activating the Power Pivot Ribbon

The Power Pivot Ribbon interface is available only when you activate it. It's important to note that the Power Pivot add-in does not install with every edition of Office. For example, if you have the Office Home edition, you will not be able to see or activate the Power Pivot add-in; thus, you will not have access to the Power Pivot Ribbon interface.

As of this writing, the Power Pivot Ribbon interface is available to you only if you have one of the following editions of Office or Excel:

Office 2013, 2016, or 2019 Professional Plus: Available through volume licensing only

Office 365 Pro Plus: Available with an ongoing subscription to Office365.com

Excel 2013, 2016, or 2019 stand-alone edition: Available for purchase through any retailer

If you have any of these editions, you can activate the Power Pivot Ribbon by following these steps:

1. **Open Excel and look for a Power Pivot tab on the Ribbon.** If you see the tab, then you can skip the remaining steps.

2. **On the Excel Ribbon, click File ⇨ Options.**

3. **Choose the Customize Ribbon option on the left.**

4. **Look in the Main Tabs list on the right and find the Power Pivot option.** Check the box next to this option and click OK.

5. **The Power Pivot tab should appear (see Figure 35.1).** If the Power Pivot tab does not appear in the Ribbon, close Excel and restart.

FIGURE 35.1

The Power Pivot Ribbon interface

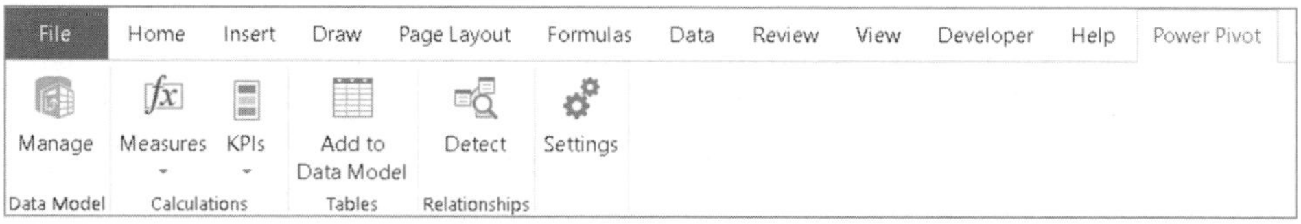

A Word on Compatibility

Since Excel 2010 was released, Microsoft has made several versions of the Power Pivot add-in available for download. Starting with Excel 2013, the Power Pivot add-in has been included natively with Excel. The bottom line is that there are different versions of Power Pivot being used today, each designed to work with different versions of Excel. This obviously leads to some compatibility considerations about which you should be aware.

You have to be careful when sharing Power Pivot workbooks in environments where some of your audience is using earlier versions of Excel (Excel 2010, for example) while others are using more recent versions of Excel. Opening and refreshing a workbook that contains a Power Pivot model created with an older version of the Power Pivot add-in will trigger an automatic upgrade of the underlying model. Once this happens, users with older versions of the add-in will no longer be able to use the workbook.

> As a general rule, Power Pivot workbooks created in a version of Excel that is equal to or less than your version should give you no problems. However, you will not be able use Power Pivot workbooks created in a version of Excel greater than your version.

Linking Excel tables to Power Pivot

The first step in using Power Pivot is to fill it with data. You can either import data from external data sources or link to Excel tables in your current workbook. For now, let's start this walk-through by linking three Excel tables to Power Pivot.

Most of the examples in this chapter are available on this book's website at www.wiley.com/go/ excel2019bible. The filename is Power Pivot Intro.xlsx.

In this scenario, we have three data sets in three different worksheets (see Figure 35.2): Customers, Invoice Header, and Invoice Details.

FIGURE 35.2

We want to use Power Pivot to analyze the data in the Customers, Invoice Header, and Invoice Details worksheets.

	A	B	C	D	E	F	G
1	CustomerID	CustomerName	Address	Country	City	State	Zip
2	DOLLISCO0001	Dollis Cove Resort	765 Kingway	Canada	Charlottetown	PEI	C1A 1W3
3	GETAWAYI0001	Getaway Inn	234 E Cannon Ave.	USA	Saginaw	MI	48605

Customers | InvoiceHeader | InvoiceDetails

	A	B	C	D
1	InvoiceDate	InvoiceNumber	CustomerID	
2	5/8/2005	ORDST1025	BAKERSEM0001	
3	4/12/2007	STDINV2251	BAKERSEM0001	

Customers | **InvoiceHeader** | InvoiceDetails

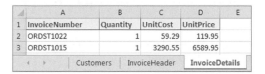

	A	B	C	D	E
1	InvoiceNumber	Quantity	UnitCost	UnitPrice	
2	ORDST1022	1	59.29	119.95	
3	ORDST1015	1	3290.55	6589.95	

Customers | InvoiceHeader | **InvoiceDetails**

The Customers data set contains basic information like Customer ID, Customer Name, Address, and so forth. The Invoice Header data set contains data that points specific invoices to specific customers. The Invoice Details data set contains the specifics of each invoice.

We want to analyze revenue by customer and month. It's clear that we'll somehow need to join these three tables together before we can do our analysis. In the past, we would have to go through a series of gyrations involving VLOOKUPs or other clever formulas. But with Power Pivot, we can build these relationships in just a few clicks.

35

Preparing your Excel tables

When linking Excel data to Power Pivot, it's a best practice first to convert your Excel data to explicitly named tables. Although not technically necessary, giving your tables friendly names helps track and manage your data in the Power Pivot data model. If you don't convert your data to tables first, Excel will do it for you and give your tables useless names like Table1, Table2, and so on.

Follow these steps to convert each data set into an Excel table:

1. **Go to the Customers tab, and click anywhere inside the data range.**

2. **Press Ctrl+T on your keyboard.** This will activate the Create Table dialog box shown in Figure 35.3.

FIGURE 35.3

Convert your data range into an Excel table.

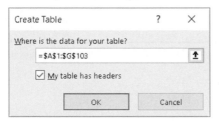

3. **In the Create Table dialog box, make sure the range for the table is correct and that the check box next to the "My table has headers" option is selected.** Click the OK button.

4. **You should now see a Table Tools Design tab on the Ribbon.** Click that tab and use the Table Name input to give your table a friendly name (see Figure 35.4). This will ensure that you will be able to recognize the table when adding it to the internal data model.

FIGURE 35.4

Give your newly created Excel table a friendly name.

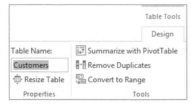

5. **Repeat steps 1–4 for the Invoice Header and Invoice Details data sets.**

Adding your Excel tables to the data model

Once you've converted your data to Excel tables, you're ready to add them to the Power Pivot data model. Follow these steps to add your newly created Excel tables to the data model using the Power Pivot tab:

1. **Click any cell inside your Customers Excel table.**

2. **Click the Power Pivot tab on the Ribbon, and click the Add to Data Model command.** Power Pivot creates a copy of your table and activates the Power Pivot window (shown in Figure 35.5).

FIGURE 35.5

The Power Pivot window shows all the data that currently exists in your data model.

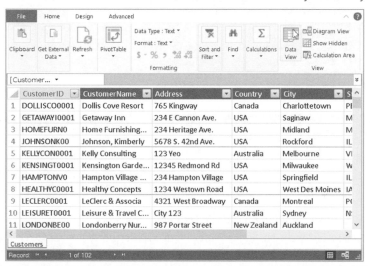

Although the Power Pivot window looks like Excel, it's actually a separate program altogether. You'll notice that the grid for the Customers table has row numbers but no column references. You'll also notice that you can't edit the data within the table. This data is simply a snapshot of the actual Excel table you imported.

Additionally, if you look at your Windows taskbar at the bottom of your screen, you'll see that Power Pivot has a separate window from Excel. You can switch between Excel and the Power Pivot window by clicking each respective program in the taskbar.

Repeat steps 1 and 2 for your other Excel tables: Invoice Header and Invoice Details. Once you have imported all your Excel tables into the data model, your Power Pivot window will show each data set on its own tab, as shown in Figure 35.6.

FIGURE 35.6

Each table you add to the data model will be placed on its own tab in Power Pivot.

	CustomerID	CustomerName	Address
1	DOLLISCO0001	Dollis Cove Resort	765 Kingway
2	GETAWAYI0001	Getaway Inn	234 E Cannon Ave.
3	HOMEFURN0	Home Furnishing...	234 Heritage Ave.
4	JOHNSONK00	Johnson, Kimberly	5678 S. 42nd Ave.
5	KELLYCON0001	Kelly Consulting	123 Yeo
6	KENSINGT0001	Kensington Garde...	12345 Redmond Rt
7	HAMPTONV0	Hampton Village ...	234 Hampton Villa;
8	HEALTHYC0001	Healthy Concepts	1234 Westown Roi
9	LECLERC0001	LeClerc & Associa	4321 West Broadw
10	LEISURET0001	Leisure & Travel C...	City 123
11	LONDONBE00	Londonberry Nur...	987 Portar Street
12	INTERNAT0001	International Mai...	8765 58th Street V
13	ISNINDUS0001	ISN Industries	987 Union Circle
14	MANCHEST00	Manchester Suites	678 W Orange Ave
15	BLUEYOND0001	Blue Yonder Airlines	P.O. Box 1234
16	COHOWINE0	Coho Wintery	234 Hickman St.

Customers | InvoiceHeader | InvoiceDetails

Record: 1 of 102

NOTE

Because the data that you just imported into Power Pivot contained in the tab is a linked Excel table, Power Pivot will pick up any changes. That is to say, even though the data is a snapshot of the data at the time you added it, the data automatically updates when you edit the source table in Excel.

Creating relationships between your Power Pivot tables

At this point in our walk-through, Power Pivot knows that we have three tables in the data model, but it has no idea how these three tables relate to one another. We'll need to connect these tables by defining relationships between the Customers, Invoice Details, and Invoice Header tables. We can do so directly within the Power Pivot window.

TIP

If you inadvertently closed the Power Pivot window, you can easily call it back up by clicking the Manage command button on the Power Pivot Ribbon tab. Alternatively, you can click the Manage Data Model command on the Data tab.

1. **Activate the Power Pivot window, and click the Diagram View command button on the Home tab.** Power Pivot will display a screen that shows a visual representation of all the tables in the data model (see Figure 35.7).

FIGURE 35.7

The Diagram view allows you to see all the tables in your data model.

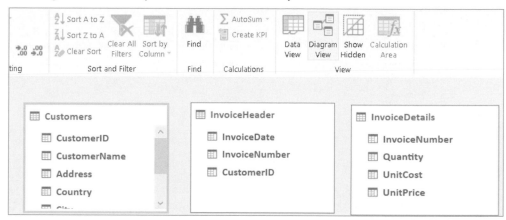

You can move the tables in the Diagram view around simply by clicking and dragging their title bars. The idea is to identify the primary index keys in each table and connect them. In this scenario, the Customers table and the Invoice Header table can be connected using the CustomerID field. The Invoice Header and Invoice Details tables can be connected using the InvoiceNumber field.

2. **Click and drag a line from the CustomerID field in the Customers table to the CustomerID field in the Invoice Header table (as demonstrated in Figure 35.8).**

FIGURE 35.8

To create a relationship, you simply click and drag a line between the fields in your tables.

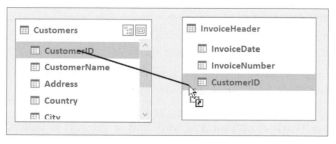

3. **Click and drag a line from the InvoiceNumber field in the Invoice Header table to the InvoiceNumber field in the Invoice Details table.**

   At this point, your diagram will look similar to Figure 35.9. Notice that Power Pivot shows a line between the tables that you just connected. In database speak, these are referred to as *joins*.

35

FIGURE 35.9

When you create relationships, the Power Pivot diagram will show join lines between your tables.

The joins in Power Pivot are one-to-many joins. This means that when a table is joined to another, one of the tables has unique records with unique index numbers, while the other can have many records where index numbers are duplicated.

Notice that the join lines have arrows pointing from a table to another table. The arrows in these join lines will always point to the table that has the nonduplicated unique index.

In this case, the Customers table contains a unique list of customers, each having its own unique identifier. No CustomerID in that table is duplicated. The Invoice header table has many rows for each CustomerID; each customer can have many invoices.

> **TIP**
> To close the diagram and get back to seeing the data tables, click the Data View command in the Power Pivot window.

Managing existing relationships

If you need to go back and edit or delete a relationship between two tables in your data model, you can do so by following these steps:

1. **Activate the Power Pivot window, select the Design tab, and then click the Manage Relationships command.**

2. **In the Manage Relationships dialog box shown in Figure 35.10, click the relationship with which you want to work and select Edit or Delete.**

FIGURE 35.10

Use the Manage Relationships dialog box to edit or delete existing relationships.

3. **Clicking Edit will open the Edit Relationship dialog box shown in Figure 35.11.**
Use the form controls presented to select the appropriate table and field names to
redefine the relationship.

FIGURE 35.11

Use the Edit Relationship dialog box to adjust the tables and field names that define
the selected relationship.

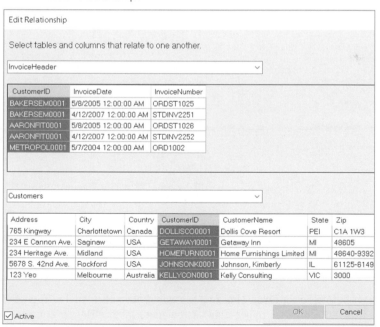

Using Power Pivot data in reporting

Once you define the relationships in your Power Pivot data model, it's essentially ready for action. In terms of Power Pivot, *action* basically means analysis with a PivotTable. In fact, all Power Pivot data is presented through the framework of PivotTables (PivotTables are covered in Chapter 29, "Introducing PivotTables," and Chapter 30, "Analyzing Data with PivotTables").

1. **Activate the Power Pivot window, select the Home tab, and then click the Pivot Table command button.**

2. **Specify whether you want the PivotTable placed on a new worksheet or an existing sheet.**

3. **Build out your needed analysis just as you would any other standard PivotTable using the PivotTable Fields list.**

The PivotTable shown in Figure 35.12 contains all the tables in the Power Pivot data model. With this configuration, we essentially have a powerful cross-table analytical engine in the form of a familiar PivotTable. Here you can see that we are calculating the average unit price by customer.

FIGURE 35.12

You now have a Power Pivot–driven PivotTable that aggregates across multiple tables.

In the days before Power Pivot, this analysis would have been tricky. You would have had to build VLOOKUP formulas to get from Customers to Invoice Header and then another set of VLOOKUPs to get from Invoice Header to Invoice Details. After all that formula building, you still would have had to find a way to aggregate the data to average the unit price per customer.

Loading Data from Other Data Sources

As you'll discover in this section, you're not limited to using only the data that already exists in your Excel workbook. Power Pivot has the ability to reach outside the workbook and import data found in external data sources. Indeed, what makes Power Pivot so powerful is its ability to consolidate data from disparate data sources and build relationships between them. This means you can theoretically create a Power Pivot data model that contains some data from a SQL Server table, some data from a Microsoft Access database, and even data from a one-off text file.

Loading data from relational databases

One of the more common data sources used by Excel analysts are relational databases. It's not difficult to find an analyst who frequently uses data from Microsoft Access, SQL Server, or Oracle databases. In this section, we'll walk through the steps for loading data from external database systems.

Loading data from SQL Server

SQL Server databases are some of the most commonly used for storing enterprise-level data. Most SQL Server databases are managed and maintained by the IT department. To connect to a SQL Server database, you'll have to work with your IT department to obtain read access to the database from which you're trying to pull data.

Once you have access to the database, open Excel and activate the Power Pivot window by selecting Power Pivot ➪ Manage.

Once activated, select the From Other Sources command button on the Home tab. This will activate the Table Import Wizard dialog box shown in Figure 35.13. Here, select the Microsoft SQL Server option and then click the Next button.

The Table Import Wizard will now ask for all the information it needs to connect to your chosen data source. This includes things such as server address, login credentials, and any other database name. The wizard will show you different fields based on the type of data source you select. The more common fields you'll see when connecting to an external data source are as follows:

Friendly Connection Name The Friendly Connection Name field allows you to specify your own name for the external source. You typically enter a name that is descriptive and easy to read.

Server Name This is the name of the server that contains the database to which you are trying to connect. You will get this from your IT department when they give you access.

Log on to the Server These are your login credentials. Depending on how your IT department gives you access, you will select either Use Windows Authentication or Use SQL Server Authentication. The Use Windows Authentication option essentially means that the server will recognize you by your Windows login. The Use SQL Server Authentication option means that the IT department created a distinct username and password for you. If you select Use SQL Server Authentication, you will need to provide a username and password. Note that you will need at least READ privileges for the target database to pull the needed data.

35

FIGURE 35.13

Activate the Table Import Wizard and select Microsoft SQL Server.

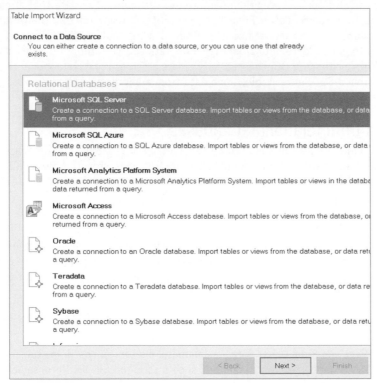

Save my Password   You can select the check box next to Save my Password if you want your username and password to be stored in the workbook. This allows your connections to remain refreshable when being used by other people. There are obviously security issues with this option because anyone can view the connection properties and see your username and password. You should use this option only if your IT department set you up with an application account (that is, an account created specifically to be used by multiple people).

Database Name   Every SQL Server can contain multiple databases. Enter the name of the database to which you are connecting. You will get this from your IT department when they give you access.

Once you enter all the pertinent information, click the Next button to get to the subsequent screen, as shown in Figure 35.14. Here you have the choice of selecting from a list of tables and views or writing your own custom query using SQL syntax. The latter involves writing your own SQL scripts. In most cases, you will choose the option to select from a list of tables.

FIGURE 35.14

Choose to select from a list of tables and views.

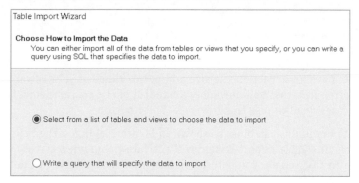

The Table Import Wizard reads the database and shows you a list of all available tables and views (see Figure 35.15). The tables will have an icon that looks like a grid, while views will have an icon that looks like a box on top of another box.

FIGURE 35.15

The Table Import Wizard will display a list of tables and views.

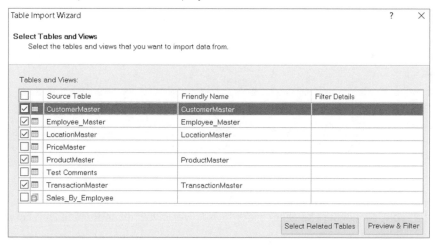

The idea is to place a check next to the tables and views that you want to import. The Friendly Name column allows you to enter a new name that will be used to reference the table in Power Pivot.

It's important to remember that importing a table imports all of the columns and records for that table. This can have an impact on the size and performance of your Power Pivot data model. You will often find that you need only a handful of the columns from the tables you import. In these cases, you can use the Preview & Filter button.

Click the table name to highlight it in blue (as shown in Figure 35.15) and then click the Preview & Filter button. The Table Import Wizard will activate the preview screen illustrated in Figure 35.16. In this screen, you will see all the columns available in the table, with a sampling of rows.

FIGURE 35.16

The Preview & Filter screen allows you to exclude columns and filter for only data you need.

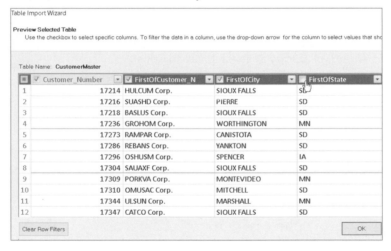

Each column header has a check box next to it, indicating that the column will be imported with the table. Removing the check mark tells Power Pivot not to include that column in the data model.

You also have the option of filtering out certain records. Clicking the drop-down arrow illustrated in Figure 35.16 activates a filter menu that allows you to specify criteria to filter out unwanted records. This works just like the standard filtering in Excel.

Once you're done selecting your data and applying any needed filters, you can click the Finish button on the Table Import Wizard to start the import process. The import log shown in Figure 35.17 displays the progress of the import and summarizes the import actions taken after completion.

FIGURE 35.17

The last screen of the Table Import Wizard shows you the progress of your import actions.

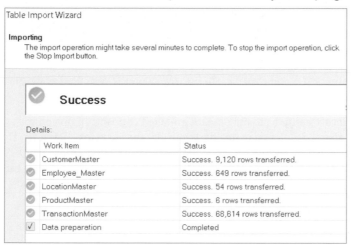

The final step in loading data from SQL Server is to review and create any needed relationships. Activate the Power Pivot window and click the Diagram View button on the Home tab. Power Pivot will display the diagram screen where you can view and edit relationships as needed (see "Creating relationships between your Power Pivot tables" earlier in this chapter).

TIP

If you find that you need to adjust the filtering you've applied to your imported data, you can call up the Preview & Filter screen again. Simply select the target table in the Power Pivot window and activate the Edit Table Properties dialog box (Design ⇨ Table Properties). You'll note that this dialog box is basically the same Preview & Filter screen that you encountered with the Import Table Wizard (see Figure 35.16). From here, you can select columns that you originally filtered out, edit record filters, clear filters, or even use a different table/view.

Loading data from other relational database systems

Whether your data lives in Microsoft Access, Oracle, dBase, or MySQL, you can load data from virtually any relational database system. As long as you have the appropriate database drivers installed, you have a way to connect Power Pivot to your data.

NOTE

To connect to any database system, you must have that system's drivers installed on your PC. SQL Server and Access are Microsoft products whose drivers are virtually guaranteed to be installed on most machines that you'll encounter. The drivers for other database systems, however, need to be installed explicitly. This is typically done by the IT department either at the time the machine is loaded with corporate software or upon demand. If you don't see the needed drivers for your database system, contact your IT department.

35

Activate the Power Pivot window, and click the From Other Sources button on the Home tab. This will activate the same Table Import Wizard as shown previously in Figure 35.13.

Select the appropriate relational database system from the plethora of options. If you need to import data from Oracle, select Oracle. If you need to import data from Sybase, select Sybase.

Connecting to any of these relational systems takes you through roughly the same steps you saw when importing SQL Server data earlier in this chapter. You may see some alternate dialog boxes, however, based on the needs of the database system you select.

Understandably, Microsoft cannot possibly create a named connection option for every database system out there. So, you may not find your database system listed. In this case, simply select the option called Others (OLEDB/ODBC). Selecting this option opens the Table Import Wizard starting with a screen asking you to enter the connection string for your database system.

Loading data from flat files

The term *flat file* refers to a file that contains some form of tabular data without any sort of structural hierarchy or relationship between records. The most common types of flat files are Excel files and text files. A ton of important data is maintained in flat files. In this section, you'll discover how to import these flat file data sources into the Power Pivot data model.

Loading data from external Excel files

Earlier in this chapter, you created linked tables by loading Power Pivot with the data contained within the same workbook. Linked tables have a distinct advantage over other types of imported data in that they immediately respond to changes in the source data within the workbook. If you change the data in one of the tables in the workbook, the linked table within the Power Pivot data model automatically changes. The real-time interactivity you get with linked tables is really nice to have.

The drawback to linked tables is that the source data must be kept in the same workbook as the Power Pivot data model. This isn't always possible. You'll encounter plenty of scenarios where you'll need to incorporate Excel data into your analysis but that data lives in another workbook. In these cases, you can use Power Pivot's Table Import Wizard to connect to external Excel files.

Activate the Power Pivot window and click the From Other Sources button on the Home tab. This will activate the Table Import Wizard dialog box. Scroll down and select the Excel File option in Figure 35.18 and then click the Next button.

The Table Import Wizard will now ask for all the information it needs to connect to your target workbook. In this screen, you'll need to provide the following:

FIGURE 35.18

Activate the Table Import Wizard and select Excel File.

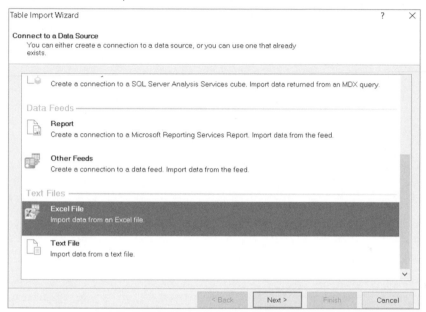

Friendly Connection Name   The Friendly Connection Name field allows you to specify your own name for the external source. You typically enter a name that is descriptive and easy to read.

Excel File Path   Enter the full path of your target Excel workbook. You can use the Browse button to search for and select the workbook from which you want to pull this information.

Use First Row as Column Headers   In most cases, your Excel data will have column headers. Be sure to select the check box next to Use First Row as Column Headers to make sure that your column headers are recognized as headers when imported.

Once you enter all the pertinent information, click the Next button to get to the next screen, as shown in Figure 35.19. Here you'll see a list of all the worksheets in the chosen Excel workbook. Place a check mark next to the worksheets you want to import. The Friendly Name column allows you to enter a new name that will be used to reference the table in Power Pivot.

35

FIGURE 35.19

Select the worksheets you want to import.

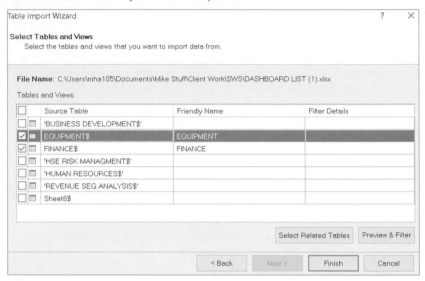

As discussed earlier in this chapter, you can use the Preview & Filter button to filter out unwanted columns and records if needed. Otherwise, continue with the Table Import Wizard to complete the import process.

As always, be sure to review and create relationships to any other tables you've loaded into the Power Pivot data model.

Loading data from text files

Text files are another type of flat file used to distribute data. These files are commonly outputs from legacy systems and websites. Excel has always been able to import text files. With Power Pivot, you can go further and integrate them with other data sources.

Activate the Power Pivot window, and click the From Other Sources button on the Home tab. This will activate the same Table Import Wizard dialog box illustrated in Figure 35.18. Select the Text File option and then click the Next button.

The Table Import Wizard will ask for all the information it needs to connect to the target text file. In this screen, you'll need to provide the following:

Friendly Connection Name   The Friendly Connection Name field allows you to specify your own name for the external source. You typically enter a name that is descriptive and easy to read.

File Path   Enter the full path of your target text file. You can use the Browse button to search for and select the file from which you want to pull this information.

Column Separator   Select the character used to separate the columns in the text file. Before you can do this, you'll need to know how the columns in your text file are delimited. For instance, a comma-delimited file will have commas separating the columns. A tab-delimited file will have tabs separating the columns. The drop-down list in the Table Import Wizard includes choices for the more common delimiters: Tab, Comma, Semicolon, Space, Colon, and Vertical Bar.

Use First Row as Column Headers   If your text file contains header rows, be sure to select the check box next to Use First Row as Column Headers. This ensures that the column headers are recognized as headers when imported.

You'll get an immediate preview of the data in the text file. As with other data sources we've covered here, you can filter out any unwanted columns simply by removing the check mark next to the column names. You can also use the drop-down arrows next to each column to apply any record filters.

Clicking the Finish button will immediately start the import process. Upon completion, the data from your text file will be part of the Power Pivot data model. As always, be sure to review and create relationships to any other tables that you've loaded into Power Pivot.

Loading data from the clipboard

Power Pivot includes an interesting option for loading data straight from the clipboard, that is, pasting data you've copied from some other place. This option is meant to be used as a one-off technique to get useful information into the Power Pivot data model quickly.

As you consider this option, keep in mind that there is no real data source. It's just you manually copying and pasting. There is no way to refresh the data, and there is no way to trace back where you actually copied the data from.

Imagine that you received a Word document showing a list of branches in a table. You'd like to include this static list of branches in your Power Pivot data model, as shown in Figure 35.20.

35

FIGURE 35.20

You can copy data straight out of Microsoft Word.

	A	B	C
1	Branch_Number	Market	Region
2	101313	FLORIDA	SOUTH
3	101419	MICHIGAN	NORTH
4	102516	TULSA	MIDWEST
5	103516	TULSA	MIDWEST
6	173901	CHARLOTTE	SOUTH
7	201605	DENVER	MIDWEST
8	201709	SEATTLE	WEST
9	201714	PHOENIX	WEST
10	201717	CALIFORNIA	WEST
11	202600	DALLAS	SOUTH
12	202605	DENVER	MIDWEST
13	202714	PHOENIX	WEST

You can copy the table and then go to the Power Pivot window and click the Paste command on the Home tab. This activates the Paste Preview dialog box illustrated in Figure 35.21, where you can review what exactly will be pasted.

FIGURE 35.21

The Paste Preview dialog box gives you a chance to see what you're pasting.

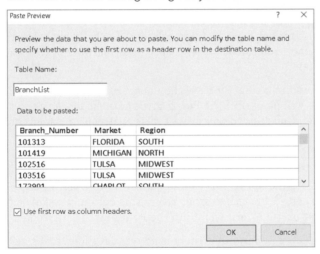

There aren't that many options here. You can specify the name that will be used to reference the table in Power Pivot, and you can specify whether the first row is a header.

Clicking the OK button will import the pasted data into Power Pivot without a lot of fanfare. At this point, you can adjust the data formatting and create the needed relationships.

Refreshing and managing external data connections

When you load data from an external data source into Power Pivot, you essentially create a static snapshot of that data source at the time of creation. Power Pivot uses that static snapshot in its internal data model.

As time goes by, the external data source may change and grow with newly added records. However, Power Pivot is still using its snapshot, so it can't incorporate any of the changes in your data source until you take another snapshot.

The action of updating the Power Pivot data model by taking another snapshot of your data source is called *refreshing your data*. You can refresh manually, or you can set up an automatic refresh.

Manually refreshing your Power Pivot data

On the Home tab of the Power Pivot window, you will see the Refresh command. Clicking the drop-down arrow below it will display two options: Refresh and Refresh All.

Use the Refresh option to refresh the Power Pivot table that's currently active. That is, if you are on the Customers tab in Power Pivot, clicking Refresh will reach out to the external data source and request an update for just the Customers table. This works nicely when you need to refresh strategically only certain data sources.

Use the Refresh All option to refresh all the tables in the Power Pivot data model.

Setting up automatic refreshing

You can configure your data sources to pull the latest data and refresh Power Pivot automatically. Go to the Data tab in the Excel Ribbon, and select the Queries & Connections command. This will activate the Queries & Connections task pane illustrated in Figure 35.22.

FIGURE 35.22

The Queries & Connections task pane

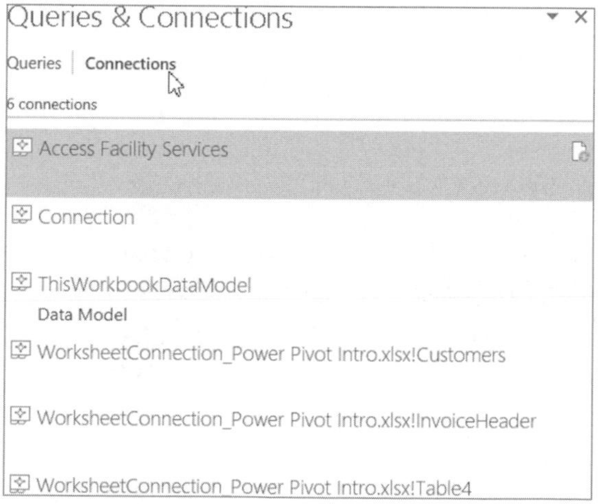

35

Click Connections at the top of the task pane and then double-click the connection with which you want to work.

With the Connection Properties dialog box open (see Figure 35.23), select the Usage tab. Here you'll find the following options:

Refresh Every X Minutes Placing a check mark next to this option tells Excel to refresh the chosen data connection automatically after a specified number of minutes. This will refresh all tables associated with that connection.

Refresh data when opening the file Placing a check mark next to this option tells Excel to refresh the chosen data connection automatically upon opening the workbook. This will refresh all tables associated with that connection as soon as the workbook is opened.

Refresh this connection on Refresh All Earlier in this section, you discovered that you can refresh all the connections that feed Power Pivot by using the Refresh All command found on the Power Pivot Home tab. If the data connection in question imports millions of lines of data from an external data source, you may not want to slow down your machine each time you trigger a Refresh All. You can remove the check mark next to the Refresh This Connection on Refresh All option. This essentially tells the connection to ignore the Refresh All command.

FIGURE 35.23

The Connection Properties dialog box lets you configure the chosen data connection to refresh automatically.

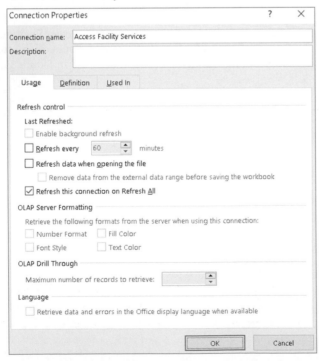

Editing your data connection

There may be instances where you need to edit your source data connection after you've already created it. Unlike refreshing, where you simply take another snapshot of the same data source, editing the source data connection allows you to go back and reconfigure the connection. Here are a few reasons that you'll need to edit a data connection:

- The location or server or data source file has changed.
- The name of the server or data source file has changed.
- You need to edit your login credentials or authentication mode.
- You need to add tables that you left out during the initial import.

In the Power Pivot window, go to the Home tab and click the Existing Connections button. The Existing Connections dialog box shown in Figure 35.24 will open. Your Power Pivot connections will be under the Power Pivot Data Connections subheading. Choose the data connection that needs editing.

FIGURE 35.24

Use the Existing Connections dialog box to reconfigure your Power Pivot source data connections.

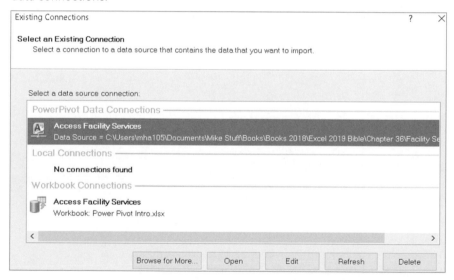

Once your target data connection is selected, look to the Edit and Open buttons. The button you click depends on what you need to change.

The Edit button Lets you reconfigure the server address, file path, and authentication settings.

The Open button Lets you import a new table from the existing connection. This is handy when you inadvertently missed a table during the initial loading of data.

35

Working Directly with the Internal Data Model

IN THIS CHAPTER

Directly feeding the internal data model

Managing relationships in the internal data model

Removing tables from the internal data model

U p until now, you used the Power Pivot Ribbon interface to work with the internal data model. As you will discover in this chapter, however, you can use a combination of PivotTables and Excel data connections to interact directly with the internal data model—without the Power Pivot Ribbon interface.

 Most of the examples in this chapter are available on this book's website at www.wiley.com/go/ excel2019bible. The filename is Internal Data Model.xlsx.

Directly Feeding the Internal Data Model

Imagine that you have the Transactions table shown in Figure 36.1. On another worksheet, you have an Employees table (see Figure 36.2) that contains information about the employee.

FIGURE 36.1

This table shows transactions by employee number.

	A	B	C	D
1	Sales_Rep	Invoice_Date	Sales_Amount	Contracted Hours
2	4416	1/5/2007	111.79	2
3	4416	1/5/2007	111.79	2
4	160006	1/5/2007	112.13	2
5	6444	1/5/2007	112.13	2
6	160006	1/5/2007	145.02	3
7	52661	1/5/2007	196.58	4
8	6444	1/5/2007	204.20	4
9	51552	1/5/2007	225.24	3
10	55662	1/6/2007	86.31	2
11	1336	1/6/2007	86.31	2
12	60224	1/6/2007	86.31	2
13	54564	1/6/2007	86.31	2
14	56146	1/6/2007	89.26	2
15	5412	1/6/2007	90.24	1

FIGURE 36.2

This table provides information on employees: first name, last name, and job title.

	A	B	C	D
1	Employee_Number	Last_Name	First_Name	Job_Title
2	21	SIOCAT	ROBERT	SERVICE REPRESENTATIVE 3
3	42	BREWN	DONNA	SERVICE REPRESENTATIVE 3
4	45	VAN HUILE	KENNETH	SERVICE REPRESENTATIVE 2
5	104	WIBB	MAURICE	SERVICE REPRESENTATIVE 2
6	106	CESTENGIAY	LUC	SERVICE REPRESENTATIVE 2
7	113	TRIDIL	ROCH	SERVICE REPRESENTATIVE 2
8	142	CETE	GUY	SERVICE REPRESENTATIVE 3
9	145	ERSINEILT	MIKE	SERVICE REPRESENTATIVE 2
10	162	GEBLE	MICHAEL	SERVICE REPRESENTATIVE 2
11	165	CERDANAL	ALAIN	SERVICE REPRESENTATIVE 3
12	201	GEIDRIOU	DOMINIC	TEAMLEAD 1

You need to create an analysis that shows sales by job title. This would normally be difficult given the fact that sales and job title are in two separate tables. But with the internal data model, it's just a matter of a few clicks.

The first thing you will need to do is to convert your data tables into Excel Table objects that the internal data model can recognize:

1. **Click inside the TransactionMaster data table and select Insert ⇨ Table.** This activates the Create Table dialog box.

2. **Select the table range and then click OK.** You will want to name your Table objects explicitly. This way, you can easily recognize your tables in the internal data model. If you don't name your tables, the internal data model shows them as Table1, Table2, and so on.

3. **Insert your cursor anywhere inside the table and select the Table Tools Design tab.** There you will find the Table Name input box in the Properties group. Enter a new name for your table (in this case, **Transactions**). At this point, you're ready to feed your table to the internal data model.

4. **Select Data ⇨ Existing Connections.**

5. **In the Existing Connections dialog box, select the Tables tab.** You will see a list of existing Table objects (see Figure 36.3).

6. **Double-click the Transactions Table object.** This will activate the Import Data dialog box shown in Figure 36.4.

7. **Select the Only Create Connection option and then click OK.**

Repeat the previous steps for the Employees table.

Once both tables are loaded into the internal data model, you can create the needed PivotTable by following these steps:

1. **Select Data ⇨ Existing Connections.**

2. **In the Existing Connections dialog box, select the Tables tab.**
3. **Double-click the Tables in Workbook Data Model entry (see Figure 36.5).**

FIGURE 36.3

The Existing Connection dialog box lists all available Table objects.

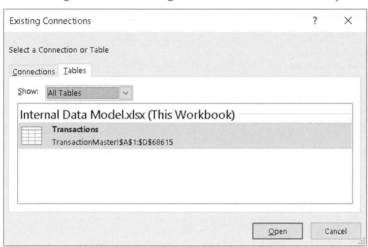

FIGURE 36.4

Use the Import Data dialog box to add the Table object to the internal data model.

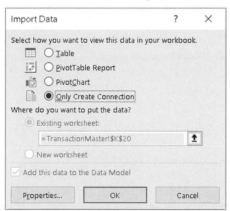

FIGURE 36.5

You can explicitly choose the internal data model as the source for a PivotTable.

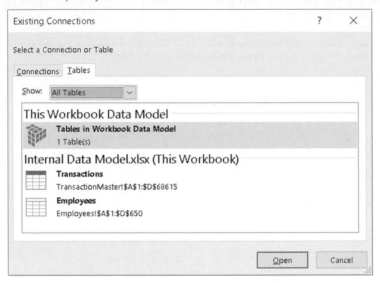

4. **The Import Data dialog box will open.** As Figure 36.6 illustrates, you will choose to create a PivotTable report on a new worksheet. Click OK to confirm.

FIGURE 36.6

Creating a new PivotTable on a new worksheet

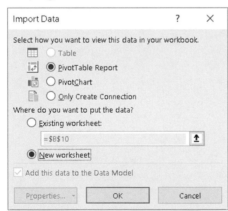

At this point, you can click the newly created PivotTable to activate the PivotTable Fields list, if necessary. Choose the All selector, as shown in Figure 36.7. This shows all available tables in the Fields list.

FIGURE 36.7

Select All in the PivotTable Fields list to see both tables in your internal data model.

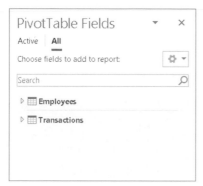

5. **Build out your PivotTable as normal.** In this case, Job_Title goes to the Rows area and Sales_Amount goes to the Values area.

   As you can see in Figure 36.8, Excel immediately recognizes that you are using two tables from your internal data model and prompts you to create a relationship between them. You have the option of letting Excel auto-detect the relationships between your tables, or you can click the Create button. It's always best to create the relationships yourself to avoid any possibility of Excel getting it wrong. Click the Create button.

6. **Excel activates the Create Relationship dialog box shown in Figure 36.9.** Here you select the tables and fields that define the relationship. In Figure 36.9, you can see that the Transactions table has a Sales_Rep field. It is related to the Employees table via the Employee_Number field.

After you create your relationship, you have a single PivotTable that effectively uses data from both tables to create the analysis you need. Figure 36.10 illustrates the final PivotTable after number formatting has been applied to the sum of the sales amount.

FIGURE 36.8

When Excel prompts you, choose to create the relationship between the two tables.

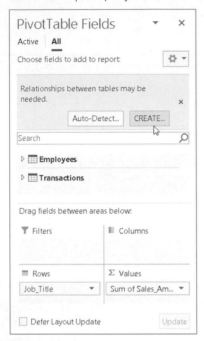

FIGURE 36.9

Build the appropriate relationship using the Table and Column drop-downs.

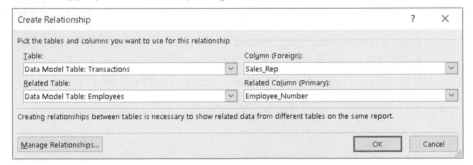

FIGURE 36.10

You have achieved your goal of showing sales by job title.

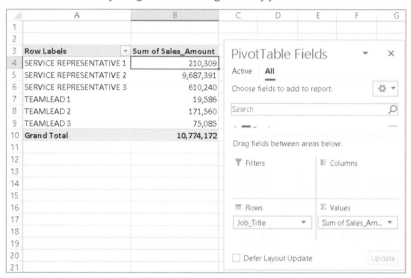

> **NOTE**
>
> In Figure 36.9, you see that the lower-right drop-down is named Related Column (Primary). The term *primary* means that the internal data model uses this field from the associated table as the primary key.
>
> A primary key is a field that contains only unique non-null values (no duplicates or blanks). Primary key fields are necessary in the data model to prevent aggregation errors and duplications. Every relationship that you create must have a field designated as the primary key.
>
> So, the Employees table (in the scenario in Figure 36.9) must have all unique values in the Employee_Number field, with no blanks or null values. This is the only way that Excel can ensure data integrity when joining multiple tables.

Managing Relationships in the Internal Data Model

After you assign tables to the internal data model, you might need to adjust the relationships between the tables. To make changes to the relationships in an internal data model, activate the Manage Relationships dialog box.

Click the Data tab in the Ribbon and select the Relationships command. The dialog box shown in Figure 36.11 displays.

FIGURE 36.11
The Manage Relationships dialog box enables you to make changes to the relationships in the internal data model.

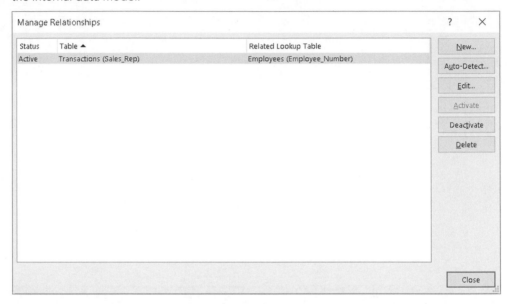

Here, you will find the following commands:

New   Create a new relationship between two tables in the internal data model.

Auto-Detect   Have Power Pivot automatically detect and create relationships based on the data in your tables.

Edit   Alter the selected relationship.

Activate   Enforce the selected relationship, telling Excel to consider the relationship when aggregating and analyzing the data in the internal data model.

Deactivate   Turn off the selected relationship, telling Excel to ignore the relationship when aggregating and analyzing the data in the internal data model.

Delete   Remove the selected relationship.

Removing a Table from the Internal Data Model

You might find that you want to remove a table or data source altogether from the internal data model. To do so, click the Data tab in the Ribbon and then click the Queries & Connections command. The Queries & Connections task pane shown in Figure 36.12 activates.

Right-click the table that you want to remove from the internal data model (Employees, in this case) and then click the Delete option. Click OK if you want to confirm the deletion.

36

FIGURE 36.12

Use the Queries & Connections task pane to remove any table from the internal data model.

Adding Formulas to Power Pivot

IN THIS CHAPTER

Creating your own calculated columns

Utilizing DAX to create calculated columns

Creating calculated measures

Using Cube functions to break out of PivotTables

W hen analyzing data with Power Pivot, you'll often find that you need to expand your analysis to include data based on calculations that are not in your original data set. Power Pivot has a robust set of functions called *data analysis expressions*, or *DAX functions*, which allow you to perform mathematical operations, recursive calculations, data lookups, and much more.

This chapter introduces you to DAX functions, and it provides the ground rules for building your own calculations in Power Pivot data models.

 Most of the examples in this chapter are available on this book's website at www.wiley.com/go/ excel2019bible. The filename is Power Pivot Formulas.xlsx.

Enhancing Power Pivot Data with Calculated Columns

Calculated columns are columns that you create to enhance a Power Pivot table with your own formulas. Calculated columns are entered directly in the Power Pivot window, becoming part of the source data you use to feed your PivotTable. Calculated columns work at the row level; that is, the formulas that you create in a calculated column perform their operations based on the data in each individual row. For example, imagine you have a Revenue column and a Cost column in your Power Pivot table. You could create a new column that calculated [Revenue] minus [Cost]. This calculation is simple and is valid for each row in the data set.

Calculated measures are used to perform more complex calculations that work on an aggregation of data. These calculations are applied directly to your PivotTable, creating a sort of virtual column that can't be seen in the Power Pivot window. Calculated measures are needed when you need to calculate based on an aggregated grouping of rows, such as the sum of [Year2] minus the sum of [Year1].

Creating your first calculated column

Creating a calculated column works very much like building formulas in an Excel table. Let's continue the walk-through with some sample data; follow these steps to create a calculated column:

1. **Open the** `Pivot Formulas.xlsx` **sample file, activate the Power Pivot window (by clicking the Manage button on the Power Pivot Ribbon tab), and then select the Invoice Details tab.**

2. **In the table, you will see an empty column on the far right labeled Add Column. Click the first blank cell in that column.**

3. **In the Formula bar (see Figure 37.1), enter the following formula:**

   `=[UnitPrice]*[Quantity]`

4. **Press Enter to see your formula populate the entire column.**

5. **Power Pivot will automatically rename the column to Calculated Column 1. Double-click the column label, and rename the column Total Revenue.**

FIGURE 37.1

Start your calculated column by entering your desired operation in the Formula bar.

	InvoiceNumber	Quantity	UnitCost	UnitPrice	Total Revenue
1	ORDST1022	1	59.29	119.95	119.95
2	ORDST1015	1	3290.55	6589.95	6589.95
3	ORDST1016	10	35	34.95	349.5
4	ORDST1017	50	91.59	189.95	9497.5
5	ORDST1018	1	59.29	119.95	119.95
6	INV1010	1	674.5	1349.95	1349.95
7	INV1011	1	91.25	189.95	189.95
8	INV1012	1	303.85	609.95	609.95
9	ORDST1020	1	59.29	119.95	119.95
10	ORDST1021	1	59.29	119.95	119.95

[Total Revenue] ▾   *fx* =[UnitPrice]*[Quantity]

NOTE

You can rename any column in the Power Pivot window by double-clicking the column name and entering a new name. Alternatively, you can right-click any column and choose the Rewname Column option.

TIP

You can build your calculated columns by clicking instead of typing. For example, instead of manually entering = [UnitPrice]*[Quantity], you can enter the equal sign (=), click the UnitPrice column, enter the asterisk (*), and then click the Quantity column. Note that you can also enter your own static data. For example, you can enter a formula to add a 10 percent tax by entering =[UnitPrice]*1.10.

Each calculated column that you create will automatically be available in any PivotTable connected to the Power Pivot data model. You don't have to take any action to get your calculated columns into the PivotTable. Figure 37.2 illustrates the Total Revenue calculated column in the PivotTable Fields list. These calculated columns can be used just as you would any other field in your PivotTable.

FIGURE 37.2

Calculated columns automatically show up in your PivotTable Fields list.

Row Labels	Sum of Total Revenue
Aaron Fitz Electrical	45668.4
Adam Park Resort	6238.5
Advanced Paper Co.	131930.45
Advanced Tech Satellite System	2278.7
American Science Museum	6357.8
Associated Insurance Company	1299.8
Astor Suites	174604.55
Atmore Retirement Center	39.95
Baker's Emporium Inc.	18418
Blue Yonder Airlines	26138.3
Boyle's Country Inn's	1829.85
Breakthrough Telemarketing	91437
Castle Inn Resort	239.9
Central Communications LTD	36816.2
Central Distributing	9637.8
Central Illinois Hospital	10229.9
Communication Connections	928.85
Computerized Phone Systems	239.9

PivotTable Fields

ACTIVE | ALL

Choose fields to add to report:

Search

▲ ⬛ InvoiceDetails
  ☐ InvoiceNumber
  ☐ Quantity
  ☐ UnitCost
  ☐ UnitPrice
  ☑ Total Revenue

▷ ⬛ InvoiceHeader

Drag fields between areas below:

▼ FILTERS   ▥ COLUMNS

 See Chapter 35, "Introducing Power Pivot," for a refresher on how to create a PivotTable from Power Pivot.

Formatting your calculated columns

You'll often need to change the formatting of your Power Pivot columns to match the data within them appropriately. For example, you might want to show numbers as currency, remove decimal places, or display dates in a certain way.

You are by no means limited to formatting just calculated columns. These steps can be used to format any column that you see in your Power Pivot window:

1. **In the Power Pivot window, click the column that you want to format.**
2. **Go to the Home tab of the Power Pivot window and find the Formatting group (see Figure 37.3).**

3. **Use the option to alter the formatting of the column as you see fit.**

FIGURE 37.3

You can use the formatting tools found on the Power Pivot window's Home tab to format any column in the data model.

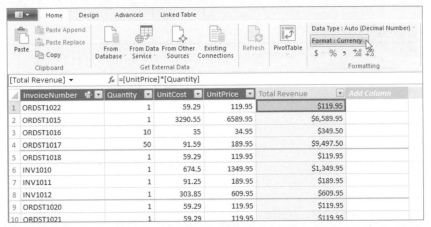

> **TIP**
>
> Veterans of Excel PivotTables know that changing PivotTable number formats one data field at a time is a pain. One fantastic feature of Power Pivot formatting is that any format you apply to your columns in the Power Pivot window will automatically be applied to all PivotTables connected to the data model!

Referencing calculated columns in other calculations

Like all calculations in Excel, Power Pivot allows you to reference a calculated column as a variable in another calculated column. Figure 37.4 illustrates this with a new calculated column called Gross Margin. Notice in the Formula bar that the calculation uses our previously created [Total Revenue] calculated column.

FIGURE 37.4

The new Gross Margin calculation uses the previously created [Total Revenue] calculated column.

fx =[Total Revenue]-([UnitCost]*[Quantity])

Quantity	UnitCost	UnitPrice	Total Revenue	Gross Margin
1	59.29	119.95	$119.95	60.66
1	3290.55	6589.95	$6,589.95	3299.4
10	35	34.95	$349.50	-0.5
50	91.59	189.95	$9,497.50	4918
1	59.29	119.95	$119.95	60.66
1	674.5	1349.95	$1,349.95	675.45
1	91.25	189.95	$189.95	98.7
1	303.85	609.95	$609.95	306.1
1	59.29	119.95	$119.95	60.66
1	59.29	119.95	$119.95	60.66

Hiding calculated columns from end users

Because calculated columns can reference each other, you can imagine creating columns simply as helper columns for other calculations. You may not want your end users to see these columns in your client tools. In this context, the term *client tools* refers to PivotTables, Power View dashboards, and Power Map.

Similar to hiding columns on an Excel worksheet, Power Pivot allows you to hide any column (it doesn't have to be a calculated column). To hide columns, simply select the columns you want hidden, right-click the selection, and then choose the Hide from Client Tools option (illustrated in Figure 37.5).

FIGURE 37.5

Right-click and select Hide from Client Tools.

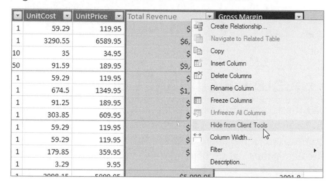

When a column is hidden, it will not show as an available selection in your PivotTable Fields list. However, if the column you are hiding is already part of the PivotTable report, meaning that you already dragged it onto the PivotTable, hiding the column in the Power Pivot window will not automatically remove it from the report. Hiding merely affects the ability to see the column in the PivotTable Fields list.

You'll note in Figure 37.6 that Power Pivot recolors columns based on their attributes. Hidden columns are subdued and grayed out, while calculated columns that are not hidden have a darker (black) header.

FIGURE 37.6

Hidden columns are grayed out, and calculated columns have a darker heading.

UnitCost	UnitPrice	Total Revenue	Gross Margin
59.29	119.95	$119.95	60.66
3290.55	6589.95	$6,589.95	3299.4
35	34.95	$349.50	-0.5
91.59	189.95	$9,497.50	4918
59.29	119.95	$119.95	60.66
674.5	1349.95	$1,349.95	675.45
91.25	189.95	$189.95	98.7
303.85	609.95	$609.95	306.1
59.29	119.95	$119.95	60.66
59.29	119.95	$119.95	60.66

> **NOTE**
> To unhide columns, select the hidden columns in the Power Pivot window, right-click the selection, and then choose the Unhide from Client Tools option.

Utilizing DAX to Create Calculated Columns

Data Analysis Expression (DAX) is essentially the formula language Power Pivot uses to perform calculations within its own construct of tables and columns. The DAX formula language comes with its own set of functions. Some of these functions can be used in calculated columns for row-level calculations, while others are designed to be used in calculated measures for aggregate operations.

In this section, we'll touch on some of the DAX functions that can be leveraged in calculated columns.

> **NOTE**
> There are more than 150 different DAX functions. The examples of DAX demonstrated in this chapter are meant to give you a sense of how calculated columns and calculated measures work. A full overview of DAX is beyond the scope of this book. If after reading this chapter you have a desire to learn more about DAX, consider picking up the book by Alberto Ferrari and Marco Russo called *The Definitive Guide to DAX* (Microsoft Press, 2015). Ferrari and Russo provide an excellent overview of DAX that is both easy to understand and comprehensive.

Identifying DAX functions safe for calculated columns

In the previous section, you used the Formula bar within the Power Pivot window to enter calculations. Next to that Formula bar, you may have noticed the Insert Function button labeled *fx*. This is similar to the Insert Function button found in Excel. Clicking this button will activate the Insert Function dialog box shown in Figure 37.7. This dialog box allows you to browse, search for, and insert the available DAX functions.

FIGURE 37.7

The Insert Function dialog box shows you all available DAX functions.

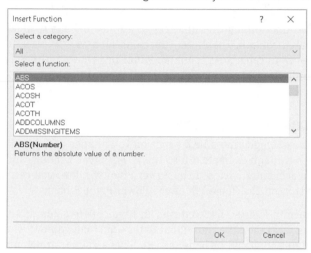

FIGURE 37.8

As you look through the list of DAX functions, you'll notice that many of them look like the Excel functions with which you are already familiar. Make no mistake, however; these are *not* Excel functions. Where Excel functions work with cells and ranges, these DAX functions are designed to work at the table and column levels.

To understand what that means, start a new calculated column on the Invoice Details tab. Click the Formula bar, and enter a good old SUM function: =SUM([Gross Margin]). Figure 37.8 shows the result.

FIGURE 37.8

The DAX SUM function can only sum the column as a whole.

As you can see, the SUM function sums the entire column. This is because Power Pivot and DAX are designed to work with tables and columns. Power Pivot has no construct for cells and ranges. It doesn't even have column letters on its grid. Where you would normally reference a range, as in an Excel SUM function, DAX basically takes the entire column.

The bottom line is not all DAX functions can be used with calculated columns. Because a calculated column evaluates at the row level, only DAX functions that evaluate single data points can be used in a calculated column.

A good rule of thumb is if the function requires an array or a range of cells as an argument, then it not viable in a calculated column. Therefore, functions such as SUM, MIN, MAX, AVERAGE, and COUNT don't work in calculated columns. Functions that require only single data point arguments work quite well in calculated columns, such as YEAR, MONTH, MID, LEFT, RIGHT, IF, and IFERROR.

Building DAX-driven calculated columns

To demonstrate the usefulness of employing a DAX function to enhance calculated columns, let's return to our walk-through example. Go to the Power Pivot window, and click the InvoiceHeader tab. If you accidentally closed the Power Pivot window, you can activate it by clicking the Manage button on the Home tab of the Power Pivot Ribbon.

The InvoiceHeader table, shown in Figure 37.9, contains an InvoiceDate column. Although this column is valuable in the raw table, the individual dates aren't convenient when analyzing the data with a PivotTable. It would be beneficial to have a column for Month and a column for Year. This way, you could aggregate and analyze your data by month and year.

FIGURE 37.9

DAX functions can help enhance the InvoiceHeader data with Year and Month time dimensions.

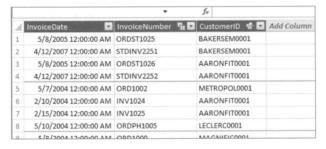

For this endeavor, you use the YEAR(), MONTH(), and FORMAT() DAX functions to add some time dimensions to your data model. Follow these steps:

1. **In the InvoiceHeader table, click the first blank cell in the empty column labeled Add Column on the far right.**

2. **In the Formula bar, type** =YEAR([InvoiceDate]), **and then press Enter.**

3. **Power Pivot will automatically rename the column to Calculated Column 1. Double-click the column label, and rename the column** Year.

4. **Starting the next column, click the first blank cell in the empty column labeled Add Column on the far right.**

5. **In the Formula bar, type** =MONTH([InvoiceDate]) **and then press Enter.**

6. **Power Pivot will automatically rename the column to Calculated Column 1. Double-click the column label, and rename the column** Month.

7. **Starting the next column, click the first blank cell in the empty column labeled Add Column on the far right.**

8. **In the Formula bar, type** =FORMAT([InvoiceDate],"mmm") **and then press Enter.**

9. **Power Pivot will automatically rename the column to Calculated Column 1. Double-click the column label and rename the column** Month Name.

After going through these steps, you should have three new calculated columns similar to the ones shown in Figure 37.10.

FIGURE 37.10

Using DAX functions to supplement a table with Year, Month, and Month Name columns

[Month Name] ▾		f_x =FORMAT([InvoiceDate],"mmm")				
InvoiceDate 🔽	InvoiceNumber 🔽	CustomerID 🔽	Year 🔽	Month 🔽	Month Name 🔽	
5/8/2005 12:00:00 AM	ORDST1025	BAKERSEM0001	2005	5	May	
4/12/2007 12:00:00 AM	STDINV2251	BAKERSEM0001	2007	4	Apr	
5/8/2005 12:00:00 AM	ORDST1026	AARONFIT0001	2005	5	May	
4/12/2007 12:00:00 AM	STDINV2252	AARONFIT0001	2007	4	Apr	
5/7/2004 12:00:00 AM	ORD1002	METROPOL0001	2004	5	May	
2/10/2004 12:00:00 AM	INV1024	AARONFIT0001	2004	2	Feb	
2/15/2004 12:00:00 AM	INV1025	AARONFIT0001	2004	2	Feb	
5/10/2004 12:00:00 AM	ORDPH1005	LECLERC0001	2004	5	May	
5/8/2004 12:00:00 AM	ORD1000	MAGNIFIC0001	2004	5	May	

As mentioned, creating calculated columns will automatically make them available through your PivotTable Fields list (see Figure 37.11).

FIGURE 37.11

DAX calculations are immediately available in any connected PivotTable.

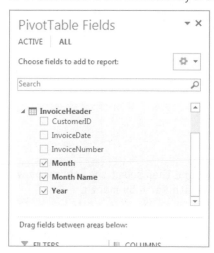

825

Month sorting in Power Pivot-driven PivotTables

One of the more annoying things about Power Pivot is that it doesn't inherently know how to sort months. Unlike standard Excel, Power Pivot doesn't use the built-in custom lists that define the order of month names. When you create a calculated column like [Month Name] and place it into your PivotTable, Power Pivot will put those months in alphabetical order (see Figure 37.12).

FIGURE 37.12

Month names in Power Pivot–driven PivotTables don't automatically sort in month order.

Row Labels	Sum of Total Revenue
⊟ Aaron Fitz Electrical	$45,668.40
Apr	$5,609.40
Feb	$13,228.00
Jan	$14,273.60
Mar	$6,948.00
May	$5,489.50
Sep	$119.90
⊟ Adam Park Resort	$6,238.50
Apr	$2,519.75
Jan	$1,199.00
May	$119.80
Sep	$2,399.95
⊟ Advanced Paper Co	$131,030.45

The fix for this is fairly easy. Activate the Power Pivot window and select the Home tab. There you will find the Sort by Column button. Upon clicking the button, the Sort by Column dialog box shown in Figure 37.13 opens.

FIGURE 37.13

The Sort by Column dialog box lets you define how your columns are sorted.

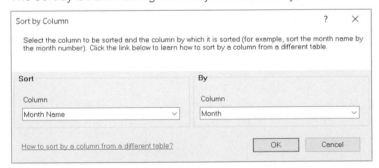

The idea is to select the column you want sorted and then select the column by which you want to sort. In this scenario, we want to sort Month Name by month.

Once you confirm the change, it will initially appear as though nothing happened. This is because the sort order that you defined is not for the Power Pivot window. The sort order is applied to your PivotTable. You can flip over to Excel and see the result in the PivotTable (see Figure 37.14).

FIGURE 37.14

Your month names now show in correct month order.

Row Labels	Sum of Total Revenue
⊟ Aaron Fitz Electrical	$45,668.40
Jan	$14,273.60
Feb	$13,228.00
Mar	$6,948.00
Apr	$5,609.40
May	$5,489.50
Sep	$119.90
⊟ Adam Park Resort	$6,238.50
Jan	$1,199.00
Apr	$2,519.75
May	$119.80
Sep	$2,399.95
⊟ Advanced Paper Co	$131,930.45

Referencing fields from other tables

Sometimes the operation you are trying to perform with a calculated column requires you to utilize fields from other tables within the Power Pivot data model. For instance, you may need to account for a customer-specific discount amount from the Customers table (see Figure 37.15) when creating a calculated column in the InvoiceDetails table.

FIGURE 37.15

The Discount Amount value in the Customers table can be used in a calculated column in another table.

	Custom...	CustomerName	Discount Amount	Address
1	DOLLISCO0001	Dollis Cove Resort	11 %	765 Kingway
2	GETAWAYI0001	Getaway Inn	10 %	234 E Cannon Ave.
3	HOMEFURN0001	Home Furnishings Limited	25 %	234 Heritage Ave.
4	JOHNSONK0001	Johnson, Kimberly	12 %	5678 S. 42nd Ave.
5	KELLYCON0001	Kelly Consulting	5 %	123 Yeo
6	KENSINGT0001	Kensington Gardens Resort	13 %	12345 Redmond Rd
7	HAMPTONV0001	Hampton Village Eatery	20 %	234 Hampton Villa
8	HEALTHYC0001	Healthy Concepts	11 %	1234 Westown Roa
9	LECLERC0001	LeClerc & Associates	8 %	4321 West Broadw
10	LEISURET0001	Leisure & Travel Consultants	6 %	City 123

To accomplish this, you can use a DAX function called RELATED. Similar to VLOOKUP in standard Excel, the RELATED function allows you to look up values from one table to use them in another.

Take a moment to follow these steps to create a new calculated column that displays a discounted revenue for each transaction in the InvoiceDetails table:

1. **In the InvoiceDetails table, click the first blank cell in the empty column labeled Add Column on the far right.**

2. **In the Formula bar, type the following:**

   ```
   =RELATED(
   ```

   As soon as you enter the open parenthesis, a menu of available fields (shown in Figure 37.16) will be displayed. Note that the items in the list represent the table name followed by the field name in brackets. In this case, we're interested in the `Customers[Discount Amount]` field.

FIGURE 37.16

Use the RELATED function to look up a field from another table.

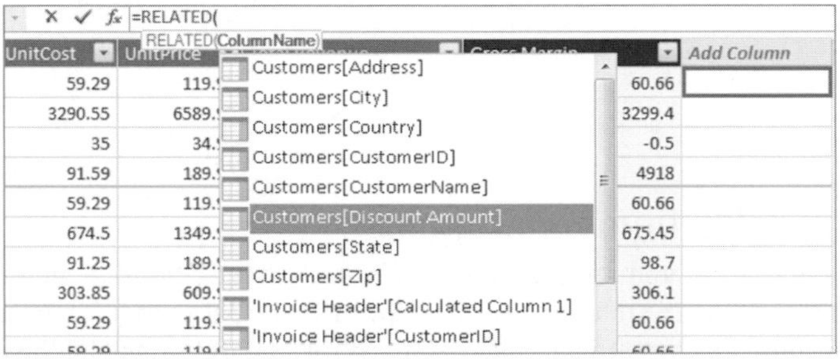

> **NOTE**
>
> The RELATED function leverages the relationships that you defined when creating the data model to perform the lookup. So, this list of choices will contain only the fields that are available based on the relationships you defined.

3. **Double-click the Customers[Discount Amount] field and then press Enter.**

4. **Power Pivot will automatically rename the column to Calculated Column 1. Double-click the column label and rename the column** `Discount%`.

5. **Starting the next column, click the first blank cell in the empty column labeled Add Column on the far right.**

6. **In the Formula bar, type**
   `=[UnitPrice]*[Quantity]*(1-[Discount%])` **and then press Enter.**

7. **Power Pivot will automatically rename the column to Calculated Column 1. Double-click the column label and rename the column** `Discounted Revenue`.

The reward for your efforts will be a new column that uses the discount percent from the Customers table to calculate discounted revenue for each transaction. Figure 37.17 illustrates the new calculated column.

FIGURE 37.17

The final Discounted Revenue calculated column using the Discount% column from the Customers table

	Total Revenue	Discount%	Discounted Revenue
9.95	$119.95	0.13	$104.36
9.95	$6,589.95	0.11	$5,865.06
4.95	$349.50	0.09	$318.05
9.95	$9,497.50	0.06	$8,927.65
9.95	$119.95	0.09	$109.15
9.95	$1,349.95	0.15	$1,147.46
9.95	$189.95	0.17	$157.66
9.95	$609.95	0.05	$579.45
9.95	$119.95	0.11	$106.76
9.95	$119.95	0.16	$100.76
9.95	$359.95	0.15	$305.96
9.95	$9.95	0.11	$8.86
9.95	$5,999.95	0.07	$5,579.95

Nesting functions

In the previous example, you first created a Discount% column using the RELATED function and then used that column in another calculated column to calculate the discounted revenue.

It's important to note that you don't necessarily have to create multiple calculated columns to accomplish a task like this. You could, instead, nest the RELATED function into the discounted revenue calculation. This would be the syntax for the nested calculation:

```
=[UnitPrice]*[Quantity]*(1-RELATED(Customers[Discount Amount]))
```

As you can see, nesting simply means embedding desired functions within a calculation. In this case, instead of using the RELATED function in a separate Discount% field, you can embed it directly in your discounted revenue calculation.

Nesting functions can definitely save time and even improve performance in larger data models. On the other hand, complicated nested functions can be harder to read and understand.

Understanding Calculated Measures

You can enhance the functionality of your Power Pivot reports with another kind of calculation called a *calculated measure*. Calculated measures are used to perform more complex calculations that work on an aggregation of data. These calculations are not applied to the Power Pivot window like calculated columns. Instead, they are applied directly to your PivotTable, creating a sort of virtual column that can't be seen in the Power Pivot window. You use calculated measures when you need to calculate based on an aggregated grouping of rows.

Imagine you wanted to show the difference in unit costs between the years 2007 and 2006 for each of your customers. Think about what technically has to be done to achieve this calculation. You'd have to figure out the sum of unit costs for 2007, then you'd have to get the sum of unit costs for 2006, and finally you'd have to subtract the sum of 2006 from the sum of 2007. This is a calculation that simply can't be done using calculated columns. Using calculated measures is the only way to get the cost variance between 2007 and 2006.

Follow these steps to create a calculated measure:

1. **Start with a PivotTable created from a Power Pivot model.**
2. **Click the Power Pivot tab in the Excel Ribbon, and select Measures ⇨ New Measure.** This will open the Measure dialog box shown in Figure 37.18.

> **NOTE**
>
> The sample file for this chapter contains a tab called Calculated Measures with a PivotTable already created.

FIGURE 37.18

Creating a new calculated measure

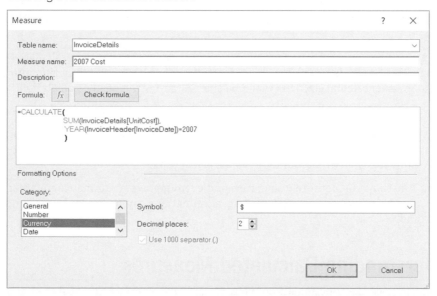

> **NOTE**
>
> You will notice in Figure 37.18 that the DAX calculation is entered with carriage returns and spaces. This is purely for readability purposes. The fact is that DAX ignores white space and is not case sensitive. So, it's very forgiving on how you structure your calculation. Given this fact, it's always best to attempt to achieve some readability with the use of carriage returns and spaces.

3. **In the Measure dialog box, input the following information:**

Table name Choose the table that you want to contain the calculated measure when looking at the PivotTable Fields list. Don't sweat this decision too much. The table you select has no bearing on how the calculation works. It's just a preference on where you want to see the new calculation within the PivotTable Fields list.

Measure name Give your calculated measure a descriptive name.

Formula Enter the DAX formula that will calculate the results of your new field.

Formatting Options Specify the formatting for the calculated measure results.

In this example, we are using the following DAX formula:

```
=CALCULATE(
    SUM(InvoiceDetails[UnitCost]),
    YEAR(InvoiceHeader[InvoiceDate])=2007
    )
```

This formula uses the CALCULATE function to sum the UnitCost column from the InvoiceDetails table, where the Year column in the InvoiceHeader is equal to 2007.

4. **Click the Check Formula button to ensure that there are no syntax errors.** If your formula is well formed, you will see the message "No errors in formula." If there are errors, you will see a full description of the errors.

5. **Click the OK button to confirm your changes and close the Measure dialog box.** You will immediately see your newly created calculated measure in the PivotTable.

6. **Repeat steps 2–5 for any other calculated measure that you need to create.**

In this example, we need a measure to show the 2006 cost:

```
=CALCULATE(
    SUM(InvoiceDetails[UnitCost]),
    YEAR(InvoiceHeader[InvoiceDate])=2006
    )
```

We will also need a measure to calculate the variance:

```
=[2007 Revenue]-[2006 Revenue]
```

Figure 37.19 illustrates the newly created calculated measures. The calculated measures are applied to each customer, displaying the variance between their 2007 and 2006 costs. As you can see, each calculated measure is available for selection in the PivotTable Fields list.

37

FIGURE 37.19

Calculated measures can be seen in the PivotTable Fields list.

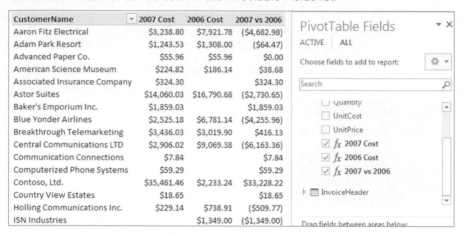

Editing and deleting calculated measures

You may find that you need either to edit or to delete a calculated measure. You can do so by following these steps:

1. **Click anywhere inside your PivotTable and then click the Power Pivot tab in the Excel Ribbon and select Measures ⇨ Manage Measures.** This will open the Measure dialog box shown in Figure 37.20.

FIGURE 37.20

The Manage Measures dialog box lets you edit or delete your calculated measures.

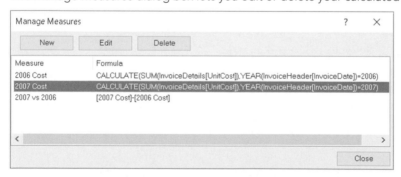

2. **Select the target calculated measure, and click either the Edit or Delete button.**

Clicking the Edit button will activate the Measure dialog box where you can make changes to the calculation setting.

Clicking the Delete button will activate a message box asking you to confirm that you want to remove the measure. After confirming with Yes, the calculated measure will be removed.

Using Cube Functions to Free Your Data

Cube functions are Excel functions that can be used to access the data in a Power Pivot data model outside the constraints of a PivotTable. Although Cube functions are technically not used to create calculations themselves, they can be used to free Power Pivot data so that it can be used with formulas that you may have in other parts of your Excel spreadsheet.

One of the easiest ways to start exploring Cube functions is to allow Excel to convert your PivotTable into Cube functions. The idea is to tell Excel to replace all cells in the PivotTable with a formula that connects back to the Power Pivot data model.

Follow these steps to create your first set of Cube functions:

1. **Start with a PivotTable created from a Power Pivot model.**

> **NOTE**
>
> The sample file for this chapter contains a tab called Cube Functions with a PivotTable already created.

2. **Select any cell inside the PivotTable and then select PivotTable Tools Analyze ⇨ OLAP Tools ⇨ Convert to Formulas, as demonstrated in Figure 37.21.**

FIGURE 37.21

Select the Convert to Formulas option to convert your PivotTable to Cube formulas.

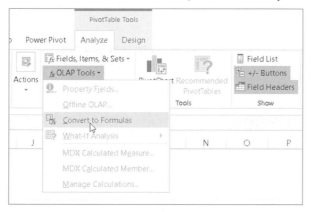

After a second or two, the cells that used to house a PivotTable are now homes for Cube formulas. The Formula bar shown in Figure 37.22 illustrates a Cube function.

FIGURE 37.22

These cells are now a series of Cube functions!

If your PivotTable contains a report filter field, the dialog box shown in Figure 37.23 activates. This dialog box gives you the option of converting your filter drop-down selectors to Cube formulas. If you select this option, the drop-down selectors are removed, leaving a static formula.

FIGURE 37.23

Excel gives you the option of converting your report filter fields.

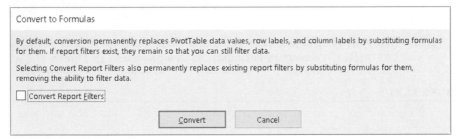

If you need to have your filter drop-down selectors intact so that you can continue to change the selections in the filter field interactively, be sure to leave the Convert Report Filters option unchecked when clicking the Convert button.

Now that the values you see are no longer part of a PivotTable object, you can insert rows and columns, you can add your own calculations, or you can combine the data with other formulas in your spreadsheet. Cube functions give you the flexibility to free your Power Pivot data from the confines of a PivotTable and use it in all sorts of ways by simply moving formulas around.

Introducing Power Query

IN THIS CHAPTER

I n information management, ETL refers to the three separate functions typically required to integrate disparate data sources: extraction, transformation, and loading. The *extraction* function refers to the reading of data from a specified source and extracting a desired subset of data. The *transformation* function refers to the cleaning, shaping, and aggregating of data to convert it to the desired structure. The *loading* function refers to the actual importing or writing of the resulting data to a target location.

Excel analysts have been manually performing ETL processes for years—although they rarely call it ETL. Every day, millions of Excel users manually pull data from some source location, manipulate that data, and integrate it into their reporting. This amounts to lots of manual effort.

Power Query enhances the ETL experience by offering an intuitive mechanism to extract data from a wide variety of sources, perform complex transformations on that data, and then load the data into a workbook or the internal data model.

In this chapter, you'll explore the basics of Power Query and get a glimpse of how it helps you save time and automate the steps needed to ensure that clean data is imported into your reporting models.

Understanding Power Query Basics

To start this basic look at Power Query, let's walk through a simple example. Imagine that you need to import Microsoft Corporation stock prices for the past 30 days using Yahoo Finance. For this scenario, you need to perform a web query to pull the data needed from Yahoo Finance.

To start your query, follow these steps:

1. **In Excel, select the Get Data command in the Get & Transform Data group on the Data tab and then select From Other Sources ⇨ From Web (see Figure 38.1).**

FIGURE 38.1

Starting a Power Query web query

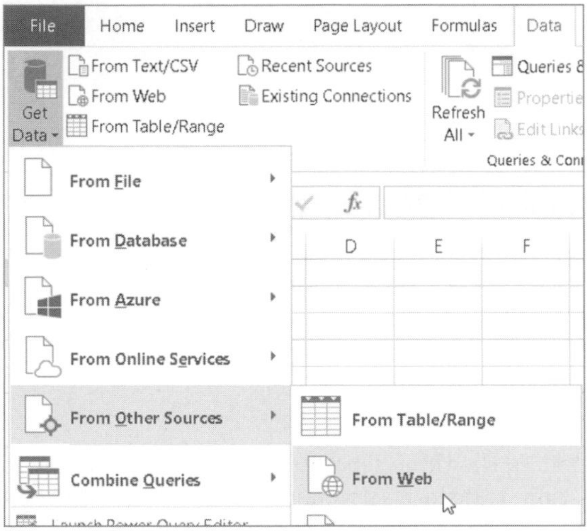

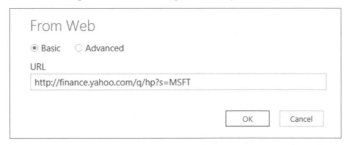

2. **In the dialog box that appears (see Figure 38.2), enter the URL for the data that you need, in this case,** `http://finance.yahoo.com/q/hp?s=MSFT`.

FIGURE 38.2

Enter the target URL containing the data you need.

After a bit of gyrating, the Navigator pane shown in Figure 38.3 appears. Here, you select the data source you want extracted. You can also click each table to see a preview of the data.

3. **In this case, the table labeled Table 2 holds the historical stock data you need, so click Table 2 and then click the Edit button.**

FIGURE 38.3

Select the correct data source and then click the Edit button.

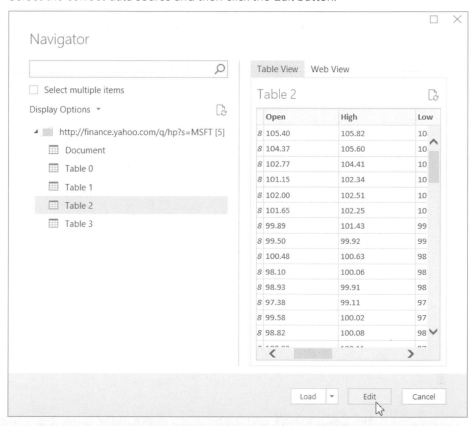

NOTE

You may have noticed that the Navigator pane shown in Figure 38.3 offers a Load button (next to the Edit button). The Load button allows you to skip any editing and import your targeted data as is. If you are sure you will not need to transform or shape your data in any way, you can opt to click the Load button to import the data directly into the data model or a spreadsheet in your workbook.

CAUTION

Excel has another From Web command button on the Data tab next to the Get Data command. This unfortunate duplicate command is actually the legacy web scraping capability found in all Excel versions going back to Excel 2000.

The Power Query version of the From Web command (found under the Get Data drop-down) goes beyond simple web scraping. Power Query is able to pull data from advanced web pages, and it is able to manipulate the data. Make sure you are using the correct feature when pulling data from the Web.

When you click the Edit button, Power Query activates a new Power Query Editor window, which contains its own Ribbon and a preview pane that shows a preview of the data (see Figure 38.4). Here, you can apply certain actions to shape, clean, and transform the data before importing.

FIGURE 38.4

The Power Query Editor window allows you to shape, clean, and transform data.

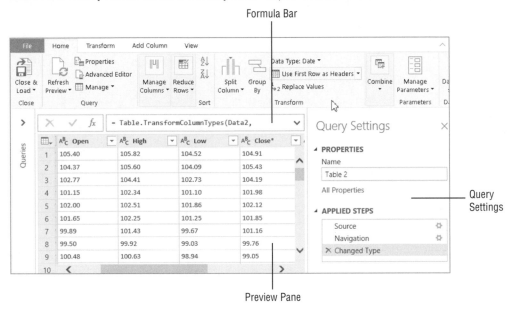

Formula Bar

Query Settings

Preview Pane

The idea is to work with each column shown in the Power Query Editor, applying the necessary actions that will give you the data and structure you need. You'll dive deeper into column actions later in this chapter. For now, you need to continue toward the goal of getting the last 30 days of stock prices for Microsoft Corporation.

4. **Right-click the Date field to see the available column actions, as shown in Figure 38.5. Select Change Type and then Date to ensure that the Date field is formatted as a proper date.**

FIGURE 38.5

Right-click the Date column and choose to change the data type to a date format.

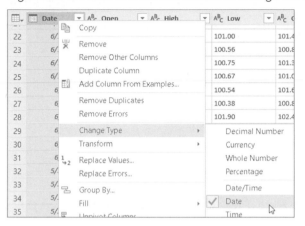

5. **Remove all the columns that you do not need by right-clicking each one and clicking Remove.** (Besides the Date field, the only other columns that you need are the High, Low, and Close fields.) Alternatively, you can hold down the Ctrl key on your keyboard, select the columns you want to keep, right-click any of the selected columns, and then choose Remove Other Columns (see Figure 38.6).

FIGURE 38.6

Select the columns you want to keep and then select Remove Other Columns to get rid of the other columns.

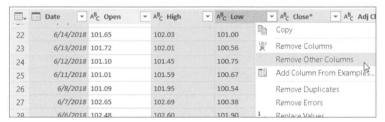

6. **Ensure that the High, Low, and Close fields are formatted as proper numbers.** To do this, hold down the Ctrl key on your keyboard, select the three columns, right-click one of the column headings, and then select Change Type ⇨ Decimal Number. After you do this, you may notice that some of the rows show the word *Error*. These are rows that contained text values that could not be converted.

7. **Remove the Error rows by selecting Remove Errors from the Column Actions list (next to the High field), as shown in Figure 38.7.**

FIGURE 38.7

You can click the Table Actions icon to select actions (such as Remove Errors) that you want applied to the entire data table.

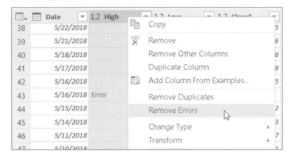

8. **Once all the errors are removed, add a Week Of field that displays the week to which each date in the table belongs.** To do this, right-click the Date field and select the Duplicate Column option. A new column (named Date -Copy) is added to the preview.

9. **Right-click the newly added column, select the Rename option, and then rename the column** Week Of.

10. **Right-click the Week Of column you just created and select the Transform ⇨ Week ⇨ Start of Week, as shown in Figure 38.8.** Excel transforms the date to display the start of the week for a given date.

FIGURE 38.8

The Power Query Editor can be used to apply transformation actions such as displaying the start of the week for a given date.

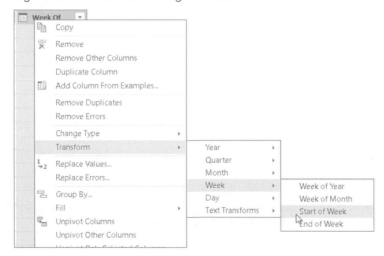

11. **When you've finished configuring your Power Query feed, save and output the results.** To do this, click the Close & Load drop-down found on the Home tab of the Power Query Ribbon to reveal the two options shown in Figure 38.9.

FIGURE 38.9

The Load To dialog box gives you more control over how the results of queries are used.

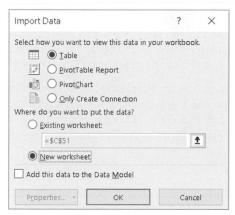

The Close & Load option saves your query and outputs the results to a new worksheet in your workbook as an Excel table. The Close & Load To option activates the Import Data dialog box, where you can choose to output the results to a specific worksheet or to the internal data model.

The Import Data dialog box also enables you to save the query as a query connection only, which means you will be able to use the query in various in-memory processes without actually needing to output the results anywhere. Select the New Worksheet option button to output your results as a table on a new worksheet in the active workbook.

At this point, you will have a table similar to the one shown in Figure 38.10, which can be used to produce the PivotTable you need.

FIGURE 38.10

Your final query pulled from the Internet: transformed, put into an Excel table, and ready to use in a PivotTable

38

Take a moment to appreciate what Power Query allowed you to do just now. With a few clicks, you searched the Internet, found some base data, shaped the data to keep only the columns you needed, and even manipulated that data to add an extra Week Of dimension to the base data. This is what Power Query is about: enabling you easily to extract, filter, and reshape data without the need for any programmatic coding skills.

Understanding query steps

Power Query uses its own formula language, known as the M language, to codify your queries. As with macro recording, each action you take when working with Power Query results in a line of code being written into a query step. Query steps are embedded M code, which allows your actions to be repeated each time you refresh your Power Query data.

You can see the query steps for your queries by activating the Query Settings pane in the Power Query Editor window (see Figure 38.11). Simply click the Query Settings command on the View tab of the Ribbon. You can also place a check in the Formula Bar option to enhance your analysis of each step with a formula bar that displays the syntax for the given step.

FIGURE 38.11

Query steps can be viewed and managed in the Applied Steps section of the Query Settings pane.

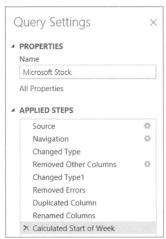

Each query step represents an action that you took to get to a data table. You can click any step to see the underlying M code in the Power Query formula bar. For example, clicking the step called Removed Errors reveals the code for that step in the Formula bar.

You can right-click any step to see a menu of options for managing your query steps. Figure 38.12 illustrates the following options:

Edit Settings   Edit the arguments or parameters that define the selected step.

Rename   Give the selected step a meaningful name.

Delete   Remove the selected step. Be aware that removing a step can cause errors if subsequent steps depend on the deleted step.

Delete Until End   Remove the selected step and all following steps.

Move Up   Move the selected step up in the order of steps.

Move Down   Move the selected step down in the order of steps.

Extract Previous   Extract all steps prior to this one into a new query.

FIGURE 38.12

Right-click any query step to edit, rename, delete, or move the step.

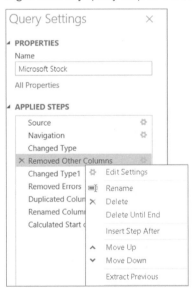

Viewing the Advanced Query Editor

Power Query gives you the option of viewing and editing a query's embedded M code directly. While in the QPower Query Editor window, click the View tab of the Ribbon and select Advanced Editor. The Advanced Editor dialog box is little more than a space for you to edit the existing M code or type your own M code. Advanced users can use the M language to extend the capabilities of Power Query by directly coding their own steps in the Advanced Editor. We'll touch on the M language in Chapter 39, "Transforming Data with Power Query."

Refreshing Power Query data

It's important to note that Power Query data is not in any way connected to the source data used to extract it. A Power Query data table is merely a snapshot. In other words, as the source data changes, Power Query will not automatically keep up with the changes; you intentionally need to refresh your query.

If you chose to load your Power Query results to an Excel table in the existing workbook, you can manually refresh by right-clicking the table and selecting the Refresh option.

If you chose to load your Power Query data to the internal data model, you need to click Data ⇨ Queries & Connections and then right-click the target query and select the Refresh option.

To get a bit more automated with the refreshing of your queries, you can configure your data sources to refresh your Power Query data automatically. To do so, follow these steps:

1. **Go to the Data tab in the Excel Ribbon, and click the Queries & Connections command.** The Queries & Connections task pane appears.
2. **Right-click the Power Query data connection that you want to refresh and then select the Properties option.**
3. **With the Properties dialog box open, select the Usage tab.**
4. **Set the options to refresh the chosen data connection:**

Refresh Every X Minutes   Placing a check next to this option tells Excel to refresh the chosen data automatically every specified number of minutes. Excel will refresh all tables associated with that connection.

Refresh Data When Opening the File   Placing a check next to this option tells Excel to refresh the chosen data connection automatically upon opening the workbook. Excel will refresh all tables associated with that connection as soon as the workbook is opened.

These refresh options are useful when you want to ensure that your customers are working with the latest data. Of course, setting these options does not preclude the ability to refresh the data manually.

Managing existing queries

As you add various queries to a workbook, you will need a way to manage them. Excel accommodates this need by offering the Queries & Connections pane, which enables you to edit, duplicate, refresh, and generally manage all of the existing queries in the workbook. Activate the Queries & Connections pane by selecting the Queries & Connections command on the Data tab of the Excel Ribbon.

You need to find the query on which you want to work and then right-click it to take any one of the following actions (see Figure 38.13):

FIGURE 38.13

Right-click any query in the Queries & Connections pane to see the available management options.

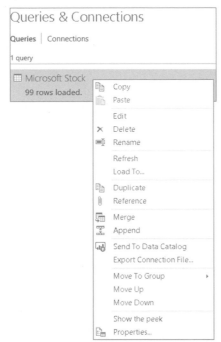

Edit   Open the Power Query Editor, where you can modify the query steps.

Delete   Delete the selected query.

Rename   Rename the selected query.

Refresh   Refresh the data in the selected query.

Load To   Open the Load To dialog box, where you can redefine where the selected query's results are used.

Duplicate   Create a copy of the query.

Reference   Create a new query that references the output of the original query.

Merge   Merge the selected query with another query in the workbook by matching specified columns.

Append   Append the results of another query in the workbook to the selected query.

Send To Data Catalog   Publish and share the selected query via a Power BI server that your IT department sets up and manages.

Export Connection File   Save an Office Data Connection (.odc) file with the connection credentials for the query's source data.

Move To Group   Move the selected query into a logical group that you create for better organization.

Move Up   Move the selected query up in the Queries & Connections pane.

Move Down   Move the selected query down in the Queries & Connections pane.

Show the Peek   Show a preview of the query results for the selected query.

Properties   Rename the query and add a friendly description.

The Queries & Connections pane is especially useful when your workbook contains several queries. Think of it as a kind of table of contents that allows you to easily find and interact with the queries in your workbook.

Understanding column-level actions

Right-clicking a column in the Power Query Editor activates a shortcut menu that shows a full list of the actions you can take. You can also apply certain actions to multiple columns at one time by selecting two or more columns before right-clicking. Figure 38.14 shows the available column-level actions, and Table 38.1 explains them, as well as a few other actions that are available only in the Power Query Editor Ribbon.

> **NOTE**
>
> Note that all the column-level actions available in Power Query are also available in the Power Query Editor Ribbon. Thus, you can either opt for the convenience of right-clicking to select an action quickly or choose to utilize the more visual Ribbon menu. There are a few useful column-level actions found only in the Ribbon (see Table 38.1).

FIGURE 38.14

Right-click any column to see the column-level actions that you can use to transform the data.

TABLE 38.1　Column-Level Actions

Action	Purpose	Available with Multiple Columns?
Remove	Remove the selected column from the Power Query data.	Yes
Remove Other Columns	Remove all nonselected columns from the Power Query data.	Yes
Duplicate Column	Create a duplicate of the selected column as a new column placed at the far right of the table. The name given to the new column is Copy of X, where X is the name of the original column.	No
Add Column From Examples	Create a custom column that combines data from other columns based on a few examples that you provide. Like the Flash Fill feature in Excel, Power Query's smart detection logic infers transformation logic based on your examples and then applies that logic to fill the new column.	Yes
Remove Duplicates	Remove all rows from the selected column where the values duplicate earlier values. The row with the first occurrence of a value is not removed.	Yes

Continues

TABLE 38.1   (continued)

Action	Purpose	Available with Multiple Columns?
Remove Errors	Remove rows containing errors in the selected column.	Yes
Change Type	Change the data type of the selected column.	Yes
Transform	Change the way values in the column are rendered. You can choose from the following options: Lowercase, Uppercase, Capitalize Each Word, Trim, Clean, Length, JSON, and XML. If the values in the column are date/time values, the options are as follows: Date, Time, Day, Month, Year, or Day of Week. If the values in the column are number values, the options are as follows: Round, Absolute Value, Factorial, Base-10 Logarithm, Natural Logarithm, Power, or Square Root.	Yes
Replace Values	Replace one value in the selected column with another specified value.	Yes
Replace Errors	Replace unsightly error values with your own friendlier text.	Yes
Group By	Aggregate data by row values. For example, you can group by state and either count the number of cities in each state or sum the population of each state.	Yes
Fill	Fill empty cells in the column with the value of the first nonempty cell. You have the option of filling up or filling down.	Yes
Unpivot Columns	Transpose the selected columns from column-oriented to row-oriented or vice versa.	Yes
Unpivot Other Columns	Transpose the unselected columns from column-oriented to row-oriented or vice versa.	Yes
Unpivot Only Selected Columns	Transpose the selected columns from column-oriented to row-oriented or vice versa. This option also retains a columns list in the current step so that the same set of columns is unpivoted on future refresh operations.	Yes
Rename	Rename the selected column to a name you specify.	No
Move	Move the selected column to a different location in the table. You have these choices for moving the column: Left, Right, To Beginning, and To End.	Yes
Drill Down	Navigate to the contents of the column. This is used with tables that contain metadata representing embedded information.	No
Add as New Query	Create a new query with the contents of the column. This is done by referencing the original query in the new one. The name of the new query is the same as the column header of the selected column.	No

Action	Purpose	Available with Multiple Columns?
Split Column (Ribbon only)	Split the value of a single column into two or more columns, based on a number of characters or a given delimiter, such as a comma, semicolon, or tab.	No
Merge Column (Ribbon only)	Merge the values of two or more columns into a single column that contains a specified delimiter, such as a comma, semicolon, or tab.	Yes

Understanding table actions

While you're in the Power Query Editor, Power Query allows you to apply certain actions to an entire data table. You can see the available table-level actions by clicking the Table Actions icon, as shown in Figure 38.15.

FIGURE 38.15

Click the Table Actions icon in the upper-left corner of the Power Query Editor Preview pane to see the table-level actions you can use to transform the data.

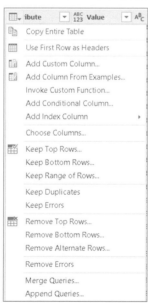

Table 38.2 lists the table-level actions and describes the primary purpose of each one.

TABLE 38.2   Table-Level Actions

Action	Purpose
Copy Entire Table	Copy the data within the current query to the Clipboard.
Use First Row as Headers	Replace each table header name with the value in the first row of each column.
Add Custom Column	Insert a new column after the last column of the table. The values in the new column are determined by the value or formula you define.
Add Column From Examples	Create a custom column that combines data from other columns based on a few examples that you provide. Like the Flash Fill feature in Excel, Power Query's smart detection logic infers transformation logic based on your examples and then applies that logic to fill the new column.
Invoke Custom Function	Insert a new column after the last column of the table and then run a user-defined function for each row in the column.
Add Conditional Column	Insert a new column after the last column of the table and then fill it with a conditional if-then-else statement that you define.
Add Index Column	Insert a new column containing a sequential list of numbers starting from 1, 0, or another specified value you define.
Choose Columns	Choose the columns you want to keep in the query results.
Keep Top Rows	Remove all but the top N number of rows. You specify the number threshold.
Keep Bottom Rows	Remove all but the bottom N number of rows. You specify the number threshold.
Keep Range of Rows	Remove all rows except the ones that fall within a range you specify.
Keep Duplicates	Remove all rows where the values in the selected columns are unique, enabling you to focus on the duplicate rows.
Keep Errors	Remove all rows that do not contain an error. This allows for the quick filtering of error values encountered during transformation.
Remove Top Rows	Remove the top N rows from the table.
Remove Bottom Rows	Remove the bottom N rows from the table.
Remove Alternate Rows	Remove alternate rows from the table, starting at the first row to remove and specifying the number of rows to remove and the number of rows to keep.
Remove Duplicates	Remove all rows where the values in the selected columns duplicate earlier values. The row with the first occurrence of a value set is not removed.
Remove Errors	Remove rows containing errors in the currently selected columns.

Action	Purpose
Merge Queries	Create a new query that merges the current table with another query in the workbook by matching specified columns.
Append Queries	Create a new query that appends the results of another query in the workbook to the current table.

NOTE

Note that all the table-level actions available in Power Query are also available in the Power Query Editor Ribbon. So, you can either opt for the convenience of right-clicking to select an action quickly or choose to utilize the more visual Ribbon menu.

Getting Data from External Sources

Microsoft has invested a great deal of time and resources in ensuring that Power Query has the ability to connect to a wide array of data sources. Whether you need to pull data from an external website, a text file, a database system, Facebook, or a web service, Power Query can accommodate most, if not all, data sources.

You can see all the available connection types by clicking the Get Data drop-down on the Data tab in the Excel Ribbon. As Figure 38.16 illustrates, Power Query offers the ability to pull from a wide array of data sources.

From File Pulls data from a specified Excel file, text file, CSV file, XML file, JSON file, or folder.

From Azure Pulls data from Microsoft's Azure Cloud service.

From Database Pulls data from databases like Microsoft Access, SQL Server, or SQL Server Analysis Services.

From Online Services Pulls data from cloud application services such as Facebook, Salesforce, and Microsoft Dynamics online.

From Other Sources Pulls data from a wide array of Internet, cloud, and other ODBC data sources. Here, you will also find the Blank Query option. Selecting Blank Query will activate the Power Query Editor in the Advanced Editor view. This is handy when you want to copy and paste M code directly into the Power Query Editor.

FIGURE 38.16

Power Query has the ability to connect to a wide array of text, database, and Internet data sources.

In the rest of this chapter, you will explore the various connection types that can be leveraged to import external data.

Importing data from files

Organizational data is often kept in files such as text files, CSV files, and even other Excel workbooks. It's not uncommon to use these kinds of files as data sources for data analysis. Power Query offers several connection types that enable the importing of data from external files.

> **NOTE**
>
> Keep in mind that the files you import don't necessarily have to be on your own PC. You can import files on network drives as well as cloud repositories such as Google Drive or Microsoft OneDrive.

Getting data from Excel workbooks

You can import data from other Excel workbooks by going to the Excel Ribbon and selecting Data ⇨ Get Data ⇨ From File ⇨ From Workbook.

Note that you can import any kind of Excel file, including macro-enabled workbooks and template workbooks. Power Query will not bring in charts, PivotTables, shapes, VBA code, or any other objects that may exist within a workbook. It simply imports the data found in the used cell ranges of the workbook.

Once you've selected your file, the Navigator pane will activate, showing you all of the data sources available in the workbook. The idea here is to select the data source you want and then either load or edit the data using the buttons at the bottom of the Navigator pane. The Load button allows you to skip any editing and import your targeted data as is. Use the Edit button if you want to transform or shape the data before completing the import.

In terms of Excel workbooks, a data source is either a worksheet or a defined named range. The icons next to each data source let you distinguish those sources that are worksheets and those that are named ranges. In Figure 38.17, the source called MyNamedRange is a defined named range, while the source called National Parks is a worksheet.

You can import multiple sources at once by clicking the Select multiple items check box and then placing a check next to each worksheet and named range that you want to import.

FIGURE 38.17

Select the data sources with which you want to work and then click the Load button.

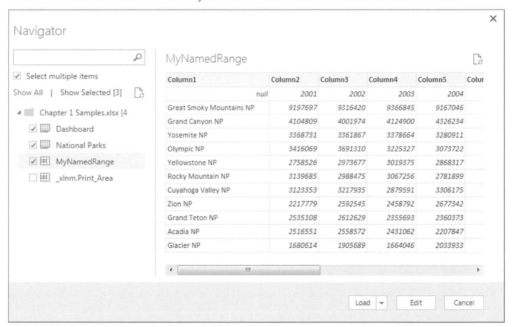

Getting data from CSV and text files

Text files are commonly used to store and distribute data because of their inherent ability to hold many thousands of bytes of data without having an inflated file size. Text files can do this by forgoing all the fancy formatting, leaving only the text.

Comma-separated value (CSV) files are text files that contain commas to delimit (separate) values into columns of data.

To import a text or CSV file, go to the Excel Ribbon and select Data ➪ Get Data ➪ From File ➪ From Text/CSV. Excel will activate the Import Data dialog box where you can browse for and select a text or CSV file.

CAUTION

Excel has another From Text/CSV button on the Data tab next to the Get Data command. This duplicate command is actually the legacy import capability found in all Excel versions.

The Power Query version is much more powerful, allowing you to shape and transform text data before importing. Make sure you are using the correct Power Query version of the From Text/CSV feature.

Power Query will open the Power Query Editor to show you the contents of the text or CSV file that you just imported. The idea here is to apply any changes you want to make to the data and then click the Close & Load command on the Home tab to complete the import.

NOTE

Some text files are structured as tab-delimited files. Similar to CSV files, tab-delimited text files contain tab characters that separate text values into columns of data. Power Query will recognize tab-delimited text files and import these files into a table that contains a separate column for each tab delimiter.

Power Query is good at recognizing the correct delimiters in CSV files and typically does a good job of importing the data correctly.

For instance, row 5 in the sample CSV file illustrated in Figure 38.18 contains the value Johnson, Kimberly. Power Query contains the intelligence to know that the comma in that value is not an actual delimiter. So, all of the columns are separated correctly.

FIGURE 38.18

CSV files are brought into the Power Query Editor where you can apply your edits and then click the Close & Load command to complete the import.

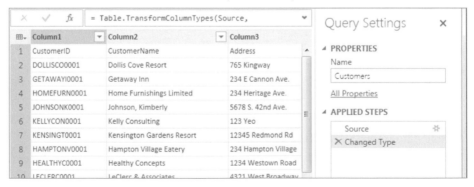

Importing data from database systems

In larger organizations, the task of data management is not performed by Excel; rather, it is primarily performed by database systems such as Microsoft Access and SQL Server. Databases like these not only store millions of rows of data but also ensure data integrity, prevent redundancy, and allow for the rapid search and retrieval of data through queries and views.

Power Query offers options to connect to a wide array of database types. Microsoft has been keen to add connection types for as many commonly used databases as it can.

Importing data from relational and OLAP databases

Click Data ➪ Get Data ➪ From Database, and you will see the list of databases to which you can connect. Power Query offers connection types for many of the popular database systems in use today: SQL Server, Microsoft Access, Oracle, MySQL, and so on.

Importing data from Azure databases

If your organization has a Microsoft Azure cloud database or a subscription to Microsoft Azure Marketplace, there is an entire set of connection types designed to import data from Azure. You can get to these connection types by clicking Data ➪ Get Data ➪ From Azure.

Importing data using ODBC connections to nonstandard databases

Some of you may be using a unique nonstandard database system that isn't popular enough to be specifically included as an option under the Get Data command. Not to worry. As long as an ODBC connection string can be used to connect to your database system, Power Query can connect to it.

Click Data ➪ Get Data ➪ From Other Sources to see a list of other connection types. Click the From ODBC option to start a connection to your unique database via an ODBC connection string.

Getting Data from Other Data Systems

In addition to ODBC, Figure 38.19 illustrates other kinds of data systems that can be leveraged by Power Query.

FIGURE 38.19

Other systems Power Query can utilize as data sources

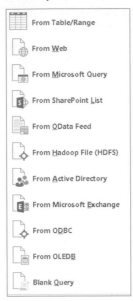

To get to the list shown in Figure 38.19, select Data ⇨ Get Data ⇨ From Other Data Sources. Some of these data systems (SharePoint, Active Directory, and Microsoft Exchange) are popular ones that are used in many organizations to store data, track sales opportunities, and manage email. Other systems like OData Feed and Hadoop are less-common services used to work with large volumes of data. These are often mentioned in conversations about "Big Data." Of course, the From Web option (demonstrated earlier in this chapter) is an integral connection type for any analyst who leverages data from the Internet.

Clicking any of these connections will activate a set of dialog boxes customized for the selected connection. These dialog boxes ask for the basic parameters that Power Query needs to connect to the specified data source; they are parameters such as file path, URL, server name, credentials, and so forth.

Each connection type requires its own unique set of parameters, so each of their dialog boxes will be different. Luckily, Power Query rarely needs more than a handful of parameters to connect to any one data source, so the dialog boxes are relatively intuitive and hassle-free.

Managing Data Source Settings

Each time you connect to any web-based data source or data source that requires some level of credentials, Power Query caches (stores) the settings for that data source.

For instance, let's say you connected to a SQL Server database, entered all of your credentials, and imported the data you needed. At the moment of successful connection, Power Query caches information about that connection in a file located on your local PC. This includes connection string, username, password, privacy settings, and so on.

The purpose of all this caching is so that you don't have to re-enter credentials each time you need to refresh your queries. That's nifty, but what happens when your credentials are changed? Well, the short answer is those queries will fail until the data source settings are updated.

Editing data source settings

You can edit data source settings by activating the Data Source Settings dialog box. To do so, click Data ⇨ Get Data ⇨ Data Source Settings.

The Data Source Settings dialog box, shown in Figure 38.20, contains a list of all credentials-based data sources previously used in queries. Select the data source you need to change and then click the Edit Permissions button.

FIGURE 38.20

Edit a data source by selecting it and clicking the Edit button.

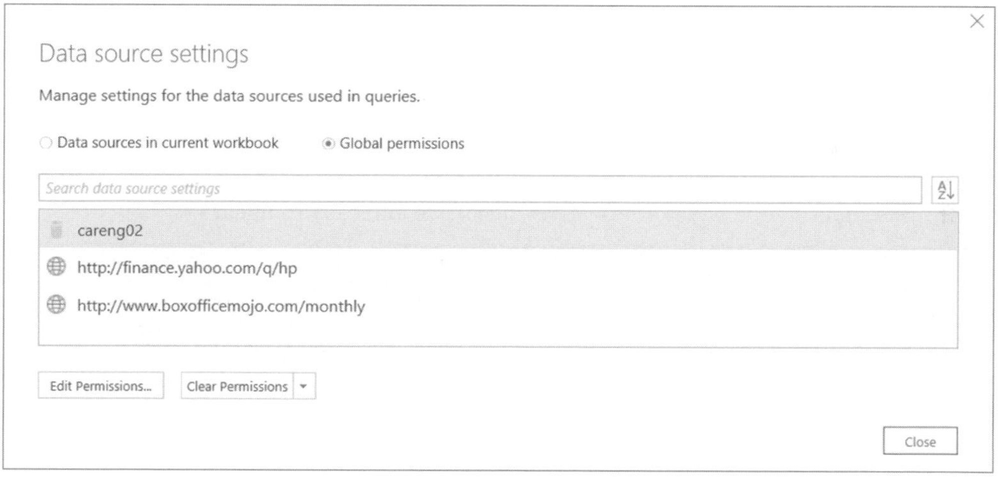

Another dialog box will pop up, this one specific to the data source you selected (see Figure 38.21). This dialog box enables you to edit credentials as well as other data privacy settings.

FIGURE 38.21

The credentials edit screen for your selected data source

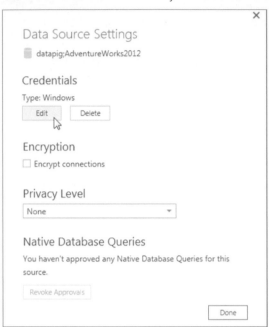

Click the Edit button to make changes to the credentials for the data source. The credentials edit screen will differ based on the data source with which you are working, but again, the input dialog boxes are relatively intuitive and easy to update.

> **NOTE**
>
> Power Query caches data source settings in a file located on your local PC. Even though you may have deleted a particular query, the data source setting is retained for possible future use. This can lead to a cluttered list of old and current data sources. You can clean out old items by selecting the data source in the Data Source Settings dialog box and clicking the Delete button.

Transforming Data with Power Query

IN THIS CHAPTER

Performing common transformations

Creating your own custom columns

Understanding data types

Understanding Power Query formulas

Applying conditional logic

D ata transformation generally entails certain actions that are meant to "clean" your data—actions such as establishing a table structure, removing duplicates, cleaning text, removing blanks, and even adding your own calculations.

In this chapter, you will be introduced to some of the tools and techniques in Power Query that make it easy for you to clean and massage your data.

 You can follow along with the examples in this chapter by downloading the `LeadList.txt` sample file at `www.wiley.com/go/excel2019bible`.

Once you've downloaded the file, you can import the sample file into Power Query (select Data ⇨ Get & Transform Data ⇨ From Text/CSV, browse to the `LeadList.txt` file, and then click the Edit button).

Performing Common Transformation Tasks

You will find that many of the unpolished data sets that come to you will require various types of transformation actions. This section covers some of the more common transformation tasks that you will have to perform.

Removing duplicate records

Duplicate records are absolute analysis killers. The effect that duplicate records have on your analysis can be far-reaching, corrupting almost every metric, summary, and analytical assessment that you produce. It is for this reason that finding and removing duplicate records should be your first priority when you receive a new data set.

Before you jump into your data set to find and remove duplicate records, it's important to consider how you define a duplicate record. To demonstrate this point, look at the table shown in Figure 39.1, where you see 11 records. Out of the 11 records, how many are duplicates?

FIGURE 39.1

Are there duplicate records in this table? It depends on how you define one.

SicCode	PostalCode	CompanyNumber	DollarPotential	City	State	Address
1389	77032	11147805	$9,517.00	houston	tx	6000 n sem heirten pkwy e
1389	77032	11147848	$9,517.00	houston	tx	43410 e herdy rd
1389	77042	11160116	$7,653.00	houston	tx	40642 rachmend ave ste 600
1389	77051	11165400	$9,517.00	houston	tx	5646 helmis rd
1389	77057	11173241	$9,517.00	houston	tx	2514 san filape st ste 6600
1389	77060	11178227	$7,653.00	houston	tx	100 n sem heirten pkwy e ste 100
1389	77073	11190514	$9,517.00	houston	tx	4660 rankan rd # 400
1389	77049	11218412	$7,653.00	houston	tx	4541 mallir read 6
1389	77040	13398882	$18,379.00	houston	tx	3643 wandfirn rd
1389	77040	13399102	$18,379.00	houston	tx	3643 wandfirn rd
1389	77077	13535097	$7,653.00	houston	tx	44160 wisthiamir rd ste 100

If you were to define a duplicate record in Figure 39.1 as a duplication of just the SicCode, you would find 10 duplicate records. That is, out of the 11 records shown, 1 record has a unique SicCode, while the other 10 are duplications. Now, if you were to expand your definition of a duplicate record to a duplication of both SicCode and PostalCode, you would find only two duplicates: the duplication of PostalCodes 77032 and 77040. Finally, if you were to define a duplicate record as a duplication of the unique value of SicCode, PostalCode, and CompanyNumber, you would find no duplicates.

This example shows that having two records with the same value in a column does not necessarily mean you have a duplicate record. It's up to you to determine which field or combination of fields will best define a unique record in your data set.

Once you have a clear idea of what field, or fields, best make up a unique record in your table, you can remove duplicates easily by using the Remove Duplicates command.

Figure 39.2 illustrates the removal of duplicate rows based on three columns. Note the importance of selecting the columns that define a duplicate. In this case, the combination of Address, CompanyNumber, and CompanyName defines a duplicate record. These columns are selected before right-clicking and selecting the Remove Duplicates command.

> **CAUTION**
>
> The Remove Duplicates command essentially looks for distinct values in the columns that you selected, and then it removes all of the records it needs to eliminate to end up with a unique list of values. If you select only one column before initiating the Remove Duplicates command, Power Query will use only the one column that you selected to determine the unique list of values. This will undoubtedly remove too many records—records that are not really duplicates. For this reason, it's important to make sure you select all of the columns that define a duplicate.

FIGURE 39.2

Removing duplicate records

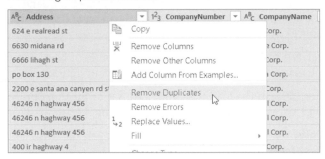

If you made a mistake and removed duplicates based on the wrong set of columns, don't worry. You can always use the Query Settings pane to delete that step. Right-click the Removed Duplicates step and select Delete (see Figure 39.3).

FIGURE 39.3

Undo the removal of records by deleting the Removed Duplicates step.

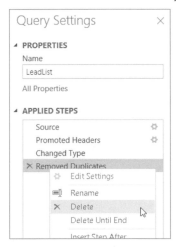

TIP

Don't see a Query Settings pane? Select View ➪ Query Settings to activate the Query Settings pane.

Filling in blank fields

It's important to note that there are actually two kinds of blank values: null and empty string. A *null* is essentially a numerical value of nothing, while an empty string is equivalent to entering two quotes ("") in a cell.

Blank fields are not necessarily a bad thing, but an excessive number of blanks in your data can lead to unexpected problems when it comes time to analyze your data.

Your job is to decide whether to leave the blanks in your data set or fill them in with an actual value. When deciding this, you should consider the following best practices:

- **Use blanks sparingly:** Working with a data set is a much less daunting task when you don't have to test for blank values constantly.
- **Use alternatives when possible:** A good practice is to represent missing values with some logical missing value code whenever possible.
- **Never use null values in number fields:** Use zeros instead of null in a currency or number field that will be used in calculations.

Power Query will show the word `null` for any null value in your data. Replacing the null values is as simple as selecting the column or columns that you want to fix, right-clicking, and then selecting the Replace Values command.

The Replace Values dialog box shown in Figure 39.4 will activate. The key here is to enter the word **null** as the Value to Find value. You can then enter the value that you want to use instead. In this case, you can enter **0** as the Replace With value.

FIGURE 39.4

Replacing null

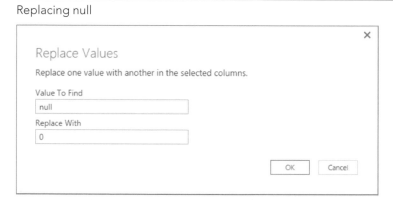

Filling in empty strings

It's always a best practice to represent missing values in a field with some logical value code whenever possible. For example, in Figure 39.5, we want to tag any record with a missing title in the ContactTitle field with the word `Undefined`.

FIGURE 39.5

Replacing empty strings with the word Undefined

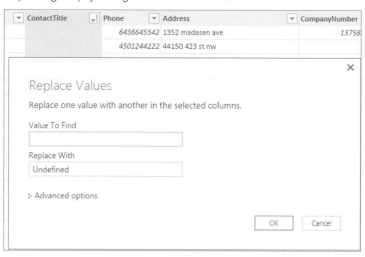

We can do so by right-clicking the ContactTitle field, selecting the Replace Values command, and then entering the word **Undefined** in the Replace With text box. As you can see in Figure 39.5, because we are replacing an empty string, there is no need to enter anything in the Value To Find text box.

> **TIP**
>
> If you need to adjust or correct the step where you replaced values, you can reactivate the Replace Values dialog box by clicking the gear icon next to the name for that step in the Query Settings pane. This is true for basically any action that requires a dialog box to complete. Clicking the gear icon next to any step name will activate the appropriate dialog box for that step.

Concatenating columns

You can easily *concatenate* (join) the values in two or more columns. In Power Query, this is achieved by using the Merge Columns command. The Merge Columns command concatenates the values in two or more fields and outputs the newly merged values into a new column.

The idea is to select the columns that you want to concatenate, right-click, and select the Merge Columns command, as shown in Figure 39.6.

This will activate the Merge Columns dialog box shown in Figure 39.7. Here, you have the option of choosing a character that will act as a separator for the concatenated values. You have all of the standard options such as comma, semicolon, space, and so forth. As you can see, you also have the option of naming the new column that will be created.

FIGURE 39.6

Merging the Type and Code fields

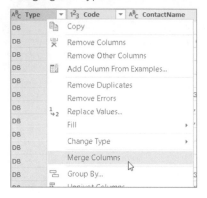

FIGURE 39.7

The Merge Columns dialog box

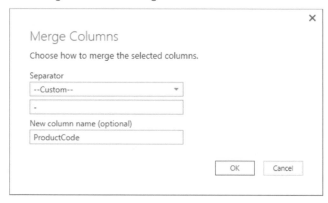

The reward for your efforts will be a new field containing the concatenated values from original column (see Figure 39.8).

This is nifty, but you will notice that Power Query removes the original Type and Code columns. There will definitely be instances when you want to concatenate values but still retain the source columns. In those instances, the answer is to create your own custom column. Later in this chapter, you'll discover how to use custom columns to solve this and other transformation problems.

FIGURE 39.8

The original columns are removed and replaced with a new merged column.

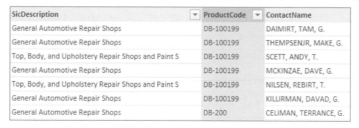

SicDescription	ProductCode	ContactName
General Automotive Repair Shops	DB-100199	DAIMIRT, TAM, G.
General Automotive Repair Shops	DB-100199	THEMPSENJR, MAKE, G.
Top, Body, and Upholstery Repair Shops and Paint S	DB-100199	SCETT, ANDY, T.
General Automotive Repair Shops	DB-100199	MCKINZAE, DAVE, G.
Top, Body, and Upholstery Repair Shops and Paint S	DB-100199	NILSEN, REBIRT, T.
General Automotive Repair Shops	DB-100199	KILLIRMAN, DAVAD, G.
General Automotive Repair Shops	DB-200	CELIMAN, TERRANCE, G.

Changing case

Making sure that the text in your data has the correct capitalization may sound trivial, but it's important. Imagine that you receive a customer table that has an address field where all the addresses are lowercase. How is that going to look on labels, form letters, or invoices? Fortunately, Power Query has a few built-in functions that make changing the case of your text a snap.

For example, the ContactName field (see Figure 39.9) contains names that are formatted in all uppercase letters. To change these names to a more appropriate, proper case, you can right-click the column and then select Transform ⇨ Capitalize Each Word.

FIGURE 39.9

Reformatting the ContactName field to proper case

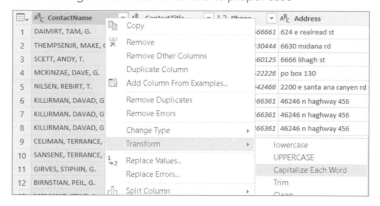

Finding and replacing specific text

Imagine that you work in a company called BLVD, Inc. One day, the president of your company informs you that the abbreviation *blvd* on all addresses is now deemed an infringement on your company's trademarked name, and it must be changed to *Boulevard* as soon as possible. How would you go about meeting this new requirement?

The Replace Values function is ideal in a situation like this. Select the Address field and then click the Replace Values command on the Home tab.

In the Replace Values dialog box (shown in Figure 39.10), simply fill in the Value To Find and the Replace With fields.

FIGURE 39.10

Replacing text values

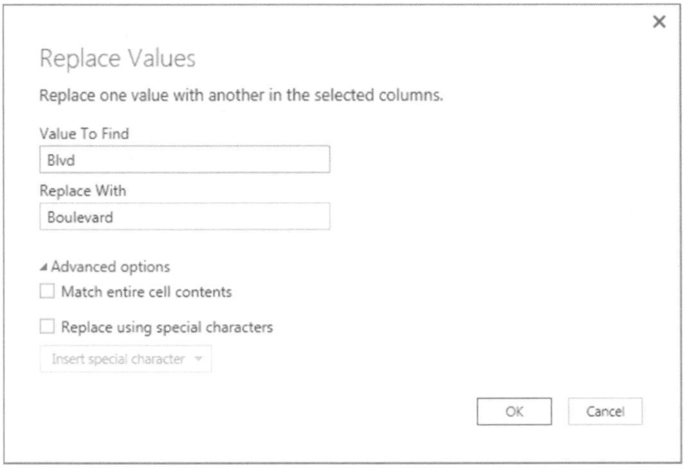

Note that clicking Advanced Options exposes two optional settings:

Match entire cell contents   Checking this option tells Power Query to replace values that contain only the text entered into the Value To Find field. This comes in handy when you want to replace zeros (0) with n/a but don't want to affect any zeros that are actually part of a number, only those that are alone in a cell.

Replace Using Special Characters   Checking this option allows you to use special invisible characters such as line feed, carriage return, or tabs as replacement text. This is useful when you want to force an indent or reposition the text so that it shows up on two lines.

Trimming and cleaning text

When you receive a data set from a mainframe system, a data warehouse, or even a text file, it is not uncommon to have field values that contain leading and trailing spaces. These spaces can cause some abnormal results, especially when you're appending values with leading and trailing spaces to other values that are clean. To demonstrate this, look at the data set in Figure 39.11.

FIGURE 39.11

Leading spaces can cause issues in analysis.

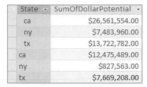

This is intended to be an aggregate view that displays the sum of the dollar potential for California, New York, and Texas. However, the leading spaces are forcing each state into two sets, preventing you from discerning the accurate totals.

You can easily remove leading and trailing spaces by using the Trim function in Power Query. Figure 39.12 demonstrates how you would update a field to remove the leading and trailing spaces by right-clicking the column and using the Transform ⇨ Trim command.

FIGURE 39.12

The Trim command

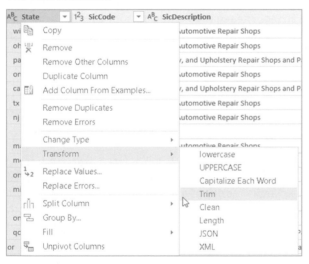

Again, the Trim command will be applied to any column or columns you select. So, you can fix multiple columns at once simply by selecting them before selecting the Trim command.

Figure 39.12 also shows the Clean command (beneath Trim). While Trim removes leading and trailing spaces, the Clean command will remove any invisible characters such as carriage returns and other nonprintable characters that may slip in from external source systems. These characters are typically rendered in Excel as a question mark or square box. But in Power Query, they show up as spaces.

If the source system that supplies your data has a nasty habit of including strange characters and leading spaces, you can apply the Trim and Clean functions to sanitize the data set.

> **NOTE**
>
> Some of you may know that the TRIM function in Excel removes the leading spaces, trailing spaces, and excess spaces within the given text. Power Query's TRIM function removes leading and trailing spaces but doesn't touch the excess spaces within the text. If excess spaces are an issue in your data, you can deal with them by using the Replace Values function to replace a given number of spaces with just one space.

Extracting the left, right, and middle values

In Excel, we have the benefit of the RIGHT function, the LEFT function, and the MID function. These functions allow you to extract portions of a string starting from different positions:

- The LEFT function returns a specified number of characters starting from the leftmost character of the string. The required arguments for the LEFT function are the text you are evaluating and the number of characters that you want returned. For example, LEFT ("70056-3504", 5) would return five characters starting from the leftmost character (70056).

- The RIGHT function returns a specified number of characters starting from the rightmost character of the string. The required arguments for the RIGHT function are the text you are evaluating and the number of characters you want returned. For example, RIGHT ("Microsoft", 4) would return four characters starting from the rightmost character (soft).

- The MID function returns a specified number of characters starting from a specified character position. The required arguments for the MID function are the text that you are evaluating, the starting position, and the number of characters you want returned. For example, MID ("Lonely", 2, 3) would return three characters starting from the second character, or character number 2 in the string (one).

Power Query has equivalent functions exposed through the Extract command found on the Transform tab (see Figure 39.13).

The options under the Extract command are as follows:

Length   Transforms a given column into numbers that represent the number of characters in each field (similar to Excel's LEN function).

First Characters   Transforms a given column to show a specified number of characters from the beginning of text in each row (similar to Excel's LEFT function).

FIGURE 39.13

The Extract command allows you to pull out parts of the text found in a column.

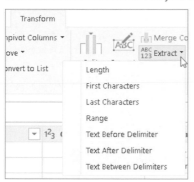

Last Characters   Transforms a given column to show a specified number of characters from the end of text in each row (similar to Excel's RIGHT function).

Range   Transforms a given column to show a specified number of characters starting from a specified character position (similar to Excel's MID function).

Text Before Delimiter   Transforms a given column to show only the text that comes before a specified delimiter.

Text After Delimiter   Transforms a given column to show only the text that comes after a specified delimiter.

Text Between Delimiters   Transforms a given column to show only the text between two specified delimiters.

> **NOTE**
>
> Applying the Extract command to a column will effectively replace the original text with the results of the operation you choose to apply. That is, the original text will not be visible in the table after applying the Extract command. For this reason, it's often useful to first copy the column and perform the extraction on the duplicate column.
>
> You can create a copy of a column by right-clicking the column and selecting Duplicate Column. When the duplicate column is created, it will be the last column (at the far right) of the table.

Extracting first and last characters

To extract the first N characters of text, highlight the column, select Extract ➪ First Characters, and then use the dialog box shown in Figure 39.14 to specify the number of characters that you want to extract. In this case, the first three characters of the Phone field will be extracted.

FIGURE 39.14

Extracting the first three characters of the Phone field

To extract the last N characters of text, highlight the column, select Extract ➪ Last Characters, and then use the dialog box to specify the number of characters you want to extract.

Extracting middle characters

To extract the middle N characters of text, highlight the column, and select Extract ➪ Range. The dialog box shown in Figure 39.15 will activate.

The idea here is to tell Power Query to extract a specific number of characters starting from a certain position in the text. For example, the SicCode field is a four-digit field. If you wanted to extract the two middle numbers of the SicCode, you would tell Power Query to start at the second character and extract two characters from there.

As you can see in Figure 39.15, Starting Index is set to 2 (starting at the second character), and Number of Characters is set to 2 (extract two characters from the starting index).

Splitting columns using character markers

Have you ever gotten a data set where two or more distinct pieces of data were jammed into one field and separated by commas? For example, a field called Address may have a text value that represents "Address, City, State, ZIP." In a proper data set, this text would be split into four fields.

In Figure 39.16, you can see that the values in the ContactName field are strings that represent "Last name, First name, Middle initial." Imagine that you need to split this column string into three separate fields.

FIGURE 39.15

Extracting the two middle characters of the SicCode

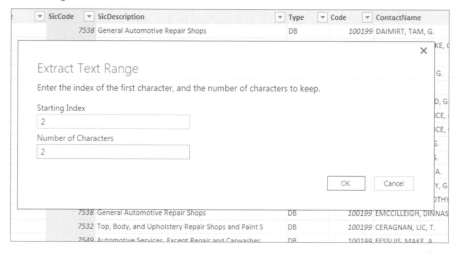

FIGURE 39.16

The Split Column command can easily split the ContactName field into three separate columns.

Although this is not a straightforward undertaking in Excel, it can be done fairly easily with the Split Column command. Simply right-click the target column and then select the Split Column option. This will reveal two options:

By Delimiter Allows you to split a column based on specific characters such as commas, semicolons, spaces, and so forth. This is useful for parsing names, addresses, or any field that contains multiple data points separated by delimiting characters.

By Number of Characters   Allows you to split a column based on a specified number of characters. This is useful for parsing uniform text at a defined character position.

In the example shown in Figure 39.16, the contact names are made up of last names, first names, and middle initials, all separated (delimited) by commas. So, the By Delimiter option is the one we'll use.

You can highlight the ContactName field, right-click, and then select Split Column ⇨ By Delimiter. This will activate the Split Column by Delimiter dialog box illustrated in Figure 39.17.

FIGURE 39.17

Splitting the ContactName column at every occurrence of a comma

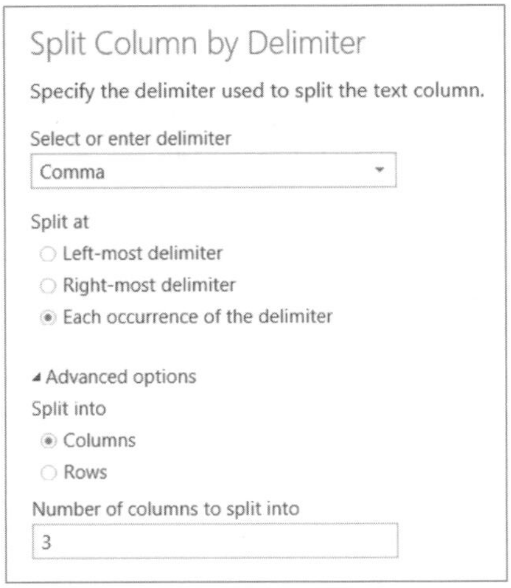

The inputs here are as follows:

Select or enter delimiter   Use the drop-down to choose the delimiter that will define where the values should be split. If your delimiter is not listed as a choice in the drop-down, you can select the Custom option and define your own.

Split   Select how you want Power Query to use the specified delimiter. Power Query can split the column only on the first occurrence of the delimiter (the leftmost delimiter), effectively creating two columns. Alternatively, you can tell Power Query to split the column only on the last occurrence of the delimiter (the rightmost delimiter), again creating two columns. The third option is to tell Power Query to split the column at each occurrence of the delimiter.

Advanced options   By default, selecting the option to split the column at each occurrence of the delimiter will create as many columns as there are delimiters. You can use the Advanced options to override the default and limit the number of columns to create.

Figure 39.18 demonstrates the new columns created after the ContactName column is split at each comma. As you can see, three new fields are created, and the original ContactName column is removed. You can rename the fields by right-clicking and selecting the Rename option.

FIGURE 39.18

The ContactName field has successfully been split into three columns.

Code	ContactName.1	ContactName.2	ContactName.3	ContactTitle
100199	DAIMIRT	TAM	G.	Manager
100199	THEMPSENJR	MAKE	G.	Manager
100199	SCETT	ANDY	T.	Owner
100199	MCKINZAE	DAVE	G.	Owner
100199	NILSEN	REBIRT	T.	Owner
100199	KILLIRMAN	DAVAD	G.	Manager
200	CELIMAN	TERRANCE	G.	Owner
null	SANSENE	TERRANCE	G.	Owner
100199	GIRVES	STIPHIN	G.	Owner
100199	BIRNSTIAN	PEIL	G.	Manager
200	MCMANIR	STIVE	A.	Plant Manager
100199	MACHAL	TIMOTHY	G.	Owner
200	YESHANEGA	TIMOTHY	A.	President

Unpivoting columns

You often encounter data sets like the one shown in Figure 39.19, where important headings (such as the month) are spread across the top of the table, pulling double duty as column labels and actual data values. This matrix layout is easy to look at in a spreadsheet, but it causes issues when attempting to perform any kind of data analysis that requires aggregation, grouping, and so on.

FIGURE 39.19

Matrix layouts are problematic for data analysis.

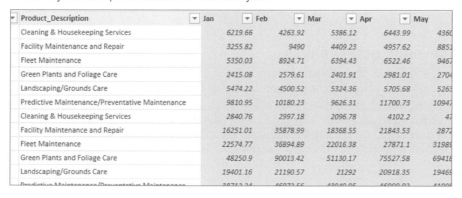

Product_Description	Jan	Feb	Mar	Apr	May
Cleaning & Housekeeping Services	6219.66	4263.92	5386.12	6443.99	4360
Facility Maintenance and Repair	3255.82	9490	4409.23	4957.62	8851
Fleet Maintenance	5350.03	8924.71	6394.43	6522.46	9467
Green Plants and Foliage Care	2415.08	2579.61	2401.91	2981.01	2704
Landscaping/Grounds Care	5474.22	4500.52	5324.36	5705.68	5263
Predictive Maintenance/Preventative Maintenance	9810.95	10180.23	9626.31	11700.73	10947
Cleaning & Housekeeping Services	2840.76	2997.18	2096.78	4102.2	47
Facility Maintenance and Repair	16251.01	35878.99	18368.55	21843.53	2872
Fleet Maintenance	22574.77	36894.89	22016.38	27871.1	31989
Green Plants and Foliage Care	48250.9	90013.42	51130.17	75527.58	69418
Landscaping/Grounds Care	19401.16	21190.57	21292	20918.35	19469
Predictive Maintenance/Preventative Maintenance	28712.24	46073.56	43040.05	45000.03	41006

39

Power Pivot offers an easy way to unpivot and pivot columns, allowing you to convert matrix-style tables to tabular data sets (and vice versa) quickly.

The Unpivot Columns command lets you select a set of columns and convert those columns into two columns: one column consisting of the column labels and another containing the column data.

 You can follow along with this example by downloading the `UnpivotExample.xlsx` sample file at www.wiley.com/go/excel2019bible.

For instance, in Figure 39.19, the month columns can be unpivoted by selecting the months and then right-clicking and selecting the Unpivot Columns command.

Figure 39.20 shows the resulting table. Note that the month labels are now an entry in a new column called Attribute. The month values are now in a new column called Value. You can, of course, rename these columns to something like Month and Revenue.

FIGURE 39.20

All months are now in a tabular format.

	Market	Product_Description	Attribute	Value
1	BUFFALO	Cleaning & Housekeeping Services	Jan	6219.66
2	BUFFALO	Cleaning & Housekeeping Services	Feb	4263.92
3	BUFFALO	Cleaning & Housekeeping Services	Mar	5386.12
4	BUFFALO	Cleaning & Housekeeping Services	Apr	6443.99
5	BUFFALO	Cleaning & Housekeeping Services	May	4360.14
6	BUFFALO	Cleaning & Housekeeping Services	Jun	5097.46
7	BUFFALO	Cleaning & Housekeeping Services	Jul	7566.19
8	BUFFALO	Cleaning & Housekeeping Services	Aug	4263.92
9	BUFFALO	Cleaning & Housekeeping Services	Sep	7245.64
10	BUFFALO	Cleaning & Housekeeping Services	Oct	3847.15
11	BUFFALO	Cleaning & Housekeeping Services	Nov	6540.21
12	BUFFALO	Cleaning & Housekeeping Services	Dec	5610.45
13	BUFFALO	Facility Maintenance and Repair	Jan	3255.82
14	BUFFALO	Facility Maintenance and Repair	Feb	9490
15	BUFFALO	Facility Maintenance and Repair	Mar	4400.33

Unpivoting other columns

As nice as the Unpivot Columns command is, there is a flaw. The flaw is that you have to explicitly select the months you want unpivoted. But what if the number of columns is ever growing? What if you unpivot January through June, but next month, a new data set will arrive with July and then August and then September? Because the Unpivot Columns command forces you essentially to hard-code the columns you want unpivoted, you'll have to redo the unpivot each and every month—that is, unless you use the Unpivot Other Columns command. This nifty command allows you to unpivot by selecting the columns you want to remain static and telling Power Query to unpivot all other columns.

For instance, Figure 39.21 demonstrates that instead of selecting the month columns, you can select the Market and Product Description columns, right-click, and then select Unpivot Other Columns.

FIGURE 39.21

Use Unpivot Other Columns when the number of matrix columns will be variable.

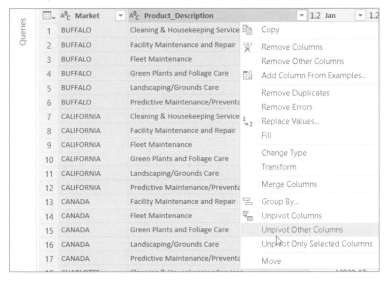

Now it doesn't matter how many new month columns are added or removed each month. Your query will always unpivot the correct columns.

TIP

It's a good idea always to use the Unpivot Other Columns option. Even if you don't anticipate new matrix columns, the Unpivot Other Columns option offers more flexibility for those unexpected changes in data.

Pivoting columns

If you find that you need to transform your data from a tabular layout to a matrix-style layout, you can use the Pivot Column command.

Simply select the columns that will make up the header labels and values for the new matrix columns and then select the Pivot Column command from the Transform Ribbon tab. Figure 39.22 illustrates an example.

FIGURE 39.22

Pivoting the Month and Revenue columns

Before finalizing the pivot operation, Power Query will activate a dialog box to confirm the value column and the aggregation method (see Figure 39.23). By default, Power Query will use the Sum operation to aggregate the data into the matrix format.

FIGURE 39.23

Confirm the aggregation operation to finalize the pivot transformation.

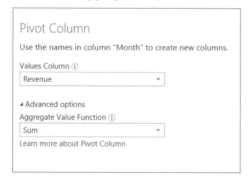

You can override this default by selecting a different operation (Count, Median, Minimum, and so on). You can even specify that you don't want any aggregation performed. Click OK to finalize the pivot operation.

Creating Custom Columns

When transforming your data, you'll sometimes have to add your own columns to extract key data points, create new dimensions, or even create your own calculations.

You start a new custom column by going to the Add Column tab and clicking the Custom Column command (see Figure 39.24). This activates the Custom Column dialog box.

FIGURE 39.24

Adding a custom column

The Custom Column dialog box (shown in Figure 39.25) is your workbench for adding your own functionality to your query through the use of Power Query formulas. When you add a new custom column, it won't do anything until you provide a formula that gives it some utility.

FIGURE 39.25

The Custom Column dialog box

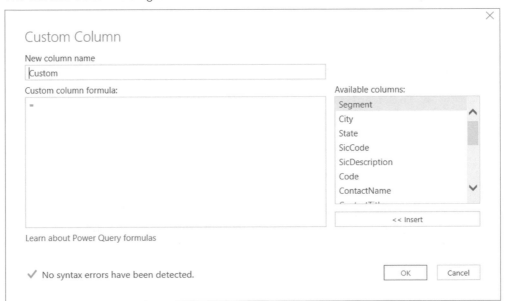

As for the Custom Column dialog box, there's not much to it. The points of input are as follows:

New column name   An input box where you enter a name for the column that you're creating.

Available columns   A list box that contains the names of all the columns in your query. Double-click any column name in this list box to place it automatically in the formula area.

Custom column formula   The area where you type your formula.

Just as in Excel, a formula can be as simple as =1 or as complicated as an IF statement that applies some conditional logic. Over the next few sections, you'll walk through a few examples of creating custom columns to go beyond the functionality provided through the user interface.

But before diving in to building Power Query formulas, it's important to understand how Power Query formulas differ from those in Excel. Here are some high-level differences of which you should be aware:

- **No cell references:** You can't point outside the Custom Column dialog box to select a range of cells. Power Query formulas work by referencing columns, not cells.
- **Excel functions don't work:** The Excel functions that you're used to won't work in Power Query. Power Query has many of the same kinds of functions as Excel, but it has its own formula language.
- **Everything is case sensitive:** In Excel, you can type in all-lowercase or all-upper-case letters and formulas will work. Not so in Power Query. To Power Query, *sum*, *Sum*, and *SUM* are three different things, and only one of them (Sum) is acceptable.
- **Data types matter:** Some fields are text fields, other fields are number fields, while others are dates. Excel does a good job at handling formulas that mix fields of differing data types. The Power Query formula language is extremely sensitive to data types. It doesn't have the built-in intelligence to handle data type mismatches gracefully. Data type issues are resolved with conversion functions covered later in this chapter.
- **No ScreenTips or intelligence help:** Excel is quick to throw up a ScreenTip or a menu of options when you start entering a new formula. Power Query has none of that. The most Power Query currently offers is a "Learn about Power Query formulas" link, taking you to a Microsoft site dedicated to Power Query.

It's not as gloomy as it sounds. Let's start with a simple custom column.

Concatenating with a custom column

Earlier in this chapter, you discovered how to concatenate values from two or more columns by using the Merge Columns command. Although the Merge Columns command is easy to use, it results in the original source columns being removed. There will definitely be instances when you will want to concatenate values but still retain the source columns.

In these instances, you can create your own custom column. Follow these steps to create a new column that merges the Type and Code columns:

1. **While in the Query Editor, click Add Column ⇨ Custom Column.**

2. **Place your cursor in the formula area after the equal sign.**

3. **Find the Type column in the Available Columns list and double-click it.** You will see [Type] pop into the formula area.

4. **After [Type], enter the following text: &"-"&.** This text will ensure that the values in the two columns are separated by a hyphen.

5. **Next, enter Number.ToText().** This Power Query function converts a number to text format on the fly so that it can be used with other text. In this case, since the Code field is formatted as a number, we'll need to convert it on the fly to join it to the Type field. You'll learn more about data type conversions later.

6. **Place your cursor between the parentheses for the Number.ToText function.**

7. **Next, find the Code column in the Available Columns list and double-click it.** You will see [Code] pop into the formula area.

8. **In the New Column Name input, enter MyFirstColumn.**

At this point, your dialog box should look similar to the one shown in Figure 39.26. Note the message at the bottom of the dialog box stating that "No syntax errors have been detected." Each time you create or adjust a formula, you'll want to ensure that this message states that no errors have been detected.

9. **Click OK to apply your custom column.**

If all went well, you have a new custom column that concatenates two fields. With this example, you get the basic foundation for how Power Query formulas work.

Understanding data type conversions

When working with formulas in Power Query, you'll inevitably need to perform some action on fields that have differing data types. Take, for example, the previous exercise where we merged the Type column (a text field) with the Code column (a numeric field). In that example, we used a conversion function to change the data type of the Code field so that it can be temporarily treated as a text field.

Conversion functions are just what they sound like. They convert data from one data type to another.

Table 39.1 lists common conversion functions. As demonstrated in the previous section, you simply wrap these functions around the columns that need converting.

```
Number.ToText([ColumnName])
```

39

FIGURE 39.26

A formula to merge the Type and Code columns

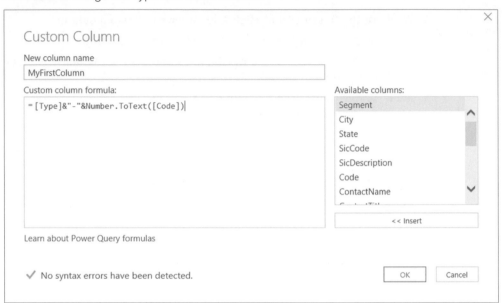

TABLE 39.1 Common Conversion Functions

Convert From	To	Function
Date	Text	`Date.ToText()`
Time	Text	`Time.ToText()`
Number	Text	`Number.ToText()`
Text	Number	`Number.FromText()`
Text Dates	Date	`Date.FromText()`
Numeric Dates	Date	`Date.From()`

All that being said, it's clear that you'll need to know the data types for the fields that you use in Power Query formulas. That way, you'll know which conversion functions to use.

To discover and change the data type for a field, place your cursor in the field and then select the Data Type drop-down on the Transform tab (see Figure 39.27). The data type at the top of the drop-down is the type for the field you're on. You can edit the data type for the field by selecting a new type from the drop-down list.

FIGURE 39.27

Use the Data Type drop-down to discover and select the data type for a given field.

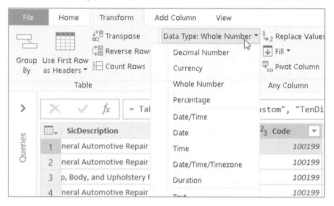

Spicing up custom columns with functions

With a few basic fundamentals and a little knowledge of Power Query functions, you can create transformations that go beyond what you can do through the Query Editor. In this example, we'll use a custom column to pad numbers with zeros.

You may encounter a situation where key fields are required to be a certain number of characters for your data to be able to interface with peripheral platforms such as ADP or SAP. For example, imagine that the CompanyNumber field must be 10 characters long. Those that are not 10 characters long must be padded with enough leading zeros to create a 10-character string.

The secret to this trick is to add 10 zeros to every company number, regardless of the current length, and then pass them through a function similar to the RIGHT function that will extract only the right 10 characters.

For example, company number 29875764 would first be converted to 000000000029875764; then it would go into a RIGHT function that extracts only the right 10 characters. This would leave you with 0029875764.

Although this is essentially two steps, you can accomplish the same thing with just one custom column. Here's how to do it:

1. **While in the Query Editor, click Add Column ⇨ Custom Column.**
2. **Place your cursor in the formula area after the equal sign.**
3. **Enter 10 zeros in quotes (as in `"0000000000"`) followed by an ampersand (&).**
4. **Next, enter `Number.ToText()`. (Do not type the period.)**
5. **Place your cursor between the parentheses for the `Number.ToText` function.**

6. **Next, find the CompanyNumber column in the Available Columns list and double-click it.** You will see [CompanyNumber] pop into the formula area.

   At this point, your formula area should contain this syntax:

   `"0000000000"&Number.ToText([CompanyNumber])`

   This formula will result in nothing more than a concatenation of 10 zeros and the CompanyNumber. The goal is to go further and extract only the right 10 characters.

   The RIGHT function is an Excel function that won't work in Power Query. However, Power Query does have an equivalent function called Text.End(). Just like the RIGHT function, the Text.End function requires a couple of parameters: the text expression and the number of characters to extract.

   `Text.End([MyText], 10)`

7. **In this scenario, the text expression will be your formula, and the number of characters to extract will be 10. Enter Text.End and a left parenthesis (before your existing formula) and then follow the formula with a comma and then the number 10 and a right parenthesis.** The final syntax is shown here:

   `Text.End("0000000000"&Number.ToText([CompanyNumber]),10)`

8. **In the New Column Name input, enter TenDigitCustNumber.**

   At this point, your dialog box should look similar to the one shown in Figure 39.28. Again, make sure that the message as the bottom of the dialog box reads "No syntax errors have been detected."

FIGURE 39.28

A formula to create a consistent CompanyNumber padded with 10 digits

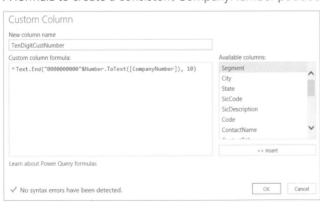

9. **Click OK to apply your custom column.**

Table 39.2 lists some other Power Query functions useful in extending the capabilities of custom columns. Take a moment to review the list of functions and note how they differ from their Excel equivalents. Remember that Power Query functions are case sensitive.

TABLE 39.2   Useful Transformation Functions

Excel Function	Power Query Function
LEFT([Text],[Number])	Text.Start([Text],[Number])
RIGHT([Text],[Number])	Text.End([Text],[Number])
MID([Text],[StartPosition],[Number])	Text.Range([Text],[StartPosition],[Number])
FIND([Find],[Within])	Text.PositionOf([Within],[Find])+1
IF([Expression],[Result1],[Result2])	if [Expression] then [Result1] else [Result2]
IFERROR([Procedure],[FailResult])	try [Procedure] otherwise [FailResult]

Adding conditional logic to custom columns

As you may have noticed from Table 39.2, Power Query has a built-in if function. The if function is designed to test for conditions and provide different outcomes based on the results of those tests. In this section, you'll see how you can control the output of your custom columns by utilizing Power Query's if function.

Just as in Excel, Power Query's if function evaluates a specific condition and returns a result based on a true or false determination:

```
if [Expression] then [Result1] else [Result2]
```

> **NOTE**
>
> In Excel, you think of the commas in an IF function as THEN and ELSE statements. In Power Query, you don't use commas.
>
> The Excel formula IF(Babies=2,"Twins","Not Twins") would translate to the following: If Babies equals 2 then "Twins" else "Not Twins".

Imagine that you need to tag customers as either large customers or small customers based on their dollar potential. You decide that you'll add a custom column that contains either "LARGE" or "SMALL" based on the revenue potential of the customer.

With the help of the if function, you can tag all customers with one custom column that uses the following formula:

```
if [2016 Potential Revenue]>=10000 then "LARGE" else "SMALL"
```

39

This function tells Power Query to evaluate the [2016 Potential Revenue] field for each record. If the potential revenue is greater than or equal to 10,000, use the word LARGE; if not, use the word SMALL.

Figure 39.29 demonstrates this if statement as it is applied in the Add Custom Column dialog box.

FIGURE 39.29

Applying an if statement in a custom column

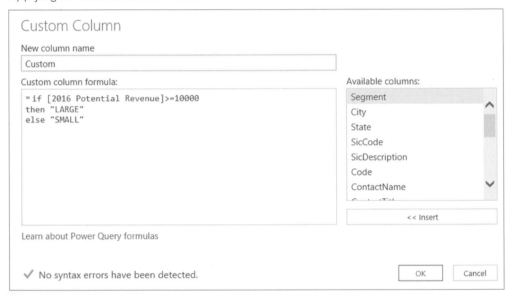

TIP

Power Query pays no attention to white space. This means you can put as many spaces and carriage returns as you'd like. As long as the correct case and spelling is used, Power Query will not complain. Figure 39.29 illustrates how separating formulas into multiple lines can make them much easier to read.

Grouping and Aggregating Data

In some cases, you may need to transform your data set into compact groups to get it into a manageable size of unique values. You may even need to summarize numerical values into an aggregate view. An aggregate view is a grouped snapshot of your data that will show sums, averages, counts, and more.

Power Query offers a Group By feature that enables you easily group to data and create aggregate views.

While in the Query Editor, select the Group By command on the Transform tab. The Group By dialog box illustrated in Figure 39.30 will open.

FIGURE 39.30

The Group By dialog configured to sum potential revenue by State and City

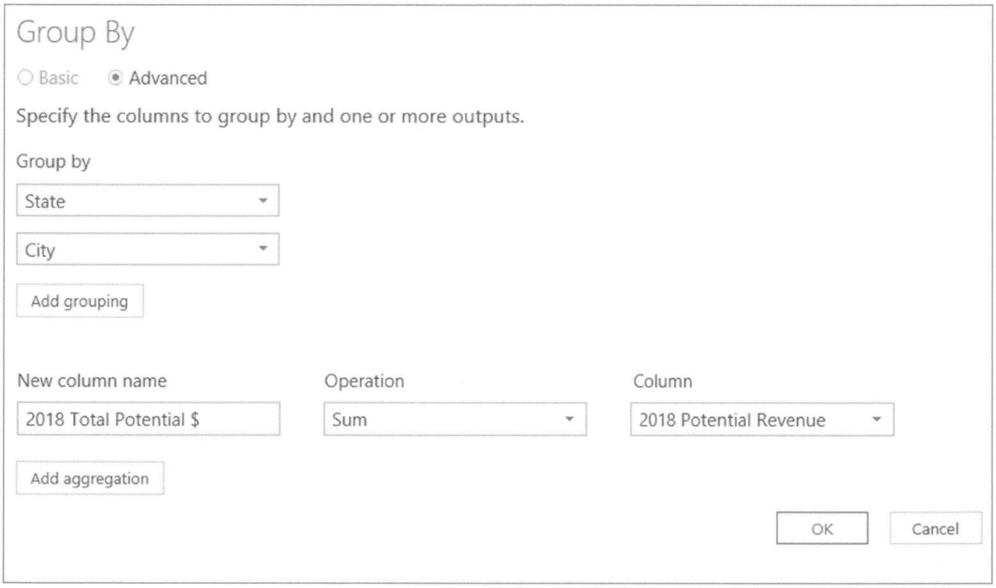

You have the option of creating a Basic grouping with only one column to group by or creating an Advanced aggregation that uses multiple group by columns.

Let's take a moment to walk through the steps for transforming data into an aggregate view by City and State:

1. **While in the Query Editor, activate the Group By dialog box (Transform ⇨ Group By).**
2. **Click the option for Advanced grouping.** This exposes the fields that we need to group by multiple columns.
3. **Use the Group by drop-down list to select the column on which you want to aggregate. Then click the Add Grouping button to add columns to the grouping.** (In Figure 39.30, State and City were selected.)
4. **Use the New column name input box to give the new aggregate column a name.**

5. **Use the Operation drop-down list to select the kind of aggregation you want to apply** (Sum, Count Rows, Average, Min, Max, **and so forth)**. In Figure 39.30, we have chosen to apply Sum.

6. **Use the Column drop-down list to choose the column that will be aggregated.** In this case, it's 2018 Potential Revenue.

7. **Click the OK button to confirm and apply your changes.**

Figure 39.31 illustrates the resulting output.

FIGURE 39.31

The resulting aggregate view by State and City

	ABC State	ABC City	123 2018 Total Potential $
260	CA	Foresthill	31453
261	CA	Fortuna	10681
262	CA	Foster City	52363
263	CA	Fountain Valley	27718
264	CA	Fremont	121340
265	CA	Fresno	116290
266	CA	Fullerton	74958
267	CA	Garden Grove	21601
268	CA	Gardena	111759
269	CA	Gilroy	50938
270	CA	Glendale	56541
271	CA	Goleta	55920

> **NOTE**
>
> When you apply the Group By feature, Power Query removes all columns that were not used when configuring the Group By dialog box. This leaves you with a clean view of just your grouped data.

Making Queries Work Together

IN THIS CHAPTER

Reusing query steps

Consolidating data with the Append feature

Understanding join types

Using the Merge feature

Data analysis is frequently done in layers, with each layer of analysis using or building on the previous layer. When you build a pivot table using the results of a Power Query output, you are layering your analysis. When you build a query based on a table created by an SQL Server view, you are also creating a layered analysis.

You'll often find the need to build queries on top of other queries to get the results you're seeking. That's what this chapter is all about. Here you'll take a look at a few ways that you can advance your data analysis by making your queries work together.

 You can follow along with the examples in this chapter by downloading these sample files from `www. wiley.com/go/excel2019bible`:

`Sales By Employee.xlsx`

`Appending_Data.xlsx`

`Merging_Data.xlsx`

Reusing Query Steps

It's common to rely on the same main data table for all kinds of analysis. Even the simple table shown in Figure 40.1 can be used to create different views: sales by employee, sales by business segment, sales by region, and so forth.

Of course, you can build separate queries, each performing different grouping and aggregation steps, but that would mean repeating all of the data cleanup steps you needed before performing any kind of analysis.

FIGURE 40.1

This data can be used as the source for various levels of aggregated analysis.

To see what this means, take a moment to follow these steps:

1. **Open the `Sales By Employee.xlsx` sample file.**

2. **Select any cell inside the table and then click Data ⇨ From Table/Range.** Power Query will open the Power Query Editor to show you a table that looks similar to Figure 40.1.

3. **Click the Filter drop-down for the Market field, and filter out the Canada market (remove the check next to Canada).**

4. **Select the Last_Name and First_Name fields, right-click either column heading, then select Merge Columns.**

5. **Use the Merge Columns dialog box to create a new Employee field, joining Last_Name and First_Name separated by a comma (see Figure 40.2).**

6. **Click the Group By command on the Transform tab to display the Group By dialog box.** The goal is to group by the Employee field to get the Sum of Sales Amount. **Name the new aggregated column `Revenue`.**

Figure 40.3 illustrates the completed Group By dialog box.

At this point, you've successfully created a view that shows total revenue by employee. As you can see in Figure 40.4, the query steps include all of the preparation work you did before grouping.

FIGURE 40.2

Merge the Last_Name and First_Name columns to create a new Employee field.

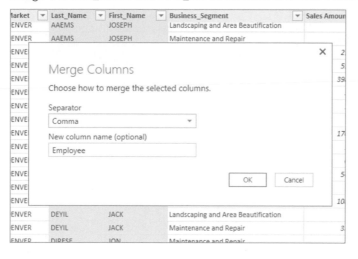

FIGURE 40.3

Group the Employee field and sum the Sales Amount column to create a new Revenue column.

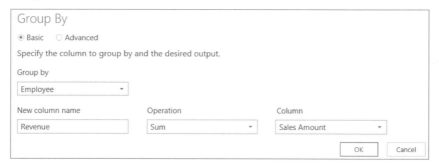

So, what if you wanted to create another analysis using the same data? For instance, what if you wanted another view that shows employee sales by business segment?

40

FIGURE 40.4

All of the query steps before Grouped Rows are needed to prepare the data for grouping.

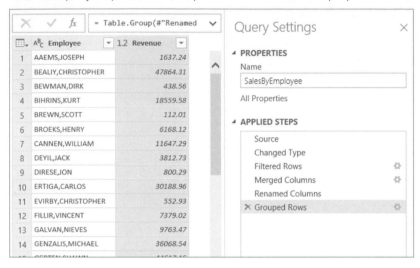

You could always start from step 1 and import another copy of the source data, but you'd have to repeat the preparation steps (the Filtered Rows and Merged Columns steps in this case).

A better way is to reuse the steps you've already created by extracting them into a new query. The idea is first to decide what steps you want to reuse and then right-click the step immediately below. In this scenario (see Figure 40.4), you want to keep all query steps up until Grouped Rows.

7. **Right-click the Grouped Rows step and select Extract Previous.**

8. **Use the Extract Steps dialog box shown in Figure 40.5 to name the new query** SalesByBusiness. **Click OK to confirm.**

FIGURE 40.5

Naming the new query SalesByBusiness

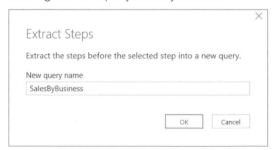

After clicking OK, Power Query does two things. First, it moves all the extracted steps to the newly created query. Then it ties the original query to the new query. That is to say, both queries are sharing the first few query steps up until the Grouped Rows step.

You can see the new SalesByBusiness query (see Figure 40.6) in the pane on the left. Notice that the query steps for the newly created SalesByBusiness query do not include the Grouped Row step. Power Query only moved the extracted steps (those before the Grouped Row step).

FIGURE 40.6

Your two queries are now sharing the extracted steps.

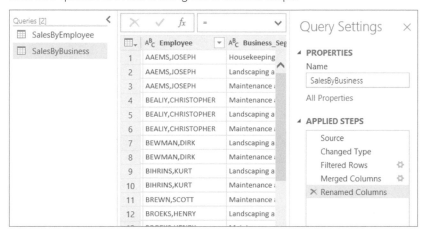

This concept of extracting steps can be a bit confusing. The bottom line is that instead of starting from square one with a new query, you're telling Power Query that you want to create a new query that utilizes the steps you've already created.

> **NOTE**
> When two or more queries share extracted steps, the query that contains the extracted steps serves as the data source for the other queries. Because of this link, the query that contains the extracted steps cannot be deleted. You'll first have to delete all dependent queries before deleting the query that holds the extracted steps.

Understanding the Append Feature

Power Query's Append feature allows you to add the rows generated from one query to the results of another query. In other words, you're essentially copying records from one query and adding them to the end of another.

The Append feature comes in handy when you need to consolidate multiple identical tables into one table. For example, if you have tables from the North, South, Midwest, and West regions, you can consolidate the data from each region into one table using the Append feature.

To understand the Append feature better, let's walk through an exercise that consolidates data from four different regions into one table. In this walk-through, we'll use the regional data found on four different tabs in the `Appending_Data.xlsx` sample file (see Figure 40.7).

FIGURE 40.7

The data found on each region tab needs to be consolidated into one table.

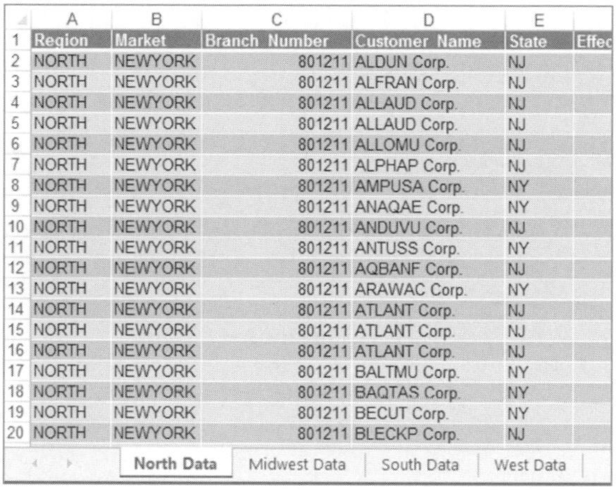

	A	B	C	D	E	
1	Region	Market	Branch Number	Customer_Name	State	Effec
2	NORTH	NEWYORK	801211	ALDUN Corp.	NJ	
3	NORTH	NEWYORK	801211	ALFRAN Corp.	NJ	
4	NORTH	NEWYORK	801211	ALLAUD Corp.	NJ	
5	NORTH	NEWYORK	801211	ALLAUD Corp.	NJ	
6	NORTH	NEWYORK	801211	ALLOMU Corp.	NJ	
7	NORTH	NEWYORK	801211	ALPHAP Corp.	NJ	
8	NORTH	NEWYORK	801211	AMPUSA Corp.	NY	
9	NORTH	NEWYORK	801211	ANAQAE Corp.	NY	
10	NORTH	NEWYORK	801211	ANDUVU Corp.	NJ	
11	NORTH	NEWYORK	801211	ANTUSS Corp.	NY	
12	NORTH	NEWYORK	801211	AQBANF Corp.	NJ	
13	NORTH	NEWYORK	801211	ARAWAC Corp.	NY	
14	NORTH	NEWYORK	801211	ATLANT Corp.	NJ	
15	NORTH	NEWYORK	801211	ATLANT Corp.	NJ	
16	NORTH	NEWYORK	801211	ATLANT Corp.	NJ	
17	NORTH	NEWYORK	801211	BALTMU Corp.	NY	
18	NORTH	NEWYORK	801211	BAQTAS Corp.	NY	
19	NORTH	NEWYORK	801211	BECUT Corp.	NY	
20	NORTH	NEWYORK	801211	BLECKP Corp.	NJ	

North Data | Midwest Data | South Data | West Data

Creating the needed base queries

It's important to understand that the Append feature works only on existing queries. That is to say, no matter what kind of data sources you have, you'll need to import them into Power Query before you can append them together. In this case, it means getting all of the region tables into queries.

Follow these steps:

1. **Go to the North Data worksheet, select any cell inside the table, and then click Data ⇨ From Table/Range.** The Power Query Editor will activate, showing you the contents of the table you just imported. To finalize the creation of the query, you'll need to use one of the Close & Load commands.

Now, because you're creating this query simply for the purpose of appending it to other queries, there is no need to use the Close & Load command on the workbook. Instead, you can choose to close and load the data as a connection only.

2. **On the Home tab of the Power Query Editor, click the drop-down arrow under the Close & Load button and select Close & Load To.**

3. **In the Import Data dialog box, choose the option Only Create Connection and then click OK.**

4. **Repeat steps 1 through 3 for the other worksheets in the workbook.**

   Once you've created queries for each region, activate the Queries & Connections pane (Data ⇨ Queries & Connections) to see all of the queries. As you can see in Figure 40.8, each query is a connection-only query.

FIGURE 40.8

Create a connection-only query for each region.

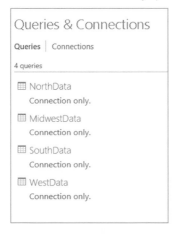

Now that your data tables have all been imported into queries, you can start appending the data.

Appending the data

Follow these steps to append data from all other queries to the NorthData query:

1. **In the Queries & Connections pane, right-click the NorthData query and select Append to activate the Append dialog box shown in Figure 40.9.**

40

FIGURE 40.9

Appending multiple queries to NorthData

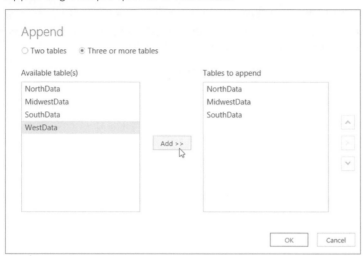

2. **Choose the Three or more tables option at the top of the dialog box.** The Append dialog box reconfigures to show two list boxes. The list on the left includes all of the existing queries in your workbook. The list on the right contains the query to which you are currently appending data (the NorthData query in this scenario).

3. **Select any query you want appended from the left and add it to the list box on the right.**

4. **Click OK to confirm your selections.** The Power Query Editor will launch, giving you the opportunity to review and edit the results.

5. **Click the Close & Load button to save and exit the Power Query Editor.**

   At this point, the NorthData query contains the data for all four regions. To see the fully consolidated table, you'll need to change the load destination of the NorthData query to a new worksheet instead of connection only.

6. **In the Queries & Connections pane, right-click the NorthData query and select Load To.** The Import Data dialog box will display.

7. **Select the option for Table and then click OK.**

   Figure 40.10 illustrates the final output. You have successfully created a consolidated table of region data.

FIGURE 40.10

The final consolidated table of all regional data

	Region	Market	Branch_Number	Customer_Name	State
31	MIDWEST	TULSA	401612	JUHNST Corp.	OK
32	MIDWEST	TULSA	401612	PRANTA Corp.	OK
33	MIDWEST	TULSA	401612	UKLAFU Corp.	OK
34	MIDWEST	TULSA	401612	UKLOHU Corp.	OK
35	SOUTH	NEWORLEANS	601310	ANTUSM Corp.	GA
36	SOUTH	NEWORLEANS	601310	SUASHU Corp.	GA
37	SOUTH	NEWORLEANS	601310	TAREPR Corp.	GA
38	SOUTH	NEWORLEANS	801607	MUDACA Corp.	MS
39	WEST	PHOENIX	201714	VANCHU Corp.	AZ
40	WEST	PHOENIX	701708	CUAQTU Corp.	NV
41	WEST	PHOENIX	701708	EASOTU Corp.	NV
42	NORTH	NEWYORK	801211	BECUT Corp.	NY
43	NORTH	NEWYORK	801211	BUYUSB Corp.	NJ

CAUTION

Note in Figure 40.9 that the NorthData query is on both the left and right list boxes. Be careful not to move the NorthData query to the right list box by mistake. If you do, you'll append the query to itself, effectively duplicating all of the records within the query. Unless you have some strange requirement where creating exact copies of records is beneficial, you will want to avoid appending the current query to itself.

Beware of Mismatched Column Labels

When you append one query to another, Power Query first scans the column labels for both queries to capture all column names. It then outputs all distinct column names and consolidates the data from both queries into the appropriate columns. It uses the column labels as a guide for knowing which data goes into which column.

If the column labels in your queries don't match, Power Query will consolidate data for any matching column and will leave null values in any columns that don't match.

For example, imagine you have one query with the column labels Region and Revenue and another query with the column labels Region and SalesAmount. Appending these two records will yield a final table with all three columns: Region, Revenue, and SalesAmount. The records from the first query will be input into the Region and Revenue fields. The records from the second query will be input into the Region and SalesAmount field. This will essentially leave you with gaps in the Revenue and SalesAmount fields.

The bottom line is to make sure the column labels in your queries are identical before appending. As long as the column labels in each query are identical, Power Query will be able to append the data correctly. Even if the columns in each query are positioned in a different sequence, Power Query is able to use the column labels to get all the data into the correct columns.

Understanding the Merge Feature

You'll often find the need to build queries that join the data between two tables. For example, you may want to join an employee table to a transaction table to create a view that contains both transaction details and information on the employees who logged those transactions.

In this section, you'll discover how you can leverage the Merge feature in Power Query to join data from multiple queries.

Understanding Power Query joins

Similar to VLOOKUP in Excel, the Merge feature joins the records from one query to the records in another by matching on some unique identifier. An example of a unique identifier would be Customer ID or Invoice Number.

There are several ways to join two data sets. The kind of join you apply is important because it will determine which records are returned from each data set.

Power Query supports six kinds of joins. As you review each kind of join listed here, feel free to glance at Figure 40.11 to get a visual understanding of each one.

FIGURE 40.11

The kinds of joins supported by Power Query

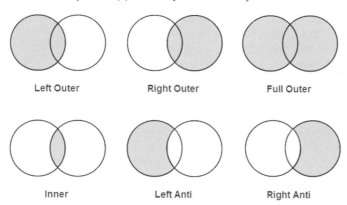

Left Outer   Right Outer   Full Outer

Inner   Left Anti   Right Anti

Left Outer   This join tells Power Query to return all of the records from the first query regardless of matching *and* only those records from the second query that have matching values in the joined field.

Right Outer   This join tells Power Query to return all of the records from the second query, regardless of matching, *and* only those records from the first query that have matching values in the joined field.

Full Outer   This join tells Power Query to return all of the records from both queries regardless of matching.

Inner   This join tells Power Query to return only those records from both queries that have matching values.

Left Anti   This join tells Power Query to return only those records from the first query that don't match any of the records from the second query.

Right Anti   This join tells Power Query to return only those records from the second query that don't match any of the records from the first query.

Merging queries

To understand the Merge feature better, let's walk through an exercise that merges interview questions and answers. In this walk-through, we'll use the interview predefined queries found in the Merging_Data.xlsx sample file.

As you can see in Figure 40.12, there are two existing queries in the Queries & Connections pane: Questions and Answers. These queries represent the questions and answers from the interview. The goal is to merge these two queries to create a new table showing the questions and answers side by side.

FIGURE 40.12

You need to merge the Questions and Answers queries into one table.

NOTE

The Merge feature can be used only with existing queries. That is to say, no matter what kind of data sources you have, you'll need to import them into Power Query before you can use them in a merge.

Follow these steps to perform the merge:

1. **Click Data ⇨ Get Data ⇨ Combine Queries ⇨ Merge (see Figure 40.13).** This will activate the Merge dialog box.

40

FIGURE 40.13

Activating the Merge dialog box

Figure 40.14 illustrates the Merge dialog box. The idea here is to use the drop-down boxes to select the queries you want to merge and then choose the columns that define the unique identifier for each record. In this case, the InterviewID and QuestionID/AnswerID fields make up the unique identifier for each record.

2. **Select the Questions query in the top drop-down box.**

3. **Hold down the Ctrl key on the keyboard and then click InterviewID and QuestionID—in that order.**

4. **Select the Answers query in the lower drop-down box.**

5. **Hold down the Ctrl key on the keyboard and then click InterviewID and AnswerID—in that order.**

6. **Use the Join Kind drop-down box to select the kind of join that you want Power Query to use.** In this case, the default Left Outer works.

7. **Click the OK button to finalize and open the Power Query Editor.**

> **CAUTION**
>
> Note the small numbers 1 and 2 in the InterviewID and QuestionID fields in Figure 40.14. These small numbers are assigned based on the order in which you selected them (see steps 3 and 5 earlier).
>
> The order you selected the unique identifiers in each query matters. The two columns tagged with the small number 1 will be joined together regardless of column labels. The two columns tagged with the small number 2 will also be joined together.

FIGURE 40.14

The completed Merge dialog box

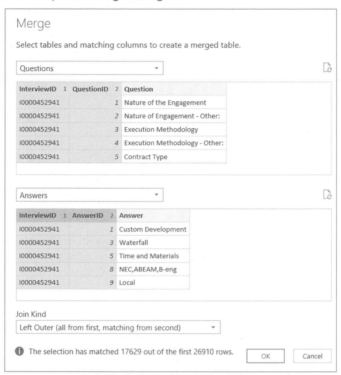

8. **With the newly merged query open in the Power Query Editor, all that is left to do is to click the Expand icon in the newly added field and choose the fields you want to be included in the final output (demonstrated in Figure 40.15).** In this case, all you need is the Answer file ID.

40

FIGURE 40.15

Expand the NewColumn field, and choose the merged fields you want output.

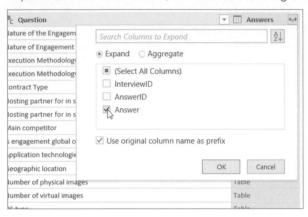

9. **At this point, you can apply more transformations if needed. When you're happy with the way things look, click the Close & Load command to output the results to the workbook.**

   Figure 40.16 illustrates the final merged query.

FIGURE 40.16

The final table with merged questions and answers

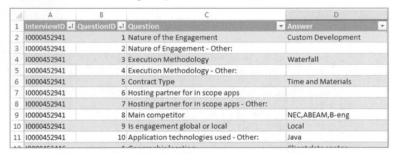

> **NOTE**
>
> When working in the Power Query Editor, you may see the word *null* wherever there are empty values. You don't need to take any special action to get rid of all of the instances of the word *null*. Excel automatically recognizes these as empty values, and it won't show them in the final worksheet.

If you find that you need to adjust or correct a merged query, right-click the query in the Queries & Connections pane and select Edit. In the Power Query Editor, click the gear icon next to the Source query step (see Figure 40.17). This will activate the Merge dialog box, where you can make the necessary changes.

FIGURE 40.17

Click the gear icon next to the Source query step to reactivate the Merge dialog box.

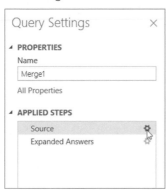

Enhancing Power Query Productivity

IN THIS CHAPTER

Organizing your queries

Saving time

Configuring Power Query options

Avoiding Power Query performance issues

T his chapter offers practical tips for organizing queries and working more efficiently with Power Query. You will also discover a few pointers for optimizing query performance.

Implementing Some Power Query Productivity Tips

Over the past few years, Microsoft has added countless features to Power Query. It has truly become a rich toolset with multiple ways to perform virtually any data transformation you can think of. This growth in functionality has paved the way for a good number of tips that can help you work more efficiently with your Power Query models.

Getting quick information about your queries

All of the Power Query queries that live in a particular workbook can be viewed in the Queries & Connections task pane. Click Data ➪ Queries & Connections to activate it.

Here, you can get some quick information about a query simply by hovering over it. You can see the data source for the query and the last time the query was refreshed, and you can get a sneak peek of the data within the query. You can even click a column hyperlink to peek at a particular column (see Figure 41.1).

FIGURE 41.1

Hover over a query to get quick information including sneak peeks of column contents.

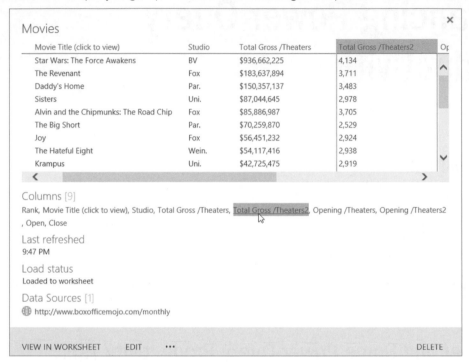

Organizing queries in groups

As you add queries to your workbook, your Queries & Connections pane may start to feel cluttered and disorganized. You can get organized by creating groups for your queries.

Figure 41.2 illustrates the kinds of groups that you can create. You can create a group for specific stages of data processing. Or how about a group for queries sourced from external databases? What about a group where you store small reference tables? Each group is collapsible, so you can neatly pack away queries that you aren't working with at present.

You can create a group by right-clicking a query in the Queries & Connections pane and selecting Move To Group ➪ New Group. Right-clicking the group name will expose a set of options for managing the group itself (see Figure 41.3). You even have the option of refreshing all of the queries within the group at once.

FIGURE 41.2

Queries can be organized into groups.

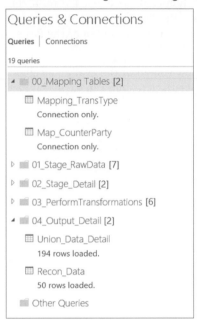

FIGURE 41.3

Group-level options

Selecting columns in your queries faster

When dealing with a large table with dozens of columns in the Query Editor, it can be a pain to find and select the right columns to work with. You can avoid all that scrolling back and forth by clicking the Choose Columns command on the Home tab of the Power Query Editor.

The dialog box in Figure 41.4 will activate and show you all of the available columns (including custom columns that you may have added). Here, you can easily find and select the columns you need.

FIGURE 41.4

Use the Choose Columns command to find and select columns faster.

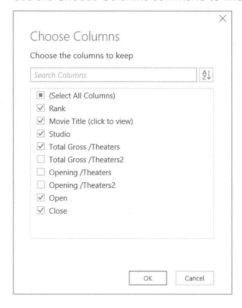

Renaming query steps

Each time you apply an action in the Query Editor, a new entry is made in the Query Settings pane (shown in Figure 41.5). Query steps serve as a kind of audit trail for all the actions you've taken on the data.

FIGURE 41.5

Right-click query steps to rename them.

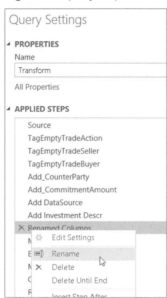

Query steps are automatically given generic names like Uppercased text or Merged Columns. Why not take the time to add some clarity on what each step is doing? You can rename your steps step by right-clicking each step and selecting Rename.

Quickly creating reference tables

There are always a handful of columns in a data set that make for fantastic reference tables. For instance, if your data set contains a column with a list of product categories, it would be useful to create a reference table of all the unique values in that column. Reference tables are often used to map data, feed menu selectors, serve as lookup values, and much more.

While in the Query Editor, you can right-click the column from which you want to create a reference table and then select Add as New Query (see Figure 41.6). A new query will be created, using the table that you just pulled from as the source. The Query Editor jumps into action, showing just the column you selected. From here, you can use the Query Editor to clean up duplicates, remove blanks, and so forth.

FIGURE 41.6

Create a new query from an existing column.

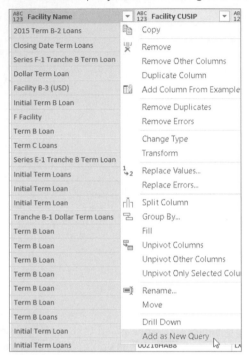

Copying queries to save time

It's always smart to reuse work whenever you can. Why reinvent the wheel when your Queries & Connections pane is full of wheels that you've already created?

Save time by duplicating the queries in your workbook. To do so, activate the Queries & Connections pane, right-click the query you want to copy, and then select Duplicate.

Setting a default load behavior

If you're working heavily with Power Pivot as well as Power Query, chances are that you're loading your Power Query queries to the internal data model a majority of the time. If you're one of those analysts who always loads to the data model, you can tweak the Power Query options to load to the data model automatically.

Click Data ⇨ Get Data ⇨ Query Options to open the dialog box shown in Figure 41.7. Select Data Load under Global and then choose to specify a custom default load setting. This enables the options to load to the worksheet or load to the data model by default.

FIGURE 41.7

Use the Global Data Load options to set a default load behavior.

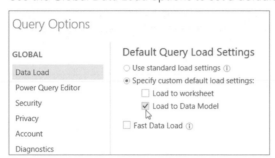

Preventing automatic data type changes

One of the more recent additions to Power Query is the ability to detect data types automatically and proactively change data types. This *type detection* is most often applied when new data is introduced to the query.

For instance, Figure 41.8 shows the query steps after importing a text file. Note the Changed Type step. This step was automatically performed by Power Query as part of its type detection feature.

FIGURE 41.8

Power Query automatically adds a step to change data types when data is imported.

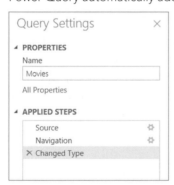

Although Power Query does a decent job at guessing what data types should be used, automatic data type changes can cause unexpected issues. Some veterans of Power Query frankly find the type detection feature annoying. If data types need to be changed, *they* want to be the ones to make that determination.

If you'd rather handle data type changes without the help from Power Query's type detection feature, you can turn it off. Click Data ➪ Get Data ➪ Query Options to open the dialog box shown in Figure 41.9. Select Data Load under Current Workbook and then uncheck the option to Automatically detect column types and headers for unstructured sources.

FIGURE 41.9

Disabling the Type Detection feature

Query Options

GLOBAL	
Data Load	
Power Query Editor	
Security	
Privacy	
Account	
Diagnostics	
CURRENT WORKBOOK	
Data Load	
Regional Settings	
Privacy	

Type Detection

☐ Automatically detect column types and headers for unstructured sources

Relationships

☑ Create relationships between tables when adding to the Data Model for the first time ⓘ

☐ Update relationships when refreshing queries loaded to the Data Model ⓘ

Background Data

☑ Allow data preview to download in the background

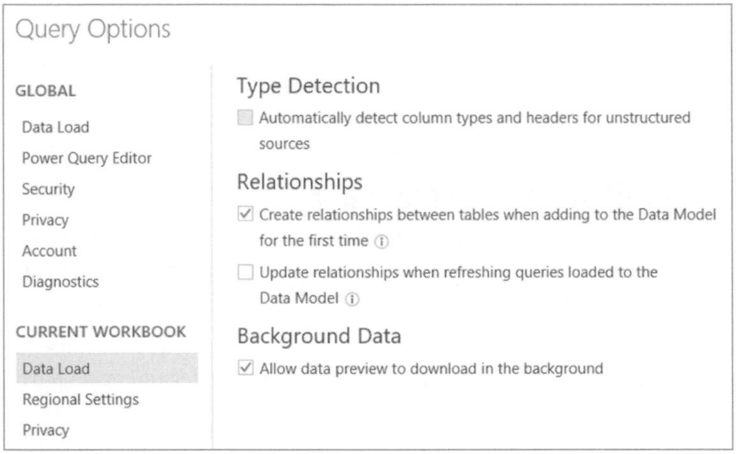

Avoiding Power Query Performance Issues

Because Power Query inherently paves the way for large amounts of data with fairly liberal restrictions, it's possible to end up with queries that are unbearably slow.

When you're wrangling a few thousand records, query performance is not an issue. However, when you are importing and crunching hundreds of thousands of records, performance becomes an issue. There is no getting around the fact that the larger the volume of data, the slower your queries will run. That being said, there are steps that you can take to optimize query performance.

Using views instead of tables

When connecting to an external database, Power Query allows you to import views as well as tables. A *view* is essentially a predefined query on the server itself.

While tables are more transparent, allowing you to see all of the raw unfiltered data, they come with all available columns and rows—whether you need them or not. This often forces you to take extra steps and processing power to remove columns and filter out data that you don't need.

Views not only provide you with cleaner, more user-friendly data, but they can help streamline your data model by limiting the amount of data you import.

Letting your back-end database servers do some crunching

Most Excel analysts who are new to Power Query have a tendency to pull raw data directly from the tables on their external database servers. Once the raw data is in Power Query, they then build transformation and aggregation steps as needed.

Why make Power Query perform transformations that the back-end server could have handled? The reality is that back-end database systems like SQL Server have the ability to shape, aggregate, clean, and transform data much more efficiently than Power Query. Why not utilize their powerful capabilities to massage and shape your data before importing into Power Query?

Instead of pulling raw table data, consider leveraging server-side functions and stored procedures to perform as much data transformation and aggregation work for you as possible. This reduces the amount of processing Power Query will have to do and will naturally improve performance.

Upgrading to 64-bit Excel

If you continue to run into performance issues, there is always the option of getting a better PC. Better, in this case, means moving to a 64-bit PC with 64-bit Excel installed.

The 64-bit version of Excel can access more of your PC's RAM, ensuring that it has the system resources needed to crunch through bigger data sets. In fact, Microsoft recommends 64-bit Excel for anyone working with data models made up of millions of rows.

Before you start installing 64-bit Excel, however, you'll need to consider a few things:

- **Do you already have 64-bit Excel installed?** To check, click File ⇨ Account ⇨ About Excel. A dialog box will activate showing either 32-bit or 64-bit at the top of the screen.
- **Are your data models large enough?** Unless you're working with large data models, the move to 64-bit may not produce a noticeable difference in your work. What's large? A general rule of thumb is that if you have workbooks that use the internal data model and have a file size upwards of 50 megabytes, you would definitely benefit from an upgrade.
- **Do you have a 64-bit operating system installed on your PC?** 64-bit Excel will not install on a 32-bit operating system. You can find out if you're running a 64-bit operating system by entering "My PC 64-bit or 32-bit" into your favorite search engine. You'll get loads of sites that will walk you through the steps to determine your version.
- **Will your other add-ins die?** If you're using other add-ins, be aware that some of them may not be compatible with 64-bit Excel. You don't want to install 64-bit Excel just to find out that your trusted add-ins don't work anymore. Contact your

add-in providers to be sure that they are 64-bit compatible. This includes add-ins for all Office products, not just Excel. When you upgrade Excel to 64-bit, you'll have to upgrade the entire Office suite with it.

Disabling privacy settings to improve performance

The privacy-level settings in Power Query are designed to protect organizational data as it gets combined with other sources. When you create a query that uses an external data source with an internal data source, Power Query stops the show to ask how you'd like to categorize the data privacy levels of each data source.

For a majority of analysts who deal solely with organizational data, the privacy level settings do little more than slow down queries and cause confusion. Fortunately, there is an option for ignoring privacy levels.

Click Data ➪ Get Data ➪ Query Options to open the dialog box shown in Figure 41.10. Select Privacy under Current Workbook and then choose the option to ignore privacy levels.

FIGURE 41.10

Disabling the privacy level settings

Query Options

GLOBAL

Data Load

Power Query Editor

Security

Privacy

Account

Diagnostics

CURRENT WORKBOOK

Data Load

Regional Settings

Privacy

Privacy Levels

○ Combine data according to your Privacy Level settings for each source

◉ Ignore the Privacy Levels and potentially improve performance ⓘ

Learn more about Privacy Levels

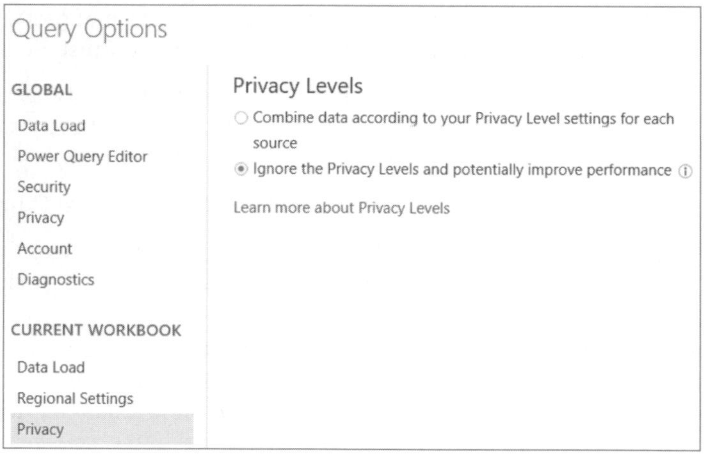

Disabling relationship detection

When building a query and choosing Load to Data Model as the output, Power Query will, by default, attempt to detect relationships between queries and create those relationships within the internal data model. The relationships between queries are primarily driven by the defined query steps. For instance, if you were to merge two queries and then load the result into the data model, a relationship is automatically created.

In larger data models with a dozen or so tables, Power Query relationship detection can affect performance and increase the time it takes to load the data model. You can avoid this hassle and even gain a performance boost by disabling relationship detection.

Click Data ⇨ Get Data ⇨ Query Options to open the dialog box shown in Figure 41.9. Select Data Load under Current Workbook and then uncheck this option: Create relationships between tables when adding to the Data Model for the first time.

41

Part VI

Automating Excel

Visual Basic for Applications (VBA) is a powerful programming language built in to Excel, which you can use to automate routine or repetitive tasks, create custom worksheet formulas, or develop Excel-based applications for other users.

IN THIS PART

Introducing Visual Basic for Applications

This chapter introduces the Visual Basic for Applications (VBA) macro language—a key component for users who want to customize and automate Excel. This chapter teaches you how to record macros and create simple macro procedures. Subsequent chapters expand upon the topics in this chapter.

Introducing VBA Macros

A macro is a sequence of instructions that automates some aspect of Excel so that you can work more efficiently and with fewer errors. You may create a macro, for example, to format and print your month-end sales report. After you write the macro, you can then execute it every month. Not only does this save you from having to repeat the formatting steps every month, it also ensures that the exact same formatting is applied.

You don't have to be a power user to create and use simple VBA macros. Once they understand a few basics, even casual users can simply turn on Excel's macro recorder, which records your actions and converts them into a VBA macro. When you execute the recorded macro, Excel performs the actions again. More advanced users, though, can write code that tells Excel to perform tasks that can't be recorded. For example, you can write procedures that display custom dialog boxes or process data in a series of workbooks and even create special-purpose add-ins.

What You Can Do with VBA

VBA is an extremely rich programming language with thousands of uses. The following list contains just a few things you can do with VBA macros. (Not all of these tasks are covered in this book.)

- **Insert boilerplate text.** If you need to enter standard text into a range of cells, you can create a macro to do the typing for you.

- **Automate procedures that you perform frequently.** For example, you may need to prepare a month-end summary. If the task is straightforward, you can develop a macro to do it for you.

- **Automate repetitive operations.** If you need to perform the same action in 12 different workbooks, you can record a macro while you perform the task once—and then let the macro repeat your action in the other workbooks.

- **Create custom commands.** For example, you can combine several Excel commands so that they're executed from a single keystroke or from a single mouse click.

- **Create a simplified "front end" for users who don't know much about Excel.** For example, you can set up a foolproof data-entry template.

- **Develop new worksheet functions.** Although Excel includes a wide assortment of built-in functions, you can create custom functions that greatly simplify your formulas.

- **Create complete macro-driven applications.** Excel macros can display custom dialog boxes and respond to new commands added to the Ribbon.

- **Create custom add-ins for Excel.** Add-ins are programs that extend Excel's capabilities.

Displaying the Developer Tab

If you plan to work with VBA macros, make sure you can see the Developer tab on the Excel Ribbon. The Developer tab, which does not appear by default, contains useful commands for VBA users (see Figure 42.1). To display this tab, follow these steps:

FIGURE 42.1

The Developer tab

1. **Right-click any Ribbon control, and select Customize the Ribbon from the shortcut menu.** The Customize Ribbon tab of the Excel Options dialog box appears.

2. **In the list box on the right, place a check mark next to Developer.**

3. **Click OK to return to Excel.**

Learning about Macro Security

Macros have the potential to cause serious damage to your computer, such as erasing files or installing malware. Consequently, Microsoft has added macro-security features to help prevent macro-related problems.

Figure 42.2 shows the Macro Settings section of the Trust Center dialog box. To display this dialog box, choose Developer ➪ Code ➪ Macro Security.

FIGURE 42.2

The Macro Settings section of the Trust Center dialog box

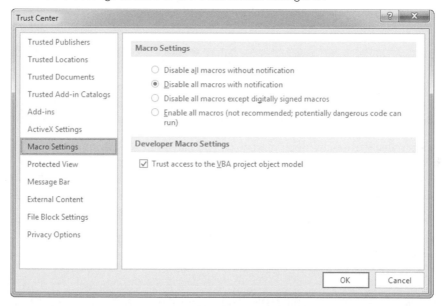

By default, Excel uses the Disable All Macros with Notification option. With this setting in effect, if you open a workbook that contains macros (and the file is not already trusted), the macros will be disabled, and Excel will display a security warning above the Formula bar (see Figure 42.3). If you're certain that the workbook comes from a trusted source, click the Enable Content button in the security warning area, and the macros will be enabled.

Excel remembers your decision; if you enable the macros, you won't see the security warning the next time you open that file.

FIGURE 42.3

Excel displays a security warning if a workbook contains macros.

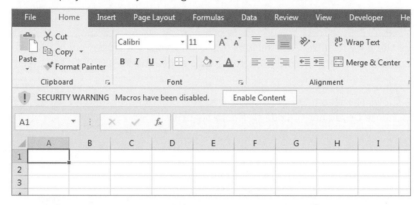

> **NOTE**
>
> If the Visual Basic Editor (VBE) window is open when you open a workbook that contains macros, Excel does not display the security warning above the Formula bar. Instead, it displays a dialog box with two buttons: Enable Macros and Disable Macros.

Rather than deal with individual workbooks, you may prefer to designate one or more folders as "trusted locations." All of the workbooks in a trusted location are opened without a macro warning. You designate trusted folders in the Trusted Locations section of the Trust Center dialog box.

Saving Workbooks That Contain Macros

If you store one or more VBA macros in a workbook, you must save the file with an .xlsm extension.

The first time you save a workbook that contains macros (or even an empty VBA module), the file format defaults to .xlsx—and this format can't contain macros. Unless you change the file format to .xlsm, Excel displays the warning shown in Figure 42.4. You need to click No and then choose Excel Macro-Enabled Workbook (*.xlsm) from the Save As Type drop-down list in the Save As dialog box.

FIGURE 42.4

Excel warns you if your workbook contains macros and you attempt to save it as a regular Excel file.

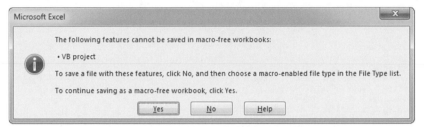

> **NOTE**
>
> Alternatively, you can save the workbook in the old Excel 97–2003 format (which uses an .xls extension) or the newer Excel binary format (which uses an .xlsb extension). Both of these file formats can contain macros.

Looking at the Two Types of VBA Macros

A VBA macro (also known as a *procedure*) is usually one of two types: a Sub or a Function. The next two sections discuss the difference.

What's New in the Visual Basic Editor?

In a word, nothing. Beginning with Excel 2007, Microsoft made many changes to Excel's user interface. However, the VBE has remained untouched and seems like outdated software. The VBA language has been updated to accommodate most of the new Excel features, but the VBE has no new features, and the toolbars and menus work as they always have.

VBA Sub procedures

You can think of a Sub procedure as a new command that either the user or another macro can execute. You can have any number of Sub procedures in an Excel workbook. Figure 42.5 shows a simple VBA Sub procedure. When this code is executed, VBA inserts the current date into the active cell, applies a number format, makes the cell bold, sets the text color to white, sets the background color to black, and adjusts the column width.

FIGURE 42.5

A simple VBA procedure

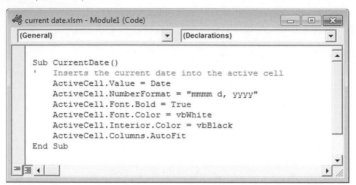

 A workbook that contains this macro is available on this book's website at www.wiley.com/go/ excel2019bible. It also includes a button that makes it easy to execute the macro. The file is named current date.xlsm.

Sub procedures always start with the keyword Sub, the macro's name (every macro must have a unique name), and then a list of arguments inside of parentheses. The parentheses are required even if the procedure doesn't use arguments, like this example. The End Sub statement signals the end of the procedure. The lines in between Sub and End Sub make up the procedure's code.

The CurrentDate macro also includes a comment. Comments are simply notes to yourself, and VBA ignores them. A comment line begins with an apostrophe. You can also put a comment in the same line as a statement. In other words, when VBA encounters an apostrophe, it ignores the rest of the text in the line.

You execute a VBA Sub procedure in any of the following ways:

- **Choose Developer ⇨ Code ⇨ Macros (or press Alt+F8) to display the Macro dialog box.** Select the procedure name from the list and then click Run.
- **Assign the macro to a control in the Quick Access toolbar or to a control in the Ribbon.**
- **Press the procedure's shortcut key combination (if it has one).**
- **Click a button or other shape that has a macro assigned to it.**
- **If the VBE is active, move the cursor anywhere within the code and press F5.**
- **Execute the procedure by calling it from another VBA procedure.**
- **Enter the procedure name in the Immediate window in the VBE.**

VBA functions

The second type of VBA procedure is a function. A function returns a single value (just as a worksheet function always returns a single value). A VBA function can be executed by other VBA procedures or used in worksheet formulas, just as you would use Excel's built-in worksheet functions.

Figure 42.6 shows a custom worksheet function. This function is named CubeRoot, and it requires a single argument. CubeRoot calculates the cube root of its argument and returns the result. A Function procedure looks much like a Sub procedure. Notice, however, that function procedures begin with the keyword Function and end with an End Function statement.

FIGURE 42.6

This VBA function returns the cube root of its argument.

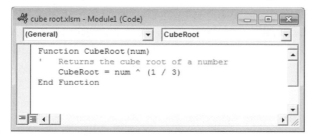

 A workbook that contains this function is available on this book's website at www.wiley.com/go/ excel2019bible. The file is named cube root.xlsm.

 Creating VBA functions that you use in worksheet formulas can simplify your formulas and enable you to perform calculations that otherwise may be impossible. Chapter 43, "Creating Custom Worksheet Functions," discusses VBA functions in greater detail.

Some Definitions

If you're new to VBA, you may be overwhelmed by the terminology. Here are some key definitions to help you keep the terms straight. These terms cover VBA and UserForms (custom dialog boxes)—two important elements that are used to customize Excel:

Code VBA instructions that are stored in a module when you record a macro or enter them manually.

Controls Objects on a UserForm (or in a worksheet) that are used to interact with the user. Examples include buttons, check boxes, and list boxes.

Function One of two types of VBA macros that you can create. (The other is a Sub procedure.) A function returns a single value. You can use VBA functions in other VBA macros or in your worksheets.

Continues

continued

Macro   A set of VBA instructions.

Method   An action taken on an object. For example, applying the Clear method to a Range object erases the contents and formatting of the cells.

Module   A container for VBA code.

Object   An element that you manipulate with VBA. Examples include ranges, charts, and drawing objects.

Procedure   Another name for a macro. A VBA procedure can be a Sub procedure or a Function procedure.

Property   A particular aspect of an object. For example, a Range object has properties, such as Height, Style, and Name.

Sub procedure   One of two types of VBA macros that you can create. The other is a Function.

UserForm   A container that holds controls for a custom dialog box and holds VBA code to manipulate the controls.

VBA   Visual Basic for Applications. The macro language that is available in Excel as well as in the other Microsoft Office applications.

VBE   Visual Basic Editor. The window (separate from Excel) that you use to create VBA macros and UserForms. Press Alt+F11 to toggle between Excel and the VBE.

 Chapter 44, "Creating UserForms," and Chapter 45, "Using UserForm Controls in a Worksheet," explain UserForms in depth.

Creating VBA Macros

Excel provides two ways to create macros:

- Turn on the macro recorder and record your actions.
- Enter the code directly into a VBA module.

The following sections describe these methods.

Recording VBA macros

In this section, we describe the basic steps that you take to record a VBA macro. In most cases, you can record your actions as a macro and then simply replay the macro; you don't need to look at the code that's automatically generated. If simply recording and playing back macros is as far as you go with VBA, you don't need to be concerned with the language itself (although a basic understanding of how things work can be helpful).

Recording your actions to create VBA code: the basics

The Excel macro recorder translates your actions into VBA code. To start the macro recorder, choose Developer ➪ Code ➪ Record Macro (or click the Record Macro icon on the left side of the status bar). The Record Macro dialog box, as shown in Figure 42.7, appears.

FIGURE 42.7

The Record Macro dialog box

The Record Macro dialog box presents several options:

Macro Name   The name of the macro. Excel proposes generic names, such as Macro1, Macro2, and so on.

Shortcut Key   You can specify a key combination that executes the macro. The key combination always uses the Ctrl key. You can also press Shift when you enter a letter. For example, pressing Shift while you press H makes the shortcut key combination Ctrl+Shift+H.

> **CAUTION**
> Shortcut keys assigned to macros take precedence over built-in shortcut keys. For example, if you assign Ctrl+S to a macro, you can't use the key combination to save your workbook when that macro is available.

Store Macro In   The location for the macro. Your choices are the current workbook, your Personal Macro Workbook (see "Storing macros in your Personal Macro Workbook" later in this chapter), or a new workbook.

Description   A description of the macro (optional).

To begin recording your actions, click OK; your actions within Excel are converted to VBA code. When you finish recording the macro, choose Developer ➪ Code ➪ Stop Recording, or you can click the Stop Recording button on the status bar. This button replaces the Start Recording button while your macro is being recorded.

> **NOTE**
>
> Recording your actions always results in a new `Sub` procedure. You can't create a `Function` procedure by using the macro recorder. You must create function procedures manually.

Recording a macro: a simple example

This example demonstrates how to record a simple macro that inserts your name into the active cell.

To create the macro, start with a new workbook and follow these steps:

1. **Select an empty cell.**

> **NOTE**
>
> Select the cell before you start recording your macro. This step is important. If you select a cell while the macro recorder is turned on, the actual cell that you select will be recorded into the macro. In such a case, the macro would always use that particular cell, and it would not be a general-purpose macro.

2. **Choose Developer ➪ Code ➪ Record Macro.** The Record Macro dialog box appears. (Refer to Figure 42.7.)
3. **Enter a new single-word name for the macro to replace the default `Macro1` name.** For example, type `MyName` as the name.
4. **Assign this macro to the shortcut key Ctrl+Shift+N by entering an uppercase N in the Shortcut Key field.**
5. **Make sure that This Workbook is selected in the Store Macro In field.**
6. **Click OK to close the Record Macro dialog box and begin recording your actions.**
7. **Type your name into the selected cell and then press Enter.**
8. **Choose Developer ➪ Code ➪ Stop Recording (or click the Stop Recording button on the status bar).**

Examining the macro

The macro was recorded in a new module named `Module1`. To view the code in this module, you must activate the VBE. You can activate the VBE in either of two ways:

- Press Alt+F11.
- Choose Developer ➪ Code ➪ Visual Basic.

In the VBE, the Project window displays a list of all open workbooks and add-ins. This list is displayed as a tree diagram, which you can expand or collapse. The code you recorded previously is stored in Module1 in the Modules folder of the current workbook. When you double-click Module1, the code in the module appears in the Code window.

NOTE

If you don't see the list of open workbooks, choose Project Explorer from the View menu or press Ctrl+R to display the Project Explorer.

Figure 42.8 shows the recorded macro, as displayed in the Code window.

FIGURE 42.8

The MyName procedure was generated by the Excel macro recorder.

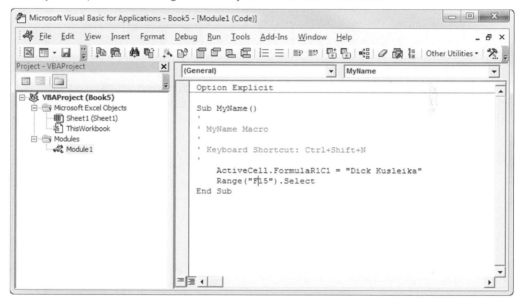

The macro should look something like this (with your name substituted in, of course):

```
Sub MyName()
'
' MyName Macro
'
' Keyboard Shortcut: Ctrl+Shift+N
'
    ActiveCell.FormulaR1C1 = "Dick Kusleika"
    Range("F15").Select
End Sub
```

The macro recorded is a Sub procedure that is named MyName. The statements tell Excel what to do when the macro is executed.

Notice that Excel inserted some comments at the top of the procedure. These comments are based on information that appeared in the Record Macro dialog box. These comment lines (which begin with an apostrophe) aren't really necessary, and deleting them has no effect on how the macro runs. If you ignore the comments, you'll see that this procedure has only two VBA statements:

```
ActiveCell.FormulaR1C1 = "Dick Kusleika"
Range("F15").Select
```

The first statement causes the name that you typed while recording the macro to be inserted into the active cell. The FormulaR1C1 part is a property of the Range object, which we'll discuss later. When you press Enter in a cell, Excel moves down one cell (unless you've change the default behavior). You can guess from this code that the active cell was F14 when the macro was recorded.

Testing the macro

Before you recorded this macro, you set an option that assigned the macro to the Ctrl+Shift+N shortcut key combination. To test the macro, return to Excel by using either of the following methods:

- Press Alt+F11.
- Click the View Microsoft Excel button on the VBE toolbar.

When Excel is active, activate a worksheet. (It can be in the workbook that contains the VBA module or in any other workbook.) Select a cell and press Ctrl+Shift+N. The macro immediately enters your name into the cell and selects cell F15.

Editing the macro

After you record a macro, you can make changes to it (although you must know what you're doing). For example, assume that you don't want to select F15, but rather you want to select the cell below the active cell. Press Alt+F11 to activate the VBE window. Then activate Module1 and change the second statement to the following:

```
ActiveCell.Offset(1, 0).Select
```

The edited macro appears as follows:

```
Sub MyName()
'
' MyName Macro
'
' Keyboard Shortcut: Ctrl+Shift+N
'
    ActiveCell.FormulaR1C1 = "Dick Kusleika"
    ActiveCell.Offset(1, 0).Select
End Sub
```

Test this new macro, and you will see that it performs as it should.

Absolute versus relative recording

If you're going to work with recorded macros, you need to understand the concept of relative versus absolute recording modes. In the previous example, we showed how even a simple macro could act unexpectedly because of an incorrect recording mode.

Normally, when you record a macro, Excel stores exact references to the cells that you select. (That is, it performs absolute recording.) If you press Enter while in cell F14 and the active cell moves down one, the recorded macro will show that you selected cell F15. Similarly, if you were to select cells B1:B10 while you're recording a macro, for example, Excel records this selection as follows:

```
Range("B1:B10").Select
```

This VBA statement means exactly what it says: "Select the cells in the range B1:B10." When you invoke the macro that contains this statement, the same cells are always selected, regardless of where the active cell is located.

In the Developer ⇨ Code group of the Ribbon there is a Use Relative References control. When you click this control, Excel changes its recording mode from absolute (the default) to relative. When recording in relative mode, selecting a range of cells is translated differently, depending on where the active cell is located. For example, if you're recording in relative mode and cell A1 is active, selecting the range B1:B10 generates the following statement:

```
ActiveCell.Offset(0, 1).Range("A1:A10").Select
```

This statement can be translated as "From the active cell, move 0 rows down and 1 column right. Then treat this new cell as if it were cell A1. Now select what would be A1:A10." In other words, a macro that is recorded in relative mode starts out by using the active cell as its starting point and then stores relative references to this cell. As a result, you get different results, depending on the location of the active cell. When you replay this macro, the cells that are selected depend on the active cell. This macro selects a range that is 10 rows by 1 column, offset from the active cell by 0 rows and 1 column.

When Excel is recording in relative mode, the Use Relative References control appears with a background color. To return to absolute recording, click the Use Relative References control again and it displays its normal state, with no background color.

Another example

In the first example, the macro behaved oddly by selecting cell F15 after it entered the name. This odd behavior didn't cause any harm or cause the macro not to execute properly. This example demonstrates how choosing the wrong recording mode can actually cause the macro to work incorrectly. You will record a macro that inserts the current date and time into the active cell. To create the macro, follow these steps:

1. **Activate an empty cell.**
2. **Choose Developer ⇨ Code ⇨ Record Macro.** The Record Macro dialog box appears.

3. **Enter a new, single-word name for the macro to replace the default Macro1 name.** A good name is `TimeStamp`.

4. **Assign this macro to the shortcut key Ctrl+Shift+T by entering an uppercase *T* in the Shortcut Key field.**

5. **Make sure that This Workbook is selected in the Store Macro In field.**

6. **Click OK to close the Record Macro dialog box.**

7. **Enter this formula into the selected cell:**

   `=NOW()`

8. **With the date cell selected, click the Copy button (or press Ctrl+C) to copy the cell to the Clipboard.**

9. **Choose Home ⇨ Clipboard ⇨ Paste ⇨ Values (V).** This step replaces the formula with static text so that the date and time do not update when the worksheet is calculated.

10. **Press Esc to cancel Copy mode.**

11. **Choose Developer ⇨ Code ⇨ Stop Recording (or click the Stop Recording button on the status bar).**

Running the macro

Activate an empty cell, and press Ctrl+Shift+T to execute the macro. There's a pretty good chance that the macro won't work!

The VBA code that is recorded in this macro depends on a setting on the Advanced tab of the Excel Options dialog box, namely, After Pressing Enter, Move Selection. If this setting is enabled (which is the default), the recorded macro won't work as intended because the active cell was changed when you pressed Enter. Even if you reactivated the date cell while recording (in step 7), the macro still fails.

Examining the macro

Activate the VBE and take a look at the recorded code. Figure 42.9 shows the recorded macro, as displayed in the Code window.

The procedure has five statements. The first inserts the `NOW()` formula into the active cell. The second statement selects cell F6—if the active cell moved to the next cell in step 7, then you had to reselect the active cell in step 8. The exact cell address depends on the location of the active cell when the macro was recorded.

The third statement copies the cell. The fourth statement, which is displayed on two lines (the underscore character means that the statement continues on the next line), pastes the Clipboard contents (as a value) to the current selection. The fifth statement cancels the dashed border around the copied cell.

FIGURE 42.9

The TimeStamp procedure was generated by the Excel macro recorder.

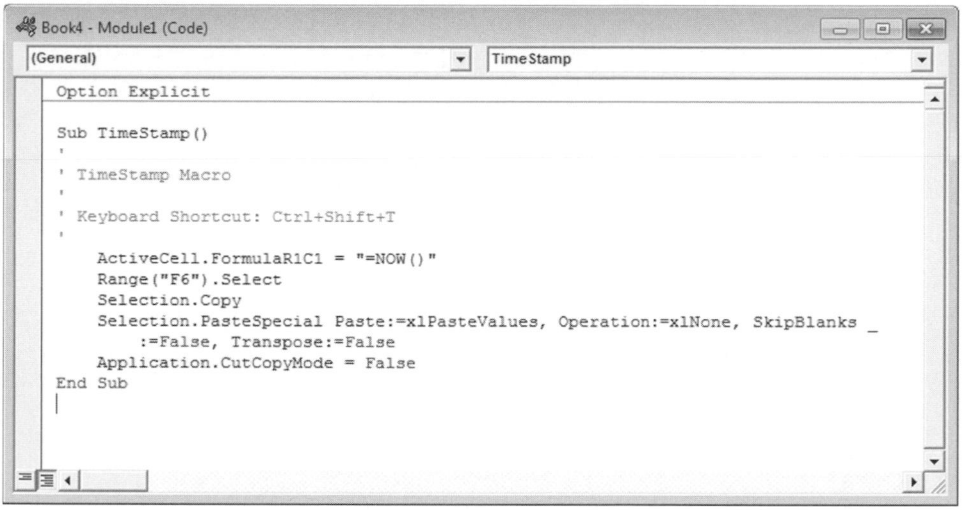

```
Book4 - Module1 (Code)

(General)                                              TimeStamp

Option Explicit

Sub TimeStamp()
'
' TimeStamp Macro
'
' Keyboard Shortcut: Ctrl+Shift+T
'
    ActiveCell.FormulaR1C1 = "=NOW()"
    Range("F6").Select
    Selection.Copy
    Selection.PasteSpecial Paste:=xlPasteValues, Operation:=xlNone, SkipBlanks _
        :=False, Transpose:=False
    Application.CutCopyMode = False
End Sub
```

42

The problem is that the macro is hard-coded to select cell F6. If you execute the macro when a different cell is active, the code always selects cell F6 before it copies the cell. This is not what you intended, and it causes the macro to fail.

> **NOTE**
>
> You'll also notice that the macro recorded some actions that you didn't make. For example, it specified several options for the `PasteSpecial` operation. Recording actions that you don't specifically make is just a by-product of the method that Excel uses to translate actions into code.

Rerecording the macro

You can fix the macro in several ways. If you understand VBA, you can edit the code so that it works properly, or you can re-record the macro using relative references.

Activate the VBA Editor, delete the existing `TimeStamp` procedure, and re-record it. Before you start recording, click the Use Relative References command in the Code group of the Developer tab.

Figure 42.10 shows the new macro, recorded with relative references in effect.

FIGURE 42.10

This TimeStamp macro works correctly.

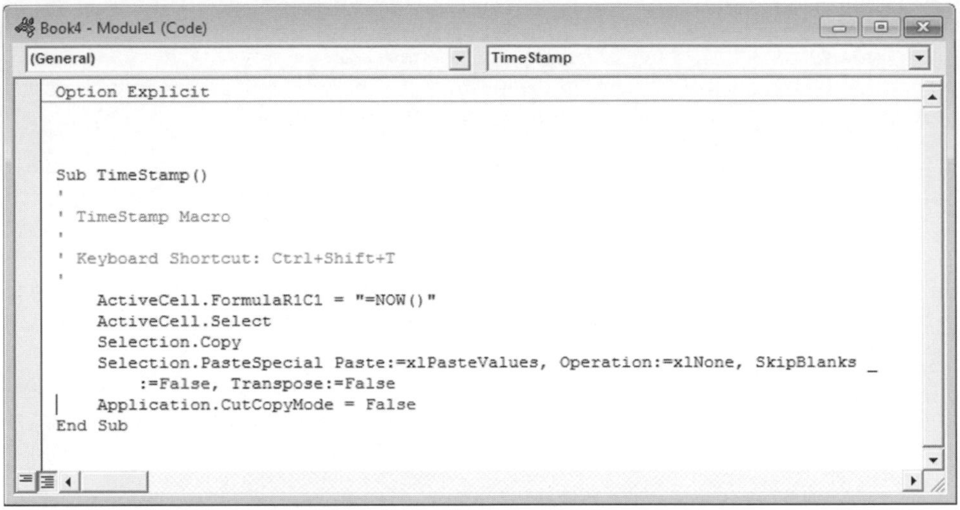

Note that the second line now says `ActiveCell.Select` instead of using a specific cell address. This solves the problem of copying and pasting the wrong cell, but why would it select a cell that's already selected? It's just one of the curiosities of recording macros. As you select cells, such as when you press Enter after keying a formula, the recorder dutifully registers every selection. In this example, when you pressed Enter in step 7, the recorder recorded this line:

```
ActiveCell.Offset(1, 0).Range("A1").Select
```

Since you didn't do anything while in that cell, however, it didn't save it. When you reselected the cell with the date in it, it replaced the line above with the one you see in the macro.

Testing the macro

When Excel is active, activate a worksheet. (The worksheet can be in the workbook that contains the VBA module or in any other workbook.) Select a cell and press Ctrl+Shift+T. The macro immediately enters the current date and time into the cell. You may need to widen the column to see the date and time.

When the result of a macro requires additional manual intervention, it's a sign that the macro could be improved. To widen the column automatically, just add this statement to the end of the macro (before the `End Sub` statement):

```
ActiveCell.EntireColumn.AutoFit
```

More about recording VBA macros

If you followed along with the preceding examples, you should have a better feel for how to record macros—and a good feel for problems that might occur with even simple macros. If you find the VBA code confusing, don't worry. You don't really have to be concerned with it as long as the macro that you record works correctly. If the macro doesn't work properly, re-recording the macro rather than editing the code is often easier.

A good way to learn about what is recorded is to set up your screen so that you can see the code that is being generated in the VBE window. To do so, make sure that the Excel window isn't maximized; then arrange the Excel window and the VBE window so that both are visible. While you're recording your actions, make sure that the VBE window is displaying the module in which the code is being recorded. (You may have to double-click the module name in the Project Explorer window.)

42

TIP

If you do a lot of work with VBA, consider adding a second monitor to your system. Then you can display Excel on one monitor and the VBE on the other.

Storing macros in your Personal Macro Workbook

Most user-created macros are designed for use in a specific workbook, but you may want to use some macros in all of your work. You can store these general-purpose macros in the Personal Macro Workbook so that they're always available to you. The Personal Macro Workbook is loaded whenever you start Excel. This file, named `personal.xlsb`, doesn't exist until you record a macro, using Personal Macro Workbook as the destination.

NOTE

The Personal Macro Workbook is normally located in a hidden window to keep it out of the way.

To record the macro in your Personal Macro Workbook, select the Personal Macro Workbook option in the Record Macro dialog box before you start recording. This option is in the Store Macro In drop-down box.

If you store macros in the Personal Macro Workbook, you don't have to remember to open the Personal Macro Workbook when you load a workbook that uses macros. When you want to exit, Excel asks whether you want to save changes to the Personal Macro Workbook.

Assigning a macro to a shortcut key

When you begin recording a macro, the Record Macro dialog box gives you an opportunity to provide a shortcut key for the macro. Here's what to do if you'd like to change the shortcut key or provide a shortcut key for a macro that doesn't have one:

1. **Choose Developer ⇨ Code ⇨ Macros (or press Alt+F8).** The Macro dialog box appears.

2. **Select the macro name from the list.**

3. **Click the Options button.** The Macro Options dialog box, shown in Figure 42.11, appears.

4. **Specify the shortcut key.** Use a single letter (for a Ctrl+letter shortcut), or press Shift and enter an uppercase letter (for a Ctrl+Shift+letter shortcut).

5. **Click OK to return to the Macro dialog box.**

6. **Click Cancel to close the Macro dialog box.**

FIGURE 42.11

Use the Macro Options dialog box to add or change a shortcut key for a macro.

Assigning a macro to a button

After you record a macro and test it, you may want to assign the macro to a button placed in a worksheet. You can follow these steps to do so:

1. **If the macro is a general-purpose one that you plan to use in more than a single workbook, make sure the macro is stored in your Personal Macro Workbook.**

2. **Choose Developer ⇨ Controls ⇨ Insert and then click the icon identified as Button (Form Control).** Figure 42.12 shows the list of controls. Move your mouse pointer over the icons, and you will see a ScreenTip that describes the control.

3. **Click the worksheet and drag to draw the button.** When you release the mouse button, the Assign Macro dialog box appears.

4. **Select the macro from the list.**

5. **Click OK to close the Assign Macro dialog box.**

6. **(Optional) Change the text that appears on the button to make it descriptive; right-click the button, choose Edit Text from the shortcut menu, and make your changes.**

FIGURE 42.12

Adding a button to a worksheet so that it can be used to execute a macro

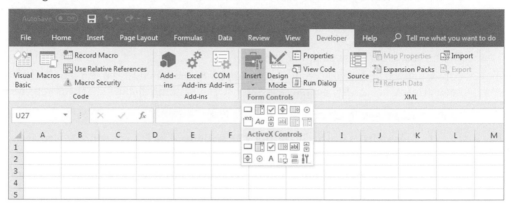

After you perform these steps, clicking the button executes the assigned macro.

Adding a macro to your Quick Access toolbar

You can also assign a macro to a button on your Quick Access toolbar:

1. **Right-click the Quick Access toolbar, and choose Customize Quick Access Toolbar from the shortcut menu.** The Quick Access Toolbar tab of the Excel Options dialog box appears.

2. **Select Macros from the drop-down list on the left.**

3. **At the top of the list on the right, choose For All Documents, or For xxx (where xxx is the active workbook's name).** This step determines whether the macro will be available for all workbooks or just the workbook that contains the macro.

4. **Select your macro and click the Add button.**

5. **To change the icon or displayed text, click the Modify button, make a selection, and click OK.**

6. **Click OK to close the Excel Options dialog box.**

After performing these steps, your Quick Access toolbar will display a button that executes your macro.

Writing VBA code

As demonstrated in the preceding sections, the easiest way to create a simple macro is to record your actions. To develop more complex macros, however, you have to enter the VBA code manually—in other words, write a program. To save time (and assist in the learning process), you can often combine recording with manual code entry.

Before you can begin writing VBA code, you must have a good understanding of such topics as objects, properties, and methods. Also, you must be familiar with common programming constructs, such as looping and If-Then statements.

This section is an introduction to VBA programming, which is essential if you want to write (rather than record) VBA macros. It isn't intended to be a complete instructional guide. Our book *Excel 2019 Power Programming with VBA* (Wiley, 2018) covers all aspects of VBA and advanced spreadsheet application development.

The basics: entering and editing code

Before you can enter code, you must insert a VBA module into the workbook. If the workbook already has a VBA module, you can use the existing module sheet for your new code.

Follow these steps to insert a new VBA module:

1. **Press Alt+F11 to activate the VBE window.** The Project window displays a list of all open workbooks and add-ins.

2. **In the Project window, locate and select the workbook you're working in.**

3. **Choose Insert ⇨ Module.** VBA inserts a new (empty) module into the workbook and displays it in the Code window.

A VBA module, which is displayed in a separate window, works like a text editor. You can move through the sheet, select text, insert text, copy, cut, paste, and so on.

VBA Coding Tips

When you enter code into a module sheet, you're free to use indenting and blank lines to make the code more readable. In fact, this is an excellent habit.

After you enter a line of code (by pressing Enter), it's evaluated for syntax errors. If none is found, the line of code is reformatted, and colors are added to keywords and identifiers. This automatic reformatting adds consistent spaces (before and after an equal sign, for example) and removes extra spaces that aren't needed. If a syntax error is found, you receive a pop-up message, and the line is displayed in a different color (red, by default). You need to correct your error before you can execute the macro.

A single statement can be as long as you need. However, you may want to break the statement into two or more lines. To do so, insert a space followed by an underscore (_). The following code, although written as two lines, is actually a single VBA statement:

```
Sheets("Sheet1").Range("B1").Value = _
   Sheets("Sheet1").Range("A1").Value
```

You can insert comments freely into your VBA code. The comment indicator is an apostrophe or single quote character ('). Any text that follows a single quote on that line is ignored. A comment can be a line by itself, or it can be inserted after a statement. The following examples show two comments:

```
' Assign the values to the variables
Rate = .085   'Rate as of November 16
```

The Excel object model

VBA is a language designed to manipulate objects. Some objects are contained in the language itself, but most of the objects that you will use when programming VBA for Excel come from the Excel object model.

At the top of the object model is the `Application` object. This object represents Excel itself, and all other objects are below it in the hierarchy. One way to think about writing code is to ask which object you'd like to change and which property or method controls that aspect of the object. For example, if you want to force users to enter data using the Formula bar as opposed to entering data directly in cells, you can change the `EditDirectlyInCell` property of the `Application` object.

If you don't know which object or property to change—and when you're just starting out you won't—you can use the macro recorder. Start recording a macro, and make the changes. Then see what the recorder came up with. If you record a macro and choose File ⇨ Options ⇨ Advanced and uncheck Allow editing directly in cells, you will see this recorded macro.

```
Sub Macro1()
'
' Macro1 Macro
'

'
    Application.EditDirectlyInCell = False
End Sub
```

Now you know that the `EditDirectlyInCell` property of the `Application` object is where that setting is stored, and you can use that in your own code.

Objects and collections

In addition to the `Application` object, there are hundreds of other objects available to use in your code, such as `Ranges`, `Charts`, and `Shapes`. These objects are arranged in a hierarchy with the `Application` object at the top.

Objects of the same type are contained in *collections*. (Collections are also an object.) Collection objects are named using the plural form of the objects that they contain. Each open workbook is a `Workbook` object, and all of the open workbooks are in the `Workbooks` collection object. Similarly, the `Shapes` collection object contains all of the objects of type `Shape`.

There are a few places where the plural collection naming convention breaks down. The `Range` object is an important exception that we'll discuss later in this chapter.

You reference a specific object by traversing the hierarchy. To reference cell A1, you might use code such as the following:

```
Application.Workbooks.Item("MyBook.xlsx").Worksheets.Item(1).
Range("A1")
```

Fortunately, VBA provides some shortcuts. Since `Application` is at the top, you can omit it, and VBA will know what you want. VBA also provides default properties for some objects. All collection objects have a default property called `Item` that's used to access one of the collections. You can shorten your code as follows:

```
Workbooks("MyBook.xlsx").Worksheets(1).Range("A1")
```

When accessing an `Item` of a collection, you can ask for it by name or by number. For the `Workbooks` collection, we passed in the name of the workbook that we wanted, and it returned the `Workbook` object with that name. For the `Worksheets` collection, however, we asked for the first `Worksheet` object in the collection regardless of its name.

Properties

The objects you work with have properties, which you can think of as attributes of the objects. For example, a `Range` object has properties, such as `Column`, `Row`, `Width`, and `Value`. A `Chart` object has properties, such as `Legend`, `ChartTitle`, and so on. `ChartTitle` is also an object, with properties such as `Font`, `Orientation`, and `Text`. Excel has many objects, and each has its own set of properties. You can write VBA code to do the following:

- Examine an object's current property setting and take some action based on it.
- Change an object's property setting.

You refer to a property in your VBA code by placing a period (a dot) and the property name after the object's name. For example, the following VBA statement sets the `Value` property of a range named frequency to 15. (That is, the statement causes the number 15 to appear in the range's cells.)

```
Range("frequency").Value = 15
```

You might have noticed that we used the dot operator to traverse the hierarchy in the previous section, and we're using it again to access properties. That's not a coincidence. Properties can contain a lot of different values, and they can also contain other objects. When we used `Application.Workbooks("MyBook.xlsx")`, we were actually accessing the `Workbooks` property of the `Application` object. That property returns a `Workbooks` collection object.

Some properties are read-only, which means you can examine the property, but you can't change the property. For a single-cell `Range` object, the `Row` and `Column` properties are read-only properties: you can determine where a cell is located (in which row and column), but you can't change the cell's location by changing these properties.

A `Range` object also has a `Formula` property, which is not read-only; that is, you can insert a formula into a cell by changing its `Formula` property. The following statement inserts a formula into cell A12 by changing the cell's `Formula` property:

```
Range("A12").Formula = "=SUM(A1:A10)"
```

> **NOTE**
>
> Contrary to what you may think, Excel doesn't have a `Cell` object. When you want to manipulate a single cell, you use the `Range` object (with only one cell in it).

The `Application` object has several useful properties that refer to where the user is in the program:

> `Application.ActiveWorkbook`: Returns the active workbook (a `Workbook` object) in Excel.
>
> `Application.ActiveSheet`: Returns the active sheet (a `Sheet` object) of the active workbook.
>
> `Application.ActiveCell`: Returns the active cell (a `Range` object) of the active window.
>
> `Application.Selection`: Returns the object that is currently selected in the active window of the `Application` object. This can be a `Range`, a `Chart`, a `Shape`, or some other selectable object.

In many cases, you can refer to the same object in a number of different ways. Assume you have a workbook named `Sales.xlsx` and that it's the only workbook open. Furthermore, assume that this workbook has one worksheet, named `Summary`. Your VBA code can refer to the `Summary` sheet in any of the following ways:

```
Workbooks("Sales.xlsx").Worksheets("Summary")

Workbooks(1).Worksheets(1)

Workbooks(1).Sheets(1)

Application.ActiveWorkbook.ActiveSheet

ActiveWorkbook.ActiveSheet

ActiveSheet
```

The method that you use is determined by how much you know about the workspace. For example, if more than one workbook is open, the second or third method isn't reliable. If you want to work with the active sheet (whatever it may be), any of the last three methods would work. To be absolutely sure you're referring to a specific sheet on a specific workbook, the first method is your best choice.

Methods

Objects also have methods. You can think of a method as an action taken with an object. Generally, methods are used to interact with the computer outside the Excel application or to modify multiple properties at once. For example, `Range` objects have a `Clear` method.

The following VBA statement clears a `Range`, an action that is equivalent to selecting the `Range` and then choosing Home ➪ Editing ➪ Clear ➪ Clear All:

```
Range("A1:C12").Clear
```

The `Clear` method involves changing several properties of the `Range` object at once. It includes setting the `Value` property to `Empty` (clearing its contents), the `Bold` property of the `Font` object to `False` (clearing all formats), and the `Comments` property to `Nothing` (deleting the cell's comment). It's doing a few other things as well.

If your code interacts with files on a disk, printers, or other aspects of your computer outside of Excel, you'll probably use a method. Each `Workbook` object has a `Name` property that's read-only. You can't change the `Name` property by setting it directly as follows:

```
Workbooks(1).Name = "xyz.xlsx"
```

That will fail. However, you can change a `Workbook`'s name by using the `SaveAs` method:

```
Workbooks(1).SaveAs "xyz.xlsx"
```

In addition to changing the name property, `SaveAs` changes a few other properties, and it also writes the file to the hard drive.

In VBA code, methods look like properties because they're connected to the object with a "dot." However, methods and properties are different concepts.

The Range object

The `Range` object is special. As you might imagine, it's central to the Excel object model. Workbooks and worksheets exist only to hold cells. But while the `Worksheets` collection holds a bunch of `Worksheet` objects and the `Shapes` collection holds a bunch of `Shape` objects, the `Range` object works differently.

A single cell is a `Range` object. A range of cells is also a `Range` object, but not a Ranges collection object. It's one of the few objects that breaks the plural naming convention of collections.

Most collection objects have a default property of `Item`. That allows you to write the following:

```
Workbooks(1)
```

instead of the following:

```
Workbooks.Item(1)
```

Generally, if an object has an `Item` property, that's the default. For objects that aren't collections, if they have a `Value` property, that's the default. For example, these two lines of VBA are identical because `Value` is the default property of `Checkbox` objects:

```
If Sheet1.CheckBox1.Value = True Then
If Sheet1.CheckBox1 = True Then
```

The Range object has both an Item property and a Value property. In some contexts, the Item property is the default, while in others, it's the Value property. The good news is that VBA does a pretty good job of picking the right one.

Variables

Like all programming languages, VBA enables you to work with variables. In VBA (unlike in some languages), you don't need to declare variables explicitly before you use them in your code (although doing so is definitely a good practice).

> **Note**
>
> If your VBA module contains an `Option Explicit` statement at the top of the module, you must declare all variables in the module. Undeclared variables will result in a compile error, and your procedures will not run.

In the following example, the value in cell A1 on Sheet1 is assigned to a variable named Rate:

```
Rate = Worksheets("Sheet1").Range("A1").Value
```

After the statement is executed, you can work with the variable Rate in other parts of your VBA code.

Controlling execution

VBA uses many constructs that are found in most other programming languages. These constructs are used to control the flow of execution. This section introduces a few of the more common programming constructs.

The If-Then construct

One of the most important control structures in VBA is the If-Then construct, which gives your applications decision-making capability. The basic syntax of the If-Then structure is as follows:

```
If condition Then statements [Else elsestatements]
```

In plain English, if a condition is true, then a group of statements will be executed. If you include the Else clause, then another group of statements will be executed if the condition is not true.

The following is an example (which doesn't use the optional Else clause). This procedure checks the active cell. If it contains a negative value, the cell's font color is changed to red. Otherwise, nothing happens:

```
Sub CheckCell()
    If ActiveCell.Value < 0 Then ActiveCell.Font.Color = vbRed
End Sub
```

Here's another multiline version of that procedure that uses an `Else` clause. Because it uses multiple lines, you must include an `End If` statement. This procedure colors the active cell text red if it's a negative value and green otherwise:

```
Sub CheckCell()
    If ActiveCell.Value < 0 Then
        ActiveCell.Font.Color = vbRed
    Else
        ActiveCell.Font.Color = vbGreen
    End If
End Sub
```

For-Next loops

You can use a `For-Next` loop to execute one or more statements a number of times. Here's an example of a `For-Next` loop:

```
Sub SumSquared()
  Total = 0
  For Num = 1 To 10
    Total = Total + (Num ^ 2)
  Next Num
  MsgBox Total
End Sub
```

This example has one statement between the `For` statement and the `Next` statement. This single statement is executed ten times. The variable `Num` takes on successive values of 1, 2, 3, and so on, up to 10. The variable `Total` stores the sum of `Num` squared added to the previous value of `Total`. The result is a value that represents the sum of the first ten integers squared. This result is displayed in a message box.

Do loops

`For-Next` loops execute a set of statements a particular number of times. Do loops execute a set of statements until a particular condition exists or stops existing.

```
Sub SumSquaredTo500()
    Total = 0
    num = 0
    Do
        num = num + 1
        Total = Total + (num ^ 2)
    Loop Until Total >= 500
    MsgBox num & Space(1) & Total
End Sub
```

This procedure keeps summing squares until the total gets above 500. With Do loops, you can check the condition on the `Do` line or the `Loop` line, but not both. The four options are as follows:

- `Do Until`
- `Do While`

- Loop Until
- Loop While

The With-End With construct

A construct that you sometimes encounter if you record macros is the With-End With construct. This is a shortcut way of dealing with several properties or methods of the same object. The following is an example:

```
Sub AlignCells()
  With Selection
    .HorizontalAlignment = xlCenter
    .VerticalAlignment = xlCenter
    .WrapText = False
    .Orientation = xlHorizontal
  End With
End Sub
```

The following macro performs the same operations but doesn't use the With-End With construct:

```
Sub AlignCells()
  Selection.HorizontalAlignment = xlCenter
  Selection.VerticalAlignment = xlCenter
  Selection.WrapText = False
  Selection.Orientation = xlHorizontal
End Sub
```

The Select Case construct

The Select Case construct is useful for choosing among two or more options. The following example demonstrates the use of a Select Case construct. In this example, the active cell is checked. If its value is less than 0, it's colored red. If it's equal to 0, it's colored blue. If the value is greater than 0, it's colored black:

```
Sub CheckCell()
  Select Case ActiveCell.Value
    Case Is < 0
      ActiveCell.Font.Color = vbRed
    Case 0
      ActiveCell.Font.Color = vbBlue
    Case Is > 0
      ActiveCell.Font.Color = vbBlack
  End Select

End Sub
```

Any number of statements can go below each Case statement, and they all are executed if the case is true.

A macro that can't be recorded

The following is a VBA macro that can't be recorded because it uses programming concepts that must be entered manually. This macro creates a list of all formulas on the active sheet. The list is stored on a new worksheet:

```
Sub ListFormulas()
' Create a range variable
    Set InputRange = ActiveSheet.UsedRange
' Add a new sheet and save in a variable
    Set OutputSheet = Worksheets.Add
' Variable for the output row
    OutputRow = 1
' Loop through the range
    For Each cell In InputRange
      If cell.HasFormula Then
        OutputSheet.Cells(OutputRow, 1) = "'" & cell.Address
        OutputSheet.Cells(OutputRow, 2) = "'" & cell.Formula
        OutputRow = OutputRow + 1
      End If
    Next Cell
End Sub
```

 A workbook that contains this example is available on this book's website at www.wiley.com/go/ excel2019bible. The file is named list formulas.xlsm.

Although this macro may look complicated, it's fairly simple when you break it down. Here's how it works:

1. The macro creates an object variable named InputRange. This variable corresponds to the used range on the active sheet (avoiding the need to check every cell).

2. It then adds a new worksheet and assigns the worksheet to an object variable named OutputSheet. The OutputRow variable is set to 1. This variable is incremented later.

3. The For-Next loop examines each cell in the InputRange. If the cell has a formula, the cell's address and formula are written to the OutputSheet. The OutputRow variable is also incremented.

Figure 42.13 shows the part of the result of running this macro—a handy list of all formulas in the worksheet.

As macros go, this example is okay, but it's certainly not perfect. It's not very flexible, and it doesn't include error handling. For example, if the workbook structure is protected, trying to add a new sheet will cause an error.

FIGURE 42.13

The ListFormulas macro creates a list of all formulas in a worksheet.

	A	B	C	D	E
1	$G$2	=B9/2			
2	$A$8	=SUM(A2:A7)			
3	$B$8	=SUM(B2:B7)			
4	$C$8	=SUM(C2:C7)			
5	$D$8	=SUM(D2:D7)			
6	$A$9	=AVERAGE(A2:A7)			
7	$B$9	=AVERAGE(B2:B7)			
8	$C$9	=AVERAGE(C2:C7)			
9	$D$9	=AVERAGE(D2:D7)			
10	$E$9	=AVERAGE(E2:E7)			
11	$A$15	=RANDBETWEEN(1,1000)			
12	$B$15	=RANDBETWEEN(1,1000)			
13	$C$15	=RANDBETWEEN(1,1000)			
14	$D$15	=RANDBETWEEN(1,1000)			
15	$E$15	=RANDBETWEEN(1,1000)			
16	$A$16	=RANDBETWEEN(1,1000)			
17	$B$16	=RANDBETWEEN(1,1000)			
18	$C$16	=RANDBETWEEN(1,1000)			
19	$D$16	=RANDBETWEEN(1,1000)			
20	$E$16	=RANDBETWEEN(1,1000)			
21	$A$17	=RANDBETWEEN(1,1000)			
22	$B$17	=RANDBETWEEN(1,1000)			
23	$C$17	=RANDBETWEEN(1,1000)			
24	$D$17	=RANDBETWEEN(1,1000)			

42

Learning More

This chapter is a basic introduction to VBA. If this is your first exposure to VBA, you might be a bit overwhelmed by objects, properties, and methods. It's frustrating when you know what you want to do but don't know which objects, properties, or methods you need to do it. Fortunately, several good ways are available to learn about objects, properties, and methods.

Read the rest of the book   Subsequent chapters in this section contain additional information and many more examples.

Record your actions   The best way to become familiar with VBA is to turn on the macro recorder and record the actions you make in Excel. You can then examine the code to gain some insights regarding the objects, properties, and methods.

Use the Help system   The main source of detailed information about Excel's objects, methods, and procedures is the VBA Help system. Help is thorough and easy to access. When you're in a VBA module, just move the cursor to a property or method and press F1. You get help that describes the word that is under the cursor. All VBA Help is online, so you must be connected to the Internet to use the Help system.

Get another book   Several books are devoted exclusively to using VBA with Excel. Our book *Excel 2019 Power Programming with VBA* (Wiley, 2018) is one of them.

Creating Custom Worksheet Functions

IN THIS CHAPTER

Getting an overview of VBA functions

Looking at function procedures

Focusing on function procedure arguments

Debugging custom functions

Pasting custom functions

A s mentioned in the preceding chapter, you can create two types of VBA procedures: Sub procedures and Function procedures. This chapter focuses on Function procedures.

Introducing VBA Functions

Function procedures that you write in VBA are quite versatile. You can use these functions in two situations:

- You can call the function from a different VBA procedure.
- You can use the function in formulas that you create in a worksheet.

This chapter focuses on creating functions for use in your formulas.

Excel includes more than 450 predefined worksheet functions. With so many from which to choose, you may be curious as to why anyone would need to develop additional functions. The main reason is that creating a custom function can greatly simplify your formulas by making them shorter, and shorter formulas are more readable and easier to work with. For example, you can often replace a complex formula with a single function. Another reason is that you can write functions to perform operations that would otherwise be impossible.

> **NOTE**
> This chapter assumes that you're familiar with entering and editing VBA code in the Visual Basic Editor (VBE).

See Chapter 42, "Introducing Visual Basic for Applications," for an overview of the VBE.

Seeing a Simple Example

Creating custom functions is relatively easy after you understand VBA. Without further ado, here's an example of a VBA function procedure. This function is stored in a VBA module, which is accessible from the VBE.

Creating a custom function

This example function, named NumSign, uses one argument. The function returns a text string of Positive if its argument is greater than zero, Negative if the argument is less than zero, and Zero if the argument is equal to zero. If the argument is nonnumeric, the function returns an empty string. Figure 43.1 shows the NumSign function.

FIGURE 43.1

A simple custom worksheet function

```
Function NumSign(num)
    If IsNumeric(num) Then
        Select Case num
            Case Is < 0
                NumSign = "Negative"
            Case 0
                NumSign = "Zero"
            Case Is > 0
                NumSign = "Positive"
        End Select
    Else
        NumSign = ""
    End If
End Function
```

You can, of course, accomplish the same effect with the following worksheet formula, which uses nested IF functions:

```
=IF(ISNUMBER(A1),IF(A1=0,"Zero",IF(A1>0,"Positive","Negative")),"")
```

Many would agree that the custom function solution is easier to understand and to edit than the worksheet formula.

Using the function in a worksheet

When you enter a formula that uses the NumSign function, Excel executes the function to get the result. This custom function works just like any built-in worksheet function. You can insert it in a formula by choosing Formulas ➪ Function Library ➪ Insert Function, which displays the Insert Function dialog box. (Custom functions are listed in the User Defined category.) When you select the function from the list, you can then use the Function Arguments dialog box to specify the arguments for the function, as shown in Figure 43.2. You can also nest custom functions and combine them with other elements in your formulas.

FIGURE 43.2

Creating a worksheet formula that uses a custom function

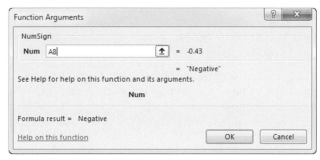

Analyzing the custom function

This section describes the NumSign function. Here again is the code:

```
Function NumSign(num)
    If IsNumeric(num) Then
        Select Case num
            Case Is < 0
                NumSign = "Negative"
            Case 0
                NumSign = "Zero"
            Case Is > 0
                NumSign = "Positive"
        End Select
    Else
        NumSign = ""
    End If
End Function
```

Notice that the procedure starts with the keyword `Function`, followed by the name of the function (`NumSign`). This custom function uses one argument (`num`), and the argument's name is enclosed in parentheses. The `num` argument represents the cell or value that is to be processed. When the function is used in a worksheet, the argument can be a cell reference (such as `A1`) or a literal value (such as `-123`). When the function is used in another procedure, the argument can be a numeric variable, a literal number, or a value that is obtained from a cell.

The first statement inside the function is an `If` statement. It starts what is known as an `If` block. An `If` block consists of an `If` statement, an `End If` statement, one or more optional `Else If` statements, and one optional `Else` statement. The previous code is indented in a way that makes it obvious that the `Else` and `End If` statements near the bottom of the function belong to the `If` statement near the top of the procedure. Indenting is optional, but you'll find your code is much easier to read if you do it.

The `If` statement contains the built-in function `IsNumeric` that returns a `True` if the argument is a number and `False` if it's not. Whenever a built-in function begins with `Is` or `Has`, it returns `True` or `False` (a Boolean value).

The `NumSign` function uses the `Select Case` construct (described in Chapter 42) to take a different action, depending on the value of `num`. If `num` is less than zero, `NumSign` is assigned the text `Negative`. If `num` is equal to zero, `NumSign` is `Zero`. If `num` is greater than zero, `NumSign` is `Positive`. The value returned by a function is always assigned to the function's name.

There is often more than one way to accomplish the same goal in VBA. Instead of using a `Select Case` construct, you could use an `If` block. The following code returns the same result as the original function but uses another `If` block with an `Else If` statement. Note how the indented code makes it easy to see which statements belong to which `If` blocks:

```
Function NumSignIfBlock(num)
    If IsNumeric(num) Then
        If num = 0 Then
            NumSign = "Zero"
        ElseIf num > 0 Then
            NumSign = "Positive"
        Else
            NumSign = "Negative"
        End If
    Else
        NumSign = ""
    End If
End Function
```

Learning about Function Procedures

A custom function has much in common with a `Sub` procedure. Function procedures have some important differences, however. Perhaps the key difference is that a function returns a value (such as a number, a date, or a text string). When writing a function, the value that's returned is the value that has been assigned to the function's name when a function is finished executing.

To create a custom function, follow these steps:

1. **Activate the VB Editor.** (Press Alt+F11.)

2. **Select the workbook in the Project Explorer (choose View ⇨ Project Explorer if it's not already visible).**

3. **Choose Insert ⇨ Module to insert a VBA module, or you can use an existing code module.** However, it must be a standard VBA module.

4. **Enter the keyword `Function` followed by the function's name and a list of the arguments (if any) in parentheses.** If the function doesn't use an argument, the VBE adds a set of empty parentheses.

5. **Type the VBA code that performs the work—and make sure that the variable corresponding to the function's name has the appropriate value when the function ends.** This is the value that the function returns.

6. **End the function with an `End Function` statement.** The VBE adds this statement automatically when you type the function statement.

> **NOTE**
>
> Step 3 is important. If you put a function procedure in a code module for `ThisWorkbook` or a worksheet (for example, `Sheet1`), the function will not be recognized in a worksheet formula. Excel will display a `#NAME?` error. Putting a function procedure in the wrong type of code module is a common mistake.

Function names that are used in worksheet formulas must adhere to the same rules as variable names.

What a Function Can't Do

Almost everyone who starts creating custom worksheet functions using VBA makes a fatal mistake: they try to get the function to do more than is possible.

A worksheet function returns a value, and the function must be completely "passive." In other words, the function can't change anything on the worksheet. For example, you can't develop a worksheet function that changes the formatting of a cell. (Every VBA programmer has tried, and not one of them has been successful!) If your function attempts to perform an action that isn't allowed, the function simply returns an error.

Nevertheless, the preceding paragraph isn't absolutely true. There are a few cases in which a VBA function used in a formula can have an effect. For example, it's possible to create a custom worksheet function that adds or deletes cell comments. For the most part, however, functions used in formulas must be passive.

VBA functions that aren't used in worksheet formulas can do anything that a regular `Sub` procedure can do, including changing cell formatting.

43

Executing Function Procedures

You can execute a Sub procedure in many ways, but you can execute a function procedure in just two ways:

- Call it from another VBA procedure.
- Use it in a worksheet formula.

Calling custom functions from a procedure

You can call custom functions from a VBA procedure just as you call built-in VBA functions. For example, after you define a function called CalcTax, you can enter a statement such as the following:

```
Tax = CalcTax(Amount, Rate)
```

This statement executes the CalcTax custom function with Amount and Rate as its arguments. The function's result is assigned to the Tax variable.

Using custom functions in a worksheet formula

You use a custom function in a worksheet formula just as you use built-in functions. However, you must ensure that Excel can locate the function. If the function procedure is in the same workbook, you don't have to do anything special. If the function is defined in a different workbook, you may have to tell Excel where to find the function. The following are the three ways in which you can do this:

Precede the function's name with a file reference For example, if you want to use a function called CountNames that's defined in a workbook named MyFunctions, you can use a reference such as the following:

```
=MyFunctions.xlsm!CountNames(A1:A1000)
```

If the workbook name contains a space, you need to add single quotes around the workbook name. Here's an example:

```
='My Functions.xlsm'!CountNames(A1:A1000)
```

If you insert the function with the Insert Function dialog box, the workbook reference is inserted automatically.

Set up a reference to the workbook If the custom function is defined in a referenced workbook, you don't need to precede the function name with the workbook name. You establish a reference to another workbook by choosing Tools ➪ References (in the VB Editor). You're presented with a list of references that includes all open workbooks. Place a check mark in the item that refers to the workbook containing the custom function. (Click the Browse button if the workbook isn't open.)

Create an add-in When you create an add-in from a workbook that has function procedures, you don't need to use the file reference when you use one of the functions in a formula; the add-in must be installed, however.

Chapter 48, "Creating Custom Excel Add-Ins," discusses add-ins.

> **NOTE**
>
> Function procedures don't appear in the Macro dialog box because you can't execute a function directly. As a result, you need to do extra, up-front work to test your functions while you're developing them. One approach is to set up a simple Sub procedure that calls the function. If the function is designed to be used in worksheet formulas, you can enter a simple formula that uses the function to test it while you're developing the function.

Using Function Procedure Arguments

Keep in mind the following about function procedure arguments:

- Arguments can be variables (including arrays), constants, literals, or expressions.
- Some functions do not have arguments.
- Some functions have a fixed number of required arguments (from 1 to 60).
- Some functions have a combination of required and optional arguments.

The following sections present a series of examples that demonstrate how to use arguments effectively with functions. Coverage of optional arguments is beyond the scope of this book.

The examples in this chapter are available on this book's website at www.wiley.com/go/excel2019bible. The file is named vba functions.xlsm.

Creating a function with no arguments

Most functions use arguments, but that's not a requirement. Excel, for example, has a few built-in worksheet functions that don't use arguments, such as RAND, TODAY, and NOW.

The following is a simple example of a function that has no arguments. This function returns the UserName property of the Application object, which is the name that appears in the Personalize section of the Excel Options dialog box. This function is simple, but it can be useful because there's no built-in function that returns the user's name:

```
Function User()
' Returns the name of the current user
  User = Application.UserName
End Function
```

When you enter the following formula into a worksheet cell, the cell displays the name of the current user:

```
=User()
```

As with Excel's built-in functions, when you use a function with no arguments, you must include a set of empty parentheses.

Creating a function with one argument

The function that follows takes a single argument and uses the Excel text-to-speech generator to "speak" the argument:

```
Function SayIt(txt)
    Application.Speech.Speak (txt)
End Function
```

> **NOTE**
>
> To hear the synthesized voice, your system must be set up to play sound.

For example, if you enter this formula, Excel will "speak" the contents of cell A1 whenever the worksheet is recalculated:

```
=SayIt(A1)
```

You can use this function in a slightly more complex formula, as shown here. In this example, the argument is a text string rather than a cell reference:

```
=IF(SUM(A:A)>1000,SayIt("Goal reached"),)
```

This formula calculates the sum of the values in Column A. If that sum exceeds 1,000, you will hear "Goal reached."

When you use the `SayIt` function in a worksheet formula, the function always returns 0 because a value is not assigned to the function's name.

Creating another function with one argument

This section contains a more complex function that is designed for a sales manager who needs to calculate the commissions earned by the sales force. The commission rate is based on the amount sold—those who sell more earn a higher commission rate. The function returns the commission amount, based on the sales made (which is the function's only argument—a required argument). The calculations in this example are based on the following table:

Monthly Sales	Commission Rate
0–$9,999	8.0%
$10,000–$19,999	10.5%
$20,000–$39,999	12.0%
$40,000+	14.0%

You can use any of several different methods to calculate commissions for various sales amounts that are entered into a worksheet. You could write a formula such as the following:

```
=IF(AND(A1>=0,A1<=9999.99),A1*0.08,IF(AND(A1>=10000,
A1<=19999.99), A1*0.105,IF(AND(A1>=20000,
A1<=39999.99),A1*0.12,IF(A1>=40000,A1*0.14,0))))
```

This approach isn't the best for a couple of reasons. First, the formula is overly complex and difficult to understand. Second, the values are hard-coded into the formula, making the formula difficult to modify if the commission structure changes.

A better solution is to use a lookup table function to compute the commissions; here's an example:

```
=VLOOKUP(A1,Table,2)*A1
```

Using the VLOOKUP function requires that you have a table of commission rates set up in your worksheet.

Another option is to create a custom function, such as the following:

```
Function Commission(Sales)
' Calculates sales commissions
  Tier1 = 0.08
  Tier2 = 0.105
  Tier3 = 0.12
  Tier4 = 0.14
  Select Case Sales
    Case 0 To 9999.99
      Commission = Sales * Tier1
    Case 10000 To 19999.99
      Commission = Sales * Tier2
    Case 20000 To 39999.99
      Commission = Sales * Tier3
    Case Is >= 40000
      Commission = Sales * Tier4
  End Select
End Function
```

After you define the Commission function in a VBA module, you can use it in a worksheet formula. Entering the following formula into a cell produces a result of 3,000. (The amount, 25,000, qualifies for a commission rate of 12%.)

```
=Commission(25000)
```

If the sales amount is in cell D23, the function's argument would be a cell reference, like this:

```
=Commission(D23)
```

Creating a function with two arguments

This example builds on the previous one. Imagine that the sales manager implements a new policy: the total commission paid is increased by 1 percent for every year that the salesperson has been with the company. For this example, the custom Commission function (defined in the preceding section) has been modified so that it takes two arguments, both of which are required arguments. Call this new function Commission2:

```
Function Commission2(Sales, Years)
'  Calculates sales commissions based on years in service
    Tier1 = 0.08
    Tier2 = 0.105
    Tier3 = 0.12
    Tier4 = 0.14
    Select Case Sales
        Case 0 To 9999.99
          Commission2 = Sales * Tier1
        Case 10000 To 19999.99
          Commission2 = Sales * Tier2
        Case 20000 To 39999.99
          Commission2 = Sales * Tier3
        Case Is >= 40000
          Commission2 = Sales * Tier4
    End Select
    Commission2 = Commission2 + (Commission2 * Years / 100)
End Function
```

The modification was quite simple. The second argument (Years) was added to the Function statement, and an additional computation was included that adjusts the commission before exiting the function.

The following is an example of how you write a formula using this function. It assumes that the sales amount is in cell A1 and that the number of years that the salesperson has worked is in cell B1:

```
=Commission2(A1,B1)
```

Creating a function with a range argument

The example in this section demonstrates how to use a worksheet range as an argument. Actually, it's not at all tricky; Excel takes care of the details behind the scenes.

Assume that you want to calculate the average of the five largest values in a range named Data. Excel doesn't have a function that can do this calculation, so you can write the following formula:

```
=(LARGE(Data,1)+LARGE(Data,2)+LARGE(Data,3)+
LARGE(Data,4)+LARGE(Data,5))/5
```

This formula uses Excel's LARGE function, which returns the nth largest value in a range. The preceding formula adds the five largest values in the range named Data and then divides the result by 5. The formula works fine, but it's rather unwieldy. Plus, what if you need to compute the average of the top six values? You'd need to rewrite the formula and make sure that all copies of the formula also get updated.

Wouldn't it be easier if Excel had a function named TopAvg? For example, you could use the following (nonexistent) function to compute the average:

```
=TopAvg (Data,5)
```

This situation is an example of when a custom function can make things much easier for you. The following is a custom VBA function, named TopAvg, which returns the average of the top n values in a range:

```
Function TopAvg(Data, Num)
' Returns the average of the highest Num values in Data
  Sum = 0
  For i = 1 To Num
    Sum = Sum + WorksheetFunction.Large(Data, i)
  Next i
  TopAvg = Sum / Num
End Function
```

This function takes two arguments: Data (which represents a range in a worksheet) and Num (the number of values to average). The code starts by initializing the Sum variable to 0. It then uses a For-Next loop to calculate the sum of the nth largest values in the range. (Note that Excel's LARGE function is used within the loop.) You can use an Excel worksheet function in VBA if you precede the function with WorksheetFunction and a period. Finally, TopAvg is assigned the value of Sum divided by Num.

You can use all Excel worksheet functions in your VBA procedures except those that have equivalents in VBA. For example, VBA has a Rnd function that returns a random number. Therefore, you can't use Excel's RAND function in a VBA procedure.

Creating a simple but useful function

Useful functions don't have to be complicated. The function in this section is essentially a wrapper for a built-in VBA function called Split. The Split function makes it easy to extract an element in a delimited string. The function is named ExtractElement:

```
Function ExtractElement(Txt, n, Separator)
' Returns the nth element of a text string, where the
' elements are separated by a specified separator character
  ExtractElement = Split(Application.Trim(Txt), Separator)(n - 1)
End Function
```

The function takes three arguments:

Txt: A delimited text string, or a reference to a cell that contains a delimited text string

n: The element number within the string

Separator: A single character that represents the separator

Here's a formula that uses the `ExtractElement` function:

```
=EXTRACTELEMENT("123-45-678",2,"-")
```

The formula returns `45`, the second element in the string that's delimited by hyphens.

The delimiter can also be a space character. Here's a formula that extracts the first name from the name in cell A1:

```
=EXTRACTELEMENT(A1,1," ")
```

Debugging Custom Functions

Debugging a function can be a bit more challenging than debugging a `Sub` procedure. If you develop a function to use in worksheet formulas, an error in the function simply results in an error display in the formula cell (usually `#VALUE!`). In other words, you don't receive the normal runtime error message that helps you locate the offending statement.

When you're debugging a worksheet formula, using only one instance of the function in your worksheet is the best technique. The following are three methods you may want to use in your debugging:

- Place `MsgBox` functions at strategic locations to monitor the value of specific variables. Fortunately, message boxes in function procedures pop up when the procedure is executed. But make sure you have only one formula in the worksheet that uses your function; otherwise, the message boxes appear for each formula that's evaluated.
- Test the procedure by calling it from a `Sub` procedure. Runtime errors display normally, and you can either fix the problem (if you know what it is) or jump right into the debugger.
- Set a breakpoint in the function, and then use the Excel debugger to step through the function. Press F9, and the statement at the cursor becomes a breakpoint. The code will stop executing, and you can step through the code line by line (by pressing F8). Consult the Help system for more information about using VBA debugging tools.

Inserting Custom Functions

The Excel Insert Function dialog box makes it easy to identify a function and insert it into a formula. This dialog box also displays custom functions written in VBA. After you select a function, the Function Arguments dialog box prompts you for the function's arguments.

You also can display a description of your custom function in the Insert Function dialog box. To do so, follow these steps:

1. **Create the function in a module by using the VBE.**
2. **Activate Excel.**
3. **Choose Developer ⇨ Code ⇨ Macros.** The Macro dialog box appears.
4. **Type the name of the function in the Macro Name field.** Notice that functions don't appear in this dialog box, so you must enter the function name yourself.
5. **Click the Options button.** The Macro Options dialog box appears, as shown in Figure 43.3.
6. **Enter a description of the function and then click OK.** The Shortcut key field is irrelevant for functions.

FIGURE 43.3

Entering a description for a custom function. This description appears in the Insert Function dialog box.

The description that you enter appears in the Insert Function dialog box.

Another way to provide a description for a custom function is to execute a VBA statement that uses the `MacroOptions` method. The `MacroOptions` method also lets you assign your function to a specific category and even provide a description of the arguments. The argument descriptions display in the Function Arguments dialog box, which appears after you select the function in the Insert Function dialog box. Excel 2010 added the ability to provide descriptions of function arguments.

Figure 43.4 shows the Function Arguments dialog box, which prompts the user to enter arguments for a custom function (TopAvg). This function appears in function category 3 (Math and Trig). We've added the description, category, and argument descriptions by executing this Sub procedure:

```
Sub CreateArgDescriptions()
  Application.MacroOptions Macro:="TopAvg", _
    Description:="Calculates the average of the top n values in a
range", _
    Category:=3, _
    ArgumentDescriptions:=Array("The range that contains the data",
"The value of n")
End Sub
```

The category numbers are listed in the VBA Help system. You execute this procedure only one time. After you execute it, the description, category, and argument descriptions are stored in the file.

FIGURE 43.4

Using the Function Arguments dialog box to insert a custom function

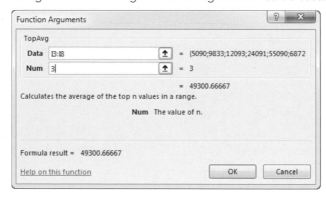

Learning More

The information in this chapter only scratches the surface when it comes to creating custom functions. It should be enough to get you started, however, if you're indeed interested in this topic.

 See Chapter 47, "Seeing Some VBA Examples," for more examples of useful VBA functions. You may be able to use the examples directly or adapt them for your needs.

Creating UserForms

Y ou can't use Excel very long without being exposed to dialog boxes. Excel, like most Windows programs, uses dialog boxes to obtain information, clarify commands, and display messages. If you develop VBA macros, you can create your own dialog boxes that work very much like those that are built in to Excel. These dialog boxes are known as *UserForms*.

Understanding Why to Create UserForms

Some macros that you create behave the same every time that you execute them. For example, you may develop a macro that enters a list of your sales regions into a worksheet range. This macro always produces the same result and requires no additional user input. You may develop other macros, however, that perform differently under different circumstances or that offer options for the user. In such cases, the macro may benefit from a custom dialog box.

The following is an example of a simple macro that makes each cell in the selected range uppercase (but skips cells that have a formula). The procedure uses VBA's built-in StrConv function:

```
Sub ChangeCase()
  For Each cell In Selection
    If Not cell.HasFormula Then
      cell.Value = StrConv(cell.Value, vbUpperCase)
    End If
  Next Cell
End Sub
```

This macro is useful, but it can be improved. For example, the macro would be more helpful if it could also change the cells to lowercase or proper case (only the first letter of each word is uppercase). This modification is not difficult to make, but if you make this change to the macro, you need some method of asking the user what type of change to make to the cells. The solution is to present a dialog box like the one shown in Figure 44.1. This dialog box is a UserForm that was created by using the Visual Basic Editor (VBE), and it's displayed by a VBA macro.

FIGURE 44.1

A UserForm that asks the user to select an option

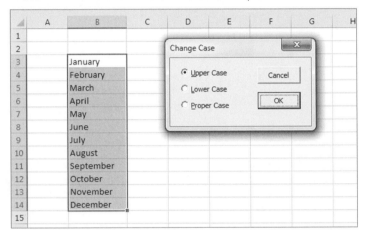

Another solution is to develop three macros—one for each type of text case change. Combining these three operations into a single macro and using a UserForm is a more efficient approach, however. We discuss this example, including how to create the UserForm, in "Seeing Another UserForm Example," later in the chapter.

Exploring UserForm Alternatives

After you get the hang of it, developing UserForms isn't difficult. But sometimes using the tools that are built into VBA is easier. For example, VBA includes two functions (InputBox and MsgBox) that enable you to display simple dialog boxes without having to create a UserForm in the VBE. You can customize these dialog boxes in some ways, but they certainly don't offer the number of options that are available in a UserForm.

Using the InputBox function

The InputBox function is useful for obtaining a single input from the user. A simplified version of the function's syntax follows:

```
InputBox(prompt[,title][,default])
```

The elements are defined as follows:

prompt (Required): Text that is displayed in the input box

title (Optional) : Text that appears in the input box's title bar

default (Optional): The default value

The following is an example of how you can use the InputBox function:

```
CName = InputBox("Customer name?","Customer Data")
```

When this VBA statement is executed, Excel displays the dialog box shown in Figure 44.2. Notice that this example uses only the first two arguments for the InputBox function and does not supply a default value. When the user enters a value and clicks OK, the value is assigned to the variable CName. Your VBA code can then use that variable.

FIGURE 44.2

This dialog box is displayed by the VBA InputBox function.

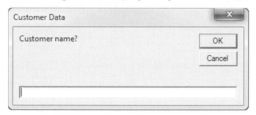

Using the MsgBox function

The VBA MsgBox function is a handy way to display information and to solicit simple input from users. We use the VBA MsgBox function in many of this book's examples to display a variable's value. A simplified version of the MsgBox syntax is as follows:

```
MsgBox(prompt[,buttons][,title])
```

The elements are defined as follows:

prompt (Required): Text that is displayed in the message box

buttons (Optional): The code for the buttons that are to appear in the message box

title (Optional): Text that appears in the message box's title bar

You can use the MsgBox function by itself or assign its result to a variable. If you use it by itself, don't include parentheses around the arguments. The following example displays a message and does not return a result:

```
Sub MsgBoxDemo()
    MsgBox "Click OK to continue"
End Sub
```

Figure 44.3 shows how this message box appears.

FIGURE 44.3

A simple message box, displayed with the VBA `MsgBox` function

To get a response from a message box, you can assign the result of the `MsgBox` function to a variable. The following code uses some built-in constants (described in Table 44.1) to make it easier to work with the values that are returned by `MsgBox`:

```
Sub GetAnswer()
  Ans = MsgBox("Continue?", vbYesNo)
  Select Case Ans
   Case vbYes
' ...[code if Ans is Yes]...
   Case vbNo
' ...[code if Ans is No]...
  End Select
End Sub
```

When this procedure is executed, the `Ans` variable contains a value that corresponds to `vbYes` or `vbNo`. The `Select Case` statement determines the action to take based on the value of `Ans`.

You can easily customize your message boxes because of the flexibility of the `buttons` argument. Table 44.1 lists the most common built-in constants that you can use for the `buttons` argument. You can specify which buttons to display, whether an icon appears, and which button is the default.

TABLE 44.1   Constants Used in the MsgBox Function

Constant	Value	Description
vbOKOnly	0	Displays OK button
vbOKCancel	1	Displays OK and Cancel buttons
vbAbortRetryIgnore	2	Displays Abort, Retry, and Ignore buttons
vbYesNoCancel	3	Displays Yes, No, and Cancel buttons
vbYesNo	4	Displays Yes and No buttons
vbRetryCancel	5	Displays Retry and Cancel buttons
vbCritical	16	Displays Critical Message icon

Constant	Value	Description
vbQuestion	32	Displays Query icon (a question mark)
VBExclamation	48	Displays Warning Message icon
vbInformation	64	Displays Information Message icon
vbDefaultButton1	0	First button is default
vbDefaultButton2	256	Second button is default
vbDefaultButton3	512	Third button is default

The following example uses a combination of constants to display a message box with a Yes button and a No button (vbYesNo) and a question mark icon (vbQuestion). The second button (the No button) is designated as the default button (vbDefaultButton2), which is the one that is executed if the user presses Enter. For simplicity, these constants are assigned to the Config variable, and Config is then used as the second argument in the MsgBox function.

```
Sub GetAnswer()
    Config = vbYesNo + vbQuestion + vbDefaultButton2
    Ans = MsgBox("Process the monthly report?", Config)
    If Ans = vbYes Then RunReport
    If Ans = vbNo Then Exit Sub
End Sub
```

Figure 44.4 shows how this message box appears when the GetAnswer procedure is executed. If the user clicks the Yes button, the routine executes the procedure named RunReport (which is not shown). If the user clicks the No button (or presses Enter), the procedure is ended with no action. Because the title argument was omitted in the MsgBox function, Excel uses the default title (Microsoft Excel).

FIGURE 44.4

The second argument of the MsgBox function determines what appears in the message box.

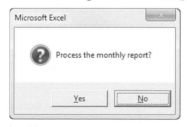

The procedure that follows is another example of using the MsgBox function:

```
Sub GetAnswer2()
    Msg = "Do you want to process the monthly report?"
```

```
      Msg = Msg & vbNewLine & vbNewLine
      Msg = Msg & "Processing the monthly report will take approximately
"
      Msg = Msg & "15 minutes. It will generate a 30-page report for all
"
      Msg = Msg & "sales offices for the current month."
      Title = "XYZ Marketing Company"
      Config = vbYesNo + vbQuestion
      Ans = MsgBox(Msg, Config, Title)
      If Ans = vbYes Then RunReport
      If Ans = vbNo Then Exit Sub
   End Sub
```

This example demonstrates an efficient way to specify a longer message in a message box. A variable (Msg) and the concatenation operator (&) are used to build the message in a series of statements. vbNewLine is a constant that represents a line break character. (Using two line breaks inserts a blank line.) The title argument is also used to display a different title in the message box. The Config variable stores the constants that generate Yes and No buttons and a question mark icon. Figure 44.5 shows how this message box appears when the procedure is executed.

FIGURE 44.5

A message box with a longer message and a title

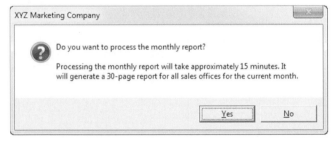

Creating UserForms: An Overview

The InputBox and MsgBox functions are adequate for many situations, but if you need to obtain more information, you need to create a UserForm.

The following is a list of the general steps that you typically take to create a UserForm:

1. **Determine exactly how the dialog box is going to be used and where it will fit into your VBA macro.**

2. **Activate the VBE and insert a new UserForm.**

3. **Add the appropriate controls to the UserForm.**

4. **Create a VBA macro to display the UserForm.** This macro goes in a normal VBA module.

5. **Create event handler VBA procedures that are executed when the user manipulates the controls (for example, when the user clicks the OK button).** These procedures go in the code module for the UserForm.

The following sections offer more details on creating a UserForm.

Working with UserForms

To create a dialog box, you must first insert a new UserForm in the VBE. To activate the VBE, choose Developer ⇨ Code ⇨ Visual Basic (or press Alt+F11). Make sure that the correct workbook is selected in the Project window and then choose Insert ⇨ UserForm. The VBE displays an empty UserForm, as shown in Figure 44.6. When you activate a UserForm, the VBE displays the Toolbox, which is used to add controls to the UserForm.

FIGURE 44.6

An empty UserForm

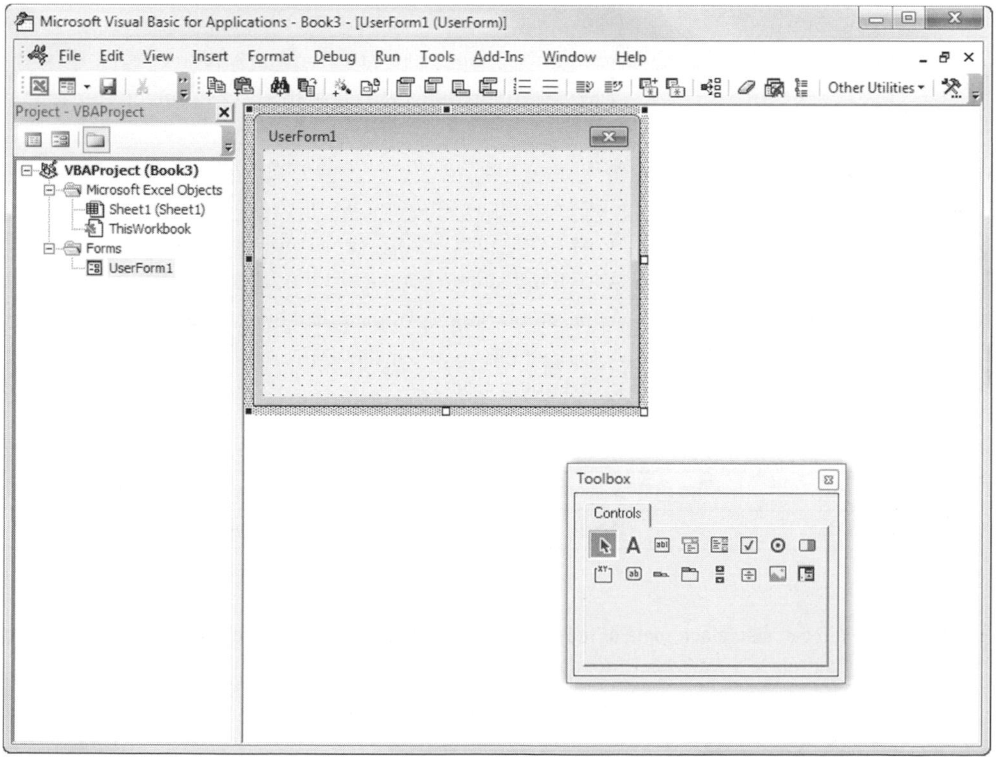

Adding controls

The Toolbox, also shown in Figure 44.6, contains various ActiveX controls that you can add to your UserForm. If the Toolbox is not visible, choose View ➪ Toolbox.

When you move the mouse pointer over a control in the Toolbox, the control's name appears. To add a control, select the control in Toolbox and either click in the form to get the default size or drag the desired size onto the form. After adding a control, you can move it or change its size.

Table 44.2 lists the Toolbox controls.

TABLE 44.2   Toolbox Controls

Control	Description
Select Objects	Lets you select other controls by dragging
Label	Adds a label (a container for text)
TextBox	Adds a text box, which allows the user to type text
ComboBox	Adds a combo box (a drop-down list)
ListBox	Adds a list box, which allows the user to select an item from a list
CheckBox	Adds a check box to control Boolean options
OptionButton	Adds an option button to allow the user to select from multiple options
ToggleButton	Adds a toggle button to control Boolean options
Frame	Adds a frame (a container for other objects)
CommandButton	Adds a command button (a clickable button)
TabStrip	Adds a tab strip (a container for other objects)
MultiPage	Adds a multipage control (a container for other objects)
ScrollBar	Adds a scrollbar, which allows the user to specify a value by dragging a bar
SpinButton	Adds a spin button, which allows the user to specify a value by clicking up or down
Image	Adds a control that can contain an image
RefEdit	Adds a reference edit control, which lets the user select a range

 You can also place some of these controls directly on your worksheet. See Chapter 45, "Using UserForm Controls in a Worksheet," for details.

Changing the properties of a control

Every control that you add to a UserForm has several properties that determine the way the control looks and behaves. You can change some of these properties (such as Height and Width) by clicking and dragging the control's border. To change other properties, use the Properties window.

To display the Properties window, choose View ⇨ Properties Window (or press F4). The Properties window displays a list of properties for the selected control. (Each control has a different set of properties.) If you click the UserForm itself, the Properties window displays properties for the form. Figure 44.7 shows the Properties window for a CommandButton control.

FIGURE 44.7

The Properties window for a CommandButton control

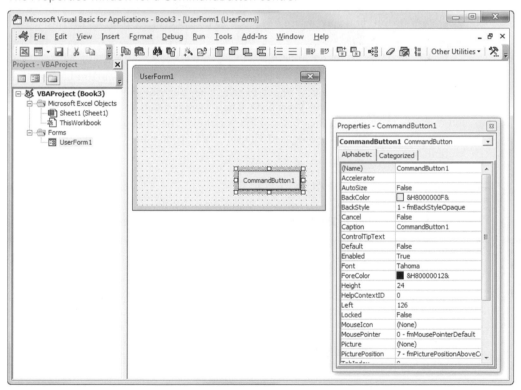

To change a property, select the property in the Properties window and then enter a new value. Some properties (such as BackColor) let you select a property from a list. The top

969

of the Properties window contains a drop-down list of all the controls on the form. You can also click a control to select it and display its properties.

When you set properties via the Properties window, you're setting properties at design time. You can also use VBA to change the properties of controls while the UserForm is displayed (that is, at run time).

A complete discussion of all of the properties is well beyond the scope of this book—and it would indeed be dull reading. To find out about a particular property, select it in the Properties window and press F1 for help.

Handling events

When you insert a UserForm, that form can also hold VBA Sub procedures to handle the events that are generated by the UserForm. An event is something that occurs when the user manipulates a control. For example, clicking a button causes a click event. Selecting an item in a list box control also triggers a click event, as well as a change event. To make a UserForm useful, you must write VBA code to do something when an event occurs.

Event handler procedures have names that combine the control with the event. The general form is the control's name, followed by an underscore and then the event name. For example, the procedure that is executed when the user clicks a button named MyButton is MyButton_Click. You don't have to remember how they're named, however. Just right-click the control and choose View Code. The Private Sub and End Sub keywords will be inserted for you, and the correct name of one of the control's events will already be constructed. Use the drop-downs at the top of the code pane to change the event from the default.

Displaying a UserForm

You also need to write a procedure to display the UserForm. You use the Show method of the UserForm object. The following procedure displays the UserForm named UserForm1:

```
Sub ShowDialog()
    UserForm1.Show
End Sub
```

This procedure should be stored in a regular VBA module (not the code module for the UserForm). If your VB project doesn't have a regular VBA module, choose Insert ⇨ Module to add one.

When the ShowDialog procedure is executed, the UserForm is displayed. What happens next depends on the event handler procedures that you create.

Looking at a UserForm Example

The preceding section is, admittedly, rudimentary. This section demonstrates, in detail, how to develop a UserForm. This example is rather simple. The UserForm displays a message to the user—something that can be accomplished more easily by using the MsgBox function. However, a UserForm gives you more flexibility in terms of formatting and layout of the message.

 This workbook is available on this book's website at www.wiley.com/go/excel2019bible. The file is named show message.xlsm..

Creating the UserForm

If you're following along on your computer, start with a new workbook. Then follow these steps:

1. **Choose Developer ⇨ Code ⇨ Visual Basic (or press Alt+F11).** The VBE appears.

2. **Click your workbook's name in the Project Explorer to activate it.**

3. **Choose Insert ⇨ UserForm.** The VBE adds an empty form named UserForm1 and displays the Toolbox.

4. **Press F4 to display the Properties window, and then change the following properties of the UserForm object:**

Property	Change to
Name	AboutBox
Caption	About This Workbook

5. **Use the Toolbox to add a Label object to the UserForm. If the Toolbox is not visible, choose View ⇨ Toolbox.**

6. **Select the Label object, and in the Properties window change the Name property to lblMessage and enter any text you want in the Caption property.**

7. **In the Properties window, click the Font property and adjust the font.** You can change the typeface, size, and so on. The changes then appear in the form. Figure 44.8 shows an example of a formatted Label control. In this example, the TextAlign property was set to the code that center aligns the text.

   2 - fmTextAlignCenter

44

FIGURE 44.8

A Label control, after changing its Font properties

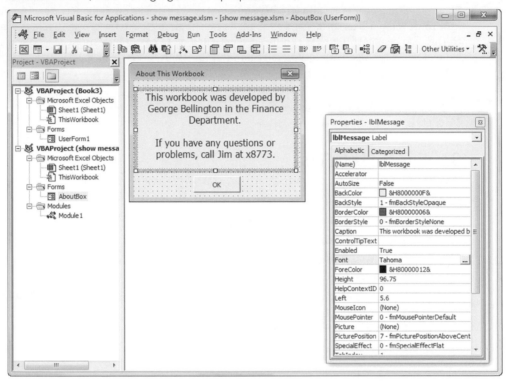

8. **Use the Toolbox and add a `CommandButton` object to the UserForm. Then use the Properties window to change the following properties for the `CommandButton`:**

Property	Change to
Name	OKButton
Caption	OK
Default	True

9. **Make other adjustments so that the form looks good to you.** You can change the size of the form or move or resize the controls.

Testing the UserForm

At this point, the UserForm has all of the necessary controls. What's missing is a way to display the UserForm. While you're developing the UserForm, you can press F5 to display it and see how it looks. To close the UserForm, click the Close button (X) in the dialog box title bar.

This section explains how to write a VBA procedure to display the UserForm when Excel is active:

1. **Insert a VBA module by choosing Insert ⇨ Module.**

2. **In the empty module, enter the following code:**

```
Sub ShowAboutBox()
    AboutBox.Show
End Sub
```

3. **Press Alt+F11 to activate Excel.**

4. **Choose Developer ⇨ Code ⇨ Macros (or press Alt+F8).** The Macro dialog box appears.

5. **Select ShowAboutBox from the list of macros, and then click Run.** The UserForm appears.

If you click the OK button, notice that it doesn't close the UserForm as you may expect. This button needs to have an event handler procedure for it to do anything when it's clicked. To dismiss the UserForm, click the Close button (X) in its title bar.

 You may prefer to display the UserForm by clicking a CommandButton on your worksheet. See Chapter 45 for details on attaching a macro to a worksheet CommandButton.

Creating an event handler procedure

An event handler procedure is executed when an event occurs. In this case, you need a procedure to handle the Click event that's generated when the user clicks the OK button.

1. **Press Alt+F11 to activate the VBE.**

2. **Activate the AboutBox UserForm by double-clicking its name in the Project window.**

3. **Double-click the CommandButton control.** The VBE activates the code module for the UserForm and inserts the Sub and End Sub statements for the button's click event, as shown in Figure 44.9.

FIGURE 44.9

The code module for the UserForm

4. **Insert the following statement before the End Sub statement:**

```
Unload Me
```

This statement simply dismisses the UserForm by using the `Unload` statement. The complete event handler procedure is as follows:

```
Private Sub OKButton_Click()
    Unload Me
End Sub
```

After you add the event procedure, clicking the OK button closes the form.

> **NOTE**
>
> The Me keyword when used in a UserForm's code module is a shortcut to refer to the UserForm itself. It's the same as coding `Unload AboutBox`, but if you decide to change the name of the form, using Me will continue to work.

Looking at Another UserForm Example

The example in this section is an enhanced version of the `ChangeCase` procedure presented at the beginning of the chapter. Recall that the original version of this macro changes the text in the selected cells to uppercase characters. This modified version asks the user what type of case change to make: uppercase, lowercase, or proper case (initial capitals).

 This workbook is available on this book's website at www.wiley.com/go/excel2019bible. The file is change case.xlsm.

Creating the UserForm

This UserForm needs one piece of information from the user: the type of change to make to the text. Because only one option can be selected, `OptionButton` controls are appropriate. Start with an empty workbook and follow these steps to create the UserForm:

1. **Press Alt+F11 to activate the VBE.**

2. **In the VBE, choose Insert ⇨ UserForm.** The VB Editor adds an empty form named `UserForm1` and displays the Toolbox.

3. **Press F4 to display the Properties window and then change the following properties of the UserForm object:**

Property	Change to
Name	UChangeCase
Caption	Change Case

4. **Add a** CommandButton **object to the UserForm and then change the following properties for the** CommandButton**:**

Property	Change to
Name	OKButton
Caption	OK
Default	True

5. **Add another** CommandButton **object and then change the following properties:**

Property	Change to
Name	CancelButton
Caption	Cancel
Cancel	True

6. **Add an** OptionButton **control and then change the following properties.** (This option is the default, so its Value property should be set to True.)

Property	Change to
Name	OptionUpper
Caption	Upper Case
Value	True

7. **Add a second** OptionButton **control and then change the following properties:**

Property	Change to
Name	OptionLower
Caption	Lower Case

8. **Add a third** OptionButton **control and then change the following properties:**

Property	Change to
Name	OptionProper
Caption	Proper Case

9. **Adjust the size and position of the controls and the form until your UserForm resembles the one shown in Figure 44.10.** Make sure that the controls do not overlap.

44

FIGURE 44.10

The UserForm after adding controls and adjusting some properties

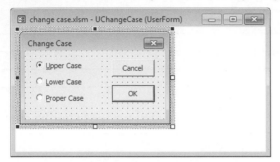

Creating event handler procedures

The next step is to create two event handler procedures: one to handle the Click event for the CancelButton CommandButton and the other to handle the Click event for the OKButton CommandButton. Event handlers for the OptionButton controls are not necessary. The VBA code can determine which of the three OptionButton controls is selected, but it does not need to react when the choice is changed—only when OK or Cancel is clicked.

Event handler procedures are stored in the UserForm code module. To create the procedure to handle the Click event for the CancelButton, follow these steps:

1. **Activate the UserForm1 form by double-clicking its name in the Project window.**
2. **Double-click the CancelButton control.** The VBE activates the code module for the UserForm and inserts an empty procedure.
3. **Insert the following statement before the End Sub statement:**

   ```
   Unload Me
   ```

That's all there is to it. The following is a listing of the entire procedure that's attached to the Click event for the CancelButton:

```
Private Sub CancelButton_Click()
    Unload Me
End Sub
```

This procedure is executed when the CancelButton is clicked. It consists of a single statement that unloads the form.

Next, add the code to handle the Click event for the OKButton control. Follow these steps:

1. **Select OKButton from the drop-down list at the top of the module or reactivate the UserForm and double-click the OKButton control.** The VBE creates a new procedure called OKButton_Click.

2. **Enter the following code.** The VBE has already entered the first and last statements for you:

```
Private Sub OKButton_Click()
'    Exit if a range is not selected
     If TypeName(Selection) <> "Range" Then Exit Sub
'    Upper case
     If Me.OptionUpper.Value Then
         For Each cell In Selection
         If Not cell.HasFormula Then
             cell.Value = StrConv(cell.Value, vbUpperCase)
         End If
         Next cell
     End If
'    Lower case
     If Me.OptionLower.Value Then
         For Each cell In Selection
         If Not cell.HasFormula Then
             cell.Value = StrConv(cell.Value, vbLowerCase)
         End If
         Next cell
     End If
'    Proper case
     If Me.OptionProper.Value Then
         For Each cell In Selection
         If Not cell.HasFormula Then
             cell.Value = StrConv(cell.Value, vbProperCase)
         End If
         Next cell
     End If
     Unload Me
End Sub
```

The macro starts by checking the type of selection. If a range is not selected, the procedure ends. The remainder of the procedure consists of three separate blocks. Only one block is executed, determined by which OptionButton is selected. The selected OptionButton has a Value of True. Finally, the UserForm is unloaded (dismissed).

Showing the UserForm

At this point, the UserForm has all of the necessary controls and event procedures. All that's left is a way to display the form. This section explains how to write a VBA procedure to display the UserForm:

1. **Make sure the VBE window is activated.**

2. **Insert a module by choosing Insert ⇨ Module.**

3. **In the empty module, enter the following code:**

```
Sub ShowUserForm()
    UChangeCase.Show
End Sub
```

4. **Choose Run ⇨ Run Sub/UserForm (or press F5).** The Excel window is activated, and the new UserForm is displayed, as shown in Figure 44.11.

FIGURE 44.11

Displaying the UserForm

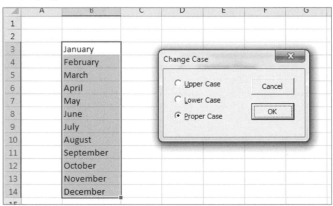

Testing the UserForm

To try the UserForm from Excel, follow these steps:

1. **Activate Excel.**

2. **Enter some text into a range of cells.**

3. **Select the range with the text.**

4. **Choose Developer ⇨ Code ⇨ Macros (or press Alt+F8).** The Macro dialog box appears.

5. **Select ShowUserForm from the list of macros and then click Run.** The UserForm appears, as shown in Figure 44.11.

6. **Make your choice, and click OK.**

Try it with a few more selections, including noncontiguous cells. Notice that if you click Cancel, the UserForm is dismissed, and no changes are made.

The code does have a problem, though: if you select one or more entire columns, the procedure processes every cell, which can take a long time. The version of the workbook on the website corrects this problem by working with a subset of the selection that intersects with the workbook's used range.

Making the macro available from a worksheet button

At this point, everything should be working properly. However, you have no quick and easy way to execute the macro. A good way to execute this macro would be from a button on the worksheet. You can use the following steps:

1. **Choose Developer ⇨ Controls ⇨ Insert and click the `Button` control in the Form Controls group.**

2. **Click and drag in the worksheet to create the button.** The Assign Macro dialog box appears.

3. **Select the ShowUserForm macro and then click OK.**

4. **(Optional) At this point, the button is still selected, so you can change the text to make it more descriptive.** You can also right-click the button at any time to change the text.

After you perform the preceding steps, clicking the button executes the macro and displays the UserForm.

 The button in this example is from the Form Controls group. Excel also provides a button in the ActiveX Controls group. See Chapter 45 for more information about the ActiveX Controls group.

Making the macro available on your Quick Access toolbar

If you'd like to use this macro while other workbooks are active, you may want to add a button to your Quick Access toolbar. Follow these steps:

1. **Make sure the workbook containing the macro is open.**

2. **Right-click anywhere on the Ribbon, and choose Customize Quick Access Toolbar from the shortcut menu.** The Excel Options dialog box appears, with the Quick Access Toolbar section selected.

3. **Choose Macros from the Choose Commands From drop-down menu on the left.** You'll see your macro listed.

44

4. **Select the macro's name, and click Add to add the item to the list on the right.**

5. **(Optional) To change the icon, click Modify and choose a new image; then click OK.** You can also change the Display Name.

6. **Click OK to close the Excel Options dialog box.** The icon appears on your Quick Access toolbar.

Enhancing UserForms

Creating UserForms can make your macros much more versatile. You can create custom commands that display dialog boxes that look exactly like those that Excel uses. This section contains some additional information to help you develop custom dialog boxes that work like those that are built in to Excel.

Adding accelerator keys

All Excel dialog boxes work well with a mouse and a keyboard because each control has an associated accelerator key. The user can press Alt plus the accelerator key to work with a specific dialog box control.

Your custom dialog boxes should also have accelerator keys for all controls. You add accelerator keys in the Properties window by entering a character for the `Accelerator` property.

Your accelerator key can be any letter, number, or punctuation, regardless of whether that character appears in the control's caption. It's a good practice to use a letter that is in the control's caption, though, because that letter will be underlined—a visual cue for the user. (See Figure 44.11 for an example of option buttons with accelerator keys.) Another common convention is to use the first letter of the control's caption. But don't duplicate accelerator keys. If the first letter is already taken, use a different letter, preferably one that is easy to associate with the word (like a hard consonant). If you have duplicate accelerator keys, the accelerator key acts on the next control in the tab order of the UserForm. Then, pressing the accelerator key again takes you to the second control with that accelerator.

Some controls (such as textboxes) don't have a Caption property and other controls (such as labels) can't have the focus. You can assign an accelerator key to a label that describes the control and put that label right before your target control in the tab order. Pressing the accelerator key for a control that can't take the focus activates the next control in the tab order.

Controlling tab order

The previous section refers to a UserForm's tab order. When you're working with a UserForm, pressing Tab and Shift+Tab cycles through the dialog box's controls. When you create a UserForm, you should make sure that the tab order is correct. Usually, it means that tabbing should move through the controls in a logical sequence.

To view or change the tab order in a UserForm, choose View ⇨ Tab Order to display the Tab Order dialog box (see Figure 44.12). You can then select a control from the list; use the Move Up and Move Down buttons to change the tab order for the selected control.

FIGURE 44.12

Adjusting the tab order in a UserForm

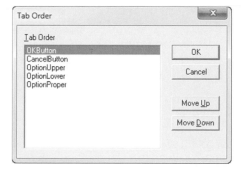

Learning More

Mastering UserForms takes practice. You should closely examine the dialog boxes that Excel uses to get a feeling for the way dialog boxes are designed. You can duplicate many of the dialog boxes that Excel uses.

The best way to learn more about creating dialog boxes is by using the VBA Help system. Pressing F1 is the quickest way to display the Help window.

44

Using UserForm Controls in a Worksheet

C hapter 44, "Creating UserForms," presented an introduction to UserForms. If you like the idea of using dialog box controls but you don't like the idea of creating a custom dialog box, this chapter is for you. It explains how to enhance your worksheet with a variety of interactive controls, such as buttons, list boxes, and option buttons.

Understanding Why to Use Controls on a Worksheet

The main reason to use controls on a worksheet is to make it easier for the user to provide input. For example, if you create a model that uses one or more input cells, you can create controls to allow the user to select values for the input cells.

Adding controls to a worksheet requires much less effort than creating a dialog box. In addition, you may not have to create any macros because you can link a control to a worksheet cell. For example, if you insert a CheckBox control on a worksheet, you can link it to a particular cell. When the CheckBox is checked, the linked cell displays TRUE. When the CheckBox is not checked, the linked cell displays FALSE.

Figure 45.1 shows an example that uses three types of controls: a Checkbox, two sets of OptionButtons, and a ScrollBar. The user's selections are used to display a loan amortization schedule on another worksheet. The workbook is interactive, but it uses no macros.

FIGURE 45.1

This worksheet uses UserForm controls.

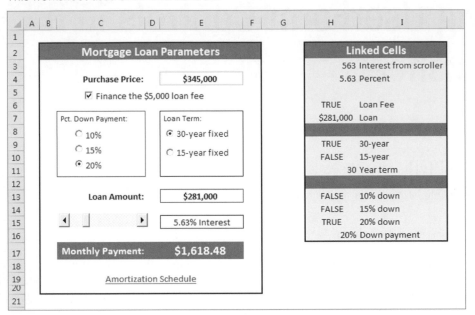

 This workbook is available on this book's website at www.wiley.com/go/excel2019bible. The
file is named mortgage loan.xlsx.

Adding controls to a worksheet can be a bit confusing because Excel offers two different
sets of controls, both of which you access by choosing Developer ➪ Controls ➪ Insert:

Form controls These controls are unique to Excel.

ActiveX controls These controls are a subset of those that are available for use on
UserForms.

Figure 45.2 shows the controls that appear when you choose Developer ➪ Controls ➪ Insert.
When you move your mouse pointer over a control, Excel displays a ScreenTip that identifies the control.

To add to the confusion, many controls are available from both sources. For example, a control named ListBox is listed in both Forms controls and ActiveX controls. However, they're
two entirely different controls. In general, Forms controls are easier to use, but ActiveX
controls provide more flexibility.

FIGURE 45.2

Excel's two sets of worksheet controls

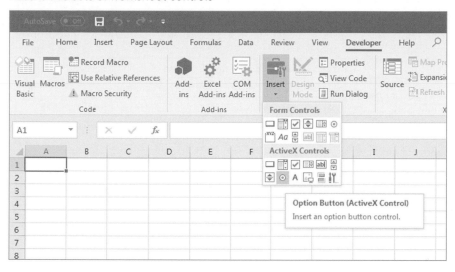

Table 45.1 describes the ActiveX controls.

TABLE 45.1 ActiveX Controls

Button	What It Does
Command Button	Inserts a CommandButton control (a clickable button).
Combo Box	Inserts a ComboBox control (a drop-down list).
Check Box	Inserts a CheckBox control (to control Boolean options).
List Box	Inserts a ListBox control (to allow the user to select an item from a list).
Text Box	Inserts a TextBox control (to allow the user to type text).
Scroll Bar	Inserts a ScrollBar control (to specify a value by dragging a bar).
Spin Button	Inserts a SpinButton control (to increment a value by clicking up or down).

Continues

45

TABLE 45.1 *(continued)*

Button	What It Does
Option Button	Inserts an `OptionButton` control (to allow a user to select from multiple options).
Label	Inserts a `Label` control (to display text).
Image	Inserts an `Image` control (to display an image).
Toggle Button	Inserts a `ToggleButton` control (to control Boolean options).
More Controls	Displays a list of other ActiveX controls that are installed on your system. Not all of these controls work with Excel.

Using Controls

Adding ActiveX controls in a worksheet is easy, but you need to learn a few basic facts about how to use them.

Adding a control

To add a control to a worksheet, choose Developer ➪ Controls ➪ Insert. From the Insert drop-down list, click the control you want to use and then drag it into the worksheet to create the control. You don't need to be too concerned about the exact size or position of the control because you can modify those properties at any time.

> **CAUTION**
>
> Make sure that you select a control from the ActiveX controls, not from the Forms controls. If you insert a Forms control, the instructions in this chapter will not apply. When you choose Developer ➪ Controls ➪ Insert, the ActiveX controls appear in the lower half of the list.

Learning about Design mode

When you add a control to a worksheet, Excel goes into Design mode. In this mode, you can adjust the properties of any controls on your worksheet, add or edit macros for the control, or change the control's size or position.

> **NOTE**
>
> When Excel is in Design mode, the Design Mode button in the Developer ➪ Controls group appears highlighted. You can click this button to toggle Design mode on and off.

When Excel is in Design mode, the controls aren't enabled. To test the controls, you must exit Design mode by clicking the Design Mode button. When you're working with controls, you'll probably need to switch in and out of Design mode frequently.

Adjusting properties

Every control that you add has various properties that determine how it looks and behaves. You can adjust these properties only when Excel is in Design mode. When you add a control to a worksheet, Excel enters Design mode automatically. If you need to change a control after you exit Design mode, click the Design Mode button in the Controls section of the Developer tab.

To change the properties for a control, follow these steps:

1. **Make sure Excel is in Design mode.**

2. **Click the control to select it.**

3. **If the Properties window isn't visible, click the Properties icon in the Controls section of the Developer tab.** The Properties window appears, as shown in Figure 45.3.

FIGURE 45.3

Use the Properties window to adjust the properties of a control—in this case, a CommandButton control.

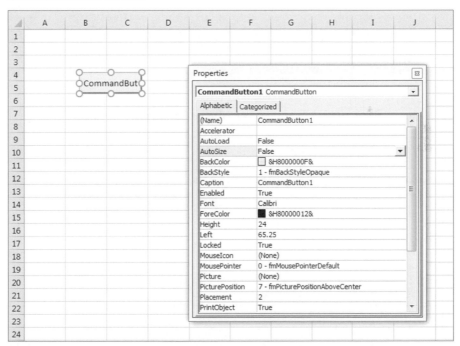

4. **Select the property and make the change.**

The manner in which you change a property depends on the property. Some properties display a drop-down list from which you can select from a list of options. Others (such as Font) provide a button that displays a dialog box when clicked. Other properties require you to type the property value. When you change a property, the change takes effect immediately.

> **TIP**
>
> To find out about a particular property, select the property in the Properties window and press F1.

The Properties window has two tabs. The Alphabetic tab displays the properties in alphabetical order. The Categorized tab displays the properties by category. Both tabs show the same properties; only the order is different.

Using common properties

Each control has its own unique set of properties. However, many controls share properties. This section describes some properties that are common to all or many controls, as set forth in Table 45.2.

> **NOTE**
>
> Some ActiveX control properties are required (for example, the Name property). In other words, you can't leave the property empty. If a required property is missing, Excel will always tell you so by displaying an error message.

TABLE 45.2   Properties Shared by Multiple Controls

Property	Description
AutoSize	If True, the control resizes itself automatically based on the text in its caption.
BackColor	The background color of the control.
BackStyle	The style of the background (either transparent or opaque) .
Caption	The text that appears on the control.
LinkedCell	A worksheet cell that contains the current value of a control.
ListFillRange	A worksheet range that contains items displayed in a ListBox or ComboBox control.
Value	The control's value.
Left and Top	Values that determine the control's position.

Property	Description
Width and Height	Values that determine the control's size.
Visible	If False, the control is hidden.
Name	The name of the control. When you add a control, Excel assigns it a name based on the control type. You can change the name to any valid name. However, each control's name must be unique on the worksheet.
Picture	Enables you to specify a graphics image to display.

Linking controls to cells

Often, you can use ActiveX controls in a worksheet without using macros. Many controls have a LinkedCell property, which specifies a worksheet cell that is linked to the control.

For example, you may add a SpinButton control and specify cell B1 as its LinkedCell property. After doing so, cell B1 contains the value of the SpinButton, and clicking the SpinButton changes the value in cell B1. You can, of course, use the value contained in the linked cell in your formulas.

NOTE

When specifying the LinkedCell property in the Properties window, you can't "point" to the linked cell in the worksheet. You must type the cell address or its name (if it has one).

Creating macros for controls

To create a macro for a control, you must use the Visual Basic Editor (VBE). The macros are stored in the code module for the sheet that contains the control. For example, if you place an ActiveX control on Sheet2, the VBA code for that control is stored in the Sheet2 code module. Each control can have a macro to handle any of its events. For example, a CommandButton control can have a macro for its Click event, its DblClick event, and various other events.

TIP

The easiest way to access the code module for a control is to double-click the control while in Design mode. Excel displays the VBE and creates an empty procedure for the control's default event. For example, the default event for a CheckBox control is the Click event. Figure 45.4 shows the autogenerated code for a control named CheckBox1, located on Sheet1.

45

FIGURE 45.4

Double-clicking a control in Design mode activates the VBE and enters an empty event-handler procedure.

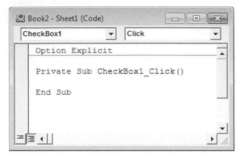

The control's name appears in the upper-left portion of the code window, and the event appears in the upper-right area. If you want to create a macro that executes when a different event occurs, select the event from the list in the upper-right area.

The following steps demonstrate how to insert a CommandButton and to create a simple macro that displays a message when the button is clicked:

1. **Choose Developer ⇨ Controls ⇨ Insert.**
2. **Click the CommandButton tool in the ActiveX Controls section.**
3. **Click and drag in the worksheet to create the button.** Excel automatically enters Design mode.
4. **Double-click the button.** The VBE is activated, and an empty procedure is created for the button's Click event.
5. **Enter the following VBA statement before the End Sub statement:**

   ```
   MsgBox "Hello, it's " & Time
   ```
6. **Press Alt+F11 to return to Excel.**
7. **(Optional) Adjust any other properties for the CommandButton using the Properties window.** Choose Developer ⇨ Controls ⇨ Properties if the Properties window isn't visible.
8. **Click the Design Mode button in the Developer ⇨ Controls section to exit design mode.**

After you perform the preceding steps, when you click the CommandButton, the message box appears and displays the current time.

> **NOTE**
>
> You must enter the VBA code manually. You can't create macros for controls using the VBA macro recorder. However, you can record a macro and then execute it from an event procedure. For example, if you've recorded a macro named FormatCells, you can type a statement with the macro's name. When that statement is executed, your recorded macro will run. Or, you can copy the recorded code and paste it to your event procedure.

Reviewing the Available ActiveX Controls

The following sections describe the ActiveX controls that are available for use in your worksheets.

 This book's website at www.wiley.com/go/excel2019bible contains a file that includes examples of all the ActiveX controls. This file is named worksheet controls.xlsm.

CheckBox

A CheckBox control is useful for getting a binary choice: yes or no, true or false, on or off, and so on. The following is a description of the most useful properties of a CheckBox control:

Accelerator A letter that enables the user to change the value of the control by using the keyboard. For example, if the accelerator is *A*, pressing Alt+A changes the value of the CheckBox control. The accelerator letter is underlined in the caption of the control.

LinkedCell The worksheet cell that's linked to the CheckBox. The cell displays TRUE if the control is checked or FALSE if the control is not checked.

ComboBox

A ComboBox control is a combination of a TextBox and a ListBox. It acts as a TextBox because the user can type in it just like a TextBox, even if what they type isn't on the list. It acts as a ListBox because when you click its drop-down arrow, a list of available items appears.

Figure 45.5 shows a ComboBox control that uses the range D1:D12 for the ListFillRange and cell A1 for the LinkedCell.

FIGURE 45.5

A ComboBox control

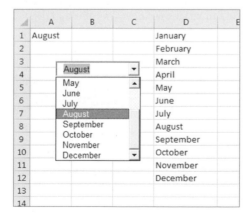

The following is a description of the most useful properties of a ComboBox control:

BoundColumn   If the ListFillRange contains multiple columns, this property determines which column contains the returned value.

ColumnCount   This specifies the number of columns to display in the list.

LinkedCell   This specifies the worksheet cell that displays the selected item.

ListFillRange   This specifies the worksheet range that contains the list items.

ListRows   This specifies the number of items to display when the list drops down.

ListStyle   This determines the appearance of the list items.

Style   This determines whether the control acts like a drop-down list or a ComboBox. A drop-down list doesn't allow the user to enter a new value.

 You can also create a drop-down list directly in a cell by using data validation. See Chapter 26, "Using Data Validation," for details.

CommandButton

A CommandButton control is used to execute a macro. When a CommandButton is clicked, it executes an event procedure with a name that consists of the CommandButton name, an underscore, and the word Click. For example, if a CommandButton is named MyButton, clicking it executes the macro named MyButton_Click. This macro is stored in the code module for the sheet that contains the CommandButton.

Image

An Image control is used to display an image. These are the most useful properties of an Image control:

AutoSize   If TRUE, the Image control is resized automatically to fit the image.

Picture   This is the path to the image file. Click the button in the Properties window, and Excel displays a dialog box so that you can locate the image. Or, copy the image to the Clipboard, select the Picture property in the Properties window, and press Ctrl+V.

PictureSizeMode   This determines how the picture is changed when the container size is different than the picture.

> **TIP**
> You can also insert an image on a worksheet by choosing Insert ⇨ Illustrations ⇨ Pictures.

Label

A Label control simply displays text. Like on a UserForm, it's used to describe other controls. You can also use its Click event to activate other controls with an accelerator key.

ListBox

A `ListBox` control presents a list of items, and the user can select an item (or multiple items). It's similar to a `ComboBox`. The main difference is that a `ListBox` doesn't require you to click a drop-down arrow to display more than one item at a time.

The following is a description of the most useful properties of a `ListBox` control:

BoundColumn   If the list contains multiple columns, this property determines which column contains the returned value.

ColumnCount   This specifies the number of columns to display in the list.

IntegralHeight   This is TRUE if the height of the `ListBox` adjusts automatically to display full lines of text when the list is scrolled vertically. If FALSE, the `ListBox` may display partial lines of text when it's scrolled vertically.

LinkedCell   This specifies the worksheet cell that displays the selected item.

ListFillRange   This specifies the worksheet range that contains the list items.

ListStyle   This determines the appearance of the list items.

MultiSelect   This determines whether the user can select multiple items from the list.

> **NOTE**
> If you use a `MultiSelect` `ListBox`, you can't specify a `LinkedCell`; you need to write a macro to determine which items are selected.

OptionButton

`OptionButton` controls are useful when the user needs to select from a small number of items. `OptionButton` controls are always used in groups of at least two.

The following are the most useful properties of an `OptionButton` control:

Accelerator   A letter that lets the user select the option by using the keyboard. For example, if the accelerator for an `OptionButton` is C, pressing Alt+C selects the control.

GroupName   A name that identifies an `OptionButton` as being associated with other `OptionButtons` with the same `GroupName` property.

LinkedCell   The worksheet cell that's linked to the `OptionButton`. The cell displays TRUE if the control is selected or FALSE if the control isn't selected.

> **NOTE**
> If your worksheet contains more than one set of `OptionButton` controls, you must ensure that each set of `OptionButtons` has a different `GroupName` property. Otherwise, all `OptionButtons` become part of the same set.

45

ScrollBar

A `ScrollBar` control is useful for specifying a cell value. Figure 45.6 shows a worksheet with three `ScrollBar` controls. These `ScrollBar` controls are used to change the color in the rectangle shape. The value of the `ScrollBar` control determines the red, green, or blue component of the rectangle's color. This example uses a few simple macros to change the colors.

FIGURE 45.6

This worksheet has three `ScrollBar` controls.

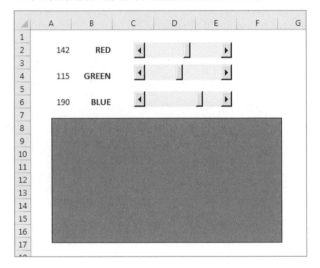

The following are the most useful properties of a `ScrollBar` control:

Value   The current value of the control

Min   The minimum value for the control

Max   The maximum value for the control

LinkedCell   The worksheet cell that displays the value of the control

SmallChange   The amount that the control's value is changed by clicking the arrows

LargeChange   The amount that the control's value is changed by clicking in the scroll area

The `ScrollBar` control is most useful for selecting a value that extends across a wide range of possible values.

SpinButton

A `SpinButton` control lets the user select a value by clicking the control, which has two arrows (one to increase the value and the other to decrease the value). A `SpinButton` can display either horizontally or vertically.

The following are the most useful properties of a `SpinButton` control:

`Value`   The current value of the control.

`Min`   The minimum value of the control.

`Max`   The maximum value of the control.

`LinkedCell`   The worksheet cell that displays the value of the control.

`SmallChange`   The amount that the control's value is changed by a click. Usually, this property is set to 1, but you can make it any value.

TextBox

On the surface, a `TextBox` control may not seem useful. After all, it simply contains text—you can usually use worksheet cells to get text input. In fact, `TextBox` controls are useful not so much for input control as for output control. Because a `TextBox` can have scrollbars, you can use a `TextBox` to display a great deal of information in a small area.

Figure 45.7 shows a `TextBox` control that contains Lincoln's Gettysburg Address. Notice the vertical scrollbar displayed using the `ScrollBars` property.

FIGURE 45.7

A `TextBox` control with a vertical scrollbar

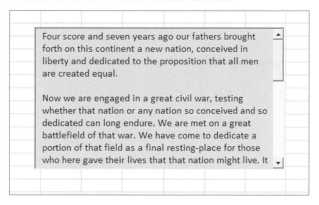

The following are the most useful properties of a `TextBox` control:

`AutoSize`   This determines whether the control adjusts its size automatically, based on the amount of text.

45

IntegralHeight   If TRUE, the height of the TextBox adjusts automatically to display full lines of text when the list is scrolled vertically. If FALSE, the ListBox may display partial lines of text when it's scrolled vertically.

MaxLength   This determines the maximum number of characters allowed in the TextBox. If 0, no limit exists on the number of characters.

MultiLine   If TRUE, the TextBox can display more than one line of text.

TextAlign   This determines the way the text is aligned in the TextBox.

WordWrap   This determines whether the control allows word wrap.

ScrollBars   This determines the type of ScrollBars for the control: horizontal, vertical, both, or none.

ToggleButton

A ToggleButton control has two states: on and off. Clicking the button toggles between these two states, and the button changes its appearance to indicate its current state. Its value is either TRUE (pressed) or FALSE (not pressed). You can often use a ToggleButton in place of a CheckBox control.

Working with Excel Events

I n the preceding chapters, we presented a few examples of VBA event-handler procedures for ActiveX controls. These procedures are the keys to making your Excel applications interactive. This chapter introduces the concept of events for Excel objects and includes many examples that you can adapt to meet your own needs.

Understanding Events

Excel monitors a variety of events and can execute your VBA code when any of these events occur. This chapter covers the following types of events:

Workbook events   These occur for a particular workbook. Examples include `Open` (the workbook is opened or created), `BeforeSave` (the workbook is about to be saved), and `NewSheet` (a new sheet is added). You must store VBA code for workbook events in the `ThisWorkbook` code module.

Worksheet events   These occur for a particular worksheet. Examples include `Change` (a cell on the sheet is changed), `SelectionChange` (the selection on the worksheet is changed), and `Calculate` (the worksheet is recalculated). VBA code for worksheet events must be stored in the code module for the worksheet (for example, the module named `Sheet1`).

Special Application events   The final category consists of two useful application-level events: `OnTime` and `OnKey`. These are different from other events because the code isn't in a class module. Rather, you set the events by calling a method of the Application object.

Many events exist at both the worksheet and workbook levels. For example, `Sheet1` has an event called `Change` that fires when any cell on `Sheet1` is changed. The workbook has an event called `SheetChange` that fires every time any cell on any sheet is changed. The workbook version of this event has an additional argument that lets you know which sheet was affected.

Entering Event-Handler VBA Code

Every event-handler procedure must reside in a specific type of code module. Code for workbook-level events is stored in the `ThisWorkbook` code module. Code for worksheet-level events is stored in the code module for the particular sheet (for example, the code module named `Sheet1`).

In addition, every event-handler procedure has a predetermined name. You can declare the procedure by typing it, but a much better approach is to let the Visual Basic Editor (VBE) do it for you by using the two drop-down controls at the top of the window.

Figure 46.1 shows the code module for the `ThisWorkbook` object. Select this code module by double-clicking it in the Project window. To insert a procedure declaration, select `Workbook` from the objects list in the upper left of the code window and then select the event from the procedures list in the upper right. When you do, you get a procedure "shell" that contains the procedure declaration line and an `End Sub` statement.

FIGURE 46.1

The best way to create an event procedure is to let the VBE do it for you.

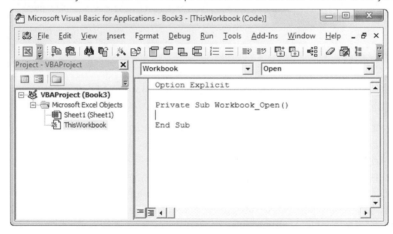

For example, if you select `Workbook` from the objects list and `Open` from the procedures list, the VBE inserts the following (empty) procedure:

```
Private Sub Workbook_Open()

End Sub
```

Your event-handler VBA code goes between these two lines.

Some event-handler procedures contain an argument list. For example, you may need to create an event-handler procedure to monitor the `SheetActivate` event for a workbook.

(This event is triggered when a user activates a different sheet.) If you use the technique described in the previous section, the VBE creates the following procedure:

```
Private Sub Workbook_SheetActivate(ByVal Sh As Object)

End Sub
```

This procedure uses one argument (Sh), which represents the activated sheet. In this case, Sh is declared as an Object data type rather than a Worksheet data type because the activated sheet also can be a chart sheet.

Your code can, of course, use information passed as an argument. The following example displays the name of the activated sheet by accessing the argument's Name property. The argument becomes either a Worksheet object or a Chart object:

```
Private Sub Workbook_SheetActivate(ByVal Sh As Object)
    MsgBox Sh.Name & " was activated."
End Sub
```

Several event-handler procedures use a Boolean argument named Cancel. For example, the declaration for a workbook's BeforePrint event is

```
Private Sub Workbook_BeforePrint(Cancel As Boolean)
```

The value of Cancel passed to the procedure is False. However, your code can set Cancel to True, which cancels the printing. The following example demonstrates this:

```
Private Sub Workbook_BeforePrint(Cancel As Boolean)
    Msg = "Have you loaded the 5164 label stock?"
    Ans = MsgBox(Msg, vbYesNo, "About to print...")
    If Ans = vbNo Then Cancel = True
End Sub
```

The Workbook_BeforePrint procedure executes before the workbook prints. This procedure displays a message box asking the user to verify that the correct paper is loaded. If the user clicks the No button, Cancel is set to True, and nothing prints.

Here's another procedure that uses the workbook's BeforePrint event. This example overcomes a deficiency in Excel's headers and footers: it's not possible to use the contents of a cell for a page header or footer. This simple procedure is triggered when the workbook is printed. It places the contents of cell A1 in the page header:

```
Private Sub Workbook_BeforePrint(Cancel As Boolean)
    ActiveSheet.PageSetup.CenterHeader = Worksheets(1).Range("A1")
End Sub
```

Using Workbook-Level Events

Workbook-level events occur for a particular workbook. Table 46.1 lists the most commonly used workbook events along with a brief description of each.

TABLE 46.1   **Workbook Events**

Event	Action That Triggers the Event
`Activate`	The workbook is activated.
`AfterSave`	The workbook was saved.
`BeforeClose`	The workbook is about to be closed.
`BeforePrint`	The workbook (or anything in it) is about to be printed.
`BeforeSave`	The workbook is about to be saved.
`Deactivate`	The workbook is deactivated.
`NewSheet`	A new sheet is created in the workbook.
`Open`	The workbook is opened.
`SheetActivate`	Any sheet in the workbook is activated.
`SheetBeforeDoubleClick`	Any worksheet in the workbook is double-clicked. This event occurs before the default double-click action.
`SheetBeforeRightClick`	Any worksheet in the workbook is right-clicked. This event occurs before the default right-click action.
`SheetChange`	Any worksheet in the workbook is changed by the user.
`SheetDeactivate`	Any sheet in the workbook is deactivated.
`SheetSelectionChange`	The selection on any worksheet in the workbook is changed.
`WindowActivate`	Any workbook window is activated.
`WindowDeactivate`	Any workbook window is deactivated.

The remainder of this section presents examples of using workbook-level events.

> **CAUTION**
>
> All the sample procedures that follow must be located in the code module for the `ThisWorkbook` object. If you put them into any other type of code module, they won't work—and you will not see an error message.

Using the Open event

One of the most common monitored events is a workbook's `Open` event. This event is triggered when the workbook opens and executes the `Workbook_Open` procedure. A `Workbook_Open` procedure is versatile, and it is often used for the following tasks:

- Displaying welcome messages
- Opening other workbooks

- Activating a specific sheet
- Ensuring that certain conditions are met; for example, a workbook may require that a particular add-in is installed

> **CAUTION**
>
> Keep in mind that there is no guarantee that your `Workbook_Open` procedure will be executed. For example, the user may choose to disable macros. And if the user holds down the Shift key while opening a workbook, the workbook's `Workbook_Open` procedure won't execute.

The following is a simple example of a `Workbook_Open` procedure. It uses the VBA `Weekday` function to determine the day of the week. If it's Friday, a message box appears to remind the user to perform a file backup. If it's not Friday, nothing happens.

```
Private Sub Workbook_Open()
    If Weekday(Now) = 6 Then
        Msg = "Make sure you do your weekly backup!"
        MsgBox Msg, vbInformation
    End If
End Sub
```

The following example performs a number of actions when the workbook is opened. It maximizes the workbook window, activates the sheet named `DataEntry`, selects the first empty cell in column A, and enters the current date into that cell. If a sheet named `DataEntry` does not exist, the code generates an error.

```
Private Sub Workbook_Open()
    ActiveWindow.WindowState = xlMaximized
    Worksheets("DataEntry").Activate
    Range("A1").End(xlDown).Offset(1,0).Select
    ActiveCell.Value = Date
End Sub
```

Using the SheetActivate event

The following procedure executes whenever the user activates a sheet in the workbook. The code simply selects cell A1. Including the `On Error Resume Next` statement causes the procedure to ignore the error that occurs if the activated sheet is a chart sheet:

```
Private Sub Workbook_SheetActivate(ByVal Sh As Object)
    On Error Resume Next
    Range("A1").Select
End Sub
```

An alternative method to handle the case of a chart sheet is to check the sheet type. Use the `Sh` argument, which is passed to the procedure:

```
Private Sub Workbook_SheetActivate(ByVal Sh As Object)
    If TypeName(Sh) = "Worksheet" Then Range("A1").Select
End Sub
```

Using the NewSheet event

The following procedure executes whenever a new sheet is added to the workbook. The sheet is passed to the procedure as an argument. Because a new sheet can be either a worksheet or a chart sheet, this procedure determines the sheet type. If it's a worksheet, it inserts a date and time stamp in cell A1:

```
Private Sub Workbook_NewSheet(ByVal Sh As Object)
  If TypeName(Sh) = "Worksheet" Then _
    Sh.Range("A1").Value = "Sheet added " & Now()
End Sub
```

Using the BeforeSave event

The BeforeSave event occurs before the workbook is actually saved. As you know, choosing File ⇨ Save sometimes brings up the Save As dialog box—for example, when the file has never been saved or was opened in read-only mode.

When the Workbook_BeforeSave procedure executes, it receives an argument that enables you to identify whether the Save As dialog box will appear. The following example demonstrates this:

```
Private Sub Workbook_BeforeSave _
  (ByVal SaveAsUI As Boolean, Cancel As Boolean)
    If SaveAsUI Then
        MsgBox "Use the new file-naming convention."
    End If
End Sub
```

When the user attempts to save the workbook, the Workbook_BeforeSave procedure executes. If the save operation brings up the Save As dialog box, the SaveAsUI variable is True. The preceding procedure checks this variable and displays a message only if the Save As dialog box is displayed. In this case, the message is a reminder about how to name the file.

The BeforeSave event procedure also has a Cancel variable in its argument list. If the procedure sets the Cancel argument to True, the file is not saved.

Using the BeforeClose event

The BeforeClose event occurs before a workbook is closed. This event is often used in conjunction with a Workbook_Open event handler. For example, use the Workbook_Open procedure to initialize items in your workbook, and use the Workbook_BeforeClose procedure to clean up or restore settings to normal before the workbook closes.

If you attempt to close a workbook that hasn't been saved, Excel displays a prompt that asks whether you want to save the workbook before it closes.

> **CAUTION**
>
> A problem can arise from this event with unsaved workbooks. By the time the user sees the prompt to save before closing, the `BeforeClose` event has already executed. If the user cancels the close at the save prompt, the workbook remains open, but your event code has already run.

Working with Worksheet Events

The events for a `Worksheet` object are some of the most useful. As you'll see, monitoring these events can make your applications perform feats that would otherwise be impossible.

Table 46.2 lists the more commonly used worksheet events with a brief description of each. Remember that these event procedures must be entered into the code module for the sheet. These code modules have default names like Sheet1, Sheet2, and so on.

TABLE 46.2 Worksheet Events

Event	Action That Triggers the Event
Activate	The worksheet is activated.
BeforeDoubleClick	The worksheet is double-clicked. This event occurs before the default double-click action.
BeforeRightClick	The worksheet is right-clicked. This event occurs before the default right-click action.
Change	Cells on the worksheet are changed by the user.
Deactivate	The worksheet is deactivated.
FollowHyperlink	A hyperlink on the worksheet was clicked.
SelectionChange	The selection on the worksheet is changed.

Using the Change event

A `Change` event is triggered when a user changes any cell in the worksheet. A `Change` event is not triggered when a calculation generates a different value for a formula or when an object (such as a chart or a shape) is added to the sheet.

When the `Worksheet_Change` procedure executes, it receives a `Range` object as its `Target` argument. This `Range` object corresponds to the changed cell or range that triggered the event. The following example displays a message box that shows the address of the `Target` range:

```
Private Sub Worksheet_Change(ByVal Target As Range)
    MsgBox "Range " & Target.Address & " was changed."
End Sub
```

To get a feel for the types of actions that generate the Change event for a worksheet, enter the preceding procedure into the code module for a Worksheet object. After you enter this procedure, activate Excel and, using various techniques, make changes to the worksheet. Every time the Change event occurs, a message box displays the address of the range that changed.

Unfortunately, the Change event doesn't always work as expected. For example,

- Changing the formatting of a cell does not trigger the Change event (as expected), but choosing Home ➪ Editing ➪ Clear ➪ Clear Formats *does*.
- Pressing Delete generates an event even if the cell is empty at the start.
- Cells changed via Excel commands may or may not trigger the Change event. For example, sorting and goal-seeking operations do not trigger the Change event. However, operations such as Find and Replace, using the AutoSum button, or adding a Total row to a table *do* trigger the event.
- If your VBA procedure changes a cell, it does trigger the Change event.

Monitoring a specific range for changes

Although the Change event occurs when any cell on the worksheet changes, most of the time you'll be concerned only with changes that are made to a specific cell or range. When the Worksheet_Change event-handler procedure is called, it receives a Range object as its argument. This Range object corresponds to the cell(s) that changed.

Assume that your worksheet has a range named InputRange, and you want your VBA code to monitor changes to this range only. No Change event exists for a Range object, but you can perform a quick check within the Worksheet_Change procedure. The following procedure demonstrates this:

```
Private Sub Worksheet_Change(ByVal Target As Range)
    Dim VRange As Range
    Set VRange = Me.Range("InputRange")
    If Union(Target, VRange).Address = VRange.Address Then
        Msgbox "The changed cell is in the input range."
    End if
End Sub
```

This example creates a Range object variable named VRange, which represents the worksheet range that you want to monitor for changes. The procedure uses the VBA Union function to determine whether VRange contains the Target range (passed to the procedure in its argument). The Union function returns an object that consists of all the cells in both its arguments. If the range address is the same as the VRange address, VRange contains Target, and a message box appears. Otherwise, the procedure ends, and nothing happens.

The preceding procedure has a potential flaw: Target may consist of a single cell or a range. For example, if the user changes more than one cell at a time, Target becomes a multicell range. As it is, all of the changed cells must be within InputRange. If you still want to act on cells within InputRange, even if some of the changes are not, you have to change the procedure to loop through all of the cells in `Target`. The following procedure checks each changed cell and displays a message box if the cell is within the desired range:

```
Private Sub Worksheet_Change(ByVal Target As Range)
    Set VRange = Me.Range("InputRange")
    For Each cell In Target.Cells
        If Union(cell, VRange).Address = VRange.Address Then
            Msgbox "The changed cell is in the input range."
        End if
    Next cell
End Sub
```

> **CAUTION**
>
> A workbook with this example is available on this book's website at `www.wiley.com/go/excel2019bible`. The file is named `monitor a range.xlsm`.

Using the SelectionChange event

The following procedure demonstrates a `SelectionChange` event. It executes whenever the user makes a new selection on the worksheet:

```
Private Sub Worksheet_SelectionChange(ByVal Target As Range)
    Me.Cells.Interior.ColorIndex = xlNone
    With Target
        .EntireRow.Interior.ColorIndex = 35
        .EntireColumn.Interior.ColorIndex = 35
    End With
End Sub
```

This procedure shades the row and column of the selected cells, making it easy to identify. The first statement removes the background color of all cells. Next, the entire rows and columns of the selected cells are shaded light green. Figure 46.2 shows the shading.

> **CAUTION**
>
> A workbook with this example is available on this book's website at `www.wiley.com/go/excel2019bible`. The file is named `selection change event.xlsm`.

> **CAUTION**
>
> You won't want to use this procedure if your worksheet contains background shading because the macro will erase it. However, if the shading is the result of a style applied to a table, the macro doesn't erase the table's background shading.

FIGURE 46.2

Selecting a cell causes the active cell's row and column to become shaded.

⊿	A	B	C	D	E	F	G	H	I
1		Mary	Bill	Joe	Frank	Carol	Pete	Nancy	
2	January	551	664	582	607	675	513	557	
3	February	548	572	577	529	500	681	635	
4	March	665	513	546	678	673	566	693	
5	April	699	667	663	562	504	626	595	
6	May	640	581	661	586	510	542	537	
7	June	649	689	569	518	591	607	625	
8	July	538	516	660	626	523	560	689	
9	August	618	533	611	681	585	641	618	
10	September	587	546	584	538	575	624	648	
11	October	573	616	612	602	696	621	620	
12	November	613	692	617	603	544	601	678	
13	December	657	518	597	630	638	602	652	
14									
15									

Using the BeforeRightClick event

Normally, when the user right-clicks in a worksheet, a shortcut menu appears. If, for some reason, you want to prevent the shortcut menu from appearing, you can trap the `RightClick` event. The following procedure sets the `Cancel` argument to `True`, which cancels the `RightClick` event—and, thus, the shortcut menu. Instead, a message box appears:

```
Private Sub Worksheet_BeforeRightClick _
  (ByVal Target As Range, Cancel As Boolean)
     Cancel = True
     MsgBox "The shortcut menu is not available."
End Sub
```

Using Special Application Events

So far, the events discussed in this chapter are associated with an object like a worksheet. This section discusses two additional events: `OnTime` and `OnKey`. These events are not associated with an object. Instead, you access them by using methods of the `Application` object.

> **NOTE**
>
> Unlike the other events discussed in this chapter, you use a standard VBA module to program the `On` events in this section.

Using the OnTime event

The OnTime event occurs at a specified time. The following example demonstrates how to program Excel to beep and then display a message at 3 p.m.:

```
Sub SetAlarm()
    Application.OnTime TimeSerial(15,0,0), "DisplayAlarm"
End Sub

Sub DisplayAlarm()
    Beep
    MsgBox "Wake up. It's time for your afternoon break!"
End Sub
```

In this example, the SetAlarm procedure uses the OnTime method of the Application object to set up the OnTime event. This method takes two arguments: the time (the TimeSerial function is an easy way to get a time, and the hour argument of 15 is 3 p.m.) and the procedure to execute when the time occurs (DisplayAlarm in the example). In the example, after SetAlarm executes, the DisplayAlarm procedure is called at 3 p.m., bringing up the message.

You could also use VBA's TimeValue function to represent the time. TimeValue converts a string that looks like a time into a value that Excel can handle. The following statement shows another way to program an event for 3 p.m.:

```
Application.OnTime TimeValue("3:00:00 pm"), "DisplayAlarm"
```

If you want to schedule an event that's relative to the current time—for example, 20 minutes from now—you can write an instruction like either of these:

```
Application.OnTime Now + TimeSerial(0, 20, 0), "DisplayAlarm"
```

```
Application.OnTime Now + TimeValue("00:20:00"), "DisplayAlarm"
```

You also can use the OnTime method to schedule a procedure on a particular day. Of course, you must keep your computer turned on, and Excel must be running.

To cancel an OnTime event, you must know the exact time the event was scheduled to run. Then you use the schedule argument of OnTime set to False. OnTime works to the nearest second. If you schedule something for 3 p.m., you can unschedule it with this code:

```
Application.OnTime TimeSerial(15, 0, 0), "DisplayAlarm", , False
```

If you scheduled something relative to the current time and want to cancel it, you need to store that time. This code will schedule the event:

```
TimeToRun = Now + TimeSerial(0, 20, 0)
Application.OnTime TimeToRun, "DisplayAlarm"
```

The TimeToRun variable can be used to unschedule it, assuming that the variable is still in scope:

```
Application.OnTime TimeToRun, "DisplayAlarm", , False
```

Using the OnKey event

While you work, Excel constantly monitors what you type. As a result, you can set up a keystroke or a key combination that, when pressed, executes a particular procedure.

The following example uses the OnKey method to set up an OnKey event. This event essentially reassigns the PgDn and PgUp keys. After the Setup_OnKey procedure executes, pressing PgDn executes the PgDn_Sub procedure, and pressing PgUp executes the PgUp_Sub procedure. The effect is that pressing PgDn moves down one row, and pressing PgUp moves up one row:

```
Sub Setup_OnKey()
  Application.OnKey "{PgDn}", "PgDn_Sub"
  Application.OnKey "{PgUp}", "PgUp_Sub"
End Sub

Sub PgDn_Sub()
  On Error Resume Next
  ActiveCell.Offset(1, 0).Activate
End Sub

Sub PgUp_Sub()
  On Error Resume Next
  ActiveCell.Offset(-1, 0).Activate
End Sub
```

> **NOTE**
>
> The key codes are enclosed in brackets, not parentheses. For a complete list of the keyboard codes, consult VBA Help. Search for OnKey.

> **TIP**
>
> The preceding examples used On Error Resume Next to ignore any errors generated. For example, if the active cell is in the first row, trying to move up one row causes an error. Furthermore, if the active sheet is a chart sheet, an error occurs because no such thing as an active cell exists in a chart sheet.

By executing the following procedure, you cancel the OnKey events, and the keys return to their normal functions:

```
Sub Cancel_OnKey()
    Application.OnKey "{PgDn}"
    Application.OnKey "{PgUp}"
End Sub
```

> **CAUTION**
>
> Contrary to what you may expect, using an empty string as the second argument for the OnKey method does *not* cancel the OnKey event. Instead, it causes Excel to ignore the keystroke and do nothing. For example, the following instruction tells Excel to ignore Alt+F4. (The percent sign represents the Alt key.)
>
> `Application.OnKey "%{F4}", ""`

Seeing Some VBA Examples

O ur philosophy about learning to write Excel macros places heavy emphasis on examples. Often, a well-thought-out example communicates a concept much better than a lengthy description of the underlying theory. In this book, space limitations don't allow us to describe every nuance of VBA, so we prepared many examples. Don't overlook the VBA Help system for specific details. To get help while working in the Visual Basic Editor (VBE), press F1. For context-sensitive help, select a VBA keyword, object name, property, or method before you press F1.

This chapter consists of several examples that demonstrate common VBA techniques. You may be able to use some examples directly, but in most cases, you must adapt them to your own needs.

Working with Ranges

Most of what you do in VBA probably involves worksheet ranges. When you work with range objects, keep the following points in mind:

- Your VBA code doesn't need to select a range to work with the range.
- If your code does select a range, its worksheet must be active.
- The macro recorder doesn't always generate the most efficient code. Often, you can use the recorder to create your macro and then edit the code to make it more efficient.
- We recommend you use named ranges in your VBA code. For example, a reference such as `Range("Total")` is better than `Range("D45")`. In the latter case, you need to modify the macro if you add a row above row 45.
- When you record macros that select ranges, pay close attention to Relative versus Absolute recording mode. The recording mode that you choose can determine whether your macro works correctly.

See Chapter 42, "Introducing Visual Basic for Applications," for more on recording modes.

- If you create a macro that loops through each cell in the current range selection, be aware that the user can select entire columns or rows. In such a case, you need to create a subset of the selection that consists only of nonblank cells. Or, you can work with cells in the worksheet's used range (by using the UsedRange property).
- Be aware that Excel allows you to select multiple ranges in a worksheet. For example, you can select a range, press Ctrl and then select another range. You can test for this in your macro and take appropriate actions.

The examples in the following sections demonstrate these points.

Copying a range

Copying a range is a frequent activity in macros. When you turn on the macro recorder (using Absolute recording mode) and copy a range from A1:A5 to B1:B5, you get a VBA macro like this:

```
Sub CopyRange()
    Range("A1:A5").Select
    Selection.Copy
    Range("B1").Select
    ActiveSheet.Paste
    Application.CutCopyMode = False
End Sub
```

This macro works, but it's not the most efficient way to copy a range. You can accomplish the same result with the following one-line macro:

```
Sub CopyRange2()
    Range("A1:A5").Copy Range("B1")
End Sub
```

This code takes advantage of the fact that the Copy method can use an argument that specifies the destination. Useful information about properties and methods is available in the Help system.

> **NOTE**
>
> Most of the examples in this chapter use unqualified object references. A *qualified object reference* is one where you explicitly tell VBA which object you want by identifying its Parent objects. For example, Range("A1") is unqualified because we haven't told VBA which worksheet it's on. The fully qualified version is Application. Workbooks("MyBook").Worksheets("MySheet").Range("A1").
>
> When you use an unqualified range reference in a standard module, VBA assumes you mean the ActiveSheet in the ActiveWorkbook. This saves you from having to type the whole string of parents if that is indeed what you mean. If you want or need to be explicit, consider using an object variable as described in "Simplifying object references" later in this chapter.

The example demonstrates that the macro recorder doesn't always generate the most efficient code. As you see, you don't have to select an object to work with it. Note that `CopyRange2` doesn't select a range; therefore, the active cell doesn't change when this macro is executed.

Copying a variable-size range

Often, you want to copy a range of cells in which the exact row and column dimensions are unknown.

Figure 47.1 shows a range on a worksheet. This range contains data that is updated weekly. Therefore, the number of rows changes. Because the exact range address is unknown at any given time, writing a macro to copy the range can be challenging.

FIGURE 47.1

This range can consist of any number of rows.

⊿	A	B	C	D
1	Week Ending	Calls	Orders	
2	4/5/2019	604	109	
3	4/12/2019	545	87	
4	4/19/2019	677	122	
5	4/26/2019	493	84	
6	5/3/2019	443	62	
7	5/10/2019	499	65	
8	5/17/2019	610	116	
9	5/24/2019	445	76	
10	5/31/2019	493	84	
11	6/7/2019	653	72	
12				

The macro that follows demonstrates how to copy this range to Sheet2 (beginning at cell A1). It uses the `CurrentRegion` property, which returns a `Range` object that corresponds to the block of used cells surrounding a particular cell. This is equivalent to choosing Home ⇨ Editing ⇨ Find & Select ⇨ Go To, clicking the Special button, and then selecting the Current Region option:

```
Sub CopyCurrentRegion()
    Range("A1").CurrentRegion.Copy Sheets("Sheet2").Range("A1")
End Sub
```

Another approach is to use a table to store the data. When you add new rows to a table, the table's range address adjusts automatically, so you can use a procedure like this:

```
Sub CopyTable()
    Range("Table1[#All]").Copy Sheets("Sheet2").Range("A1")
End Sub
```

47

A workbook that contains these macros is available on this book's website at www.wiley.com/go/ excel2019bible. The file is named range copy.xlsm.

Selecting to the end of a row or column

You're probably in the habit of using key combinations, such as pressing Ctrl+Shift+→ and Ctrl+Shift+↓, to select from the active cell to the end of a row or column. When you record these actions in Excel (using Relative recording mode), you'll find that the resulting code works as you would expect.

The following VBA procedure selects the range that begins at the active cell and extends down to the last cell in the column (or to the first empty cell, whichever comes first). When the range is selected, you can do whatever you want with it—copy it, move it, format it, and so on:

```
Sub SelectDown()
   Range(ActiveCell, ActiveCell.End(xlDown)).Select
End Sub
```

Notice that the Range property has two arguments. These arguments represent the upper-left and lower-right cells in a range.

This example uses the End method of the Range object, which returns a Range object. The End method takes one argument, which can be any of the following constants: xlUp, xlDown, xlToLeft, or xlToRight.

A workbook that contains this macro is available on this book's website at www.wiley.com/go/ excel2019bible. The file is named select cells.xlsm.

Selecting a row or column

The macro that follows demonstrates how to select the column of the active cell. It uses the EntireColumn property, which returns a range that consists of a column:

```
Sub SelectColumn()
   ActiveCell.EntireColumn.Select
End Sub
```

As you may suspect, an EntireRow property also is available, which returns a range that consists of a row.

If you want to perform an operation on all cells in the selected row or column, you don't need to select the row or column. For example, when the following procedure is executed, all cells in the row that contains the active cell are made bold:

```
Sub MakeRowBold()
   ActiveCell.EntireRow.Font.Bold = True
End Sub
```

Moving a range

Moving a range consists of cutting it to the Clipboard and then pasting it to another area. If you record your actions while performing a move operation, the macro recorder generates code as follows:

```
Sub MoveRange()
  Range("A1:C6").Select
  Selection.Cut
  Range("A10").Select
  ActiveSheet.Paste
End Sub
```

As demonstrated with copying earlier in this chapter (see "Copying a range"), this method is not the most efficient way to move a range of cells. In fact, you can do it with a single VBA statement as follows:

```
Sub MoveRange2()
 Range("A1:C6").Cut Range("A10")
End Sub
```

This statement takes advantage of the fact that the Cut method can use an argument that specifies the destination.

 A workbook that contains this macro is available on this book's website at www.wiley.com/go/ excel2019bible. **The file is named** range move.xlsm.

Looping through a range efficiently

Many macros perform an operation on each cell in a range, or they may perform selective actions based on the content of each cell. These operations usually involve a For-Next loop that processes each cell in the range.

The following example demonstrates how to loop through all of the cells in a range. In this case, the range is the current selection. In this example, Cell is a variable name that refers to the cell being processed. (Notice that this variable is declared as a Range object.) Within the For-Next loop, the single statement evaluates the cell. If the cell is negative, it's converted to a positive value:

```
Sub ProcessCells()
  Dim Cell As Range
  For Each Cell In Selection.Cells
    If Cell.Value < 0 Then Cell.Value = Cell.Value * -1
  Next Cell
End Sub
```

The preceding example works, but what if the selection consists of an entire column or an entire range? This is not uncommon because Excel lets you perform operations on entire columns or rows. In this case, though, the macro seems to take forever because it loops through each cell—even those that are blank. What's needed is a way to process only the nonblank cells.

You can accomplish this task by using the `SpecialCells` method. In the following example, the `SpecialCells` method is used to create a new object: the subset of the selection that consists of cells with constants (as opposed to formulas). This subset is processed, with the net effect of skipping all blank cells and all formula cells:

```
Sub ProcessCells2()
    Dim ConstantCells As Range
    Dim Cell As Range
'    Ignore errors
    On Error Resume Next
'    Process the constants
    Set ConstantCells = Selection.SpecialCells(xlConstants,
xlNumbers)
    For Each Cell In ConstantCells
        If Cell.Value < 0 Then Cell.Value = Cell.Value * -1
    Next Cell
End Sub
```

The `ProcessCells2` procedure works fast, regardless of what is selected. For example, you can select the range, select all columns in the range, select all rows in the range, or even select the entire worksheet. In all of these cases, only the cells that contain constants are processed inside the loop. This procedure is a vast improvement over the `ProcessCells` procedure presented earlier in this section.

Notice that the following statement is used in the procedure:

```
On Error Resume Next
```

This statement causes Excel to ignore any errors that occur and simply process the next statement. This statement is necessary because the `SpecialCells` method produces an error if no cells qualify and because the numerical comparison will fail if a cell contains an error value. Normal error checking is resumed when the procedure ends. To return to normal error-checking mode inside a procedure, use the following statement:

```
On Error GoTo 0
```

 This macro is available on this book's website at www.wiley.com/go/excel2019bible. The file is named skip blanks while looping.xlsm.

Prompting for a cell value

As discussed in Chapter 44, "Creating UserForms," you can take advantage of the VBA `InputBox` function to ask the user to enter a value. Figure 47.2 shows an example.

FIGURE 47.2

Using the VBA InputBox function to get a value from the user

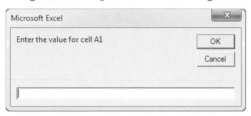

You can assign this value to a variable and use it in your procedure. Often, however, you want to place the value into a cell. The following procedure demonstrates how to ask the user for a value and place it into cell A1 of the active worksheet, using only one statement:

```
Sub GetValue()
    Range("A1").Value = InputBox("Enter the value for cell A1")
End Sub
```

This procedure has a problem, however: if the user clicks Cancel, the contents of cell A1 are replaced with an empty string. Here's a modified version in which the InputBox entry is assigned to a variable named UserVal. The code checks this variable and takes action only if the variable is not empty:

```
Sub GetValue()
    UserVal = InputBox("Enter the value for cell A1")
    If UserVal <> "" Then Range("A1").Value = UserVal
End Sub
```

Here's a variation that accepts only a numeric value. If the user enters a non-number, the InputBox keeps appearing until a number is entered. Only when a number is entered does the code exit the Do Loop, and the value is entered into A1. Another line inside the loop allows the user to click Cancel and get out of the procedure:

```
Sub GetValue()

  Do
    UserVal = InputBox("Enter a numeric value for cell A1")
    If UserVal = "" Then Exit Sub
  Loop Until IsNumeric(UserVal)

  Range("A1").Value = UserVal

End Sub
```

Determining the type of selection

If your macro is designed to work with a selected range, you need to determine that a range is actually selected. Otherwise, the macro most likely fails. The following procedure identifies the type of object selected:

```
Sub SelectionType()
  MsgBox TypeName(Selection)
End Sub
```

 A workbook that contains this macro is available on this book's website at www.wiley.com/go/ excel2019bible. The file is named selection type.xlsm. For objects that let you enter text, the macro won't work in Edit mode. If you click the button and nothing happens, press the Esc key to exit Edit mode.

If a cell or a range is selected, the MsgBox displays Range. If your macro is designed to work only with ranges, you can use an If statement to ensure that a range is actually selected. The following is an example that displays a message if the current selection is not a Range object:

```
Sub CheckSelection()
  If TypeName(Selection) = "Range" Then
    ' ... [Other statements go here]
  Else
    MsgBox "Select a range."

  End If
End Sub
```

Identifying a multiple selection

Excel enables you to make a multiple selection by pressing Ctrl while you select objects or ranges. This method can cause problems with some macros; for example, you can't copy a multiple selection that consists of nonadjacent ranges. The following macro demonstrates how to determine whether the user has made a multiple selection:

```
Sub MultipleSelection()
  If Selection.Areas.Count = 1 Then
    ' ... [Other statements go here]
  Else
    MsgBox "Multiple selections not allowed."
  End If
End Sub
```

This example uses the Areas method, which returns a collection of all Range objects in the selection. The Count property returns the number of objects that are in the collection.

You may want to work with multiple selections rather than just ignore them, for example, if you want to copy the selection. You can loop through the `Areas` collection of the `Range` object as this example shows:

```
Sub LoopAreas()

  Dim Area As Range
  Dim Cell As Range

  For Each Area In Selection.Areas
    'copy each selection 10 columns to the right
    Area.Copy Area.Offset(0, 10)
  Next Area

End Sub
```

Counting selected cells

You can create a macro that works with the selected range of cells. Use the `Count` property of the `Range` object to determine how many cells are contained in a range selection (or any range, for that matter). For example, the following statement displays a message box that contains the number of cells in the current selection:

```
MsgBox Selection.Count
```

CAUTION

With the larger worksheet size introduced in Excel 2007, the `Count` property can generate an error. The `Count` property uses the `Long` data type, so the largest value that it can store is $2,147,483,647$. For example, if the user selects 2,048 complete columns (2,147,483,648 cells), the `Count` property generates an error. Fortunately, Microsoft added a new property, `CountLarge`, which uses the `Double` data type that can handle values up to $1.79+E^308$.

For more on VBA data types, see Table 47.1.

Bottom line? In the majority of situations, the `Count` property will work fine. If there's a chance that you may need to count more cells (such as all cells in a worksheet), use `CountLarge` instead of `Count`.

If the active sheet contains a range named `data`, the following statement assigns the number of cells in the data range to a variable named `CellCount`:

```
CellCount = Range("data").Count
```

You can also determine how many rows or columns are contained in a range. The following expression calculates the number of columns in the currently selected range:

```
Selection.Columns.Count
```

And, of course, you can use the Rows property to determine the number of rows in a range. The following statement counts the number of rows in a range named data and assigns the number to a variable named RowCount:

```
RowCount = Range("data").Rows.Count
```

Working with Workbooks

The examples in this section demonstrate various ways to use VBA to work with workbooks.

Saving all workbooks

The following procedure loops through all workbooks in the Workbooks collection and saves each file that has been saved previously:

```
Public Sub SaveAllWorkbooks()
    Dim Book As Workbook
    For Each Book In Workbooks
        If Book.Path <> "" Then Book.Save
    Next Book
End Sub
```

Notice the use of the Path property. If a workbook's Path property is empty, the file has never been saved. (It's a new workbook.) This procedure ignores such workbooks and saves only the workbooks that have a nonempty Path property.

Saving and closing all workbooks

The following procedure loops through the Workbooks collection. The code saves and closes all workbooks:

```
Sub CloseAllWorkbooks()
    Dim Book As Workbook
    For Each Book In Workbooks
        If Book.Name <> ThisWorkbook.Name Then
            Book.Close SaveChanges:=True
        End If
    Next Book
    ThisWorkbook.Close SaveChanges:=True
End Sub
```

The procedure uses an If statement within the For-Next loop to determine whether the workbook is the one that contains the code. This is necessary because closing the workbook that contains the procedure would end the code, and subsequent workbooks would not be affected.

Working with Charts

Manipulating charts with VBA can be confusing, mainly because of the large number of objects involved. To get a feel for working with charts, turn on the macro recorder, create a chart, and perform some routine chart editing. You may be surprised by the amount of code that's generated.

When you understand the way that objects function in a chart, however, you can create some useful macros. This section presents a few macros that deal with charts. When you write macros that manipulate charts, you need to understand some terminology. An *embedded chart* on a worksheet is a `ChartObject` object, and the `ChartObject` contains the actual `Chart` object. A *chart* on a chart sheet, on the other hand, does not have a `ChartObject` container.

It's often useful to create an object reference to a chart. (See "Simplifying object references" later in this chapter.) For example, the following statements declare an object variable (`MyChart`) and assign the embedded chart named Chart 1 on the active sheet to it:

```
Dim MyChart As Chart
Set MyChart = ActiveSheet.ChartObjects("Chart 1").Chart
```

The following sections contain examples of macros that work with charts.

 These macros are available on this book's website at www.wiley.com/go/excel2019bible. **The file is named** chart macros.xlsm.

Modifying the chart type

The following example changes the chart type of every embedded chart on the active sheet. It makes each chart a clustered column chart by adjusting the `ChartType` property of the `Chart` object. A built-in constant, `xlColumnClustered`, represents a standard column chart:

```
Sub ChartType()
    Dim ChtObj As ChartObject
    For Each ChtObj In ActiveSheet.ChartObjects
        ChtObj.Chart.ChartType = xlColumnClustered
    Next ChtObj
End Sub
```

The preceding example uses a `For-Next` loop to cycle through all of the `ChartObject` objects on the active sheet. Within the loop, the chart type is assigned a new value, making it a column chart.

The following macro performs the same function but works on all chart sheets in the active workbook:

```
Sub ChartType2()
    Dim Cht As Chart
```

```
        For Each Cht In ActiveWorkbook.Charts
            Cht.ChartType = xlColumnClustered
        Next Cht
    End Sub
```

Modifying chart properties

The following example changes the legend font for all charts that are on the active sheet. It uses a `For-Next` loop to process all `ChartObject` objects and sets the `HasLegend` property to `True`. The code then adjusts the properties of the `Font` object contained in the `Legend` object:

```
Sub LegendMod()
    Dim ChtObj As ChartObject
    For Each ChtObj In ActiveSheet.ChartObjects
        ChtObj.Chart.HasLegend = True
        With ChtObj.Chart.Legend.Font
          .Name = "Arial"
          .FontStyle = "Bold"
          .Size = 8
        End With
    Next ChtObj
End Sub
```

Applying chart formatting

This example applies several formatting types to the specified chart (in this case, Chart 1 on the active sheet):

```
Sub ChartMods()
    With ActiveSheet.ChartObjects("Chart 1").Chart
        .ChartType = xlColumnClustered
        .ChartTitle.Text = "XYZ Corporation"
        .ChartArea.Font.Name = "Arial"
        .ChartArea.Font.FontStyle = "Regular"
        .ChartArea.Font.Size = 9
        .PlotArea.Interior.ColorIndex = 6
        .Axes(xlValue).TickLabels.Font.Bold = True
        .Axes(xlCategory).TickLabels.Font.Bold = True
    End With
End Sub
```

The best way to learn about the objects, properties, and methods that you need to code for charts is to record a macro while you create or apply various changes to a chart.

VBA Speed Tips

VBA is fast, but it's often not fast enough. This section presents programming examples that you can use to help speed your macros.

Turning off screen updating

You've probably noticed that when you execute a macro, you can watch everything that occurs in the macro. Sometimes this view is instructive, but after you get the macro working properly, it can be annoying and slow things considerably.

Fortunately, you can disable the normal screen updating that occurs when you execute a macro. Insert the following statement to turn off screen updating:

```
Application.ScreenUpdating = False
```

If at any point during the macro's execution you want the user to see the results of the macro, use the following statement to turn screen updating back on:

```
Application.ScreenUpdating = True
```

When the macro completes, Excel automatically turns screen updating back on.

Preventing alert messages

One benefit of using a macro is that you can perform a series of actions automatically. You can start a macro and then get a cup of coffee while Excel does its thing. Some operations cause Excel to display messages that must be addressed, however. For example, if your macro deletes a sheet, you see the message that is shown in the dialog box in Figure 47.3. These types of messages mean that you can't execute your macro unattended.

FIGURE 47.3

You can instruct Excel not to display these types of alerts while a macro is running.

To avoid these alert messages (and automatically choose the default response), insert the following VBA statement:

```
Application.DisplayAlerts = False
```

To turn alerts back on, use this statement:

```
Application.DisplayAlerts = True
```

As with screen updating, Excel turns alerts back on when the macro is done.

Simplifying object references

As you may have discovered, references to objects can get lengthy—especially if your code refers to an object that's not on the active sheet or in the active workbook. For example, a fully qualified reference to a `Range` object may look like this:

```
Workbooks("MyBook.xlsx").Worksheets("Sheet1").Range("IntRate")
```

If your macro uses this range frequently, you may want to use the `Set` command to create an object variable. For example, to assign this `Range` object to an object variable named `Rate`, use the following statement:

```
Set Rate = Workbooks("MyBook.xlsx").Worksheets("Sheet1").
Range("IntRate")
```

After this variable is defined, you can use the object variable `Rate` instead of the lengthy reference. Here's an example:

```
Rate.Font.Bold = True
Rate.Value = .0725
```

Besides simplifying your coding, using object variables speeds your macros quite a bit. We've seen complex macros execute twice as fast after creating object variables.

Declaring variable types

Usually, you don't have to worry about the type of data that's assigned to a variable. Excel handles all these details behind the scenes. For example, if you have a variable named `MyVar`, you can assign a number of any type to it. You can even assign a text string to it later in the procedure.

If you want your procedures to execute as fast as possible, though, you should tell Excel in advance what type of data is going be assigned to each of your variables. Providing this information in your VBA procedure is known as declaring a variable's type.

Table 47.1 lists all of the data types that VBA supports. This table also lists the number of bytes that each type uses and the approximate range of possible values.

TABLE 47.1   VBA Data Types

Data Type	Bytes Used	Approximate Range of Values
`Byte`	1	0 to 255
`Boolean`	2	True or False
`Integer`	2	–32,768 to 32,767
`Long` (long integer)	4	–2,147,483,648 to 2,147,483,647
`Single` (single-precision floating-point)	4	–3.4E38 to –1.4E–45 for negative values; 1.4E–45 to 4E38 for positive values

Data Type	Bytes Used	Approximate Range of Values
Double (double-precision floating-point)	8	–1.7E308 to –4.9E–324 for negative values; 4.9E–324 to .7E308 for positive values
Currency (scaled integer)	8	–9.2E14 to 9.2E14
Decimal	14	+/–7.9E28 with no decimal point
Date	8	January 1, 100 to December 31, 9999
Object	4	Any object reference
String (variable length)	10 + string length	0 to approximately 2 billion
String (fixed length)	Length of string	1 to approximately 65,400
Variant (with numbers)	16	Any numeric value up to the range of a Double
Variant (with characters)	22 + string length	Same range as for variable-length String
User-defined (using Type)	Number required by elements	Range of each element is the same as the range of its data type

If you don't declare a variable, Excel uses the Variant data type. In general, the best approach is to use the data type that uses the smallest number of bytes yet one that can still handle all of the data assigned to it. An exception is when you're performing floating-point calculations. In such a case, it's always best to use the Double data type (rather than the Single data type) to maintain maximum precision. Another exception involves the Integer data type. Although the Long data type uses more bytes, it usually results in faster performance.

When VBA works with data, execution speed is a function of the number of bytes that VBA has at its disposal. In other words, the fewer bytes that data uses, the faster that VBA can access and manipulate the data.

To declare a variable, use the Dim statement before you use the variable for the first time. For example, to declare the variable Units as a Long data type, use the following statement:

```
Dim Units As Long
```

To declare the variable UserName as a string, use the following statement:

```
Dim UserName As String
```

If you declare a variable within a procedure, the declaration is valid only within that procedure. If you declare a variable outside of any procedures (but before the first procedure), the variable is valid in all procedures in the module.

If you use an object variable (as described in "Simplifying object references" earlier in this chapter), you can declare the variable as the appropriate object data type. Here is an example:

```
Dim Rate As Range
Set Rate = Workbooks("MyBook.xlsx").Worksheets("Sheet1").
Range("IntRate")
```

To force yourself to declare all of the variables that you use, insert the following statement at the top of your module:

```
Option Explicit
```

If you use this statement and Excel encounters a variable that hasn't been declared, Excel displays an error message. After you get into the habit of correctly declaring all of your variables, you'll find that it not only can speed up code execution, but it helps eliminate errors and simplifies spotting errors.

Creating Custom Excel Add-Ins

For developers, one of the most useful features in Excel is the capability to create add-ins. This chapter discusses this concept and provides a practical example of creating an add-in.

Understanding Add-Ins

Generally speaking, an *add-in* is something that's added to software to give it additional functionality. Excel includes several add-ins, including the Analysis ToolPak and Solver. Ideally, the new features blend in well with the original interface so that they appear to be part of the program.

Excel's approach to add-ins is quite powerful: any knowledgeable Excel user can create add-ins from workbooks. The type of add-in covered in this chapter is basically a different form of a workbook file. Any Excel workbook can be converted into an add-in, but not every workbook is a good candidate for an add-in.

What distinguishes an add-in from a normal workbook? Add-ins, by default, have an `.xlam` extension. In addition, add-ins are always hidden, so you can't display worksheets or chart sheets that are contained in an add-in. However, you can access its VBA procedures and display dialog boxes that are contained on UserForms.

The following are some typical uses for Excel add-ins:

Store one or more custom worksheet functions When the add-in is loaded, you can use the functions like any built-in worksheet function.

Store Excel utilities VBA is ideal for creating general-purpose utilities that extend the power of Excel.

Store proprietary macros If you don't want end users to see (or modify) your macros, store the macros in an add-in and protect the VBA project with a password. Users can use the macros, but they can't view or change them unless they know the password. An additional benefit is that the add-in doesn't display a workbook window, which can be distracting.

As previously noted, Excel ships with several useful add-ins, and you can acquire other add-ins from third-party vendors or online. In addition, Excel includes the tools that enable you to create your own add-ins. We explain this process later in this chapter (see "Creating Add-Ins").

Working with Add-Ins

The best way to work with add-ins is to use the Excel Add-In Manager. To display the Add-In Manager, follow these steps:

1. **Choose File ⇨ Options.** The Excel Options dialog box appears.

2. **Select the Add-Ins category.**

3. **At the bottom of the dialog box, select Excel Add-Ins from the Manage list and then click Go.**

The Add-Ins dialog box appears, as shown in Figure 48.1. The dialog box contains all the add-ins that Excel knows about, which varies from computer to computer. The add-ins that are checked are open. You can open and close add-ins from this dialog box by selecting or deselecting the check boxes.

FIGURE 48.1

The Add-Ins dialog box

48

TIP

Pressing Alt+T followed by I is a much faster way to display the Add-Ins dialog box. Or, if the Developer tab is visible, choose Developer ⇨ Add-Ins ⇨ Excel Add-Ins.

CAUTION

You can also open most add-in files by opening the file using File ⇨ Open. After an add-in is opened, however, you can't choose File ⇨ Close to close it. The only way to remove the add-in is to exit and restart Excel or to write a macro to close the add-in. Therefore, you're usually better off opening the add-ins by using the Add-Ins dialog box.

The user interface for some add-ins (including those included with Excel) may be integrated into the Ribbon. For example, when you open the Analysis ToolPak add-in, you access these tools by choosing Data ⇨ Analysis ⇨ Data Analysis.

NOTE

If you open an add-in created in a version prior to Excel 2007 (an *.xla file), any user interface modifications made by the add-in will not appear as intended. Instead, you must access the user interface items (menus and toolbars) by choosing Add-Ins ⇨ Menu Commands or Add-Ins ⇨ Custom Toolbars. The Add-ins tab will show on the Ribbon only if an add-in is loaded that uses the old menu and CommandBar user interface.

Understanding Why to Create Add-Ins

Most Excel users have no need to create add-ins. However, if you develop spreadsheets for others—or if you simply want to get the most out of Excel—you may be interested in pursuing this topic further.

Here are some reasons why you may want to convert your Excel workbook application to an add-in:

To avoid confusion   If an end user loads your application as an add-in, the file isn't visible in a window—and, therefore, is less likely to confuse novice users or get in the way. Unlike a hidden workbook window, an add-in can't be unhidden.

To simplify access to worksheet functions   Custom worksheet functions stored in an add-in don't require the workbook name qualifier. For example, if you have a custom function named MOVAVG stored in a workbook named Newfuncs.xlsm, you have to use syntax such as the following to use this function in a different workbook:

```
=NEWFUNCS.XLSM!MOVAVG(A1:A50)
```

If this function is stored in an add-in file that's open, however, the syntax is much simpler because you don't need to include the file reference:

```
=MOVAVG(A1:A50)
```

To provide easier access   After you identify the location of your add-in, it appears in the Add-Ins dialog box and can display a friendly name and a description of what it does.

To permit better loading control   You can automatically open add-ins when Excel starts, regardless of the directory in which they're stored.

To omit prompts when unloading   When an add-in is closed, the user never sees the Save Change In prompt because changes to add-ins aren't saved unless you specifically do so from the VB Editor window.

Creating Add-Ins

Technically, you can convert any workbook to an add-in. Not all workbooks benefit from this conversion, though. In fact, workbooks that consist only of worksheets (that is, no macros or custom dialog boxes) become unusable because add-ins are hidden.

Workbooks that benefit from conversion to an add-in are those with macros. For example, you may have a workbook that consists of general-purpose macros and functions. This type of workbook makes an ideal add-in.

The following steps describe how to create an add-in from a workbook:

1. **Develop your application, and make sure that everything works properly.**

2. **(Optional) Add a title and description for your add-in. Choose File ⇨ Info, and click Show All Properties at the bottom of the right panel. Enter a brief descriptive title in the Title field and then enter a longer description in the Comments field.** Although this step isn't required, it makes installing and identifying the add-in easier.

3. **(Optional) Lock the VBA project.** This step protects the VBA code and UserForms from being viewed. You do this in the Visual Basic Editor (VBE) by choosing Tools ⇨ <Project Name> Properties (where *<Project Name>* corresponds to your VB project name). In the dialog box, click the Protection tab and select Lock Project for Viewing. If you like, you can specify a password to prevent others from viewing your code.

4. **Save the workbook as an add-in file by choosing File ⇨ Save As and selecting Excel Add-In (*.xlam) from the Save As Type drop-down list.** By default, Excel saves your add-in to your AddIns directory. You can override this location and choose any directory that you like.

> **NOTE**
>
> After you save the workbook as an add-in, the original (non-add-in) workbook remains active. If you're going to install the add-in and test it, you should close this file to avoid having two macros with the same name.

After you create the add-in, you need to install it:

1. **Choose File ⇨ Options ⇨ Add-Ins.**

2. **Select Excel Add-Ins from the Manage drop-down list and then click Go.** The Add-Ins dialog box appears.

3. **Click the Browse button to locate the XLAM file that you created, which installs the add-in.** The Add-Ins dialog box uses the descriptive title that you provided for the Title field in the Show All Properties panel.

> **NOTE**
> You can continue to modify the macros and UserForms in the XLAM version of your file. Because the add-in doesn't appear in the Excel window, you save your changes in the VB Editor by choosing File ⇨ Save.

Looking at an Add-In Example

This section discusses the steps required to create a useful add-in from the `change case.xlsm` workbook that we covered in Chapter 44, "Creating UserForms." This workbook contains a UserForm that displays options that change the text case of selected cells (uppercase, lowercase, or proper case). Figure 48.2 shows the add-in in action.

FIGURE 48.2

This dialog box enables the user to change the case of text in the selected cells.

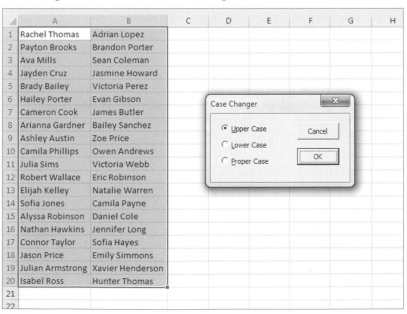

This book's website at www.wiley.com/go/excel2019bible contains the original version of the workbook (change case.xlsm), plus a version after it was converted to an add-in (called (addin)change case.xlam). Neither file is locked, so you have full access to the VBA code and UserForm.

This workbook contains one worksheet, which is empty. Although the worksheet is not used, it must be present because every workbook must have at least one sheet. It also contains one VBA module and one UserForm.

Learning about Module1

The Module1 code module contains one procedure that displays the UserForm. The ShowChangeCaseUserForm procedure checks the type of selection. If a range is selected, the dialog box in UserForm1 appears. If anything other than a range is selected, a message box is displayed:

```
Sub ShowChangeCaseUserForm ()
    If TypeName(Selection) = "Range" Then
        UserForm1.Show
    Else
        MsgBox "Select some cells."
    End If
End Sub
```

 For information on how to navigate the Visual Basic Editor, including using the Project Explorer to find modules, see Chapter 42, "Introducing Visual Basic for Applications."

Learning about the UserForm

Figure 48.3 shows the UserForm1 form, which has five controls: three OptionButton controls and two CommandButton controls. The controls have descriptive names, and the Accelerator property is set so that the controls display an accelerator key (for keyboard users). The option button with the Upper Case caption has its Value property set to TRUE, which makes it the default option.

 Refer to Chapter 44 for details about how the code works.

Testing the workbook

Before you convert a workbook to an add-in, test it when a different workbook is active to simulate what happens when the workbook is an add-in. Remember that an add-in is never the active workbook, and it never displays any of its worksheets.

To test it, save the XLSM version of the workbook, close it, and then reopen it. With the workbook open, activate a different workbook, select some cells that contain text, and then press Alt+F8 to display the Macros dialog box. Execute the `ShowChangeCaseUserForm` macro and try all of the options.

FIGURE 48.3

The custom dialog box

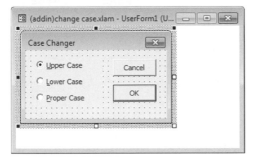

Adding descriptive information

Adding descriptive information is recommended but not necessary. Choose File ➪ Info and click Show All Properties at the bottom of the right panel (see Figure 48.4). Enter a title for the add-in in the Title field. This text appears in the Add-Ins dialog box. In the Comments field, enter a description. This information appears at the bottom of the Add-Ins dialog box when the add-in is selected.

FIGURE 48.4

Adding descriptive information about your add-in

Creating the user interface for your add-in macro

At this point, the future add-in is missing one key component: a way to execute the macro that displays the UserForm. The easiest solution is to provide a shortcut key that executes the macro. Ctrl+Shift+C is a good key combination. Here's how to do it:

1. **In Excel, choose Developer ⇨ Code ⇨ Macros (or press Alt+F8).** The Macro dialog box appears.
2. **In the Macro Name list, select the macro named ShowChangeCaseUserForm.**
3. **Click the Options button.** The Macro Options dialog box appears.
4. **Specify Ctrl+Shift+C as the shortcut key and click OK.**
5. **Click Cancel to close the Macro dialog box.**

Make sure you save the workbook after making this change.

Protecting the project

In some situations (such as a commercial product), you may want to protect your project so that others can't see the source code. To protect the project, follow these steps:

1. **Activate the VBE.**
2. **In the Project window, click the project.**
3. **Choose Tools ⇨ *<Project Name>* Properties.** The VBE displays its Project Properties dialog box.
4. **Select the Protection tab (as shown in Figure 48.5).**

FIGURE 48.5

The Protection tab of the Project Properties dialog box

5. **Select the Lock Project for Viewing check box.**

6. **Enter a password (twice) for the project.**

7. **Click OK.**

Creating the add-in

To save the workbook as an add-in, follow these steps:

1. **Switch to the Excel window, and activate your workbook.**

2. **Choose File ⇨ Save As.**

3. **Select Microsoft Excel Add-In (*.xlam) from the Save as Type drop-down list.**

4. **Enter a name for the add-in file and then click Save.** By default, Excel saves the add-in in your AddIns directory, but you can choose a different directory if you like.

Installing the add-in

Now it's time to try the add-in. Make sure the XLSM version of the workbook is not open and then follow these steps:

1. **Choose File ⇨ Options ⇨ Add-Ins.**

2. **Select Excel Add-Ins from the Manage drop-down list and click Go.** The Add-Ins dialog box appears.

3. **Click the Browse button, and locate and select the** change case.xlam **add-in that you just created. Click OK.** The Add-Ins dialog box displays the add-in in its list. Notice that the information that you provided in the Show All Properties panel appears here.

4. **Click OK to close the dialog box and open the add-in.**

When the add-in is installed, you can access it by pressing Ctrl+Shift+C. Another option is to add a new item to your Quick Access toolbar or to the Ribbon.

 See Chapter 8, "Customizing the Excel User Interface," for information about customizing Excel's user interface.

Index

Symbols

! (exclamation point)
    in link formula syntax, 638
    when referencing cells in other workbooks, 224
    when referencing cells in other worksheets, 223
" (quote), in workbook filenames, 161
(hash) marks
    cells filled with, 50, 68, 425
    in formula errors, 229
& (ampersand), entering in text, 189
& (concatenation) operator, 189, 208, 210, 225, 255
' (comment indicator), 936
() (parentheses)
    nesting within formulas, 210–211
    overriding Excel's built-in precedence, 210–211
– (negation) operator, 430, 431
– (subtraction) operator, 208, 210, 431
>= (greater than or equal to) operator, 208
> (greater than) operator
    in condition arguments, 296
    as formula operator, 208, 210
    in workbook names, 161
<= (less than or equal to), 208, 209
< (less than) symbol
    as formula operator, 208, 210
    in workbook names, 161
* (asterisk)
    in condition arguments, 306
    searching for, 81
    in workbook names, 161
    in worksheet names, 57
* (multiplication) operator, 207, 208, 209, 211
+ (addition) operator, 207, 208, 210
+ (plus sign), in worksheet outlines, 634
, (comma)
    in automatic number formatting, 46
    in function arguments, 213
    as list separator, 214
    as one-dimensional horizontal array list separator, 404
    as one-dimensional vertical array list separator, 405
    as range reference operator, 214, 235
    as two-dimensional horizontal array list separator, 405
- (minus sign), 634
/ (division) operator, 208, 209
/ (slash)
    in workbook names, 161
    in worksheet names, 56
: (colon)
    in range addresses, 29, 71
    as range reference operator, 235
    in workbook names, 161
    in worksheet names, 56
; (semicolon)
    in custom number formats, 50
    as list separator, 214, 404
    in number formatting strings, 541, 542
    as two-dimensional vertical array list separator, 405
    when suppressing zeros, 543
= (equal sign)
    as formula operator, 208, 209, 210, 214, 216
    in condition arguments, 296
    in named arrays, 407
    precedence, 210
? (question mark)
    in condition arguments, 306
    searching for, 81
    in workbook names, 161
    in worksheet names, 57
[] (square brackets)
    in column names, 226, 229
    in link formula syntax, 638
    when applying custom format colors, 554
    in workbook names, 224
    in worksheet names, 56
\ (backslash), in worksheet names, 56
^ (exponentiation) operator, 208, 209, 310
{} (curly brackets)
    in array constants, 403, 407
    in array formulas, 408, 409
    in formula names, 401
    in named arrays, 407

creating, 400–401

creating array constants from values in a range, 411–412

creating arrays from values in a range, 411

creating arrays of consecutive integers, 415–416

expanding, 410

transposing arrays, 414–415

using functions with arrays, 413

MultiLine property, TextBox control, 996

multiple selection, 73

multiplication (*) operator, 207, 208, 209, 211

Multiply option, Paste Special dialog box, 92–93

MultiSelect property, ListBox control, 993

N

#N/A errors, 230, 428

Name box, 94

name box, Excel window, 5, 6

Name Manager, 97–98

#NAME? errors, 230, 428

named styles, 143

applying, 143–144

controlling with templates, 146

creating, 145–146

merging from other workbooks, 146

modifying, 144–145

overview, 143

named views, creating, 193–194

names

array constants, 407–408

constants, 233

formulas, 233–234

range names

deleting, problems with, 428

pasting into formulas, 216

sheet tabs, 56

worksheets, 56–57

negative values, fixing trailing minus signs, 609

net present value, calculating, 356–358

NETWORKDAYS function, 277–278

NETWORKDAYS.INTL function, 278

New Formatting Rule dialog box, 132–133

creating formula-based rules, 137

customizing colors, 133

customizing icon sets, 135

highlighting values based on dates, 393–398

highlighting values based on value of another cell, 367–369

highlighting values in one list and another, 391–393

highlighting values in one list but not another, 389–391

highlighting values with lower values than hard-coded value, 366–367

New Name dialog box, 94–95

New Sheet button, 5, 6

New Sheet control, adding worksheets to workbooks, 55

New Table Style command, 114

NewSheet workbook event, 1000, 1002

NOMINAL function, 343–345

nonleveraged interquatile ranges, 381

Normal Probability option, Regression dialog box, 766

Normal view, printing in, 174, 175

NOW function, 275–276

nper argument

PMT function, 346

PV function, 355

NPV function, 356–358

#NULL! errors, 230, 428–429

#NUM! errors, 230, 429

Num Lock key, 8–9

number bases, converting between, 597–598

Number number format, 50

numbers

formatting, 537

automatic, 46

custom number formatting, 50, 540–546

for dashboards, 576

Format Cells dialog box, 48–50, 539–540

hiding zeros, 543–544

number format strings, 540–546

numbers in millions, 543

numbers in thousands, 542–543

overview, 44–45

using Ribbon buttons, 46, 537–538

shortcut keys for, 46, 538–539

suppressing zeros, 543–544

in text strings, 266–268

identified as text, 254

padding with zeros, 266

quarter numbers, calculating, 286

random number generation tool, 763–765

rounding, 247

to nearest penny, 247–248

to significant digits, 248–250

using formulas, 247

U